D1563288

EMPIRES OF IDEAS

Empires of Ideas

Creating *the* Modern University *from* Germany *to* America *to* China

WILLIAM C. KIRBY

THE BELKNAP PRESS OF HARVARD UNIVERSITY PRESS
Cambridge, Massachusetts & London, England
2022

First printing

Library of Congress Cataloging-in-Publication Data
Names: Kirby, William C., author.
Title: Empires of ideas : creating the modern university from Germany to America to
    China / William C. Kirby.
Description: Cambridge, Massachusetts : The Belknap Press of Harvard University Press,
    2022. | Includes bibliographical references and index.
Identifiers: LCCN 2021049001 | ISBN 9780674737716 (hardcover)
Subjects: LCSH: Universities and colleges—Germany—History. | Universities and
    colleges—United States—History. | Universities and colleges—China—History. |
    Education, Higher—Germany—History. | Education, Higher—United States—
    German influences. | Education, Higher—China—History.
Classification: LCC LA728 .K54 2022 | DDC 378.43—dc23/eng/20211129
LC record available at https://lccn.loc.gov/2021049001

Contents

Preface

子曰，學而時習之，不亦說乎？

The Master said: To study, and at due times to practice
what one has studied, is this not a pleasure?

This first line of the Confucian *Analects,* set down somewhere between the
fifth and third centuries BCE, captures better than any I know the challenges and rewards of the modern university. It reflects, too, my own path to
this book as a historian, teacher, and dean.

I have had the pleasure of learning and practicing in colleges and universities since I was eighteen. Studying as an undergraduate at Dartmouth and
Wellesley, and in Mainz, I learned to value an education in the liberal arts
and sciences, with an international dimension. In graduate studies in Berlin
and at Harvard, I sought to acquire the skills to apprentice as a professor. At
Washington University and at Harvard, I learned to practice what I had
studied, both as a scholar and as an official.

Along the way I learned gradually of the richness and complexity of our
world of universities from Europe to America to Asia. This book owes much
to the experience, collegiality, and assistance of individuals and institutions
on three continents.

At Washington University in St. Louis, a jewel among American universities, I could see how the good and principled leadership of William H.
Danforth and later Mark S. Wrighton could transform an institution in a
matter of decades while maintaining collegiate and clear governance. I owe

everything to my mentors there in the History Department and University College. Arriving at Harvard in the early 1990s, I had the opportunity of working under a remarkable dean, Jeremy R. Knowles, and a professor's president, the eloquently persuasive Neil L. Rudenstine, in what was, in retrospect, a golden decade for that university. In my own research abroad, in establishing international research partnerships, and in serving on advisory boards to Chinese and European universities, I came to appreciate the dynamism of China's resurgent universities and the impetus for renewal in Europe. From the institution-building of Chen Jining and Qiu Yong at Tsinghua University; Chen Jia'er, Wang Enge, and Hao Ping at Peking University; Victor Fung and Peter Mathieson at the University of Hong Kong; Susanne Weigelin-Schwiedrzik, first at Heidelberg and then Vienna; Marijk van den Wende, of Amsterdam University College and then Utrecht; and Mechthild Leutner and Peter-André Alt at Free University of Berlin, I learned a great deal. To these friends and colleagues, I am deeply grateful.

This book would not have been possible without the generous research funds received from Harvard Business School (HBS) during the tenure of Dean Nitin Nohria, who, like his predecessor Jay Light, gave unstinting support. My colleagues at the Harvard China Fund and the Harvard Center Shanghai, Julia Cai, Yi Wang, and Nancy Dai, provided critical logistical and research assistance.

The HBS case method has shaped this book, but my remarkable HBS research associates have helped to shape it further still. Joycelyn W. Eby provided extraordinary support for the American and Chinese sections, accompanied me on multiple interviews, and co-authored with me HBS cases on Berkeley, Tsinghua, and the University of Hong Kong that were early drafts of the final chapters. Yuanzhuo Wang co-authored the HBS case on Duke University and provided critical assistance in our research visit to Nanjing University. John McHugh and Joyce Kim did invaluable work in bringing the manuscript to completion, with their expertise on the Chinese and American scenes, respectively, and their deep commitment to the project. Mareike-Christin Bues helped to conceptualize the German cases, and Carolyn Taratko strengthened them greatly for the final submission. Noah Truwit assisted with post-submission updates and references. Ava Russell, my HBS faculty support specialist during the years this project was under way, kept us on budget and (somewhat) on time. Her successor, Alice Foster McCallum, reviewed the copyedited manuscript. For the assistance, advice, and support of these colleagues I could not be more grateful.

I have had the pleasure of working with two outstanding editors at Harvard University Press. Elizabeth Knoll originally signed me to the project and has given good counsel ever since. Andrew Kinney—a historian with deep knowledge of higher education—offered strong advice and edits of the entire manuscript, which he made shorter and better. Penelope Perkins, of Pen & Ink, gave every line of the manuscript a most rigorous editing and proofreading. Jenny Korte provided superb copyediting, Angela Piliouras oversaw final copyediting and typesetting, and Mary Mortensen prepared the index. I am indebted also to Joy de Menil, director of Belknap Publishing, and to two directors of Harvard University Press, Bill Sisler and George Andreou, who watched the project grow from idea to manuscript. I am most grateful for the comments and suggestions made by our two anonymous readers of this book.

A study such as this must rely on a wide variety of sources: published, archival, and oral. I am the beneficiary of the knowledge and assistance of archivists at Humboldt University; Free University of Berlin; Duke University; the University of California, Berkeley; Tsinghua University; Nanjing University; and the University of Hong Kong. For the remarkable access to materials past and present at Duke, I am especially grateful to University Librarian Deborah Jakubs and former provost Peter Lange.

I had the privilege of interviewing nearly one hundred leaders, past and present, of the institutions studied in the book. I was pleased, often amazed, by the candor with which these presidents, provosts, professors, and senior administrators addressed the issues confronting their universities. I cannot list them all here, but even a short list is a form of "who's who" of German, American, and Chinese higher education.

In Germany, I learned from the insights and experience of Presidents Heinrich Fink, Christoph Markschies, and Jan-Hendrik Olbertz of Humboldt University as well as their senior colleagues in administration and teaching such as Eva Inés Obergfell and Peter Frensch. I learned much from Heinz-Elmar Tenorth and the many colleagues who contributed to his magisterial history of the university's first two hundred years.

My research at Free University was made possible by the cooperation of President Alt, Vice President Klaus Mühlhahn, Herbert Grieshop, Matthias Dannenberg, Chancellor Andrea Bör, and the former chancellor, the incomparable Peter Lange. (One of two incomparable Peter Langes in this book.) I gained much from the advice of Hans Weiler and other members of Free University's International Advisory Committee, which advised the university on its strategy in Germany's Excellence Initiative.

At Harvard, of course, I had no shortage of colleagues to torment with interviews, former presidents Neil Rudenstine and Drew Faust, and future president Lawrence Bacow, chief among them. Former deans William Graham, Barry Bloom, and Venkatesh Narayanamurti, and former provost Steven Hyman gave unfiltered accounts of their tenures. Provost Alan Garber and Dean Frank Doyle addressed the challenges of engineering in a town where MIT resides, while Douglas Melton, leader of the Harvard Stem Cell Institute, looked farther west to identify Harvard's chief competitor.

At Berkeley, Chancellor Nicholas Dirks and his team shared with me the ambitions, tensions, and fiscal constraints that have marked Berkeley's recent history. Former chancellor Robert Birgeneau and future chancellor Carol Christ helped me grasp the university's distinctive culture, while former provost George Breslauer gave detailed context to Berkeley's endurance in the wake of the financial crisis of 2008. Another remarkable former provost, Judd King, graciously hosted me at Berkeley's Center for Studies in Higher Education. My fellow historians Wen-hsin Yeh and Sheldon Rothblatt, both great scholar-citizens of Berkeley, provided invaluable insight.

At Duke, the hospitality and openness of the entire institution followed the example set by President Richard Brodhead. Former president Nannerl Keohane provided important background. Provosts Peter Lange and Sally Kornbluth gave extensive interviews and provided access to a wealth of the university's planning documents. Executive Vice President James Roberts and Treasurer Tallman Trask III helped me unpack the financial picture, while Vice President Michael Merson set out Duke's international ambitions. To understand the ambitions and challenges of Duke Kunshan University in China, I am indebted to Blair Sheppard, Mary Brown Bullock, Haiyan Gao, Noah Pickus, Wendy Kuran, William Johnson, and, in particular, Nora Bynum. Kunshan Party Secretary Guan Aiguo and Vice Mayors Jin Naibing and Jin Ming provided important context on site in China.

At Tsinghua University I am grateful for the perspectives of Presidents Chen Jining and Qiu Yong; Party Secretary Chen Xu; Vice President Yang Bin; Deans Qian Yingyi, David Daokui Li, Xue Lan, and David Pan; and Professors Xie Zheping and Wang Hui. On Tsinghua's Schwarzman Scholars program, I learned firsthand from its founding trustee, Stephen A. Schwarzman, and its indefatigable CEO, Amy Stursberg. I thank friends and colleagues at Tsinghua's neighbor and rival, Peking University, for their broad perspective on Chinese higher education: Presidents Wan Enge and Lin Jianhua and Professors Jin Li and Yuan Ming, in particular.

My work at Nanjing University was aided by its remarkable modern historians Zhang Xianwen, Chen Qianping, and Jiang Liangqin, who provided deep background and arranged access to both archives and interviews. For their assistance I thank Party Secretaries Zhang Yibin and Hu Jinbo, Executive Vice Chancellor Yang Zhong, Vice President Wang Zhenlin, Professor He Chengzhou, and Professor Neil Kubler, the former co-director of the Hopkins-Nanjing Center.

Finally, I had the opportunity to research in Hong Kong at a time of comparative openness and much tension. I could not have pursued my work at the University of Hong Kong without the help of Presidents Peter Mathieson and Xiang Zhang, Provosts Roland Chin and Paul Tam, Pro-Vice Chancellors Amy Tsui and John Malpas, Deans Ian Holiday and Gabriel Leung, and Professors Xu Guoqi, Yang Rui, and (especially) John Carroll. Former and current council chairs Victor Fung and Arthur Li gave clarifying accounts of their tenures. On the promise and problems of the broader educational scene in Hong Kong, I learned directly from my colleagues on Hong Kong's University Grants Committee.

As always in a study such as this, only some of these archival and interview encounters will have made their way into the final book, but collectively they did a great deal to shape it.

I owe a particular debt of gratitude to Director Miaw-fen Lu and the Institute of Modern History of the Academia Sinica in Taiwan. I had the honor of presenting there an overview of this project as the 2017 Kuo Tingyee Memorial Lectures.[1]

One word on the romanization of Chinese names: I have used the standard *pinyin* romanization of the People's Republic of China, with the family name first, except when individuals were widely known or preferred to be known by another form.

An author whose work takes him so frequently abroad can succeed only with the help of a wonderful family at home. I am blessed by my son Ted, my daughter Elizabeth, my sister Katherine, and above all by my wife and fellow historian, Yvette Sheahan Kirby, whose patience is matched only by her experience in the world of universities. To her is this book dedicated.

Introduction

The "World-Class" University

W<span></span>E LIVE in a world of universities. At least 30,000 institutions call themselves universities, some 1,400 of which are ranked in the *Times Higher Education World University Rankings*. Who is in the lead? By sheer numbers of higher education institutions, the answer may be India, with 1,043 universities and 42,343 colleges in 2020,[1] far outdistancing the United States with its nearly 4,000 degree-granting colleges and universities. China's Ministry of Education counted 3,012 higher education institutions in 2021. Israel has 63 and Palestine 25. North Korea has 3 by one assessment and 300 by another.[2] Even Greenland, Djibouti, and Monaco have 1 university, each.[3]

It is, of course, a world of rather different universities. There are Oxford and Cambridge—two of the world's oldest and still leading universities by any measure—and then there is the happily defunct and corrupt "Trump University," which like its namesake, is currently dethroned and out of business. And then there are the self-promoters of a different sort: the readers of this book will be able to name many institutions that once were "schools" or "colleges" that today recruit students as "universities." Sheldon Rothblatt, a distinguished historian of higher education, made this point in discussing "the history of the idea that a university derives its identity from an idea": throughout the centuries in which universities have existed, a "single idea of a university has never truly existed."[4] The offerings of some universities are capacious. Others are narrowly specialized. Universities in the former Soviet bloc were paragons of applied knowledge, their students graduating

1

directly into preselected state enterprises. There are, as we shall see, rather different national systems of higher education, but not all are systematic. Universities may exist as form before there is function: think of the American neo-Gothic campuses that preceded the academic excellence later found in them.

The world of universities is not far removed from the world of power politics. Whom, after all, do universities serve? The individual? The community? The state? The Party? These are old questions of contemporary importance. The *Doktorvater* of all modern research universities, the University of Berlin, was founded to strengthen a defeated Prussian state, substituting the power of knowledge for lost land. Harvard, we will see, was a "state" university for much of its undistinguished first century, but it is now a famously private university with a strong sense of public purpose. The University of California, Berkeley, was, from its founding, a proud public university serving the state of California, but it is now increasingly a privately funded institution, still with the aspiration of serving a broad public. Tsinghua University was founded with a foreign policy mission: to bind the United States and China closer together by sending Tsinghua graduates to the United States. Today, Tsinghua is the recipient of American and other international talent as it climbs the ranks of the world's most admired institutions.

Yet the world of universities is singularly absent from many influential studies of power politics and of the rise and demise of nations. Paul Kennedy focuses on economic change and military conflict in his classic *Rise and Fall of the Great Powers*. David Landes, assessing *The Wealth and Poverty of Nations,* pays more attention to clocks and watches than to education in any form. In *Why Nations Fail,* Daron Acemoglu and James Robinson dig deep into the origins of power, prosperity, and poverty, but "education" is not to be found in the index. And my colleague Charles Maier, who is deeply knowledgeable about the state of higher education in general and at Harvard in particular, has little room for universities in his tour de force that looks at American ascendancy, *Among Empires*.[5] Yet in these analyses of the wealth and power among nations, at least Landes quotes one merchant banker from a Persian Gulf country at the height of the oil boom, pondering the nature of true wealth: *"Rich* is education . . . expertise . . . technology. *Rich* is knowing. We have money, yes. But we are not *rich.*"[6]

"A rich country cannot have poor farmers." That was the lesson imparted to my Harvard Business School students by Dhanin Chearavanont, senior chairman of C. P. Group and leader of one of the world's most innovative agribusiness firms, when I taught a case about C. P.'s work in China. I believe it is also true that an enduring rich country cannot have, as a rule, poor universities. The capacity of a nation may be measured more precisely in gross domestic product or in military might, but if we cannot imagine equally precise calculations of the quality of higher education, it does not mean that it is unimportant.

The foremost global political and economic powers of the past three centuries have also been powerful leaders in scholarship and learning. In the seventeenth and eighteenth centuries, France dominated Europe more enduringly by the power of ideas than by its military prowess. In Asia the great Qing Empire, then at its height, defined what it meant to be learned and civilized in much of the East Asian world and was admired as such in Europe. In the nineteenth century, as first Britain, then France, and then Germany rose to be world powers, their power was accompanied by the global allure of their leading schools and universities. In Britain, elites from the British Empire (and later from the Commonwealth) would be educated at Cambridge or Oxford or at the many British-modeled institutions in the colonial world. The *grandes écoles* of France have not (until recently) been welcoming to international audiences, but they could be the educational venue of first choice for elites from *la France d'outre-mer*. German universities, by contrast, became the destination of choice for scholars the world around because they redefined what universities could be—and in an era of growing German national strength. And if American universities gained global prestige and increasing numbers of international students and scholars over the course of the twentieth century, this was closely tied to the ascent of the United States in an "American century." In 2022, as Chinese universities climb quickly in global rankings and attract more than a half-million international students to their campuses, this cannot easily be separated from China's return to a position of global power and influence.

This is not a book about geopolitics, but it is a book about the roles, historically and in prospect, of universities in a global context. This book is about the modern *research* university in three of its most powerful settings: Germany, the United States, and China. It is about the future of the university, in light of its past. I examine three leading global centers of higher education in the twenty-first century from a historian's perspective: I explore how they have grown, assess their greatest challenges today, and estimate which system (if any single one) is likely to set global standards in the twenty-first century.

German universities set in place the foundations of modern universities everywhere in the nineteenth century. American universities had enormous international influence by the end of the twentieth century. I pose a simple question: What, then, are the prospects for *Chinese* leadership in the twenty-first century? Simply to ask this question is to demand some level of comparative research on German, American, and Chinese universities.

In 2022 nearly every major ranking of global universities shows American institutions in leading positions. Yet we know this was not the case in 1922, and there is no reason to assume it will be true in 2122. American leadership in higher education—as in other areas—is today under great stress, particularly in its public universities but also in the realm of private research universities. Meanwhile, nowhere on earth have recent decades seen more revolutionary change in higher education than in the People's Republic of China. In 1977 Chinese universities were just reopening after the catastrophe of the Cultural Revolution. Today they are poised for positions of international leadership in research and education.

The rapid, recent growth of Chinese universities (with now more than forty million students enrolled) has outpaced the great postwar expansion in the United States or the growth of mass-enrollment universities in Europe in the 1970s and 1980s. Square acreage of universities in China has grown fivefold in the past two decades. And unlike the American expansion of the 1950s and the European growth of the 1970s, this growth has elements that are self-consciously elitist, with the aim of building a significant number of "world-class universities." The best of these are investing enormously in research, and the most innovative of these are also experimenting creatively with conceptions of "liberal education" that have both German and American antecedents.

My broader study, then, is an investigation, past and present, of three realms of higher education that have defined, or promise to define, excellence: those of Germany, the United States, and China over the past two centuries. I realize, of course, that there is often seemingly little "system" to the many varied institutions in Germany, the United States, and China. I have pursued this study not as a series of comprehensive, national studies, but through case studies of individual universities, from which we may draw lessons. Within the field of education, researchers have long used the case study to address "critical problems of practice" and to extend knowledge of the diversity of educational experiences.[7] In this book, each university, to be sure, is rooted in a larger system, but each has its own, distinctive narrative, its own character, and its own concerns. Each is its own drama, but with lessons, I hope, for a larger audience.

I have taught at Harvard University now for three decades, but in the last fifteen years also at Harvard Business School (HBS). I have seen how case studies and, in teaching, the case method, can illuminate the whole while focusing on the particular. Teaching an HBS case study has been described as "the art of managing uncertainty."[8] Our cases are primarily vehicles for teaching, with multiple possible outcomes: good stories that lead one to think about broader principles, not the other way around. The case studies in this book are not meant to build toward a single set of conclusions, but rather to enrich the readers' experience and lead them to contemplate, from multiple immersions into the lives of different universities, central themes common and distinct to the world's leading research universities.

For each university I will discuss, in the course of the narratives, factors that may make for excellence or decline: the leadership of presidents, chancellors, and rectors; the quality of faculty and students; and the capacity of financial resources, among others. I will pay particular attention to three interlocking phenomena that may be traced to the founding of the University of Berlin in 1810: The first is the concept of a university devoted to scientific research at the highest level—*Wissenschaft*, be it in philosophy or physics. The second is a commitment to foster a culture of education in the liberal arts and sciences that stresses, in its most basic sense, *Bildung* (the education of the whole person), as distinct from *Übung* (more practical training). In Chinese, this is the distinction between a broad-based education, or *jiaoyu*, and *xunlian*, a narrower, more repetitive schooling. In this combination, this idealized "German model" would remake American higher education from the second half of the nineteenth century to the present; and today it is this model (now often viewed as "American") that is becoming part of the system of higher education in contemporary China.

A third, and defining, aspiration of the *moderne Original*, as today's Humboldt University likes to describe itself, is in the realm of governance, specifically governance that accords the university the autonomy to make its own appointments and set its own priorities, insulated to a high degree from political winds. In the making or breaking of great global universities, perhaps no criterion is more important than the quality of governance.

For Germany our cases are the University of Berlin, the mother of all modern research universities, known over time also as Friedrich Wilhelm University and later Humboldt University; and Free University of

Berlin, founded with American foundation support at the onset of the Cold War.

In the United States, the cases are Harvard, which I know well from thirty years as a faculty member and, more intimately, as a department chair, center director, and dean of its Faculty of Arts and Sciences in the 1990s and early 2000s; the University of California, Berkeley, the once-premier public university in the United States, now undergoing painful transitions; and Duke University, a rapidly rising private university whose global ambitions outstrip those of either Harvard or Berkeley.

In China we focus on Tsinghua University, founded in 1911 as an American-funded preparatory school in the arts and sciences, now China's premier institution of science, engineering, and economics; Nanjing University, the former National Central University of China's Nationalist government, founded on the model of the University of Berlin; and the University of Hong Kong, a British imperial university that aspires to be "Asia's Global University."

Disclosures

These universities are, of course, well known around the world, and they might be natural choices for any such book. I have chosen them also because I know them well from personal experience with each of them over the course of several decades. As a young scholar of German history, I studied in Berlin after college, receiving a German Academic Exchange Service fellowship to study at Free University of Berlin. Later, as a doctoral student and assistant professor in the field of modern Chinese history, I corresponded with and came to know well the outstanding cadre of sinologists at Humboldt University. Later still, I served on the International Advisory Board of Free University and studied the Berlin academic landscape more deeply. In the United States, apart from my time as a graduate student and (much later) a faculty member at Harvard, I served on multiple review committees for Berkeley, our peer and competitor in China studies and home to a leading Center for Higher Education Research, where I spent part of a semester as I began work on this book. I served as Senior Advisor on China for Duke University at its campus in Kunshan, China, and was frequently resident both in Durham and in Kunshan. I chaired the Academic Advisory Committee for the Schwarzman Scholars program at Tsinghua University and now sit on its board. I have visited Nanjing University and its nearby national archives of the pre-Communist era periodically since 1984. In Hong Kong, I served several terms on that city's University Grants Committee, which oversees its universities, and I was recently part of a major and controversial governance review of the University of Hong Kong.

So, I know these places well. That does not mean I study them uncritically. Above all, this book has emerged from my career as a historian—first of Germany and then of China—and as a practitioner of higher education, largely in the United States. As a young professor in my first position, at Washington University in St. Louis, I came to see how excellent leadership, strong but collegial governance, and a community of outstanding students and scholars could make a powerful difference in the life of an institution. When I accepted a deanship at Washington University, one of my doctoral advisers back at Harvard, John King Fairbank, wrote to me to say that he hoped it would prove "an early inoculation" from academic administration. That was not to be, and I have been fascinated with the making of academic excellence ever since.

Reasonable readers may wonder: How can a book on "the world of universities" leave out its oldest (Bologna); two of its most ancient, venerable, and still absolute best (Oxford and Cambridge); or the fast-growing and dynamic institutions that may be found in contemporary India? Of course, the excellence of Oxford and Cambridge long predated the rise of the research university in Germany. But it was only with the rise of the German model in the nineteenth century that Oxbridge scholars returning from Germany began to incorporate a research emphasis in their collegiate system.[9] Compared to China, India, with its vast, sprawling array of higher education institutions, does not have a robust arm of government to develop national higher education policy for quality assurance and funding.[10] Perhaps taking a page from China, only in 2020 did the Indian government launch an ambitious twenty-year plan to double its higher education capacity.[11]

In any event, no single book can do everything. Since my purpose is to explore both the leading sites and systems that clearly set global standards in the nineteenth, twentieth, and (possibly) twenty-first centuries, the choice of Germany, the United States, and China is compelling. The German, American, and Chinese universities studied in this book have all been, or aspire to be, global leaders. Throughout the book there will be references to how universities measure success and, in particular, how they have come to measure success against each other. This is the story of what we today call "rankings" or "league tables." It is the story of the quest for and measurement of leadership, the effort to be, or remain, world-class universities. So perhaps we should begin by investigating what it means to be "world class."

Rankings and Reputations in Global Higher Education

Contemporary government leaders, academic administrators, parents, and students have been concerned with understanding and identifying world-class universities. As nations race to develop innovation-driven economies, they find themselves in a global competition to nurture, attract, and retain top talent. Universities are seen as a key means to accomplishing this goal.[12] Nowhere is this more apparent than in China, where the central government has poured funding into its most elite institutions with the explicit goal of achieving world-class status. University administrations took the goal very seriously as well. For example, the 2011–2015 development plan of Tsinghua University included the phrase "world-class university" twenty-seven times.[13]

But what does "world class" mean? Philip Altbach, an American expert who has written widely on international higher education, recognized: "Everyone wants a world-class university. No country feels it can do without one. The problem is that no one knows what a world-class university is, and no one has figured out how to get one."[14] Scholars and the media have long tried to classify and quantify what makes a university great. No clear agreement has emerged, but there are common threads. Assessments of the quality of universities have taken many forms, but one type in particular stands out for its longevity and popularity: ranking tables. Widely disseminated and quick to read, national and international ranking tables became one of the most popular ways to quantify "world-class" achievement. Today, everything from fine wine to hotels to dishwashers is given grades or ranks. Why not universities?

The American (Now Global) Obsession with Rankings

Rankings began as an American pastime. One of the earliest examples of college rankings in the United States grew out of a more general project on the backgrounds of outstanding thinkers, led by psychologist James McKeen Cattell.[15] As part of a larger project on outstanding scholars, in 1910 Cattell compiled a list of the one thousand most distinguished "American Men of Science," fully ranked and grouped by deciles. He then aggregated information on where these men had attended school and worked, and he devel-

Table I.1. Top ten institutions by faculty (absolute) (0.5 faculty indicates an emeritus or part-time faculty member) (Source: James McKeen Cattell, ed., *American Men of Science: A Biographical Directory,* 2nd ed. [New York: The Science Press, 1910], 589.)

Rank	Institution	Number of "Men of Science" faculty
1	Harvard	79.5
2	Columbia	48
3	Chicago	47.5
4	Yale	38
5	Cornell	35
6	Johns Hopkins	33.5
7	Wisconsin	30
8	Department of Agriculture	28
9	Geological Survey	25.5
10	MIT	25

oped lists of institutions according to total number of distinguished faculty, total number of distinguished alumni, and ratio of distinguished faculty to the entire faculty body. Most important, one of his closing analyses listed the universities according to number of currently employed "Men of Science"—that is, faculty who did real research—weighted by each man's (and they were all men, then) individual ranking among his peers.

The importance of balancing the use of absolute and relative statistics was apparent from this first ranking: had Cattell ordered his chart according to the *ratio* of total number of faculty to number of "Men of Science," we would get a rather different outcome. For example, in 1910 Clark University—the Caltech of its day—was, pound for pound, far more distinguished in research than Harvard.

Cattell's work laid out the choices and trade-offs that have continued to confound ranking systems. Cattell's effort is an early example of one of the methodological pillars of rankings today: outcome-based analysis.[16] Outcome-based analyses judge universities on the basis of the various outputs and outcomes of their operations, such as famous alumni produced, prize-winning professors employed, or research papers published.

In 1924 chemist Raymond Hughes piloted a study that introduced the other pillar of modern ranking methodology: reputation-based analysis.[17] At the behest of the North Central Association of Schools and Colleges, he

Table I.2. Top ten institutions by faculty (relative) (Data source: James McKeen Cattell, ed., *American Men of Science: A Biographical Directory*, 2nd ed. [New York: The Science Press, 1910], 589.)

Rank	Institution	Ratio of total faculty: "Men of Science" faculty
1	Clark	2
2	Johns Hopkins	5.6
3	Chicago	6
4	Stanford	6.9
5	Harvard	7.8
6	Bryn Mawr	7.8
7	Wesleyan	8.5
8	Case	8.8
9	Princeton	9.8
10	MIT	10.1

surveyed faculty members at Miami University, asking them to rate twenty disciplines at thirty-six universities on a scale of one to five, and then aggregated these ratings into a comprehensive list. In the next iteration of his survey in 1934, Hughes surveyed respondents from a broader spread of universities, but he made aggregated results available only in alphabetical order, for his intention was not to determine a ranking. His work laid the foundation for a proliferation of reputation-based graduate program ranking systems in the 1950s and 1960s.

But it was not until 1983, with the first "America's Best Colleges" report by *U.S. News and World Report* (USNWR) that the general public gained access to and took interest in university rankings. *U.S. News and World Report* was a minor and failing newsweekly, outflanked by *Time* and *Newsweek*. It needed another mission, and it found one. "America's Best Colleges" began as a purely reputational survey and produced a ranking solely based on the opinions of university presidents. In response to criticism of its methodology, USNWR shifted its approach in 1988 to develop a ranking that was 25 percent reputational and 75 percent based on absolute data, including admissions and graduation rates, faculty performance, and so on. From then on, the USNWR ranking dominated the sphere of US university rankings at both the undergraduate and then graduate and professional levels, all now published annually.[18]

According to David S. Webster, "Just as democracy, according to Winston Churchill, is the worst form of government except for all the others, so quality rankings are the worst device for comparing the quality of American colleges and universities, except for all the others."[19] By the early 2000s, however, domestic US rankings were no longer the only ones that were debated. As faculty, students, jobs, and information became more globally mobile, universities found themselves in an increasingly internationalized marketplace. Globalization and the universal aspiration to world-class status led to a proliferation of ranking systems that compared institutions across national borders. This made a hard job even harder. It was difficult enough to try to objectively compare universities with a wide range of schools, specializations, and missions within even a single country like the United States.

But, despite the limitations of the rankings—and there are many—and the misgivings of university administrators and critics of higher education, who bemoan their ubiquity and their influence, the ranking systems did help establish a consensus for evaluation and comparison. Each system—*U.S. News and World Report*, the Shanghai Jiao Tong University Academic Ranking of World Universities (ARWU), *Times Higher Education World University Rankings*, and Quacquarelli Symonds (QS) World University Rankings—tended to place primary importance on the research produced at each university, perhaps the most easily quantifiable output. Outside the ranking systems, scholars and administrators established more nuanced definitions of greatness that incorporated abstract concepts such as academic freedom and institutional autonomy as well as measurable outputs such as faculty citations and prizes won by alumni. The common ground among the many definitions of "world class" lay in the consistent emphasis on excellence in three areas: faculty, students, and administration. More recently, and in China in particular, the definition of "world class" often also includes international and cultural exchange.

Faculty

A faculty of the highest quality that produces plentiful research is key in almost every conception of "world class." As Henry Rosovsky, former dean of the Faculty of Arts and Sciences at Harvard, argued, the best schools "correctly assume that the quality of the faculty is the most important factor in maintaining their reputation and position. The best faculty attracts the finest students, produces the highest-quality research, gains the most outside support."[20] But what policies attract high-quality faculty members?

How do universities ensure that an exemplary scholar continues to produce research?

The most basic requirement for plentiful, high-quality research output from faculty is academic autonomy. The concepts of "freedom to teach" (*Lehrfreiheit*) and "freedom to learn" (*Lernfreiheit*) were central to the world's first research university, the University of Berlin. As the model of the research university spread and evolved in Europe and the United States, the value of academic freedom allowed professors, as experts in their fields, to pursue research in areas to the extent that their interests and resources allowed. This expanded freedom of research (never perfect to be sure) allowed universities to become centers of innovation and discovery. The protection of academic freedom was linked to an implicit social contract between the professoriat and society at large—those afforded the time and space to carry out research had a duty to share their findings with society and work toward the greater good.[21]

Of course, much is missing in the rankings game. Rankings rank only what can be measured. They privilege research publication in select (largely English-language) international journals. Criteria such as citation indexes may be critical to the field of economics but rather unhelpful in Celtic language studies. International rankings can focus on major research prizes, and universities glory in having on their faculty Nobel laureates, taking credit for work often done decades earlier at another university.

As a rule, rankings studiously ignore teaching, education, and curriculum, let alone mentoring or inspiration. Universities have to evaluate teaching on their own, and they do so unevenly. Few universities actively reward good teaching professionally or financially. In principle, outstanding teaching can connect cutting-edge faculty research with the nurturing of talented students. But even the best teaching and mentorship may be only vaguely represented in rankings by other measures, such as faculty-to-student ratios.

The centrality of faculty to the creation of world-class universities can be a financial and organizational burden for university administrations. Attracting the best faculty who are distinguished in research can mean entering a bidding war not unlike that in European football. Who would not want the Lionel Messi of the life sciences? Recruitment of the best requires outsized compensation, extraordinary resources, and facilities (often new), not to mention time *off* from teaching. Tenure systems, begun in part as a means to ensure academic autonomy, are now inextricably linked with competition among universities. To recruit or retain the very best in an international, competitive environment, universities have to offer lifelong tenure. Today, no national system of higher education is recruiting more vigorously across national borders than that of China. But China's Thousand Talents Program is but the latest example of a recruitment game long tested in the West.

Students

Universities would not exist without students. The ability to attract top students and nurture exceptional and productive graduates (however these may be defined) is another key facet of a world-class university. A world-class university needs admissions mechanisms that allow it to recruit and admit students with the highest potential. Once admitted, students are exposed to new ideas and inspiring research. While the quality of faculty certainly affects the development of students, equally important is the quality of fellow students and, not the least, the nature of the curriculum.

In discussions of global excellence in universities, a curriculum based in the liberal arts (often in the form of general education requirements) is frequently cited as the central means to nurture students' future potential as citizens. The late president of the University of Iowa and Dartmouth College, James O. Freedman, one of the most articulate American advocates for an education in the liberal arts and sciences, stressed the public purpose of undergraduate education: "A liberal education seeks to strengthen students' capacities to deal with the world's and the nation's agendas, to expand their horizons, enrich their intellect, and deepen their spirit. It asks them to accept responsibility for their actions and for the welfare of others."[22] A 2013 report of the American Academy of Arts and Sciences, *The Heart of the Matter,* argued that an education in the humanities and social sciences was a national imperative for the United States, essential "1) to educate Americans in the knowledge, skills, and understanding they will need to thrive in a twenty-first-century democracy; 2) to foster a society that is innovative, competitive, and strong; and 3) to equip the nation for leadership in an interconnected world. These goals cannot be achieved by [natural] science alone."[23]

To be sure, exhortations to bolster the liberal arts are more than matched by academic hand-wringing about how their perceived virtues (e.g., teaching critical thinking, building character, educating for citizenship) are absent in practice.[24] Further, there is no consensus on how the liberal arts ought best be taught. As I recall from Harvard's own review of undergraduate education in the first decade of the 2000s, when, as dean, I commissioned sets of faculty and student essays on general education, there is no shortage of imaginative and quite divergent views on what an education in the liberal arts and sciences entails.[25]

Still, the idea remains powerful and global. In the early twenty-first century, European and Chinese universities began to emulate the practices of American liberal arts colleges, often in the form of elite honors colleges within research universities. Aspiring world-class universities sought ways to balance the holistic development of their students with the depth of their specialist knowledge.

Governance

Universities commonly deemed "world class" may be said to have another distinguishing trait: they enjoy flexible and effective governance systems, largely insulated from political interference in their appointments and education, and with sufficient resources to implement their visions. This was the nineteenth-century Humboldtian vision, seldom realized perfectly anywhere. In the United States, most universities developed a governance system led by a president, at the top of an administrative hierarchy, and a board of trustees. Ideally this management structure allowed even publicly funded universities to (mostly) base decisions on the best interests of the institution, without being swept up in the political tides. But as the eminent scholar of American higher education Jonathan Cole, the former provost of Columbia University, argues, among the greatest threats faced by universities today is "government intrusion into the freedom of academic inquiry."[26]

Yet governments are essential to the lives and livelihoods of universities. Jamil Salmi, a leading scholar of international higher education, argues that in the current globalized world, "it is unlikely that a world-class university can be rapidly created without a favorable policy environment and direct public initiative and support."[27] A challenge for aspiring world-class universities today, as for German, American, and Chinese universities over the past two centuries, is to foster cooperative relationships with supportive, but not stifling, governments. Finding a relationship with the state that, as Goldilocks might say, is "just right," turns out not to be easy.

Regardless of political influences from outside the university, world-class universities also need effective systems of governance within their walls. For example, in most leading American universities, key budgeting or potentially contentious decisions are made by appointed deans, provosts, or other administrators rather than by faculty committees. German universities, by contrast, have traditions of elected deans and presidents, a process that Henry Rosovsky suggests "ensures that leadership is weak."[28] Chinese universities have experimented with every conceivable model over the last century, but today the growing role of the Communist Party in university administration brings the prospect of strong but perhaps not responsive leadership.

Internationalization

While found in only three out of the four main ranking systems, international engagement is frequently cited as a criterion for world-class universities, especially in China. International engagement appears in many different ways on university campuses, including an internationally diverse faculty and student body, international academic exchange programs, and the founding of stand-alone or joint-venture international branch campuses. The current internationalization of universities has both responded to and led economic globalization, as universities compete to host a "global community of future leaders," as Tsinghua University claims for one of its flagship programs.[29] This, too, is not new: the leading universities studied in this book have each been the product of several centuries of academic internationalization.

The Rule of Rankings

As discussions of world-class universities became an academic cottage industry in the twenty-first century, definitions of the term grew complex and, at times, contradictory. Chinese officials tended to emphasize contribution to the public good as a defining mark of a world-class university.[30] Others stressed the role of a university in innovation, while a few argued instead for the centrality of tradition.[31] It was unclear whether definitions would converge on a few key ideas or become more diverse over time.

Perhaps the debate over the meaning of "world class" was in part a reaction to the worship of rankings, which could drive universities to focus only on that which was ranked, rather than on a broad mission of academic exploration and discovery. Might not rankings—all of which measured past activity—in fact impede creativity in the building of new or renewed institutions? Yet the presidents, provosts, and deans around the world who ritually denounced the tyranny of rankings to their governing boards still did their best every day to rise in them.

And rankings do show, however imperfectly, the shifting tectonic plates of global leadership in higher education. Had rankings such as those issued by Shanghai Jiao Tong University (the ARWU ranking), read today by deans and presidents around the world, existed a century ago, German universities would still have held pride of place. Harvard University, which ranks very well at the present, would not have been in the top ten, perhaps not in the top twenty; it became a research university worthy of the name only in the late nineteenth century by emulating the practices of the University of Berlin. Today, at least according to the QS rankings, Peking University and Tsinghua University outperform *every* German university. Times change.

CHAPTER ONE

The University in Germany

A Historical Introduction

A T THE center of Berlin, on the central avenue Unter den Linden, sits an armory, or *Zeughaus*, built by Frederick III, Elector of Brandenburg, in the late seventeenth and early eighteenth centuries. It became a military museum in 1875 under the unified Prussian-German Empire. In 1943 it was the site of a failed attempt to assassinate Adolf Hitler. Today it is home to the German Historical Museum.

Visitors entering the museum are introduced not to the story of "Germany," which as a political entity did not exist before 1870, but to the history of German-speaking peoples in a European context, whether under Prussian, Polish, Austrian, or French rule. Visitors progress through exhibits from late Roman times through to the Middle Ages. They experience the Reformation and the Thirty Years' War from alternative perspectives; dynastic rivalries between the Bourbons and the Habsburgs; the French Revolution and Napoleonic conquests; the abortive revolutions of 1848; Germany's unification and its defeat in World War I; the Weimar experiment; Hitler's rise, genocide, and Germany's demise in World War II. Then at 1949, the exhibit divides, and visitors must decide: to go left is to be greeted by a Trabant, the spunky socialist fiberglass auto, and to enter the German Democratic Republic; to go right is to be escorted by a Volkswagen bug to the Western world of the German Federal Republic. When visitors reach 1990, the exhibit, like Germany, reunites.

Like the path of German history, the story of German universities is not linear. As with the landscape traversed by the museum, some German-founded universities are no longer in the territory of any German-speaking state. The East Prussian University of Königsberg, for example, where Immanuel Kant taught and served as rector in the late eighteenth century, lies now in the Russian Federation, the site of a federal university recently renamed for Kant by Vladimir Putin. Today the University of Heidelberg calls itself "Germany's oldest university," but that is true only if one limits German geography to the present Federal Republic.[1] Scattered across the lands of the Holy Roman Empire, the medieval and early modern establishments that called themselves "universities" bore little resemblance to the research institutions that would transform the world of universities in the nineteenth century and beyond.

With papal blessing, Emperor Charles IV, who was also king of Bohemia, founded the University of Prague in 1348 to educate Bohemians, Bavarians, Poles, and Saxons, although it took the university more than a decade to produce its first graduate. His son-in-law, Rudolf IV, Duke of Austria, followed suit in 1365 with the University of Vienna. Divisions in Christianity fed the establishment of new institutions. The Western Schism of 1378 and ensuing confrontation led to the founding of the universities of Heidelberg (1386), Cologne (1388), and Erfurt (1392), as existing ecclesiastical institutions were enlarged into universities. A regional bishop typically administered the university, which was, in principle, subject only to the Emperor. After the establishment of universities in Greifswald in 1456 and Freiburg (Breisgau) in 1457, it was common practice to possess the "privileges" of the emperor, such as certain exemptions from taxation and military service, in addition to the one given by the pope. German universities had a public character from birth.

German universities grew in number, if not distinction, when the Protestant Reformation of the sixteenth century increased demand for institutions whose religious affiliations aligned with those of a sovereign: *cuius regio, eius religio* ("whose realm, his religion"). Before the Reformation, there were fifteen universities in German-speaking lands; by 1700 this number had doubled.

These were universally small institutions reliant on imperial, papal, or princely patronage. Enrollment and teaching positions fluctuated considerably; some universities came close to extinction. Enrollment at the best-regarded institutions ranged between one thousand and twelve hundred students, but the smallest universities had but eighty to one hundred attendees. Reputations rose and fell. No single university dominated the landscape. In the early fifteenth century, Erfurt and Cologne were among the largest and most eminent. A century later, Leipzig and Ingolstadt rose to prominence. Humanism and the Reformation gave Wittenberg and Leipzig, as well as Helmstedt, Frankfurt an der Oder, Jena, and Ingolstadt their days in the sun. During the Thirty Years' War, Königsberg, Rostock, and Cologne became comparatively large universities, with students fleeing war conflict zones and—in the best tradition of university students of any era—avoiding military conscription.

German universities in the eighteenth century trained men for professions, such as in medicine, the clergy, or (by studying law) the government. Universities were, in principle, the apogee of a variegated system of schools of highly uneven quality. Most of these served different segments of society for very specific functions. Cadet schools trained officers for the military, while seminaries graduated pastors. Aristocratic families sent young men to what we may call "knight schools"—the *Ritterakademien*—that became popular in the late sixteenth century as places to learn military and courtly manners. Sons of artisans and merchants studied at Latin schools for several years before learning a trade. These schools were not part of any systematic hierarchy, and, as a result, there was no single path to university. Whatever their type, these schools were mostly "ill-equipped, poorly run, and badly attended."[2]

The behavior of students did not enhance the reputation of universities. Eighteenth-century versions of *National Lampoon's Animal House* made universities infamous for intoxication and immorality—with brawling accompanied by swordplay (although the *Schmisse,* or dueling scar, would not become popular until the nineteenth century). The late-eighteenth century educational reformer Joachim Heinrich Campe asked rhetorically, "Do universities do more good than harm?" His answer was no. "The best young people are, if not destroyed completely, at least made wild at universities and return from them weakened in body and soul, lost to themselves and the world."[3]

Even—or perhaps especially—in the century of Enlightenment, German universities had a simply awful reputation. While in Paris and Oxford university life flourished, attracting scholars from across Europe, in Germany universities remained largely provincial. It was not a compliment when they were called "medieval." They were considered sites of rote learning, imparted to students by a professoriat reciting ancient texts and largely beholden to church and sovereign.[4] Professors lectured and (on occasion) published in Latin. Leading intellectuals largely made their reputations apart from university life. The great mathematician and philosopher Gottfried Wilhelm Leibniz thought of universities as monasteries with "sterile fancies."[5] He convinced the Elector of Brandenburg *not* to establish a new university, but to found instead (in 1700) a *Societät der Wissenschaften*, which became the Royal Prussian Academy of Sciences.

There were, however, attempts in the eighteenth century to reform the potential of German universities. The practical needs of the state with a growing bureaucracy, as well as early Enlightenment currents, gave impetus to rethinking the role of the university. The University of Halle was founded in 1694 by the same, reformist Elector of Brandenburg (Frederick III). It was built on the grounds of an existing *Ritterakademie*, to which were added faculties of theology and law. Early Enlightenment figures, like Christian Thomasius in Halle, sought to transform universities from places of orthodoxy and dogma and into havens for reflection and free speech well suited to the modern state. Thomasius began to lecture at Halle in the German vernacular, rather than in Latin. He brought together the medieval with the modern, in a curriculum that covered riding, fencing, and preparation for the Prussian civil service. Halle was also a business success, competing successfully for the offspring of the nobility (who paid higher fees than others) by combining an early modern "general education" with a contemporary legal education.[6]

Halle's early success (it would not last) inspired competition from the House of Hanover, now in union with Great Britain and a rival of Prussia. Founded in 1737 by George II of England and Elector of Hanover, the University of Göttingen foreshadowed in some ways the coming of the modern research university. It was nonsectarian; the state confirmed professorial appointments; it recruited talent from across German Europe by paying high salaries; it developed a strong *Philosophische Fakultät*, encompassing the arts and sciences; and, for eminently practical reasons, it brought together a superb law faculty. As a leading figure in Göttingen's rise, the Hanoverian official Gerlach Adolf von Münchhausen, noted, "That the legal faculty be filled with famous and excellent men is necessary above all, because that faculty must induce many rich and distinguished students to study in Göttingen."[7] Göttingen cultivated an enviable, internal esprit de corps. When in 1789 the Prussian minister Friedrich Gedike reported to King Frederick William II on the state of German universities, he wrote this about Göttingen: "Nowhere else have I found as much fondness for their university on the part of professors as here. They seem to take it as a foregone conclusion that their university is the best in Germany. They often speak of other universities with disdain or pity. It's as if they are all intoxicated with pride in the university's merits—partly real, partly alleged, and partly imagined." At least from a Prussian point of view, Göttingen was a scholarly paradise. Gedike found little of the "factionalization, envy, backbiting, and need to diminish one another's accomplishments" that was ubiquitous in other universities. "Or, at least, they are less apparent here."[8]

The University of Jena was another beacon of excellence. Located in the duchy of Saxe-Weimar, it reached its height in the second half of the eighteenth century under the Duke Karl August, who was Goethe's patron. It was a center of German idealism, where at different times the faculty included Fichte, Hegel, Schelling, and Schlegel. Even Schiller taught there briefly.

Yet the German university "system," to the degree one can describe it as such, still suffered from stasis and educated the privileged few at the turn of the nineteenth century. It remained polycentric, still (despite Göttingen's pretensions) with no single leading institution. It relied on princely patronage and the high tuition charged to noble and elite families, but its audience was shrinking, not growing. German universities outside Austria enrolled in toto, at most, nine thousand students in 1700. A century later, enrollments had fallen by at least one-third, to less than six thousand. Other estimates put the number as low as thirty-seven hundred in 1780.[9] To the degree that innovation had occurred at all, it was in the newer institutions of Halle and Göttingen, not in the large majority of institutions, where a lethargic and privileged professoriat defended its historical practices. In the view of educational reformers such as Campe, it was too late to reform: "To change the nature of the universities means to abolish them."[10] At the turn of the nineteenth century, the Prussian minister responsible for higher education proposed just that: the total elimination of the university as an institution.[11]

That this did not happen was in no small measure the result of the efforts generously attributed to a home-schooled man who never finished his university studies at Frankfurt an der Oder and Göttingen: Wilhelm von Humboldt. His story, and that of the University of Berlin, which he initiated in

1810 and which became the exemplar of the modern research university, is the subject of Chapter 2. Here we might simply set out several themes that endured from the pre-Humboldtian world of German universities to the world of universities today.

First, even after the ascendance of the University of Berlin over the course of the nineteenth century to a position of national and international eminence, German higher education remained decentralized, in the hands of the various political entities governing German-speaking lands. Despite several German unifications (1870, 1938, 1990) there would be no "national university." Today, it is still the individual states (*Länder*) of the Federal Republic that oversee German universities. Universities rose and fell in prestige and in competition one with another: if in the eighteenth century this was a competition for students, in the twenty-first century it is a race for recognition in an "Excellence Initiative."

Second, modern German universities inherited from their medieval and early modern ancestors certain traditions of institutional autonomy, initially as corporations, which set their own procedures of governance and were guarded jealously. Whereas in the eighteenth century this often fostered a defensive insularity and a stultifying pedantry, the self-regulating capacity of a renewed professoriat in the nineteenth century to set new standards of research and teaching would differentiate the German university from anything else. And disputes over internal governance would nearly bring German universities to their knees in the 1960s.

Third, from early modern times to nearly the present, governance meant the rule not just of professors, but of *Ordinarien,* of full professors. Nineteenth century reforms formally established the *Ordinarienuniversität,* or a university of chaired professors, as the norm. There were three basic ranks of faculty: the *Ordinarius,* or *ordentlicher* (full) *Professor,* who held a chair, or *Lehrstuhl;* what we might translate as associate professor, appropriately named *Extraordinarius,* or *außerordentlicher Professor,* whose only hope at a professorship was to be "called" to another university; and below that, the ranks of the *Privatdozent,* the learned scholar with a doctorate and a post-doctorate *Habilitation,* who was not formally a member of the faculty and was not a civil servant. This was (and is still today) no "tenure-track" system. Chaired professors ruled in their area of expertise; faculties were built around seminars or institutes, each headed by a chaired professor with an assemblage of academic help.[12] German universities created both a tradition of senior faculty rule and a class of permanently adjunct faculty.

Fourth, as a result, academic leadership of an institution seldom came from the top. A dean was seldom more than a coordinator of chairs. The rector, a chaired professor who nominally headed the university, was primus inter pares, representing the chairs externally. The rector was elected from among the chaired professors for a two-year term; and for the University of Berlin, it was a *nonrenewable* term until the 1930s. Only in the second half of the twentieth century was the position renamed "president." Presidents were officers who did not have to be professors nor members of the university, although normally they were.

Fifth, while professorial self-governance, an eventually rigorous appointment process, and generous funding of professorial chairs helped to make German universities extraordinary innovators in research in the nineteenth century, the absence of strong administrative leadership in the university meant that the states that funded German universities could, and at times would, have a decisive voice in determining their direction. Examples include the founding of the University of Berlin in 1810, its eminence in the natural sciences under the guidance of a strong Prussian minister in the late nineteenth century, and its Nazification in 1933.

Sixth, although German universities became global models in the nineteenth and early twentieth centuries, dissatisfaction with their limits spawned the growth of external research organizations. Just as Leibniz convinced the Elector of Brandenburg to found an Academy of Sciences in 1700, so two centuries later would Emperor William II establish the scientific societies that we today know as the Max Planck institutes—powerful engines of research but connected to German universities only along dotted lines. And in Communist East Germany, a revived Academy of Sciences (now on a Soviet model) competed with universities for funding and talent.

Finally, traditions of student independence and assertive behavior would endure as German universities matured in the nineteenth century and massified in the late twentieth. Dueling scars would be a badge of honor in German universities until the Nazis outlawed the practice in the 1930s. But it was political activism on the part of students that would repeatedly test institutions and governments. Nationalist student fraternities (*Burschenschaften*) would be banned in the era of Metternichian repression after 1819. Students would challenge the communization of the University of Berlin in 1948 and found their own, "free" university that same year. Twenty years later, students at Free University became poster children for the global left as they disrupted classes and sought to defenestrate professors.

These continuities matter, but they must not obscure the point. As Daniel Fallon has written in his study of *The German University*, the reinvention of the university in the nineteenth century was a radical act: "Perhaps the most remarkable fact about the widely admired German university of the nineteenth century is that it had no clear precedent." The idea of a *research* university was struck de novo.[13]

Contemplate the changing fate of German universities. By 1800 German universities were at once ancient and outmoded, ripe for abolition. A half-century later, the first president of the University of Michigan, Henry Philip Tappan, wrote: "The system of public instruction adopted by the State of Michigan is copied from the Prussian, acknowledged to be the most perfect in the world." By the late nineteenth century, the president of Clark University, then a leading institution of engineering and applied science in the United States, wrote: "The German University is today the freest spot on earth. . . . Nowhere has the passion to push on to the frontier of human knowledge been so general." Two world wars later, the former president of Harvard and the former American ambassador to West Germany, James B. Conant, was nostalgic as he called the German university "the best in the world—for the nineteenth century."[14]

Few would argue that German universities are the "best in the world" today. But they once were, and they are striving toward revival. In contemporary league tables, no matter what the ranking system, no German university enters the top twenty, and only a handful are listed in the top one hundred. The first ARWU ranking of 2003 prompted soul searching in Germany, as not a single German university was to be found among the top fifty.[15] It prompted, too, strategies for a return to "excellence."

As we shall see, in recent years German politicians and administrators have puzzled over how to claw their way back to the top, how to reignite dynamic research and recruit top international researchers. Europe-wide higher education reforms officially introduced in 1999 called the "Bologna Process" led German universities to streamline antiquated and idiosyncratic degree systems, making them more accessible to international students. The popular Erasmus program—a European Union–wide student exchange program—increased mobility and internationalization. Universities pooled resources to attract and retain talent. Three rounds of funding to reward distinctive, especially high-potential programming in the form of a nationwide "Excellence Initiative" propelled certain institutions forward, equipping them for research and teaching in the twenty-first century.

The best way to understand the rise, destruction, and revival of German higher education is to take a closer look at two universities. Although they are both located in the Prussian (now German) capital of Berlin, in many respects they are from two different worlds. Chapters 2 and 3 chart the histories of Humboldt University and Free University in Berlin. They provide case studies that allow a revealing look into the past and future of German higher education.

CHAPTER TWO

The Modern Original

The University of Berlin

A s you enter the gates of today's Humboldt University, you pass the marble statues of the two men who became the university's namesakes. One was the scholar and statesman Wilhelm von Humboldt; the other, his great naturalist brother, Alexander. Located on Unter den Linden in the heart of Berlin, the main building once was home to the younger brother of Frederick the Great. Across the street from the university sits the Stadtschloß, the magnificent urban palace of the Hohenzollern monarchs that dates from the fifteenth century, was blown up by the Communists in the mid-twentieth century, and has now been reconstructed and reconceived in the twenty-first century as a cultural center at the heart of Germany's, and in some sense Europe's, capital.

Entering the university's *Hauptgebäude*, or main building, you find yourself in a grand foyer of red marble from East German mines. A grand staircase leads you to a landing with a large quotation in gold letters by one of the university's most famous alumni, Karl Marx. "Philosophers have only interpreted the world in various ways; the point, however, is to change it." The Communist regime had ordered the installation of Marx's epigrammatic eleventh thesis on Feuerbach in 1953, when the university was convulsed in change. Today, the stairs leading up to Marx's call to action are adorned with a satirical art installation. Each step forward warns: *"Vorsicht Stufe"* ("Beware of the step").

Arriving on the second level of the *Hauptgebäude*, the portraits of the university's twenty-nine Nobel laureates greet you. Among them are Fritz

Figure 2.1. Main building of Humboldt University. Beek100/Wikimedia Commons/CC BY-SA 3.0.

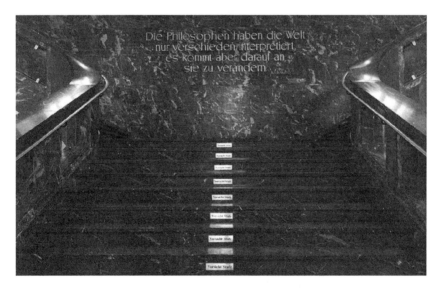

Figure 2.2. Karl Marx quote at Humboldt University. Photograph © William C. Kirby.

Haber, whose work made possible the production of reactive nitrogen, used in fertilizers; Theodor Mommsen, the renowned classical scholar, historian, and jurist; Robert Koch, who discovered the pathogens that cause infectious diseases; Otto Hahn, who conducted the first nuclear fission experiment; Max Planck, the founder of quantum theory; and, most famously, Albert Einstein.

From the red marble staircase, the way to the president's office leads down a long and wide corridor characteristic of eighteenth century neoclassical architecture. More impressive is the height of the ceilings, which makes it nearly impossible to cool the offices in summer or heat them in winter. Solitude and freedom, Wilhelm von Humboldt noted, were necessary to the proper functioning of the university. But in the case of Humboldt's recent leaders, solitude could feel more like isolation.

The University of Berlin was founded on the promise of change. As the world's first modern research university, it was a global model of innovation in research, teaching, and governance. In 2021, its president, Sabine Kunst, confronted the challenge of energizing an institution burdened by its history and enervated by a governance structure that has become belatedly (and perhaps too) democratic. After all, her predecessor declined his candidacy for a second term after failed attempts to change the university's leadership structure. Indeed, none of her predecessors since the fall of the Berlin Wall in 1989 completed more than a single term. Kunst came into office aware of the many challenges facing her: from a severely constrained financial situation, to the overdue professionalization of administration, to the pressure to be successful in the ongoing national "Excellence Initiative."

The experience of one of her recent predecessors, Christoph Markschies, was not promising. When greeting an international assembly of scholars (of which this author was one) to mark the two hundredth anniversary of the founding of the University at Berlin, Markschies noted that the university was home to "Humboldt's model." But what did that mean? Was it, he wondered, the "kind of university which developed into the Prussian State University in the middle of the nineteenth century . . . which was to be perverted by National Socialism and anti-Semitism, which finally degenerated at the hands of a petty bourgeoisie masquerading as Marxist"? In all these contexts, he noted, the university had been a model, "at first with worldwide recognition, then in the 'Großdeutsches Reich,' and finally, in East Germany."[1]

But what was the university today? In the two centuries that separated Humboldt from Markschies, the ambitions of the new university and its leadership had been repeatedly frustrated by political turmoil, restrictions on academic freedom, and cycles of financial hardship. In his welcoming address to this international conference on "Humboldt's Model," Markschies, in one of his final speeches as university president, told the assembled and astonished guests, "Today nobody anywhere in the world is prepared to take this university, which is financially and otherwise in the hands of one of the poorest States in the Federal Republic, as a model."[2]

Founding the Modern Research University, 1810–1848

The University of Berlin, predecessor to the modern Humboldt University and to Free University of Berlin, was heir to multiple and mixed legacies. For its first century and more, it was literally and figuratively in the shadow of the palace, in the direct service of the Prussian-German state. It was home to the birth of modern scientific research in a university setting. It witnessed political battles for Germany's and the university's soul.

The University of Berlin was an upstart in comparison with venerable institutions such as Bologna (founded in 1088), Salamanca (1164), Oxford (1167), and Cambridge (1209). In German-speaking lands, Vienna (1365), Heidelberg (1386), Leipzig (1409), and Rostock (1419) all held pride of place. Yet Berlin would outdo them all by reimagining what a university could be. Within decades of its founding in 1810, the university developed into one of the world's leading institutions of higher education. It would lead Germany and eventually the world in creating a modern system of research-driven higher education.

In the beginning was Napoleon.[3] Two weeks after Napoleon and his army defeated Prussia at the battlefield outside Jena on October 14, 1806, French forces marched through the Brandenburg Gate, occupying and plundering Berlin. Remnant Prussian forces and King Frederick William III retreated to the East Prussian stronghold of Königsberg. The following year the Treaty of Tilsit brought a harsh peace. Prussia lost not only more than half of its territory but also its six universities west of the Elbe River. The French Revolution and Napoleon's conquests left Europe's university landscape devastated: in 1815, 60 of the 143 European universities that had existed before 1789 were closed. In the German states, 18 out of 34 universities were shuttered.[4] The University of Halle (established in 1694), Prussia's leading university at the time and a center of the eighteenth-century German Enlightenment, was among them. The French occupiers first turned the university into a military hospital; later its main building became a slaughterhouse. When a delegation of faculty from Halle visited King Frederick William III, he agreed to open a "general educational institution" (*allgemeine Lehranstalt*) in Berlin. "The state," the king reasoned, in a phrase seldom heard from political leaders, "must replace with intellectual strength what it has lost in physical strength."[5]

At the turn of the nineteenth century, Berlin was home to around 170,000 inhabitants and, despite being home to a vibrant, cosmopolitan community of intellectuals, doctors, lawyers, and artists, the city continued to suffer from a reputation as a garrison city. The Prussian capital could not rival Vienna in cultural terms. Furthermore, there was no university in the city. King Frederick William III's decision to establish new universities stimulated debate among educational reform thinkers such as Johann Gottlieb Fichte, Friedrich Schleiermacher, and Friedrich August Wolf. The critical move took place, however, when Friedrich Wilhelm Christian Karl Ferdinand Freiherr von Humboldt (Wilhelm von Humboldt) was appointed Director of the Section for Ecclesiastical Affairs and Education at the Ministry of the Interior in 1810.

Figure 2.3. Wilhelm von Humboldt, 1767–1835. Humboldt-Universität zu Berlin, Universitätsbibliothek.

Wilhelm von Humboldt was a man of letters of the German Enlightenment and a lifelong friend of Friedrich Schiller. He became a philosopher, linguist, philologist, diplomat, and, very briefly, a reformer of education. His work in each of these fields was notable, but he is known best for the sixteen months he spent in Berlin, in between diplomatic postings to the Vatican and Vienna. There he set out plans to reform all levels of public education: reshaping elementary schools to focus on individual growth and founding a new type of secondary school, the *Gymnasium*. And there he oversaw the founding of the University of Berlin. While his administrative commitment was limited in time, it was time well spent. The "Humboldtian" model largely shaped the world of modern universities.

What were German universities like before Humboldt? As we have seen, they were small, scattered, and largely undistinguished. There were but a few thousand students in *all* German universities by 1780. Many families could not afford the "idle time" for their sons.[6] The professoriat was paid poorly enough that most had second jobs or other income. Nepotism was rampant. As Charles McClelland notes, "Had the princely bureaucracies listened to whatever there was of public opinion in the late eighteenth century, they probably would have abolished the universities along with serfdom and other relics of the Middle Ages."[7]

Two institutions, Halle and Göttingen, sought to raise the quality of their faculty by being pioneers in recruiting "stars" from elsewhere and paying them more. Universities were largely preprofessional in training for medicine, theology, and law, the latter of which was a stepping-stone to government service. By the end of the eighteenth century, many German states required some level of university education as a prerequisite to an official position.[8]

The idea that universities might serve and strengthen the state was thus not new, but with the founding of the University of Berlin this idea took a different form. Under the Stein-Hardenberg policies—named for the ministers who oversaw them—Prussia began its transformation into a modern administrative state. Government finances and administration were rationalized and gradually professionalized; municipalities were given powers of self-government, in part to create a broader interest in public affairs; the army was rebuilt; serfdom was abolished; Jews were "emancipated" from a wide range of discriminatory laws; and education was thoroughly reformed.

What was the role of the university in Prussia's renewal? Humboldt had already set to paper in 1792 (although not published) his theory of "The

Limits of State Action." Universities, Humboldt believed, would serve the state best *indirectly*. Just as his reforms of primary schools were designed to produce "well informed human beings and citizens" who could learn their vocations later, his vision of the university was one centered on the cultivation of individual capacities that, if allowed to develop freely, would best serve state and society.[9] His conception of *Bildung*, as the historian David Sorkin has argued, had both inward and civic dimensions: inward in the making of a learned, moral personality with "inner refinement"; civic in the engagement of educated men in society.[10]

Humboldt's conception of the new University of Berlin was part of a movement for "national education" (*Nationalerziehung*) led by the philosopher Johann Gottlieb Fichte, but one that should not be, in Humboldt's view, instrumentally nationalistic. Humboldt's reforms cut across social divides. He radically proposed that education should not be shaped by one's occupational or social standing, but that, "the lowest wage worker and the finest educated man must be equal in their dispositions (*Gemüt*)."[11] To achieve this, he recommended a common curriculum for all. Elementary schools would teach basic skills. High schools (*Gymnasien*) would teach not only *what* to learn but *how* to learn, and impart a degree of intellectual independence. There students would receive a "general education" (*allgemeine Menschenbildung*) in the classics, history, and mathematics.[12]

Humboldt spoke of the university as a community of teachers and students who would "devote themselves to science."[13] *Wissenschaft* incorporated learning, knowing, scholarship, and "science" in the broadest sense, including—especially—the humanities. The university would conduct scientific research at the highest level, emphasizing the transmission of knowledge to the next generation. Students would be selected on the basis of talent more than hereditary lineage; general education was offered to all on an equal basis. The university would foster a culture of liberal education that stressed education (in the sense of *Bildung*) as a progression of personal development distinct from practical training (*Übung*) in the professions.

Like other humanists of the day, Humboldt wanted to do away with what Schiller had called *Brotstudium* for careerist "bread students" seeking a moneymaking job. The aim was instead to foster the full self-development of a student's interests, capacities, and personality.[14] Humboldt convinced King Frederick William III to build on the liberal ideas of Friedrich Schleiermacher, who had petitioned the monarch to create a university, not to stress the practical, but "to stimulate the idea of science in the minds of the students, to encourage them to take account of the fundamental laws of science in all their thinking."[15]

Humboldt laid forth a new model for a university. It had three core principles. The first was the principle of the unity of research and teaching. It confirmed professors' responsibility to produce and disseminate original research for their teaching, which was quite new in 1810. At the same time, it introduced students to methods of research—for example, by supplementing lectures with small seminars and encouraging research-based study.

The second principle was the protection of academic freedom. Students were at liberty to pursue any curriculum of their choosing. Professors, in turn, had freedom of unrestricted inquiry in their teaching. *Lehrfreiheit,* the freedom to teach, and *Lernfreiheit,* the freedom to learn, became fundamentally intertwined principles. The state's role with regard to the university was to protect its freedom, not to impede it. To that end, Humboldt proposed that the university be financially independent, with its own endowment, making it a truly national institution at arm's length from the government.

The third principle was the centrality in the university of the *Philosophische Fakultät,* what in the United States today would be called the Faculty of Arts and Sciences. All students had to start their studies with arts and sciences and only then continue in specialized subjects. An education that would form creative individuals by the pursuit of knowledge would be, in time, the greatest contribution to the state that a university could make.[16]

These are principles echoed today in every college or university that professes to value the liberal arts and sciences. They would be difficult to achieve from the start.

When the university opened its doors for the winter semester of 1810, a commission led by Schleiermacher called fifty-three of Germany's most eminent scholars to Berlin. Humboldt understood that the selection of an outstanding faculty was, at the beginning and end of the day, "the crux of the matter."[17] These 53 men taught 256 students, largely, as Humboldt had intended, from non-aristocratic backgrounds. The first rector, the jurist Theodor Schmalz, was named in 1810, and he lasted but a year, having fought (and won) the first battle against censorship in the university.

Johann Gottlieb Fichte, the Idealist philosopher known best at the time for his patriotic *Reden an die deutsche Nation* at the height of the Napoleonic humiliation, became the first elected rector in July 1811. In his inaugural address to the university, he assured his audience of notables, professors, and students of the university's lofty goals in preserving the progress of humanity, and "that at no university in the world is academic freedom more secure and firmly in place as right here at this university."[18] He quickly came at odds with student groups, who—perhaps not surprisingly—were more interested in learning a profession and forging social ties than they were invested in the university's liberal curriculum.

Fichte, too, witnessed the university's first faculty controversy over student behavior. A Jewish student who had been challenged to a duel by a Christian student and member of a *Burschenschaft*, a nationalist student fraternity, declined and thereafter suffered public humiliation and ultimately an attack with a hunting whip in broad daylight.[19] The incident epitomized the way that rigid social customs among the student organizations terrorized perceived outsiders. Fichte resolved to make an example of the case. Yet his attempt to pursue the matter was prevented by the university senate. Instead, the affair was tried before a student "court of honor" with a severe punishment for the victim. As a result of this conflict and the ensuing bitterness, Fichte resolved to resign; he left office by February 1812.[20] The administrative half-life of the leaders of modern universities was, from the beginning, short.

The university grew and thrived, albeit in ways different than Humboldt had imagined. In its first decades it expanded by integrating existing institutions and infrastructure. The Charité, founded by Frederick the Great in 1726 as a "plague" hospital to treat the poor and infirm, became the Faculty of Medicine. A school of animal medicine became the Faculty of Veterinary Medicine. The royal library served as the university's first library.

To secure the university's independence, Humboldt suggested the university be provided with an endowment in the form of a large grant of royal land, but this plan was abandoned by his successors. Not only in finances, but also in governance, the university was intimately tied to the powers of the state. The state recruited students by limiting enrollment to graduates of the selective state-controlled *Gymnasien*. A state commission recruited and appointed the faculty. This relationship gave a monopoly to universities over the training of state officials and provided the state with academically trained civil servants. The close relationship between crown and gown was symbolized by the university's location at the very heart of Prussia's capital, surrounded by the Prussian Academy, the State Library, and the State Opera House. To house the university's central functions, the king donated the former palace of Prince Heinrich of Prussia—a gift from his brother Frederick the Great—to be the location of the university on Unter den Linden. In 1828 the university was renamed the Friedrich Wilhelm University in honor of its founding monarch, the formal name that it would retain until 1945.

Bildung, Humboldt believed, had the potential to "inoculate the Germans with the Greek spirit" and to "humanize the state."[21] But to realize that ideal he needed Prussian bureaucracy. Professors, after all, could not be counted on to run the university alone. "To direct a group of scholars," he wrote in a letter to his wife, "is not much better than to have a troop of comedians under you."[22] The appointment of professors was "the prerogative of the state . . . [for] the nature of the university is too closely tied to the vital interests of the state."[23] The accommodation of the two parties in this marriage required a constant process of negotiation between state control and liberal ideals.

The ideals of the new university would be tested severely in the era of restoration and reaction that followed the Napoleonic years. The Austrian statesman Klemens von Metternich dominated Central European politics from 1815 to 1848. He oversaw a constriction of academic discourse that began with the Carlsbad Decrees of 1819, enacted following the murder, by a radical student, of a Prussian diplomat and writer, August von Kotzebue. The decrees, enacted by the new German Confederation of states, aimed to limit liberal and nationalistic voices in the German-speaking world. Student organizations—the *Burschenschaften,* or fraternities—were restricted. Newspapers and periodicals were subject to state censorship. A state-selected "curator" was to be placed in each university—a kind of early nineteenth-century Party secretary. Although the decrees would not be repealed until the revolutions of 1848, their enforcement by the states of the loose and weak German Confederation (including Prussia) was uneven at best. In Göttingen, the "*Göttinger Sieben,*" seven professors (including the Brothers Grimm) who refused to swear loyalty to the new king after he moved to annul the kingdom's constitution, were removed from their university posts and became academic martyrs. In Berlin, the theologian Wilhelm de Wette was dismissed in 1819 for his liberal sympathies. But de Wette's ouster was protested by faculty of all political persuasions, and he soon found another post in Basel.

Even in an era of repression, most of the Humboldtian reforms endured in Berlin, and the Berlin model of a serious research university spread across Germany. It was already a famously serious place. Ludwig Feuerbach, later known best for Marx's "theses" on his work, was a student at Berlin in 1826 when he wrote, "Compared to this temple of work, the other universities appear like public houses."[24]

The university attracted an astonishing cadre of talent. The founding generation of Schleiermacher and Fichte was joined in the university's first decades by Georg Friedrich Wilhelm Hegel, the legal scholar Friedrich Carl von Savigny, the philosopher Arthur Schopenhauer, and the natural philosopher Friedrich von Schelling. Being a professor, in particular a full, or *ordentlicher Professor*, especially at Berlin, became a mark of singular social and cultural prestige. As Hegel wrote to a friend in 1816, a university post had become "an almost indispensable condition" for influence as a philosopher.[25]

The full professoriat, with a *Lehrstuhl*, or chair, was well funded but limited in numbers. They alone could not account for the "explosion of research and publication activities" in German universities in the nineteenth century.[26] For that—at Berlin and elsewhere—another innovation was critical: the growth of an academic underclass, what we would call today the "adjunct" faculty. Beyond the ranks of *ordentliche Professoren* grew a large cadre of *außerordentliche Professoren* and *Privatdozenten*—university teaching positions that brought with them prestige but little, if any, salary and no voting rights. This was a class of professors-in-waiting. In the university's 1816 statute, the *Habilitation* process, a procedure following the doctorate, which entitled the holder to hold lectures, was mentioned. Although this practice had existed before, over the course of the nineteenth and twentieth centuries it became formalized to a greater degree across German-speaking lands.[27] By the mid-nineteenth century across German universities, this distinguished adjunct faculty—increasingly composed of scholars with doctorates—well outnumbered the *Ordinarien*.[28]

The Revolution of 1848 took place in Berlin within earshot of the university: students and faculty must have heard the shooting on the Schloßplatz on March 18, which led to the promise, later betrayed, of a liberal democratic polity in Prussia and elsewhere in Germany. The university was not unaffected by the events of the following year, but neither was it a central actor. It was itself riven by disputes between the *Privatdozenten*, who sought their "corporate rights," and a conservative professoriat, which, together with the government, denied them.[29]

Liberal Education in an Illiberal Polity, 1848–1909

One of the most important developments in the first half of the nineteenth century was the professionalization of university careers. Professors became state officials and, gradually, formed an elite that derived its status not from birthright, but from scholarship.[30] By the time of the convulsions of 1848, professors had become "notables," and as a group competed well in the elections of that democratic spring. Thus, the Frankfurt National Assembly—the first freely elected representative body for all of Germany, which aspired to a democratic unification of German states—became known as the "parliament of professors." Their efforts failed, but the constitution that parliament wrote would have an afterlife in that of the Weimar and Federal Republics. And the revolution's reversal did no apparent damage to the high prestige of German academics.[31]

The University of Berlin became part of the German nation-state that emerged in 1870. Members of the nation's ruling class spent their formative years in its lecture halls, training in disciplines such as political science or law, which were typical for the civil servants who administered the new nation-state. Much of the radical promise of the Humboldtian *Bildungs*-ideal gave way to cultivating and preserving a new ruling class. This also involved keeping certain people out. In 1878 Chancellor Otto von Bismarck passed anti-socialist legislation, which remained in effect until 1890. It banned socialists' meetings and newspapers, and deep prejudices and control over appointments effectively kept members of the Social Democratic Party (SPD) out of the higher ranks of the *Ordinarien*. Although party membership grew steadily over the late nineteenth and early twentieth centuries and was the largest in the Reichstag after 1912, before 1918 not a single Social Democrat could be found among the professors or teaching staff at German universities.[32] After passing a new law in 1898, the Prussian state permitted itself enhanced powers to remove instructors who were deemed politically unacceptable.[33]

With a strong administrative state, the university took on a more conservative role in cultivating the next generation of bureaucrats and advisors. Germany consolidated power on the world stage between 1870 and 1914 and became widely admired for its efficiency in technology and learning. Yet it retained elements of an illiberal political culture, with a complementary university structure, in which the fundamental decisions—not the least of which were war and peace—lay in a few hands. It was in the context of assertiveness abroad and conservatism at home that German universities became leaders.

In addition to their role in training the administrative and political class, in the last decades of the nineteenth century universities became subject to national education policies that stressed the importance of natural sciences and technology as instruments for national economic strength. German industrial enterprises and the military required scientific knowledge and results. By 1880 the number of students in the natural sciences in Berlin had grown rapidly, from 3 percent in 1867 to 18 percent in 1880.[34] And a second university was established in 1879 for this more applied purpose: the Royal Technical University (today the Technical University of Berlin). Like their Chinese counterparts a century later, a growing emphasis on technology and natural science made the Berlin universities engines for national industrial strength and military power. As Emperor William II declared at the onset of the twentieth century, with an unintended swipe at Humboldt, "The new century will be determined by the sciences, including technology, unlike the previous century determined by philosophy."[35]

In the rise of German science in the nineteenth and twentieth centuries, universities played a central, perhaps *the* central, role. They became the locus of scientific research and the beneficiaries of new levels of state support. *Bildung* was now linked directly to *Forschung,* a "research imperative" that prized originality and discovery across the arts and sciences.[36] The comparative amateurism of Humboldt's day gave way to an era of professional specialists that is with us still. No place was more central to all of this than Berlin. The University of Berlin produced groundbreaking discoveries in physics, chemistry, and medicine. Before the end of the First World War, approximately one-third of Nobel Prizes were awarded to German researchers. Around half of them (fourteen) were awarded to researchers associated with the University of Berlin. In the years before the onset of World War I, the University of Berlin received 15 percent of all Nobel Prizes.[37]

Many universities have been defined by their presidents or rectors. Not so the University of Berlin, where until 1933 rectors served, on average, a term of but one year, serving in a largely honorific capacity. Humboldt had "founded" the university not as rector but as a government official. When the university grew to be the academic crown jewel of a unified and industrializing Germany in the second half of the nineteenth century, the key figure was an official named Friedrich Althoff, who defined the university and much of Prussian higher education by what was later dubbed the "System

Figure 2.4. Left to right: Nobel Prize winners (all affiliated with the University of Berlin) Walther Nernst, Albert Einstein, Max Planck, Robert A. Millikan, and Max von Laue in the latter's apartment, around 1930. Nationaal Archief, Den Haag/Wikimedia Commons.

Althoff." Althoff was an associate professor of civil law at the University of Strasbourg who came to Prussia in 1882 to head the University Department of the Prussian Ministry for Education. He stayed in that position for a quarter century, a leader of the *Berufsbeamtentum*, the permanent civil service that stayed in place while ministers and rectors came and went. His aim was to concentrate excellence and specialization in a very few institutions. As a not-so-modest "czar" for Prussian universities, he pursued a strategic, unconventional *Wissenschaftspolitik,* in which he mobilized new funds for higher education, particularly for the University of Berlin. During his tenure, the number of institutes at the University of Berlin increased from thirty-eight to eighty-one. The university clinic Charité became a modern hospital, and the city's libraries coalesced into a network of specialized sites that cooperated with each other, facilitating lending and acquisitions. And he himself recruited, retained, and reprimanded faculty, playing an extraordinary personal role in calling to Berlin Adolf von Harnack, Max Planck, Walther Nernst, Paul Ehrlich, Robert Koch, and Ferdinand von Richthofen, among others—sometimes ignoring the faculty's own recommendations. Althoff did not shy away from reminding faculty of their status as state employees and of his role in deciding their fates. Those who were not his favorites received no "call." Althoff's long dominance and his disregard for normal bureaucratic procedure diminished professorial self-governance, even as it made the university unparalleled in academic strength.[38]

While it remained a politically conservative institution, the University of Berlin took a mild step ahead on another front. In 1896 Prussia adapted its laws to accept women as guest auditors at universities. Prior to the new legislation, women needed a dispensation by the Minister of Education in Prussia to be accepted to audit lectures. Some lectures, like anatomy classes, remained exclusively for men. The University of Berlin had a comparatively high percentage of women auditing lectures, many of whom were Jewish women who had immigrated to Berlin from Russia. In 1899 Elsa Neumann obtained special approval from the Ministry of Education to receive a doctoral degree. She became the first woman to complete her doctoral studies in physics. Regular enrollment for women began only in 1908 and made up but 5 percent of the student body in that year. Yet one-third of the total number of women students in Germany were enrolled in Berlin.[39]

By the end of the nineteenth century, the University of Berlin was by some measure Germany's leading center of scholarship, outshining older venues such as Göttingen, Heidelberg, and Munich. It, without question, set the standards for research universities the world over. Berlin became a mecca for scholars and scientists and the center of a thriving academic community. It was the apex of a professorial career to receive a "call" to Berlin. Full professors in Berlin were therefore particularly old: in 1907 the average Berlin professor was almost sixty years old, whereas elsewhere in Prussia professors were, on average, six years younger.[40] Berlin offered not only prestige but good compensation. Then, as now, it paid to pay well. The average salaries in Berlin in 1905 and 1906 were 30 percent higher than academic salaries elsewhere in Prussia.[41]

Berlin—and by extension German universities as a whole—had become a model for the world. There were no comparable institutions in the United States, and access to British universities was severely restricted. An estimated nine thousand Americans had studied at German universities in the nineteenth century and were trained in the new scientific methods taught there. The reputation of the University of Berlin grew in tandem with that of Germany, which was at the height of what we today would call its "soft power." As Christopher Lasch has pointed out, for a generation of American progressives before 1914, Germany "stood for nothing if not progress."[42] For example, modeling itself after the University of Berlin, Johns Hopkins University established the first graduate school in the United States under the guidance of Daniel Coit Gilman in 1876. Most of its fifty-three faculty members had studied at German universities, and thirteen had received German doctorates.

Beginning a Second Century, 1910–1932

The centenary of 1910 marked at once a high point and a decisive turn in the history of the university. The jubilee was marked by pomp and circumstance: Emperor William II and his empress attended the opening reception on October 11, 1910. It was a time of congratulatory myth-making: for the first time in a sustained way, the "Humboldtian ideals" that underlay the university's founding were celebrated and mythologized, often in unrecognizable form. And it was a time for reflection on what the university had become.[43]

The contrast with the fledgling institution of 1810 could not have been starker. The university had been founded in an era of defeat; its centenary was hailed in a triumphalist "culture of victory." At home and abroad, the university was "the most famous address in the world of research and learning."[44] Founded with the promise of autonomy from the state (and of an endowment to fund it), the university was now well supported, but exclusively by the state, and was inseparably part of the political culture of Wilhelmine Germany. In founding the university in the aftermath of military catastrophe, King Frederick William III aimed in 1810 to "replace with intellectual strength what it [the state] has lost in physical strength." Now the speeches in 1910 celebrated the university in martial metaphors: it was "Germany's first intellectual parade-ground." The Minister of Culture August von Trott zu Solz proclaimed it "an intellectual fortress for the protection of the Fatherland" and "the arsenal of its scientific weapons."[45] To these assertions there was no rejoinder, for at a university that had prized intellectual originality and witnessed firsthand the debates of the Napoleonic, Metternichian, and *Vormärz* eras, there now ruled a "graveyard peace" (*Friedhofsruhe*) in the realm of politics.[46]

Other developments of that anniversary year called into question founding concepts. While over the past century the university (as opposed to the court or academies of science) had cemented its status as the arbiter and home of the modern sciences, the founding of independent research institutions slowly shifted this balance. Again it was Althoff, sometimes described as the "Bismarck of German higher education," who before his death in 1908 had initiated the founding of the *Kaiser-Wilhelm-Gesellschaft* (KWG, later renamed the *Max-Planck-Gesellschaft*), which was inaugurated at the centenary. This society was an umbrella organization that housed the first independent graduate research institutions in Germany, with the central purpose to foster basic research in the natural sciences. They were joint ventures between industry and government, outside the walls of a university, albeit connected often by joint appointments. The KWG undid the universities' monopoly on research but manifested the state's support for German industry, so long as it helped to pay for it. A group of industrial enterprises, banks, and agricultural businesses provided the KWG with its initial funding. The state endowed the KWG with property in Berlin-Dahlem and created civil service posts for its directors. The establishment of twenty new KWG institutes between 1911 and 1933 forged a new, powerful alliance between the state, the economy, and science. For the University of Berlin, however, this development precipitated the search for a new identity. First, the university no longer held a monopoly on high-quality research in Berlin. Second, it now had to compete for leading faculty and public resources. Positions at the KWG institutes were particularly attractive to professors because they were institutes of advanced research, unencumbered by students.

In other words, in the centenary year in which the university celebrated an increasingly imaginary continuity with Humboldtian values, such as the unity of teaching and research, it began to turn in new directions. The centrality of the *Philosophische Fakultät*, in which research in the "pure" (not applied) sciences had been housed, was now diminished, for in addition to the establishment of the KWG, a new body of polytechnic schools emerged with the rank of university.[47]

Still, given Germany's rise, growing strength, and preeminence in higher education, the university seemed poised to lead in what promised to be the "German century." Students and professors reacted euphorically when the war broke out in 1914.

"War semesters are victorious semesters," the theologian Adolf Deißmann argued, with reference to the enormous support for the war effort at the university.[48] The departments of chemistry and physics were mobilized to support German forces. In 1915 a special unit led by the chemist Fritz Haber (winner of the Nobel Prize in Chemistry in 1918) worked to develop weaponized chlorine and other poisonous gases.

The Berlin professoriat before the war was overwhelmingly conservative, monarchist, and patriotic. As such it enjoyed influence and still a considerable degree of autonomy in the handling of its own affairs—within the limits of an illiberal polity, academic appointments in Wilhelmine Germany were based on merit, but also, implicitly, on *Gesinnung,* or ideology. The Berlin philosopher Friedrich Paulsen asserted that academic freedom remained "generally . . . a recognized and undisputed right at German universities," but within boundaries. Max Weber was harsher: "The 'freedom of science' exists in Germany within the limits of ecclesiastical and political acceptability. Outside these limits there is none."[49]

By the end of the war, 57 members of the faculty and 997 students had been killed. Yet for women, World War I presented new opportunities at the university. With young men at war, women finally received academic attention. By 1918, the beginning of the Weimar Republic, around 10 percent of the student body was female. By the end of the era of the Weimar Republic, this number grew slowly but steadily to around 20 percent.[50]

Darkness: The University in the National Socialist Era, 1933–1945

Germany's descent from a nation of "poets and thinkers" (*Dichter und Denker*) to one of "judges and hangmen" (*Richter und Henker*)[51] came at the cost of its leadership in higher education. The impact of the Nazi regime that came to power in January 1933 became manifest on May 10 of that year, when the members of the German Student Union—among them many students from the University of Berlin—publicly piled and burned books from public libraries on the streets of Berlin's *Opernplatz,* the square opposite the university's main building. A crowd of seventy thousand, including students, professors, and members of the SA and SS—storm troopers for National Socialism—watched as thousands of volumes were torched.[52]

The university locked arms with the new regime. In the spring of 1933 student agitators spread pamphlets agitating for purges of "non-national" elements within the universities. The university rector at the time, Eduard Kohlrausch, found the agitators problematic. However, it was not the anti-Semitic content of their invective that he took issue with, but rather the agitators' choice of method of distributing pamphlets and posters at the university, including forcibly hanging a poster calling for "action against the un-German spirit" on campus.[53] Approval—whether tacit, or, as among the more opportunistic professors, more vocal—for the National Socialist's 1933 "Law for the Restoration of the Professional Civil Service," which expelled Jewish faculty, was the order of the day. Protests remained the exception, as many professors greeted the dismissal of Jewish colleagues as an opportunity for advancement and as a legitimate pursuit of national goals. Prominent faculty, including the agronomist Konrad Meyer and jurist Carl Schmitt, as well as anthropologist Eugen Fischer, who served as rector of the university between 1933 and 1935, enthusiastically contributed to National Socialist crimes and plans for domination and extermination.[54]

In short order the Nazi regime purged universities of non-Aryan and dissident members. Universities lost any capacity for self-government. The University of Berlin increasingly abandoned its own traditions of teaching and research. Scholarship serving truth for truth's sake was jettisoned for scholarship in service of the "Volk." The natural sciences as well as the departments of classics, theology, and literature were all affected and exploited by the dogma of "blood, soil, and race." Many German scholars eagerly embraced National Socialism and its ideology; more than a third of Berlin's faculty joined the Nazi Party. Perhaps one of the most extreme examples of the university's involvement in National Socialism was Konrad Meyer, professor of agriculture, who was named by Heinrich Himmler as the chief planner of the SS's infamous *Generalplan Ost,*" a plan to resettle occupied Poland with Germans while expelling, enslaving, and exterminating hundreds of thousands of Poles living in that area.

Nazi policies and the spread of anti-Semitism led to a sizeable intellectual migration to Britain and America. But beyond the famous names such as Albert Einstein, then of the Prussian Academy of Sciences, who was in the United States when Hitler came to power, there were many more who were denied asylum—for anti-Semitism was not a German monopoly in the 1930s.[55] One fortunate scholar was Hajo Holborn, a student at Berlin of the eminent historian Friedrich Meinecke. He was dismissed from his academic post in Berlin in 1933 and made his way to America, where he would become Sterling Professor of History at Yale and president of the American Historical Society. The architect Walter Gropius was another, having moved to Berlin from Dessau only to flee the city in 1934, making his way eventually to the United States, where he would chair the Department of Architecture at Harvard's Graduate School of Design and personally design the new Harvard Graduate Center. Not for the last time—as we shall see—the United States was a fortunate recipient of exiled intellectuals.

Resistance in the university to Nazi rule was limited. A famous exception was Dietrich Bonhoeffer, Protestant theologian and assistant professor at the University of Berlin. In the 1930s he helped organize the Confessing Church in opposition to the state church controlled by the Nazis. At the outbreak of World War II, he joined the resistance movement surrounding Admiral Wilhelm Canaris in the *Abwehr,* a military intelligence group that was intent on overthrowing and later assassinating Hitler. The Nazis hanged him naked during the last weeks of the war in the concentration camp Flossenbürg.

By the end of the war, various estimates put the loss of faculty across Germany at 40 percent of their prewar numbers. Although the statistics vary somewhat, it is clear that the war devastated the ranks of university faculty.[56] Berlin was hit particularly hard as 280 faculty members were forced to leave the university. The majority of these dismissals were for "racial" anti-Semitic reasons. As central Berlin became a target of Allied bombing in 1943 and 1944, the university operated at reduced capacity before ceasing to function altogether in October 1944.

From Public University to SED University: Higher Education in a Socialist World Order, 1946–1989

In 1945 the University of Berlin, like most German universities, lay in ruins: 50 percent of the university's buildings were destroyed, including its main building and the medical department, Charité. Somehow the university library remained mostly intact. Berlin was divided among the victorious allies, and the university found itself in the Soviet sector. The Soviets decided to reopen the university only eight months after the war had ended.

At the ceremony celebrating the return of activity to the university, its leadership proudly declared that "the reopening is not only a matter of taking up the work and preserving received traditions, but it involves a total renewal of the external and, even more so, the internal character of the university."[57] Soviet authorities began a period of denazification, including purges among faculty and students, to distance themselves from the Nazi and militaristic past. The Soviet authorities viewed the professoriat with suspicion and held it partly responsible for the implementation of Nazi dictatorship and the preparation for war. As the university reopened, nearly 85 percent of its professors were dismissed on the grounds of their active collaboration with National Socialism.[58] Authorities feared the influence that accompanied these posts. The reorganization of the university in accordance with Soviet political principles followed soon after, aiming to transform students from bourgeois specialists to working socialists. The formal mission of educating the whole person—already long in retreat—was quickly replaced with creating a cadre of ideologically faithful socialists.

Soon social democratic, liberal, and conservative students, who had returned in small numbers after the fall of the Nazi regime, were suspended from the university, at times even arrested. In April 1948 a coalition of students, professors, and the American military governor in Berlin, General Lucius D. Clay, initiated a new university in the western sector of the city. This "Free University of Berlin," which we will encounter in detail in Chapter 3, was founded in the institutes of the old *Kaiser-Wilhelm-Gesellschaft* in Dahlem and claimed to be the true heir of the original university. Berlin was now two cities, housing two universities divided along the ideological lines of the Cold War, instantiating the increasing tensions between the Soviets and the West in the following decades.

On February 8, 1949, shortly after the foundation of Free University, the University of Berlin, which in 1946 had dropped "Friedrich Wilhelm" from its masthead, was renamed the "Humboldt University of Berlin" in honor of the Humboldt brothers. The reality, however, little reflected Humboldt's ideals of academic freedom and liberal education. The SED (Socialist Unity Party of Germany), the governing party of the German Democratic Republic (GDR), intended to create a socialist elite university, closely aligned with the party's ideology. These intentions affected the university's faculty. For example, the first five women in the university's history to take up full professorships were appointed in the immediate postwar years, but by 1948 all but one had left because of ever-tightening ideological controls.

Students took required classes in Marxism-Leninism and historical materialism, memorizing the new socialist catechism with the *Kadavergehorsamkeit* (the obedience of corpses) for which Prussia was once famous. Their summers involved obligatory labor service and duty. The university's leadership team was remodeled into a double structure of party and academic staff, the party having the final word in all essential decisions. Heinrich Fink, a theology professor who became the university's first president after reunification, recalled, "The president never decided anything without the party. The orders came from above."[59]

In the summer of 1961 the building of the Berlin Wall interrupted any contact between students and faculty and the West. The sixteen million inhabitants of the GDR were not allowed to travel and were held under strict police control. Between January and November 1961, 623 university members left the GDR, 379 of whom escaped secretly after the Wall was built.[60] The state security service ("Stasi") appointed a department with seventeen full-time members to supervise the university. The university in turn also participated actively in the GDR's surveillance system. For example, the university created a degree program in "Criminalistic," designed to be an unofficial entryway for a career with the Stasi. Beyond this there was no shortage of "IM," short for *inoffizielle Mitarbeiter,* or unofficial collaborators, at the university who collected and forwarded information on students and faculty to the Stasi. Between 1950 and 1989 an estimated 620,000 GDR citizens served as IM.[61] Faculty who dared to question the premises of the GDR regime or to advocate reforms were expelled.

Despite being walled off from the West, the university was not unaffected by the pivotal "year 1968," when political and societal debates in the West and in Poland, Yugoslavia, and Czechoslovakia sparked great interest. Many students entertained sympathies for the "Prague Spring" in 1968 and objected to its suppression. However, open opposition and demonstrative actions among students remained rare. Only eighteen students were subjected to disciplinary proceedings by the university.[62] Whether through fear or belief, students, faculty, and administration stayed loyal to the party line.[63]

Until the fall of the Wall in 1989, the university struggled with the effects of the scarcity of resources that was ubiquitous in the GDR. Overall, the university was characterized by academic stagnation, political control, and ideological paternalism. Nevertheless, outstanding research was still produced, particularly in medicine and the natural sciences. The university also looked across borders, establishing important exchange relationships with other institutions of higher education behind the Iron Curtain, and especially with the Soviet Union, as well as with socialist countries in Africa, Asia, and South America. As the largest university in the GDR, it still commanded international respect. Humboldt also opened up to students with worker family backgrounds and explicitly welcomed women. In 1989, 51.2 percent of the GDR's university students were female, one of the highest rates in the world.[64] Additionally, the university put more emphasis on the importance of teaching: the faculty-student ratio was around one-to-seven in 1989.[65] The university also established strong international research and exchange links with other universities in the "socialist brother countries" and gained distinctive strength in Russian/Soviet and Chinese studies.[66]

Refounding Humboldt University in the Capital of a Reunited Germany, after 1990

The peaceful reunification of the two parts of Germany signified yet another turning point for Humboldt University and was, after the fascist and communist dictatorships, the third disruption it faced in the twentieth century. At first there was euphoria and then reality. As reform efforts from within failed, the university was redesigned by the initiative of the Senate of Berlin. Within a few years, the university was restructured and reorganized in a way that left little unchanged. The process resembled a new founding, except that the university continued its teaching and research operations throughout this phase.

As the first freely elected rector, or president, in the history of the University of Berlin, Heinrich Fink, recalled, "Everyone, from the lowest student to the university president, was in the spirit of Humboldt. You know the Humboldt spirit? Total science. And in the Humboldt spirit, without, and free from, ideology, we wanted to renew ourselves. We initiated a new program of study. We elected new committees. We had a newly elected, freely elected university president. . . . Then the West Berlin Senate said no, no, not like that. . . . You have too many professors and too many Marxists."[67]

Curricula were assessed and redefined, institutes and departments were merged and regrouped into three campuses, namely Campus Mitte, Campus Nord, and Campus Adlershof. Professors had to reapply for their positions and had to compete with colleagues from the West to keep their jobs. Former president Fink noted, "There was great tension above all among the staff, who suddenly found themselves being evaluated and who were not going to be [automatically] employed again."[68] To the purges of 1933 (against Jews and liberals) and 1945–1946 (against Nazi members, conservatives, and liberals) was now added the purge *nach der Wende* (literally, "after the turn") of 1989. Between 1990 and 1994, 477 professors were newly appointed. Among 2,755 employees in 1989, only 16.4 percent remained in the workforce by 1997.[69] Some viewed the evaluation of the faculty and academic employees as a necessary step for the decommunization of the university, while others called it an academic "colonization" from Western Germany, for the new appointees were almost entirely from the West.

At Humboldt University's archives are files of those dismissed in the 1990s. One was Roland Felber, the GDR's leading historian of modern China. He had studied in China at Peking University in the 1950s; received his doctorate at Leipzig; assumed the chair in Chinese history at Berlin in 1977; and was a widely respected scholar in Europe, North America, and Asia. Promoted to vice dean at Humboldt University in 1990, he was then interrogated and forced to fill out forms—loosely adapted from the denazification forms of the 1940s—on all that he had done under GDR rule. Did he work for the Stasi? (No.) Had he been paid by the Stasi? (No.) Was he a functionary of the SED? (No.) Was he a member of the SED? (Yes.) And so on. He was forced to reapply for his professorship only to be told that he had come in number two on the appointment list, to a much more junior scholar from Western Germany. Then, in 1993, he was summarily cashiered. His health broken, he was permitted to continue in a limited capacity until 2000.[70] Humboldt University has been undistinguished in this field ever since.

Berlin now housed three large universities: Humboldt University, Free University, and Technical University. Plans to form one large university in the capital of Germany—a national university—were quickly abandoned. Before 1990 the universities had been recipients of generous state funding from the competing East and West German governments. Now a united but poorer Berlin had to pay for them itself. With Free University (FU) in particular, a new phase of competition and collaboration began. In 1997–1998 the hospitals of Free University (Virchow Hospital) and Humboldt University (Charité) were merged to form the largest university hospital in Europe. At the same time, these two universities increasingly competed for resources and recognition from the Berlin Senate. Between 1995 and 2001 Berlin reduced its spending on higher education by 16.5 percent; between 1992 and 2000 grants for Humboldt University through the state of Berlin were cut by 14.5 percent.[71]

Governance: From Authoritarianism to Anarchism

Slowly Humboldt University renewed itself, starting with its governance. The university metamorphosed from an SED-dominated university into a democratic, self-governed university. University laws very similar to those formed in the 1960s and 1970s in Western Germany were implemented, giving faculty and staff enormous agency, including the right to elect their leaders.

At the top was the president, a position that replaced that of the rector and was meant to give the university much stronger administrative leadership. Three vice presidents with designated areas of administration—the Vice President of Academic Affairs, the Vice President of Research, and the Vice President of Finance, Personnel, and Technical Matters—completed the Presidential Board. The members of this board were individually elected for five-year terms.[72] The Presidential Board governed the university in collaboration with three central administrative bodies: the Academic Senate, the Council, and the Board of Trustees.

The Academic Senate (AS) was entrusted with making decisions on myriad issues ranging from day-to-day matters to the university's strategic orientation. The AS was composed of twenty-five members with voting power who were elected for two-year terms. They represented four different constituencies of the university: academic employees, nonacademic employees, students, and professors. The first three of these subgroups each had four representatives, while professors were granted thirteen representatives, allowing the faculty a thin majority when acting unanimously. Ten additional groups held privileges to speak and make proposals during meetings of the AS.[73] The university's medical school, Charité, which operated in partnership with Free University, had a senate of its own.

The Council was, in principle, the university's highest governing body. In addition to the election of the Presidential Board, the Council was responsible for other fundamental decisions, such as enacting the university's constitution and electoral regulations, and debating the Presidential Board's annual report.[74] The Council had sixty-one members, elected for two years, consisting of the twenty-five members of the Academic Senate in addition to members from the same four subgroups that made up the AS. In toto, the Council comprised thirty-one professors, ten academic employees, ten nonacademic employees, and ten students. Elections for both the Academic Senate and the Council were held in one electoral process, in which all university members were both eligible and entitled to vote for members of their subgroups.

The Presidential Board reported to the Board of Trustees, consisting of nine voting members. The president and the Berlin senator responsible for universities were members ex officio.[75] The remaining seven members were elected by the Academic Senate.[76] The Board of Trustees advised the university in strategic questions and in decisions concerning public matters. It was also involved in electing the university president and vice presidents. The election or reelection to the Presidential Board required three steps. First, the Board of Trustees formed a search committee (with half of its eight members from the Council and the other half from the Board of Trustees) to identify candidates. Second, the search committee proposed candidates to the Council. Finally, the Council elected a candidate with an absolute majority vote.[77]

This ultrademocratic approach to governance was cherished by faculty, staff, and students and generally loathed by presidents because it often led to significant resistance to institutional changes.[78] As part of a renewed university with an altogether new professoriat after 1990, "Humboldtian" faculty identified strongly with their institution and its founding ideals.

The challenges in administration were greater given an unusual inheritance from German reunification in the 1990s. While the original professoriat was replaced by hundreds of professors from the West, the administrative staff, which in 2020, thirty years *nach der Wende* comprised around fifteen hundred people, remained basically intact and, given its voice in governance, self-perpetuating.[79] Differing values between a new faculty and an older bureaucracy entangled presidents, professors, and staff in endless battles.

A university with such a flat governance structure made decision-making often impossible. President Jan-Hendrik Olbertz stated at the end of his tenure, "The culture of democracy entails that elected officials are given a mandate, controlled of course [by university institutions]. This mandate is temporary and one has to legitimize [elected authority] with responsibility and results. It is however not possible to allow everybody the same right to vote on important questions; otherwise we would have no structure."[80]

But almost everybody *did* have a vote. Approval by the Academic Senate was essential for any major initiative. On the positive side, as Peter Frensch, Vice President for Research, noted, "Once you have a decision in the Academic Senate, then it is a done deal."[81] But from the president's office the view was different: Humboldt University was a place where "everybody takes part in decisions, but only a very small number of members of the university take part in responsibility."[82] And the most prestigious faculty members, as a rule, did not seek positions in the Academic Senate to "not get their hands dirty."[83]

Adding to leadership woes was the absence of a centralized budget and professional financial administration. The vice president for finance, personnel, and technical matters was not chosen by the president but elected from, and largely by, the faculty. During his presidency, Olbertz aimed to professionalize a cumbersome financial administration by installing—as was the norm in many German universities—a professional "chancellor" skilled in financial management in lieu of an academic vice president. Olbertz remarked, "I needed somebody at my side who is a professional in administration and who is a member of my team. But you are absolutely unable to create any reform in an encompassing way [in the current system]. That's why we are so behind on very important steps toward a modern administration.[84]

Before his presidency, Olbertz himself held the position of vice president for finance, personnel, and technical matters for six months, and he knew the challenges of a disconnected leadership corps. Olbertz wanted his own team. But after wrenching public debate, he failed to convince the Academic Senate of the need for change. When he declined to stand for reelection as president in 2016, he joined a distinguished list of his predecessors since 1990, not one of whom had completed a second term.

Competing for Faculty

Humboldt University's bureaucratic silos perhaps contributed to making the university a place that was widely appreciated by the faculty for its individuality, creativity, collegiality, and freedom of thought. Olbertz, despite his frustration with the organization of his institution, considered this intellectual culture one of the university's main assets. "Sometimes," he stated, "I am afraid when I am looking for more structure and calculability that it is a danger for our intellectual atmosphere, our very high level of creativity, and openness to the interdisciplinarity. Would I kill this atmosphere by instituting a professional structure and administration?"[85] Overall, the university had great appeal to faculty members. A "call" to Berlin was not what it once was, but the reunified city itself was a big attraction. According to a high-ranking university administrator, the university was successful in hiring or retaining faculty in 70 to 80 percent of cases, an outstanding ratio illustrating its competitiveness vis-à-vis other German universities.[86]

Nevertheless, recruitment was not easy, given Berlin's budget constraints. This was true especially for international scholars. Professors were civil servants in Germany and their basic salaries were fixed by the states, not by the universities; salaries were not increased according to seniority. In 2020 Berlin's Senate granted a basic salary for full professors between €73,000 (US$86,370) and €84,000 (around US$99,380); junior professors earned a basic salary of around €56,000 (US$66,200).[87] Beyond that, candidates could negotiate a bonus and other academic benefits (research assistants, research budgets), especially when the candidate had competing job offers. But salaries were hardly competitive internationally. Even within Germany, richer states had more generous compensation policies. With nine hours of teaching per week, the teaching requirements for faculty in Berlin were high compared to international standards.[88] The teaching load and the budget were tied in such a way that the number of teaching hours determined the number of students to be admitted; the admitted students in turn determined the size of the budget granted by Berlin's Senate. It was difficult for Humboldt University to hire international faculty at the height of their careers because the mandated retirement age in Berlin began at age sixty-five (and could only be extended to age sixty-eight).

In 2020 the faculty consisted of a total of 440 professors. Although nearly 20 percent of the positions were funded by external (third-party) sources in 2020, the rest were funded entirely (and inadequately) by the state.[89] The faculty was largely full professors, with the exception of fifty-one so-called junior professors. Junior professorships were created in Germany on a national level in 2002 to enable postdoctoral fellows to gain professorial appointments without being required to write the second dissertation, or *Habilitation*.[90]

Junior professors were initially appointed for three or four years, and, after an evaluation, their professorship could be extended to a total of six years. The creation of junior professorships was also an attempt to address the problem of underrepresentation of women in Germany's faculties by making the academic career path more flexible and hence more attractive. The demographic makeup of Humboldt University signaled the problem. While in 2020, 58 percent of the students were female, and over 50 percent of the academic employees that were not part of the professoriat were female, only 35 percent of Humboldt's professors (including junior professors) were women.[91] Still, compared to the German average of 24.7 percent (in 2018), the percentage at Humboldt was significantly higher.[92] In fact, in comparison with other German states, the state of Berlin had the highest percentage of female professors in 2018, while Bavaria had the lowest with around 20 percent.[93]

Massification: The Student Body

With 35,981 students (excluding about 8,200 students at Charité) enrolled, Humboldt University was one of the largest German universities in 2019–2020.[94] Since the mid-1990s student enrollment at Humboldt had grown five times as fast as faculty expansion,[95] and faster than the overall growth of students at Berlin universities.[96] Humboldt's students were enrolled in nine schools in a total of 172 degree programs. Women made up 57 percent of the student body, a number higher than the German average of 48 percent.[97] With 57 percent of students coming from local backgrounds (as of 2015 data), the university maintained the character of a regional state university.[98] Markschies described the difficulty of balancing access with excellence: "This is the consensus of a great coalition of old political parties in Germany: Every university should at the same time welcome all students of its local state and also satisfy the demands of being an elite university."[99]

Compared with their American and British counterparts, German universities were much less selective when it came to admission. In Berlin in particular, universities followed a strong egalitarian tradition. Nonselective admission policies were protected by Berlin's Senate, which also determined the total intake of students every year.[100] Similar to other German public universities, the only internal selection criterion at Humboldt was the so-called *Numerus Clausus* (NC). The NC is a classification policy based on final scores in the German *Abitur* examination. It is used at German universities to restrict admissions for sought-after areas of study by determining the lowest admitted grade. In 2014–2015, the acceptance rate in majors that had an NC, such as biology and economics, was around 15 percent.[101] Markschies described the problem: "In my farewell speech as president I addressed the mayor of Berlin and said to him, 'give us freedom to select our students and also the number of students.' He laughed at me, saying, 'never, ever, in my lifetime.'"[102]

Reengaging the World

The University of Berlin was once the place to which scholars from around the world flocked to learn what a university could be. In GDR times, it sent its own students abroad, mostly eastward, toward Moscow and the "socialist brother countries." Those ties atrophied (although they did not die entirely) with the fall of the Wall. By 2017 it had become attractive to new generations of international students, perhaps as much for Berlin as for the university. International enrollment at Humboldt University was 17.5 percent (the average at German universities was 12.3 percent).[103] With over two-thirds of international students hailing from European countries (41 percent from the European Union; 13 from the rest of Europe), Humboldt University's source of internationalization was primarily European. Asian students made up 14 percent of the international students, and North, Central, and South America together had a share of 28 percent of the international students.[104] Whereas Russian had been an international lingua franca for the university in GDR times, by 2020 the university offered thirty-three English-language degree programs.[105] In comparison with other German universities, Humboldt's faculty was also more international: 14 percent came from countries other than Germany, while the average for full-time academic employees and professors from outside Germany was around 7 percent.[106]

Within the context of the Bologna Process, Humboldt University, along with all other German higher education institutions, introduced a series of wide-ranging measures designed to reform the structure of the university in accordance with guidelines from the European Union. The Bologna Process officially began in 1999 with the signing of the Bologna Declaration and has been an ongoing series of ministerial conferences that aim to bring coherence and quality standardization of higher education across forty-eight European countries. Since 2003 this reform at Humboldt has aimed to establish internationally accepted degrees, improve the quality of courses of study, and enhance students' employability and mobility. Furthermore, the reform aspired to enhance the attractiveness of German institutions of higher education for students and young academics from abroad. Among the most debated reform measures was the introduction of a system of comprehensible and comparable degrees (with three-year bachelor's and two-year master's degree programs), which was a departure from the five-year bachelor's system in Germany.[107]

For Humboldt—a university that once set international standards—these Europe-wide efforts meant now adopting foreign models, such as the US baccalaureate. The Bologna Process aimed to make higher education in Europe a continental-wide enterprise, with mobility not only of students but also of faculty and staff, in part to compete with larger and more competitive systems of higher education in the United States and China.

But in the formal adoption of the baccalaureate, there was little interest in the educational values that have defined the bachelor of arts degree in many American colleges, which stressed, in the original spirit of Humboldt, a broad undergraduate education in the liberal arts and sciences. The "key competencies" for lifelong learning recommended by the European Parliament in 2006 quite appropriately include language learning; information and communication technologies; and math, science, and technology but not the humanities.

Humboldt University's own "International Agenda 2015" set out a modest strategy built around a limited series of international partnerships.[108] Before Humboldt launched this strategy, the first collaboration to support undergraduate, graduate student, and faculty exchanges was established with Princeton University in 2012. It supported research and teaching projects between the two institutions with a joint fund in the amount of €300,000 (US$390,000) per year. The academic partnership was complemented by a staff mobility program for administrative employees.[109] Other strategic partnerships were built with the National University of Singapore and Universidade de São Paulo.[110] Funded by money from the Excellence Initiative, a program called "KOSMOS" was designed to rebuild relations with the old Soviet bloc, inviting young academics from Eastern Europe and Russia to Humboldt University for limited periods.

The Limits of Public Funding

Historically and today, universities in Germany are mainly public and funded by the public purse. There are a number of small private professional schools, but they enroll less than 5 percent of German students of university age. With its federal system, Germany's sixteen states are principally responsible for higher education. As a result, universities in poorer states (mostly former GDR states in Eastern Germany) receive less money than universities in wealthier states.

In the case of Humboldt University, the city-state of Berlin allocated an annual budget, which was supplemented by additional money from other, also mostly public, sources. In 2020 Humboldt University's total budget was just over US$520 million (or close to €461 million), including salaries for professors, who are civil servants in Germany. In 2016 third-party funds, mostly government money from the German Research Foundation, accounted for 28 percent of the university's budget.[111] Donations from the private sector were but a small source of additional funding for Humboldt and remained below 10 percent.[112] Humboldt had neither tradition nor capacity to gain financial support among alumni, who largely lacked a history of philanthropy. Potential industrial partners preferred to invest in the Technical University of Berlin.

Like most German universities, Humboldt was structurally underfunded. Therefore, when Germany's constitutional court overturned a 1976 law prohibiting tuition fees in 2005, many universities introduced annual charges (laws limited the fees to US$1,058 [or €1,000]). Berlin however, never introduced fees, and by 2014 all states had abolished fees in the wake of student protests and political pressure. For the most part, the states compensated the universities for the income lost when fees were abolished. But where fees were never levied, as in Berlin, compensation was never paid. In 2020 the total fees at Humboldt University were US$357 (or €316) per semester, including a public transport ticket for Berlin and Brandenburg whose value alone accounted for two-thirds of the fees. At different times since 1990, budget deficits forced the university to cut back on faculty and other staff members. In 1998 only 10 percent of midlevel academics who had been employed as of 1993 remained at the university.[113] In 2004 nearly eighty professorships (along with their academic employees, secretaries, and technical staff), constituting around 20 percent of the workforce, were axed for budgetary reasons.[114]

Competing for Preeminence: The Excellence Initiative, 2005–2020

In the early 2000s policymakers in Germany were increasingly worried about the state of German universities, in particular their weak showing in international rankings, in spite of well-founded and often-voiced reservations against rankings in general among German policymakers and university administrators.[115] None of the German universities managed to enter the top twenty, and only a handful were listed in the top one hundred in influential global rankings such as the *Times Higher Education,* QS World University Rankings, and the Academic Ranking of World Universities.

At home, German universities faced increasing competition from nonuniversity research institutes, such as the Max Planck Society, the Leibniz Association, and the Helmholtz Association of German Research Centers. Many high-profile scientists found the independent institutes to be more attractive workplaces compared to universities: there was no teaching and more money. Perhaps even more problematic for Germany's universities was the "brain drain." Since the 1990s thousands of researchers had left Germany for other countries, mainly for the United States. This phenomenon is well illustrated by the fact that the four German Nobel Prize winners between 1998 and 2001 had transferred to American universities by the time their Nobel Prizes were awarded.[116]

The national Excellence Initiative (*Exzellenzinitiative*), begun in 2005, was an attempt to steer higher education in Germany in a new direction. In a period when public funding for universities decreased steadily in England and the United States, the tax-funded budget for higher education in Germany increased notably, even during the years after the 2008 financial crisis. Federal and state funding for higher education was US$19.5 (or €18.4) billion in 2005, rising more than 50 percent to US$30.5 (or €28.7) billion by 2015.[117] With the so-called Higher Education Pacts I and II, the federal government allocated US$8.5 (or €8) billion between 2007 and 2015 to the states to fund 425,000 student spots. Over its first twelve years, the Excellence Initiative allocated almost US$5 billion of funding, three-quarters of which was funded by the federal government and one-quarter by the sixteen states.[118]

German federal and state governments launched the initiative in 2005 to help a handful of German universities join the ranks of the global research elite. The German Research Foundation (*Deutsche Forschungsgemeinschaft*, or DFG), which together with the German Council of Science and Humanities (*Deutscher Wissenschaftsrat*) jointly ran the Excellence Initiative, defined the broader goal of the initiative as "mak[ing] Germany a more attractive research location, making it more internationally competitive, and focusing attention on the outstanding achievements of German universities and the German scientific community."[119] And indeed, the initiative did pay off for certain universities.

The Excellence Initiative's first funding round ran from 2006 to 2011. Competition for funding was divided into three lines: first, "graduate schools" to support young graduate researchers; second, "clusters of excellence" to promote collaborative projects within universities and with other scientific institutions (such as Max Planck institutes); and third, "institutional strategies" to provide promising research universities with extra funding on an institutional basis. In the first line of funding, the initiative sought to create more than fifty graduate schools for more integrated doctoral programs and enhanced research groups than could be found in the traditional disciplines or in a *Lehrstuhl* overseen by a single professor. The clusters of excellence promoted interdisciplinary cooperation across different realms of research.

Finally, the initiative aimed to bolster the long-term development of high-level research for German universities via the institutional strategies line of funding. To become a "University of Excellence" the applicant institution had to win at least one Cluster of Excellence and one Graduate School award. The institution also had to demonstrate a coherent overall strategy for building up its research profile. In the first round there were 319 proposals from 74 universities overall.[120]

In the first funding round, US$2.5 billion was made available for a five-year period beginning in 2006, with, as noted, the federal government providing the lion's share and the states funding the rest. The money was, of course, an important motivator for Germany's underfinanced universities. Equally valuable was the galvanizing of German higher education institutions to rethink their priorities and to come up with strategies of world-class excellence.

Humboldt University was humiliated in the first round. But Humboldt's offspring, Free University, would now be known as a "University of Excellence," having established itself as a national leader in the humanities. Humboldt entered the second competition with trepidation, but it ultimately gained entry into the circle of elite universities, in part by partnering with Free University and the Max Planck institutes on a research cluster. For the university "and its institutional self-confidence this was very, very important," former President Olbertz recalled.[121]

For the third round of funding of the Excellence Initiative, the results of which were announced in 2019, there were only two, instead of the prior three lines of funding. One line was for clusters of excellence and the other was a new line called "universities of excellence," which encouraged institutions to apply jointly. Humboldt put all its eggs in a collaborative basket in a joint proposal for a "Berlin University Alliance" along with Free University, Charité, and the Technical University of Berlin. This joint strategy represented a resounding success, and the integrated research agenda received funding in both lines of funding.

Critics of the Excellence Initiative have pointed out that, compared to the funding of leading research institutions in other countries, the money distributed since the launch of the Excellence Initiative has had little significance in financial terms. The annual budget of the Excellence Initiative, around US$530 (or €500) million, was distributed among ten to twelve universities. Had Humboldt University received the entire sum of annual nationwide funding of the initiative, its budget would have been but 17 percent of Stanford University's, but with Humboldt having around twice as many students.[122]

Yet this comparatively modest financial incentive made a big difference in attitudes. Even most critics conceded that the Excellence Initiative had changed Germany's higher education landscape. For the first time, German universities were spurred to compete for funding *and* to develop formal strategies to position themselves nationally and internationally. According to a recent study by the International Expert Commission on the Excellence Initiative ("Imboden report"), led by emeritus Professor Dieter Imboden of ETH Zurich, the initiative "succeeded in initiating a structural change at the universities."[123] Members of Humboldt University's leadership team, often stymied by the university's convoluted governance structure, described the initiative as a catalyst to set strategies. Olbertz recalled that the Excellence Initiative "brought enormous dynamism to the university."[124]

"Excellence" was measured, above all, by research. Indeed, data on citation impact of the eleven universities selected for institutional funding suggest that their research was cited more frequently than German universities in general. The proportion of papers from these eleven universities in the world's top 10 percent by citation grew from one-sixth in 2003 to nearly one-quarter in 2015. Yet data also showed that other universities less favored by the Excellence Initiative managed to keep pace when it came to highly cited papers.[125] These positive effects may also be partly explained by the general increase of research funding across Germany over the past decade. Still, even the top German universities ranked poorly against the world's leading institutions, and Humboldt University was no exception.

In the latest round of the Excellence Initiative competition in 2019, the Berlin partnership made great strides toward putting Humboldt University back on the map as part of a Berlin-wide academic "ecosystem."[126] The alliance strove to unite the research competencies of the institutions and to create networks of professional exchange and continuing education. The plan not only enabled the universities to compete nationally but also allowed them to act more nimbly on the international stage. In 2017, in the wake of Brexit, the Berlin universities partnered with Oxford to become its German counterpart for exchange and collaboration and to mitigate the effects of Britain's withdrawal from the EU on students and research.[127] As Humboldt President Sabine Kunst said, "Through collaboration with a top British university, we hope to put together a targeted collective strategy in order to circumvent any possible consequences of Brexit."[128] The alliance formalized a number of reciprocal visiting arrangements, cooperation with museums and libraries, and common research agendas, as well as set out plans for physical centers to be constructed in the near future to support intense collaboration and attract third-party funding. By making use of the city's existing institutional structures resulting from Berlin's patchwork history along with its reputation as an attractive place to live and conduct research, the alliance finally allowed Humboldt to put its best foot forward.

Humboldt's Future, in the Light of its Past

At its bicentennial jubilee in 2010, as Humboldt University organized a conference to celebrate itself as "the modern original," the university could reflect on its past and contemplate its future. As a public university, its history was deeply intertwined with the history of Berlin. The university had outlasted five political regimes—the Kingdom of Prussia, the German Empire, the Weimar Republic, Nazi Germany, and the German Democratic Republic—to find itself in the Federal Republic of Germany, perhaps the only one truly receptive to the ideas of *Lehr- und Lernfreiheit* that had so animated Wilhelm von Humboldt. Through its tumultuous history, the university also showed an exceptional resilience.

For the first time since the early years in the history of the university, liberal education in the spirit of Humboldt was possible. But with democratization came also budget constraints and a nearly tenfold increase in the student body (today nearly thirty-six thousand). A student-faculty ratio of seven-to-one in GDR times was now fifteen-to-one.[129] If Nazism and Communism had suppressed any pretense of free and open inquiry at the university, the massification of the student body and the overwhelming obsession with research—as distinct from teaching and mentorship—in the era of the Excellence Initiative may ensure that Humboldtian ideals will be practiced as an exception rather than the rule in the classroom.

After nearly 180 years under authoritarian governance, Humboldt University embraced participatory democracy in its contemporary governance. An Academic Senate was composed of faculty, staff, and students who held veto power over major decisions of the university leadership. This is surely one reason for the extraordinarily short tenures of Humboldt's presidents. When President Sabine Kunst resigned in October 2021, less than a year into her second term, she was part of a lineage of post-1989 presidents for whom one term proved more than enough. After more than a century of

Prussian-German rule, twelve years of Nazism, and forty years of Communism, Humboldt University had become truly democratic in governance, and as a result also rudderless, until recently without clear academic direction and distinction, compared to the height of its glory. Physically surrounded by Berlin's great museums—including a new one in the rebuilt Hohenzollern Stadtschloß—Humboldt University is today a living museum of a university, striving to return to distinction. What is beyond doubt, however, is that the mother of all research universities was now but one among many, and by no means the most distinguished, even in Germany.

CHAPTER THREE

Truth, Justice, and Freedom in a Cold War World

Free University of Berlin

O N JUNE 26, 1963, nearly two years after the erection of the Berlin Wall, John F. Kennedy flew to West Berlin. Before a cheering throng of 450,000, the American president delivered the most memorable speech of the Cold War. "All free men," he said as he closed his oration, "wherever they may live, are citizens of Berlin, and, therefore, as a free man, I take pride in the words '*Ich bin ein Berliner.*'"[1]

Hours later, Kennedy addressed twenty thousand faculty and students gathered on the campus of the Freie Universität Berlin (Free University, or FU). Receiving an honorary degree, he was "honored to become an instant graduate of this distinguished university." But was the word "free" not redundant? "The fact of the matter is," he argued, "that any university, if it is a university, is free." But not necessarily in Berlin. This was the challenge of those studying at Free University: "This school is not interested in turning out merely corporation lawyers or skilled accountants. What it is interested in . . . is in turning out citizens of the world . . . who are willing to commit their energies to the advancement of a free society. That is why you are here, and that is why this school was founded." Evoking Free University's motto of *veritas, iustitia, libertas,* Kennedy concluded, "The scholar, the teacher, the intellectual have a higher duty than any of the others, for society has trained you to think as well as to do. This community has committed itself to that objective, and you have a special obligation to think and to help forge the future of this city in terms of truth and justice and liberty."[2]

Humboldt could not have said it better. Twenty-six years after Kennedy's visit, the Berlin Wall fell, and the several parts of Berlin (and soon Germany)

Figure 3.1. John F. Kennedy speaking at Free University of Berlin, 1963.
Courtesy of Peter-André Alt.

were reunited. After another three decades, Free University found itself primus inter pares among Berlin universities and an exemplar of "excellence" in the Federal Republic. Yet its Cold War origins remained everywhere visible. The offices of the university president and leading administrators were housed in the building of the Allied Kommandatura—the governing body of immediate postwar Berlin—in Berlin-Dahlem, a Weimar-era edifice built in an aggressive modern style. In the corridor outside the president's office, pictures and documents of Kennedy's visit welcome visitors. Not far from the president's office sits the beautifully renovated Henry Ford Building, financed by the Ford Foundation and designed to be the *Hauptgebäude,* or main building, of the university to rival that of the original university in East Berlin. An imposing structure of two hundred thousand square feet, it is encased in glass and bathed in light, symbolizing the freedom, openness, and transparency that were founding hallmarks of Free University. The architect's client, the university denotes, was "democracy."[3]

More than fifty years after Kennedy's seismic speeches, President Peter-André Alt stepped out of his office in the old Kommandatura and reflected on the unexpected transformations of his university during his lifetime. By the time Alt assumed the presidency in 2010, FU, as it is colloquially called, had reinvented itself yet again as a modern, international university, rooted in the humanities in the Humboldtian tradition. In the twenty-first century, FU acquired national and international renown and was now one of eleven members of the "Excellence Initiative," a prestigious coalition of Germany's leading institutions of higher education. Under Alt's tenure, FU had outdone and outranked its more famous neighbor, named for Humboldt, in the east of the city. But this was a university that had experienced multiple moments of distinction and nearly as many near-death experiences. Alt knew his presidency was coming to a close, and that a colleague at FU, Günter Ziegler, would assume his role in July 2018. Reflecting on his eight years in the Kommandatura, Alt wondered, What would guarantee the future of modern Germany's most experimental university?

"A Severely Tested Youth": Origin Stories, 1945–1948

Berlin, Germany's capital city, had been a focal point for Allied attacks during the Second World War. By the end of the war, the center of the city surrounding the Stadtschloß and the university was in rubble. Soon Berlin, like the rest of Germany, was divided into four sectors. The *Mitte* district, where most of the government ministries and the bulk of the university buildings were located, came under Soviet control. The rest of Berlin was then occupied by the three Western Allied powers: France, Great Britain, and the United States. The University of Berlin (today's Humboldt), located in the Soviet sector, was not subordinate to the Allied Kommandatura, the official governing body for the whole city, but came under Soviet control.

Berlin's unique situation—a city half-controlled by Western forces in the middle of the Soviet Occupation Zone of Germany—made it a natural focal point in the Cold War after 1947. The city was initially governed by a four-power Allied Control Council with a leadership that rotated monthly. However, as East-West relations deteriorated, the Soviets withdrew from the council and began governing their sector independently. The Control Council maintained the rotating leadership policy, although now involving only the three Western Allies.

The University of Berlin itself lay in ruins, with 90 percent of its buildings destroyed. Teaching had ceased altogether in 1944. Much of the faculty had emigrated, had been expelled, or were executed. Between 1933 and 1945 over a third of Berlin's faculty was forcibly removed from the university, representing one of the highest expulsion rates among German universities.

With Soviet permission, the University of Berlin reopened in January 1946. Five other universities in the Soviet sector also reopened at that time: Jena, Halle-Wittenberg, Leipzig, Greifswald, and Rostock. At all of these universities, the Soviets enforced a rigorous process of denazification, with the goal of eliminating the old fascist elites and "forming a generation capable of definitively establishing Communism."[4] All employees at every German university had to reapply for their positions. The University of Berlin subsequently employed only 120 of its 700 original professors and lecturers. The newly reestablished university admitted twenty-eight hundred students from more than nine thousand applicants.[5] When academic instruction resumed, professors and students had to prove that they were either victims of fascism or had ideologically distanced themselves from the Nazi regime. The surest way to do so was to join the Socialist Unity Party of Germany (SED), an amalgam of the former Social Democrats and Communists, although utterly dominated by the latter.

With the ultimate goal of forming a socialist "people's university," education in the Soviet sector was dominated by themes of class struggle. As in the Soviet Union—and later throughout the Soviet bloc, including China—

obligatory courses in all degree programs instructed students in Marxist-Leninist philosophy and political economy, à la Stalin. This system aimed to "proletarianize" universities and change the social makeup of the students and faculty. It also severely curbed academic freedom. It soon became apparent that the University of Berlin was intended by the Soviet leadership to be a training ground for future SED cadres. Admissions, and success, became tied to political orientation. In response, protests arose among a group of democratically inclined students who felt that the obligatory lectures offered little more than indoctrination in the tenets of Marxism-Leninism. Some voiced critiques against the role of the Soviets and the SED at the university and beyond.

Student activism led to rapid repression. In March 1947 Soviet police arrested Georg Wrazidlo, a medical student who was head of the student council, as he met with fellow students in Berlin's famous coffeehouse Café Kranzler. Two months later, five other students disappeared in a similar fashion. In a secret session, a Soviet court found Wrazidlo and several others guilty of "covert fascist activities." The students received prison sentences of between ten and twenty-five years. Wrazidlo had survived incarceration in Buchenwald under the Nazis. Now he found himself in a camp at Sachsenhausen under the Communists. He was forty when he was released from the camp in 1956.[6]

Yet dissident students who avoided arrest continued their resistance. A handful of particularly outspoken students, including Otto Hess, Joachim Schwarz, and Otto Stolz, declared, "Freedom, humanity and the rights of man are for us of inestimable worth, and we shall fight unrelentingly against anyone who attempts to infringe upon them. . . . This we wish to state quite openly: . . . we shall criticize anything that is worthy of criticism."[7]

By the end of 1947 the student activists were increasingly critical about the state of the university and its students. Hess wrote, "In Berlin the great majority of students obviously do not have the energy and courage anymore to represent their views, instead they allow themselves to be terrorized by a tiny minority without showing any resistance."[8] To these discouraged young reformers, it seemed more and more unlikely that it would be possible to change the old university. Because it was illegal under the occupation agreements to criticize Soviet authorities directly, dissidents could only seek to discredit the German SED authorities, while chronicling the demise of democratic institutions at universities in the Soviet zone. In a heavy-handed response, the central administration and the rector of the university expelled Stolz, Hess, and Schwarz in mid-April 1948 "because of publishing activities which act counter to the good manners and dignity of a student."[9]

Even though dozens of students had already received similar dismissals, having subsequently been placed under arrest or gone elsewhere to study, the latest expulsions electrified the dissident members of the student body. Immediately, different student groups organized a strike. On April 23, 1948, two thousand student protesters appeared at the Hotel Esplanade on Potsdamer Platz, located in the British sector in Western Berlin, only 150 feet away from the Soviet zone. There, students Erich Weber, from the University of Jena, and Otto Stolz announced an idea that was previously inconceivable: the establishment of a new university in the Western part of Berlin, one where students could study free of repression and ideological encroachment.

A young American journalist named Kendall Foss, who was on staff at the American-sponsored *Neue Zeitung*, had written about the events at the University of Berlin and witnessed the demonstration at the Esplanade. Impressed by Stolz's ardor, Foss offered to connect the students with the American authorities. Foss called on American General Lucius D. Clay, the American High Commissioner for Germany, and Herman Wells, the president of Indiana University, who had taken leave to be cultural adviser to the Allied Military Government. Wells hired Foss to serve as a special assistant to explore the establishment of a new university in the West: "Foss understood the situation and seemed to have the drive and competence."[10] A preparatory committee was formed, consisting of sympathetic German professors, politicians, and students seeking to establish a counter-university in Western Berlin. Foss and his committee submitted their findings to General Clay in May 1948. Foss was at pains to ensure it would not be an "American" university: "The committee believes that the project as it is developing will be (and should be) fundamentally German in its initiation and relation. U.S. participation can properly be confined to moral and material support of a worthy German idea."[11]

Seldom if ever has a university been started so quickly. At the urging of a now-enthusiastic General Clay, assisted by the German-American political scientist Carl J. Friedrich, who took leave from Harvard to serve as Clay's advisor, the preparatory committee concluded that a new university could start within six months and be up and running by autumn 1948. Recruitment of faculty was, to be sure, a challenge, but sixty of the sixty-six professors at the University of Berlin already lived in the West, and—in a bit of arrogance—it was felt that "a staff the equal of the present Berlin University could surely be found."[12] As the preparatory committee, now chaired by the governing mayor of Berlin, Ernst Reuter, began to take concrete steps, the students, too, planned for the establishment of the new university.

Across town, two-thirds of the student council of the University of Berlin had resigned their positions and formed their own preparatory committee. Their expectations in many ways defined the new university in both the immediate and distant future. As Otto Hess wrote in July 1948, "If a new university is to be more than merely an attempt to preserve honorable but outmoded traditions, then courage must be evident to go in new directions." Every generation had the right "to find its own way."[13]

Never has application to a new university been easier: students could apply by postcard, giving their academic history in the briefest form. University of Berlin students sat on the admissions committees in choosing the first cohort. By October 5,500 applications had yielded an inaugural class of 2,140.[14]

The appeal to raise support for the new university sought to place it in the tradition of the brothers Alexander and Wilhelm von Humboldt: "It is about the establishment of a free university, which serves truth for its own sake. Every student should know that this is a place where, in the spirit of true democracy, one's individuality can freely evolve and not become an object of one-sided propaganda."[15]

The original University of Berlin was founded by the king; Free University of Berlin was founded by students. At the least, without their combination of energy, idealism, and entrepreneurialism, no new university was conceivable in the Berlin of 1948. It followed, therefore, that the governing structure of the university entrusted students with a remarkable degree of influence. In what became known as the Berlin Model of university governance, students served as voting members of committees and on the highest authority of the university, its Board of Regents (*Kuratorium*). In direct contrast to what was, by 1949, called Humboldt University—and indeed to any German university—students ran "student affairs": they helped to set admissions criteria; they took part in student discipline; and they sat in the University Senate, where—for the first time in the history of German universities—students voted on professorial appointments. With this authority came responsibility, a significant workload, and, above all in the early years of FU, a sense of common purpose. As the constitution of the university stated, Free University would be "a community of scholars and teachers."[16]

The new university was distinguished also by establishing, partly on an American model, its own Board of Trustees, with authority to set budgets and major policies. Governing Mayor Ernst Reuter chaired the Board, but the structure argued for greater autonomy from the state than that enjoyed by any modern German university.

But even democracies need leaders, and before its inauguration, the university sought a "notable," a figure of eminence, to lead it. Edwin Redslob, a well-known art historian and early leader of the nascent faculty, argued that the new university had to be "built up from the top down," and its first rector should be a "celebrated personality." Celebrated personalities without compromised pasts were not easy to find in immediate postwar Berlin, but Ernst Reuter convinced the aging, ill, and increasingly deaf historian Friedrich Meinecke to assume the position. The octogenarian was widely regarded as the leading German historian alive. A man of centrist to moderate liberal politics, his work had contrasted the values of cosmopolitanism with those of the national state. The Nazis had dismissed him from his decades-long editorship of the *Historische Zeitschrift*, the world's most prestigious journal of historical research, in 1935. Meinecke took up the post on two conditions: that there be an executive vice rector (*Geschäftsführender Rektor*)—Edwin Redslob—to handle university administration and that Reuter get more electricity to Meinecke's apartment, so the old man could read.[17]

The *Gründungsfeier* inaugurating Free University took place on December 4, 1948. Bad weather and a bad cold kept Rector Meinecke home and in bed. Restricted transportation limited participation of rectors and academic leaders from other universities. Without facilities of its own, the university borrowed a public hall that was available on that date. But by all accounts the ceremony was unforgettable. Speaking from his home by RIAS (Radio in the American Sector), Meinecke began, "With joy I hear the voice of youth, and I welcome its call for a new university, for a true sanctuary of science (*Wissenschaft*) and its teaching." This was, he noted, "a new university rising directly from the passionate demands of a severely tested youth," and as "the oldest in the Faculty" and in a "grandfatherly relationship," he took "the outstretched hand of youth." He called for competition, not conflict, between Berlin's now two universities: "May the day come when we can be reunited."[18]

Survival and Sustainability, 1949–1961

Lectures at FU had actually started in mid-November, before the *Gründungsfeier* was celebrated and just seven months after the three students had been expelled from the old university. Meinecke's hopes for the future notwithstanding, Berlin was now divided academically as it was politically. One day after the official ceremonies, elections for Berlin's municipal government were held in the Western sectors of Berlin, boycotted by the SED. But West Berlin had already become an isolated extension of the West.

The university was founded at the height of the Berlin blockade—the Soviet effort to make life in a separate, Allied-occupied West Berlin unsustainable. In response to Allied efforts to fuse the American, French, and British sectors of Western Germany into one political entity by initiating a new currency, the Soviets had blocked all ground access—railway, road, and canal—to the Western sectors of Berlin on June 26, 1948. The American and British air forces engaged in a massive logistical effort to supply the western part of the city through an audacious *Luftbrücke*, or "air bridge"—the Berlin Airlift.

The airlift was a heroic effort by the Americans, their allies, and the Berlin citizens who persevered through a winter of cold and dearth. The blockade lasted almost a year. With its extraordinary scale (270,000 flights to supply West Berlin for 11 months) and Allied solidarity (the French built a new airport in their sector in 90 days), the airlift made anything else seem possible, including the lightning founding of a new university.

Free University lacked everything from buildings to furniture to books; the medical faculty was short of basic equipment. The city of Berlin could provide moral and legal support, less so financial support. Among the Western occupation forces, only the United States actively supported the founding of the university. Free University quickly became a symbol of German-American friendship. The American occupying power subsidized the university during its first months of existence with earnings from newspapers issued in the American sector. In its founding months in 1948, Free University received approximately US$500,000 from the Americans.[19] They even carved out of the airlift shipments special allocations for Free University. This aid would grow significantly over time, as Berlin became a central battlefield in the global Cold War. From its founding through 1963, FU received US$5.7 million from the US government. The Ford Foundation, then in the heyday of its international engagement, awarded the university US$3.175 million, including the funds for Benjamin Franklin University Hospital and

Figure 3.2. Henry Ford Building. Times/Wikimedia Commons/CC BY-SA 3.0.

for the iconic Henry Ford Building that defined the early campus.[20] The early university was designed to have a residential campus in the American sense; this already distinguished it from other universities in Germany.

The university's location in Berlin-Dahlem spoke to its ambitions. In the beginning of the twentieth century, Dahlem had been chosen by Prussian authorities to become a "city of science." It was home to many scientific institutions, such as state archives and museums. Most famously, the *Kaiser-Wilhelm-Gesellschaft* (KWG), precursor of the Max Planck Society, was founded there in 1911 as a "German Oxford" (a rather strange metaphor given Berlin's dominance over Oxford in the sciences at that time). It was here in Dahlem, not in the downtown campus, that Nobel laureates Albert Einstein, Werner Heisenberg, and Max Planck made their names. After World War II these institutes belonged formally to Humboldt University. In 1949 the American authorities transferred the administration of these institutes to Free University, which (bizarrely, since legal ownership remained to be determined) paid rent to Humboldt University. But ultimately this was an appropriation of major facilities in the natural and medical sciences. Two years later, Humboldt University's faculty of veterinary medicine defected en masse to FU.

The 2,140 students enrolled in the inaugural class were taught in three faculties: the Philosophical Faculty, the Faculty of Law and Economics, and the Medical Faculty. The senior faculty of *ordentliche Professoren* numbered but forty-three, including the rector, deans, and "honorary professors" who lent their names to the enterprise. These were augmented by junior scholars and visiting faculty from American universities, including Stanford and Yale. In following years, the faculty grew by recruiting scholars disaffected with East German universities and, more gradually, as the university grew in size and reputation, from West German institutions. In the winter semester of 1948–1949, approximately 70 percent of the non-first-year students had studied at the University of Berlin downtown, and another 20 percent at other East German universities. Nine percent came from West German universities, joined by thirty international students.

The university grew steadily through the 1950s and 1960s to six thousand students in 1954, twelve thousand by 1960, and nearly fifteen thousand in 1968.[21] Budgets and faculty recruiting grew accordingly. With generous support from Bonn, Berlin, and the United States, the budget grew 30 percent annually between 1958 and 1968. By 1968 the university had 396 professors, offered 77 degrees, and housed 155 institutes.[22] It was a major university.

For its first decade, at least, FU retained much of the idealism and energy that had led to its founding. As intended in the Berlin Model, students played an important role in supportive governance, and—at a time before FU's reputation as a research university was established—faculty devoted their energies largely to undergraduate education. To the standard *Vorlesungen,* or lecture courses, was added the first tutorial system on an Anglo-American model. Begun as a form of remedial reentry point for students from East German universities, it gained a life of its own and external funding from the Ford Foundation. To this was added a program—equally innovative for a German university—of general education. In a system in which students were still admitted to study in a particular discipline or profession, general education borrowed from the recent American experience (e.g., at Harvard) to broaden the scope of inquiry toward contemporary social, political, and cultural affairs. And the new university reached out to the city that had given it life: its *Funk-Universität,* or radio university, began to broadcast basic courses for Berlin citizens as early as the summer of 1949—here again the first German university to do so. An in-person Evening University was added for the general public in 1952. The strong sense of collective resolve that had united students and faculty and the university with the city in 1948 endured—for a time.[23]

Navigating the Global 1960s and After: Protest and Reform, 1962–1989

After its humble beginnings marked by economic austerity, Free University reached a status comparable to other West German institutions of higher learning by the early 1960s. While FU was widely known as a "reform" university, its West German peers resisted innovation and aimed for a "restoration" of German academic excellence of the pre-Nazi period.[24] As it recruited faculty and students now almost exclusively from West Germany, gradually, almost invisibly, FU was becoming part of a national system that was at once undynamic and unreformed.

Meanwhile, West Berlin was changing, gaining ever more of an original identity. The building of the Berlin Wall in 1961 made its western half, now surrounded with concrete barriers and watchtowers, even more of a Cold War island. It was deep in East Germany but deliberately distinct from the German Democratic Republic that encircled it. West Berlin was tied to the Federal Republic in the West, which bankrolled it substantially as a vibrant Western showcase, in comparison to the drab grayness (in Western eyes) *drüben*, "over there," in the East.

Once a great industrial city, Berlin grew to be an increasingly edgy cultural center, known for music and the arts and, increasingly, education. Independent-minded students who sought a university seemingly at the cutting edge, at the heart of global affairs, and in a city known for *Kinos und Kneipen* (movie houses and bars) chose Berlin. And for young men of draft age who studied in Berlin there was an additional incentive: residents of the former *Hauptstadt* were exempt from conscription into the West German *Bundeswehr*, since Berlin was not (yet) legally part of the Federal Republic. From a besieged Cold War city (which, in real terms, it still was), West Berlin became a cool, countercultural, subsidized alternative to Frankfurt, Hamburg, Stuttgart, and other materialist vanguards of the West German economic miracle.

President Kennedy's 1963 visit set the high water mark for pro-Western and pro-American sentiment in Berlin. His assassination later that year and American distraction toward Asia (Vietnam) seemed to dash hopes that the

Wall, and Berlin's division, would be short lived. Seeds of anti-American sentiment had been laid by FU students in the late 1950s protesting the proliferation of atomic weapons and the American rearmament of West Germany. Young Germans born after the war began to confront Germany's militarist past, spurred on by revisionist historians such as Fritz Fischer, whose 1961 book, *Griff nach der Weltmacht,* (published in English as *Germany's Aims in the First World War*) set out a powerful case for German war guilt in both world wars. Within two years of Kennedy's triumphal appearance, FU found itself facing a seemingly endless series of internal crises. A "free speech" movement akin to that at the University of California, Berkeley, challenged the right of administrators to approve external speakers. A junior faculty member accused the rector of proactive censorship in another case. Students gathered en masse to call for the rector's resignation. Within weeks, the historian James Tent has written, FU moved "from an apparently normally functioning urban university into a crisis-ridden institution whose very basis was being questioned."[25]

By 1966 the Berlin Model of faculty-student comity was on life support. Leftist students formed their own student groups that demanded *Mitbestimmung,* or full co-representation, as if they were a labor union in a major firm. With growing outrage over the American war in Vietnam, anti-American demonstrations (for example, against the Berlin visit of Vice President Hubert Humphrey in 1967) became numerous and turbulent. When in 1967 FU student Benno Ohnesorg was shot in the head by Berlin police while protesting the visit of the Shah of Iran, an American ally, on a state visit to Berlin, the outrage was universal, but the lessons drawn were generational. Fifteen thousand attended the services on FU campus in the Henry Ford Building for Ohnesorg, the first but not last victim of a cultural revolution at Free University.[26] The murder set off weeks of mass demonstrations in West Germany and radicalized the student movement. Ohnesorg's death also led to the resignation of the president of the police, the interior senator of Berlin, and the mayor of West Berlin, all of whom were forced to confront the brutality of the offending police officer. The officer himself was eventually acquitted, and subsequent investigations revealed that he and several witnesses had made false statements in an attempt to cover up the affair. The 2009 revelation that the officer in question was working as a Stasi-IM at the time further complicated the story, yet no evidence has been found that his intention in firing was to sow dissent in West Berlin.

Figure 3.3. Student sit-in on April 19–20, 1967, in the lobby of the Henry Ford Building. Courtesy of Bernard Larsson.

A university founded as a reaction to leftist extremism now found itself at the center of radical political movements that were spreading across the globe. In Paris, May 1968 saw the onset of student-led demonstrations that led to a general strike and nearly brought down the French government. In the United States, divisions over the Vietnam War roiled American campuses. In China, the Maoist Cultural Revolution disrupted and closed universities, while a loosely understood "Maoism" found favor among Western leftists. And in Berlin, a university that was the beneficiary of American largesse became a target for anti-American politics.

By the early 1970s the student movement had radicalized further and splintered into well-organized student groups, threatening the freedom of teaching and learning with agitprop techniques. The university became intensely politicized. The Academic Senate and the rector's office were periodically occupied by protesting students. Political graffiti adorned buildings old and new. In 1970 a part-time FU instructor, Ulrike Meinhof, masterminded the escape of a convicted political arsonist, Andreas Baader, and the consequent "Baader-Meinhof Gang" became synonymous with domestic terrorism. The nonfatal shooting of charismatic student movement leader Rudi Dutschke a year later brought matters to a boiling point.

All this gave rise to a movement for governance reform that would build on the original Berlin Model and take it further still, to incorporate (and ideally focus) student energies on the working of the university. An early advocate of what would become the new University Law of 1969 was the political scientist Alexander Schwan, who believed in *Mitbestimmung* and bringing students further into the running of the university. The new law did precisely that, institutionalizing radical student groups in university committees and programs. By 1971 Schwan had had enough and called the reformed law a mistake. The response by Maoist students was to attempt to defenestrate him—that is, to throw him out the window of his seminar in the Otto Suhr Institute, the home of political science at FU. Amid an intense physical struggle, Schwan was saved by a group of moderate students and by his wife, the young assistant professor Gesine Schwan.[27]

I was a student at Free University in 1972–1973, a postgraduate recipient of a DAAD (German Academic Exchange Service) grant and a *Luftbrückendankstipendium* (Airlift Thank-you Fellowship) from the city of Berlin. I was a student of history at the Friedrich Meinecke Institute, where I heard rumors of the near-defenestration of another scholar, Friedrich Zipfel, a historian of the Nazi era whose lectures I audited. In the winter semester the new Rostlaube building was opened, housing courses on history and political science. Before a single class could meet, its rusty exterior was covered in red and yellow political slogans. There I took a seminar on Marx in the Otto Suhr Institute. It was taught by Gesine Schwan, who would outlive her husband and all FU's disorder to become a major scholar and a political figure in Germany's Social Democratic Party. Schwan was then very early in her teaching career, and no seminar could have been more challenging. Among the fifteen or so students in our class, there were at least six different Communist parties or factions. Perhaps Marx has never been so thoroughly examined: from the vantage point of Maoists, of Stalinists, of Marxian anarchists, not to mention those who believed that little Albania practiced Marxism in its purist form. We the students read Marx collaboratively (more or less) in *Arbeitsgruppen,* or work groups, albeit usually in the friendly confines of a Berlin *Kneipe.* Because I was the only one among us who could cross the Wall as a citizen of an Allied power, I had the special task of buying our texts on the cheap in East Berlin. Schwan, whose every utterance in seminar was interrupted by one faction or the other, wins my vote for the Iron Cross in endurance and patience.

The university had reached the point of breakdown in the early 1970s. Berlin city officials lamented that the university's patent inability to govern itself meant that the state had to intervene. The Berlin Model of the university's early days was by then a distant memory, and revisions to the university law in 1974 and an altogether new legislation in 1978 restored the majority rule of the professoriat and strengthened the position of the president. These measures were carried further in the 1980s. As James Tent, whose political history of the first three decades of FU remains the standard account, wrote, "For a short time the Free University operated under a system so democratic as to excite the astonishment of any Communist-bloc nation or institution." The results were so polarizing as to invite an inevitable reaction. As political movements and university laws came and went, the original Free University of Berlin disappeared. Here again, Tent said, "The blunt fact was that no amount of tinkering with laws and constitutions could restore [what] had once made the Free University a unique institution for nearly a generation."[28]

Throughout this period, perhaps in an effort to coopt the university's radicalization, government spending on education increased, but curricula were altered to prepare students better for the job market, not for revolution. The revised Berlin University Law of 1978 focused not on the "whole person education" that had defined the founding years of both Berlin universities, but rather on "the needs of professional practice."[29] But the decade of turmoil at FU had made the university a less attractive place, perhaps especially to the practically minded. By the mid-1970s, the quality of the faculty and student body had decreased significantly. The number of students, however, increased dramatically. During the 1970s and 1980s the university—like many in Germany—became a mass university (*Massenuniversität*). Students came young and stayed late—in part because of the exemption from military service and because limits on time-to-degree were seldom enforced. Political pressures on the Berlin government led to ever-greater expansion. Since university budgets were determined in large measure by the number of students, there was a mutual incentive on the part of government and university to grow. And so the university bloated. The size of the student body rose from 15,778 in 1968 to 27,892 in 1973, to 61,198 in 1988, on the eve of the fall of the Berlin Wall.[30] Earlier concepts of small-group learning in tutorials and broader initiatives in general education atrophied.

In the 1980s, with a return to academic normalcy across the western world, moderating influences prevailed at FU. But as the university moved away from its politicized past, it grew undistinguished. It was now "a normal German university,"[31] but in an era when the global reputation of German universities was a distant memory. When state budgets inevitably became tight again, FU had to institute a hiring freeze; its medical clinic, Westend, closed. One compensating factor—and an auspicious sign for the future—was that the university began to attract third-party resources in Germany in a serious way. Between 1978 and 1985 the amount of independent support doubled to DM 56 million.[32] This enabled the university's Office of International Affairs to maintain the international programs that from its early days had defined FU as a university with special ties to America, and now beyond.

Nach der Wende: Retrenchment, 1989–2000

With the fall of the Wall and the formal reunification of Germany eleven months later, the original raison d'être of Free University ceased to exist. FU and Humboldt University had begun minor areas of cooperation before 1989, but they would soon enter into a competitive struggle for survival.

Berlin was again to be the capital of a united Germany. It was inconceivable that Humboldt University, located in what again would be the real *Mitte* of Berlin, would cease to exist. Rather, as we have seen, immediate efforts were made to decommunize it and to give it more democratic governance. The question was, should Humboldt be *the* university in Berlin once more? And should a newly reunited country with a reunited capital not aspire further? German universities historically were funded by the states in which they were situated. Was it not time for a truly *national* university?

The answer was no. German reunification was going to be expensive enough, and there was neither the will nor the budget to build a national university. The newly unified Berlin was proud but broke. The West German funds that had subsidized West Berlin during the Cold War would be discontinued, and the city would have to fund higher education largely on its own, as Berlin became one of the sixteen states of Germany and one of the poorest.

The question then was this: Should Humboldt take over FU, and perhaps also the Technical University, to have one, huge, comprehensive university for Berlin in multiple parts of the city, with an elite core in the city center? The name Humboldt, after all, was world renowned, as was the legacy of the University of Berlin. The upstart FU had fewer claims to fame and had perhaps served its historic purpose. Berlin's Senator for Science Manfred Erhardt imagined a renewed, elite Humboldt whose influence would spread far beyond the city. The West German universities, he argued, were seen internationally as anything but a model, and the *Massenuniversitäten* of Free and Technical Universities had so many problems that it would take years of reform before they would enjoy a significant external reputation.[33]

That both Humboldt and FU survived, joined also by the Technical University, is testament to the power of inertia, of bureaucratic passive (and at times active) resistance on the part of the existing institutions; the absence of a vision of what a united university would look like; and, again, a lack of money. Ultimately, administrators and the Senate decided to keep both Humboldt and Free Universities in the hope that this would foster healthy intercollegiate competition, ultimately improving the teaching and research at both institutions.[34]

In the first years *nach der Wende,* after the fall of the Wall, a great number of students from the former East Germany sought to start or continue their studies at Free University. Enrollment increased and the number of students at FU exceeded sixty-two thousand. But as Berlin's budgetary realities hit home, and with fewer subsidies from the German federal government, the budget of FU was reduced considerably in the 1990s.

In 1988 FU had proposed to Berlin's Senate a structural plan that had envisaged a decade of university investment and stability in the 1990s.[35] That plan was now worthless. The Senate's 1993 University Structural Plan reduced funding for Berlin's universities by DM 1 billion (approximately US$600 million) over the next decade. The costs to FU were disproportionately great, for as Humboldt was being built back up, FU was seemingly drawn and quartered to help pay for it. The number of fully funded student seats at FU decreased by half: from nearly 40,000 in 1992, to 26,000 in 2001, and then to 21,000 in 2003. The number of professors in the same period declined even more radically: from approximately 700 (outside of medical fields) in 1990, to 440 in 1999, and to 368 in 2003.[36] Annually, between 1992 and 1999, the number of faculty departures far outweighed faculty appointments.

The cuts hit hardest at the core academic missions. The university could not downsize everywhere. Because nonacademic employees were largely permanent, with contracts that could not be nullified, many academic employees were laid off, while the nonacademic staff retained their positions in the university's bureaucracy. Beyond this, degree programs that were offered by both FU and Humboldt were subject to cutbacks. A number of smaller institutes were transferred from FU to Humboldt, including the institutes for library science, sports science, Scandinavian studies, and Slavic studies. The medical school, including the dental clinic and the pediatric clinic, was transferred to Humboldt University, leaving the future of the life sciences at FU in doubt. In 1996 the Berlin Senate reduced drastically the budget at both university libraries. In April 1996 and in the winter semester of 1997–1998, these cutbacks resulted in widespread student demonstrations and strikes. In an echo of the 1960s the offices of the FU president were once again occupied by students.

Reinvention and Renewal in the Twenty-First Century

In the twenty-first century, Free University would have to reconceive itself yet again. The mass university had to shed students, faculty, and decades of accumulated fat and memory. That it would emerge a leaner, fitter, more competitive enterprise to compete with the resurrected Humboldt University—this no one could have imagined at the turn of the century.

Yet by 2017 the *Times Higher Education* ranked FU as one of the top five (out of more than one hundred) German research universities, and among the top twenty in the world in the humanities. And it had built on its early history of internationalization—being the product of a global Cold War—to be the leading German university in the realms of international studies and global partnerships. Spread across three modern campuses in Berlin, the university in 2020 had eleven academic units, now a joint medical school (Charité) with Humboldt University, as well as three international institutes that offered degrees in Eastern European, Latin American, and North American studies. In all, Free University offered some 180 bachelor's and master's degree programs as well as around 50 doctoral programs. It was known above all for its programs in the humanities and social sciences, but increasingly also for the natural and life sciences.

Free University made a remarkable comeback in the twenty-first century. How did it do it?

Governance: The Capacity for Leadership

Part of the answer must lie in governance. Formally, many aspects of the governance of Free University today seem similar to the governance structures found at Humboldt and other German universities. Its Academic Senate (AS), led by the president, comprises twenty-five members, who are elected for two-year terms. The AS consists of four groups representing different interests at the university: thirteen professors and four representatives each from the student body, the academic staff, and the nonacademic staff. The professors hold an absolute majority, but only by one vote, and only if they voted unanimously. The AS passes resolutions on matters including university development and equipment plans and establishes basic principles applicable to instruction, studies, and research at the university. It confirms the number of students admitted each year. It is also involved in the establishment and elimination of courses of study and issues a position statement on the draft budget every year. Since FU is a public university, Berlin's Senate continues to function as an influential stakeholder. It negotiates the annual basic funding with Free University, and—more than the Academic Senate—determines the number of students admitted every year, since it is the Berlin Senate that pays for them.

As at Humboldt University, Free University is led by a president who serves for a term of four years and could be reelected. The president and the executive vice president are elected by a majority vote of the extended Academic Senate, which includes thirty-six additional members, on nomination by the same governing body. Together with the Academic Senate, the president proposes three additional vice presidents, who are responsible for different areas of administration and finance.

Compared with Humboldt University, the FU president has greater agency in choosing the FU leadership team. And perhaps because of the gravity of the crisis of the 1990s, the Academic Senate and university leadership work in comparative harmony. Unlike Humboldt University, where none of the presidents after 1989 served a full second term, the leadership at FU has much more continuity and de facto authority. The average presidential tenure in office is seven years. The president is part of an executive board, which also includes the chancellor, the executive vice president, and the vice presidents. It approves the draft budget and proposes structural and development plans. It also implements resolutions of the AS, such as the establishment and elimination of courses of study.

Of course, it is not just the positions but the people who hold them that matter. FU's history in the twenty-first century is testimony to the importance of continuity and quality of presidential leadership in a university. Despite, or more likely because of, FU's tumultuous experience in the past, presidents were accorded—and they asserted—more authority than was common for German universities. The legal scholar Johann Wilhelm Gerlach led the university from 1991 to 1999, resisting fiercely the attempted merger of FU with Humboldt University, encouraging student protests over budget cuts, and using court procedures to defend the university's institutional autonomy. Dieter Lenzen, a scholar of educational philosophy, was elected FU's sixth president in 2003, coming to office after having taught at Stanford, Columbia, and Tokyo, among other distinguished international universities. Lenzen's vision and drive led FU to build on its international strengths and to reform its administration, which led to its distinction in the first round of Excellence Initiative funding.[37] By all accounts a force of nature, Lenzen spearheaded FU's efforts in its first competition in the nationwide Excellence Initiative before leaving to preside over the University of Hamburg in 2010. And the distinguished scholar of German literature (eighteen monographs) Peter-André Alt led FU with a gentle disposition and iron backbone from 2010 until 2018, taking it to stunning success in the second and third rounds of Germany's Excellence competitions. He was succeeded by the internationally renowned mathematician Günter M. Ziegler, an MIT PhD who had founded the Berlin Mathematical School, a joint graduate program of the three major (including the Technical University) Berlin universities.

The Iron Chancellor

Presidents are, or ought to be, central to the direction of any university. Equally important at FU was the role of professional administration. At Humboldt University, as we have seen, the *Berufsbeamtentum,* or professional civil service, was initially held over from GDR days. At FU, strength in administrative leadership was a key factor in the university's renewal.

Second to the role of the president at FU is the *Kanzler.* The *Kanzler* is chancellor—as in Britain's Chancellor of the Exchequer—and formally in charge of the budget. (It was the absence of this position at Humboldt University that would so frustrate its presidents.) At FU, the Board of Trustees elects the chancellor upon nomination of the president, and then the Berlin

Senate formally appoints the chancellor for a ten-year term. With responsibilities that have grown far beyond the budget, the chancellor plays a critical role at FU. The chancellor's term has outlasted that of any president, and the chancellor has had unique power and knowledge of the purse in times of dearth (such as the 1990s) or reinvestment (as in the 2010s).

The iron chancellor of the modern FU was Peter Lange. Peter Lange (pronounced *Lahn-ge*, and not to be confused with Peter Lange, the longtime provost of Duke, whom we shall meet in Chapter 7), began his association with FU in 1976 as a student of economics pedagogy and retired forty years later, having served as research associate and lecturer, then managing director for the Academic Senate, then as head of the presidential office for a decade, and, for his final fifteen years, as chancellor. Lange was the embodiment of administrative continuity in the turbulent and transformative quarter-century after the fall of the Wall. His coordination of FU's structural reform in the 1990s, his deft touch in working with the Berlin Senate, mastery of budgets and budgetary politics, and keen collaboration with a series of presidents all helped to ensure that as FU became smaller and leaner, it grasped the opportunity to become, pound-for-pound, much better. He contributed mightily to the raising of FU's profile domestically and internationally and above all to its successes in the Excellence Initiative. He also oversaw the development of the university's physical plant, as the client for Lord Norman Foster's Philological Library, which opened in 2005, and for the gracious complex completed in 2015 for the *Kleine Fächer*, or small departments, in the humanities and social sciences that were at the heart of FU's renewal—today the largest building on the campus.

Over his long tenure, Lange was the most enduringly powerful and least visible leader of the university. A student publication wrote in 2011 about its search for a "Phantom": "At the FU there rules an Invisible Man." Chancellor Peter Lange was among "the most influential" people, yet "hardly anyone on campus knows him."[38] Indeed, he would become widely and publicly feted only on retirement. President Peter-André Alt remarked at the retirement gathering for Lange in December 2015, when Lange's portrait was hung in the Henry Ford Building, that Lange was "the universalist" among chancellors. "What does this chancellor do?" Alt asked a large audience. "Almost everything. Budgets and personnel. Controls. Planning with academic departments on their goals. Coordination of centralized and decentralized processes. Construction and campus development. Energy and IT. Hiring of tenured faculty. Third-party funding. Research fit-outs. Li-

Figure 3.4. The Philological Library, designed by Norman Foster. senhormario/flickr/CC BY 2.0.

braries. Learning and teaching." Unlike other chancellors at German universities who focused solely on budgets, Lange "does it all. He takes on everything himself and is never haughty." Lange had "firm control" over the two thousand colleagues in the FU administration because "he knows what is to be done."[39]

When Lange retired, he was asked what he was most proud of: "The success of the Free University. To see a university, which in the reunited city [of Berlin] was repeatedly given no chance, develop so grandly after the painful cuts of the 1990s. This outcome is the result of a great many medium, large, and a few huge successes, all of which had to be pursued tirelessly—accompanied to be sure by setbacks. And as former chancellor I am naturally proud that we have succeeded in building one of the most modern and efficient university administrations in Germany."[40]

Funding from the Outside

Lange and the presidents he served found success in an economy of scarcity, where priorities had to be set carefully. Berlin's fiscal crisis after the fall of the Wall led to vast cuts in state funding. The Berlin Senate shifted resources from FU and Technical University to Humboldt University, cutting FU's budget in half. Tuition fees could have served to compensate for the cutbacks in state funding, but even the contemplation of them in the 1990s led to massive student demonstrations at the Brandenburg Gate. In any event, the traditionally left-leaning Senate of Berlin was fundamentally against the idea of tuition, and it remained opposed even when tuition fees were first allowed by the German Supreme Court in 2005. By 2014 Germany's sixteen states had all abolished tuition charges for undergraduates. "In retrospect," President Alt would later lament, "we lost an opportunity to enhance our financial support and budget situations. We could have invested much more and done much more."[41] In 2020 student fees at FU were but US$340 per semester, two-thirds of which paid for a highly discounted public transit pass for greater Berlin.

To make things more difficult, German universities had a terrible record of raising money from private donors and industry. FU was no exception. As Alt analyzed the situation, "Since higher education is left to politics, there is no consciousness to support higher education. Private donors are a very small group when it comes to university funding. There has been a massive increase in private wealth. Maybe this will cause a change in the system, but this will need time, at least ten years from now." Private donations to FU totaled but US$1.1 million in 2016.[42]

The Senate of Berlin provided the main source of income for the university. In 2017 it designated a total of US$306 million. The funding was negotiated every three years in "university treaties" that were first established for all public universities in Berlin in 1997. Universities only received public funding under the condition that they complied with certain performance indicators, including the number of accepted students, faculty diversity, and internationalization. The university treaty gave FU planning stability, especially when it came to the appointment of new professors. Moreover, these funds were supplemented by salary and other support by partner institutions such as the Max Planck Society. Still, the funds provided by the Senate of Berlin were never sufficient for the university's expenses. FU's Structural Plan of 2015 described the funding situation as one of "forced structural overload."[43]

The federal government stepped in to provide additional public funding through its Higher Education Pact 2020. The initiative gave Free University additional funds, but only under the condition of increased enrollment. In 2017 these federal resources amounted to almost 12 percent of the university's total basic funding.

In recent years, Free University concentrated its efforts on raising *Drittmittel,* or third-party funds. Although the name "third-party funds" may suggest otherwise, these funds were largely public, taken from other sections of the federal education budget and the European Union. The difference between third-party funds and the general funds was that the universities had to compete for the third-party resources, which were linked to specific research projects. Between 1989 and 1995 third-party funds had doubled (from US$46 million to US$89 million) as state funding was slashed but were still ancillary to the regular state budget.[44] By 2017, however, third-party funds amounted to nearly 40 percent of the total funding of the university. The German Research Foundation (*Deutsche Forschungsgemeinschaft,* or DFG), found that FU was one of the strongest universities when it came to attracting third-party funds for research. In the reporting period 2014–2016, FU secured almost US$300 million in research funds from the DFG, ranking fifth among all German universities. In the humanities and social sciences, FU secured more third-party funds than any other German university.

Third-party funds made the university nationally competitive and internationally visible. They also created new pressures. The university was increasingly dependent on acquiring third-party funds, not the least because the funded projects were mostly short-term. Many research activities, especially new PhD programs, relied almost entirely on these resources and their prospect for renewal. That FU has attracted funding for new graduate degree programs is a vote of confidence in FU's judgment as to where academic fields are headed. The capacity to attract third-party funding became a major criterion for hiring decisions. It made the university at once more entrepreneurial (in seeking support) and more managerial (in using it). Full professors already had the task of running their *Lehrstuhl;* now they sought and managed sizeable external projects as well. And—as in leading research universities everywhere—third-party funds accentuated the already strong tendency to value research over teaching.

All that said, the necessary search for external support gave FU ever more of a start-up culture. And its early successes with DFG and other foundations proved to be preconditions for its performance in the most prestigious competition of all, the Excellence Initiative.

A New Call to Berlin: Faculty and Students

Competitive success in any research university depends ultimately on the faculty. Through good times and bad, Free University's faculty has consisted of a dedicated body of scholars that produced world-renowned research. Since 1948 five Nobel laureates have taught at FU. The faculty also included seventeen Leibniz Prize winners, the highest endowed award in Germany; seven Max Planck research award winners; and fifteen members of the German National Academy of Sciences, Leopoldina, one of the oldest associations of scholars of natural science and medicine in Germany. For scholars and researchers of natural sciences, being elected a member of Leopoldina was considered one of the highest distinctions granted by any institution in Germany.

In the past decade, FU's faculty has experienced a surge. A "call" to Berlin—now to FU—was again a mark of great prestige. But beyond the "full" professoriat, whose numbers were limited by the Berlin Senate, several hundred new positions were created by other means. Between 2018 and 2022 FU planned to raise the percentage of academic personnel with permanent careers to 35 percent by adding a variety of new professorships and a tentative step toward a tenure-track path.[45] These include endowed professorships, Excellence Initiative professorships, joint professorships with other research institutions, and junior professorships. Junior professorships, a category established in 2002, are term-limited to six years, at which point scholars are expected to apply for professorships *elsewhere*. By 2020 their ranks had expanded to 96.

FU recruited well and retained well. Between 2000 and 2017 the average rate of success in retention negotiations was 82 percent.[46] In cases in which the university was not able to retain faculty members, the main area of contention was often salary. Compared to the other German states, the salaries for professors in Berlin had been relatively low (as indeed had been the cost of living). In 2016 the salary for a professor in Berlin was approximately 10 percent less than the highest paying German state, Baden-Württemberg.[47] Compared to the United States, the salaries at FU were especially low. Except for appointments of foreign professors, the average base salary for full professors at FU in 2017 was US$107,000. For the highest rank (W3) professor, the average salary (including bonuses) was US$144,000 in 2018.[48] Another issue was the high teaching load. Universities in Berlin required their professors to teach nine hours per week. As anywhere, faculty devised means to reduce those numbers, but the load was still comparatively high.[49]

In 2018 FU had 358 full professors, with forty-eight of them holding joint appointments, or "extraordinary professorships," with other higher education institutions in and around Berlin. In addition, there were 127 junior and other fixed-term professors, and 4,450 nonprofessorial staff members who supported teaching, research, and operations. The forty-eight so-called extraordinary professorships included, but were not limited to, the four major independent research institutions in Germany that were also publicly funded: the Max Planck Society, the Fraunhofer Society, the Helmholtz Association, and the Leibniz Association. Costs for the jointly appointed professors were distributed among the institutions. These partnerships intensified cooperation with nonuniversity institutions, particularly the Max Planck Society, that were nationally and internationally renowned for their research.

The teaching staff of 3,798 taught in 2018 some 33,000 undergraduate and master's level students and 4,000 doctoral candidates.[50] Faculty diversity was an issue: a faculty that was 63 percent male instructed an undergraduate population that was 59 percent female.[51] With 7,975 international students in 2018, about 13 percent of the undergraduate body and 26 percent of the master's students were from outside Germany.[52] Approximately 14 percent of the faculty was international.[53] In addition, approximately 600 international visiting scholars and scientists came to the university each year to serve in teaching and research roles.[54]

Vanguard of Internationalization

From its origin, a centrally distinguishing feature of Free University was its international profile. Internationalization would distinguish the university again in the twenty-first century.

Founded with American support, FU's first partnerships were naturally with American universities. But Free University had established connections with universities all over the world to remain academically relevant from its isolated position in West Berlin. While Humboldt University limited its international partnerships after World War II to universities in the "socialist brother countries," which became fewer after splits within the Soviet bloc, FU established partnerships with universities first in the West then, in the era of détente, with institutions in Eastern Europe, the Soviet Union, and China.

In 1968 FU established an exchange partnership with Leningrad State University (today's Saint Petersburg State University).[55] Partnerships with universities in Eastern Europe followed. In 1981 FU forged a partnership with Peking University, West Germany's first in China since the Communist takeover there. The following decades saw many more alliances, primarily with institutions in North America, Eastern Europe, and East Asia, most visibly in the humanities and social sciences.

By 2017 FU maintained more than 100 university-wide, bilateral partnerships and more than 330 university partnerships within the network of the Erasmus program, a European Union-sponsored exchange program that provides opportunities for students to gain study or work experience in a different European country and funds joint European degree programs. In addition, among the university's various departments and research institutes, more than fifty partner agreements with other higher education institutions had formed.

Of course, many universities boast a roster of international connections. It is easy for presidents to ink dozens of MOUs (memoranda of understanding) without much understanding of what, if anything, they may lead to. It is something else to maintain long-standing international alliances and to focus on the ones that make a difference. Over the past decade Free University has been active in all corners of the world, but also focused on six major strategic partnerships based on academic excellence, geographical diversity, and potential for future growth. In 2011 and 2012 FU initiated three strategic partnerships with the Hebrew University of Jerusalem, Peking

University, and Saint Petersburg State University. In 2014 the University of British Columbia and in 2016 the University of California, Berkeley, were added to the list of strategic partners. In 2017 they were joined by the University of Zurich. Partnership with Peking University led to the establishment of Germany's first Confucius Institute, which trains Chinese language teachers and hosts conferences and workshops (a number of which I have attended) as an extension of the university under the leadership of a distinguished FU sinologist, Mechthild Leutner.

A parallel focus of FU's internationalization strategy was the establishment of liaison offices across the globe. These offices aimed to increase FU's visibility outside of Germany, foster relationships with existing partnerships in the region, and serve as sites to recruit students and researchers for the university. By 2020 the international network of FU encompassed seven offices, the highest number for any university in Germany.[56] Given its historical ties with the United States, FU set up the first office in New York City in 2005 in cooperation with the Ludwig Maximilian University of Munich. This "German University Alliance," housed in an office facing the United Nations building in New York, sought to "build a bridge over the Atlantic and strengthen [FU's] international integration into the scientific community."[57] Offices in Brussels, Cairo, Moscow, New Delhi, Beijing, and Sao Paulo followed, each with a region-specific focus. These were modest, often shoestring, operations, but they planted FU's flag on five continents and lent credibility to the university's international ambitions. One result, according to the German Academic Exchange Service (DAAD) in 2016, was that FU received the most external funding of all German universities for international projects.

Free University was also by far the most popular destination in Germany for international students. A study published by the DAAD, *Wissenschaft Weltoffen 2019*, showed that FU also had the second highest number (761) of participants in the Erasmus program in Germany.[58] In 2016, 20 percent of FU's students came from foreign countries; this percentage was even higher for doctoral students (34 percent).[59] FU was a prized destination also for international research scholars. The Alexander von Humboldt Foundation (AvH) was one of the most prestigious sources of funding for international scholars, maintaining a worldwide network of more than 28,000 Humboldtians from all disciplines in more than 140 countries, including fifty-four Nobel Prize winners. Every year, the foundation enabled 2,000 researchers from around the world to conduct collaborative research in Germany. FU led all German universities as a destination, with 15 percent of Humboldtians landing there. Between 2014 and 2018 FU attracted 265 scholars for research stays longer than one month.[60]

In 2019 the European Commission launched the European Universities Initiative to strengthen strategic partnerships and increase the international competitiveness of European universities. This initiative included seventeen university alliances. FU was selected to be part of one of these alliances, the University Alliance Europa (UNA Europa), which was colloquially called the "University of the Future."[61] The goal was for universities within this alliance to focus their research and education on the interdisciplinary topics of European studies, data science and artificial intelligence, and cultural heritage to spur social innovation and internationalization.

In the twenty-first century, then, Free University was fast becoming an internationally networked university. It was about to be formally recognized as such.

Creating a German "Ivy League": FU in the Excellence Initiative

Although Germany had been home to the world's best universities in the nineteenth and early twentieth centuries, that was a distant memory at the onset of the twenty-first century. Seldom did any German university appear in the top fifty of institutions ranked by the major university ranking systems. The limitations on funding, which came primarily from regional governments; the lack of revenue-generating tuition or academic philanthropy (as in the United States); and the outsourcing of prestigious research projects to institutions such as the Max Planck Society (research often involving university faculty but externally credited to the Max Planck institutes) all led to a massive underperformance in the research rankings of German universities. As we have seen, it was in response to this situation in 2005 that the federal and state governments, in cooperation with the German Council of Science and Humanities and the DFG, launched the Excellence Initiative, with the goal of selecting a small number of German universities to become internationally competitive higher education institutions.

With nine funded projects (some in collaboration with other universities), Free University was the most successful university during the first funding period. It was recognized as a "University of Excellence," building on its institutional strategy as an "International Network University." Developing this strategy entailed creating research alliances, promoting young researchers, and bolstering international collaboration through the creation of three centers: the Center for Research Strategy; the Dahlem Research School, which fostered an integrated cross-field set of doctoral programs for junior scholars; and the Center for International Collaboration. FU was awarded four clusters of excellence. Five graduate schools at FU also received funding. In addition, FU created two administrative bodies to oversee FU's Excellence Initiative efforts. One was the Excellence Council, an internal advisory board of twenty distinguished professors from across FU that advised the university's strategic research priorities within the Excellence Strategy. The other was the International Council, an external advisory body of twenty-one experts from twelve countries with international experience in university management and higher education policy.[62] (I served on the latter body from 2012 to 2018.)

In short, in the first round, following a university-wide, all-hands-on-deck planning effort overseen by President Lenzen and Chancellor Lange, FU vaulted to the top ranks of German universities. Lenzen's acumen channeled much of the funding into a robust administrative apparatus that equipped the university for competition in the twenty-first century while supporting its research agenda. In mid-2009 the federal and state governments decided to continue the Excellence Initiative for another five-year period from 2012 to 2017, now with more than US$3.5 billion in funding. In the second round, new proposals competed with prior applications for additional funding. Funding was awarded to forty-five graduate schools and forty-three clusters of excellence. President Alt now led FU to Excellence status once more. In June 2012 the "International Network University" Institutional Strategy was again funded. Three Excellence Clusters received further funding and two additional graduate schools were founded and funded. By 2012, under the umbrella of the Dahlem Research School, there were nine newly formed graduate schools.

We have seen that the first two rounds of the Excellence Initiative made dramatic changes to the university landscape in Germany, less because of the money itself (in the first two rounds FU's additional intake was less than US$300 million) than because of the spirt of academic entrepreneurship and ambition that the initiative encouraged. But when in fall 2018, the Excellence Initiative announced a third round, it encouraged less institutional risk-taking and seemed to promote consolidation across the higher education sector. There were two lines of funding: one again for clusters of excellence, and the other for a broader level of support for "universities of excellence," which would provide the institutions themselves with additional funding. For the first time, universities were encouraged to apply together in consortia under the universities of excellence funding line.

Given the long and complex history of the universities in Berlin, and the Berlin Senate's begrudging approval to maintain three institutions after 1989, it is not surprising that FU was strongly encouraged to apply in a consortium with its fellow Berlin institutions. Although in financial and reputational terms this was not obviously to the advantage of FU, it joined a Berlin University Alliance with Humboldt University, Technical University, and Charité Berlin University of Medicine (the reorganized Charité) in the Universities of Excellence funding competition through the strategy "Crossing Boundaries Towards an Integrated Research Environment."

The Excellence Initiative announced in July 2019 that the Berlin University Alliance would be one of thirteen German universities awarded Excellence status. The status came with a US$212 million award over a seven-year period for the alliance.[63] The consortium also won funding for four Excellence Clusters. Between the four institutions, there were over thirty international partnerships, liaison offices, and international campuses. As Alt reflected on FU's success in the Excellence Initiative, he called the strategic international partnerships one of "the most important elements of the general development of the university in this decade that may define the general progress of the institution."[64]

Facing the Future

Despite the success of the third Excellence Initiative funding round, by investing in a more regional strategy through the Berlin University Alliance, there were questions to be raised. Was FU compromising its individual international efforts? Would the historically competitive dynamics between Humboldt and Free Universities limit their common success? Would the remarkable differences in administrative systems among the institutions that made up the Berlin University Alliance impede implementation of new research projects and hinder the transformation of these new projects into more sustainable, permanent structures? Would the Berlin Senate move toward an ever-greater integration or even consolidation of its universities?

By 2020 the Excellence Initiative had boosted research production and raised the international profile of German universities. The forty-five universities that received initiative funding received 76 percent of all third-party funds raised by German higher education institutions in 2012. Almost a quarter (23 percent) of academic staff in the graduate schools and clusters of excellence were recruited from outside Germany by 2015. German universities were beginning again to be a magnet for global talent.

When Free University of Berlin was founded in 1948, it envisioned itself as returning to the Humboldtian ideal of a university, providing a space to form and educate young people in an environment free of ideological commitments. The obstacles facing the university had primarily been political and economic, namely the institution's dependence on the support of Western Germany and the United States, as well as its struggle for funding, faculty, and recognition in devastated postwar Berlin.

During the first two decades of the twenty-first century, FU carved out a space for itself not just within the landscape of German higher education but also as a European institution. The 2016 Brexit referendum sent shockwaves through higher education, as students and researchers struggled to imagine a future of curtailed mobility. As the United Kingdom has sought to distance itself from the European project, Germany has stepped in and redoubled its commitment. This can be seen in its universities, and especially at FU, where Erasmus enrollments continue to increase yearly, making it among the most sought-after places to study and research, with new degree programs, many of which are offered in English and take advantage of the city's unique historical and cultural heritage. These rich offerings in higher education have in no small part contributed to Berlin's reputation as a truly European capital.

When President Alt left the university to become president of the German Rectors' Conference in 2018, Free University faced a different set of challenges. Over the previous decade, the institution had developed into a leading German university in one of Europe's most vibrant cities. Now it faced competition from other higher education institutions in Berlin, Germany, and overseas. And it faced the challenge of linking its destiny to those of the other Berlin universities.

Like his predecessor, President Günter M. Ziegler was an internal administrative appointment who had served as a faculty member in the Institute of Mathematics since 2011. Like Alt, he had a successful career in academia. Having established and run the Berlin Mathematical School, Ziegler also knew firsthand the challenge of cooperation in strengthening Berlin's higher education system. To that end, the latest Excellence Initiative / Strategy had not only provided additional university funding but also forced FU to re-align its own academic mission in a greater spirit of cooperation with Humboldt University and the Technical University. How that would affect the university's autonomy and development remained to be seen.

Protesting is a contemporary ritual in Berlin. But today, instead of the unruly student demonstrations of 1968 protesting against the inherent conservatism of universities or overseas entanglements, new solidarities have waxed and waned. From March 2019 young and old (but primarily young) Berliners congregated at open plazas as part of the global "Fridays for Future" climate strike, protesting the continued negligence of meaningful climate policy in Germany and all over the world. These gatherings also made their mark on FU. Free University was founded in political controversy and has at times (in the Cold War and in the leftist movements of the 1960s) been defined by it. Today, the topic of focus has become the environment, as the threat to the natural world seeps into the life of the university. In December 2019, over a year into Ziegler's presidency, FU declared a state of climate emergency.[65] The university announced it would aim to be climate neutral by 2025 and design curricula to center around topics of sustainability and climate protection. A new steering committee, comprising students, professors, and other university members, was formed to help plan the university's efforts to increase energy efficiency and expand the campus's renewable energy sources. This announcement built on FU's prior commitment toward sustainability efforts. Between 2001 and 2018 FU reduced its power and heat consumption by 25 percent and its carbon dioxide emissions by 75 percent. Reflecting on this announcement, Ziegler stated, "We as universities have a special responsibility. . . . Our task is not only to improve scientific knowledge and communicate this to society, but to also act in an exemplary way within our areas of responsibility."[66] This effort reflected Ziegler's view that universities should function as society's "living labs" (*Zukunftswerkstätten*) or dynamic environments that lead cutting-edge research and teaching to address society's most pressing issues.

I believe that John F. Kennedy would have agreed, for he asserted long ago that Free University of Berlin had a special mission. Its graduates were to be "citizens of the world" who had "a special obligation to think and to help forge the future."[67] Free University had for seven decades served as a "living lab" in the pursuit of *veritas, iustitia, libertas*. As the most experimental and international of German universities, it prepared to meet more challenges still.

CHAPTER FOUR

The Rise and Challenges of American Research Universities

TODAY, AMERICAN universities outrank their German counterparts in every global ranking system. And yet a century and a half ago the concept of the research university was completely foreign to the higher education institutions of the United States, including the ones that had deemed themselves universities in name. "During the nineteenth century German universities led the world in erudition and scientific investigation, and their great professors attracted many students from all parts of the world in quest of higher education. But times are altered." So declared Henry W. Diederich, U.S. Consul to Germany in an article in *Science* in 1904. He continued, "Despite all our imperfections one can not [*sic*] but admire the great upward strides which the American system of education, from the humble district school up, has been making during the last few decades."[1] The shifting tides of dominance in higher education were not just apparent on one side of the Atlantic. Speaking at the University Teachers' Day in Leipzig in 1909, the historian Karl Lamprecht warned his audience, "We are no longer atop the universities of the world. France and America have left us far behind."[2]

Time has demonstrated the prescience of Diederich and Lamprecht. How did this shift in the center of gravity in the research world happen? How did the trends that Diederich and Lamprecht observed at the turn of the twentieth century snowball into a broadly acknowledged American dominance in higher education over the course of the next century?

The German Obsession and the Struggle for Greatness

By the early nineteenth century, higher education had a firmly established, if relatively small, presence in the United States. Nine colleges had been established prior to American independence in 1776. Cambridge and Oxford provided the original models for these colonial colleges. Even the charter establishing Harvard bore the phrase *pro modo Academiarum in Anglia* ("according to the manner of universities in England").[3] Yet, in each of these colonial colleges, the founders realized that differences in the physical and social environments of the American context precipitated unanticipated modifications to the English model.[4] By 1820 there were fifty-two American degree-granting institutions.[5]

The earliest higher education institutions were insular. As soon as Harvard had enough graduates from which to appoint presidents and professors, it looked no further than its own Yard for faculty.[6] By contrast, when establishing the University of Virginia in 1819, Thomas Jefferson's first instinct was to recruit talent from other American institutions, but, unable to poach faculty such as George Ticknor, who was at Harvard, he turned to recruitment of European professors.[7]

As the United States grew into its nationhood and engaged in its own right with European countries, there was an increasing awareness of the strengths of European, and particularly German, universities. In 1815 the Harvard Corporation, one of the governing boards of Harvard University, decided that before hiring Edward Everett as professor of Greek literature, they would send him and future Harvard professor George Ticknor to Germany for advanced study. Studying at Göttingen, Everett became the first American to earn a PhD at a German university, initiating a century-long pattern of top American scholars seeking their credentials at German institutions.

After studying at German universities, most scholars returned to the United States, bringing back with them conceptions of *Lehrfreiheit, Lernfreiheit,* and, above all, a commitment to *Wissenschaft* and the advancement of learning in all realms through research and discovery. Several generations of German-trained scholars transformed the American system from one in which generalist learned men educated students through recitations, lectures, and disputations to one in which specialist scholars furthered knowledge in their fields of interest through research while also training students in the latest developments in their disciplines.

In 1861 Yale University awarded the first American doctoral degrees, but it was not until 1876 that the first, true research university was founded in the United States. In 1873 six trustees of the estate of Baltimore financier Johns Hopkins reached out to three top leaders in higher education (Charles Eliot of Harvard, James Angell of the University of Michigan, and Andrew White of Cornell) for advice on how to use Hopkins's bequest of $7 million for a university. According to higher education historian Edwin Slosson, "With remarkable unanimity all three of these gentlemen answered that a university was a very different thing from the institutions over which they presided, and that Daniel C. Gilman [then the president of the University of California] should be president of it."[8] Under Gilman's leadership, Johns Hopkins University was established on a German model, with graduate seminars, doctoral programs, and a strong emphasis on research and the sciences that it has retained to this day.

Some leaders remained skeptical of the appropriateness of the German model in the United States—Harvard President Charles Eliot reportedly commented that the German model "would fit Harvard freshmen 'about as well as a barnyard would suit a whale.'"[9] Still, by the end of the century, most universities were inspired by the Johns Hopkins model (and staffed by Johns Hopkins alumni), and colleges around the country were transformed into universities by investing heavily in research-based graduate programs. The number of nonprofessional graduate schools grew from eight in 1850 to around four hundred in 1876 to over five thousand in 1910.[10]

American professors also began to make the German model their own. As one of the leading scholars of America higher education, Jonathan Cole, has noted, the laboratory of the famous developmental biologist Thomas Hunt Morgan established the "new standard in most academic disciplines" of a more democratic, less hierarchical lab environment in which graduate students worked closely with faculty members.[11] Edwin Slosson remarked upon the advantages and benefits of the emerging American model, or, as he called it, that "peculiar combination which has developed in the United States of instruction and research, graduate and undergraduate students, letters and technology."[12]

This shift in the nature of scholarship occurred in tandem with fundamental changes in the American economy and society that complemented and accelerated research and applied learning in American higher education. Industrialization, urbanization, and the further mechanization of agriculture resulted in higher demand for an educated workforce and citizenry. The need became great enough that the federal government, heretofore removed from higher education, made the development of new, public universities a priority when it passed the Morrill Act of 1862. This act donated federal lands in each state for the establishment of higher education institutions with a particular focus on agriculture and the mechanical arts. Many of the great American public universities, such as the universities of California and Wisconsin, and a few of the top private ones, such as Cornell and MIT, were founded (or significantly expanded) through the largess of the Morrill Act. The technical and scientific focus of the Morrill Act also promoted disciplines in the applied sciences and engineering against the backdrop of traditional liberal arts curricula.

Industrialization created a new class of American tycoons and a new culture of private philanthropy in support of higher education, particularly research universities. John D. Rockefeller referred to his gift establishing the University of Chicago in 1890 as "the best investment I ever made."[13] When Leland and Jane Stanford sought to establish an institution in memory of their son, they weighed the merits of different kinds of schools before founding Leland Stanford Jr. University in 1891.[14]

Even as the research capacity of American universities grew, undergraduate education remained a priority for many institutions. The broad liberal arts model of undergraduate education that had evolved in the colonial colleges had become an indelible part of higher education in America. Those institutions that chose to not emphasize their undergraduate education programs did so at their future peril. Johns Hopkins and Clark Universities, both known for their excellent German-style graduate research programs, watched their national reputations fall in the early twentieth century. Undergraduate education became an important driver of intellectual curiosity and a passion of the faculty.

In the less than three decades between the founding of Johns Hopkins and the observations of Diederich and Lamprecht, American universities gained a place on the global stage as exciting institutions that, in a manner that Humboldt would have admired, integrated teaching and research. It was the global political and institutional ramifications of the twentieth century's two world wars, however, that connected American research universities with an influx of international talent and expanded funding from government and industry, resources that in turn catapulted American research universities forward.

The Morrill Act provided federal government support for the establishment and expansion of universities, but it was the establishment of the National Research Council in 1916 that began to connect university research
with government funding and priorities. The Council connected government
resources and laboratories with university researchers and industrial production managers to create and manufacture new technology that supported
the American effort in World War I.[15] Universities and the federal government found further partnership in programs such as the Student Army
Training Corp, which trained students for the military on campus, both
meeting the government's need for trained soldiers and, because they were
given federal funding to run such programs, the universities' need for funding
in the face of drastic enrollment drops. With the US entry into the war, enrollments at top universities dropped by as much as 40 percent. This early
effort at federal government-university partnership laid the foundation for a
much higher level of cooperation during the next world war.[16]

By the time the federal government again turned to university partnership to support the war effort in the 1940s, it found a university sector newly
invigorated by the arrival of academic refugees from Europe in general and
Germany in particular. As we have seen, the increasing militarization and
then Nazification of German universities ended their status as global leaders
and led to an exodus of talent, to the benefit of other countries, especially
the United States. The numbers would have been larger still if not for the
anti-immigrant and anti-Semitic attitudes in English-speaking countries.
This influx of highly skilled humanists, social scientists, and, especially,
scholars of the physical universe propelled American university research forward almost immediately, just as the federal government again began to
turn to universities to support a new war effort.

Postwar Booms

Following World War II, American higher education massified, as enrollment in higher education institutions in the United States surged from 1.5
million in 1940 to 2.4 million in 1950.[17] College and university enrollments
reached 3.6 million in 1960, 8 million in 1970, and 11.6 million in 1980.[18]
By 1980 the number of students attending college was eight times higher
than it was before the beginning of World War II.[19] State universities in particular gave more students access to higher education, and there a cultural

fascination with "collegiate life" grew.[20] Despite this expansion, higher education, particularly at the best research institutions, remained the province of a socially elite few. Harvard, Yale, and Princeton retained their esoteric admissions processes that heavily favored (white, Anglo-Saxon, Protestant) preparatory high school graduates.

The proponents of the Servicemen's Readjustment Act (commonly known as the GI Bill) estimated that only 8 to 10 percent of soldiers returning from service in World War II would take advantage of the act's education provision, which offered significant financial subsidies for discharged servicemen to pursue higher education. These estimates turned out to be incorrect. Instead, between the passing of the act in 1944 and 1950, 16 percent of eligible veterans (over two million out of fourteen million) took advantage of these provisions.[21] In 1947, at the height of veteran enrollment, veterans made up 49 percent of all students admitted to college.[22]

Students and professors were backed by new levels of government and industry support. Wartime cooperation between the academe and the government was managed by the Office of Scientific Research and Development (OSRD), established in 1941 by President Franklin D. Roosevelt and led by Vannevar Bush. As the end of the war drew near, Bush feared the end of government support for basic scientific research that had paid such dividends during the war.[23] In his 1947 manifesto, *Science: The Endless Frontier*, Bush argued that government, industry, and national economic development were dependent upon the basic research carried out in university labs and that such research should be supported (but not dictated) by a new government agency.[24] Following the Second World War, Bush argued for an academic declaration of independence from Germany: "We can no longer count on ravaged Europe as a source of fundamental knowledge. . . . We must pay increased attention to discovering this knowledge for ourselves."[25] This document precipitated the founding of the National Science Foundation—the American equivalent of the Kaiser Wilhelm / Max Planck Society—and the initiation of a new age of government-funded university research in peacetime.

Expanded engagement with the federal government meant not only new sources of funding but also increased oversight and efforts at control. The apex (or, if you will, nadir) of government intrusion into university campuses came during the McCarthy era, when universities across the country struggled with how to balance the anti-communist demands and political winds with principles of academic and institutional freedom that had been strengthened over the previous century of German influence. Concern over the relationship between the government and universities did not end with the downfall of Senator Joseph McCarthy but continued in a variety of forms. In his farewell address from the presidency of the United States in 1961, Dwight D. Eisenhower, who had served as Columbia University's president, warned against the growing strength of the military-industrial complex and the potential ramifications of the growing dependence of "the free university" on "Federal employment, project allocations, and the power of money."[26] The intense political activism on university campuses in the 1960s offered an even stronger critique of government intrusion in higher education. But government funding for and engagement with American higher education was now a permanent part of the academic landscape.

A Hybrid System

The second half of the twentieth century saw the sustained rise—in terms of the size of individual institutions, the system overall, and general reputation—of the American research university. One of the great strengths of higher education in America is its institutional diversity.[27] The modern American research university was thus built upon a foundation of three diverse elements: an undergraduate liberal arts education in the tradition of the colonial colleges; participatory research evolved from the German tradition of the nineteenth century; and twentieth century engagement with government, industry, and private philanthropy.

As we look at American higher education from a global perspective in the twenty-first century, it is useful to clarify what American higher education is not. First, in spite of the common features listed previously, there is no American higher education *system*. There is no national university. Higher education institutions and policies differ from state to state, and each state may contain a diverse array of institutions—public and private, baccalaureate and doctoral, elite and massive. Many scholars have noted that this nonsystemized diversity has allowed American higher education to reach such a high level of quality, as institutions sought to maximize their comparative advantages in an open, competitive marketplace for the best faculty, students, and financial support.[28]

Yet, for all its lack of system, there are similarities that tie these diverse institutions together. "Universities tend to reflect, echo, and codify their national societies and culture," James Axtell has noted.[29] American ideals of democracy, equal opportunity, and individualism color American universities in various ways. More concretely, the competition among American universities has led to some basic structural similarities in governance, faculty policy, and finance.

Governance

American universities tend to have similar overarching governance structures, although the relative power and influence of each of the bodies composing the structure vary greatly across institutions.[30] Typically, a board of trustees serves as the legal representative of the university. Trustees, who are often (particularly at private universities) alumni of the institution, are expected to bring their administrative and financial experience to bear in supporting (and monitoring) the work of the university president, whom they are also responsible for selecting.

University presidents are the apex of the academic leadership team, usually supported by a provost and a series of deans focused on different specific areas of academic and campus life. Former President of Harvard Derek Bok observed that administrative and fundraising duties increasingly dominate the time of university presidents, and, consequently, "presidents today tend to delegate most of the responsibility over academic affairs to provosts and deans."[31] American deans are faculty members, either chosen from existing faculty or recruited from other institutions for a specific decanal role. Unlike their European counterparts, American deans are not elected (or deposed) by their peers but generally serve for specific terms or at the pleasure of their university presidents.

The relative balances of power between the board and the president, between the president and the provost, and between the president and deans vary greatly across institutions. Differences in power structure are not clearly aligned with private versus public institutions. Harvard, for example, is (in)famously decentralized, with a large amount of money and power resting in the deans of its twelve schools, while relatively little is retained by the central administration. The central administration at Duke University, by contrast, maintains much more control, which it uses to guide the institution's strategic planning process. Balances of power among administrative bodies are functions of tradition and university cultures as well as of the personalities of individual leaders.

Beyond serving as a pool from which to draw deans and presidents, the faculty as a whole often plays a role in university governance through an academic senate or similar body. In general, this kind of collective faculty body has less power in the United States than analogous bodies do in European universities, where (as at Humboldt University) such a body would be charged with making key academic administrative appointments. Still, academic senates or meetings of faculty have proven able to influence decision making at key points in the history of many universities. As Bok noted, "as a practical matter, regardless of the formal organization, ultimate power resides with those who are most difficult to replace."[32] At elite research universities, which compete fiercely to gain and retain top professors, the faculty, when united, can prove extraordinarily powerful.

Faculty

Faculty members at American research universities are protected not only by the power inherent in their importance to the university but also through "tenure" systems. This is a variant on the German *Lehrstuhl*, albeit typically with individually less prestige and resources, as the number of "full" professors in an American university is rather larger than at any German institution. American professors, even in state universities, are not *Beamten*, or permanent civil servants, in the German tradition. The tenure process, which essentially offers continuous employment to academics who have proven their worth through a series of rigorous reviews of their publications and (sometimes) teaching, was designed in principle to protect professors and guarantee their freedom to explore any topic they deem to have value. Most universities implement "up or out" tenure processes—denial of tenure for a candidate means not only that the candidate fails to move "up" into the company of tenured faculty but also that they will be sent "out" of the institution. The process not only stands as a significant hurdle to establishing a career in academia but also represents the high level of expected commitment to the faculty member from the university and vice versa.

There are two basic paths through which universities can improve the quality of their faculty. The first is through lateral hiring, or the recruiting of full tenured (and, often, star) professors from other universities. The second is through investing resources into the development of young, tenure-track faculty, ideally to reap the benefit of their subsequent scholarship.

The balance with which universities employ these two methods depends on institutional traditions and culture as well as available resources.

Another facet of the lives of university faculty in the United States is the sabbatical. Tenure-track and tenured faculty in research universities generally receive sabbaticals—regular, paid leaves of absences after six years of service so that the seventh might provide them with an opportunity to spend more time on research. The sabbatical system evolved out of the inadequacy of American-based advanced academic training in the early nineteenth century. Faculty (or potential future faculty) were granted study leaves to pursue advanced training in European (especially English and German) universities.[33] In 1880 Harvard University President Charles Eliot systematized sabbaticals for faculty for the first time, and by 1900 ten universities had adopted the practice. By 1920 at least fifty leading liberal arts colleges and universities, both public and private, had established sabbatical policies.[34] Now a common practice, the system is acknowledged to have a variety of benefits—both personal and institutional. Certainly few faculty members decline one.[35]

Funding

American universities, whether public or private, receive funding from a combination of sources, including earned revenue (tuition), government funding, and private philanthropy. The largest portion of federal funding for universities is allocated through Pell Grants, need-based financial aid awards offered by the federal government. In 2019, of the $75.6 billion in federal funding for higher education, Pell Grants accounted for nearly $30 billion. Federal research grants accounted for around one-third of total federal higher education spending ($24.6 billion).[36] Research funding is generally garnered through competitive grant processes and is given for specific research objectives. Both public and private universities receive federal funding. Additionally, public universities receive funding from their state governments. This state funding, in theory at least, allows public universities to charge lower tuition for local students.

Government support of research and higher education was one of the major factors enabling American research universities to reach such a prominent global position. Today that funding is in jeopardy. From 2010 to 2019 federal funding for research and development declined (in constant dollars) 28.9 percent.[37] State funding for public universities also decreased dramatically. In 2017, after adjusting for inflation, overall state funding for public two-year and four-year colleges was almost $9 billion below the 2008 level.[38] Currently, America's premier public research universities often receive less than 10 percent of their funding from the state.[39]

Government appropriations, of course, are not the only source of funding for American universities. Private philanthropy has played an important role in shaping the higher education landscape. According to the Council for Aid to Education, philanthropic giving to higher education totaled over $46.7 billion in 2018, the largest amount since the agency began collecting information in 1957.[40] This philanthropy was highly targeted. The increase in overall funds was driven by large gifts given to a small number of institutions—29 percent of philanthropic gifts were made to less than 1 percent of universities and colleges. Ten universities raised over $500 million each, and two, Stanford and Harvard, raised over $1 billion each.[41]

These impressive donations bolster already-substantial endowment coffers. Stanford and Harvard, for example, had endowments worth $27.7 and $40.9 billion, respectively, at the end of the 2019 fiscal year. The distribution of endowment funds across American universities and colleges has been skewed for quite some time. The 1990 National Association of College and University Business Officers Endowment Report showed that in that year, the top five university endowments (those of Harvard, Yale, the University of Texas system, Princeton, and Stanford) accounted for about 25 percent of the endowment value of all institutions surveyed. That remained true nearly thirty years later.[42] In short, the finances of American universities mirrored the country's growing disparities of wealth and income.

The change in magnitude of endowments at the highest end of the spectrum was significant. In 1990 the value of the top five US university endowments was equivalent to 0.26 percent of US gross domestic product. By 2019 this percentage had jumped to 0.72 percent.[43] Managers of these largest endowments moved increasing portions of their assets into alternative investment strategies: less liquid, high-risk, high-return vehicles, including private equity, hedge funds, venture capital, and energy and natural resources. This last category in particular began to draw protests from students in 2015 and after, as they advocated for divestment from fossil fuels.

Of course, the spectacular growth of university endowments in the 1990s and into the twenty-first century reflected the growth in value of the US stock market, and as much as universities benefited from market upswings, they were also vulnerable to its downturns. This was amply demonstrated in the financial crisis of 2008. Recovery from that crisis has proceeded in fits and starts. Through most of the 2010s low returns on investments drove down ten-year returns across American university endowments.[44] By 2020, however, university endowments' long-term average return had reached 8.4 percent on the back of a strong stock market performance.[45] But not everyone knew where to put their money: the richest university, Harvard, suffered from poor endowment returns in this period: in constant dollars its endowment was worth no more in 2020 than it had been in 2008.

Beyond reduced returns from endowments, American universities faced diminished funding from government (federal and state) in the first two decades of the twenty-first century. The primary remaining financial lever was tuition, which for decades had increased well in excess of inflation. With high scrutiny of diversity (both ethnic and socioeconomic), top universities increased tuition while also rapidly increasing student financial aid packages. Yet, the ability to provide such packages rested with elite institutions. In 2018 the fabulously wealthy businessman and former New York City mayor Michael Bloomberg gave a $1.8 billion gift to his alma mater, Johns Hopkins. In a *New York Times* op-ed, he explained that the main motivation for this gift was for financial aid for "qualified low- and middle-income students," because "there may be no better investment that we can make in the future of the American dream."[46] This was the largest donation given to an American university to date.[47]

There are growing questions about whether higher education can remain an effective vehicle for promoting social mobility and access to the "American dream." In the mid-twentieth century, higher education was seen as a public good, and society bore much of the cost through state taxes that supported public university budgets. By the 1980s the costs of financing higher education, even at public universities, were placed increasingly on students and their families, as higher education came to be seen as more of a "private good."[48]

International Universities?

One of the enduring advantages of American research universities has been their welcoming of foreign scholars and students. In 1910 historian Edwin Slosson predicted that "greater and more influential than a State or a national university will be the international university of the future."[49] Today students from around the world seek out graduate and undergraduate education in the United States. In the 2018–2019 academic year 1,095,229 international students were enrolled in American higher education institutions, contributing $41 billion to the US economy, and supporting over 450,000 American jobs.[50] Still, the presence of these students, which enriched the diversity of perspective on campus and, often, institutional bottom lines, was not a given. As academic and other markets in their home countries became more promising for international students with advanced degrees (for example, for students from China), the capacity of American universities to attract and retain the top international scholars was diminished. These concerns were further heightened under the nativist administration of President Donald J. Trump, whose visa and other restrictions made the United States a distinctly less welcoming destination.

In the postwar period, American universities became leading centers of international and area studies. As we shall see, this emerged initially out of the need for wartime research under the government's Office of Strategic Services, a predecessor of the Central Intelligence Agency. The need remained during the Cold War era. In 1958 the US government authorized the National Defense Education Act (NDEA), which provided funding to foster expertise in international studies, area studies, and world cultures and languages. The impetus for this authorization was the government's own embarrassment that its ranks lacked broad or deep expertise on the many parts of the world in which the United States was now engaged. Expertise was particularly thin in the study of Cold War adversaries such as the Soviet Union and Maoist China. (Out of thirty-eight Soviet analysts in the Central Intelligence Agency in 1948, two-thirds spoke no Russian.[51]) Funding was given at the highest level to study the most "dangerous" parts of the world, hence the enduring strength in American universities of Russian and Chinese studies, compared to, say, South Asian studies. As the Cold War progressed, government leadership was matched by private groups, such as the Ford Foundation, which supported American-friendly institutions abroad (such as Free University of Berlin) and area studies at home. The international dimensions of the NDEA were reauthorized as part of the Higher Education Act of 1965, which is today responsible for funding National Resource Centers (NRCs) in universities across the United States. As of 2018 the U.S. Department of Education supported (albeit with diminishing dollars) over one hundred NRCs, across public and private higher education institutions, that seek to build knowledge capacity on the different regions of Asia, Russia and Eastern Europe, Latin America, and even such perilous places as Canada.[52]

US universities have also been increasing their physical presence abroad. Six US universities, including Northwestern and Cornell, established campuses in Qatar's government-supported "Education City," a large complex in which top universities receive facilities and funding in exchange for the establishment of programs on par with those at their home campuses.[53] At the start of the 2010s New York University opened campuses in Abu Dhabi and Shanghai. Duke University opened a campus in Kunshan, China, in 2013. Some universities partnered with universities in other countries to found centers focused on specific research areas, like the Tsinghua-Berkeley Shenzhen Institute, based in Shenzhen, China, which focused on fields that drew on both schools' strengths, including information technology, new energy, and precision medicine. Other universities, like Harvard, established research outposts to support the work of faculty and students abroad. Perhaps, as Slosson had predicted, the "international university" would indeed be the "university of the future."[54] At the very least, it seemed that every American university had to have an international strategy for the twenty-first century.

With global flows of faculty and students also came viruses. At the start of a new decade in 2020, with internationalization at a high point, a global pandemic set in. Emerging in Wuhan, China, COVID-19, an infectious disease that often caused severe respiratory illness, spread across the world. Beginning in March 2020 universities in the United States moved their classes online. Students' study abroad programs were cut short. Many international students returned home. As cities and states issued shelter-in-place advisories, many universities went completely online for the remainder of the spring 2020 semester. As the pandemic continued, all facets of the university were affected—including admissions, teaching, research, student and faculty mobility, and finances. While universities "reopened" in fall 2020, most did so from a distance, relying again on virtual learning. US institutions, which had been a magnet for international students, were looking at a much lower yield rate for incoming international students. Was the internationalization of American universities past its peak?

American Exceptionalism?

Perhaps more than anything else, it was the diversity of the American experience in higher education—diversity of institutions, goals, thought, faculty, students, governance, funding sources, and more—that distinguished it from both its European ancestors and the many institutions around the world that seek to emulate its success. Historian David Labaree has argued that America's higher education success and its "unlikely ascendancy" resulted from five key traits: institutional autonomy, sensitivity to consumers, appeal to a broad array of constituencies, structural ambiguity, and organizational complexity.[55] These traits derived from dynamic market forces and an overall low dependence on the state and begot a "motley collection of 4,700 American colleges and universities."[56] Clark Kerr, who served as president of the University of California and as the first chancellor of the University of California, Berkeley, argued in his classic study, *The Uses of the University*, that there was a simpler explanation for the unlikely ascendance of American higher education. It came from the unique fusion of three models: (1) the English college, which focused on undergraduate liberal arts education; (2) the German research university, which emphasized research at the graduate level; and (3) the American land-grant college, which centered on vocational education and providing applied solutions to public problems.[57] The "modern American university" that emerged, he argued, "is not Oxford nor is it Berlin; it is a new type of institution in the world. As a new type of institution, it is not really private and it is not really public; it is neither entirely of the world nor entirely apart from it. It is unique."[58]

In Chapters 5 through 7, we will examine three unique American universities that reflect the diverse strengths and challenges of the American scene. Harvard University, the oldest higher education institution in America, was originally modeled after the English university and later remodeled on the German pattern. It is probably the best-known university on Earth today and is an example of enduring excellence in higher education. The University of California, Berkeley, a land-grant university, is the most highly regarded public university in the country. It is one of the world's top-ranked research universities and the crown jewel of the University of California system, which has been arguably the best system of public higher education in the world. Now, however, Berkeley faces the challenge of remaining a public university while depending on private funding. Finally, Duke University, with a strong research trajectory and an ambitious international agenda, is, I will argue, the fastest-rising research university in America, in part because it is the one that has planned most explicitly for its future.

These examples will, I hope, help to address this question: American universities came to lead the world in the second half of the twentieth century—but will they continue to do so into the twenty-first?

CHAPTER FIVE

Rising through Change and through Storm

Harvard University

Fair Harvard! ~~thy sons to~~ <u>we join in</u> thy Jubilee throng,
And with blessings surrender thee o'er
By these Festival-rites, from the Age that is past,
To the Age that is waiting before.
O Relic and Type of our ancestors' worth,
That hast long kept their memory warm,
First flow'r of their wilderness! Star of their night!
Calm rising thro' change and thro' storm.
. . .
Let not moss-covered Error moor thee at its side,
As the world on Truth's current glides by,
Be the herald of Light, and the bearer of Love,
Till the ~~stock of the Puritans~~ <u>the stars in the firmament</u> die.

—Fair Harvard, *1836, by Samuel Gilman, class of 1811, original*
lyrics and revisions, 1997, 2018

1836

When *Fair Harvard* was composed by Reverend Gilman for the university's
two hundredth anniversary in 1836, Harvard was an institution still firmly
rooted in New England, of "Puritan stock." As it approached its four hundredth birthday in the twenty-first century, with a more inclusive anthem,

its ambitions had become otherworldly—an institution of earthly fame and eternal life. That might have surprised Reverend Gilman and his twenty-fifth reunion classmates at Harvard's bicentennial in 1836.

Two years earlier, on a late May evening in 1834, Harvard undergraduates torched a recitation room and threw chairs out its window. In the continuing pandemonium, they set off firecrackers in the chapel and hanged an effigy of Josiah Quincy, the president of Harvard, from the Rebellion Tree in Harvard Yard. The riot was a culmination of Quincy's ironclad enforcement of discipline that was wildly unpopular with students. Quincy responded by expelling the entire sophomore class. Two hundred years after the university's founding, Harvard's class of 1836 was the smallest to graduate since 1809, with enrollments much lower than those of Yale, Princeton, and even Dartmouth.[1]

A former Congressman and six-term mayor of Boston, Josiah Quincy had been instated as president of Harvard in 1829. Drawing on Puritan sensibilities, Quincy's "heart's desire," noted by his son, "was to make the College a nursery of high-minded, high-principled, well-taught, well-conducted, well-bred gentlemen."[2] Undergraduates may have had misgivings about the steely president's obsession with order. Student "recitations" of an inherited, required, and utterly stultifying curriculum were graded daily on a scale of 1 to 8, and Quincy himself read students' report cards weekly. An ideal course, Quincy believed, was a "thorough drilling."[3] But Quincy did begin the process of offering "elective" classes for upperclassmen in the new fields that had begun to define German scholarship: history, chemistry, geology, and astronomy, among others. In later inaugurating the university's astronomical observatory, he created Harvard's first research unit. He became a defender of *Lehrfreiheit* on the part of the faculty and, slowly, grudgingly, partially, of *Lernfreiheit* on the part of undergraduates. It was in Quincy's tenure that the word *veritas* was formally added to the university's shield. Harvard was still a parochial place, but by its bicentennial, the university was poised to grow beyond its pioneering origins.

1936

For Harvard's bicentennial in 1836, only the presidents of other New England colleges were invited, and only one of them came. A century later, Harvard President James Bryant Conant welcomed presidents and representatives from 502 colleges, universities, and learned societies, along with the president of the United States, to its tercentenary. The ceremony was preceded by a two-week Conference of Arts and Sciences for scholars—including eleven Nobel Prize recipients—from across the globe. The emphasis was on the natural sciences (Conant was a distinguished chemist) and the growth of individual scientific disciplines. Specialization, Conant proclaimed, was the key to the advancement of scientific knowledge.[4]

When in 1936 Harvard, "the Mother of American Colleges," promised to be "a new center for the world's culture," according to the president of another American university, it had done so in large measure by adopting German models of scientific research in distinct disciplines. Yet 1936 was not a proud moment for the German academy, and only one German scholar attended. President Franklin D. Roosevelt declared that Harvard's and America's challenges were as much abroad as they were at home: "In this day of modern witch-burning, when freedom of thought has been exiled from the many lands which were once its home, it is the part of Harvard and America to stand for the freedom of the human mind and to carry the torch of truth."[5]

In the spirit of Roosevelt's internationalism, one representative from China's Peking University took part in the tercentenary and was granted an honorary degree. His name was Hu Shi. As a faculty member of Peking University after 1917, he became a leading figure in China's "New Culture" movement and an eloquent proponent of liberalism in China. Hu Shi's inscription on the marble stele that he presented to Harvard connected scholarly excellence with national strength: "It is by virtue of its culture that a nation arises, but truly it is due to learning that a culture flourishes." The stele graces Harvard Yard to this day.

With nearly one thousand Chinese alumni by 1936, Harvard was on its way to being more than a place of Puritan stock. Yet it was hardly inclusive. Not one of the eighty-six scholars invited to the tercentenary conference was a woman. The main ceremony was held on the High Holiday of Rosh Hashanah—befitting an era of institutional anti-Semitism—and was sternly Christian from invocation to benediction.[6]

In 1836 President Quincy had "adjourned" the assembly of alumni until "to meet again at this place" a century later.[7] In 1936, as the threat of a second world war loomed, the vice chancellor of Oxford doubted very much that, a century hence, another such celebration could take place.

Figure 5.1. Harvard tercentenary stele. Reproduced from *Notes on the Harvard Tercentenary,* edited by David T. W. McCord and published by Harvard University Press in 1936.

President Conant himself had his doubts. Would modern universities with their newfound wealth, giving faculty and students "facilities never before at the disposal of any body of scholars," retain "that popular admiration and respect which alone can guarantee their survival?" Would Harvard "escape the curse which has so often plagued large human enterprises well established by a significant history—the curse of complacent mediocrity?" "What," Conant wondered, "will be the role of the university, particularly the privately endowed university, when the four hundredth celebration draws near in the winter of 2036?"[8]

2036?

From Harvard's tercentenary to the present, the university achieved a reputation equal to, if not greater than, that of the University of Berlin in the nineteenth century. As it rose to national prominence in the twentieth century, universities across the United States vied to be the "Harvard of the South" (Duke, Vanderbilt, Rice), the "Harvard of the Midwest" (Michigan, Northwestern, Washington University), and the "Harvard of the West" (Stanford, once upon a time).[9]

Harvard's global reputation appears to have grown further, the greater the distance from Cambridge, Massachusetts. In China, for example, the State Administration for Industry and Trademark database recorded 375 attempts to register the name "Harvard" (*hafo*) as a trademark between 1997 and 2017. When Harvard established its Harvard Center Shanghai in 2010, it was initially told that it could open its doors, but it could not use the name "Harvard," for a "Harvard University" was already registered in the city. Today, the "Harvards" of China include an automobile (a best-selling SUV), a professional training center, a child-care center, a quick-service restaurant, a "Harvard Baby" disinfectant, and even a "Harvard Exam Sitters" company (*Hafo qiangshou*), which you pay to take your college entrance exams for you. They embrace, too, one of the world's best-selling books on higher education, *Harvard Girl Liu Yiting: A Character-Training Record* (*Hafo nühai Liu Yiting: suzhi peixun jishi*), which chronicles how tiger-parents Liu Weihua and Zhang Xinwu raised their daughter, Liu Yiting, to be disciplined and independent of mind. Yiting was accepted to Harvard in 1999. Published in 2000, this "how-to-get-into-Harvard manual" became an instant sensation and spawned an industry of copycats: *Cornell Girl, How We Got Our Child into Yale,* and (the least of these) *Our Dumb Little Son Goes to Cambridge.*[10]

Eighteen years short of Harvard's four hundredth anniversary, Harvard's president was not of an old Boston family like Josiah Quincy. Nor was he a descendent of early Massachusetts Bay settlers like James Bryant Conant. Lawrence S. Bacow was born in Detroit, Michigan, to an Auschwitz survivor mother and an Eastern European refugee father. He went on to attend the Massachusetts Institute of Technology as an undergraduate and Harvard, where he earned three graduate degrees (JD, MPP, and PhD). After graduate school, he taught at MIT for twenty-four years before becoming the institution's chair of faculty and then chancellor. He then served as the twelfth president of Tufts University for a decade. When on July 1, 2018,

Bacow began his tenure as Harvard's president, he arrived with more experience in academic leadership than any of his predecessors over the previous 382 years.

Harvard was both empowered and encumbered by its history. There was much to contemplate. Bacow inherited an institution more admired abroad than at home, in an era of public critique of American higher education; a university with an endowment so large that it begged to be taxed; and a formidable set of schools led by quasi-autonomous deans, several of whom controlled more resources than the president. He faced a daunting set of overlapping institutional priorities, including the growth of a new engineering school—this in a town where there was another institution rather more famous in that realm, one of several institutional rivals that now threatened the leadership of "America's University."[11] Harvard did not have the luxury of specialization. Its was the burden of doing more things, better, than anyone else.

When a global pandemic broke out during the second year of his presidency, Bacow's leadership was tested. The COVID-19 crisis was a watershed moment in higher education. On March 10, 2020, Bacow announced that all classes would move online. Following his announcement, many universities across the United States and across the world also closed their physical spaces.

For nearly four centuries, the decisions and actions of Harvard set the tone for American higher education, from President Henry Dunster's adoption of the abandoned British terms "freshman," "sophomore," "junior," and "senior" in 1640, to President Charles William Eliot's creation of an elective-based curriculum in 1886, to President James Bryant Conant's role in developing the SAT as a common admissions tool in the 1940s. Harvard had made big bets on bold ideas throughout its long history. But no institution stays on top by standing still. How would Harvard continue to lead the American higher education sector in the twenty-first century? Or would it?

Foundations

The first British settlers of New England came from a society that had a long tradition of higher education, both for religious leaders and professionals in law and medicine. The ability to produce a supply of well-educated men to fill such roles in the newly established colony was of immediate concern to the settlers. When the Great and General Court of Massachusetts, whose forty-three members included six University of Cambridge alumni and one Trinity College, Dublin, alumnus and was led by the Oxford alumnus Governor Harry Vane, convened on October 28, 1636, they passed a legislative act to found a "scholae or colledge" in Newtowne, today's Cambridge.[12] Just what kind of men the institution would nurture, however, proved difficult to agree upon, and progress in establishing the institution was stymied by religious factionalism. Not until one year after the Court's original proclamation were they able to appoint the first "Overseers of the College," who quickly moved to recruit the recently immigrated Trinity College, Cambridge, and Dutch-educated Nathanial Eaton as the first master of the new college.

It was likely sometime during the summer of 1638, shortly after Eaton began teaching the first class of students, that he was visited by another recent immigrant, John Harvard, a graduate of Emmanuel College, Cambridge. Shortly thereafter, as John Harvard was dying of tuberculosis at the age of thirty, he dictated an oral will leaving his four-hundred-volume library and half of his estate to the new college. In what has turned out to be perhaps the best value in donor recognition of all time, the college was named Harvard in recognition of this gift in 1639.

Connecting John Harvard with the college was Eaton's greatest contribution to the school, but successful fundraisers are seldom remembered. Eaton was ousted from his position after just one year upon accusations of undue brutality against pupils and his wife's inadequate provision of beef and beer for the students. The young institution languished without a master for a year, before Henry Dunster, a thirty-year-old graduate of the University of Cambridge who had just landed in Boston, was assigned the new title of president on August 27, 1640.

Dunster sought to establish Harvard in the tradition of, and with legitimacy equal to, English institutions such as Eton College and the Oxbridge colleges: a residential setting for students and "masters," supported by endowment income.[13] Dunster focused on building Harvard's first student-scholar residences while initially serving as the primary instructor for all students. The curriculum he established, which remained largely in place until the early eighteenth century, was a further continuation of English tradition. It prescribed set courses in the Seven Liberal Arts and the Three Philosophies, reading of a classical canon, and the study of the so-called learned tongues, including Greek and Hebrew for reading of biblical texts.

The curriculum is a clue to the question, why was Harvard founded? It was not, as frequently has been asserted, simply to train preaching ministers. It *did* graduate ministers (some 50 percent of its seventeenth-century graduates), but its mission from the outset was the broader one of educating leaders in all professions for its New World. The tercentenary historian of Harvard, Samuel Eliot Morison, may have gone too far when he claimed that Harvard was founded to provide a broad "*liberal* education" for young gentlemen, but he was correct in writing that it was no divinity school.[14]

For that purpose, it began life as a public institution. Its founder was not John Harvard but the General Court of Massachusetts. It was supported in the seventeenth century by taxes and "contributions" from as far south as New Haven, at times levied in corn, and by the revenues of the Charlestown ferry that connected Cambridge to Boston, paid in wampumpeag (the currency of the Massachusetts Bay Colony). Other sources of early income included gifts (many from England), bequests, and student tuition, which was often paid in commodities such as beef, eggs, cheese, turnips, apples, and even boots and shoes, until the colony began to use its own form of currency. Even then, presidents could be well paid: it was reported in 1654 that Dunster had run the College for years on an average annual budget of £175, of which he retained £55 for his own salary.[15]

Dunster's tenure set many precedents. His assumed title of "president" would be handed down to the large majority of higher education institutions in the United States. More important, despite its legal and financial ties to the state, which supported Harvard into the nineteenth century, the College was both a public institution and an independent corporation. It was early on assumed that, like English colleges, Harvard would be run by its resident teachers. These being in short supply, a reorganized Board of Overseers was made a permanent institution by the General Court in 1642 to serve as an external board to run the College until the resident faculty could muster the strength. But when the College was formally chartered by the General Court in 1650, it formally established the "President and Fellows of Harvard College," also called the "Corporation," which owned the institution. The Corporation consisted of the president, the treasurer, and five fellows, who were initially teaching staff but later included outside community members. But in practice it would be overshadowed until the 1680s by the Board of Overseers, which continued to function. Thus Harvard's governance was complex and confusing right from the start.

In the first quarter of the eighteenth century, the role of the faculty in running the university was overshadowed by the growing role of the Corporation, with its Fellows acting as trustees, who were respected in the community in various fields but outside of the university. Governance by a president in conjunction with an external board has remained a characteristic common to most American higher education institutions.[16] As the president and Corporation governed the institution with considerable autonomy, the Overseers were placed in the advisory and subsidiary role they still occupy today. This structure of governance by external boards could at times buffer the College from the direct interference of the state. At the same time, it severely constrained the prospect of governance by faculty fellows that was at the heart of the English system. To this day, Harvard has no university-wide faculty body in a governance role.

Harvard was founded as a college with the pretense of a university. It was not called a "university" (except informally), but it appropriated the powers of one in order to grant its first bachelor's degrees in 1642. A final precedent set by Harvard in its early days was that a stand-alone college could function and give degrees that in England and Europe had historically been the prerogative of universities. (This right was formalized by the College's second charter of 1692, which gave the Corporation the right to "grant and admit to Academical Degrees, as in the Universities in England.")[17] The later explosive growth of liberal arts colleges in the United States—a truly distinctive element of American higher education—was one result. Another was the centrality of the undergraduate college, known as "Harvard College," within Harvard itself. As Harvard added professional and graduate schools in the eighteenth, nineteenth, and twentieth centuries, unlike many universities it did not subdivide undergraduate education by subject. For those studying literature, history, economics, engineering, or life sciences, there was a single admissions process to a single undergraduate college of liberal arts and sciences, taught by a single faculty, the Faculty of Arts and Sciences (FAS), which has been, and strives to remain, the center of the university.

Throughout the eighteenth and nineteenth centuries, Harvard strengthened its advanced offerings in professional disciplines, establishing the Medical School in 1782, formalizing the Divinity School in 1816, and adding the Law School in 1817. During this time, the school began to grow in both size and renown, but some outside New England saw it as a playground for the rich. Sixteen-year-old Benjamin Franklin, publishing under the pseudonym "Silence Dogood" in 1722, lambasted Harvard and, in particular "[the] extreme folly of those Parents, who, blind to their Children's Dulness, and insensible to the Solidarity of their Skulls, because they think their Purses can afford it, will needs send them to the Temple of Learning, where, for want of a suitable Genius, they learn little more than how to carry themselves handsomely, and enter a Room genteely (which might as well be acquired at a Dancing-School), and from whence they return, after abundance of trouble and Charges, as great Blockheads as ever, only more proud and self-conceited."[18]

A German-English Hybrid

For nearly two hundred years, and despite the significant influence of traditional British educational structures on the establishment of Harvard, no Harvard faculty member had attended university in Europe. Harvard professors were born of Harvard men; no other qualification was desired. This changed in 1814, when future president Edward Everett was hired as professor of Greek literature, with the opportunity to spend the first two years of his salaried employment studying abroad in Europe. Everett wisely took advantage of this unprecedented opportunity, and, along with George Ticknor, Joseph Cogswell, and George Bancroft, all Harvard-affiliated scholars, studied at the University of Göttingen.[19]

The time spent in Europe profoundly influenced all four of these men. Ticknor, who while in Europe was appointed to a senior chair at Harvard, was particularly tenacious in the fight to remake education at Harvard based on the German model. The first hint of reform came in 1825, with the passage of a new regulation at Harvard that began to break up the hated recitation model by allowing students to attend and progress through classes according to ability.[20] Ticknor also advocated for improving the library as a tool of scholarship and brought foreign scholars into Harvard's faculty ranks. The increasing proportion of German-trained scholars helped to infuse Harvard with the German mentality of *Lernfreiheit* that had undergirded the growth and fame of the University of Berlin and other German universities as centers for research and discovery.[21]

Still, Harvard was then better known for its longevity than for outstanding academic achievement. Morison, the university historian, noted: "In the nineteenth century it was a saying that all a Harvard man had to do for his master's degree was to pay five dollars and stay out of jail."[22] Peer institutions like Yale, Princeton, Columbia, and Johns Hopkins were drawing in excellent scholars and leaders, while, spurred on by the Morrill Land-Grant Acts of 1862 and 1890, state universities in California, Wisconsin, and Michigan were also establishing themselves as centers for scholarship beyond the East Coast. In New England, meanwhile, the percentage of people attending college actually dropped between 1838 and 1869.[23] Harvard itself lacked strong direction. Between Josiah Quincy's retirement in 1845 and Charles Eliot's appointment in 1869, the university went through eight failed or acting presidencies, the longest of which was that of James Walker (1853–1860), who, according to Morison, was "stone deaf and totally devoid of aesthetic sense" yet founded Harvard's music curriculum.[24]

Harvard became a university worthy of the name under—and because of—the leadership of Charles William Eliot, without question "the greatest man in the history of Harvard."[25] His darkened portrait presides today over every meeting of the Faculty of Arts and Sciences, peering out from the wall behind the president's chair in the Faculty Room. At his inaugural address as president, on October 19, 1869, his remarks over the course of an hour and three-quarters were full of one-liners, some of which may be seen as offensive today, such as "The world knows next to nothing about the natural mental capacities of the female sex." He did not seek to ingratiate himself with the professoriat, noting that "very few Americans of eminent abilities are attracted to this profession," and (my favorite line as a dean) "[t]o see every day the evil fruit of a bad appointment must be the cruelest of official torments." Yet he noted that "the poverty of scholars is of inestimable worth in this money-getting nation." But his most telling statement, in retrospect, was this: "The inertia of a massive University is formidable. A good past is positively dangerous, if it makes us content with the present and so unprepared for the future."[26]

Eliot understood how far behind Harvard had fallen. Yale, not Harvard, had established the first graduate school in New England. Johns Hopkins was recruiting scholars from Germany. Where was Harvard? As Morison writes, "Harvard College was hidebound, the Harvard Law School senescent, the Medical School ineffective, and the [comparatively new] Lawrence Scientific School 'the resort of shirks and stragglers.'"[27]

Eliot was the consummate insider who took an outsider's view of things. He was the grandson of the donor who had endowed the Eliot professorship at Harvard; he was the son of a former university treasurer (and member of the Corporation); and he was first cousin to an Overseer who helped elect him president. He was also a former assistant professor of chemistry and mathematics, unloved by students and colleagues alike, and passed over for promotion. He sojourned to Europe and studied the academic landscape there, particularly in Germany. He returned in 1865 as professor of chemistry at the newly incorporated MIT and was elected a Harvard Overseer in 1868. When the Harvard presidency became open that same year, the man who was first offered the position declined. Eliot "was far from being everybody's second choice," but he was chosen when the alternatives to this middling chemist seemed worse.[28]

Eliot, who took the presidency at the age of thirty-five, wasted no time in establishing a vision for Harvard along the lines of the great universities that he had visited for two years in Europe. At his inauguration, he announced his intentions to improve academic standing across all disciplines, develop innovative pedagogical methods, recruit faculty from Europe, expand access to Harvard College for lower-income students, and generally update the practices of American universities, which he found to be "literally centuries behind the precept of the best thinkers upon education."[29]

Over his forty-year presidency, Eliot dominated Harvard. A professor of Greek history remarked that, having seen Eliot in action, he understood how Pericles held sway over Athenian assemblies.[30] In 1870 Eliot proclaimed in his commencement address, "We mean to build here, securely and slowly, a university in the largest sense."[31] He began by delegating some authority, appointing the first dean of the College faculty that year, and in 1890 he established the Faculty of Arts and Sciences. However, throughout his four decades as president, he alone made the final appointment and promotion decisions. With the founding of the Faculty of Arts and Sciences came Harvard's first, formal, academic departments, largely organized along the lines of German *Fachbereiche*.

His tenure saw the establishment of the Graduate School of Arts and Sciences in 1872, allowing students to receive advanced degrees in the sciences and humanities at Harvard for the first time. Building on Ticknor's reforms, Eliot further divided the faculty by subject and specialization. He also quickly expanded the College from 23 faculty members teaching 529 undergraduates in 1869 to 61 faculty members teaching 1,080 students in 1886. The graduation of Harvard's first African American student, Richard Theodore Greener (who transferred from Oberlin College), in 1870 and the beginning of the inclusion of women through the opening of the Harvard Annex (later Radcliffe College) in 1879 occurred during Eliot's tenure.

Despite Eliot's goal of increasing access for the less well off, between 1870 and 1890 the proportion of the entering freshman class that had graduated from public high schools declined from 38 percent to 23 percent. Moreover, membership in elitist social clubs and integration with Boston high society became an increasingly important part of student life.[32] Harvard was more elite than ever.

In undergraduate education, Eliot was democratic, gradually making the curriculum almost entirely elective. By 1885 Harvard had no undergraduate requirements save for English composition and either French or German. In short, he treated students as adults for the first time: "[A] well-instructed youth of eighteen can select for himself . . . a better course of study than any college faculty."[33] And they would be motivated to do so by the pursuit of "honors," as conferred by the faculty, a system of "seductive stimuli" for the "*élite* of brains and character" to find "self-fulfillment and social utility." Eventually even compulsory chapel was abolished, and, as Donald Fleming writes, "God had become an elective at Harvard."[34]

Innovations could be found in several forms. The growth of a research university demanded more books, which could hardly be contained in the existing setup of the College library. The answer was the bookstack: "the most flexible, compact, and accessible form of shelving books that had ever been known" as well as the creation of a "public card catalogue," for greater accessibility to the library.[35] Harvard's unquestioned leadership in university libraries dates from Eliot's time. So, too, did Harvard's eminence in football, even though Eliot despised the sport. He oversaw the building of Harvard Stadium (1903), witness to the first sustained wave of sports fanaticism in American colleges. From the curricular to the extracurricular, by the end of Eliot's presidency, Harvard itself had become the leading model of a comprehensive, distinctly American university.[36]

It was even famous internationally. In 1912 then president emeritus Eliot was approached by the government of the new Republic of China to dispatch an advisor to help write a constitution for the first republic in Asia. He sent Frank Goodnow, the first president of the American Political Science Association and later president of Johns Hopkins. In China, Goodnow's constitutional draft helped make China's strongman, Yuan Shikai, president for life. (Yuan's life was mercifully short, for he might well otherwise have become emperor.[37]) Such was Harvard's contribution to Chinese democracy.

By the time Eliot retired in May 1909, Harvard had become *Harvard*, a university as well as a college, with a national reputation and the largest,

Figure 5.2. Portrait of Charles Eliot. Harvard University Portrait Collection, Gift by subscription from students and various Harvard clubs to the trustees of the Harvard Union, 1907, photo © President and Fellows of Harvard College, H192.

most famous faculty in the land. Of the leading one thousand scientists in the United States, one-quarter had studied at Harvard. Shortly before he died in 1924, Eliot remarked, "The best is yet to come. Let us hail the coming time."[38]

Harvard's Long Twentieth Century

Harvard's rise to academic distinction was accompanied by a succession of long-serving and impactful presidents: Charles Eliot for forty years, Abbott Lawrence Lowell for twenty-four, James Conant for twenty, Nathan Pusey for eighteen, Derek Bok for twenty, and Neil Rudenstine for ten (a long tenure by the late twentieth century). Each put a distinctive stamp on the place.

If Eliot was the architect of intellectual expansion at Harvard, his successor, Abbott Lawrence Lowell, led its physical remaking. If Eliot's foreign models for a modern university were to be found on the Continent, Lowell was an Anglophile. If Eliot let students liberally choose their courses, Lowell believed in structures and requirements. If Eliot was (for his time) open-minded on questions of faith and race, Lowell was (even for his time) a bigot.

In 1909 Lowell came to the helm of a Harvard with students divided, largely along socioeconomic lines, between private apartments and Harvard's own insufficient facilities. To promote cohesion among the student body and to transform the Harvard experience into something more akin to the Oxbridge model of colleges that blended study and student life, Lowell established new residences: first for freshmen, and then, toward the end of his presidency, for all upperclassmen in "the Houses," or residential colleges, made possible by the then-largest donation (and by a Yale graduate) in the university's history. To this was added an Oxbridge-style tutorial system.[39]

Lest his attempts to reform campus life be seen as progressive, Lowell was content to make this newly integrated academic-social campus scene available only to some. To him, the "stock of the Puritans" was a serious matter. Lowell tried to keep African American students out of the dormitories and established an unofficial cap on Jewish student enrollments.[40] In a letter to the father of a Black Harvard freshman, Lowell wrote, "I am sorry to have to tell you in the Freshman Halls, where residence is compulsory, we have felt from the beginning the necessity of not including colored men. . . . We have not thought it possible to compel men of different races to reside together."[41] Lowell sought to place a hard quota (12 percent) on Jewish freshmen, but the faculty rejected any formal quota. So an informal one took hold. During Lowell's tenure, the percentage of Jewish freshman at Harvard went from 27.6 percent in 1925 to less than 15 percent in 1933 when he retired.[42] As Lowell explained to a faculty colleague, "The summer hotel that is ruined by admitting Jews meets its fate, not because the Jews it admits are of bad character, but because they drive away the Gentiles."[43]

Of course, the most complete form of discrimination at Harvard took place against women. Radcliffe College was a distinct educational entity, even if the instructors were Harvard faculty. Radcliffe undergraduates could use Widener Library, the great temple of learning that opened in 1916, if they stayed confined to a small reading room. When Lamont Library was constructed after World War II as an undergraduate collection, it was off limits to women. Before Conant's time, only one of Harvard's graduate schools

(Education) admitted women, and it would have been out of business without them. The Law, Medical, and Business Schools "were all but unique" among their peers in excluding women.[44]

Lowell's focus on student life was accompanied by a rolling back of the curricular freedom beloved by Eliot. Lowell established a system of "Concentration and Distribution," which once again set the tone of higher education across America as almost all universities began to implement systems of majoring and minoring in certain subjects.[45]

With the curricular foundation set for another generation, it was Harvard's next president, James Bryant Conant, who propelled Harvard to the status of a research university of national and global stature, seeing Harvard's American peers more as Chicago, Hopkins, Columbia, and Berkeley, only one of which was part of the old Eastern academic world. From his inauguration in 1933, Conant focused on improving Harvard's profile as a research-driven institution: "If we have in each department of the university the most distinguished faculty which it is possible to obtain, we need have little worry about the future."[46] The problem was half of the Harvard faculty did not clear that bar in his view. Promotion reviews became more rigorous in an "up or out" tenure system. He similarly sought students from a wider range of means, talents, and geographies beyond the well-established Boston-New York axis. As the first Harvard president to espouse openly concepts of meritocracy in student admissions and the financial aid to support it, he founded the Harvard National Scholarships to "keep the way clear for the gifted youth of limited means."[47]

University and Nation (I)

It was in Conant's tenure that Harvard—perhaps more than at any time since 1775, when sixteen hundred colonial troops were housed in Harvard Yard—came to be identified ever more closely with the American national mission. For Conant, meritocracy was linked to democracy and to some degree with what we might today call social justice. Unlike much of his alumni, he admired the administration of Franklin D. Roosevelt. Unlike some of his faculty, he was a staunch interventionist in the years before World War II.

Like their German counterparts when nationalist and patriotic spirit swept the University of Berlin in 1914, Harvard and its professoriat embraced war when it came in 1941. The day after Pearl Harbor, Conant gathered the student body to hear Roosevelt's "Day of Infamy" speech to Congress. Conant pledged Harvard's full resources toward the war effort. Soldiers—largely officers in training—again were housed on campus (some of their "temporary" dorms remain today).

Harvard faculty served the military effort in multiple ways. They developed advanced torpedoes for submarine warfare and the napalm used in the firebombing of enemy cities, and they assisted in creating the first atom bomb. They also provided intelligence. Numerous Harvard scholars joined the Office of Strategic Services (OSS), the precursor to the Central Intelligence Agency (CIA). William Langer, the doyen of diplomatic history in the United States, oversaw the OSS's research division.[48] Langer recruited an extraordinary cadre of young historians: the intellectual historian H. Stuart Hughes; historian of the Balkans Robert Lee Wolff; Crane Brinton, the iconic scholar of the French Revolution; John Clive, historian of Britain and its empire; John K. Fairbank, who would return from the war to lead Harvard's study of China; and the future dean of the Faculty of Arts and Sciences, Franklin Ford, whose OSS work focused on Germany. All would, in time, become senior faculty at Harvard. Their collective work at OSS, organized in regional departments, formed the foundation of postwar "area studies" at Harvard and across the United States, supported by the Department of Defense.

The enlarged relationship between university and nation was strengthened postwar by the influx of former soldiers attending college through the GI Bill. Harvard College enrollment increased from around thirty-five hundred before WWII to fifty-five hundred in 1946. Harvard had never been terribly selective in undergraduate admissions to that point, normally admitting two of every three applicants. Briefly, it had to choose one out of fifteen. That surge did not last, although it would return decades later. A more enduring legacy of the GI Bill was in the students. The large majority had always come from private schools, but by 1952, more than half of entering freshmen had attended public high schools, a trend that would not be reversed.[49]

Conant, like his predecessors, also left his mark on the undergraduate curriculum in a way designed to influence American education at large. In 1945 a stellar faculty committee, convened by Conant to review the undergraduate curriculum in light of a student body pulled from increasingly diverse secondary education backgrounds, published its final report: *General Education in a Free Society*. Known as the "Redbook," because of the color of its cover (it was, in fact, the faded purple that passes for Harvard "crimson"), the report laid out a comprehensive treatise on the roles of secondary and tertiary institutions in educating American citizens. Seeking for students what Conant called "a common . . . understanding of the society which they will possess in common," the Harvard undergraduate curriculum was reformed once again such that one-fourth of the courses taken by an undergraduate were required to be newly created general education courses to provide a broad, interdisciplinary foundation for learning *and citizenship.* "General Education" remains today in the DNA of a Harvard education.

While leading the way in undergraduate curriculum development, Harvard was no pacesetter in its social policies. Harvard sustained its rich history of discrimination. While the discriminatory, unofficial quotas limiting the enrollment of Jewish students had been abandoned by the 1950s, women were still not eligible to attend Harvard College or many of the Harvard professional schools. In 1960 only 4 out of 427 full professorships across the university were held by women.[50] During that decade, women attending Radcliffe were given permission to attend any class at Harvard, and in 1963 Radcliffe students were granted Harvard diplomas (although still signed by the Radcliffe president).[51] The proportion of African American students remained extremely low in the 1950s and 1960s, despite the lack of any particular policy barriers. Only later in the 1960s did the university more proactively seek diversity of ethnicity and gender in the student and faculty body.

However conventional at home, Harvard's external reputation continued to grow, even in a more competitive postwar world, with its massive expansion of higher education. In a list of academic rankings of graduate schools cited by David Webster, a scholar of American higher education, not a single ranking between 1925 and 1982 placed Harvard lower than third-best in the nation.[52] Popular opinion abroad was no less supportive. A poll at the United States pavilion at the 1958 Brussels World's Fair asked where participants would like to send their son to college; over thirty-two thousand pavilion visitors responded "Harvard." "MIT" was the next most popular, with only half the number of responses.[53]

Harvard continued to grow in size and reputation in the second half of the twentieth century, albeit not without contention. As the College and faculty expanded and slowly diversified, the larger professional schools grew in wealth and autonomy, and the undergraduates challenged authority. It was a measure of Harvard's insularity in previous presidential searches that the appointments of the non-Bostonian Nathan Marsh Pusey (1953–1971) and

Derek C. Bok (1971–1991), who did not attend Harvard College, could be seen as breaks with tradition.

Money Matters: The Development State

"Harvard was always poor, strapped by a meager endowment," wrote Oscar Handlin of the university's first centuries.[54] No one could believe that after the presidency of Nathan Pusey. Plucked from comparative obscurity as the president of Lawrence College, a liberal arts college and music conservatory in Appleton, Wisconsin, Pusey became the prototype of the modern university president as fundraiser-in-chief. He deputed the administrative oversight of Harvard College and the Faculty of Arts and Sciences to the newly empowered dean of FAS, in this case, the formidable political scientist McGeorge Bundy.

In the postwar era, government—and especially foundation—grants (the American version of *Drittmittel*) grew in importance, but there Harvard was but one recipient among many. Large private gifts had come to Harvard before (for example, George F. Baker's single-handed funding of the new Harvard Business School campus in 1924), but a comprehensive "campaign" on the scale of the Program for Harvard College that was launched in 1957 had not been seen. Its goal of $82.4 million would be reached over four years, and it would set the stage for many repeat performances. Harvard alumni as a group were by no means among the most philanthropic of their peers. But the pockets of some Harvard alumni (the banker Thomas Lamont, AB 1892, for example—the namesake of Harvard's main undergraduate library) were deeper than others, and they partially emptied them when solicited.

That campaign and other gifts gave Harvard a newly modernist look: Le Corbusier's Center for the Visual Arts, Stubbins's Loeb Drama Center, Yamasaki's William James Hall, and Sert's Holyoke Center were among the thirty-three new buildings begun by Pusey. They nestled among the structures of the colonial and early federal campus, the late nineteenth century elegance of Richardson, and the early twentieth century obsession with neo-Georgian. The campaign was just the beginning of many more. Campaigns for the Business School, the Medical School, the Law School, and indeed every school of the university often competed for donations from the same group of donors. Thus began the combination of entrepreneurialism, competition, and bureaucratic Darwinism that has made Harvard fundraising so chaotic and so successful ever since. By 1964 the university's endowment had doubled in a decade and passed the magical mark of $1 billion.[55]

University and Nation (II)

President John F. Kennedy (class of 1940) visited Harvard for the last time in October 1963, four months after his triumphal visit to Berlin and one month before his assassination. As in Berlin, where 1963 marked the height of pro-American sentiment at Free University, so at Harvard it was the high point of the university's relations with the US government. Dean of FAS McGeorge Bundy had become JFK's national security adviser; Arthur Schlesinger, Jr. (AB '38) became Kennedy's special assistant; David Bell (MA '41) was budget director; and Harvard Professors John Kenneth Galbraith and Edwin Reischauer (PhD '39) were ambassadors to India and Japan, respectively.

As at Free University, within four years Harvard was in political turmoil, generated in part by the muscular foreign policy that Kennedy had begun in Southeast Asia. Defense Secretary Robert S. McNamara (MBA 1939), on campus for a visit, escaped a confrontation with students via underground steam tunnels in 1966. Corporate recruiters tied to defense industries were barricaded in buildings the following year. Student demonstrations against the war, imperialism, racism, and simply against Harvard (as the incarnation of all these things with its CIA ties, officer-training programs, and corporate donors) multiplied, culminating in the student takeover, in the spring of 1969, of University Hall, the staid Bullfinch masterpiece at the center of Harvard Yard that housed the offices of the dean of the faculty.

Pusey had (mostly) defended the university against right-wing government intrusion at the height of the McCarthyite furor of the 1950s, and now he refused to yield to the left. The occupation of University Hall lasted less than 24 hours, with the 184 occupiers violently displaced by 400 state troopers and local police. And with that "Bust," as it was called, Harvard fell apart. FAS Dean Franklin Ford, who was among those evicted by students, suffered a stroke and later resigned. Pusey stayed on, but his presidency was over.

Amid the subsequent years of student strikes, faculty debates, and internal rebuilding, Harvard recalibrated its relationship with government, canceling the ROTC officers' training program on campus, forbidding government-classified research contracts and federal grants to support the salaries of tenured faculty, and limiting at least the outward appearance of too many ties to the CIA.

(Old habits die hard, however. When I was a doctoral student about to begin a Fulbright year in Taiwan in 1977, I was invited to meet with the director of the Office of Career Services. I was happy to do so, for I knew that upon return from my dissertation research, I would face a dismal academic job market, and I wanted to ask about opportunities in the "real world." The director surprised me, however, by asking if I might have some free time to do some ancillary research on Taiwan for an [unnamed] agency. At the time of my departure, the United States was withdrawing troops from Taiwan and contemplating diplomatic recognition of mainland China; anti-Americanism was growing in Nationalist government circles. There would be much to research. But I declined, politely, noting in passing that the last I looked, Taiwan was an island, and I was a poor swimmer. In retrospect, I should not have been surprised by the overture, for both of my mentors, Franklin Ford and John Fairbank, had served in the OSS during World War II. One of them must have thought this was a good idea.)

Derek Bok, who succeeded Pusey and served as president for the following two decades, sought to reengage the university with public affairs by building on Pusey's plans to remake a sleepy School of Public Administration into the Kennedy School of Government, now built on riverside land in modern structures, if clad in old-fashioned brick. It would prepare graduate students for public service and be a (less radical?) focal point for undergraduate engagement with the political world. It would also (re)train active public servants and serve as a way station for politicians on the way up, or (more commonly) on their loss of office. Led for most of Bok's tenure by a passionate dean, Graham Allison, the Kennedy School became what it still is today: a leading center for the study *and* practice of government.

Yet by the time he retired from the presidency in 1991, Bok lamented the enduring unmooring of the university from state and society. If in the 1950s "America and its universities were united in a common resolve to build a system of scientific research preeminent in the world and to expand our colleges to embrace . . . a much larger segment of the nation's youth," that understanding was long gone. He warned, in words that ring more strongly true today: "Unless society appreciates the contributions of its universities, it will continue to reduce them to the status of another interest group by gradually stripping away the protections and support they need to stay preeminent in the world."[56]

A Golden Decade

Bok was succeeded by Neil Rudenstine, whose presidency during the 1990s was perhaps the most understated yet impactful of any decade in Harvard's modern history. A true intellectual, an erudite writer and speaker, gracious and curious, but with a backbone of steel gained from a decade of service as Princeton's provost, he was beloved by the faculty. His task was to prepare in a comparatively short time (he took office at age fifty-six—the oldest since President Walker on the eve of the Civil War) for a different, larger, yet more unified university, engaged in and far beyond the United States.

His challenges were formidable. Princeton was a highly centralized university, in which academic and budgetary authority was rooted in the president and provost. Harvard had no provost, and almost all of the spendable money was now in the hands of the deans. The "every tub on its own bottom" model of finance was designed to make the schools fiscally responsible. It made some of them also very rich. Rudenstine's challenge (not unlike that of Duke under Nannerl Keohane) was to gradually but steadily bring more resources to the center while not undoing the entrepreneurialism that underlay the schools' success. This he did by (1) taxation for infrastructure and (2) raising a then-ungodly amount of money.

Harvard was hardly poor, but it was not *that* much richer than its competitors. (Pound for pound, Princeton, with an endowment and student body then about the size of Harvard's Faculty of Arts and Sciences, was and remains the best endowed of all.) At the financial low point of the Bok years, endowment contributed but 18 percent of Harvard's revenues; today it contributes double that. But the 1990s was the decade when Harvard truly took off. Rudenstine's decade saw Harvard distance itself dramatically from other comprehensive research universities, as the Harvard endowment more than quadrupled from $4.7 billion in 1990 to $19.2 billion in 2000, supported by strong market conditions; the remarkable leadership of Jack Meyer, president and CEO of the Harvard Management Company (HMC), the entity founded in 1974 to manage Harvard's endowment; and an influx of largesse through "development," as fundraising was now called.

The University Campaign, led brilliantly by Rudenstine, was Harvard's first comprehensive university-wide fundraising effort. It was also Harvard's first—and, so far, last—endeavor at university-wide academic planning. It was linked to extensive processes of strategic planning in each school, while making room also for cross-university initiatives. Chaired by Rudenstine's close partner, Robert Stone, the Senior Fellow of the Corporation, the campaign raised $1 million a day and ended with $2.6 billion in gifts, exceeding its goal by half a billion.[57]

The Rudenstine years also witnessed a remarkable expansion of Harvard's physical footprint. The university had no place to grow in Cambridge. It rented land, for a time, in neighboring Watertown. For the longer haul, Harvard accelerated its purchase of land across the Charles River from Cambridge's Harvard Yard in the Allston neighborhood of Boston, home then only to the Business School and the athletic fields. On his rationale for this decision, Rudenstine recalled, "The idea was to think Harvard is going to need land over the next century, and we don't know exactly what will emerge, and so . . . we ought to leave a lot of land flexible to see what happened."[58] By 1997 Harvard had purchased 52.6 acres of land in Allston, bringing its total landholdings there to 192 acres (even while facing some discontent from the local community), compared with its 215 acres in Cambridge.[59] By 2017 the majority of Harvard's land holdings had shifted to Allston, where the university controlled 358 acres.[60]

The financial and physical expansion of the university during Rudenstine's tenure undergirded his overarching goal of increasing cooperation and integration (if not unification) across Harvard's many "tubs," which had grown increasingly autonomous over the Conant, Pusey, and Bok years. (In one reputed episode from 1994, the commanding and long-serving dean of Harvard Business School, John McArthur, engineered the merger of two Harvard-affiliated hospitals, Brigham and Women's, whose board he chaired, with Massachusetts General Hospital, leading to the creation of Partners Health-Care, of which he was a founding co-chair. McArthur apparently told the president of the university about the merger the night before its public announcement. The next year, HBS had a new dean.)

Rudenstine established the role of provost, the position he had filled at Princeton and from which he had been recruited to lead Harvard, to improve the capacity of a woefully understaffed central administration. He forged cross- and inter-disciplinary "inter-faculty initiatives" on the environment, health policy, ethics, and mind/brain/behavior. He drove (and led the fundraising for) major initiatives in international studies: the creation of the university-wide David Rockefeller Center for Latin American Studies and the Harvard University Asia Center. And he founded the Radcliffe Institute for Advanced Study as the successor to Radcliffe College and in the process recruited a future president.

In addition to using the carrot of new opportunities, Rudenstine used the stick of funding: deans were told to work together and critique each other's plans before they were accepted into the university-wide campaign.[61] Looking to fund expansion in Allston, he led the deans of Harvard's schools, who normally voted on nothing together, to endorse implementing an annual "tax" of 0.5 percent on each school's endowment.[62]

Rudenstine was clear-eyed about the idiosyncrasies of Harvard. He once compared for me the challenges of leading Princeton and Harvard. Princeton, he said, when it all worked well, was like conducting a symphony orchestra. Harvard, at its best, was a splendid collection of soloists. Yet he left the soloists with better instruments than he found them, and in a more collegial, prosperous, and expansive concert hall—all done in the most optimistic of spirits. Not bad for a decade's work. There is a reason Neil Rudenstine's lustrous portrait now sits over the main entrance to the Faculty Room in University Hall.

Figure 5.3. Portrait of Neil Rudenstine by Everett Raymond Kinstler. Harvard University Portrait Collection, Commissioned by the Faculty of Arts and Sciences, 2006, © Everett Raymond Kinstler Estate, H814.

Early Twenty-First Century Trials

From Eliot through Rudenstine, Harvard had the good fortune of more than a century and a quarter of long-serving, impactful presidents. Between 2000 and 2006, by contrast, four individuals sat in the president's office in Massachusetts Hall. The governance structures of the university came under stress as its largest faculty voted "no confidence" in a president while the ancient Corporation—still composed, as in 1650, of its five "fellows," the treasurer, and the president—labored to give direction to a modern, decentralized, and disputatious university. Finances were mismanaged, and the (still largest in the word) university endowment lagged others in performance. Harvard's "new campus" across the Charles River remained desolate, with not a single academic building completed in its first quarter-century. And a university that had come to set national standards in teaching and research found itself with serious competition in an era of technological revolution and globalization. If by 2020 Harvard could still be primus inter pares in the world of universities, it was a measure of the power of its disparate schools and the capacity for renewal at the center.

When in October 2001 Lawrence Summers sat for his inauguration in the creaky, uncomfortable, three-legged "Holyoke Chair," a British relic from the sixteenth century, the former Harvard professor of economics and US Treasury secretary had a full agenda in mind for Harvard's twenty-first century. He would oversee, as Conant and Bok had in their tenures, a major reform in undergraduate education, seeking to ensure that Harvard College remained the heart of an expanding, decentralized, research university. He would maintain, as Conant had, a leadership position in the sciences. And he would build on Rudenstine's internationalist agenda to make Harvard more global still. In so doing, Harvard would expand physically and become more coherent internally. Altogether this was a compelling, indeed energizing, vision for Harvard's faculty and students (and was the central reason I, having served as chair of the history department and director of the Asia Center, agreed to be the dean of the Faculty of Arts and Sciences).

Four and a half years later, in February 2006, Summers announced his resignation. His would be the shortest Harvard presidency since that of Cornelius Conway Felton (1860–1862), who died in office. In some ways, the tensions of Summers's tenure were cultural in foundation. Summers was direct and plainspoken to a degree not experienced in a university still steeped in New England traditions of courtly nonconfrontation (at least in public).

After the "troubles" of the 1960s, meetings of the Faculty of Arts and Sciences had been constrained by rules of procedure meant to limit debate, and as a result had become somnambulant affairs. Not so in Summers's time. A faculty that had grown used to being reassured that it was the best in the world found itself confronted and challenged by a president/agitator who believed with the certainty of a modern economist that it could do better. Rudenstine could turn down a senior appointment yet leave a department chair feeling better having had the discussion with him. Summers could approve an offer of tenure and leave the nominating department bruised and insulted. In those days, the president and dean presided over some forty half-day tenure meetings per year, at which multiple faculty colleagues "testified"; so, the opportunities for discord were many.

Despite the tensions emanating from what was euphemistically called the president's "managerial style," Summers set important initiatives in motion during his short tenure. His ambitious plans for Allston, which included a five-hundred-thousand-square-foot science complex, new homes for the Schools of Public Health and Education, and new undergraduate houses promised a radical transformation of the campus. He pressed the deans of the separate schools to collaborate in hiring and doctoral education—with notable success in the historically siloed life sciences. He pushed hard to ensure that Harvard scientists would have a major role in the new Broad Institute, a biomedical and genomic research center that had emerged from MIT's Whitehead Institute. And, with most enduring impact, he worked with me as dean to earmark and raise funds to alter dramatically the scope of financial aid offered to Harvard College students. In 2004 we announced that Harvard would be cost-free for families with incomes below $40,000 (in 2020 that figure was $65,000), with much-reduced costs for those with family incomes up to $150,000. The message was simple: you did not need to be rich to go to Harvard. The message was well received, but the messenger was in increasing conflict on other matters—with the faculty (especially in FAS) and with multiple deans.

"A single spark can start a prairie fire," Mao Zedong once wrote. By the time that Summers, in the January of his fourth year as president, made his now-infamous comments on women in science, in which he speculated that the underrepresentation of female scientists may have been a result of "innate differences" between genders, the tinder at Harvard was very dry.[63] At the FAS faculty meeting on February 7, 2005, the reform of undergraduate education was the central, docketed item. It would not be passed for two more years, and then under an acting president. Instead the faculty erupted in a verbal assault on the president, the likes of which had not been seen even in the 1960s.

University Hall, designed in 1813 by Charles Bullfinch, the primary architect of the United States Capitol, is a neoclassical masterpiece of the early Federal period. The former chapel that dominates its second floor is today the Faculty Room, home to FAS faculty meetings. It is a room surrounded with history, dominated by portraits of Eliot, Lowell, Conant, and Bok (and today Rudenstine), but also spiced with images of lesser luminaries, such as the seventeenth-century wooden image of William Stoughton, an early donor and the only magistrate of the Salem witch trials never to repent.

The Faculty Room can seat two hundred people uncomfortably. Twice that number came in February 2005 to speak bitterness against the president, face to face. By tradition, the president chairs the FAS faculty meetings for, as the Philosophical Faculty in Humboldt's sense, FAS is at the center of the university. That same tradition exposes the president to any question that a colleague may wish to ask, or any statement. They were fast and furious in coming, and from the most senior faculty. The anthropologist Arthur Kleinman accused Summers of uttering "reckless and undigested words based in half-baked sociological prejudices." Theda Skocpol, the sociologist, wondered, "How do we want to proceed in addressing the pathologies of leadership that are undermining the honor, the competitive effectiveness, and the collegial governance of Harvard University?" The master of Lowell House, Diana Eck, asked how Summers would respond to "what is clearly a widening crisis of confidence in your fitness to lead our University?" Stephen Owen, a University Professor (Harvard's highest professorial rank), asked, "Mr. President, when did I cease being your colleague and start being your employee?" These were among the more restrained comments in a meeting that would be continued, in two further and larger sessions, for more than a month, before concluding at the largest venue available at Harvard for such a gathering: the Loeb Drama Center. On a stage that later that evening would host Christopher Marlowe's play, *Dido, Queen of Carthage*, about a woman's rule over a haven of civilization, the faculty passed a resolution—unprecedented in Harvard's history—of no confidence in the president.[64]

Although he would stay in office for another year, Summers's presidency effectively ended that afternoon. Initiatives ground to a halt. Allston planning was put on ice. The Harvard Corporation, that senior governing body which under Summers had become increasingly disengaged from the task of governance, came under intense critique. A year later, Derek Bok was back as interim president, and the search for new leadership for the twenty-first century resumed.

In turning to Drew Gilpin Faust, founding dean of the Radcliffe Institute, a chastened Corporation at once looked back to the Rudenstine era (Neil Rudenstine had recruited her, and Drew Faust shared his diplomatic skills) and looked forward to a leader who was creative and collaborative, compelling but not combative in argument. She preferred not to be known primarily as Harvard's first woman president: she was simply its twenty-eighth president. Harvard was by no means in the forefront of appointing women to presidencies: MIT, Princeton, and Penn had done so some years earlier. But at an old place still steeped in traditions of discrimination, Faust's appointment was widely celebrated.

Faust was barely in her third year as president when a major crisis of the twenty-first century unfolded. Just before the 2008 financial crisis, the Harvard endowment had reached a value of $36.9 billion. It would lose $10 billion in value in a matter of weeks. Seemingly overnight, 27.3 percent of the endowment was lost.[65] This was a performance lagging that of every peer.[66] What was worse, overnight $1.8 billion *in cash* of Harvard's everyday expenses disappeared.[67] Every university with an endowment saw a huge drop in value that autumn. Only Harvard managed to lose not only more than a quarter of its "savings account," that is, the endowment, *but also* most of its "checking account": the short-term reserves of every school.

This large-scale financial mismanagement tells us much about Harvard's governance and internal funding model. Each school is expected to be fiscally self-sufficient, but each school has a different funding model. Older schools (FAS and Divinity, for example) are heavily endowment-dependent. Younger ones (Education, Public Health) count heavily on tuition or external grants. The President's Office, by contrast, has neither tuition nor (much) endowment to count on, and so the center of the world's richest university is much poorer than any of Harvard's major schools. The funds from the President's Office rely on modest taxation of the individual schools and the investment of their annual, short-term reserves into a "central bank." When Summers was president, he sought (rightly, in my view) to enhance the Central Bank's financial capacity by investing those reserves, rather than simply holding them. By investing Harvard's cash holdings from its General Operating Account (GOA) into comparatively riskier instruments, alongside the endowment, he hoped to boost returns and bring more of the university's

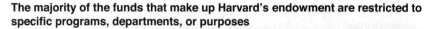

The majority of the funds that make up Harvard's endowment are restricted to specific programs, departments, or purposes

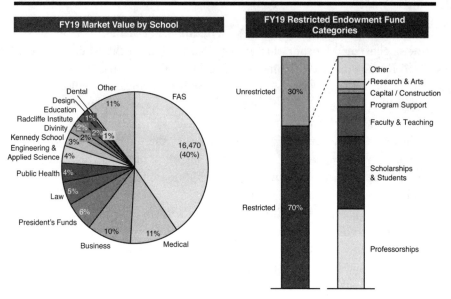

Figure 5.4. FY 2019 Harvard endowment breakdown graph. Faculty of Arts and Sciences, Harvard University.

resources to the central administration. Had Summers remained as president, my guess is that he would have known when to get the university out of those investments. But two years after he left, there were few who had the memory or expertise to understand the potential risks that would cost the university nearly $2 billion in cash.[68] The Corporation, responsible for the university's finances, was uninformed and inattentive. The dean of the School of Public Health, for example, had nurtured a reserve of nearly $100 million. It was gone in a flash. The financial crisis led to the largest percentage financial decline in forty years for Harvard.[69] Larry Bacow, who joined the Corporation in 2011 and chaired its finance committee, recalled his surprise: "Harvard had zero capacity to plan, and not only that, the endowment was being managed completely independently from the operating budget. . . . When I got there, I couldn't believe what I saw."[70] Even as the economy improved, the effects of the Great Recession were long-lasting. Not until 2021 would the endowment be worth more, in real dollars, than it had been in 2008.

The sudden financial crisis left Harvard in a panicked scramble to make ends meet. Harvard had to rush out and borrow $2.5 billion at comparatively high interest rates, and annual interest expense alone grew to $265 million by 2010. Over the same period, the endowment distribution for annual operating expenses declined by $300 million. Early retirement incentive programs and layoffs were put in place, leading to more than eight hundred employees leaving in May 2009.[71] The Faculty of Arts and Sciences, which had begun a plan to expand its faculty, froze positions, and it has not grown since. Construction of an enormous life sciences complex in Allston was stopped and abandoned, even though the $400 million, four-story-deep foundation had already been poured, giving new meaning to the term "sunk cost." One major goal of Faust's tenure was creating more unity across Harvard's various schools, transforming them into "One Harvard." In the immediate wake of the financial crisis, however, it was *sauve qui peut,* as Harvard's schools were ever more consumed with self-reliance.

Harvard in 2020

Despite an extraordinarily inauspicious start to the twenty-first century, the Harvard of 2020 remained one of the most highly regarded universities in the world. Many of its individual professional schools topped global rankings, while the university as a whole had been ranked the best university in the world by the Shanghai Academic Ranking of World Universities every year since the inception of that ranking system in 2003.

Harvard's over 371,000 living alumni could be found in 202 countries, helping to solidify its reputation around the world. However, it was Harvard's enduring ability to attract outstanding faculty and students—and ensure that somehow they learned, one from another—that kept it on or near the top.

Faculty

Over time, the Harvard faculty has included fifty-two Nobel laureates and forty-four Pulitzer Prize winners. It was not always so. Through Lowell's presidency, Harvard's research reputation trailed that of Chicago and Columbia. Its most famous faculty were teaching, not research, stars, and long-term lecturers outnumbered tenured faculty. Conant, who believed that it was "mistaken philanthropy to keep a mediocre man in a university," inaugurated the tenure "clock" in 1939. The clock stopped at eight years, after which it was "up" to a tenured appointment or "out" of the university. In 1942 Conant also inaugurated the iconic Harvard way to review tenure cases: the ad hoc committee. Unlike most of its peer institutions, Harvard has no standing committee on appointments or promotions. Rather, for each tenure case, a separate committee consisting of scholars from outside Harvard (the majority of members) and from disparate departments within the university is assembled to review the case and advise the dean and the president, who has the final say, on the appointment.[72]

By the twenty-first century, the ad hoc committee was the final stage in a famously laborious sequence. Departments were permitted to "search" for a tenured appointment, be it an internal promotion or an external recruitment, and would send out "blind" letters asking colleagues from outside the university to review a list of names that did not indicate which was the preferred candidate. If, on receipt of the responses from these reviewers, the department voted in favor of promotion, all tenured department members then had to write confidential letters to the dean to say *why* they had voted the way they had. The dean would then review the case with his or her academic advisory group, and, if the dean approved, the case would go to the president and in time to the ad hoc interrogation, which would normally last at least three hours. Cumbersome and time consuming, the procedure ensured a high degree of external scrutiny even as it ensured that deans and presidents would remain current in their grasp of different academic disciplines. Above all (and especially when tenure was awarded only at the full professorial level after the 1960s), it ensured fewer "mistakes."

Harvard being Harvard, this ad hoc system was applied across the university in an ad hoc way. It was required for FAS and the smaller schools (e.g., Divinity and Education) and less stringently for the large and powerful professional Schools of Law, Business, and Medicine. But the need for presidential approval of any tenured appointment remained absolute.

Those were its strengths. Its weakness was to diminish mightily the prospect of promotion for "junior" faculty, as the untenured were called by their seniors. Judith Singer, the James Bryant Conant Professor of Education, noted that when she was hired at the Graduate School of Education in 1984, she was told, "Assume you will not get tenure."[73] From the 1970s to the early 2000s, an assistant professorship in the humanities and social sciences at Harvard was essentially a folding chair. The social and professional distance between the tenured faculty and the day laborers of assistant professors grew to be as great as could be found in any nineteenth-century German university. With recruitment of stars from the outside prized over the development of young talent at home, the best young scholars tended not to accept Harvard offers or to leave early, while the externally recruited tenured faculty in many fields were older, whiter, and more male than their counterparts at "tenure-track" universities. External recruits were on average ten years older than internal promotions, and their reputations were already well established. The risk was this: Had they already done their best work, elsewhere? They may have been known for explosive scholarship, but were they, as FAS Dean Jeremy Knowles worried in the 1990s, "extinct volcanoes"?

This appointment culture could limit a great department's capacity for self-renewal. Take the case of my own Department of History. In the third quarter of the twentieth century, Harvard's history department enjoyed a towering reputation. Its faculty (many of them having participated in OSS during the Second World War) were both learned and worldly. Its leadership in so many fields from American to European to Russian to Chinese history set the foundation for multiple regional research centers at Harvard. Yet it lacked the ambition of self-renewal, for who was good enough to join such a club? How could the current faculty be replaced? And so it missed dynamic revolutions in historical study, be they in the history of race, class, gender, or society. This was the kind of attitude that must have motivated Henry Rosovsky, surely the most accomplished dean ever to preside over the Faculty of Arts and Sciences (he served from 1973 to 1984 and again in 1990–1991) to place in his University Hall office that sober reckoning sometimes attributed to Charles de Gaulle: "The graveyards are full of indispensable men."

When I joined the History Department in 1992, it had 31 tenured colleagues, 1.5 of whom were female. (One was a joint appointment.) An external review committee had recently found History to be "a department in crisis." Appointments languished, for every senior scholar had a *liberum veto* on candidates in their field. When *The Harvard Crimson*, the undergraduate paper, published its *Confi Guide* to courses in 1993, the pages on the History Department opened with a large photo of the *Hindenburg* consumed in flames. American history, once the pride of the department, had withered to insignificance: no one had been tenured from within the department in American history since the Eisenhower administration. And great scholar-teachers, such as the twentieth-century political historian Alan Brinkley, had been let go. The *Crimson* still recommended the department to students, "You won't have to do much schoolwork. Most of the courses are work and grade guts." And so, they advised their fellow students, "You don't need to transfer to Yale, especially if you really don't care about the New Deal."[74]

Today a remarkably different, diverse, and talented department—44 percent female among its senior ranks—leads the study of history at Harvard. Assistant professors are hired only if they have the promise, with time and support, to be serious candidates for tenure. This turnabout was the result not of happenstance but of several department chairs, myself included, making old guards uncomfortable, recruiting new generations of leaders from without and within, all with the strong support of a president (Rudenstine) and dean (Knowles) who simply would not stand by and witness academic decay.

The lessons of the History Department's renewal formed the background for changes across FAS when I assumed the FAS deanship in 2002. Bizarre as it sounds, the formal procedures for promotion and tenure had never been made public. Department chairs had copies, and sometimes shared them with their untenured colleagues, but many younger colleagues simply had no clue. Procedures for a rigorous "tenure track" were drawn up, revised, and put online. Search processes across the multitude of FAS departments were monitored by University Hall. Tenure review letters were no longer "blind." Harvard began to focus more resources on the orientation, development, and retention of young faculty members. In other words, in its search for talent, Harvard was becoming a normal American university—albeit one with a higher degree of success in recruitment and retention.

Between 2004 and 2014 the number of tenured faculty grew by 22 percent, while tenure-track faculty shrank by 12 percent, which the Harvard Faculty Development and Diversity 2013–2014 Annual Report called "a result of all-time high internal promotion rates."[75] By 2010 a majority of university tenure appointments were made through internal promotion rather than external recruitment.[76]

Like the faculties of many top-tier universities in the United States, Harvard's was not known for its diversity. It was nearly three hundred years after the establishment of the university when in 1919 Alice Hamilton became the first woman to hold a faculty position at Harvard. In the Faculty of Arts and Sciences, there were no women until 1947, when a donor endowed a professorship *on the condition* that the holder of the chair be female. In 1985 just 45 out of 898 tenured faculty members across the university were female.[77] By 2020 this proportion had increased but remained well below gender parity levels—31 percent of Harvard faculty were female, up from 26 percent in 2004.[78]

Still, each department in FAS and each unit across the university retained elements of its individual culture, some of which were historically inimical to concepts of diversity. Economics was for years a "young boys' club." And Mathematics resisted the idea that colleagues may be promoted to tenure, nor did it hire female faculty from the outside. As a result, it has remained, until very recently, entirely male. (When President Drew Faust pronounced several years ago a *Verbot* on single-sex social organizations at Harvard—she was targeting the "Final Clubs," or fancy fraternities—I suggested she start with the Math Department.)

Some progress has been made in increasing the representation of minorities in the faculty. By 2019, 24 percent of Harvard faculty were members of minority groups, a 1 percent increase from 2004. This already-small group was disproportionately Asian (around 60 percent); Blacks, Latinx, and multiracial individuals made up just 10 percent of the faculty.

Despite the variability across schools and disciplines, in the first part of the twenty-first century an offer to teach at Harvard remained the most prestigious (if not always the most remunerative) offer a scholar might entertain. It was, still, the twenty-first century "call to Berlin." Negotiation of the terms of hiring a senior scholar (from within or outside) was, as anywhere, a courtship. But once the faculty member was hired, the courtship became a marriage. Harvard would co-invest in housing, helping scholars live in a pricey environment while incurring limited personal costs. It would invest in the education of faculty children by offering interest-free loans wherever they chose to study. These were both attractions and a set of golden handcuffs to retain faculty.

Of course, Harvard could and did lose faculty to peer institutions. After all, you don't want a faculty member that no one else wants. I recall that my last hours as dean, many time zones removed from Cambridge, were spent trying to dissuade a wonderful colleague from decamping to Stanford. I did not succeed, but Harvard's overall divorce rate remained remarkably low.

Students: Admissions and Athletics

I used to tell my faculty colleagues when we were considering reform to undergraduate education, "You know, without the students, none of us would be here." That was surely true, for Harvard was founded as a teaching institution that grafted research onto its mission. It was never a rarefied institute of advanced study—a Max Planck, for example. And as a university, Harvard is defined as much by its students, and its alumni, as it is by its faculty.

One measure of the prestige of a university is how desperate people are to get into it. By this calculation Harvard remains the admissions gold standard for college students (and for business, law, and medical students). I have been asked in all corners of the world, "How do I (or my daughter or son) get into Harvard?" For this I have a ready answer: "Apply. If you don't apply, you really won't get in." But that counsel elides the point. *How does one get into Harvard?* One external view is by money. Several years ago, when I was at our Harvard Center Shanghai, three individuals came to see me to offer stunningly generous "donations" to Harvard, each at about $5 million. In each case, as I asked what prompted this admirable sense of philanthropy, it turned out that there was a family member in an admissions pool in one or another of Harvard's schools. And in each case, I thanked the would-be philanthropists for their generous spirit. Unfortunately, I informed them, we could not accept the funds because, I told them, "We would not want others to misunderstand your good intentions."

The reasons for the attempted bribery in Shanghai (but it could have been anywhere) were clear: admission to Harvard College had become insanely competitive in the early twenty-first century. The percentage of applicants admitted had fallen from around 10 percent in 2000 to less than 4 percent for the class of 2025. The College's yield of admitted students generally hovered around 80 percent, compared with yields of around 70 percent at Yale and Princeton.[79] Harvard's admissions statistics were almost perfectly matched by Stanford, which admitted 4.36 percent of applicants to its class of 2022 and reported an 82.4 percent yield rate.[80]

The increasing competitiveness of university admissions, especially in the most selective universities, has led prospective students and their parents to do whatever it takes to gain admission, even in unlawful ways. On March 12, 2019, US Attorney General Andrew Lelling announced the results of a national investigation internally nicknamed "Operation Varsity Blues." This criminal conspiracy entailed at least thirty-three parents paying a total of more than $25 million to William Rick Singer to bribe college admissions officials and provide fraudulent standardized testing scores. Many elite universities, including Stanford, Georgetown, and Yale, were implicated in this scandal. Although Harvard was not centrally involved in Operation Varsity Blues, it faced its own admissions scandal. That July, Harvard dismissed its fencing coach, Peter Brand, for a conflict of interest violation, in which his house was sold for nearly twice its estimated value to a parent of two fencers, one a Harvard undergraduate and the other an applicant to the College.[81]

Given the combined, intertwined pressures of admissions and athletics, it is almost a miracle that Harvard had not (yet) had a Varsity Blues-like scandal. For this, the university is indebted to the decades-long, principled partnership between Harvard's former athletic director, Robert Scalise, and its dean for admissions, William Fitzsimmons. Such people are rare in any institution. (Even the fencing scandal was avoidable. At Harvard, athletics, like admissions, reports to the dean of the Faculty of Arts and Sciences. When I was dean, I wanted to invest in new athletic facilities and make an older facility, the Malkin Athletic Center [MAC], into a student center. Among the complicated issues was the future of the fencing team, whose practices took a great deal of space in the MAC. Their relocation was not easy. I wondered openly if we actually needed a fencing team, but I learned quickly the risks of challenging college athletics, not the least in a sport where the students carry weapons.)

Athletics matter at Harvard far more than is widely known outside the university. Harvard has forty-two Division I intercollegiate National Collegiate Athletic Association (NCAA) sports, more than any college in the country, and so it has more varsity athletes than any college in the country. Harvard's athletes are *recruited* athletes. "Walk-ons" are a mythological species. Harvard's obsession with athletics began, as elsewhere in the United States, in the second half of the nineteenth century. Through the first quarter of the twentieth century, Harvard was a major player in big-time intercollegiate sports. Harvard football won nine national championships between 1890 and 1920, the last one capped off by crushing Oregon, 7–6, in the Rose Bowl. Harvard Stadium, built in 1903 as the first major reinforced concrete structure in the United States, is America's oldest stadium. Its physical layout, with stands coming right to the field, helped to determine the field size and rules of modern American football.

In more recent history, academics has taken precedence over athletics at Harvard, but sports still matter. The Ivy League, after all, is, in formal terms, simply an athletic conference. The number of championships that Harvard has held may have declined (save in squash and lightweight crew programs), but the number of sports, coaches, and recruited athletes is at an all-time high. In 2019 about twelve hundred undergraduates, nearly 20 percent of the student body, were intercollegiate athletes.[82] Their path to admission is easier: according to Harvard's Office of Institutional Research, athletes with high academic scores had an acceptance rate of 83 percent compared to 16 percent for non-athletes.[83] And while Ivy League schools officially give no "athletic scholarships," Harvard offers need-based scholarships to athletes that are ironclad: they remain intact even when an athlete is off the team.

Beyond athletes, of course, legacies—the offspring of alumni—also make up a significant proportion of the Harvard undergraduate population. The Harvard of 2020 may not be "your father's Harvard," but the class of 2022 was still 36.8 percent legacy students, about the same percentage as at Georgetown University.[84] Legacy admissions is another distinguishing feature of many elite American universities, with a much longer history of preferences than that of athletics. A 2013 analysis commissioned by the Office of Institutional Research demonstrated that legacy status granted applicants a forty-percentage-point advantage of being accepted over non-legacy applicants.[85] That is, children of alumni were six times more likely to be admitted than others.[86] Broadly speaking, admitted legacy students, like recruited athletes to Harvard, are academically competitive. But other great research universities, such as MIT, the California Institute of Technology, and Johns Hopkins, have shown that they can grow to greatness without any such preferences.

Diversity

Not only was Harvard College increasingly selective, it was also becoming more diverse in ethnicity and socioeconomic status in the twenty-first century. For example, in 2013 Harvard launched the "Harvard College Connection," an admissions outreach program that sought to encourage low-income students to apply to Harvard and other elite schools while also increasing their understanding of opportunities for financial aid.[87] Over one-quarter of the class of 2023 identified as African American, Latinx, or Native American, with an additional 25.6 percent of the class identifying as Asian American.[88] Among all Harvard College students in 2019, 20 percent paid no tuition at all, under Harvard's financial aid policy that required no tuition contribution from families with a total income of less than $65,000.[89] For families with incomes above $65,000, expected contributions were calculated on a generous sliding scale—90 percent of students at Harvard would pay an equal amount or more for tuition at a state school.[90] In the 2017–2018 academic year, 16 percent of Harvard undergraduate students were Pell Grant recipients, compared with 16 percent at Yale, 19 percent at Princeton, and 16 percent at Stanford.[91] This was a sharp increase even from 2008, when only 6.5 percent of Harvard undergraduates received Pell Grants.[92]

Maintaining diversity was a highly political exercise. A 2014 lawsuit alleged that Harvard discriminated against Asian Americans by favoring Black and Latinx applicants. Two lower courts ruled in Harvard's favor. As of November 2021 the Supreme Court had yet to determine if it would hear the case.

Curriculum

Students who put enormous effort into gaining admission to elite universities such as Harvard are, by and large, remarkably incurious about what it is they will learn once they get there. Perhaps that is because the curriculum keeps changing. In its modern history, Harvard College has often been at the cutting edge of undergraduate curriculum development, from Eliot's libertarian approach, to Lowell's more constrained program, to Conant's General Education of the 1940s, and the "Core Curriculum" inaugurated by Dean Henry Rosovsky in the 1970s. Each of these reforms made their mark in their day, and each became stale in time. They and their twenty-first century successors had several things in common, however. First was a grounding in some commonality in the undergraduate educational experience, but not a fully required curriculum, as in the "Great Books" approach of Columbia and Chicago. Second—this was and remains a distinguishing feature of Harvard—the teaching of "GenEd" or "Core" classes was not a burden to be assigned to the newest assistant professor but a privilege given to Harvard's leading faculty, who had to apply or be invited to teach in the program. This has been in the educational DNA of the place for at least a century, and it is one reason undergraduate education is still taken so seriously by the faculty.

I was stunned when, as dean, I began a review of undergraduate education and sought the participation of faculty colleagues. Of the one hundred colleagues I approached to assist with our review, only one turned me down. Those one hundred or so did not, of course, always agree with each other, but they were deeply committed to meeting the challenge of making a Harvard College education equal to that of the best small colleges in teaching and inspiration, while surpassing them by virtue of being at the heart of a great research university. These aspirations, articulated in multiple reports and faculty essays, had resonance well beyond Harvard. I recall the visit of the president of a major Chinese university. He wanted to study our soon-to-be-revamped Core Curriculum. When I told him we were getting rid of it, he changed his mind. Our subsequent reports on curricular reform were read at least as carefully in Beijing as they were in Boston.

Harvard's General Education program in 2020 is a product of accumulated history. It draws on the influence of Conant and the Redbook and his conviction that general education should address "that part of a student's whole education which looks first of all to his life as a responsible human being and citizen."[93] It agrees with Lowell's belief that the well-educated student should know "a little of everything and something well."[94] And it tips its hat to Eliot, who emphasized the power and importance of curricular choice in students' personal and professional development.

Curricular reviews certainly have their challenges. Bok once compared it to "moving a graveyard." And certainly there is no perfect curriculum for any given place or time. By far the most important thing, in my view—and here Harvard has succeeded in each iteration of undergraduate education—is to ensure that the current generation of faculty creates and owns the foundations of an undergraduate education. Great courses taught by imaginative teachers to welcoming undergraduates—these are much more important than any sets of rules, procedures, and categories. When in 2007 the FAS finally voted on the first iteration of curricular reform, it had debated long and hard (including with President Summers, who sought to shape it) for three years. When it finally passed with near unanimity, I was reminded of a major meeting in Chinese Communist Party history, which the minutes summarized: "The resolution passed unanimously, even though many Comrades were opposed." That has always been my best hope for a faculty meeting.

Governance, Challenged

As the oldest university in the United States, Harvard had once set standards for university governance. It would ensure institutional autonomy by placing authority in independent boards. The Harvard Corporation and Board of Overseers performed that function since 1650. But as other American universities developed more sophisticated, responsive, and professional boards in the nineteenth and twentieth centuries, Harvard's remained untouched. The small Corporation, to which almost all power accrued, was self-contained and self-nominating. The Overseers became elegant wallpaper. This structure could work well enough as long as extraordinary people led the Corporation, such as the longtime Senior Fellow of the Corporation, Robert Stone, in the last quarter of the twentieth century. But for difficult times, as in the early 2000s, the seven-member Corporation was too remote, too uninformed, and simply too small to comprehend the challenges of governing a now massive and divided university. No major university or college in the country was governed by such a small body.

Shaken by the faculty revolt against Summers and then by the financial crisis of 2008, a besieged Corporation created a Governance Review Committee to undertake a review of its practices and responsibilities. The committee proposed and enacted a series of changes that pointed toward an increased emphasis on strategic planning and stronger coordination between the Corporation and the Board of Overseers. Most immediately, the seven-person Corporation was nearly doubled in size to include twelve members plus the president. Subcommittees, of a kind to be found in every other university's board of trustees, were established to focus on specific areas such as finance and facilities, to enable the body to more effectively evaluate projects. This was a welcome change.

The reorganized Corporation was to work even more closely with the second governing body, the Board of Overseers. The Board of Overseers comprised thirty members, elected by all Harvard degree holders for staggered, six-year terms, plus the president and treasurer of Harvard as ex officio members. In practice, the Corporation still ran the show, and the Overseers saw over the university from a considerable distance.

Both boards are managed by an Office of the Governing Boards, good people whose mission in life is to maintain the stability and secrecy of the work of the Governing Boards. My best analogy for the Office of the Governing Boards is that of the Japanese Imperial Household. Things *can* change, but change must come in imperceptible increments.

So, in formal governance terms, Harvard is an extraordinarily conservative institution, with a small governing center. Unlike most American universities, there is no university-wide body of faculty (e.g., academic senate) that can address university-wide issues. When the university has moved forward in recent decades, it has more often than not been at the impetus of its schools, all of which, in principle, report to the president and provost, but all of which have been, in fact, famously autonomous.

I have described earlier a history of Harvard as one of presidential reigns. And those do matter. But from the 1930s on, the role of Harvard's deans has been equally if not more important. Paul Buck, FAS dean under Conant, was the real author of the Redbook. McGeorge Bundy, Franklin Ford, and, especially, Henry Rosovsky left indelible marks on the Faculty of Arts and Sciences.

Take the case of Harvard Business School, one of the university's newer professional schools. HBS was founded amid a financial crisis in 1908 and able to celebrate its centenary in 2008 just in time for another. It has had many strong deans, but none more independent and more creatively idiosyncratic than its seventh, John McArthur, who served from 1979 to 1995. His leadership vaulted HBS to the top rank among management schools; he expanded its endowment sixfold; and he had an outsized influence on health care in the broader Boston metropolitan area. He also kept HBS healthily separate from the rest of the university: building its own gymnasium and even its own chapel! (For the latter act, he was summoned to report to the Corporation, one of only two occasions when he was asked to meet with his putative bosses.) His successors Kim Clark and Jay Light would make HBS the most international of Harvard's faculties. HBS's dean from 2010 to 2020, Nitin Nohria, was a leader in McArthur's mold, but he took the school from strength to strength not by isolating HBS across the moat of the Charles River, but by becoming, by some measure, the leading university citizen among all of Harvard's deans.

The story of Harvard's modern success, in short, is found not in the Corporation nor the Office of the Governing Boards, but above all in the deans and schools responsible for all the teaching and research, much of the fundraising, and nearly all the innovation to be found at Harvard.

That success can be measured also by the contributions of what one might call Harvard's *Berufsbeamtentum,* or permanent civil service. Executive and associate deans of FAS, HBS, and other large schools oversaw research, physical facilities, labs, and concert halls. And they kept to budgets. Names such as Laura Fisher and Angela Crispi will be known only to Harvard insiders, but they are the heart and the memory of the institution. The faculty at Harvard are generally excellent. The students are terrific. The professional staff is better still, including—especially—its unionized members.

Funding

Excellence costs money. Lots of money. Despite the financial mismanagement of 2008, Harvard remained rich by any conceivable standard. The total operating revenue for Harvard in the 2020–2021 fiscal year was $5.2 billion.[95]

The largest source of revenue was endowment income, which provided 39 percent of funds for the university overall, although this proportion ranged across the twelve schools and institutes from 80 percent and 72 percent at the Radcliffe Institute for Advanced Study and the Divinity School, respectively, to just 23 percent and 20 percent at the Business School and the T.H. Chan School of Public Health, respectively.[96] Other sources of operating revenue for the university included income from tuition and student fees (17 percent), sponsored support (18 percent), and gifts for current use (10 percent), with the remaining 16 percent from other sources. The largest category of Harvard's $5 billion reported operating expenses was salaries, wages, and employee benefits, which accounted for $2.7 billion, or approximately 54 percent of all expenses.[97] Although Harvard's financial reports were reported at a university-wide level, financial decisions were made by each school autonomously.

The value of Harvard's endowment in 2021 ($53.2 billion) was greater than the nominal GDP of one hundred countries. From 1974 to 2021 the endowment had garnered annualized returns of more than 11 percent.[98] The endowment was not a single entity, however, but rather a large collection of gifts accumulated over nearly four hundred years, often tied to specific or limited uses, many of which are constraining. And all the money in the world could not make a department strong.

Let me give you an example. The Department of Celtic Languages and Literatures is the best department of Celtic Studies in the United States. Indeed, it is the *only* such department in the United States. It exists today (and it is an excellent department) because its three senior professorships are all fully endowed chairs. But there is an existential scramble on the part of the department any time one of its senior chairs is open—so few are the potential candidates. As dean, I explored whether Celtic might not find more applicants were it part of our English Department. This was another fencing lesson, for I learned quickly enough why the Irish and the English need to be in different buildings.

Harvard and the World

Harvard has always been an insular institution. Its first students came from somewhere else, and they did not want to go back. Even as international studies grew in strength and reputation in the twentieth century, the undergraduate experience was local, not global. Sustained by the mentality of "what place could possibly offer more than here?" for many years an extremely low proportion of Harvard undergraduate students studied abroad—for example, just 170 in the fall semester of 2000.[99] One can hardly blame those students who stayed home, for in order to study abroad, first they had to find the study abroad office, which was located in a windowless basement of the Office of Career Services. They then had to petition to withdraw both from their undergraduate House and from Harvard College. Then they had to write an essay to explain why studying abroad was not something you could do in Cambridge. If students had not graduated by the time these protracted steps were taken, they were likely to be given permission, although not promised academic credit for coursework elsewhere.

Old habits die hard, and Harvard undergraduates still stick close to home during the academic year. One result of the curricular reform of the early 2000s, however, was a broadening of international opportunities through some thirty Harvard Summer Schools abroad, robust global internship programs, and support of international public service and research. In that reform, undertaken when I was dean, we toyed with the idea of requiring an "international experience" of eight weeks or more for all undergraduates. Instead we made an international experience an "expectation," for students, leaving the rest to their sense of duty. About 80 percent have since been dutiful.

For the university as a whole, however, much of the world was terra incognita. In the early twenty-first century, American universities rushed to develop an "international strategy." Not Harvard. I recall that when I served as Duke University's Senior Advisor on China, Duke President Richard Brodhead asked each of his deans to report on the international strategy of a peer institution. The one tasked with talking about Harvard said, "This will be short, because as far as I can see there is none."

That was not entirely true, for there were as many international strategies as there were faculties and schools, just none for Harvard as a whole. Other universities took the lead. New York University set up fourteen Global Academic Centers and two full campuses, one each in Shanghai and Abu Dhabi. Duke established first a joint medical school with the National University of Singapore (NUS) and then a liberal arts campus in Kunshan, China. Both NYU and Duke had robust central offices, global programs, and strategies. Harvard did not create the position of vice provost for international affairs until 2005, and left it underresourced. Only when Yale University President Richard Levin announced in 2010 the establishment of Yale-NUS, a college of the liberal arts and sciences in Singapore, did Harvard convene an International Strategy Working Group to study—and reject—the idea of an international campus.[100]

It is worth noting that Harvard had established schools abroad in the past: the Harvard Medical School of China was in operation from 1911 to 1916; and the Harvard Business School played a role in the establishment of new business schools in Switzerland and France in the 1950s and 1960s. These efforts proved impermanent, but neither school was hurt by trying. Modern Harvard was more risk-averse.

In lieu of a campus, and under some alumni pressure to do something to match its peers (Faust wondered: "Are we missing something?"[101]), Harvard experimented with a new approach, a Harvard Global Institute (HGI), in 2015. This was an effort to focus on extending the research, not the teaching, mission of the university to different corners of the world. The idea was to bring together the decentralized schools and institutes of Harvard toward a single, signature global research program. But it relied entirely on external funding. Its first five years were funded by Wang Jianlin, the founder of the Dalian Wanda Group, a large Chinese real estate company.[102] The one major project funded was to investigate sustainability and climate change in China. HGI still awaits a second gift.

By 2020 Harvard had inadvertently committed to a different kind of international strategy that better fit its feudal structure. Individual schools had established their own presences in various locations—HBS, for example, had established a Global Initiative in 1996, which boasted eight research centers around the world by 2016. This decentralized approach was not without risk. But that risk was as much at home as abroad. Barry Bloom, the intrepid former dean of the Harvard School of Public Health (HSPH), prioritized international engagement. He increased dramatically the number of international students and put the school to work on tackling crises in global health. He successfully applied for a federal grant to have HSPH administer parts of the US President's Emergency Plan for AIDS Relief (PEPFAR), which largely operated in Africa—an effort that would in time make an enormous difference in the control of AIDS on that continent. He was far ahead of the university leadership, however. He recalled later the traumatic experience:

> I got called out of a meeting . . . into the president's office where I thought I was going to get a big hug for bagging the biggest grant in

the history of the university. Instead I got my ass torn out for putting the university at total risk at every level, financial, reputational. It reflected the lack of understanding of the assets of the university to make a difference in the world, and its lack of interest in doing so. I came to believe that Harvard is not a university, it's a brand. And everything that was done in the best interests of the university, in my view during that period, was to protect the brand.[103]

In time, after years of "bottom-up" internationalization initiatives across the schools, Harvard was now present, in one form or another, on at least five continents. By 2020 Harvard had twenty-two distinctive institutional centers and programs across the world. And it would take an increasingly vocal role in support of internationalization in the United States.

This was not the least because of the rapidly growing importance of international talent at Harvard. As of 2019 there were 791 international students at Harvard College, only about 12 percent of the undergraduate population.[104] But there were more than 10,000 international students and scholars from 155 countries across the university. Since the middle of the twentieth century, the university had grown in talent and research reputation in good measure because of its capacity to attract the best in talent irrespective of national background.

The COVID-19 crisis and the anti-immigrant policies of the Trump Administration challenged these connections. When in July 2020 the US government sought to bar international students from entering or remaining in the United States, it was Harvard's president, Larry Bacow, who took the courageous lead in criticizing a "cruel and reckless" policy that would affect Harvard students from 155 countries.[105] Harvard and MIT filed a lawsuit that was supported by over two hundred universities across the United States.[106] A week later, the US government backed down.

At home, then, as much as abroad, Harvard's future depended on deepened internationalization. As Mark Elliott, the university's vice provost of international affairs, stated, "Our future is at stake. American higher education is the undisputed global leader because of our ability to attract hardworking and creative students and scholars from all over the world to our institutions. . . . Without international students in our institutions of higher learning, contributing to academic discourse, furthering the research enterprise, and driving the growth of new businesses and industries, we are collectively much, much less well-off."[107]

The opportunities and risks of international engagement were nowhere clearer than in relations with China. For decades, Harvard had a symbiotic relationship with China. From educating the country's leaders to supporting the modernization of Chinese universities through capacity building and training academics, Harvard's reach and reputation has been great within Chinese higher education. For example, Ji Chaozhu, who served as a bridge between the two countries, was born in China and grew up primarily in the United States. He attended Harvard (and would have graduated in the class of 1952) until the Korean War broke out; he returned home in 1950 and attended Tsinghua University. He served as an interpreter for China's leaders, including Mao Zedong and Deng Xiaoping. He was an indispensable interlocutor during Henry A. Kissinger's 1971 secret visit to Beijing, which laid the foundation for President Richard Nixon to become the first American president to visit mainland China.

Harvard had established the Harvard Medical School of China in 1911 (it failed after a few years) and did not return in an institutional way for nearly a century when in 2010 the Harvard Center Shanghai (HCS) was established. This initiative, led by HBS Dean Jay Light and me as chair of the Harvard China Fund under the Provost's Office, established a platform upon which all parts of the university could further their engagement with China through teaching, research, conferences, and internships.[108] HBS—again the university citizen—was the "anchor tenant" for this and other global initiatives. The opening of HCS in 2010 capped off Harvard's most international decade so far, with the establishment of a record eight international centers, to be followed by ten more in the next decade.[109]

If, as Drew Faust declared at the launch of HCS, we were "in a world of universities without borders," where better to expand than China? By 2020 every school at Harvard had active research and related programs in China and programs at HCS. Well over one hundred faculty members visited annually, and over two hundred listed China as a place of serious research. Over four hundred undergraduates had participated in the Harvard China Summer Internship Program and hundreds more in the Harvard Beijing Academy for advanced Chinese language work. Back home, Harvard was now home to close to one thousand Chinese students and scores of visiting Chinese scholars across the university each year. Bottom-up internationalization at Harvard still fit the entrepreneurial spirit of its schools, but HCS was a hub that accelerated their engagement in the fastest growing sector of higher education in the world.

Beginning with Rudenstine, who in 1998 was the first sitting Harvard president to visit mainland China, every Harvard president since has visited to meet with the country's head of state and speak at its top universities. During a visit in 2002, accompanied by thirteen Harvard faculty, Summers spoke at Tsinghua University and announced a program that would train Chinese civil servants at Harvard's Kennedy School.[110] Faust met with President Xi Jinping and spoke at Tsinghua University on the importance of US and Chinese universities working together to address climate change in March 2015.[111] In the first year of his tenure in March 2019, Larry Bacow met with President Xi and gave a major address at Peking University, where he emphasized that universities were places "where the value of an idea is discussed and debated—not suppressed or silenced."[112]

Increased international engagement, especially in China, could also translate into tension. In January 2020 the FBI knocked on the door of Harvard professor Charles Lieber, the chair of the university's chemistry department, as part of a crackdown on alleged academic espionage, claiming that Lieber received substantial funds from China (in part to set up a lab there) and lied about it.[113]

Lieber's arrest came at a time when a nativist US administration sought to limit foreign ties on the part of universities. In February 2020 the US Education Department opened federal investigations into Harvard and Yale to see if the universities failed to report at least $375 million from countries including China, Russia, and Saudi Arabia.[114] Harvard had endured one "Red Scare" in the McCarthy era of the 1950s. It would now need to defend itself from another.

Harvard Extended and Online

Harvard had extended the reach of its education at home for more than a century through the Harvard Extension School, offering courses in evenings and summers, and enrolling some fourteen thousand students in 2020—more than any other Harvard school. The Extension School was the first at Harvard to venture into online learning, setting a foundation for a larger effort.

Harvard was no first-mover in recognizing the potential of massive, open, online courses, but in 2012 it hitched itself to the bandwagon of MIT, a pioneer in the field, to establish edX, an online platform offering free courses to the general public on a technological platform developed by MIT.[115] Harvard, MIT, and partner institutions used the platform to offer courses to learners around the world under their own "institutionX" brands (for example, HarvardX). As a nonprofit institution, edX offered its courses for free, with an option for students to pay for a course completion certificate.

By 2019 more than ninety institutions around the world had developed over twenty-four hundred courses for the edX platform, with more than seventy million students enrolled. Faculty from 10 Harvard schools developed 140 courses. My own course, "ChinaX," created with my colleague and then-Vice Provost for Advances in Learning, Peter Bol, explores three thousand years of Chinese history, culture, economy, and society in ten mini-courses, and it has had more than a half million participants, including tens of thousands in China.

By 2016 edX was recognized as one of the "Big Three" players in online course offerings but was the only nonprofit among them. Its financial future seemed uncertain. Unlike the Extension School, which collected tuition and paid faculty well for their teaching, HarvardX had no significant income to distribute in its first years. The first faculty who taught in it did so essentially as volunteers. Even for the best citizens in the faculty, this was not a sustainable approach, which is why the Harvard Business School set up its own "HBX" (today, Harvard Business School Online), with a real business model. In online learning as in other realms, there would be no "One Harvard." In 2021 MIT and Harvard sold edX to a private tech startup, 2U, Inc., and for the first time began to outsource their educational offerings. For the Harvard faculty who participated in it, edX proved to be useful basic training when the world of universities went suddenly and completely online with the onset of COVID-19 in 2020.

The Next Big Thing: Harvard and Engineering

By the twenty-first century, Harvard was known for excellence in multiple fields: literary and historical studies, political science and the history of science, economics and ecological science, stem cell research, and human evolution. Its big professional schools of law, business, and medicine seemed without peer. No one could say that about Harvard engineering, however. Yet making a mark in engineering was Harvard's big, multi-billion dollar bet for the twenty-first century. This was a huge bet, not the least because there already existed a world-class engineering institute in Cambridge, Massachusetts, and it was not Harvard.

Engineering and the applied sciences had always struggled to have a defined place within the academic structures at Harvard. Applied scientific disciplines first became a part of Harvard with the founding of the Lawrence Scientific School (LSS) in 1847, upon the receipt of the first (but not last) precedent-shattering donation for engineering at Harvard—$50,000 from prominent Massachusetts industrialist Abbott Lawrence, grandfather of Harvard's twenty-second president, Abbott Lawrence Lowell. Despite well-funded beginnings, LSS "never fulfilled the expectation of its founders," particularly after the establishment of neighboring MIT.[116] President Eliot, himself a former professor at MIT, recognized the inability of LSS to compete with MIT. He made multiple unsuccessful attempts to combine the two.[117] In 1905, after a long courtship, the union was favored by the corporations of both institutions, but the marriage was never consummated.

Instead, LSS was broken up into various programs that were scattered around Harvard in different ways, including a graduate-focused Harvard Engineering School, until 1949, when all levels of engineering and applied sciences education were brought together as the Division of Engineering and Applied Sciences (DEAS) under FAS. Despite a significant endowment, the division struggled in the more pure science-focused Harvard for the next fifty years. It was joined at the hip to FAS, for half of its faculty held joint appointments in the FAS physical science departments. Virginia Postrel, a columnist for *Bloomberg*, noted, "Harvard has never been the Harvard—or even the University of Pennsylvania—of engineering."[118] Harvard's most famous alumni in engineering and applied sciences founded great companies— Edwin Land (Polaroid), Morris Chang (Taiwan Semiconductor), Bill Gates (Microsoft), and Mark Zuckerberg (Facebook)—but they never bothered to complete their degrees.

The previously underappreciated role of DEAS within Harvard, however, began to change rapidly in the early twenty-first century. The demands of the modern job market, as well as competition from MIT and a quickly rising Stanford, made it clear that, in the words of former Harvard College dean and former interim dean of the School of Engineering and Applied Sciences (SEAS) Harry Lewis, "Harvard could not be a great university in the 21st century if it didn't have a great engineering school."[119] In 2007 Harvard announced that DEAS would officially become SEAS, still under the umbrella of FAS and maintaining its strong commitment to a liberal arts education. This, the founding dean of SEAS, Venkatesh "Venky" Narayanamurti, noted, would produce "Renaissance engineers."

Between 2007 and 2016 the profile of SEAS within Harvard continued to grow. The number of undergraduate concentrators, Harvard's term for "majors," in SEAS nearly tripled in just eight years, growing from 291 in 2008 to 887 in 2016.[120] In the 2013–2014 school year, the number of SEAS concentrators surpassed that of Arts and Humanities concentrators for the first time.[121] By 2019 SEAS concentrators made up 20 percent of Harvard College students.[122] In fall 2014, 12 percent of all students at Harvard College were enrolled in what the *Harvard Crimson* called "as much a campus cultural phenomenon as a class": SEAS's Introduction to Computer Science I (CS50).[123] The next year, CS50 lectures were live streamed to Yale, whose undergraduates could enroll in the course as Introduction to Computing and Programming. Students from both schools participated in joint activities like hackathons, and Yale students even came to the Harvard campus to attend professors' office hours.[124] CS50 became (by far) the most popular course among Harvard's online offerings.

For all this effort, in 2020 Harvard's engineering program was still ranked number twenty-five nationally, compared to the number one ranking of that other institution down the Charles River.[125] Harvard's School of Engineering and Applied Sciences was a small school, about the size of Caltech, but Caltech was the only small engineering school to rank among the leaders. For the rest, size mattered.

In 2015 John A. Paulson, the billionaire hedge fund manager and HBS graduate, made his historic gift of $400 million to endow what is now known as the Harvard John A. Paulson School of Engineering and Applied Sciences. In under ten years, SEAS found itself newly named and endowed, with a new dean, Frank Doyle—the first engineer to head engineering at Harvard—new professorships, a skyrocketing number of students, and a new engineering complex under construction in Allston.

Can Harvard Lead?

For nearly four hundred years, Harvard had been at the forefront of higher education in America, spurred on by healthy rivalries with an increasing number of outstanding American universities. Harvard's global standing, however, was a relatively recent development. With concerted efforts by governments around the world to establish "world-class" universities, would Harvard be able to maintain its status as a global leader?

By the third decade of the twenty-first century, challenges seemed everywhere. With its extraordinary and unmatched libraries, Harvard had led in the information technology of the nineteenth and twentieth centuries. No university was remotely close. But the digitization of books and journals leveled the playing field, and Harvard was not (yet) cutting edge in the next age of information technology.

Its domestic rivals—Yale, Princeton, Stanford, and Duke among them— were all much more centralized institutions, capable of thinking of the future as whole universities. Some of them even *planned* for their future in regular and rigorous ways. Harvard, with its strong schools and weak center, lacked either the capacity or the appetite for strategic planning across the university.

The story of the Allston land is a case in point. When it was announced in 2013, in a decisive move by Provost Alan Garber, that the Engineering School would relocate to Allston in substantial measure, the idea was publicly opposed, in oral and written statements, by all the senior associate deans of the school.[126]

I recall a blizzard of prospective plans for the Allston Promised Land in my time as dean and after. They foresaw a cross-river campus integrated by new pathways and bridges—one designed to be expanded like the Ponte Vecchio in Florence, adorned by shops on either side. There were plans for new modes of transport: train tunnels, monorails, and even canals, absent gondolas. In the most radical concept, the landmass of Harvard would be brought together like a modern Pangaea by moving the Charles River.

None of this happened. External planning czars for Allston came and went and came again. By 2018 Harvard finally decided to outsource Allston. It created the Allston Land Company to oversee construction of a thirty-six-acre commercial "enterprise research campus" separate from the academic enterprises of the engineering and science departments.[127] The future could not and would not be planned by Harvard alone, but in a series of prospective private partnerships. Business partnerships now mattered in the world of universities. The *Times Higher Education World University Rankings* saw Harvard drop steadily from number one in 2011 down to number seven in 2020. A central reason for this drop was the ranking's factor of "Industry Income."[128]

Harvard's competition was no longer primarily with Ivy League schools or even with great research centers such as the University of Chicago and Johns Hopkins. It was with MIT, Caltech, Cambridge, and, especially, Stanford. Much of Stanford's success has been attributed to its entrepreneurial culture, leading to an illustrious alumni base including the founders of several Fortune 500 companies such as Google, Nike, and HP. Doug Melton, a University Professor and the former faculty dean of Eliot House, remarked:

> Stanford is far and away Harvard's challenge. If I had to place money on it, I would bet on Stanford. . . . I would say that Stanford has a couple of advantages which are significant. One is, despite what we say here, Stanford feels unbound by tradition. They really don't worry so much. You would never hear people there saying, "I wonder what the alumni would think" or "what the corporation would think." They just don't think like that. Our job is to build the future. We are not honoring the past. The second thing is, and I'm sorry to say this but it's a fact of American life, money matters. There is an enormous amount of wealth that has come out of Stanford itself and for other reasons that is now located on the West Coast.[129]

President Larry Bacow was, by contrast, an optimist: "Allston will be Greater Boston's next epicenter of research, discovery, and innovation. . . . Its work will have a long-lasting impact on the development of our campus—and the broader community—and spark and shape future enterprises that will change the world in ways that none of us could predict."[130] As former chancellor of MIT, Bacow knew how strengthening ties to industry could have strong benefits to a university. Kendall Square, the neighborhood encompassing MIT, was once known as a "dustbowl" with rundown parking lots and old factories.[131] Over the decades, the neighborhood became one of the world's leader centers of biotechnology and attracted an influx of tech companies, including tech giants Google, Facebook, and Microsoft, transforming into a vibrant innovation hub that collaborated with MIT.

Matching the success of Kendall Square (or for that matter Palo Alto) would not be easy. Much time had been lost. The photos below show Kendall Square and Allston in earlier decades, when both were desolate; and Kendall Square and Allston today, when one is a leading global center of innovation and the other is, well, pretty much the same as it was.

In November 2017 there was a "topping-off" ceremony for the last steel beam of the new engineering and science building in Allston to be put into place.[132] The crane rose to place the beam, a moment decades in the making. Then the crane broke. There would be no topping off. The new engineering building was scheduled to open in fall of 2020. However, in spring 2020

Figure 5.5. Kendall Square in 1966. "Transportation Systems Center Construction Site at Kendall Square, Looking East," ca. 1966; Records of the Research and Innovative Technology Administration [Transportation], 1965–2002, Record Group 467; National Archives and Records Administration at Boston.

Figure 5.6. Kendall Square present day. Les Vants Aerial Photos.

Figure 5.7. Allston in 1929. Aero Scenic Airviews Co./Boston Pictoral Archive/Boston Public Library/CC BY-NC-ND.

Figure 5.8. Allston present day. Courtesy of Steve Dunwell.

another delay emerged in the form of the COVID-19 global pandemic. The opening of the building was postponed again to August 2021.[133] Harvard may not have topped off, but with luck it had bottomed out in Allston.

As the oldest university in the United States, Harvard reflects as well as any institution the country of its origin. Born of immigrants, it remade its identity on these shores, while continuing to import the best ideas and people from abroad. It carries a belief, like so many Americans, of the virtues of limited government, and as a result it has the smallest and least intrusive central administration of any major American university and is undistinguished in central planning. Its faculties and schools enjoy what used to be called "states' rights," and they defend their autonomy and (the rich ones) their endowments with tenacity. It is a place, like the contemporary United States, of real income inequality across its schools, even as its students are recruited from every sector of American life. Like the United States, it has enviable resources, and it manages to exhaust almost all of them. It is a place of unmatched academic entrepreneurialism, in the future perhaps matched ever more directly with entrepreneurs from the world of commerce. It has survived a revolution, a civil war, and multiple periods of domestic unrest, and it has shown a remarkable capacity for self-renewal. As the historian of higher education David Labaree has written, "Everyone wants to be Harvard."[134] But can this systemically decentralized Harvard continue to be the "Harvard" of the twenty-first century? It will need to, somehow, if it is to continue to lead the world of universities.

CHAPTER SIX

Public Mission, Private Funding

The University of California, Berkeley

> We stand at a crossroads. At stake is not our existence, per se, but the idea that society as a whole benefits when access to a world-class education is based on merit, not privilege or financial circumstances; that the private sector must not be allowed to become the sole repository of excellence; that research conducted in the public's interest is distinct from inquiry driven by the pursuit of profit; and that the deep commitment to making the world a better place that animates our campus is no accident.
>
> —*Nicholas Dirks, Former Chancellor of the University of California, Berkeley*

CAROL CHRIST, chancellor of the University of California, Berkeley, approached the podium to give the Chancellor's Installation Speech in 2017. Since first arriving on campus in 1970, Christ had watched Berkeley change over the decades and was intimately familiar with the history, culture, and legacy of America's premier public university. The following year would be Berkeley's sesquicentennial, or 150th anniversary. She wondered what the founders of the university envisioned in 1868 and asked what that meant for a twenty-first century university. In her remarks she paraphrased the former Berkeley chancellor and system president, Clark Kerr: "Universities can aim no higher than to be as British as possible in regard to undergraduate education, for universities like Oxford and Cambridge offered the model for residential liberal arts colleges; as German as possible in regard to graduate education and research, for Germany had developed the model of the research university; and as American as possible in regard to the public at large." This, she argued, was "Berkeley's founding synthesis, and one important to keep in mind as we begin our second one hundred and fifty years." She continued her speech by looking ahead, where she saw a more challenging landscape: "We stand, I believe, at a moment of transformation as great as any in Berkeley's history. Given the decline in state support, we must reimagine the financial model for the campus."[1]

Christ's predecessor, Nicholas Dirks, had begun to make headway on Berkeley's structural deficit before his resignation on June 1, 2017. He had announced plans that would reduce a $150 million deficit by $85 million by that summer.[2] Unfortunately, as difficult as were the budgetary issues confronting the university, even greater challenges loomed in Dirks's departing shadow. For many of the factors that had brought Berkeley distinction were now among its most intractable weaknesses.

At its heart, Berkeley was a public university dedicated to offering the citizens of California a world-class education. The 1960 Master Plan for Higher Education in California laid out a division of labor for the state's public institutions that for many years coordinated the efforts of the University of California (UC) and California State University (CSU) campuses, along with many California community colleges. Berkeley's identity as an engine of upward social mobility for the people of California remained deeply ingrained in the ethos of the university's community, long driving and inspiring the work of its members.

However, after a period of rapid growth and demographic shifts, California now looked very different than it had when the Master Plan was written. The state, its citizens, and the Berkeley community struggled to balance the Berkeley ideal of equitable access and the pursuit of excellence in the context of dramatic demographic shifts and ethnic diversity. More important, unlike in the era when the Master Plan was adopted, the state had—like so many US states—massively disinvested in public higher education: forty-four out of fifty US states spent less per student in 2017 than in 2008.[3] Berkeley, the state's flagship institution, received only 13 percent of its budget from the state in 2020, compared to 50 percent in 1990.[4] (From 1919 to 1968 the state had provided 95 percent of Berkeley's budget.[5]) Frequent student protests on campus and pronouncements from the Regents, the UC system's governing board, fought against tuition hikes, limiting the tools at the Berkeley administration's disposal to address diminishing state funding. Beyond funding, remarks by former California Governor Jerry Brown, disparaging Berkeley because "ordinary, normal students" were "getting frozen out," pointed toward a diminished state commitment to Berkeley as an exceptional institution.[6] Brown's successor, Governor Gavin Newsom, indicated early in his tenure that he saw value in UC, initially proposing an increase in funding for 2020–2021. But after the 2020 outbreak of COVID-19, he instead slashed higher education spending by 10 percent.[7] And yet, Berkeley faculty and students largely still operated under an assumption of entitlement to public funding, even in the face of years of evidence of declining support. The public mission that had made Berkeley so exceptional during the good times of state support now constrained its responses to, or even its acknowledgement of, reality during bad times.

The passion and dedication of the faculty to the governance of Berkeley was another long-standing institutional strength. But as growing financial constraints required increasingly tough decisions about resource allocation, Berkeley's model of faculty participation in governance, through highly democratic and equally inefficient mechanisms, often impeded the university's leadership and its capacity to move forward.

The legacy of Berkeley's mission and model remained renowned and a source of envy and emulation at public institutions in other states. Now, however, would the enduring squeeze on Berkeley's budget force its history of greatness to recede into myth? With Berkeley so long the gold standard of public higher education in America, the eyes of state university presidents across the country would be trained on its response to the challenge of what it meant to be a privately funded, public university in the United States.

From Gold Rush to Gold Standard

The stories of both the University of California system and its Berkeley campus begin with the story of the College of California—a small academic outpost in the newly formed state of California. Higher education was so valued by the residents of what became California that discussions explored building a university even before achieving statehood. Initially, private institutions such as the College of California, founded by Yale alumni and incorporated in 1855, served citizens' demands for higher education.

Seven years later, in 1862, the US government passed the Morrill Act, which incentivized state governments to develop public higher education institutions by offering public lands to states that would use them to found (or fund) the establishment of colleges for agriculture and mechanics. A wave of new institutions—the so-called land-grant universities, such as Purdue and Cornell—were established in states across the country under the auspices of this act. Californians were eager to take advantage of the federal program and to build the public university they had long desired. However, recognizing the value of the foundation—both literal and figurative—built by the College of California, it was decided that, on the condition that the new institution would include a college of letters and science in addition to colleges of agriculture and mechanics, the land grant institution could be built on the campus of the College of California. On March 23, 1868, this new science and letters-land grant hybrid was christened the University of California.

Since 1868 UC—then one campus and now eleven—has been led by a president under the direction of a Board of Regents, a leadership structure codified in the California State Constitution, ratified on May 17, 1879. Today, the Board of Regents is composed of twenty-six members, including eighteen members appointed to twelve-year terms by the governor of California, one student representative, and seven ex officio members, including the governor, the lieutenant governor, the speaker of the assembly, the state superintendent of public instruction, the president and vice president of the alumni associations of the University of California, and the president of the university.[8] From its early years, the Board of Regents helped foster UC's inclusive and diverse demeanor, allowing women to attend beginning in 1870 and welcoming international students in the same period as well.

For the first decade of its existence, UC struggled to forge an identity acceptable to both the letters and science-oriented Yale descendants and the Morrill Act-inspired agriculture and mechanics faction.[9] At this key moment, UC was led by one of several particularly consequential presidents: Daniel Coit Gilman. Initially, Gilman was excited by the prospect of building UC. Comparing UC to German and New England models, he remarked, "It is not the University of Berlin nor of New Haven which we are to copy . . . but it is the University of this State. It must be adapted to this people, to their public and private schools, to their peculiar geographical position, to the requirements of their new society and their undeveloped resources."[10] Gilman served as UC president for only three years (1872–1875), during which he was often frustrated by political and financial difficulties and after which he left to become the founding president of Johns Hopkins University, where he established the first graduate university on the Berlin model.[11] Still, during his short tenure, he managed to overcome the disagreements about the nature of UC, and he moved it in the direction of a comprehensive academic institution.

Even as a young institution, UC struggled with its relationship to the state government. When California held its second constitutional convention in 1878, an important item of discussion was university-government relations. Thanks in part to the disenchantment of the convention's delegates with the state legislature and in part to the impassioned defense of institutional autonomy for universities by delegate Joseph Winans, the 1878 California constitution established the university as an autonomous institution that was "entirely independent of all political or sectarian influence, and kept free therefrom in the appointment of its regents and in the administration of its affairs."[12] UC's institutional independence was in principle so complete that it was sometimes referred to as the fourth branch of the California state government.

Asserting institutional autonomy is one thing. Exercising it as a public university that is funded by the state is quite another. UC began to flourish under the presidency of Benjamin Ide Wheeler, who served the university from 1899 to 1919. Wheeler's tenure established the UC president as a strong, central leader, as he gradually convinced the regents to cede decision-making rights on certain issues to the Office of the President (OP). By the end of Wheeler's tenure, the UC president was in charge of faculty hiring decisions as well as budgeting. This amount of power lay in stark contrast to the powers of Wheeler's immediate predecessor, Martin Kellogg, whose major victory in expanding presidential power had been gaining the right to hire, fire, and regulate janitors.[13]

Wheeler studied at several of the top higher education institutions in Germany and received a PhD from the University of Heidelberg. Like so many of his contemporaries, he was heavily influenced and inspired by the German model of a comprehensive research university. It was under Wheeler's tenure that UC began to develop multiple academic disciplines as well as a stronger orientation toward research. When Edwin Slosson observed the university for his 1910 volume, *Great American Universities,* he found that the conflict between the College of California's academic orientation and the Morrill Act's practical orientation had largely been resolved: "I know of no other university which cultivates both mechanics and metaphysics with such equal success, or which looks so far into space, and, at the same time, comes so close to the lives of the people."[14] Slosson also lauded UC for its egalitarian student body, composed of learners from a wide range of economic and ethnic backgrounds.

Wheeler's transformative tenure was not unlike that of Eliot at Harvard. And he was not without critics. Wheeler exercised so much power as president that when he retired, the Academic Senate carried out Berkeley's first faculty revolt, demanding that more power over academic and faculty affairs be placed in the hands of the faculty themselves, through the Academic Senate. This concerted effort during a power vacuum after Wheeler's retirement resulted in the strengthening of the powers of the UC Academic Senate to such an extent that, even in 2016, the Berkeley Division of the Academic Senate was still among the most influential governing bodies of any American university. The legacy of faculty involvement in and responsibility for academic decision-making became a lasting hallmark of the UC system and a central, distinguishing feature of Berkeley's governance.

Master Planning and Insurgent Students

Just as the post-Wheeler faculty revolution was taking place, California's dramatic growth allowed the University of California to grow from its founding campus in Berkeley to be a multi-campus system spanning the state. With the discovery of oil in the southern part of the state at the turn of the twentieth century, the population, wealth, and influence of Southern California expanded; regents from Southern California pushed to upgrade local institutions to become part of UC. In 1919 the southern branch of UC (later, UCLA) was formally established in Los Angeles, based on the foundation of the Los Angeles Normal School. With the addition of a new campus, the UC governance structure remained largely unchanged. It was still led by the Board of Regents and a president, whose office remained housed on the UC Berkeley campus. The president remained the administrator in control of both institutions.

Throughout the early twentieth century, Berkeley continued to grow, even as California's educational resources were distributed across a broader and broader range of state higher education institutions. The student population of UC grew from 2,600 in 1899 to over 12,000 in 1919.[15] With 14,061 students in 1923, the University of California (all campuses) was the largest university in the United States and the world.[16] This rapid expansion in institutional size did not dilute the quality of Berkeley as an institution; rather, its reputation rose as it grew in size. From the first appearance of national ratings and rankings of US universities in 1906 to the global university rankings of 2019, Berkeley was consistently near the top of the league tables.

Clark Kerr

By the end of the Second World War, Berkeley and its sister UC campuses were well established and well regarded. Still, the extraordinary postwar boom—both in the population of the state of California and in the number of students seeking admission to UC institutions—made it clear that California needed a higher education system that was larger still and better organized. Fortunately for California, UC had just the man for such a monumental logistical and intellectual challenge. Clark Kerr had received his doctorate from and spent much of his subsequent career at Berkeley. In 1952 when the Board of Regents recognized that it was increasingly untenable for all UC campuses to be managed by a single central administrator, they established chancellorships at Berkeley and UCLA to share in the administrative burden. Kerr became the inaugural chancellor at Berkeley. His key duties began with defining his newly created role in the context of a UC president who was reluctant to relinquish control. Kerr slowly re-centered administration and decision-making at the campus, rather than the UC, level. Kerr's experience as chancellor confirmed his understanding of the need for administrative flexibility and authority at local campuses, and it informed his subsequent role as president of UC from 1958 to 1967. He moved to make the campuses more independent against the influence of the center and the professoriat more independent from the campus administration by initiating UC's first "continuous tenure" system, which was adopted by the Regents in December 1958.[17] He later noted that the gradual decentralization of power to each of the campuses was one of the great successes of the system, because it allowed campuses to compete with one another and thus all achieve a higher standard, rather than elevating one or two campuses to an elite status and leaving the rest to founder. That said, Berkeley—later joined by UCLA—was the flagship of the system, and, as Nicolas Dirks would discover, Kerr's successors as system presidents would at times try to reverse the decentralization of authority.

Of Kerr's many contributions to Berkeley and higher education in California, the best known was his leading role in the development of the 1960 Master Plan for Higher Education in California. Under the Master Plan, any qualified student, defined as any student who graduated from a California high school, would have access to three tiers of higher education. The top one-eighth of high school graduates would be admitted to a UC campus, while the top one-third would be guaranteed admission into the California State College (today, State University, or CSU) system, and the remaining graduates would have places in community colleges. The UC and CSU universities would reserve a significant number of spots in their junior classes for transfer students from the community colleges. By contrast, when Harvard admitted one transfer student from a community college in 2019, it was national news.[18] The state government and the administrators of the relevant institutions united behind this plan, which for many years served the state of California as a powerful engine for social mobility even as the state itself went through significant demographic shifts, with an increasing proportion of the state's growing population made up of minorities (particularly Asian and Latinx), and widening income inequality.[19] It is not an overstatement to say that, under Kerr, California developed the leading system of public higher education in the world.

Lernfreiheit, *California Style*

In the latter half of the twentieth century, more than any other university in the United States, Berkeley became synonymous with political activism and unrest. While Berkeley's best-known political struggle was the student-led Free Speech Movement, which began in 1964, political unrest stirred the campus as early as 1949, when the anti-communist sentiment that had been building on university campuses and in government halls across the country led UC President Robert Sproul and the Board of Regents to require faculty to sign a loyalty oath. Faculty response to this requirement was swift and contentious, and it became, in Kerr's words, "the greatest single confrontation between a university faculty and its board of trustees in American history."[20] Of the sixty-nine politically motivated faculty dismissals at US universities during the McCarthy era, thirty-one occurred at UC.[21] The conflict inaugurated an extended period of tense relations and mistrust between the university faculty and administration.

This storm was followed by the Free Speech Movement of 1964 and after, in which students won rights of free expression that were guaranteed in the United States Constitution but, until then, not permitted at Berkeley or on most American college campuses. This inaugurated years of intense campus politicization, which—as in Berlin, Boston, and Beijing—pitted students against university and state administration. Perhaps because Berkeley was so clearly in the forefront of the American student movement, the counter-revolution came sooner there. In 1966 the actor Ronald Reagan ran for governor of California on a platform of quelling the "student revolt at Berkeley."[22] His election brought to power a state government at odds with Kerr's leadership. In 1967 Kerr was fired from the UC presidency. Kerr was a man known for his wit and frankness. (He once famously quipped, "I find that the three major administrative problems on a campus are sex for the students, athletics for the alumni, and parking for the faculty.")[23] When he left office, he recalled, "The fact was that I had left the presidency of the university as I had entered it: 'fired with enthusiasm'; my own on the way in, that of certain others on my way out."[24]

Kerr was ousted, but Berkeley, and the higher education system of California that Kerr did so much to advance, continued to follow the trajectory of growth that he had established in the Master Plan. Growth continued even through increasingly uneven levels of financial and political support from California's governors and despite the growing number of UC campuses that further divided the pie of state funding and reduced Berkeley's special place in the UC system. Through it all, Berkeley remained an elite university. The biggest logistical, financial, and existential challenge, however, was yet to come.

Struggles for Survival

By 2008 Berkeley had been through many financial ups and downs, but—as at Harvard, but more enduringly—none of these experiences compared to the 2008 financial crisis. The implosion of US financial markets not only wreaked havoc on Berkeley's endowment, which dropped over 20 percent from $2.9 billion in 2007 to $2.3 billion in 2009, and pension investments, but also had an even greater, deleterious impact on the state of California's budget.[25] Given recent trends in California legislation that had seen increased amounts of dedicated funding for earmarked purposes, the UC budget was one of the few areas in which government funds were not precommitted. Facing a state budget crisis, the legislature passed brutal cuts on to the universities; in 2008 the UC system had to decrease its budget by 20 percent.[26]

Although universities across the country confronted significantly reduced endowments and investment returns, few faced as severe a burden of funding loss as the UC campuses, which were hit both by the crash of their own investments and by the sudden elimination of much state funding. Berkeley found itself doing everything from cutting library hours and implementing faculty and staff furloughs to reducing new faculty positions by 90 percent to align expenses with a greatly diminished budget.[27] University departments around the country began to circle the Berkeley faculty, believing the time had finally come to poach academic stars from the institution.

Robert Birgeneau, Berkeley's chancellor from 2004 to 2013, did remarkably well in an impossible situation. He had to decide how to manage a world-class institution facing crises on almost every front. Former Executive Vice Chancellor and Provost George Breslauer recalled Birgeneau's fortitude: "He said he's never played defense in his life, and he didn't intend to come here and play defense. He told us, 'Go for it. We've got to come out of this with glory.'"[28]

Birgeneau and Breslauer approached their decimated budget strategically. Berkeley had never been as strong in financial management as, for example, Duke, because in the past it had not needed to. Even before the onset of the crisis, Birgeneau had taken groundbreaking steps toward the professionalization of financial management on the campus by hiring Nathan Brostrom, former J. P. Morgan Managing Director, as vice chancellor for administration in 2006.

Birgeneau also strengthened the financial holdings of the center of the university by directing funds received to endow a chair partially back to the center: 50 percent of the yield from chair endowments would return to the university budget in support of the chair faculty member's salary. This was a big symbolic step for Berkeley, where chairs had long been deemed the responsibility of the state to fund. While at other universities, such as Harvard, the income from an endowed chair would be returned entirely to the school administration, named chairs at Berkeley historically supported only the research, not the salary, of a professor.

Even the best financial management could not print money. Prior to the crisis, Breslauer had been responsible for allocating the Provost's office budget of about $45 million. Of this total budget, around $5 million served as a discretionary fund, which he used to support various projects across the university, such as new faculty positions. He recalled, "After the financial collapse of 2008, the fun was over." Determined to approach his budgeting strategically, Breslauer refrained from making uniform cuts across the campus. Rather, he evaluated all the units reporting to him using an extensive set of criteria, then stratified them into four tiers and made different kinds of cuts to each tier. Breslauer completed most of this process himself: "The crash was so severe and the cut from the state was so severe that . . . time just didn't seem to be on our side, and one thing I know about committees is that they take forever." Still, he focused on transparency and consultation, in the hope that, while painful, the cuts he proposed would have "credibility and legitimacy."[29]

By most accounts, Birgeneau's crisis management strategy, including professionalization of finance, strategic allocation of resources, and belated but concerted fundraising efforts through a capital campaign and pursuit of major grants and competitions, succeeded initially. At the worst point of the crisis, Berkeley lost fourteen faculty members in one year but quickly returned to its traditionally strong faculty retention rate and gradually found itself on steadier footing.[30]

It was with a spirit of optimism, then, that Birgeneau's successor, Nicholas Dirks, came to Berkeley in 2013. His was a distinguished record of scholarship and academic leadership; he had served as executive vice president for the arts and sciences and dean of the faculty at Columbia University. When he began his chancellorship, still in the aftermath of the global financial crisis of 2008, Berkeley was beginning to find firm enough footing to dedicate serious time and energy to thinking about its strategy for the future. The financial picture remained challenging, but Berkeley had endured. Dirks recalled, "There was a sense that the place had survived and now everybody could get back to work."[31]

Given freedom to set an agenda, Dirks focused on three strategic priorities: the undergraduate experience, interdisciplinary initiatives, and global partnerships. A team of administrators reviewed ways to enhance undergraduate life, not just in the classroom but also through stronger residential programs and campus activities. Interdisciplinary initiatives such as a data science initiative and the Social Science Matrix—an institute for cross-disciplinary social science research—promoted cooperation across departments and worked against departmental isolation. Global partnerships, as

exemplified by a new Global Campus, would strengthen Berkeley's cooperation with institutions around the world. Yet, by his third year in office,
Dirks found himself caught in an increasingly small space between an un-
supportive governor, an active UC system president, and an engaged (and
sometimes enraged) faculty.

The Crisis of Berkeley's "New Normal"

Springtime was historically a time of protest on the Berkeley campus. The
spring of 2016 would prove no exception. True, the university had survived
the 2008 crisis and, with Dirks's appointment, appeared reinvigorated and
ready to innovate. Berkeley was still home to 170 academic departments and
programs housed in fourteen colleges and schools, attended by 27,000 undergraduate and 10,000 graduate students, led by 1,620 full-time faculty. But
its state funding was now at just 57 percent of its 2007 level. Dirks launched
a strategic planning initiative in February 2016 to finally confront what had
become a permanent structural deficit. Dirks noted that "some of the changes
we will undergo will be painful," but he concluded that these changes would
in no way be "an abandonment of our commitment to a public mission."
Rather, a transformed Berkeley would, he believed, embody "a fundamental
defense of the concept of the public university, a concept that we must reinvent in order to preserve."[32]

But the optimistic tone of Dirks's announcement was at odds with an un-
pleasant reality: Berkeley was indeed playing defense. Moreover, the structural deficit Berkeley faced was not simply the result of the diminution of
state spending. The deficit now approached $150 million as a result of the
university's huge capital expenditures outside the academic realm. These included the rebuilding of California Memorial Stadium, home to Berkeley's
football games. The complex relationship between athletics, fundraising, and
funding was divisive on many American university campuses, and Berkeley
was no exception.

California Memorial Stadium, built in 1922, is a wonderful, neoclassical
structure. Unlike Harvard, Berkeley in the twenty-first century was still determined to play ball with the big guys and was a member of the PAC-12,
one of the premier conferences in intercollegiate sports ("athletics for the
alumni," as Clark Kerr said). The problem was that the stadium sat directly
on top of the Hayward Fault, which made it susceptible to devastating earth-
quakes. The initial cost of retrofitting the stadium to make it safe was put at

$14 million. The budgeted cost in 2010 was $445 million, to be paid for in debt, initially to be financed by the selling of special seats—so good would "Cal football" be in a new stadium. But Cal football, despite producing great quarterbacks like Aaron Rodgers and Jared Goff, was never *that* good. The team was 1–11 in 2013, and it has lost as many games as it has won since the stadium's rebuilding. The seats didn't sell, and in 2012 the *Wall Street Journal* estimated that Berkeley's total financial obligation for the stadium would likely exceed $1 billion.[33] It was estimated that Berkeley would not even begin to pay off the principal on the loans associated with the stadium until 2032.[34] Fundraising and spending related to athletics were continued irritants between the faculty, which largely opposed them, and the administration.

But the stadium was now a sunk cost, and no state funds supported it. So strategic planning at Berkeley would have to include significant strategic cutting elsewhere. There was no other way. Dirks established Berkeley's first Office of Strategic Initiatives (OSI) to lead and coordinate this painful process.

Despite the efforts that began in Birgeneau's time, serious, cross-campus, strategic planning had never been Berkeley's practice or culture. Now it was an emergency measure. The process proved to be painful indeed, and

Figure 6.1. California Memorial Stadium. Kilfmuny/Wikimedia Commons/ CC BY-SA 4.0.

it reawakened faculty activists in the Academic Senate who continued to believe in the mission of Berkeley as a publicly funded institution (and the Senate's central role in guiding it) even in an era in which the state had effectively abdicated its role as funder. Never mind that the Academic Senate itself, with its long history of academic activism, was an enormous body which included every rank of faculty from instructors to professors emeriti (even retired colleagues could vote) and was in no position to undertake serious planning.

At the same time, another tempest arose. The overdue explosion against widespread sexual harassment that roiled tens of American campuses in 2015–2016 also led to strenuous conflict at Berkeley. The campus became embroiled in numerous harassment allegations, including several against prominent administrators and professors. In one case, when chemist Graham Fleming resigned from his position as vice chancellor for research after allegations of harassment were made by his assistant in April 2015, over one hundred faculty members signed a letter in support of Fleming and in critique of the investigatory process led by OP.[35] Fleming was subsequently appointed to a less conspicuous administrative role overseeing the development of global alliances for the Berkeley Global Campus. In March 2016, however, in an extraordinary step, UC President Janet Napolitano publicly overruled the chancellor and all but ordered Dirks to fire Fleming—who still enjoyed the support of his faculty colleagues—from his remaining administrative posts.[36]

Meanwhile, as Berkeley's administration began to move forward with the strategic planning process, faculty and staff anger grew over the perceived top-down nature of Dirks's initiatives. He had promised that his administration would avoid the lack of staff consultation that had led to faculty criticism of Birgeneau's crisis planning.[37] But "consultation" with the Academic Senate leadership, which advised the chancellor to keep discussion to small groups, would prove the death of Dirks's planning.

Suddenly other attacks against Dirks began. The construction of a $700,000 fence around the chancellor's residence on the Berkeley campus had begun in response to serious security concerns. Yet it drew widespread criticism, including a letter from the Academic Senate, for not being in keeping with Berkeley's open culture. But the house, sitting right at the edge of the campus, and thus an easy target for assault from inside or outside the university, was otherwise defenseless. Even this fence was more symbolic than secure; it would not keep out anyone who was determined to get in. The house had been subject to repeated, sometimes violent, demonstrations under Dirks's predecessors. During the tenure of former Chancellor Chang-

Figure 6.2. $700,000 fence around the chancellor's residence. Photograph © William C. Kirby.

Lin Tien, an armed woman forced her way into the residence and was shot and killed by police.[38] Still, Dirks, whose office in California Hall was at the center of the campus and a ten-minute walk from the residence, was pilloried for "fencing himself off" from Berkeley.

At the central level, Dirks's administrative team began to crumble in the face of public faculty attacks. In April 2016 Executive Vice Chancellor and Provost Claude Steele—the only senior executive whom Dirks had recruited from the outside—was criticized for his handling of another sexual harassment case. He announced his immediate resignation, followed days later by the announcement that Vice Provost of Strategic Academic and Facilities Planning Andrew Szeri would resign at the end of June 2016.[39]

Facing a furiously energized faculty with an increasingly thin administrative team reduced by resignations, retirements, and reshuffling, Dirks took to the podium at the spring meeting of the Academic Senate. "This has been a very deeply challenging year here at Berkeley," he began. "And I want to acknowledge that. I also want to assure you all, as members, as colleagues in the Academic Senate, that I've been hearing your concerns and I've been hearing your advice. . . . I appreciate the urgency with which you have offered both, and I am today resetting our strategic efforts in several fundamental dimensions."[40]

Dirks went on to announce a series of measures that diminished central power and strengthened faculty leadership, including the dissolution of his newly established Office of Strategic Initiatives, curtailment of the centralized Campus Shared Services program (a widely acknowledged failure begun under Birgeneau's administration), and an increased role for the Academic Senate in academic and financial planning.[41] He also announced plans for his office to be more directly involved with the handling of sexual harassment case findings.

Still, none of this academic politicking did anything to solve Berkeley's enduring financial and organizational challenges, nor did it save Dirks from being the convenient target of resentment in the community. Berkeley was broke. Dirks was willing to admit it. His unusual openness to discussing Berkeley's deficit and his willingness to put anything on the table had made him a lightning rod for discontent in an era of high faculty anxiety and insecurity. Dirks finally had had enough. On August 16, 2016, Chancellor Dirks notified UC President Napolitano that he intended to resign. In doing so, this Berkeley outsider honored one of Berkeley's oldest traditions: Daniel Gilman, the second UC president and one of Berkeley's most influential early leaders, also ended his term after just three years, "beset by financial difficulties and political harassment."[42] Dirks's two immediate predecessors, both, like him, recruited from the outside, had left office after some measure of faculty discontent as well.

Governing Chaos and Disinvestment

Berkeley's ongoing Kulturkampf—not unlike that of the contemporary Humboldt University with its revolving-door presidencies—was rooted in part in its higher participatory governance structure. On the Berkeley campus itself, governance was shared between the senior administration, led by the chancellor, and Berkeley's uniquely strong Academic Senate. One faculty member noted, "The Academic Senate's role in everyday affairs is rather supreme . . . [it] has really total control of the curriculum and ninety-five percent control over all hiring, promotions, and advancements."[43] Formally a division of the UC Academic Senate, the Berkeley Academic Senate took its role "more seriously than [comparable institutions] anywhere else in the country."[44] Although the full Academic Senate was normally convened only a few times per year, forty Senate committees were organized by eight elected faculty members on (what else?) the Committee on Committees.

Of course, Berkeley was a campus within a larger university system, and thus the campus-level administrative structures made up only one of two tiers of governance, the other being the UC system-wide governance. The UC system had its Board of Regents, but unlike Harvard and Duke, the flagship Berkeley campus had no governing board of its own, limiting the chancellor's sources of advice and support. The president of the UC system was supposed to serve as the advocate for all the campuses vis-à-vis the state government. OP, therefore, was responsible for both negotiating with the state for funding and disbursing the funding to the ten campuses. The president also retained control over senior administrator compensation. If Dirks needed to recruit a new member for his administration, he first had to negotiate the compensation offer with UC President Napolitano. Other important issues that fell under the mandate of OP included setting tuition and the ratio of in-state to out-of-state students. The state could therefore dictate the intake of students and limit Berkeley's capacity to charge them. Dirks noted, "You have to get approval from OP for many, many things that would seem to be within the discretion of any president of a private university."[45]

The work and success of the president of the UC system—and, by extension, of Berkeley—were influenced also by the priorities of the governor of California. Breslauer recognized support from governors as one of the five main factors that historically had allowed Berkeley to achieve institutional eminence. He further argued that throughout the history of the state, with the famous exception of Reagan, governors chose to support Berkeley in difficult times because of the persuasive leadership of the UC president.[46] After continued and nearly disastrous state disinvestment in the university, some hoped that the 2013 appointment of Napolitano, a former governor of Arizona, might help UC to have a stronger relationship with the governor. Napolitano and then-governor Jerry Brown began to work together closely, in what was referred to as "CO2," short for Committee of Two. One former administrator hoped that Napolitano could "stand up to [Governor Jerry Brown] and speak to him in his own terms and exercise power in a way that an academic in that position [would have trouble doing] unless you had a Clark Kerr."[47] (In August 2020 the former president of Ohio State University, Michael V. Drake, succeeded Napolitano and became the UC's first Black president, giving California another leader with experience managing university-state relations elsewhere.)

Nonetheless, even as the state recovered from the Great Recession and re-filled its treasury, state support for UC showed only the most modest annual increases. Taking inflation and increased enrollment into account, state support had been halved over the past decades. During the 1990–1991 fiscal year, state funding for UC averaged $19,929 per student, or 78 percent of total education expenditures. From 2017–2018, state support was a mere $7,730 per student, or 37 percent of education expenditures.[48]

Gradual state disinvestment throughout the 1990s and early 2000s, followed by a steep drop in state funding in 2008, resulted in a University of California that was public in mission but not in primary funding. The passage of Proposition 30 in 2012, which approved increased personal income taxes to prevent cuts in the state education budget, indicated a potentially renewed interest of the California citizenry in funding education, and by 2013 Berkeley seemed headed toward more stable financial footing.[49]

The Berkeley 2013–2014 budget plan proposed revenues of about $2.35 billion and expenses of around $2.14 billion, with an additional $240 million in account fund balance transfers for debt service and capital investment.[50] The Berkeley administration had limited options to increase revenue—the Regents had committed to freezing student tuition (28 percent of Berkeley's revenue) in exchange for a slight increase in state support, which at that time provided 14 percent of revenue. Federal government contracts and grants, as well as other contracts and grants and nonoperating revenue, represented a further 32 percent of revenue that was not mutable by any action of Berkeley. Altogether, this meant that 73 percent of total revenue was constrained. If Berkeley were to need to cover increased costs—and it could expect regular, incremental increases in operating costs such as health care plan payments, facilities maintenance, and more—these would have to be financed through nongovernmental, nontuition sources of revenue, such as private philanthropy or corporate partnerships. "Time is not on our side," John Wilton, the Vice Chancellor of Administration and Finance, warned: in the absence of a concerted effort to shore up these revenue sources, Berkeley would face an unsustainable operating deficit.[51]

Berkeley began to explore new funding pathways. In a speech at the Times Higher Education World Academic Summit, Dirks expressed his commitment to increasing the engagement of the private sector in partnering with and funding public higher education institutions.[52] Berkeley already had a history of such partnerships, although they were often initially fraught with concern over how to maintain academic freedom in the face of corporate interests. The 2007 announcement of the Energy Biosciences Institute, a joint new energy technology research project between Berkeley, British Petroleum (BP), the University of Illinois at Urbana-Champaign, and Lawrence Berkeley National Laboratory, funded by an initial $500 million commitment from BP, initially drew fierce criticism from the faculty.[53] Similar controversy surrounded a partnership between Novartis and Berkeley's Department of Plant and Microbiology from 1998 to 2003.[54] Private sector partnerships were possible, but they were met routinely with skepticism on the part of vocal faculty members.

A Nondevelopment State

Dirks had inherited an institution with a terrible record of private fundraising. None of the UC campuses, Berkeley in particular, had been prepared to wean themselves from the state as had other leading public universities, such as the University of Wisconsin or the University of Michigan, which in the early 1960s was the first public university to launch a large fundraising campaign. Within California, UCLA regularly outfundraised Berkeley, and both of these institutions fell far behind the University of Wisconsin-Madison, which raised an average of 31 percent more than Berkeley every year from 2008 to 2018.[55] While as a research university Berkeley regularly ranked among the top five universities in the world, it seldom was among the top twenty universities in the United States for fundraising. In reflecting on Berkeley's financial situation, Dirks stated, "I came to a university that was thirteen percent funded by the state. I'm not privatizing. *It has been privatized.*"[56]

The good news was how much room there was for improvement. After all, Berkeley was located in one of the wealthiest urban areas in the world. And while its alumni, like their alma mater, were known for their social consciousness, that had not stopped many of them from becoming enormously rich. A 2019 study ranked Berkeley's alumni base as the twelfth wealthiest of any university based on aggregate wealth of ultra-high net worth alumni, and a 2014 report found that Berkeley undergraduates had produced the eighth most billionaires among undergraduate alumni.[57] Based in the Bay Area, near the heart of Silicon Valley, Berkeley and its alumni were well placed to participate in the lucrative technology industry, and the alumni did so in droves. These statistics drive home that old adage about fundraising: Why do people give? Because they are *asked*. And if, as in Berkeley's case, you haven't asked, you haven't received.

Dirks therefore sought to enhance private giving, especially from alumni. In the 2016 academic year, Dirks led Berkeley to raise almost $480 million from nearly 100,000 gifts made by over 65,000 donors—new Berkeley records both for total amount raised and number of gifts. The new level of fundraising represented significant efforts to engage a wide variety of donors. Initiatives such as the "Big Give"—a 24-hour fundraising blitz timed to coincide with the "Big Game," that is, the annual football match between Berkeley and Stanford—appealed to a broad donor base. At the same time, Berkeley's fundraising operation also targeted larger gifts, recording a record number of gifts of over $1 million from 2015 to 2016.[58]

Dirks's successor, Chancellor Carol Christ, built on this momentum by publicly launching Berkeley's largest capital campaign ever in 2020. Begun quietly under Dirks in 2014, the "Light the Way" campaign's priorities included "expanding faculty and graduate student fellowships; improving the undergraduate experience; supporting multidisciplinary research initiatives aimed at solving the grand challenges of our time; and building better facilities for housing, athletics, and teaching and research."[59] Its launch event included the announcement of an anonymous $252 million gift, the largest in university history, toward the construction of a complex for Berkeley's Computing, Data Science, and Society division.[60] After the conclusion of the 2019–2020 fiscal year, Christ announced that Berkeley had raised $1.04 billion dollars, its most successful fundraising cycle ever.[61] But decades of overreliance on the state and neglect of its potentially philanthropic alumni meant that Berkeley was still playing catch-up. In 2019 Berkeley's combined endowment of private and public funds, worth $4.8 billion, was just a bit more than one-third of the University of Michigan's $12.4 billion endowment.

The Operational Excellence (OE) program was another effort to bridge Berkeley's funding gap. Launched under Birgeneau's chancellorship, the program focused on finding new ways to streamline administrative costs without sacrificing operational quality, with the ultimate goal of saving $75 million in operating costs annually. OE sought to meet this goal through projects like stronger campus-wide initiatives in budgeting and procurement, the creation of new online administrative tools to make important information accessible to students and faculty, and the centralization of administrative support. The OE program also included a Revenue Generation Program, through which OE program office staff worked with various campus units to launch revenue-generating projects that would also support academic goals.[62] The program, however, met with frosty faculty reception. Although John Wilton recognized the significant cost savings made through OE, faculty and staff remained suspicious of how the program determined layoffs.[63]

Wilton warned, "Expenses cannot be cut to balance the books without lasting impact on both the access to higher education and the standards achieved. The very metrics that we want to improve—time to degree, how many students graduate, debt levels, etc.—will worsen. Something has to happen on the revenue side as well as the cost side. There is no other real solution."[64] But neither state funding nor the aspirations of external fundraising had proven to be close to enough.

Cultures of Excellence and Rebellion: Faculty and Students

Berkeley's long-term investment in faculty hiring meant that the campus had a dedicated body of scholars that produced world-renowned research. In 2021 Berkeley boasted a faculty that included ten active Nobel laureates, thirty-three MacArthur Fellows, one Fields Medal winner, four Pulitzer Prize winners, three A. M. Turing Award winners, 251 fellows of the American Academy of Arts and Sciences, and 144 members of the National Academy of Sciences.[65]

(A quick detour on parking: Clark Kerr had noted, rightly, that parking was an obsession with the faculty, and Berkeley was physically constrained in this area. How then to reward the most distinguished faculty? Berkeley has had twenty-two Nobel laureates among its faculty. Initially, Berkeley rewarded the Nobel winners with a new lab, or even a new building. That got expensive. Today, Nobel laureates receive neither a lab nor a building, but they do get their own dedicated parking spot on campus, marked with "NL." At this writing, it seems that there are many more "NL" parking spots on campus than there are Nobel laureates to use them, but perhaps that is just good marketing.)

A hallmark of Berkeley was the high level of faculty engagement and autonomy in driving the campus forward. Since 1919 the Academic Senate was responsible for the oversight and approval of faculty hiring, a process that involved input from many colleagues and which was taken very seriously. Dirks noted, "When [faculty] have a job search, they all read the work

Figure 6.3. Nobel laureate parking signs. Jose Camões Silva/flickr/CC BY 2.0.

together. They go to the job talks. It is really not just a collegial but a collective investment in trying to make these decisions."[66] Clark Kerr had credited many of the outstanding research achievements of Berkeley to the thorough and consultative hiring process administered by the Senate.[67]

Berkeley's hiring practices at the assistant professor level were among the most rigorous in the nation, perhaps in part because finances mitigated against the recruitment of external senior faculty. One result was that a large percentage of the faculty was promoted to tenure from within. Approximately 80 percent of assistant professors who joined Berkeley between 1985 and 2011 in the humanities, social sciences, physical sciences, engineering, technology, and mathematics ultimately achieved tenure.[68] Once they made it through the hiring process, faculty members were likely to remain at Berkeley. Berkeley faculty were notoriously difficult to lure away to work at other institutions, even when other institutions were able to offer significantly higher salaries. Birgeneau noted, "During the darkest days, our retention went up. . . . It was the best period for retention, when the largest number of our faculty had offers from private universities."[69] A senior administrator recalled:

[A professor] was making $150,000 base salary . . . Duke offered him $450,000 to leave Berkeley and come there. . . . The dean brought him into my office, and we tried to talk sense to him. What we said to him was, "You have to understand there's no way we're going to even come close to what Duke is offering you . . . what number are you willing to settle for?" And I said, "Make sure it doesn't start with a three or a four." That's when he realized that if he was not careful about what he said, we might just let him go.[70]

Faculty and administrators at Berkeley could point to several reasons why the university was able to have such strong retaining power. First and foremost was the sense of camaraderie, equality, and responsibility among faculty members. Dirks found that faculty "wanted to stay here for reasons having to do with colleagues more than anything else . . . they find the depth and the kind of ethos of thought of their colleagues incomparable."[71] Unlike Harvard, with its historically huge social distance between senior faculty and everyone else, Berkeley made assistant professors colleagues.

Another reason was the dedication on the part of the faculty to Berkeley's public, social mission. Breslauer noted, "Some of [the faculty's desire to stay] comes from the sense and satisfaction about being a public university, and certainly an engine of upward mobility." Part of the appeal of this public mission was getting to work with students from a wide variety of socioeconomic backgrounds, including Berkeley's many first-generation college students and students from families with low incomes. Breslauer added, "When you ask most faculty, 'Why do you stay here?' they say, 'My colleagues, my students. I love them.'"[72]

This dedication could be a double-edged sword. Berkeley reaped the benefits of nurturing young scholars through the tenure process and maintaining their loyalty throughout their careers. This process produced faculty members who were proudly committed to Berkeley's culture but also inward looking. They could be suspicious of leaders hired from other institutions. As Dirks would discover, administrators who had not spent their careers at Berkeley were accused of "not really get[ting] what Berkeley is all about."[73]

While Berkeley excelled at retaining faculty, financial constraints had made hiring faculty difficult. From the early 1990s to 2018 the number of tenured faculty had stayed almost completely flat, falling to 1,133 in 2018 from 1,147 in 1993. During the same twenty-five-year period, the student population increased from just over 30,000 to 45,183.[74] The university increasingly relied on lower-ranked, non-tenured, non-tenure-track lecturers, whose numbers increased sevenfold from 54 in 1993 to 379 in 2018. At the same time, student demands for levels of service commensurate with the increasingly high tuition costs grew, as did political demands for regulatory compliance. University staff expanded to meet the demands of this changing environment—full-time administrative and managerial staff doubled from 306 in 1993 to 638 in 2011. By 2018 the staff in university management, business and financial operations, and office and administrative support occupations totaled nearly 3,000.[75] Thus, while the total number of tenured faculty had remained constant, they were becoming a smaller proportion of overall university employees. To some faculty, this seemed like a fundamental shift in the nature of the university.

Even the best faculty members have their limits. The faculty attacks on the university's leadership seem in retrospect less about their targets than a reflection of the combination of anger and insecurity that by 2010 had come to mark the faculty of America's premier public university. I noticed this firsthand when I chaired an external review committee of Berkeley's Institute of East Asian Studies. I had done this before, and with pleasure, because this institute, together with Harvard's Asia Center, was one of the two leading centers of East Asian studies in the United States and indeed in the world. It had a long and continuing history of distinguished faculty leadership. Like almost all such transregional operations, there were built-in tensions, as the study of each country reflected its status: thus China studies was overpopulated with faculty, compared to others, and under resourced, while Japanese studies was rich, but with few faculty members to spend its money on, and Korean studies was simply ignored until recently. Still, the institute was world renowned. With the enduring budget crisis after 2008, however, something seemed to snap.

When I visited in 2011–2012, in contrast to earlier visits, I found a faculty fatigued, fearful, and at the edge of civil war. Our report noted that we were at a time of "deep austerity and high anxiety across the Berkeley campus" that (and this was a big understatement) "tested the limits of collegiality" within the faculty. Our review of salaries showed how poorly paid were the excellent Berkeley faculty compared to their comrades elsewhere. And the esprit de corps that had once defined an underpaid but mission-driven faculty was gone. People were bitter and backbiting. They indulged in conspiracy theories ("there is money hidden away that *they* are not telling us about") both about the administration and their own colleagues. They believed the worst, not the best, about the motives of others. They believed things that were demonstrably not true. This, it struck me, was a great program and a great university, both in existential crisis.[76] My experience in the Institute of East Asian Studies can surely be multiplied many times across the campus over the past decade.

For a large and seemingly impersonal research university, it is refreshing to note that one of Berkeley's enduring strengths is its student body. The students at Berkeley have consistently stood out from their public university peers in terms of both excellence and diversity. Berkeley's overall graduation rate also stood out favorably compared with its public peers. By 2019 Berkeley undergraduates had a four-year graduation rate of 75.8 percent, up from 66 percent in 2008. This figure is comparable to the rate at the University of Michigan-Ann Arbor (79 percent), and well above that of the University of Wisconsin-Madison (62 percent) and the University of Texas-Austin (61 percent).[77] From 2012 to 2015 Berkeley had both the highest cumulative number of undergraduate program alumni receiving National Science Foundation (NSF) fellowships for graduate study as well as the highest number of graduate students on NSF fellowships.[78]

Earlier and better than any US private university, Berkeley demonstrated a strong commitment to helping a socioeconomically and ethnically diverse student community access its excellent undergraduate education. In 2018, 8,684 Berkeley undergraduates received Pell Grants, within throwing distance of all eight Ivy League institutions combined (11,001) and almost eight times as many as at local rival Stanford. These 8,684 students represented 28 percent of all Berkeley undergraduates, in comparison with the 1,133 Pell Grant recipients at Stanford who represented just 16 percent of that university's undergraduate population.[79] Berkeley was the first public university to have a comprehensive financial aid plan for middle-income students, as well as the first university, public or private, in the United States to offer comprehensive financial aid to undocumented students. In 2020, 23 percent of Berkeley freshmen were first-generation college students.[80] In 2019 underrepresented minorities made up 19.4 percent of the undergraduate population.[81] Berkeley even had a comprehensive support program for former foster children. In 2020 Christ also announced that Berkeley had committed to becoming a Hispanic-Serving Institution (HSI), a U.S. Department of Education designation, which meant that at least a quarter of its full-time enrolled students were Hispanic.[82]

Berkeley's students, like the Berkeley faculty, were distinguished also by what some called their "insurgent citizenship." It was students, after all, who had led the Free Speech Movement in the 1960s, and the student body remained vocal about various campus and social causes into the twenty-first century. Toward the end of the 1960s, Berkeley was home to some of the first nationwide protests that evolved into the establishment of ethnic studies departments across the United States. After the creation of the Third World Liberation Front (TWLF), a coalition of African American, Latin American, Asian American, and Native American students, at neighboring San Francisco State University in 1968, minority students at Berkeley created their own TWLF in early 1969.[83] The TWLF demanded the creation of a "Third World College" to create academic departments geared toward students of color. After ten weeks of strikes, the Academic Senate voted with a significant majority to establish an Ethnic Studies Department on the campus.[84] Berkeley's student activism reverberated across the country to Duke, where President Nannerl Keohane would later allude to the events at Berkeley as a precursor to the creation of Duke's Black Studies Department in 1969, and later its Latino/a and Asian American Studies programs.[85]

The call for shifts in curricula was not the only cause for student advocacy. A growing chorus of student protests against tuition hikes and budget cuts that began in 2009 culminated in a dramatic student "occupation" of Berkeley's Sproul Plaza in November 2011. Chancellor Birgeneau's handling of the incident recalled that of Nathan Pusey at Harvard, academic generations earlier. Birgeneau called on police, who used aggressive physical confrontation to break up the one-thousand-person demonstration, drawing even more protests and calls for his resignation.[86]

Figure 6.4. 2009 Sproul Plaza protest. Steve McConnell/UC Berkeley, © 2009 UC Regents.

Like their faculty mentors, the more politically active Berkeley students were deeply invested in the culture of their institution and their role in maintaining it. After years of student advocacy, several buildings were renamed because students alleged that their original namesakes perpetuated racist views. One notable building with a revoked name was Boalt Hall. Its nineteenth-century namesake, John Boalt, had called for the halt of Chinese immigration in the United States and espoused racist beliefs against Blacks and Native Americans. This was a big step because the term "Boalt Hall" had long been the de facto name of Berkeley's law school, and that was how it was known.

Dirks made improvement of the undergraduate experience one of the major goals for his chancellorship. The Chancellor's Undergraduate Initiative sought to create a more cohesive undergraduate experience across the university. The initiative had four major components: transforming the undergraduate program of the College of Letters and Science through a "College at Berkeley" liberal arts degree program; updating the undergraduate curriculum, particularly for first- and second-year students, to make it more cohesive and interdisciplinary; renewing physical spaces for the undergraduates; and developing a whole-student educational philosophy.[87] Dirks, from his background at Columbia with its strong commitment to the liberal arts and sciences, hoped to create an undergraduate program that would create a more shared curriculum, linking learning with Berkeley's research culture and integrating education with residential life.[88] All these efforts would stall in the crisis of Dirks's chancellorship.

Berkeley, like the other UC campuses, sought to maintain a level of ethnic diversity among its students that reflected that of the state of California's. This, however, was increasingly at odds with the mandate of the Master Plan, which required UC schools to first admit the top 12.5 percent of California's high school graduates, without reference to race or ethnicity. This became a greater challenge still when, in 1996, California voters approved Proposition 209, which effectively banned the use of affirmative action in public education. Demographic projections estimated that of California's college age cohort, almost half of the population would be Hispanic or Latinx by 2040.[89] Of undergraduates enrolled at Berkeley in 2019 only 11.5 percent identified as Hispanic or Latinx.[90] Berkeley faced difficult decisions about how to balance access and excellence in an equitable way.

The complexity of admissions decisions was compounded when out-of-state and international students were included. With in-state student tuition frozen by the Board of Regents, raising out-of-state tuition and increasing the proportion of out-of-state or international students was one of the few ways for Berkeley to increase tuition revenue. At the same time, the citizens of California were very sensitive to increases in admission of out-of-state and international students at a time when admissions at universities across the country were becoming increasingly competitive. Still, internationalization in higher education was a broader trend that Berkeley could not ignore.

Cooperation and Competition Abroad and at Home

Berkeley had a long history of international engagement, from its early welcoming of international students to the establishment of the UC system-wide Education Abroad Program in 1962. Even the university's first philanthropic gift, from attorney and university regent Edward Tomkins in 1872, was for a professorship in "Oriental Languages and Literatures" to prepare students for expanded commerce between the United States and Asia. In a letter to his fellow regents of the university before establishing the professorship, Tomkins wrote that he felt "deeply the humiliation" of seeing students from East Asia who came to study in the United States "pass by us in almost daily procession to the other side of the continent, in search of that intellectual hospitality that we are not yet enlightened enough to extend to them."[91] Since then, Berkeley has maintained a strong commitment to international engagement at the individual and institutional level. In 2019, 1,555 students from ninety-four countries were admitted to Berkeley's freshman class.[92] Total international student enrollment at all levels more than doubled from 2005 to 2019.[93]

All that was good enough, but in an era when other American universities were establishing campuses (NYU, Duke) or centers (Harvard, Stanford, Chicago, Columbia) abroad—many of these in China—how could a cash-strapped state university with a mission to serve the residents of California compete? Dirks had a brilliant answer: he would build his international campus at home. One of his central projects was the planning of the Berkeley Global Campus in Richmond Bay, on prime, largely empty real estate along San Francisco Bay that was the university's to use. Announced by Dirks at a meeting of the Academic Senate on October 29, 2014, the campus was to provide a physical location for international partnerships between Berkeley and universities around the world. The first program to be established on the campus would be a graduate-level global citizenship curriculum. In Dirks's plans for the campus, this curriculum would be joined by a variety of other interdisciplinary, globally relevant teaching and research programs.[94] In October 2015 Dirks, joined by the leaders of the University of Cambridge and the National University of Singapore, announced a commitment to establish a global alliance between their three institutions, some of whose projects would be based on the new Richmond campus.[95]

These international initiatives represented a commitment to the trend of globalization and internationalization that was coming to dominate higher education, but at the same time, signified a departure from the export model that most universities had thus far employed to achieve "globalization." Berkeley's imported global campus would bring the world to California in a way that Dirks felt was better aligned with Berkeley's dual identity as a globally relevant, locally supported, public university.[96] And he believed (not wrongly) that many rising international universities would pay top dollar to co-locate research programs at Berkeley. For Berkeley itself, the initial investment would be minimal. Before his resignation, Dirks had neared completion of negotiations with several major international universities to co-locate research programs on the Global Campus.

But even a modest investment seemed too much to vocal faculty convinced that this was a diversion from the core and underfunded mission of the university. In the storm that was building in 2016, Dirks was forced to step back from his globalizing ambition. He was forced to say, "We are not investing," and repeat, "We are not investing any campus funds in the Richmond campus." With a faculty rebellion at home, an initiative that once had pride of place as a cornerstone in Dirks's vision for Berkeley and his chancellorship could no longer be a primary concern. By 2020 Berkeley's Richmond campus, in the absence of a compelling new vision, lay in a state of benign neglect.

But Dirks and his successor, Christ, recognized that in an increasingly globalized academic market, Berkeley needed to compete globally for talent and, as an institution that received 87 percent of its funding from nonstate sources, for resources.[97] While Berkeley still ranked very highly on every global higher education league table, rankings were lagging indicators. Universities that were not globally competitive in 2019 could quickly become so by successfully competing for key resources like talented faculty.

The global competition for talent was already beginning to affect young faculty recruitment; one particularly fierce competitor in this regard was

China. In the early twenty-first century, China introduced national government policies and funding schemes that supported international recruitment of outstanding university faculty, with a particular emphasis on encouraging Chinese scholars who had studied or begun their careers abroad to return to the Chinese mainland. Former chancellor Birgeneau told me that two of his students had chosen not to apply to entry-level faculty positions open in their fields at both Berkeley and MIT, choosing instead to return to top universities in China. "[China's talent recruitment] strategy is actually working. . . . A decade ago, there's no chance [these students] would've gone back to China."[98] Plentiful funding, immediate full professorships, and cultural and emotional arguments were just a few of the appealing factors drawing American-educated Chinese graduate students back to China. Tsinghua University alone boasted forty senior faculty members who had received their PhDs from Berkeley. Tsinghua had also been able to attract tenured faculty members from Berkeley to high-profile academic leadership positions: Qian Yingyi became dean of the Tsinghua School of Economics and Management after becoming a tenured professor at Berkeley, and Peng Kaiping, a tenured faculty member in the psychology department, served as the founding chair of Tsinghua's department of psychology.

At least one Berkeley school was entrepreneurial enough to venture out on its own with an international presence. With Dirks's blessing, the College of Engineering partnered with Tsinghua and the dynamic southern Chinese city of Shenzhen to build "TBSI," the Tsinghua-Berkeley Shenzhen Institute for research and education in engineering and the applied sciences. Shenzhen, home to several of the world's most dynamic companies (Tencent, Huawei), but without a well-known university of its own, footed the $220 million bill for construction. Tsinghua contributed $1 per year. And Berkeley, for whose faculty even that figure might have seemed too much, paid nothing.

Competition Down the Road and Downstate

Some of Berkeley's fiercest competitors were also its closest neighbors. When Leland Stanford Junior University was founded just forty miles away from Berkeley in 1885, there was fear that the then-fledgling state would be unable to support two comprehensive research institutions. Instead, the founding and growth of Stanford has made the San Francisco Bay area the premiere bastion of academia west of the Mississippi River and helped establish a critical mass of scholars in the state. While Berkeley and Stanford remained rivals, their competition on the academic, as well as athletic, fields appeared to benefit both institutions. Like Harvard and Yale, or Tsinghua and Peking Universities, these two giants on either side of San Francisco Bay cooperated in almost nothing.

In its early days, UCLA was shrouded in a haze of Southern Californian angst over a perceived unequal distribution of state resources that purportedly favored Berkeley. There had been distinct growing pains as UCLA grew into an ever-stronger institution and gained more support from the state, but by 1960 UCLA had achieved prestige equal to that of Berkeley and received as much government support. Friendly competition between the two campuses spurred on their growth. Contentious relations between the state and UC, however, had the power to either strengthen or weaken this relationship. In 2020 many of the challenges that Berkeley faced—responding to state disinvestment, managing tuition levels, balancing ethnic diversity, determining out-of-state admissions—were faced also by UCLA, which, however, had been more nimble in fundraising and had built a larger endowment.

Berkeley contended not just with California-based institutions but also with many strong universities throughout the United States. Still, Berkeley was competitive with these institutions on several grounds, including overall academic excellence. In terms of national competition for faculty, Birgeneau recognized that Berkeley had a "huge competitive advantage" because of the appeal of its mission and role as a public university. "If [faculty] want to be at a public university, and they're of the caliber that they can get an offer from [the country's top universities], then it's going to be the elite private universities over there and one public [Berkeley] over here."[99] For California students, low in-state tuition ($14,312 in 2020–2021) remained a strong pull over elite private universities such as those in the Ivy League, which all had perceived costs of attendance (before financial aid) of more than $60,000 per year. The recruitment advantage of being a uniquely excellent public university was one reason for Berkeley to maintain its identity as a public institution even as state funding continued to decline as a percentage of revenue.

The Postpandemic World

Shortly after Dirks declared Berkeley's "new normal" in 2016, Carol Christ was named the eleventh chancellor of Berkeley in March 2017, becoming the first woman to hold the position. She brought with her ample experience in higher education administration and was no stranger to the campus. A scholar of Victorian literature, Christ first came to Berkeley in 1970 as an assistant professor and became chair of the English department in 1985. For over three decades, she had served as a professor and an administrator, with roles ranging from dean to provost. In 2002 she left Berkeley to become the president of Smith College, where she stayed until 2013. She returned to Berkeley in 2015, where she held several leadership roles, including interim executive vice chancellor, before ultimately becoming chancellor. Her appointment was met with enthusiasm as she was a known and proven actor, an insider with outside experience, with a reputation for being community-oriented and consultative in her leadership style. Political science professor and the outgoing Academic Senate Chair Robert Powell said that faculty members appreciated Christ's leadership and called her style "consultative in a meaningful way."[100]

Yet the challenges that followed Dirks's departure did not leave with him. Immediate dilemmas included the budget deficit, new controversies surrounding the old topic of "free speech," and a student housing crisis. Christ reduced her inherited deficit to $56 million by June 2018.[101] Through the advocacy of students, alumni, and administrators, Governor Jerry Brown signed a 2018–2019 budget that included a $346.9 million funding increase, with $98.1 million as a permanent increase from the 2017–2018 budget and $25 million as one-time funding toward Berkeley's deficit. By September 2019 Berkeley reached a balanced budget and raised $1.2 billion in two consecutive, record-breaking fundraising years.[102] In response to sometimes-violent protests against right-wing activists, Christ also established a "Free-Speech Commission" and launched a "free speech year" to bring together students, faculty, and staff to engage in dialogue around what free speech meant for a university that had founded the Free Speech Movement.[103] Christ even took a stab at addressing Berkeley's university housing shortage. Out of all the schools in the UC system, Berkeley had the smallest housing capacity. Christ proposed nine new sites for expanded university housing, including one in Richmond where Dirks had planned to build the global campus.

Despite Christ's early successes, in the wake of sustained budget cuts and the steady loss of faculty members, Berkeley's position in university league tables declined. In the 2018 Quacquarelli Symonds survey, Berkeley slipped in eighty categories. In 2018 UCLA tied with Berkeley in the *U.S. News and World Report* rankings, making it the first time in almost twenty years that Berkeley was not the sole top public university in the United States.[104] Berkeley even was initially unranked in the 2019 edition of the USNWR because the university misreported the 2016 alumni giving rate, stating it was 11.6 percent instead of the true (and miserable) rate of 7.9 percent.[105] After rectifying this misreporting, Berkeley went back in the USNWR rankings, where its position dropped behind UCLA's in both 2019 and 2020.[106]

Dirks's term of "new normal" then took on new meaning in the 2019–2020 school year. COVID-19 sparked a global pandemic and brought on unexpected changes heralding an internationally felt "new normal." At Berkeley, this had profound implications for the university. After finally reaching a balanced budget, because of short-term revenue loss as well as deep and long-term cuts in state support, Berkeley again faced a projected budget deficit between $170 and $400 million.[107] Overall state budget cuts were also predicted to be as much as $53.4 billion over the next two years, which would further reduce state funding for the UC system.[108] In June 2020 Christ announced that Berkeley would have a hybrid fall semester, including small in-person classes; a "Semester in the Cloud," or online offerings for large survey courses; and staggered student arrivals along with restricted student housing of up to sixty-five hundred students.[109] To mitigate challenges brought on for California's public higher education systems, Governor Gavin Newsom organized a California Higher Education Recovery with Equity Taskforce in August 2020.[110] Former Provost Breslauer had believed that Berkeley's worst case scenario was if "the state doesn't come through, the competition gets wealthier and wealthier" leading the university "to get blown out of the water."[111] Would the COVID-19 pandemic prove his words prophetic?

A time of crisis had returned, and the toughest questions remained unanswered: What did it mean to be a "public" institution, when the vast majority of institutional funding came from private sources? What were Berkeley's obligations to the citizens, taxpayers, and children of the state of California, which no longer funded it in a sustainable fashion? Could Berkeley meet these regional expectations while remaining one of the best universities in the world? As Christ proclaimed, "This may be a perilous time, but so, too, is it a time of creative ferment and possibility."[112] How would the university's high-minded and vocal faculty, students, and staff respond to yet another crisis in an age of enduring austerity? Had one of Berkeley's historic strengths, faculty governance, made it impossible to face inevitably difficult choices? Had Berkeley—home to the Free Speech Movement, long traditions of academic autonomy, and insurgent citizenship—finally become both ungovernable and insolvent in the face of the multiple "new normals" bearing down on it?

CHAPTER SEVEN

Outrageous Ambitions

Duke University

I N MAY 2017, nearly thirteen years after assuming Duke's presidency, Richard Brodhead found himself in the city of Kunshan, in Jiangsu Province of the People's Republic of China. He spoke to the Advisory Board of Duke Kunshan University (DKU), Duke's most ambitious international initiative, just weeks before he would step down as president. He recalled that when he assumed the presidency, he had spent his "whole adult life" at Yale, first as a student, then as a distinguished scholar of English literature, and then, for eleven years, as dean of Yale College. Many in New Haven could not imagine that he would abandon Yale for Duke. He was reminded of one student, who complained: "See, it was like Dean Brodhead was married to Yale—and now we learn he is leaving us for someone younger and more athletic."[1]

Duke was indeed younger and, in the early twenty-first century, considerably more athletic than the Ivy League schools it once measured itself against. Its famous men's basketball team had won five national championships—two during Brodhead's tenure—playing in Cameron Indoor Stadium, which Brodhead called "the boisterous home of Duke school spirit, where fans go crazy and foes wish they could just go home."[2] But it was Duke's academic athleticism—its relentless planning and its comparative lack of constraint in crossing intellectual and international boundaries—that made it an institution at once accomplished and aspiring, perhaps the most dynamic of American research universities.

Brodhead surveyed the stunningly modern DKU campus designed by Gensler & Associates and constructed by Kunshan, China's most entrepreneurial city.[3] Having just signed an agreement for the construction of the second phase of DKU's two-hundred-acre residential campus, Brodhead reflected on how far he and the university had come. Here he was, 18 hours (by air) from home, and 179 years removed from the founding of the institution that would become Duke University. Duke was establishing a liberal arts college, on American standards, in China—the first such Sino-American venture since the founding in 1919 of Yenching University, now the site of Peking University. Duke was investing academic capital aggressively into China, which was home to the fastest-growing system of higher education, in quality as well as quantity, in the world. China was home also to a major political crackdown on views deemed unorthodox by the ruling Chinese Communist Party.

As he left Kunshan at three hundred kilometers per hour by high-speed train back to Shanghai, and then by a familiar set of flights home to Durham, North Carolina, Brodhead thought about the legacy he would be leaving his successor, Vincent Price, who would assume office on July 1. DKU had been yet another daring move for Duke—perhaps the boldest yet of any American university in China—but it had not been without its challenges. Duke's Board of Trustees had called it a "one-hundred-year decision." Would it prove, for the new president, and for Duke, a mark of global leadership, distinguishing it from less determined American competitors? Or was it a risk too far, even for a university known, in the words of an earlier president, Terry Sanford, for "outrageous ambition"?[4] It was, in any event, one of the boldest ventures yet by a young university that less than a century ago was far removed from the forefront of higher education.

Rural Origins and Homegrown Endowment

It was fitting that Duke would place its newest campus in what had been, until recent decades, a small city in the countryside outside Shanghai. By 2020 Duke University had become a leading private American research university with twelve schools, nearly sixteen thousand students, and over thirty-eight hundred faculty members spread over one thousand acres in Durham.[5] Its graduate and professional schools—in medicine, business, law, public policy, and the environment, among others—were regularly ranked among the top institutions in their fields. Its undergraduate college was among the most selective in the land, and its graduates were among the most highly regarded by employers.[6] But Duke traced its origins to Brown's Schoolhouse, a one-room school built by Methodist and Quaker families in rural North Carolina. Duke, Brodhead once said, was founded "in the hinterland of what was one of the South's least developed states. But no place is so poor that its people can't care about education, and no group is ever so deprived that it can't take steps to acquire this good."[7]

The school evolved into a normal school, training teachers, and then a small college that took the name Trinity College in 1859. It abandoned Trinity, North Carolina (the town was named for the college), in 1892 for the more urban and industrial setting of Durham. Overseeing the transition was an early Yale transplant, President John F. Crowell, who envisioned (what else?) a university on a German model that would be committed to research as well as teaching. Crowell was first disheartened by what he saw at Trinity, to the point he almost resigned and returned to the north. He began to put into motion reforms, including the development of the college's

Figure 7.1. Brown's Schoolhouse, 1892. David M. Rubenstein Rare Book & Manuscript Library, Duke University.

first general library. His plans were not only academic. He was a big proponent of athletics as a way to unify a student body that was divided across
geographical and class lines and as a way to challenge the nearby state university at Chapel Hill.[8]

Late nineteenth-century Durham was a railway junction and the center
of the American tobacco trade. North Carolina tobacco had become famous
in the United States in the aftermath of the Civil War, when occupying
Union troops became enamored of its sweet aroma. Washington Duke, a pioneer in the industry, was among those whose support lured Trinity College to Durham. His son, James Buchanan Duke, revolutionized the industry
with the introduction of the cigarette-rolling machine. By the turn of the
twentieth century, the Dukes' American Tobacco Company had a near monopoly of the American cigarette market and was well on its way, through alliance
with British partners, to addicting a large part of the world to nicotine. The
firm produced and sold some 55 billion cigarettes in China by 1930, establishing a male smoking culture there that endures to this day.[9]

In the 1890s Trinity College received support from Washington Duke and
Julian S. Carr sufficient to construct a new campus at the site of today's East
Campus to host the newly ambitious and now coeducational institution,
where women, according to the terms of Washington Duke's gift, would be
"on equal footing with men."[10] Recruiting faculty from the newly established
graduate schools to the north, such as those of Johns Hopkins and Columbia,
Trinity became in the early twentieth century a leading liberal arts college
in the American south.[11]

The foundation of today's Duke University was laid under the long presidency of William Preston Few, who served from 1910 until his death in 1940.
Then, as now, good fundraising took patience and fortitude. It was after at
least a decade of pursuit that Few convinced James Buchanan Duke, who
famously liked to "think big," to support Few's vision to build a "national"
and "major" university, renamed in honor of Washington Duke.[12] Funded
in 1924 with $40 million from a larger Duke endowment in support of edu-
cation and health, Trinity was rebuilt in Georgian style in the 1920s to house
the university's Women's College, while a spectacular neo-Gothic campus
was conceived and constructed as the West Campus about a mile away.[13]
Within a decade of Duke's gift, Trinity College had become Duke University, with a Graduate School, Divinity School, Medical School, and Nursing
School, and with Schools of Engineering and Forestry soon to follow.

The locus and symbol of Duke's metamorphosis was the new West Campus, a refined design of a soaring chapel and flanking quadrangles, all in Collegiate Gothic, and all the design of the African American architect Julian Francis Abele of the Philadelphia firm of Horace Trumbauer. It is a telling story about the Duke University of those days that Abele, who designed for the university for a quarter-century, could not or would not visit North Carolina in that racist and segregationist age. The man who imagined modern Duke University's campus never set eyes on his creation.

In 1925, his last year of life, James B. Duke made another gift to the university: $4 million to establish the Duke School of Medicine, the School of Nursing, and Duke Hospital. His vision was then regional, hoping that Duke would become the greatest medical center between Baltimore and New Orleans. The medical campus and hospital were built just steps from West Campus.[14] Their physical proximity to the heart of Duke reflected the integral role they would come to play in the university life, operations, and aspirations. After opening in 1930, the nascent medical center quickly saw great success. By 1935 it entered the ranks of the nation's top twenty medical schools, according to the American Medical Association. Demand for the hospital's services grew rapidly, and a new hospital wing was added in 1940 to increase capacity.[15]

Duke's commitment to the public health of North Carolina continues today, bolstered in 1998 with the creation of the Duke University Health System (DUHS) that integrated Duke Regional Hospital with Raleigh Community Hospital and other nearby medical service providers to establish a single "academic health care system" for the region.[16] As we will see later, this regionally focused medical center was to become a first mover in Duke's ambitious internationalization with its 2005 partnership with the National University of Singapore to found Duke-NUS Medical School.

When the English novelist and philosopher Aldous Huxley visited North Carolina in 1937, he described traveling through forests "where one would never expect anything in particular to happen. And then, all of a sudden, something does happen. . . . There, astonishingly, is by far the largest Gothic building one has ever seen. . . . [T]his huge and fantastic structure which now houses a large university . . . is the most successful essay in neo-Gothic that I know."[17] In one architectural stroke, Duke was now the Collegiate Gothic equal of Princeton, the University of Chicago, and Washington University.

Figure 7.2. Aerial view of the Duke campus. Duke Today Staff.

Figure 7.3. The scholarly steps of Duke's Chapel. Photograph © William C. Kirby.

There was no little pretense in its design—the stone stairs leading down from Duke Chapel were preternaturally worn, as if centuries of scholars had trod upon them. But as Duke's first comprehensive planning report noted in 1959, "The building of a magnificent plant was not itself an answer" to the question of what "the new University might become and achieve."[18] How, in short, would Duke create a university as good as its architecture?

A Culture of Planning

Every university pretends to plan for its future. Some, like our Berlin universities, do so because the government mandates it in "treaties," or requires it in the context of the Excellence Initiative. Private American institutions such as Harvard do so mostly when launching fundraising campaigns: Why *should* we ask alumni for more funds? Individual schools in research universities necessarily plan for the next cycle of faculty appointments and capital projects, but very few institutions plan as a whole for long-term strategic direction. Duke was different. Even Duke's prologue to its 2006 *Making a Difference* strategic plan stated, "In many universities, strategic planning is an unromantic prospect, a bureaucratic exercise. . . . At Duke, strategic planning is exciting to undertake because it actually makes a difference." By the 1950s Duke already looked like a great university; it would need decades of serious planning to become one.

Taking Stock, 1958–1964

Serious, university-wide academic planning began in the 1950s. In 1958 the Executive Committee of the Board of Trustees at Duke approved a "Statement of Procedure for Long-Range Planning" drafted by Vice President Paul M. Gross (the equivalent of provost at the time). President A. Hollis Edens posed three simple questions for the committee: Where was Duke lagging behind? What direction should Duke emphasize? What ought Duke to be in the future?[19] Gross's report forced Duke to decide: Would Duke aspire to be a research university on a national scale? The answer was yes, even if conflicted: As President Edens shared the report with the faculty, he noted that the (re)founders of Duke in the 1930s had "not set out to build a provincial university, though they were in sympathy with the need to render special service to the South."[20]

Duke's *First Progress Report* in 1959 provided a frank and, at times, brutal assessment of the university, its several schools, and the challenges ahead. The undergraduate college, it noted, was "in a strong position in the Southern region," but it fell "far short of the best national standards."[21] The Graduate School lacked "dynamic progress toward real educational leadership in the national and international sense."[22] Duke, with its four thousand largely southern, exclusively white undergraduate students, twelve hundred graduate and professional students of uneven quality, and eight hundred faculty members, was much more a reputable regional university in a segregated South than a contender for national distinction.[23] Duke did not desegregate until 1961, and it enrolled its first five undergraduate African American students in 1963.[24]

Duke was also well behind leading schools of the day in terms of financial resources. In 1958 direct instructional expenditures for the 5,612 full-time students at Duke totaled $4.9 million ($868 per student), compared to $24 million ($2,318 per student) for 10,536 students at Harvard.[25] Duke's endowment in 1960 stood at less than one-tenth of Harvard's: $60 million versus $625 million.[26]

The *Second Progress Report* and *Third Progress Report* on long-range planning in 1960 and 1961, respectively, continued to highlight the university's inadequacies. The *Second Progress Report*, in particular, called for improving Duke's undergraduate student body. Duke lagged behind its aspirational peers in SAT scores and other measures.[27] The report determined to raise the academic bar for admission in test scores, math, and foreign language preparation.

These three progress reports set the stage for the *Fifth Decade* report in 1964, which brought this six-year-long strategic planning process to a conclusion. Duke's fifth decade, it declared, would witness faculty recruitment and faculty salaries at a national scale, spending of at least $100 million (greater than the size of the endowment) on new facilities, and increased tuition to help pay for all this.[28] If Duke were to be a national university, it needed to start charging like one.

Only with this planning behind it did Duke engage in its *Fifth Decade* campaign, which raised $105 million by May 1971, the most by any school located in the American South at the time.[29] The funds raised supported twenty-four building projects that significantly expanded Duke's scientific research facilities, library, student housing, and recreational facilities.[30] It also created newly endowed professorships in chemistry, business administration, international affairs, and medicine to recruit a new generation of academic leaders.[31]

Not all of Duke's new recruits came without controversy. The Duke Lemur Center (DLC) was founded in 1966 by John Buettner-Janusch, a Yale anthropologist who relocated to Duke along with his lemurs, and Peter Klopfer, a Duke biologist.[32] Located on eighty acres of the Duke Forest, close to the main campus, this is an open-air primate facility to study and protect lemurs, the most endangered mammals on the planet. With some 230 lemurs from 14 species, the DLC today boasts the most diverse lemur population outside Madagascar.[33] The DLC was home to one of the world's most famous lemurs, Jovian, star of the PBS KIDS show *Zoboomafoo*.

Even the most charming recruitment story can have its dark side. After establishing the DLC, Buettner-Janusch left Duke in 1973 when NYU offered him a higher salary. While at NYU, he was convicted in 1980 of using his lab as a "drug factory" after federal agents found evidence of LSD and other drugs.[34] In 1987, a few years after his release from prison, he sent poisoned chocolates to the judge who convicted him and to a former Duke colleague.[35] The judge's wife ate the chocolates. She survived, and the lemurs were fine, too. Today the Duke Lemur Center draws over thirty-five thousand yearly patrons to this sanctuary for these magnetic mammals with hypnotic eyes.[36]

One lesson of the *Fifth Decade* campaign—that strong strategic planning could lead to successful capital campaigns—was not lost on Duke's subsequent leaders. However, future plans would also go well beyond outlining capital needs to defining Duke's ambitions.

"Outrageous Ambitions" in the 1970s

When Duke unveiled its next strategic plan, eight years after its *Fifth Decade* report, it did so as a rapidly rising university under the leadership of a national political figure, Terry Sanford. In an address to the faculty on October 25, 1984, President Sanford proclaimed:

> This is not an Ivy League school. We are not of any flock or tribe. I quote from my inaugural speech: "I do not propose that we seek for ourselves a homogenized pattern of the half-dozen great private universities of the nation of which we are one, or that we try to 'catch up' or follow any university, no matter what its prestigious position. Simply

to do as some other university does, to teach as it teaches, to operate as it operates, to accept it as our model, would make our best success but a carbon copy. We strive to be Duke University, an institution seeking the highest scholarly attainment, and using to the fullest its own peculiar resources and creative capabilities."[37]

Like campuses from Berlin to Berkeley, Duke in the late 1960s was a site of protests in favor of civil rights and against the Vietnam War. President Douglas Knight was forced to resign in 1969 after African American students occupied the Allen Administration Building and tear gas was fired by police into a crowd of student onlookers.[38] Duke, like Harvard, Free University of Berlin, and, as we shall see, Tsinghua, found itself in the crosshairs of a generational revolution.

After Knight's departure, Terry Sanford, a progressive Democrat who supported desegregation and had doubled state spending for public schools while serving as governor of North Carolina from 1961 to 1965, was brought in by Duke's board to restore peace on campus and push the university forward as a national institution.[39] This ambition fitted an ambitious man. While president of Duke, Sanford would twice run for the presidency of the United States and eventually became a US senator after his departure from Duke. On his death, he would be entombed in the Duke University Chapel. During his tenure as president, he put Duke indelibly on the map.

Since its last strategic plan, much had improved. By 1972 undergraduates were now in the top 9 percent of all US college students as measured by average SAT scores, although Duke was still behind thirty-five to forty schools in terms of tested student quality.[40] Duke's professional schools were getting better fast. The Schools of Medicine and Law were now in the top ten nationally.[41] Duke's School of Business, founded in 1969, planned to expand its endowment fivefold to $5 million.[42]

Sanford's 1972 report aimed to push further and faster, with a key focus on undergraduate education. The rigor of the undergraduate curriculum was increased in the 1968–1969 academic year to help address "the lack of intellectual climate" at Duke and to engage students more directly in research.[43] Significant external resources were sought to improve financial aid and student diversity, with the aim that 10 percent of the undergraduate student body be minority students.[44]

In graduate education, because the majority of Duke's graduate school programs were already ranked in the top thirty nationally, the bar was raised to get most programs into the top twenty. To achieve this, the report called for the establishment of fifty new endowed professorships in addition to the forty-eight James B. Duke and other named professorships already in place.[45]

Focused Excellence in the 1980s

Duke's rise since the 1950s had taken place in an era of largely continuous growth in the American economy. But in the aftermath of the stagflation of the late 1970s, Duke's 1980 plan, *Directions for Progress,* declared that Duke, like other private research universities, had to "plan for retrenchment, not growth."[46]

All of Duke's earlier plans had looked unsentimentally at existing programs, with an eye to reducing those that no longer showed promise. *Directions for Progress* went further to argue for substantial cuts.[47] Several programs improved their financial standing and survived the cuts. These included the School of Forestry and Environmental Studies as well as the Duke University Marine Lab which combined to form a new School of the Environment in 1991.[48]

Directions for Progress also proposed sweeping reforms in academic appointments to improve Duke's competitiveness, with stress on stricter tenure policy. Eighty percent of Duke's faculty outside of the Medical Center was tenured, a percentage that posed "significant risk of stagnation" for the university.[49] Tenured appointments were to be reserved for "leading scholars" who would be "excellent by every national standard." The university could no longer afford to "confuse conscientious service with potential greatness."[50]

When economic growth returned in the late 1980s, Duke's selective and aggressive hiring had paid off. The Academic Plan of 1987 confidently called on Duke to "carve out a distinctive niche in the top echelon of research universities" and create its own "peaks of excellence."[51] This had already begun in many areas. John Hope Franklin, a leading historian of the United States and of the African American experience, was awarded a James B. Duke professorship in 1982. Duke's Humanities Institute would be founded in his name and his honor in 1999. Joel Fleishman, a prominent law scholar, was recruited from Yale in 1971 to head the Institute of Policy Sciences and Public Affairs, which would evolve into today's Sanford School of Public Policy. Phillip Griffiths gave up an endowed chair at Harvard to become provost at Duke in 1984.[52] And to chair the English Department, Duke recruited in 1986 a bold academic entrepreneur and literary theorist, Stanley Fish, who was said to have taken "a respectable but staid Southern English department and transform[ed] it into the professional powerhouse of the day."[53]

The strategic planning efforts in the 1970s and 1980s were supported by two capital campaigns under Sanford, expanding research and student support, adding new facilities, and funding the recruitment of a national student body. The percentage of undergraduates from North Carolina and other Southeastern states decreased from 55 percent in 1958 to 35 percent in 1983; 48 percent of the students were now from the Northeast, and 15 percent were from the Midwest and Pacific coast.[54] The trend toward diversity intensified under Sanford's successor, Keith Brodie. The proportion of African American students at Duke increased from 4 percent in 1985 to 9 percent in 1993.[55] The percentage of undergraduates receiving financial aid at the school increased from 20 percent to 40 percent in the same period.[56] Fourteen percent of Duke undergrads received Pell Grants.[57]

Coach K and Beyond

Also in the 1980s the roots for one of Duke's trademark programs were planted: the men's basketball team. From 1980 to 2022 Mike Krzyzewski served as head coach of this team, leading Duke to five national championships and twelve Final Fours by 2021. He holds the record for the most career wins in men's college basketball's most demanding division. Named after the coach, Krzyzewskiville, or K-ville, is an enduring Duke tradition that began in 1986 when students camped out in tents for days to get tickets to the annual game between the Duke "Blue Devils" and their blood rivals, the "Tar Heels" of the University of North Carolina, Chapel Hill. Now, K-ville has evolved into a phenomenon where students take turns camping out in tents to get tickets for basketball games anywhere from three to eight *weeks* before the game. Athletics, especially basketball, became a central part of Duke undergraduate culture. More students decide to study abroad during the fall semester than in the spring in order to be on campus for the basketball season in winter and spring. Athletics also brings in millions of dollars in revenue. For the 2018–2019 school year, Duke men's basketball brought in revenue of $35,489,891 and over $13 million in profit.[58]

It is difficult for an outsider to overstate the all-permeating and, I have to say, broadly positive impact of basketball on the Duke campus. As with football at Notre Dame, it is today part of a common culture among students, staff, faculty, and administration. I was on the Duke campus when the men's basketball team won the 2015 national championship. The next day, the 9,314 seats at Cameron Indoor Stadium were filled with students and fans from all corners of the university community to welcome home the team and its redoubtable coach.

When, several years earlier, I was invited to Duke to give an academic talk on China, I was hosted by Claire Conceison, a remarkable scholar and practitioner of Chinese drama and member of Duke's Asian/Pacific Studies Institute. (Today she is Professor of Chinese Culture and Theater Studies at MIT.) Claire taught a course at Duke called "Sports as Performance." It was very popular, I understood, with the basketball team. As I waited for her in her office in the hour before my lecture, one student after another dropped off their papers for her course. Each student was taller than the last. These were, by some measure, the tallest group of undergraduates I had ever set eyes on. As their papers piled up, I knew it would be wrong of me to take a look at them. In the end I could not resist and started reading. They were very good. I was impressed by the students, by Claire (who clearly drove them hard), and indirectly by Coach K, whose program has been untainted by academic scandal.

Figure 7.4. Coach K and the Duke 2015 National Champions men's basketball team. Duke Sports Information.

By 2019 student-athletes, or students on varsity sports teams, made up about 10 percent of the undergraduate student population—less than the percentage at Harvard (with fewer varsity sports), but more preprofessional in their aspirations in certain sports.[59] For sports was a tool for Duke's advancement as a university. Over the last three decades, no serious sports fan in the United States could credibly be unaware of Duke's extraordinary rise in basketball and, by extension, in other areas.

Yet, as elsewhere, there were dark suspicions about the prominence of athletics at Duke. In March 2006 charges of rape, kidnapping, and sexual offense allegations were raised by a Black student at North Carolina Central University, who worked as an exotic dancer on the side, and was hired to perform at an off-campus house party by the Duke men's lacrosse team over spring break.[60] The case drew national attention, and many believed that the culture of athletics had gotten out of hand. As the investigation progressed, the men's lacrosse team, which had been favored to be the national champions that year, was suspended. A year later, after contradictions from the accuser's story and mishandling of evidence by the Durham district attorney emerged, the three young men accused were declared innocent of all charges.[61] Yet the non-scandal scandal lingered in and beyond the university because so many believed it could have easily been true. In its time, the Duke lacrosse incident raised questions on the role of race, class, and elite sports within the nation's top universities—questions that have hardly gone away. Gone, however, is the house in which the incident was alleged to have occurred: it was torn down by the university as it had become a tourist attraction.

By the time Terry Sanford ended his transformative presidency (1969–1985), Duke was at once distinguished and differentiated in multiple areas of the academy. The size of the faculty had increased by 44 percent (in numbers from 984 to 1,424) from 1970 to 1985, but its perceived quality and interconnection had grown faster still. In a 1982 national ranking of biological sciences, Duke received third place, above both UC Berkeley and Harvard.[62] As a welcome external validation of Duke's rise, the university was ranked sixth among American universities by *U.S. News and World Report* in 1985, in the early days of the college-ranking business. Duke would remain in the top ten on the USNWR rankings of national universities every year save one between 1985 and 2020.[63]

Sanford said, in his final annual address to the faculty, "Everyone is seeking excellence, or claims to be. I sometimes think we have misused the word or weakened it by overuse. Excellence is not a brand of cheese. It is not even a place. It is more like a path or a guiding star. . . . It is a spirit; it is a determination; it is a set of personal and institutional values."[64]

Shaping Duke's Future in the 1990s

Nannerl Keohane, president of Duke University from 1993 to 2004, described the Duke she inherited as a "flotilla" of schools. The strategic plans signaled directions and destinations to all ships in the flotilla, as Duke sought to rid itself of "Ivy envy" in competing with and surpassing other major research universities. Duke's admirals, commodores, and captains who followed the signals of the flagship received more resources.

But as Duke's professional schools became more distinguished and better funded, focusing the university's resources grew more challenging. When Keohane took office in 1993, she discovered that as president she had little more than $1 million in truly discretionary funds.[65] While the provost had more resources through his Common Fund and Academic Priorities Pool, these resources did not exceed $3.5 million per year.[66]

In 1992 *A Duke Plan: Positioning Duke for the 21st Century* was released. After Keohane's arrival in 1993, a new strategic plan, *Shaping Our Future*, was unveiled in 1994. In part to fund *Shaping Our Future*, a program of "Virtual Equity" was set up in 1994. Virtual Equity was an institutional reinvestment account (IRA) or an "internal bank," where Duke's different schools deposited their cash reserves to be invested by DUMAC, the Duke University Management Company, which managed Duke University's endowment. (The concept was similar to, but in time much better managed than, that of Harvard's Central Bank.) The schools were guaranteed a return equal to the thirty-day T-bill rate. When the generated returns exceeded 6 percent of the fund's liabilities, the funds were redirected to the central administration to fund strategic initiatives. By 2001 $60 million had accumulated, and future income was projected at $9 million annually.[67]

As before, after planning came campaigns: The Campaign for Duke, launched in 1996, raised $2.36 billion from 250,000 donors, making it at the time the fifth-largest single campaign in the history of American higher education.[68] Duke's endowment, which stood at approximately $700 million in 1994, increased to more than $3 billion by the end of 2003.[69] The success of the Campaign for Duke and the drafting of a new campus master plan (the first since the 1920s) just before the publication of *Shaping Our Future*, allowed the construction of more than forty buildings over the course of Keohane's tenure.[70]

Controlled Chaos and Strategic Planning in Twenty-First Century Duke

Why was planning so successful at Duke? How did plans get traction and legitimacy? Reflecting on Duke's planning processes, Brodhead recalled, "Every unit participated in the planning exercise and there was high-level coordination of the themes that touched everybody. . . . When I read the Strategic Investment Plan, the way it identified funds by which to fund the plan—this was something I had never seen anywhere else." Duke's twenty-first century plans offer the best examples.

By the early twenty-first century, planning was in Duke's DNA. Success in planning was directly related to Duke's governance. While Duke's president was the "chief educational and administrative officer" of the university, the position of provost was a powerful "executive officer under the president responsible for all educational affairs and activities of the University," including strategic planning.[71] Just as Duke benefited from a series of long and successful presidencies, it was shaped also by its provosts. Peter Lange, who became provost in 1999 and remained in the position for fifteen years, stewarded the 2001 *Building on Excellence* and 2006 *Making a Difference* strategic plans.

If Free University of Berlin's Peter Lange was its Iron Chancellor, then Duke's Peter Lange was its Iron Provost. Both were strong forces of continuity and progress for their universities over the tenure of several presidencies. But while FU's Peter Lange played his formidable role noiselessly, largely outside the public eye, Duke's Peter Lange was omnipresent, with a hearty public presence and an energetic ambition to bring into alignment the stars of Duke's firmament. He had the (rare in these positions) capacity to see the big picture of university-wide development and the telling detail of trouble at the department level. The scope of the job of provost at Duke is officially quite simple and quite powerful: "The Provost is the chief academic officer of Duke University, responsible to the President for the University's teaching and research mission." The provost's office at Duke had much greater authority than that at Harvard, where it played a coordinating role, or at Berkeley, with its diminished resources and long tradition of student and faculty revolts. Reporting directly to the provost were Duke's eight schools (and their deans); its eleven interdisciplinary initiatives; six vice provosts over-seeing undergraduate education, academic affairs, finance, and more; and other offices such as those for admissions and research. As always in high-level administrative roles, other duties emerged. Once, in the midst of foot-ball season, Lange received an email stating that in a drumming class with thirteen students, seven were football players. A further concern was that the class had no syllabus. Knowing that the press was searching for instances like these in the wake of an academic fraud scandal at the neighboring University of North Carolina at Chapel Hill, Lange quickly took steps to meet with the relevant dean. In three days, the students were transferred to other classes and the potential crisis was mitigated. As Lange recalled, it was an "example of oversight." In taking on this role and serving for fifteen years, it surely helped that Duke's Peter Lange was a scholar of comparative politics. He became a compelling practitioner, too. Take, again, the case of planning.

Strategic planning under Lange took the form of democratic centralism (or "controlled chaos," in Lange's own words)—with goals set out by the lead-ership—yet with a fair amount of democracy. While individual schools submitted their planning documents to the center, Lange articulated stra-tegic themes that would help to define the overall university plan.[72] A steering committee for the plan facilitated dialogue between the provost's office, the deans, and faculty members, with the latter involved through the elected Ac-ademic Council—a strong, university-wide faculty body with power to ap-prove academic programs—and its subcommittees.

Proposals from schools and institutes were "graded" like student essays (A, B, C, etc.) based on the seriousness of their self-assessments, their vi-sion (or lack thereof), and the extent to which they aligned with the themes outlined by the provost.[73] Cross-school thematic working groups, where fac-ulty could provide input, were created in consultation with the deans of the several schools.[74]

Once the university-wide strategic plan was drafted, it faced formal re-view, first by the Academic Council and then by Duke's Board of Trustees, which had the final responsibility to review strategic plans.[75] For *Making a Difference,* the entire planning process from its beginning to approval by the Board of Trustees took two years.[76]

Lange provided the "control" in the "chaos" of feedback and participation from the broader campus community. Yet some level of "chaos" was indis-pensable to the planning process as it allowed new perspectives to be heard and incorporated, created support from multiple stakeholders, and ensured that goals outlined by the plan reflected the realities of the schools' capabilities and interests. As Lange recalled, "Controlled chaos means that we [senior leadership] create the framework, the boxes that need to be filled. And it's going to be very hard for the planning process to add or change the boxes. But then it is up to the faculty, with our overview, to fill in the content of the boxes."[77] Provost Sally Kornbluth, who succeeded Lange, recalled that "part of the reason the previous plans looked so prescient is that they actually captured what was going on. You can't lead anybody anywhere without organic growth and a lot of faculty buy-in."[78]

Building on Excellence with Deeper Pockets

A critical foundation of recent planning at Duke was its Strategic Investment Plan (SIP), which allowed the central administration to finance major initiatives for the university. Through the SIP and other means, resources were gradually gathered from the periphery and moved to the center of the university. Duke's leadership was fortunate in having among its ranks a second, long-serving administrator: its treasurer and executive vice president, Tallman Trask III, who served as the university's chief administrative and fiscal officer. Trask was responsible for an extraordinary range of activities, including the budget, finances, procurement, debt, campus planning, architecture, maintenance and construction, human resources, academic and administrative computing, and more. Gradually, steadily, but surely, Trask brought financial capacity to the center of the university. Trask had one ironclad rule in managing Duke's complex finances for strategic purposes: "Never take from people money that they *know* they have."[79]

In May 2000 Duke's Board of Trustees approved a new spending rate and distribution structure for income from Duke University's endowment. The resulting change generated $45 million over a five-year period for strategic investments by the deans of Duke's different schools with the agreement of the provost.[80] Combined with another $10 million from other unassigned and unrestricted income sources and income from the Virtual Equity program created in 1994, a total of $160 million was placed at the disposal of Duke's president and provost between fiscal year (FY) 2000–2001 and FY 2004–2005 to fund strategic initiatives; this was a sharply higher figure than the approximately $4.5 million annually available in 1994 when *Shaping Our Future* was drafted.

Lange was charged with spending these funds well. He achieved this through the SIP created in *Building on Excellence*. Combined with school resources, the SIP amounted to $727 million in spending over the course of five years. Duke had already gained recognition as one of the top ten universities in the country; the strategic initiatives outlined in the plan were meant to help it become one "among the small number of institutions that define what is best in American higher education."[81] Above all, as Lange recalled, "We decided in 1999–2000 that Duke could not be the national university leader we aspired to be in the twenty-first century with the 'boutique' engineering school we had then."[82] This led to major strategic investments in engineering and in what would become, thanks to a lead gift by Ed Pratt, a Duke alumnus who was chairman and CEO of Pfizer, Duke's renamed and expanded Pratt School of Engineering.

Although central financial resources accounted for only 22 percent ($160 million) of the entire SIP, these central funds encouraged schools to follow the university's central priorities. "Only a small percentage of academic funding was in the strategic programs," reflected Brodhead, but "the strategic initiatives meant that the autonomous units had massive self-interest in collaborating to win the small margin."[83]

Making a Difference in 2006

Building on Excellence was followed by *Making a Difference* in 2006. Duke's "enduring themes"—now central to the university's identity—were explicitly called out in *Making a Difference*. In addition to interdisciplinarity, internationalization, and diversity, new leitmotifs such as "knowledge in the service of society" were added to reinforce the plan to "make a difference."[84] *Building on Excellence* had emphasized science and engineering; *Making a Difference* now added "the centrality of the humanities and interpretative social sciences" as an enduring commitment. "Affordability and access" remained a central goal. Already offering need-blind admissions, Duke followed Harvard's lead by eliminating parental contributions for students from families making less than $60,000 per year and eliminating loans for families making less than $40,000 per year in the 2008–2009 academic year.[85] As with *Building on Excellence*, goals for *Making a Difference* were backed up by the SIP, with a planned $1.3 billion expenditure over the course of six to eight years.

But all of Duke's planning could not foresee the Great Recession that began in 2008. Implementation of the SIP was interrupted. In March 2009 Brodhead acknowledged in a letter to members of the Duke community that "the disappearance of short-term investment returns [had] removed a significant source of revenue for strategic initiatives."[86] Duke's endowment, which stood at $6.1 billion in June 2008, shrank by 20 percent, which was projected to decrease the university's operating budget by $100–125 million by 2012.[87]

To minimize damage, university leadership froze salaries for all Duke employees making more than $50,000 per year.[88] Hundreds of jobs were eliminated by voluntary retirement programs; tight controls were placed on vacancies and overtime.[89] Planning for construction continued but construction of new buildings was delayed.[90] In April 2009 Lange told the deans of Duke's various schools to review their school-level strategic plans to further prioritize scarce resources.[91] Thanks in part to these measures, the long-term trajectory of the university did not appear to be fundamentally affected. Duke's endowment, which had bottomed out at $4.4 billion in 2008–2009, returned to growth, passing the $7 billion mark in 2013–2014, and reaching $8.6 billion at the end of 2019. By July 2021, Duke's endowment stood at $12.7 billion.[92]

Duke managed its way through the crisis without a financial meltdown (or a liquidity crisis like Harvard) and with its sense of mission intact. Peter Lange drafted a letter to the faculty: "At times like this, it is sometimes useful to draw upon history. Duke was born and began to thrive in the midst of this country's deepest economic despair. Through skill, vision, hard work, and an entrepreneurial spirit, our university rapidly exceeded even the most optimistic expectation to assume a position of leadership in the nation and the world."[93]

Despite the financial crisis, the *Making a Difference* plan of 2006 still allowed university administrators to (as Brodhead put it) "build the architecture of the Duke Forward campaign [launched in 2012] on a very richly orchestrated consensus among the schools." The campaign reached its goal of $3.25 billion in July 2016, a year ahead of schedule.[94]

The newly enduring theme of "knowledge in the service of society" took root. Launched in 2007, DukeEngage allowed 4,800 Duke students to volunteer more than 1.6 million hours in six hundred community organizations in forty-six US cities and eighty-four countries by summer 2019.[95] The Sanford Institute for Public Policy was upgraded to a school in 2009, demonstrating commitment to using interdisciplinary approaches to address policy issues and provide service to society.

Together with interdisciplinarity and internationalization, civic engagement had become a part of Duke's signature branding. Noah Pickus, former Associate Provost and former Director of the Kenan Institute for Ethics at Duke, observed that "when you ask Duke students on their applications why they choose Duke, everyone always used to say, great school, basketball. Now in principle they say, great school, DukeEngage, civic engagement."[96]

Planning Interdisciplinarity

Every university talks about "interdisciplinarity" as a key to academic innovation: How do we get colleagues from different fields to work together on common problems? How might the insights of disciplines as distinct as psychology and economics be focused? Or, simply, how can universities get around the sclerotic organizational rigidity of long-standing departments in which appointments are rooted? As a younger and hungrier institution, Duke saw interdisciplinarity as a differentiator. Major administrative changes were made in the 1990s to stimulate interdisciplinary programs. An Office of the Vice Provost for Interdisciplinary Studies (OVPIS) was created, and money followed. Interdisciplinary initiatives expanded in 2001 under *Building on Excellence,* with over $150 million of the $727 million Strategic Investment Plan devoted to distinctive programs such as the John Hope Franklin Humanities Institute, the Institute for Genome Sciences and Policy, and the Social Science Initiative.[97]

Duke's passion for the interdisciplinary accelerated under *Making a Difference.* The Duke Global Health Institute was founded with a big aim: to reduce health disparities in communities worldwide based on collaboration between medicine, economics, political science, and other fields.[98] Brodhead lured to Duke his old Yale colleague, Michael Merson, then Dean of Public Health at Yale's School of Medicine. Merson energized the new Duke effort, leading it to national prominence and, unusually, embedding its activities and (often joint) faculty appointments in nearly every school at Duke. Other initiatives and institutes launched between 2006 and 2016 spanned areas of brain science, health policy, energy, entrepreneurship, and big data.

Together these formed what became known as Duke's UICs, or "Signature University Institutes and Centers."

The UICs proved to be a magnet to attract talent to Duke. *Making a Difference* stressed the need for joint and "cluster" hiring of faculty drawn to interdisciplinary work of strategic importance at Duke.[99] The UICs offered centrally financed research funds and encouraged joint appointments across the university.[100] Joint appointments almost anywhere can sound better than they are, and younger faculty in particular worry about "falling between two stools" in multi-school appointments. To energize the effort, Provost Lange set up a Joint School-UIC Tenure/Tenure Track Faculty Hiring Program, which provided funds over a nine-year period for joint hiring of faculty appointed half-time in a UIC.[101] By 2018 there were a total of 104 joint faculty appointments across different schools and UICs at Duke.[102]

The UICs gave administrative support, physical space, and technical training and services to interdisciplinary efforts, by 2018 managing $33 million in internal and external faculty grants.[103] The Duke Center for Genomic and Computational Biology offered customized genetic sequencing for labs in biological sciences, biomedical engineering, and the School of Medicine.[104] The Social Science Research Institute sponsored workshops on quantitative methods in social sciences across multiple social science disciplines.[105] Being in competition with older and better endowed universities, the centralization of services across different schools and disciplines built serious economies of scale, enabling Duke, as Provost Sally Kornbluth explained, "to do more with less."[106]

Planned interdisciplinarity emerged as a major part of Duke's identity. In Brodhead's opinion, Duke had achieved "a deeper understanding that interdisciplinarity wasn't just a cool thing" but engendered "new forms of intelligence that are going to be needed to solve problems in a successor generation."[107] According to Lange, Duke's UICs became central to faculty recruitment and retention and "put a stamp on Duke as an interdisciplinary place," even for colleagues who were not associated with the institutes.[108] Haiyan Gao, a distinguished physicist, observed that while interdisciplinary research was "pretty fashionable" when she joined the faculty in 2002, after over a decade of investment, interdisciplinary research was "becoming a part of the Duke DNA" since most of the faculty she knew were involved, "consciously or subconsciously," in interdisciplinary research or teaching.[109] Kornbluth thought Duke's willingness to cross disciplinary boundaries had helped the school put together "combinations" that became "unique niches that other people later wish they had been in," which in turn helped Duke to "punch above its weight."[110]

But—to extend the boxing metaphor—what weight class was Duke in? Lange recalled that when he first joined the Duke faculty in 1981, "we still had a lot of Ivy envy. And I would say that one of the biggest changes in Duke over the last twenty years is that we don't have Ivy envy anymore. Really." It was, Lange felt, particularly in its interdisciplinary drive, beginning with the *Crossing Boundaries* plan, that Duke came to realize that "Our success is dependent on not being exactly like [those guys]. We have assets that allow us to be different than those northeast guys, and we need to employ those assets to be different, not similar." Even the undergraduates, with whom there was "a shitload of Ivy envy" twenty years ago, had come to realize that Duke was a compellingly singular place.[111]

Together Duke 2017

Duke kicked off a new round of strategic planning in December 2014 under the leadership of Provost Kornbluth. The draft plan, which in 2017 was named *Together Duke: Advancing Excellence through Community*, recalled Duke's now "strong foundations" of interdisciplinarity, globalization, and knowledge in service of society.[112] The strategic plan had four goals, backed by an additional $132 million of centrally mobilized resources.

When university-wide strategic planning began at Duke in 1959, Duke was an all-white university in the American South, celebrating its regional excellence while becoming aware of the distance it had to go to achieve national prominence. In 2019, 57 percent of Duke's nearly sixteen thousand students were racial or ethnic minorities or were from another country. It was a top ten university in the United States, and it ranked among the top thirty universities in the world.[113]

In the flotilla of Duke's schools, the School of Medicine was ranked in the top fifteen in the United States in 2019 along with the School of Law.[114] The School of Nursing, which was phased out by the *Directions for Progress* plan in 1980, was reorganized and revived in 1985 to focus on graduate education and research. By 2019 it ranked number two for graduate nursing programs in the United States.[115] In 2019 USNWR ranked the Fuqua School of Business tenth best among business schools.[116] Thanks to the Nicholas School of the Environment, Duke was ranked sixth in the world for programs in environment and ecology.[117]

Duke was now unquestionably successful at home, with a growing international reputation. It determined now to make its mark abroad, particularly in Asia.

Planning Internationalization

The first significant reference at Duke to internationalization occurred in the 1972 strategic plan. Duke was by then a national, American university, but only marginally global in reach or intent. It had some academic presence in international studies, the most successful being its (British) Commonwealth Studies and South Asia programs.[118] In the early 1970s only 1 percent of undergraduates studied abroad.[119] The foreign nationals studying at Duke consisted of less than 1 percent and 11 percent of the undergraduate and graduate student bodies, respectively.[120]

Only two decades later did active planning begin to internationalize Duke. In 1992 Peter Lange chaired a faculty committee urging Duke's internationalization abroad and on campus. In 1994 President Keohane appointed Lange as the first Vice Provost for Academic Affairs and International Education (later renamed to Vice President and Vice Provost for Global Affairs) to mobilize Duke's internationalization.[121] Lange's ambitions, reflected in Duke's 1994 *Shaping Our Future* strategic plan, called for Duke to become "a leading international university and be recognized as such."[122] *Shaping Our Future* asked Duke's leaders to "become visible bearers" of the university's commitment to internationalize and build its international reputation by actively establishing partnerships abroad.[123]

Internationalization gained traction in the schools. For example, in 1996 Duke's Fuqua School of Business launched a Global Executive MBA program, which allowed executives who lived anywhere in the world to obtain an MBA with courses on the internet coupled with "residencies" in multiple sites: Dubai, London, New Delhi, Shanghai, St. Petersburg, and Johannesburg, in addition to Durham itself.[124] A Cross Continent MBA program was launched in 2000 for early and mid-career professionals.[125]

By 2001 Duke had formed two hundred academic partnerships across the globe.[126] The *Building on Excellence* strategic plan called also for increasing the number of international students at Duke and encouraging Duke students to study in non-English-speaking countries.[127]

Internationalization accelerated when Brodhead became president in 2004 and was formalized as an enduring theme in the 2006 plan, *Making a Dif-*

ference. Under Brodhead, internationalization intersected with interdiscipli-narity and civic engagement. DukeEngage and another program, Duke Immerse, allowed undergraduates to collaborate closely with faculty and conduct interdisciplinary research that was then tested in practice in sites around the world. In his 2011 address to faculty, Brodhead stated, "Intellectual work is increasingly done collaboratively, in partnerships not limited by physical location. The university that fails to build connectivity to a broad array of high-end partners will be the backwater of tomorrow." Duke students could now also study abroad with the forty-three programs administered by Duke; 47 percent of the class of 2020 students chose to do.[128]

In Durham, Duke's twelve international and area studies centers provided interdisciplinary teaching to students, as well as research expertise and linkages to different regions around the globe. Duke's interdisciplinary UICs sponsored their own international activities, with internationalization a central component of their strategic plans. In 2017 the Global Health Institute alone hosted 115 students in twenty-five countries around the world for field work.[129]

Duke–NUS Medical School

It is one thing to internationalize at home; it is quite another to build campuses around the world. Along with New York University, Duke became a first mover among contemporary American universities in building a physical presence abroad. In 2005 Duke entered into an agreement with the National University of Singapore (NUS) with strong backing from the government of Singapore, which was determined to make Singapore the biomedical hub of Asia. This American-style graduate medical school was designed both to train physicians and to produce leaders in biomedical sciences for Singapore and beyond. The school's 26,000-square-meter Khoo Teck Puat Building was finished three years ahead of schedule and became operational in May 2009 under the name of Duke-NUS Graduate Medical School (Duke-NUS). The curriculum was modeled on that of Duke's School of Medicine, and Duke retained decision-making power on academic affairs. At the time, the CEO of DUHS, Victor Dzau, said, "The success of Duke-NUS is integral to the success of Duke Medicine's mission of transforming medicine and health to improve peoples' lives around the world."[130] Better health care for Americans now started in Singapore.

Duke-NUS was Duke's first permanent physical presence abroad and was an unqualified success. The project validated a main reason for making internationalization a strategic priority—the recruitment of talent. The access to Asian patients for clinical research in an American medical school setting and to unique understudied diseases in Southeast Asia proved attractive for many potential Duke faculty recruits. Duke expanded the reach of its faculty through its presence in Singapore and additional partnerships in Asia built through Duke-NUS.[131] The collaborative agreement between Duke and NUS was extended in 2010 and again in 2016. The success of Duke-NUS engendered further ambition—this time in China.

Duke Kunshan University

The pioneering origins of Duke University can be traced to its founding in rural North Carolina. Its signature international venture would be found in a place once part of the Chinese countryside. Until the late twentieth century, Kunshan was more famous for its "hairy crabs," which could be found on every Shanghai plate in autumn, than it was for business, let alone for education. Kunshan had been a center of learning in the Ming (1368–1644) and Qing (1644–1912) dynasties. But in modern times, Kunshan had become a backwater, a forgotten town between the big industrial cities of Shanghai and Suzhou.

All that changed with China's "opening and reform" that began in 1979. Under the dynamic and business-savvy leadership of its local government, Kunshan became a center of foreign direct investment from Taiwan and Singapore, and a center of global electronics manufacturing. This self-starting city became a national model in China for rapid and sustainable development. It was the wealthiest small city in China by the 2010s.

By the time Kunshan approached Duke University in 2006–2007 to explore the possibility of building a joint-venture campus, its government, led by its energetic mayor and Party secretary, Guan Aiguo, imagined a future with Kunshan as the Silicon Valley of China, focused on education, research, and development. Eager to attract a renowned research university as a potential magnet for talent, Kunshan offered Duke free land and agreed to pay for the construction of a two-hundred-acre residential campus.[132] It has been estimated that if the first phase (one-third) of the campus had been built in Durham, it would have cost as much as $260 million.[133]

Guan Aiguo found his entrepreneurial partner in Blair Sheppard, the incoming dean of Duke's Fuqua School of Business. Sheppard had spearheaded the creation of Fuqua's Global Executive MBA and Cross Continent MBA programs. He was CEO of Duke Corporate Education (one of the leading executive education programs in the United States) when he was asked to lead Fuqua. A visionary and innovative dean, Sheppard planned a series of global campuses for Fuqua in order to offer truly international business education and to differentiate Fuqua among leading American business schools. He visited Kunshan in 2006 and 2007 and reached a framework agreement with lightning speed.

The faculty at Fuqua—ranked in the top ten American business schools—was not used to moving with lightning speed, and they resisted Sheppard's global vision. But Duke's leadership, Brodhead and Lange, embraced the challenge on behalf of the university. When a Cooperation Agreement was signed between Duke University and the government of Kunshan in 2010, Fuqua would still take part in the project, offering one of the several planned master's degrees, but Duke's vision was bolder still: to establish, in Kunshan, an undergraduate college in the arts and sciences at Duke's standards.

Partnering with Wuhan University, China's oldest comprehensive university, located in a city bearing the same name in China's central province of Hubei, Duke signed a "Cooperation Principles Statement" in January 2011. The project was now officially known as "Duke Kunshan University" (DKU), and "Kunshan Duke University" in Chinese translation. Duke's investment in the first phase of the DKU project was approximately $42.5 million, which included a $5.5 million initial investment and an estimated $37 million over six years to cover 52 percent of DKU's operating costs.[134] The City of Kunshan agreed to provide the land, the construction, and the other 48 percent of operating costs.[135]

Wuhan University was a fitting partner for China's most prestigious joint-venture university. Wuhan and the surrounding province of Hubei have long been leading centers of commerce, scholarship, and political leadership. It was the great reforming Governor-General Zhang Zhidong who founded in 1893—five years before Peking University was established—the "Self-Strengthening Institute" that would become Wuhan University. The Self-Strengthening Institute initially focused instrumentally on the study of those subjects that would bring about China's return to "wealth and power," primarily mathematics, science, and business, although not initially at the expense of China's educational tradition. Zhang's famous *Exhortation to Study*, published in 1898, argued that "Chinese learning" (education in the classics) had to remain the foundation, while "Western learning" was for "practical matters." By 1928, however, Wuhan University had become one of China's first comprehensive, national universities, with a distinguished and internationalized Faculty of Arts to match those in Law, Science, and Engineering. After 1949 the university was reordered on Soviet models and then became one of the national centers of strife and bloodshed during the Cultural Revolution. Today it is again a major comprehensive university, with a faculty of four thousand teaching a student body of thirty-four thousand undergraduates and twenty-one thousand graduate students and regularly ranked as fourth among Chinese universities. Duke's prospective partner in China had seen it all.

Duke's culture of strategic planning helped it launch DKU, which became a university-wide endeavor at Duke, mobilizing deans, vice presidents, and faculty, organized into multiple committees. The faculty-led Academic Council and Board of Trustees had final authority on curriculum and major commitments. In September 2012 Duke appointed Liu Jingnan and Mary Brown Bullock to serve as chancellor and executive vice chancellor, respectively, of DKU. Liu had been the president of Wuhan University from 2003 to 2008, and Bullock was the president of Agnes Scott College from 1995 to 2006. This combination of leaders from China and the United States, the former with a background in the engineering sciences and the latter in Chinese history and the liberal arts, represented the multifaceted goal of DKU to be a world-class, comprehensive university, rooted in the liberal arts, in one of the most commercial cities in China.[136]

To address concerns about intellectual freedom in China—where the ruling Communist Party was at once powerful and powerfully insecure—and to ensure Duke's control over a project that carried significant reputational risk for the university, DKU's final Joint Venture Agreement vested the "highest authority" at the school in an independent Board of Trustees on which Duke had full veto power. Senior administrators from Duke, including its provost, were ex-officio members. Internet access, which was censored by the infamous "Great Firewall" in China, would be unrestricted on DKU's campus through a virtual private network (VPN) with servers in Singapore.[137]

Duke had limited liability financially for DKU, except for the amount it agreed to contribute to its operations, and it had the right to withdraw its name from DKU should it feel necessary. An advisory board of distinguished global business leaders and retired Chinese officials was established to provide counsel, financial support, and political insulation.

A total of 137 students from eleven countries were enrolled in DKU's inaugural master's and undergraduate programs in 2014 when DKU opened. These were curtain-raisers for the larger enterprise of a four-year, liberal arts degree program that began in 2018.

A Liberal Arts Education in China?

Duke had a long history of connection with China. In 1881 Charlie Soong, patriarch of one of modern China's most influential families, attended Trinity College as the school's first international student, returning to China as a missionary, during which time he lived in Kunshan for several years. Still, given the damage that China's universities had sustained during the first decades of the People's Republic, and especially during the Cultural Revolution, the challenges of introducing (or, more accurately, reintroducing) an education in the liberal arts in China could not be underestimated. By the early twenty-first century, however, the belief that a liberal arts education could be a driver in China of innovation and entrepreneurship (as was believed in America) was widely held among presidents of Chinese universities and, indeed, by the Communist Party Secretary and mayor of Kunshan.

For its part, Duke's faculty, which had been conducting research and teaching in China for decades, now had the opportunity of a lifetime: to create an entirely new undergraduate curriculum for a university as yet unencumbered by either full-time students or faculty. A Liberal Arts in China Committee (LACC) was formed in Durham in 2014. According to Professor Haiyan Gao, a member of the committee and Vice Chancellor for Academic Affairs at DKU, committee members spent two years researching global experiments in the liberal arts and sciences and visiting multiple Chinese universities.[138] Their final curriculum promoted integrative and international learning that (in the Duke tradition) de-emphasized disciplinary boundaries. It stressed an education of "rooted globalism," with the mission "to cultivate informed and engaged citizens who are knowledgeable about each other's histories, traditions of thought and affiliations, and skilled in navigating local, national, and global identities and commitments with an international perspective."[139] To stress Duke's responsibility for the graduates of its newest school, DKU students would receive a Duke University degree.

After two years of intense discussion over the scale of the operation, China's potential restrictions on academic freedom, and reputational risks for Duke, the Academic Council of Duke's faculty overwhelmingly approved the DKU curriculum in November 2016. The result of the vote was the fruit of assiduous outreach by Duke's leadership to convince its faculty to embrace a strategically important but "high risk, high reward" proposition for the school. Brodhead and Kornbluth met with representatives from every school and many more members of the university's various governance committees to answer any questions they had regarding Duke's plans in China. Testimonies by Duke's faculty members who had worked at DKU that they encountered only unimpeded freedom to engage in discussion of even controversial subjects on DKU's campus were also crucial in alleviating faculty concerns. At the Academic Council meeting in October 2016, Brodhead made perhaps the strongest argument: "China is a part of every issue involving global health, global environment, global economics, global security, global information security, and everything else. . . . A university that can't find a way to engage in China will be a university that is unable to give its students the kind of education that will help them understand the world they need to be actors in." The Board of Trustees approved the degree program unanimously the following month.[140]

This was, in my view (and I was, by this time, Duke's Senior Advisor on China), university governance at its best. Brodhead and Lange (and later Kornbluth) established multiple layers of faculty oversight committees both to gain advice and to make the faculty part of the creative process of DKU. Budgetary figures (and risks) were shared openly and fully. Debate was robust, especially in the elected Academic Council. There were, as diplomats say, full and frank exchanges of views within the Academic Council. Duke's Board of Trustees—a larger and much more professional governance body than the Harvard Corporation of the early twenty-first century—studied the multiple proposals for DKU in both committees and plenary sessions. (It may have helped that the board was led by G. Richard "Rick" Wagoner, Jr., the former chairman and CEO of General Motors, who had personally negotiated the joint ventures in China that saved GM as a company.) At the end of the day, the faculty voted overwhelmingly and the trustees unanimously for the full establishment of DKU.

The support DKU received from the Duke community ran in contrast to the establishment of the first joint Chinese-American university in the People's Republic of China: NYU Shanghai.[141] Headed by the former president of Cornell, Jeffrey Lehman, NYU Shanghai has been an extraordinary success. But while Duke led a determined and transparent campaign of consultation with faculty on the development of DKU, NYU faculty criticized President John Sexton of pushing through NYU's international campuses by fiat. Sexton eventually departed after faculty passed the fourth vote of no confidence in his leadership. (NYU's experience would still benefit Duke: the executive vice chancellor for DKU in 2021 was Alfred Bloom, the founding vice chancellor of NYU Abu Dhabi.)

Meanwhile, in Kunshan, DKU's first master's programs and research centers, established in 2014, had attracted talent and research funding to the city and had further raised its profile internationally. Upon Duke's approval of the undergraduate program, Kunshan agreed in May 2017 to fund a second, larger phase of construction. There would still be financial challenges for DKU's operating costs, which it would have to meet by tuition and other income.[142] Duke's contribution to DKU's operating costs was capped at $5 million per year,[143] plus an additional $1 million annually to fund research or educational projects for Duke faculty in Kunshan.[144]

Duke's determination to build Duke Kunshan University proved to be a compelling, but not an easy, investment. A spectacular campus, in a style at once local and global, was in place to welcome its first undergraduates in the liberal arts and sciences. The Jiangnan (lower Yangzi) region in which Kunshan is located is marked by "water towns," of which the old center of Kunshan is one. The DKU campus was designed with water at its center, organized around a large man-made lake, with buildings and residences connected by bridges and walkways. Clad both in glass and in the distinctive white stone of Jiangnan, its terraces and pavilions offer calming water views for classrooms and conferences. To be sure, not all of the construction went smoothly. Duke erred by not sending its own facilities people to oversee construction in the first years, with resultant problems of delay and redesign. Kunshan, after all, had never constructed a campus for a "world-class" university. And so, when the first undergraduate students arrived, they and the faculty were housed in a downtown Kunshan hotel. (That necessary experiment went very well, for I recall a senior Duke faculty member who taught in Kunshan that term telling me with enthusiasm, "Now I know that a university is not a set of buildings.") By August 2019, however, phase one of the

Figure 7.5. Academic Building on the Duke Kunshan University campus. Dove Feng/Wikimedia Commons/CC BY-SA 4.0.

campus, which comprised six buildings, including the university's Innovation Center, was complete.[145] Construction for phase two, which would add twenty-two additional buildings, was set to finish by 2022.

Now that we have built it, Brodhead wondered, would they come? How would DKU, like its ancestor in Durham, form a university as fine as its architecture?

Into the Future

When Duke's latest strategic plan was approved by the Academic Council in May 2017, Richard Brodhead's term as president was coming to an end. In December 2016 Duke's Board of Trustees had elected Vincent Price as the tenth president of Duke University. Price, the provost and chief academic officer of the University of Pennsylvania since 2009, seemed ideally suited to lead Duke. He had academic appointments across Penn (as the Steven H. Chaffee Professor of Communication in the Annenberg School for Communication and Professor of Political Science in the School of Arts and Sciences), and he served as a trustee of the Wistar Institute, a nonprofit biomedical research institute, as well as on the executive planning group for University of Pennsylvania Health System. These positions left him prepared to oversee Duke University's own powerful health system.[146] As provost, Price also led Penn's global strategy, hiring the university's first Vice Provost for Global Initiatives and spearheading the creation of the Penn Wharton China Center in Beijing, which opened in 2015.[147] After Price became Duke's tenth president in 2017, he looked to the future, toward "Duke's Second Century" by outlining a strategic framework with five core areas: "empowering people, transforming education, building community, forging partnerships, and engaging our network."[148] He oversaw the launch of DKU's four-year undergraduate program in August 2018. That year, DKU welcomed an inaugural class of 266, larger than the planned-for 225 because of a particularly successful recruitment season. They hailed from 27 countries, with 175 coming from mainland China, 10 from Taiwan, 39 from the United States, and 42 from elsewhere. Former President Brodhead spoke at DKU's first undergraduate convocation, telling his audience that "the partnership [between Duke and Kunshan] has worked because the contributors share an essential attribute, a commitment to plan for the long term."[149]

In early 2020 Duke and its ambitious internationalization faced a new challenge. COVID-19 emerged first in Wuhan, home to DKU's Chinese university partner, Wuhan University, about five hundred miles from the DKU campus. As of August 2020 there had been nearly 90,000 confirmed cases and an official death toll of 4,715 in China, but because of the country's relative success (after an initial cover-up) in containing the virus, it was not in the top thirty countries globally in total number of infections.[150] China's initial virus outbreak forced DKU into emergency actions. As with other universities in China, DKU followed the Chinese Ministry of Education's direction to move classes online. Yet moving a whole liberal arts campus to a remote, online format set out a significant challenge during a time when DKU was recruiting its third class.[151] Then in May 2020, after China controlled the virus, DKU fully reopened and welcomed staff back to campus. After being closed for nearly a semester, this was a joyous occasion.[152] Meanwhile, across the world and especially in the United States, the virus spread like wildfire, eventually to the home campus.

Like many American universities, Duke in Durham attempted a hybrid reopening of campus in fall 2020. Only freshmen and sophomores, as well as select students requiring campus housing, were welcomed back into on-campus residences. Those on campus could attend courses in person, but

President Price noted that all students should expect to "complete much of their course work remotely."[153] As at other US universities, international students were unable to enter the United States during the pandemic, but here DKU gave Duke an advantage. Unlike Duke in Durham, DKU welcomed to campus all students who were in, or able to enter, China. DKU thus opened its doors to 160 stranded students from Duke and other US universities.[154] Duke students studying at DKU would receive full credit from classes there for their Duke degrees.[155] While many viewed DKU as a risk at first, a robust overseas physical presence, particularly in China—the top country of origin for Duke's international students—was now an obvious asset in a world where international travel and connectivity were no longer a given. In the autumn of 2020 the safest Duke campus for teaching and learning was not East or West Campus, but its watery *Far Eastern* campus at Kunshan, the only place in the world where all Duke instruction could be held in person and in one time zone.

In his inaugural address as president, Brodhead had marveled at Duke's enduring capacity of metamorphosis, that willingness to "remake itself in sometimes fairly drastic ways to the end of becoming better." In private discussions, Brodhead contrasted Duke with more established universities, such as the Yale he knew so well. In such places it was "very hard for the school to want to do anything except to continue to extend the things the school was excellent in doing." Theirs, he said, in a telling phrase, was the "inertia of excellence." Duke, by contrast (in the words of Nancy Andrews, Dean of the School of Medicine from 2007 to 2016), was "inspired by its traditions but not determined by them."[156]

The challenge for Brodhead's successor would be to continue with innovation rooted in relentless planning so that Duke would grow as a research and global university on its own terms. "My anxiety for Duke," Brodhead said, "has always been that it would enter a phase of complacency. That it would tell itself that it was reaching for the stars when it was actually only reaching for the nearest shiny thing."[157]

In 2020 Duke faced a trifecta of challenges: a public health crisis, another global recession, and rising US-China tensions. A university that had planned its way toward interdisciplinary innovation and internationalization faced the prospect of an era of deglobalization. Meanwhile, "inspection teams" from the Chinese Communist Party's disciplinary enforcement body were paying visits to leading Chinese universities seeking to root out "corruption" of the ideological sort. They had yet to visit DKU. Yet as several Duke colleagues had pointed out during the Academic Council's debate on the DKU curriculum, these political challenges were confirmation of how important it was for Duke to remain engaged and, indeed, to be a leader in China and there, as at home, to set global standards.[158] After all, building an institution that might one day serve as a model for teaching and learning for forty million students in the world's second-largest economy was nothing less than an outrageous ambition.

CHAPTER EIGHT

A Chinese Century?

The Revival and Rise of Chinese Universities

I N   T H E   twenty-first century, it is China that has the greatest ambitions for higher education, and its rise has been truly staggering. In 1978, after a decade of mostly closed universities, Chinese universities enrolled approximately 860,000 students.[1] This number increased gradually until 2000, with enrollment of about seven million at that time. The government subsequently accelerated the pace of expansion, and by the year 2010, over thirty million students were enrolled in Chinese universities. In 2020 there were more than forty million students in Chinese institutions of higher learning.[2]

In 1998 Chinese colleges and universities graduated 830,000 students annually; by 2010 the number was 6 million.[3] In 2000 China had approximately half the number of university students as the United States; by 2020 it had more than twice the number.[4] In 2000 there were 1,041 colleges and universities in China.[5] A decade later there were more than twice as many: 2,358.[6] From 1999 to 2009 Chinese institutions of higher education hired nearly 900,000 new, full-time faculty members.[7]

For most of the history of the People's Republic, higher education was an opportunity afforded to the very few. Now China has moved toward mass higher education. The gross enrollment ratio (college participation rate) of eighteen- to twenty-two-year-olds was 3 percent in 1999; it was 30 percent in 2013.[8] By 2020 over 50 percent of young adults in this age cohort were enrolled in colleges or universities.[9]

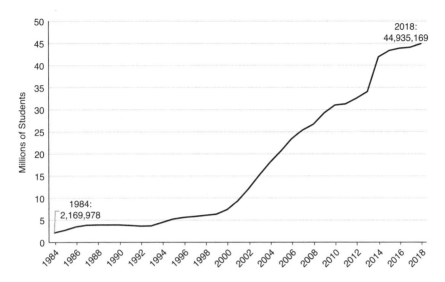

Figure 8.1. Tertiary education enrollment in China, 1984–2018 (in millions of students). Data source: UNESCO Institute for Statistics http://data.uis.unesco.org/#, accessed August 22, 2020.

This expansion of higher education is altogether new in its scope, but it is also a modern manifestation of centuries of dedication to advanced learning. To understand the Chinese higher education sector today, we must first look back at its foundations in imperial and Republican China.

Legacies of Learning

China is home to the world's longest continuous civilization, with the longest continuing sets of philosophical and literary traditions. Before the introduction of Western-style higher education in the late nineteenth and early twentieth centuries, the study of these traditions defined not only what it meant to be a scholar but also what it meant to be powerful. Imperial China's civil service examination was the gateway to elite status. The educational system that prepared candidates for the test focused not on statecraft or tax collection but instead on what we would today call the humanities: the classics of Chinese civilization that set out principles of human behavior that servants of the state were to follow.

There has seldom been a higher academic ideal: good people embarking on the living study of great books in order to do good work in government for the benefit of society. As Song dynasty Emperor Zhenzong (968–1022) wrote, in his poem "Urge to Study," "When a man wishes to fulfill the ambition of his life / He only needs to diligently study the six classics by the window."[10] In imperial China, higher learning could transform one's destiny. The classical canon tested by the civil service examination was created during the Song era (960–1279) to include the Four Books (*Great Learning* and the *Doctrine of the Mean*—which were both originally from the *Book of Rites*—the Confucian *Analects* and *Mencius*) and the Five Classics (*Classic of Poetry, Book of Documents, Book of Rites, I Ching,* and the *Spring and Autumn Annals*).[11] The examination also required candidates to demonstrate knowledge of past and present government policies and the ability to write in good literary style.

Aspiring officials sat through tiers of examinations at the district, prefectural, provincial, and national levels. Candidates would enter the examination compounds with much ceremony, bringing with them only food, water, and their personal bucket for human waste. Test-takers would remain in their own examination cell until the multiday examination was complete; the only way out before a cannon shot signaled the end of the exam was as a corpse, thrown over the compound wall.

In navigating these brutal examinations, would-be scholar-officials rose through a system of local, provincial, and national examinations and preparatory institutions, at the pinnacle of which was the Imperial Academy (*taixue,* later known as *guozijian*) located in the capital of the empire.[12] Those who achieved high enough results on the examination could become members of the Hanlin Academy at the court and act as researchers, consultants to the emperor, and overseers of the examination system.[13] Complementing this formal, government-run system was an elite local system of academies, or *shuyuan,* run by scholars or academic societies. By late imperial times, *shuyuan* were increasingly associated with civil service examination preparation, but at times offered radical or differing interpretations of the body of literature found in the examinations.[14]

The civil service examination, like the imperial educational system that flowed from it, was the meritocratic bedrock upon which several of the world's greatest empires were built. It allowed—theoretically, at least—for social mobility in an otherwise hierarchical society, elevating only the truly educated into positions of power. Yet, as Benjamin Elman has shown, social mobility was never its purpose—a modest amount of it was instead an "unexpected consequence."[15] And there were practical limits to this system in more modern times: the absence of the study of mathematics, science, and practical affairs in the examinations did not mean that the empire was thereby better governed. Their absence arguably contributed to the empire's feeble capacity in the nineteenth century to respond to a militarized, industrialized, and otherwise energized West in a series of humiliations that would spell the end of a two-thousand-year-old imperial tradition. By the end of the nineteenth century, the system was admired more abroad than at home.

As Western powers encroached upon China in the nineteenth century, the Qing court attempted to modernize the civil service examination, broadening the tests to include subjects such as mathematics in 1887.[16] Some regional *shuyuan* began to offer courses in mathematics, Western languages, science, world geography, and world history by the 1890s.[17] At the same time, both the court and private citizens set up new modern training institutes to enable China to study and compete with the West. The empire fell in 1912, but the more important date in education is 1905, when the ancient examination system was abolished. It would be replaced by an emerging system of higher education that would educate several "new Chinas."

Foreign Models for a Modern China

Taking the place of the examination system and the academies associated with it was a set of new colleges and universities on international models founded in late Qing and early Republican times. Theirs was the complex and often contradictory challenge that Wilhelm von Humboldt would have recognized: to bring global knowledge and international standards of higher education to China, while still serving the state and nation. The emergence of a Western-style university system in China began in Wuhan, a center of learning in imperial times, and the site of the founding of China's first modern university: the Self-Strengthening Institute (later Wuhan University) in 1893. Led by Governor-General Zhang Zhidong, its early, instrumentalist focus was toward the study of those subjects that would bring about China's return to "wealth and power," primarily mathematics, science, and business, although not at the expense of China's educational tradition.

What began in Wuhan soon spread throughout China, as a diverse crop of institutions sprouted up, heavily influenced by the higher education systems of Europe, Japan, and the United States. Public universities developed strong ties to foreign entities. Tsinghua University was founded in 1911 with

Boxer Indemnity funds returned by the United States. Tongji University in Shanghai grew into a private and then public university in the 1920s out of its origins as the German Medical School founded in 1907, and it has maintained its German connections to this day. Foreign influence was evident also in the universities and colleges established by various missionary groups, including St. John's University in Shanghai, founded by American Anglicans; Aurora University, founded by French Jesuits in Shanghai; and Yenching University, founded in Beijing by American Methodist Episcopalians and Congregationalists. Facing a mainland already dominated by foreign counterparts, the British raced to wield their educational influence by establishing the University of Hong Kong in 1911.

The influence of foreign models in reshaping education in China comes as no surprise, for modern Chinese history is inescapably international. During the eras of the First (1912), Second (1927), and Third (1949) Chinese Republics, each republic sought legitimacy in the form of one or another internationally authenticated "ism," from constitutionalism to communism. If the civil service examination had been a foundation of the Chinese empire's strength, international partnerships in higher education have energized modern China's century-plus long rise.

As international institutions introduced new models of higher education to China, returning Chinese scholars educated abroad helped them to flourish and endure. Faculty, deans, and presidents were recruited from the growing number of young Chinese studying internationally. The best early example of this trend was Cai Yuanpei, who served multiple terms as president of Peking University and studied in Germany and France from 1906 to 1910 and again from 1912 to 1916.

Prior to his European studies, Cai had passed the highest level (*jinshi*) of the imperial civil service examinations. Named in 1912 as the first Minister of Education of the new Republic, Cai issued an official opinion that universities should not simply serve government but should be granted institutional autonomy and be places for an "education with a worldview" (*shijieguan jiaoyu*), that is, an education with global perspective. Cai's reforms were deeply influenced by the German model of higher education. For instance, he believed in the separation of universities and technical schools, and he explicitly stressed the importance of *Bildung*, of broad, humanistic learning as the foundation of both teaching and scientific research (in the sense of *Wissenschaft*).[18]

When Cai Yuanpei assumed the presidency of Peking University in 1917, he introduced a broad range of international practices into Chinese higher education. He declared in his inaugural address: "People outside the university . . . observe that all who study here have it in their minds to become officials and get rich." Students, he said, should devote themselves to learning, not in narrow specializations but in the humanities and natural sciences. Cai's presidency saw the rapid growth of the humanities at "Beida," as Peking University became popularly called, and he phased out the business and engineering divisions. Cai famously stressed that:

> The modern principle of freedom of thought has already been publicly accepted, but the ability to make this happen rests solely with the university. The expression of thought by university teachers is not only free of restriction by religion or political parties but also free of constraints imposed by renowned scholars. . . . This is what makes a true institution of higher learning. . . . We must follow the general rule of freedom of thought and freedom of expression, and not allow any one branch of philosophy or any one tenet of religion to confine our minds.[19]

Cai recruited to the Peking University faculty the scholars Chen Duxiu and Li Dazhao, who would be instrumental in introducing Marxism to China. He recruited also China's leading proponent of liberalism, the philosopher Hu Shi, a student of John Dewey at Columbia, who had written, "For a country to lack a navy or an army is not a cause for shame; [but] a country without a university, a national library, museum, or art gallery, should be ashamed."[20] It was in the tradition of this intellectually vibrant and diverse Peking University that its students would play dramatic roles in challenging successive Chinese governments in the liberal and patriotic public demonstrations of 1919, 1935, and, eventually, 1989. Cai's presence is still felt today on the Beida campus, where a statue of his likeness stands not far from the liberal arts college named for him.

China's internationalization in higher education was at the center of the most transformative age in modern Chinese culture, the roughly ten years from 1915 to 1925, now known as the "May Fourth era." It was a cultural revolution more profound and enduring than the so-called Great Proletarian Cultural Revolution of Mao Zedong. The May Fourth Movement, unlike Mao's, focused on renewing Chinese society, rather than razing it. Its most famous moment occurred on May 4, 1919 (giving the era its name), when patriotic students protesting the Treaty of Versailles, which transferred Germany's territorial concession in China to Japan, rather than returning it to

China, poured out of the modern Red Building of Peking University to demonstrate at the nearby Forbidden City. Just a few thousand students took part, but they brought China's new universities to the forefront of Chinese political life.

In 1922 China's government sought to adopt what Ruth Hayhoe, a leading scholar of Chinese higher education, has called an "American ethos" in primary and secondary education.[21] Legislation broadened the definition of "university" to include not just institutions dedicated to theoretical studies but also those focused on professional or applied fields. This represented a shift from the German-influenced model, which drew a sharp distinction between universities and technical schools, toward a more inclusive American conception. The legislation also introduced the system of credits, which allowed students greater freedom to customize their studies. Reflecting the ambitions of the state, the legislation established a board of managers to make administrative decisions at universities, seeking to limit the role of professors in university governance.

This system-wide American influence was short-lived. As the Nationalist government consolidated power in Nanjing after 1927, it began also to exercise more centralized control over higher education.[22] In the 1930s it reorganized the higher education system according to recommendations from a League of Nations commission led by former Prussian Minister of Education C. H. Becker.[23] Reforms, made with the encouragement of the commission and heavily influenced by Prussian models, led to increased government control over a nationalized system of higher education. Political authorities favored more comprehensive universities in the 1920s, but the 1930s saw emphasis once again placed on science, mathematics, and engineering.[24]

Internationalization also took architectural form. In the twentieth century, the old examination compounds gave way to leafy campuses modeled after American and European universities. Tsinghua's campus reflects its American and (later) Soviet partners. National Central University in Nanjing channeled the University of Berlin. Alternatively, one can admire the *jingyuan* at Peking University, a lovely campus in Chinese style, built for its predecessor institution on that site, Yenching University—and designed by a New York architectural firm.

When war with Japan struck in the 1930s, Chinese universities chose to relocate and reimagine themselves during this period of tumult. As the Japanese army encroached upon Chinese borders and occupied urban centers, universities sought refuge in unoccupied areas. This movement began with the relocation of Dongbei University from Japanese-occupied Manchuria to Beijing in 1931, but it became larger in scale after 1937 when the Japanese army gained control of major cities such as Beijing and Shanghai. By 1938, 54 higher education institutions out of 114 had been damaged or destroyed by Japanese forces, and by 1941, in a heroic and patriotic migration across China, 77 institutions had relocated to temporary, safer locations.[25] At the apex of the wartime higher education system was the National Southwest Associated University (*Guoli xinan lianhe daxue*), a union of Tsinghua, Peking, and Nankai universities that remained a bastion of liberal thought and academic work despite its wartime surroundings. John Israel, an American historian who has written on *Lianda*, as it was called for short, argued that the chaotic political environment left universities free to flourish, much as they had under the less organized central governance of the 1920s.[26] This changed, however, as the war of resistance gave way to civil war and then to a new political regime, by which time most universities had returned to their original locations on China's eastern coast.

Before 1949 China had developed a vibrant and diverse, if small, system of higher education on international standards. Its leading scholars were internationally minded and often internationally educated. Its students were trained according to pedagogies and curricula broadly aligned with those at leading Western universities. In short, the intellectual and architectural foundations of every major Chinese university were international in origin.

Restructuring and Destruction, 1949–1978

The Communist takeover prompted a sizeable flow of academic emigration from China's leading universities to Taiwan, Hong Kong, and, especially, the United States. After 1949 mainland Chinese universities ceased cooperation with Western partners but redirected their international efforts East: collaboration now took place with the Soviet Union and its East European allies, as Chinese higher education was restructured to support a planned economy on a Stalinist model. Management of higher education was centralized (as it had been under the Nationalists) under a national Ministry of Education, which initially recommended gradual reform. However, as the Soviet Union consolidated its influence in China in the early 1950s, the higher education system changed dramatically to emulate Soviet approaches. Institutions were reorganized to focus on specific tasks and subjects, often separating theoretical areas of study from related practical fields. In these sovietized institutions, there was a marked separation of teaching and research: universities were to be dedicated to the teaching and transmission of knowledge, while research activities were largely housed at separate academies that existed outside the higher education system.[27]

Throughout the 1950s and 1960s, the higher education system became at once ever more controlled and compartmentalized. In the 1950s Communist Party organs were established in every university to ensure ideological orthodoxy. Governance decisions were made within increasingly smaller units within university departments. Students entered into one of an expanding panorama of specializations (from 249 in 1953 to 627 in 1962 to over 1,000 in the 1980s), and they studied a uniform curriculum within their specialization. The goal of education was to serve the state and the Chinese Communist Party (CCP), not necessarily in that order; enrollment quotas for academic departments were decided according to the needs of national economic development plans, and universities were charged with political, not just academic, education.[28]

Mao Zedong's "Cultural Revolution," unleashed in 1966, nearly destroyed Chinese higher education.[29] From 1966 to 1969 enrollment of new students was stopped completely, intellectuals were persecuted, and several universities became political and military battlegrounds between competing Party factions. When reinstated in 1970, admissions were based on "mass recommendations" and political credentials, rather than the national college entrance examination (*gaokao*). Candidates were to be recommended by "the masses" (in practice by a "work unit," or place of employment), approved by leaders, and reviewed by the schools.[30] In principle, students were to be admitted in the first instance from the ranks of "workers, peasants, and soldiers," thereby upending the traditional structures of privilege. In practice, this system produced a cohort of university students with wildly divergent levels of academic preparation, while the lack of formal entrance exams favored the politically well connected.[31] Only with Mao's death and the ousting of his loyal "Gang of Four" in 1976 was the stage set for the restoration of China's universities, once again as part of a global world of universities.

The Contemporary Chinese University System

Deng Xiaoping, who emerged as China's paramount leader in the post-Mao years, never attended university. But his father had studied at an early Chinese university, and, at the age of fifteen, Deng Xiaoping was shipped abroad to a work-study program in France, where he joined the Chinese Communist Party. He would later study briefly in Moscow. By the 1970s as a vice-premier having survived (barely) the Cultural Revolution, Deng was an early and vigorous supporter of reviving higher education. His beliefs that "scientific and technological development are the keys to modernization" and that "education is the basis of cultivating science and technology" were cited to justify reforms within higher education during a brief period of liberalization in the early 1970s.[32] Universities saw such statements as signs that higher education would soon be formally restored, and they began eliminating Cultural Revolution-era practices of their own accord by the mid-1970s.[33] The State Council affirmed this trajectory when it announced the *gaokao* would resume in October 1977.[34] The Party's recognition that China needed a new approach to national development after the catastrophe of Maoist rule underpinned the fast pace and wide scope of early reforms in higher education.

When universities reopened fully in 1978, the State Council moved swiftly to clear the wreckage of the Cultural Revolution. It established a long-lasting strategy of funneling extra resources into elite universities. It labeled eighty-eight universities as "key," with Peking, Tsinghua, and Fudan Universities selected as the top three institutions.[35] Key universities acted as the vanguards of the system, offering new degree programs, increasing their research, and garnering high levels of government funding. To supplement its own support for universities, the Chinese government sought foreign aid for this effort. In fact, the World Bank's first loan to the People's Republic of China (PRC) was $200 million to support the development of science and engineering departments at twenty-six universities in 1980.[36] A small number of elite institutions were run under the direct supervision of (and received more funding from) the central government, either through the Ministry of Education or another relevant department. Provincial and municipal governments were left to supervise and at least partially fund the remaining public colleges and universities.

During the 1980s the government experimented with a return to the principles guiding Chinese higher education in the early Republic, affording institutions greater intellectual autonomy and administrative control. Government leaders recognized that to develop growth-enhancing science and technology, Chinese intellectuals required space to set their own research agendas.[37] In 1982 constitutional reforms included legal protections for intellectual work, and the 1985 "Decision on Education Reform" went so far as to declare that "the key to restructuring higher education will lie in eliminating excessive government control over institutions of higher education."[38] That same year, government policy called for universities to become centers of both teaching and research, undoing the bifurcation of the Soviet model in the 1950s and 1960s. In brief, universities were deemed essential components in China's overall "opening and reform" agenda.

Yet during the early years of the reform era, Chinese higher education failed to meet the state's great expectations. Universities produced a glut of graduates who struggled to find jobs in China's still emerging economy.[39] Economic discontent combined with political protest in the huge and prolonged demonstrations—in which university students played a catalytic role—that took place in multiple cities in the spring of 1989, most famously in Beijing's Tiananmen Square. Deng Xiaoping's decision to crush the demonstrations by force led to the death of hundreds of students, the arrest and exile of thousands more, and enduring tensions between universities and the state. As a nationwide crackdown unfolded in the summer and autumn of 1989, the government reversed its position on political interference in academia. Deng Xiaoping now declared that "the biggest mistake of the decade was in education, particularly in regards to ideological and political education."[40] As in 1949 academic repression led to another wave of intellectual migration, largely to the United States and Europe. (One of my own doctoral students, the historian Wang Dan, had been a Peking University student leader of the Tiananmen protests. He served multiple prison terms in China before being exiled to continue his studies at Harvard. He came to us with stellar and proud recommendations from Peking University faculty. He remains active in the overseas movement for democratic reform in China.)

Tiananmen convinced Chinese political leaders that higher education should, first, be subservient to the Party and state and, second, serve China's developmental aspirations. In the early 1990s caps were placed on the growth of university enrollment to prevent the system from expanding further while officials debated how to proceed.[41] Soon, new restrictions were placed on teaching and research in the humanities and social sciences, reflecting the government's belief that these disciplines required greater ideological supervision. Yet higher education was again prioritized and liberalized when economic reforms restarted in 1992. And the system overall continued to grow. From 1999 to 2006 the total number of Chinese higher education institutions grew from 1,071 to 1,867.[42]

In 1993 the State Council announced that, throughout all levels of government, spending on universities should reach 4 percent of GNP by the year

2000. Actual expenditures on education hovered around 2.5 percent of GNP until 1997,[43] when an external shock, the Asian financial crisis, galvanized the government to increase infrastructure investment, including the construction of new university campuses, raising enrollment caps to fill these institutions. This was at once an investment in the future and a means of keeping unemployed young Chinese off the streets for an additional four years. From 2000 to 2003 the government's appropriations for higher education jumped by at least 20 percent each year and continued to increase by at least 10 percent annually until the financial crisis in 2008.[44]

Between 1998 and 2003 enrollment in Chinese universities tripled. In 1999 alone enrollment increased by 510,000 students.[45] The state-set target enrollment rate for the university-age population was raised from under 10 percent in 1998 to 15 percent by 2002. As China entered the new millennium, its universities were poised to play an even greater role in the country's economic and social development.

By the summer of 2020 there were 2,688 higher education institutions in China, including 1,265 four-year universities.[46] Of the four-year universities, 76 reported to the Ministry of Education; 38 to other central government,

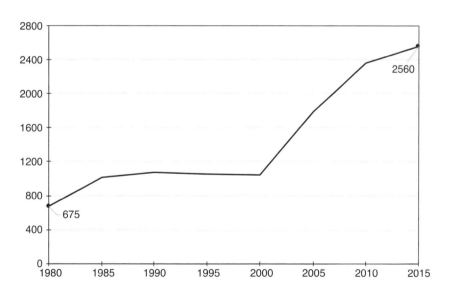

Figure 8.2. Total number of regular tertiary institutions in China, 1980–2015. Data source: China Statistical Yearbook 2018, http://www.stats.gov.cn /tjsj/ndsj/2018/indexeh.htm, accessed August 22, 2019.

CCP, or military organs; and 708 to provincial authorities.[47] Another 434 were classified as private institutions. Of these, over half (275) were so-called independent colleges, founded by public universities as a means to extend their outreach, enrollments, and, especially, income, for they could charge "private university" tuition rates.

Despite the fact that private ownership and administration of tertiary educational institutions were legalized only in 1982, the sector expanded rapidly, especially in the first two decades of the twenty-first century. Whereas private higher education institutions made up 6 percent of the higher education sector in 2002, by 2013 they accounted for over 30 percent of four-year institutions and 19.7 percent of student enrollment in higher education.[48] The number of four-year, degree-granting private institutions rose from 30 in 2007 to 423 in 2015, an increase of over 1,300 percent. One such institution can be found in the city of Xi'an, an ancient Chinese capital, where entrepreneurs worked with local officials to make that city China's capital of private higher education. Xi'an International University (*Xi'an waishi xueyuan*), founded in 1992 as an examination prep center, is now one of China's largest private universities, with a student body of thirty-four thousand. Its graduates enjoy better job placement rates than those of Peking or Tsinghua Universities. Unlike university presidents the world over, Xi'an's president, Huang Teng, does not worry about his tenure: he owns 55 percent of the university. President Huang has looked to establish branch campuses elsewhere in China and in North America.[49]

Large companies are also getting into the higher education game. Alibaba's Taobao unit launched "Taobao University" to train e-business owners, managers, salesmen, and professionals, and in time to extend business education to more than one million online students seeking the skills to start and sustain small- and medium-sized businesses. Taobao University made plans also to enroll some twenty thousand students "offline," that is, in person.[50]

Other forms of private institutions include new Sino-foreign joint-venture universities, which were established in China for the first time since the Communist revolution. Nine such institutions, whose foreign partners include universities from both the United States and the United Kingdom, have brought higher education and research centers beyond the plans of the Ministry of Education.[51] Modern British universities pioneered this movement, with the establishment in 2004 of the University of Nottingham Ningbo China, in partnership with a private Chinese education company. It offers liberal arts, engineering, and business education to eight thousand students in one of China's leading business cities. Its main structure is an architectural emulation of the elegant Trent Building on the Nottingham campus. The University of Liverpool partnered with Xi'an Jiaotong University to establish in 2008 a campus in the eastern industrial city of Suzhou, with a mission to "educate technical and managerial professionals with international perspectives and competitive capabilities."[52] In 2013 New York University established NYU Shanghai as a vertical university (that is, in a high-rise) as part of its global network and in partnership with one of China's most creative universities, East China Normal University. And, as we have seen, Duke University's two-hundred-acre residential campus in Kunshan, China's richest and most entrepreneurial town, located just west of Shanghai, opened its doors in 2014 as Duke Kunshan University.[53]

For all this expansion, land and capital have been made available by a variety of means. Land in China is owned by the state, specifically local governments, who have broad authority to expropriate it and to pay little in compensation to its historical inhabitants, often farmers. The result has been a quintupling in the acreage of Chinese universities since 2000. Old universities have built stunning new campuses. Zhejiang University, which was founded in 1897, houses its fifty thousand students across seven large campuses. Chongqing University, established in 1929, has opened beautifully landscaped new university grounds as part of an eight-university *daxuecheng*, or "university city." Until recently, higher education institutions had been concentrated in but a few areas, Beijing and the lower Yangzi region chief among them. Today cities and provinces never known for higher education compete to found, build, and expand colleges and universities—often within new science and technology zones—as part of their competitive strategies for growth, development, and prestige.

Unlike the growth of American universities in the 1950s and the extraordinary expansion of European institutions that began in the 1970s, the development of higher education in China has been elitist, focusing the majority of resources on a small subset of institutions favored by the state, as well as massive. The government-supervised higher education system was keen on tracking and comparing the performance of universities identified as nationally significant. The first university league tables, produced by the Chinese Academy of Management Sciences for publication in the state-run *Science and Technology Daily*, ranked the research performance in science, engineering, agriculture, and medical sciences of only eighty-six "key" universities.[54] Universities important enough to be measured for their contributions to key disciplines began to win rewards for subjecting themselves to such scrutiny in the 1990s. In 1995 the Ministry of Education launched "Project 211" to enhance the quality of about one hundred universities. It was followed in 1998 by "Project 985" to support thirty-nine elite universities, of which nine—China's so-called Ivy League—would be developed as "world-class" institutions (*guoji yiliu daxue*), defined as being "cradles" of high-level, creative researchers; frontiers of scientific research; forces of transformative research and innovation; and bridges for international exchange. To that end, Chinese central, provincial, and local governments, supplemented by university foundations and private philanthropy, have provided enormous revenues to the leading institutions, well outspending the (very significant) rewards given in recent European competitions, such as the Excellence Initiative in Germany.

In 2018, 44.94 million students were enrolled in some form of higher education institution in China.[55] The diversity, scale, and resources of the higher education landscape in China have left room for significant differentiation between its most and least elite institutions. Chinese universities have become deeply embedded in international networks of knowledge production and dissemination, seeking to emulate standards set by leaders in global higher education. At the same time, they remain shaped to at least an equal measure by national policies and priorities on university governance, funding, faculty, and students.

Governance

In the post-Mao era, the government transferred an increasing amount of decision-making powers back to universities. In 1985 university presidents were given authority to make most decisions, save those of a political nature, which still fell under the jurisdiction of the university Party secretary.[56] The Higher Education Law of 1998 went further and specified seven areas in which higher education institutions had autonomy. These included both administrative areas, such as financial and property management, international structure, and personnel management, and academic programming decisions, including research and service, international exchange and cooperation, student admissions, teaching affairs, and the establishment of new specializations. In reality, most universities had to maintain close working relationships with the government, in what some have called a "state-supervised" model, in contrast with the "state-controlled" model of the pre-reform era.[57]

This changed with Xi Jinping's ascent to power. In 2014 the CCP reemphasized that public university governance in China occurred under "a system where the university president was responsible *under the leadership of the [university's] CCP Committee*" (italics added).[58] The university's Party secretary headed the university Party committee, while the president normally served as the first-ranked vice secretary. The rest of the committee would consist of other senior school administrators, including vice Party secretaries, vice presidents, and the secretary of the university's CCP discipline inspection commission, which was in charge of anti-corruption probes and, increasingly, "political discipline." The central role of the Party committee in decision-making, and the need for all Party members to "emulate" and "look to the [CCP leadership] core" has been reinforced in recent years in government departments, state-owned enterprises, and all public (and now even private) institutions, as well as universities.

The Party secretaries and presidents of the thirty-one most important Chinese universities (including Tsinghua and Peking) had administrative ranks equivalent to that of a government vice minister. Like all officials at or above vice minister rank in China, they were appointed to their roles by the Organization Department of the CCP Central Committee. With few exceptions, these leaders had to adhere to the mandatory retirement age of sixty-three for vice minister–ranked officials. Other senior leaders at these universities and the top leaders of other universities reporting to central government or Party organs were, in most cases, appointed by the Ministry of Education. Similarly, leaders of provincial universities were either appointed by the Organization Department of the province's CCP committee or its government's Department of Education, depending on their administrative ranks.

As of 2007 approximately one hundred universities (of which twenty were private) had formed boards of directors. However, unlike the boards of American universities, which often carry out governance or supervisory functions and are the legal representatives of universities, boards of public Chinese universities are limited in mandate and tend to focus on fundraising and building connections with industry. Chinese university presidents serve as the legal representatives of their institutions, and sometimes serve on boards. Overall board involvement in university affairs is minimal where Party committees are in charge.

Some private universities in China have taken governance boards more seriously. In 2015 several leading Chinese scholars planned a privately financed institution that could one day become China's Caltech. The result was Westlake University, located in the eastern city of Hangzhou and led by President Shi Yigong. Shi was elected by and responsible to a Board of Trustees chaired by Qian Yingyi, former dean of Tsinghua University's School of Economics and Management. The other nineteen members of the board included Nobel laureate and Caltech president emeritus David Baltimore, current and former leaders of leading Chinese universities, titans of industry and philanthropy, a representative of the Hangzhou city government, and the secretary of the university's Communist Party Committee. In private entrepreneurial universities such as Xi'an International University, boards may serve more as window dressing. As the president of one such institution once told me, "Yes, of course, we have a Board, but I make all the decisions."

A Chinese Excellence Initiative

Growth in the higher education sector during the 1990s and the first decade of the 2000s was accompanied by the expansion and diversification of funding sources. By the end of this period, university funding came primarily from three sources: government, tuition fees, and commercial income.[59] As philanthropic efforts gained traction in China, donations became an increasingly important source of university income as well. By 2008, 108 higher education institutions had established fundraising foundations.[60]

Funding from various strata of government accounted for the largest portion of the budget of many universities, although this proportion was decreasing. Continuing patterns of funding established in the 1950s and 1960s and renewed in the post-Mao era, the government tended to funnel resources to a few select institutions in order to foster centers of excellence.[61] Funding for these elite universities came through two major government projects, the previously mentioned Project 211 and Project 985. Starting in 1995, Project 211 allocated approximately $2.2 billion to approximately one hundred top universities to support curricular and academic development within the disciplines as well as physical infrastructure. Universities applying for Project 211 funding submitted plans for how they would use the money to raise research and educational standards for consideration by the interministerial working group, which included leaders from the Ministry of Education (then the State Education Commission), the National Development and Reform Commission (then the State Planning Commission), and the Ministry of Finance. This working group assessed applications for Project 211 funding against the initiative's principles of "improving the level of national higher education, accelerating the development of the national economy, promoting the development of science and technology, enhancing comprehensive national strength and international competitiveness, and realizing high-level talent cultivation in China."[62]

Subsequently, the government launched Project 985 in 1998 at the centennial celebration of Peking University. Although structured similarly to Project 211, this project focused on allocating funding to a much smaller number of institutions—initially just two, later expanded to nine—but provided them with much larger sums. Both Tsinghua and Peking Universities, the original two universities chosen to participate, received a total of $225 million in the project's first three years. In 2003 the research labs at Project 985-funded universities received nearly half of the annual research funds for higher education despite their universities enrolling only 1 percent of the total students in higher education.[63] The initiative also gave birth to China's Ivy League equivalent, the "C9" group, which is composed of the nine universities that received early Project 985 funding.[64] The government has since expanded the project to provide funding for a total of thirty-nine universities. Between 2015 and 2017 funding under Project 211 and Project 985 was replaced by the Double First Class Universities Program, with "Double First Class" (DFC) standing for "first-class universities" and "first-class academic disciplines."

Universities' funding strategies were shaped also by the state's innovation and industrial policies. Since the higher education system's reestablishment, the state believed universities to be critical for fostering China's scientific and technological development. With the number of higher education institutions rapidly expanding at the start of the twenty-first century, the government experimented with new incentives for universities to focus their research on priority technologies. An early example was the State Council's 2001 announcement of a pilot for-profit enterprise program at Tsinghua and Peking Universities, which allowed them to operate revenue-generating companies that "further promote the industrialization of scientific and technological achievements in universities."[65] Municipal governments also began funding university-based research institutes that aligned with industrial policy priorities, one example being the Beijing-Tsinghua Industrial Development Institute in 1998. As China's industrial policy priorities evolved, so did the research programs universities were encouraged to contribute to. In 2015 the Ministry of Education advised universities that to solve "the poor employment prospects" of their graduates, they should focus on "innovation-driven development, Made in China 2025, Internet+, mass entrepreneurship and innovation, and the 'One Belt, One Road,' and other major national strategies to . . . truly enhance local universities to serve regional economic and social development."[66] As long as they agreed to incubate China's industrial policies, universities were promised greater latitude to develop new sources of income.

For universities outside the reach of these elite government projects, nongovernmental funding became increasingly important. In 1989 the state began to collect some tuition and fees from students, and from 1994, universities themselves were allowed to charge tuition, gaining a way to recoup costs for the first time. By 2001 tuition and fees covered over 50 percent of the total higher education expenditure, although elite universities still tended to have more diversified sources of income.[67] Facing the need for more funding and responding to the government's push to increase enrollment, many universities established affiliated "independent" colleges, as noted previously. These schools enjoyed lower prestige and higher tuition than their parent institutions. Generally, public universities charged the lowest tuition, while private, independent, and joint-venture institutions charged much higher fees.[68]

Support from provincial and local governments became increasingly important for Ministry of Education universities outside of Beijing. The "joint-building" or joint-funding of these universities with local governments became common in the late 1990s. Hoping to attract talent that could, in turn, attract high-tech companies and their investments, local governments launched ambitious projects to build new universities with both domestic and international partners. In 2011 the city of Shanghai partnered with the Chinese Academy of Sciences (CAS) to build ShanghaiTech University. The city spent over $700 million building ShanghaiTech's campus and contributed in part to an additional $3 billion to build surrounding key national laboratories, which were staffed and run with the help of CAS. The co-location of the university with key national laboratories was inspired by the example of the Lawrence Berkeley National Laboratory near the University of California, Berkeley. The teaching and research model at ShanghaiTech was inspired by Caltech. Shanghai municipality provided the land, the start-up funding for the university, and, as of 2018, 98 percent of the university's budget.[69]

Faculty

The Ministry of Education set a goal in 2005 to raise the proportion of faculty members with graduate degrees to 80 percent of all faculty, with PhDs accounting for at least 30 percent.[70] This was an ambitious goal, for even among China's most elite institutions, the proportion of faculty with PhDs at that time was significantly lower than their American counterparts. At Tsinghua University in 2006, PhDs made up 62.7 percent of total faculty, while that year at Yale University, 91 percent held a doctorate. Still, Tsinghua's 62.7 percent represented a rapid increase from 1995, when only 15 percent of the faculty held doctorate degrees.[71]

To improve the diversity within and quality of institutions, the Ministry of Education also sought to break the tradition of "faculty inbreeding," through which faculty members completed their entire academic careers—from undergraduate student to senior faculty—at a single institution. The Ministry stipulated the goal that 70 percent or more of faculty should have completed at least one of their degrees at a different school or in a different department than the one in which they were employed. However, sample data collected by Beijing Normal University in 2009 showed that, although these efforts were starting to show progress, among the universities under the jurisdiction of the Ministry of Education, 57 percent of faculty could be classified as "inbred."[72]

Government policy supported the achievement of these quality improvement and diversification goals: in 2008 the central government launched the Thousand Talents Program, which attracted from overseas sixteen hundred scholars and entrepreneurs, mostly of Chinese descent. This success was followed by the Thousand Foreign Experts program in 2011. Both programs were designed to draw overseas research and innovation talent to China, with a particular focus on entrepreneurs and academics.[73]

Chinese university recruiting efforts overseas achieved highly publicized successes for recruiting both Chinese and non-Chinese scholars. Scholars were attracted to Chinese universities by supportive terms and unique opportunities. In 2007 the former President of Cornell University, Jeffrey Lehman, became the founding dean of the Peking University School of Transnational Law.[74] In 2012 he became vice chancellor of NYU Shanghai. In 2008 Tsinghua University convinced Professor Shi Yigong, then a prominent scientist at Princeton, to give up an endowed chair and turn down a $10 million grant from the Howard Hughes Medical Institute to take up the deanship of Tsinghua's School of Life Sciences.[75] As noted, Shi would later become president of Westlake University, showing Chinese higher education as a system attractive enough to recruit and retain international talent. The halls of top-tier Chinese universities were increasingly filled with scholars who had left tenured positions abroad to participate in the extraordinary growth—in quality as in quantity—of Chinese higher education.

Admissions

Who gets into Chinese universities? As in the time of the imperial civil service examination, success in examination still determines the fate of students. One lone criterion—a high school student's score on the *gaokao*—largely dictates admission into university. Although the *gaokao* is officially titled the National Higher Education Entrance Examination, there have been significant regional differences in the test papers administered in various provinces. While from 1978 to 1987, the exam was standard across the nation, legislation in 1987 allowed each province to adjust the test according to local situations. Whereas each province's exams continued to cover similar subjects, by 2005 only sixteen out of China's thirty-one provinces used the national standard exam papers.[76] The examination usually comprised tests in Chinese, mathematics, and English as well as a set of three other subjects, either in the science track (physics, chemistry, and biology) or the humanities track (geography, history, and politics). The examination was infamous for its complexity, both in terms of the sheer depth of knowledge it required as well as the opacity of its questions.

In most regions, only students with an official residence permit (*hukou*) were allowed to sit for that region's test, despite the increasing number of migrant children who grow up and attend schools far away from their officially registered residences. Apart from the logistical and financial barriers associated with traveling to their (often rural) official residences for an exam, students faced a more fundamental obstacle: universities were allowed to determine regional admission quotas and set the lowest qualifying *gaokao* score for admission. This was ostensibly to give priority at each school to local students. However, since institutional quality varied greatly across the country, this gave distinct advantages to students who were born and raised in the big cities that house the country's flagship institutions. For example, Peking University and Tsinghua University are widely acknowledged to be the best universities in China. They are both located in Beijing. Data from 2013 showed that prospective students from Beijing were 30 times more likely to be accepted at Tsinghua than were *gaokao* takers from Guangdong.[77]

Reforms for this system were announced in late 2014. In the new system, students would be able to take examinations in a wider variety of subjects spread over multiple years of high school, rather than in a two-day national testing blitz.[78] The central government also planned for a greater level of standardization at the national level eventually. Finally, the government asked universities to incorporate other measures of performance beyond test scores to evaluate students' potential, while also moving to eliminate the often-exploited opportunities for students to score additional test points for extracurricular talents.

Still, public universities in China continued to admit students primarily on the basis of their test scores. Private colleges and universities, which were often considerably more expensive and less prestigious than the public institutions, mainly served students whose test scores did not reach the threshold for admittance to public universities. Independent colleges affiliated with public institutions did the same.

A Return to the Liberal Arts?

As higher education institutions moved away from the Soviet-style specialization model and broadened their disciplinary offerings, institutions reconceived their undergraduate curricula. Chinese universities have long had general education (*tongshi jiaoyu*) programs of a certain sort, such as required classes (*bixiu ke*) in Marxism-Leninism-Mao Zedong Thought. And like required courses everywhere, students loathe and endure them. Over the past decade, however, mainland universities, together with those in Hong Kong and Taiwan, have competed to introduce general and liberal education programs that open opportunities for learning across the humanities and social sciences.

The idea of a "liberal education," that concept of German origin now with its deepest roots in North America, has begun to reestablish itself in Chinese thinking about the purpose of higher education as well. Just as many American educators believe (not wrongly) that young Chinese students are better educated in math and science than their American counterparts, many Chinese educators believe that it is the West, and particularly the Americans, who are "innovative" and "creative thinkers" while the Chinese people (despite all their ancient inventions and modern revolutions) remain "traditional," "rule bound," and "rote learners." For this, some blame the tortured path to university admission through the *gaokao*. How can students so completely focused on test scores to enter university possibly be innovators when they get there?

Leading American institutions claim to believe that for a truly liberal education, a study of the humanities is essential. Despite—or because of—a century-long obsession with engineering, this view is shared increasingly today in China's premier universities. Pacesetting Chinese universities believe that China's next generation of leaders should be broadly educated in the humanities and social sciences as well as in the sciences. In 2001 Peking University inaugurated the Yuanpei Program (now Yuanpei College) as part of a broad reform of undergraduate education to foster "a new generation of talented individuals with higher creativity as well as international competence so as to meet the needs of our present age." As we will see, Tsinghua University's School of Economics and Management, under the leadership of Dean Qian Yingyi, who received his doctorate at Harvard and held a professorship at UC Berkeley, has implemented one of the most imaginative programs in liberal arts and general education to be found in any Chinese university—and this in a professional school. Renmin University in Beijing, founded as the "People's University" on a Soviet model, now houses several of China's leading centers for classical studies and Chinese history.

Internationalization

The early twenty-first century has been a time of expansion, outreach, and experimentation in Chinese higher education. These developments in China have promoted cooperation and competition across the realm of "Greater China": Hong Kong, Taiwan, and Singapore all compete with Beijing and Shanghai to be the educational center of the Chinese-speaking world.

While institutions internally sought out international best practices in undergraduate curriculum development, many also became increasingly intertwined in more explicit external partnerships with foreign institutions. Apart from the Sino-foreign universities discussed previously, the hugely successful China Europe International Business School, a joint venture with the European Union, ranks regularly as the top business school in China and among the top twenty-five worldwide.

Meanwhile, nearly every leading international university today believes that it needs to have a "China strategy" and to be somehow involved in the rapid growth of higher education in China. This has given rise to a healthy set of experiments and alternative models of engagement. Apart from formal campuses, Columbia University and the University of Chicago have opened an office and a center, respectively, in Beijing. Stanford University has built a courtyard center within the campus of Peking University. The Harvard Center Shanghai promotes research, student internships, conferences, and executive education in China.[79] Yet currently the Chinese government gives its international educational partners conflicting signals. New cooperative ventures in higher education are praised at the same time that the Ministry of Education terminated more than two hundred cooperative agreements, more than 20 percent of the total, with foreign universities.[80] Still, "Improving how Sino-foreign universities are run" was among the "China Education Modernization 2035" plan's top priorities.[81]

Internationalization is not a one-way street. The Ministry of Education reported that in 2018, over 1.5 million Chinese students were studying abroad.[82] Chinese students accounted for over 30 percent of foreign undergraduate students in the United States and composed the largest group of foreign students in countries as diverse as Finland, Italy, and South Korea.[83] Chinese institutions were internationalizing as well: in June 2015 Tsinghua University announced a partnership with the University of Washington and Microsoft to establish a graduate school for innovation in technology and has recently opened partnerships in Italy, Indonesia, and Chile.[84, 85] Peking University established a business school in Oxford. Xiamen University opened a $300 million campus in Malaysia in 2015, with plans for five thousand undergraduate and graduate students.[86] And Fudan University announced in 2021 its determination to open a campus in Hungary in 2024.[87] These are the first, and surely not last, examples of Chinese universities expanding beyond China's borders.

World-Class Challenges

A little over forty years since the reestablishment of the college entrance examination, Chinese higher education had made great strides in expanding both quantity and quality of education. Long-term investments, such as those in faculty quality and state-of-the-art laboratories, were paying off: the academic reputation of Chinese universities, particularly top-tier institutions, was rising rapidly. In 2008 no Chinese university ranked above two hundredth place on Shanghai Jiao Tong University's Academic Ranking of World

Universities. By 2018 three were in the top one hundred. In 2021 Tsinghua and Peking Universities were ranked fifteenth and twenty-third, respectively, by the QS World University Rankings, the highest levels yet by Chinese universities in any international ranking. Tsinghua ranked above all but two of the American Ivy League schools.[88]

The Chinese government launched the Double First Class Universities Program in 2015 to boost further the standing of Chinese universities in the world. The program was built around a core group of forty-two leading Chinese universities considered either "well on their way" (Type A) or "have the potential" (Type B) to become world-leading universities. All of these forty-two universities were also part of either Project 211 or Project 985 or both. Ninety-five additional Chinese universities were selected as part of the program to become "first class in the world" in specific academic disciplines where they had existing strengths. Among the 110 academic disciplines being targeted, 36 percent were in engineering and technology fields where, by some measures, Chinese universities such as Tsinghua were already first class or even world leading.[89] Universities selected for the program that failed to perform well could be removed from the program and lose preferential funding.

Given the size and diversity of China's higher education sector, it is not surprising that there is a gulf between those who oversee Chinese universities (the central government and the Party-State at various levels) and those responsible for their day-to-day operation. "Education is the cornerstone of national rejuvenation," according to the preamble of China's 2010 National Plan for Medium and Long-Term Education Reform and Development.[90] From the central government's perspective, education takes as its goal the building of *national* strength, developing talent for the collective good, not primarily for individual merit. This viewpoint is in obvious tension with programs of general education at top Chinese universities that aim, like their American counterparts, also to liberate and educate the *individual* to be a critical thinker.

While the central government sees education as serving national strategies, making the best strategic use of the enormous funding now coming from all levels of government, the local and provincial officials who are the main funders of universities often have a shorter-term, more utilitarian viewpoint. They seek to spur economic growth, to enhance the job opportunities of people in their late teens and twenties, and to take advantage of the cheap credit offered by state banks for the expansion of higher education.

Equity and Access

If there is a "China model" for universities, it is not a particularly Communist one. As the historian Zhang Jishun, the former Party secretary of East China Normal University, has argued, just because enrollments have grown does not mean that access and equity have increased in equal measure. Take the case of tuition. There used to be none in Chinese universities. In 2020 a student majoring in the sciences, for example, would pay annual tuition of around $850 at Tsinghua University, a leading public university; $926 at Zhejiang University City College, an independent institution affiliated with the public Zhejiang University; $3,861 at the private Xi'an International University (although many times that in its preparatory programs); and $30,890 to attend NYU Shanghai.[91] While these figures are not high by American standards, the cost of attending a public university could easily exceed one-third of the disposable income of rural residents in China.[92] Tuition at private Chinese universities can be many times their annual income. This has led to a situation in which the poorest students, usually from rural areas, often end up at private universities, which are the most expensive, while wealthier and well-connected students from urban backgrounds have much better access to elite public institutions, which are among the least expensive.

We can see this in statistics of rural students attending Chinese universities. Nationwide, about 50 percent of university students hail from rural families (with a generous definition of what constitutes a rural family), but at the elite universities such as Peking and Tsinghua, only about 20 percent of the student body is made up of students from rural areas. In 2020 the higher education enrollment ratios in China's twelve most rural provinces were on average thirteen points lower than in China's eleven east coast provinces.[93] The Chinese government has now promised "universal higher education."[94] But for China's rural and poor, the army and public security bureaus offer better means of social mobility than do China's mass universities.

Finally, take the case of examinations and admissions. The *gaokao* persists, as did the old imperial examinations, because it has the appearance of rewarding merit and is one of the few national institutions that people believe is fair and honest. In principle, only the best, determined by competitive examination, are admitted. But the limitations of the *gaokao* have long been known, and elite universities are the leaders in setting patterns for alternative portals of entry through additional tests, interviews, "Olympic-style" prizes, and other mechanisms that privilege those of means and position who went to the best schools. The long-standing admissions quota system that favors local over out-of-province students contributes to inequality but also has proven difficult to reform. In May 2016 when the Ministry of Education attempted to increase the number of out-of-province student spots at certain universities, parents in four provinces garnered international media attention with their vocal protests.[95]

China's fifty-five officially recognized ethnic minority communities, which together compose about 8.5 percent of the PRC's population, have also faced barriers to full participation in higher education. But the share of minority enrollment in universities has grown significantly in the last decade, rising over 45 percent from 6.76 percent in 2010[96] to 9.86 percent in 2020.[97] The government has instituted affirmative action–style policies that give China's ethnic minorities a boost in university admissions, generally by lowering the *gaokao* score needed for a minority student to be accepted. At China's most elite universities, Tsinghua and Beida, this strategy seems to have worked, with ethnic minority students making up 9.7 percent of Tsinghua's 2020 freshmen class and about 12 percent of Beida's.[98] While minority representation in Chinese undergraduate programs has been enhanced, minorities represent only 5.47 percent of the postgraduate student body.[99]

Politics

In 2013 the presidents from Fudan, Nanjing, and the rest of China's elite C9 institutions, along with the Association of American Universities and Australia's Group of Eight, cosigned the "Hefei Statement on the Ten Characteristics of Contemporary Research Universities."[100] The signers agreed that "the responsible exercise of academic freedom" is a tenet of contemporary university life.

These ideals have proven difficult to uphold. Perhaps the greatest challenges to the rise of Chinese universities lie in the realms of governance and politics. The hierarchical governance structures of Chinese universities leave many decisions to a very few people. Chinese universities are overseen by Party committees, and the university Party secretary normally outranks, and frequently outflanks, the president. A few extraordinary Party secretaries are key to their university's successes, but as a rule this system of parallel governance limits rather than enhances the flow of ideas. Few Party secretaries—like few presidents of American universities—look favorably upon the prospect of unbridled faculty governance. But the freedom of faculty to pursue ideas wherever they may lead is essential for sustained innovation. Where, after all, do the best ideas come from in universities? Deans and presidents everywhere must make decisions and set priorities. In practice, however, many of the best ideas— those that deans and presidents will be compelled to support on their intellectual merits—will come up from the mistakenly named "bottom": that is, from faculty at the top of their fields. Having an institutional structure to support this is rare anywhere, and in Chinese universities today it is rarer still. By any comparative measure of leading international universities, faculty in Chinese institutions have little role in governance.

It was not a good sign when China's Vice President (and President-designate) Xi Jinping visited China's leading universities in June 2012 to call for increased Party supervision of higher education. Indeed, the visit was a harbinger of the increasing emphasis on government control over the classroom under President Xi's tenure. A communiqué, known as Document 9, which was circulated among Party members in 2013 and later leaked to the media, enumerated seven forbidden topics of discussion, namely the promotion of Western constitutional democracy, "universal values," civil society, neoliberalism, Western (read: independent) journalism, historical nihilism, and, finally, any "Questioning Reform and Opening and the socialist nature of socialism with Chinese characteristics."[101] This weighty list was followed by Document 30, never made public, which called for stronger ideological control in higher education.

Taking the cue from the top, Minister of Education Yuan Guiren railed against the inclusion of "Western" values and ideas in Chinese university teaching. His pronouncements threatened a tightening of the academic freedom that had been expanding on university campuses. At a number of leading institutions, the Chinese Communist Party sought to reassert ideological discipline in the (still) required courses on Marxism-Leninism-Mao Zedong Thought as well as in other realms of the humanities and social sciences. At Peking University, the Party summarily dismissed President Wang Enge, a deeply respected scholar. As Peking University's assertive (now former) Party Secretary Zhu Shanlu wrote:

> We must grasp the right to the leadership, management, and discussion of ideological work tightly in our hands, and we can never put it to the side at any moment, or we will have committed an irrevocable and historic error. Universities are an important battleground for the production and confluence of ideology, and have an important role as leaders, models, and spreaders of ideas to all of society. Only by

firmly grasping the active authority of ideological work in universities will we be able to further strengthen the cohesiveness and appeal of the Party in high intellectual circles, and only then will we win over the youth and win the future.[102]

As a part of Xi Jinping's extensive anti-corruption campaign, "inspection teams" from the CCP's Central Discipline Inspection Commission were sent in 2017 across the country, including to leading universities. There they scrutinized university finances and the political loyalties of their leaders and faculty members. Heads of leading universities were accused of lax enforcement of ideological norms and inadequate work in strengthening Party organizations on campus. The inspection teams also warned that "clues" gathered during the inspection regarding individual disciplinary violations would be passed on to higher investigative organs.

On October 23, 2018, in meetings held on their individual campuses, representatives from the CCP's Central Organization Department announced a series of personnel changes at Peking and Nanjing Universities. Having reached the age of sixty-three, President Lin Jianhua of Peking University, it was announced, was suddenly going into retirement—the second Peking University president to be replaced in three years. He was succeeded by Peking University Party Secretary Hao Ping, who now served as vice Party secretary. Judge Qiu Shuiping became the university's new Party secretary and first in command. Qiu, a Peking University law graduate, spent his early career in local government in Beijing before serving as one of the city's top judicial and security officials, including briefly as the Party secretary of the city's State Security Bureau. Qiu was summoned back to Peking University from the position of president (chief judge) of the Shanxi Provincial High Court. This was not quite the equivalent of academic martial law, but close.

In November 2018 the Ministry of Education released "10 Guidelines for the Professional Behavior of Teachers in Colleges and Universities in the New Era," which underscored the Party's view that universities and their faculty must not cross political red lines. In President Xi Jinping's self-proclaimed "new era," professors were to meet "new and higher requirements . . . to implement the fundamental task of establishing morality." What were these requirements? At the top of the list were "no words and deeds that harm the authority of the Party Central Committee."[103]

Meanwhile the Party increased its authority over university governance. Between 2013 and 2017, 109 universities publicly published their institutional charters for the first time.[104] To varying degrees, these documents pledged that universities would adhere to the Party's leadership and follow its political prerogatives. In late 2019 three universities released revised charters further elevating the position of the Party in their institutions. Fudan University, one of China's most renowned institutions, removed references to academic independence and freedom of thought in favor of language supporting Party governance and patriotism.[105]

Challenges to Chinese universities' world-class aspirations came not just from within but also, and increasingly, from without. As the US-China economic clash over technology and innovation grew, Chinese universities and their international exchanges became caught in the crossfire. Cutting-edge research in engineering and the applied sciences relies on access to the latest software and hardware. The US government, particularly under the Trump administration, viewed Chinese universities' research in these areas as aiding the Party-State's military-civil fusion (MCF) strategy. Begun in 2015 MCF provided incentives for institutions throughout the Chinese economic and social landscape, including universities, to aid the People's Liberation Army in developing technology for military end uses.

To be sure, this policy is not unlike the many agreements between the U.S. Department of Defense and American institutions of higher education and private firms. Still, in May 2020 the Trump administration issued an executive order that would block the students, graduates, and affiliates of "Chinese entities that support China's MCF strategy" from entering the United States on certain visas often used to support academic and cultural exchanges.[106] Then in September the US government revoked over one thousand visas for Chinese students and researchers suspected of having ties to the Chinese military.[107] The US government also put, for the first time, two Chinese universities (Harbin Institute of Technology and Harbin Engineering University) on the U.S. Department of Commerce's "Entity List," which requires American firms to receive US government approval to sell their technology to targeted organizations.

Cases

Let us turn now to three case studies of leading universities in greater China. At various points in time, all three have led in higher education in greater China and aim to lead again. First, I will examine Tsinghua, often referred to as China's MIT but which, in recent years, has become China's most globally competitive comprehensive university. Second, I present Nanjing University, the modern incarnation of the institution known during the Republican period as National Central University, itself modeled on the University of Berlin. Geographically and, at times, intellectually distant from the national government, Nanjing University is today a battleground in the Communist Party's campaign for control over higher education. Finally, we turn to the University of Hong Kong, which has the distinction of being the best university in the Chinese-speaking world that is not—at least not yet—under the direct leadership of the Chinese Communist Party.

All three of these institutions have legacies that span the history of modern higher education in China. All three have histories of partnership and cooperation with universities and experts outside of China's borders. Do these three have the potential to lead the world of higher education in the twenty-first century?

CHAPTER NINE

From Preparatory Academy to National Flagship

Tsinghua University

O N SUNDAY, April 21, 2013, a crowd gathered at the Great Hall of the People on Tiananmen Square in central Beijing to inaugurate a new college at Tsinghua University. Letters from Chinese President Xi Jinping and US President Barack Obama were read aloud, followed by video testimonials from past and present American secretaries of state: Henry Kissinger, Colin Powell, and John Kerry. Together with Chinese Vice Premier Liu Yandong, who hosted the meeting, all identified the founding of Schwarzman College at Tsinghua as a landmark in the history of US-China relations and in the ascent of Chinese universities. The vision of Tsinghua and of the new college's benefactor, the American businessman and philanthropist Stephen A. Schwarzman, was to build a residential college that would house and educate, in China, the global leaders of the twenty-first century. Schwarzman College and its resident Schwarzman Scholars program would match in ambition and endowment the Rhodes Scholarships at Oxford University, which for more than a century have been committed to educating those "with potential for leadership."[1]

The dynamic president of Tsinghua University, Chen Jining (a rising star who would go on to become China's Minister of Environmental Protection and then mayor of Beijing), noted that the new college and program were part of Tsinghua's long history of internationalization. But whereas the university once prepared Chinese citizens to study in the United States, Tsinghua was now to be the educational destination of top postgraduate students from America, Europe, Asia, and beyond. With the celebration of the new program,

Tsinghua, already at the apex of China's rapidly expanding domestic higher education system, was announcing its arrival onto the global higher education stage.

Wars, Revolutions, and the Evolution of Tsinghua

Tsinghua University today is one of China's two leading universities and one of the world's elite schools in terms of admission. China and the world of Chinese higher education have come a long way since Tsinghua was founded in 1911, the *xinhai* year of the Xuantong Emperor (that is, the last year of the last emperor of the last imperial dynasty, which was overthrown in 1912). The history of Tsinghua mirrors the story of higher education in modern China.

Tsinghua, like the University of Berlin, was founded in the aftermath of catastrophic military defeat. In the summer of 1900 the ruling Qing Empress Dowager Cixi declared war on the world, or at least on Great Britain, the United States, Russia, Japan, France, Germany, Italy, Spain, Austria-Hungary, the Netherlands, and even Belgium, bowing to a powerful antiforeign movement known as the Boxer Uprising. In the subsequent "Fifty-five Days in Peking," a small contingent of foreigners (led by Charlton Heston and Ava Gardner in the Hollywood version) held out in their legations in Beijing before an expeditionary force of eight nations came to their rescue. Just 20,000 foreign troops subdued an empire of 400 million. The subsequent peace brought with it a crushing indemnity ($10 billion in 2018 prices) to be paid over the next four decades.

The humiliation of the Qing Empire was complete, but in its final decade—the first decade of the twentieth century—it restarted a series of "self-strengthening" reforms, not the least in education. Tsinghua, founded by the Qing court as *Tsinghua xuetang* (Tsinghua Academy), began as a preparatory school for students selected to study in the United States. At the urging of then-president of the University of Illinois, Edmund J. James, US President Theodore Roosevelt remitted a large portion of America's Boxer Indemnity funds for the education of Chinese in the United States and the establishment of Tsinghua. China, James wrote to Roosevelt, was on the edge of revolution. "The nation which succeeds in educating the young Chinese of the present generation," he wrote, "will reap the largest possible returns in moral, intellectual, and commercial influence."[2]

In its first decade, Tsinghua built up an American-style campus—its Jeffersonian Grand Auditorium inspired by the auditorium at Urbana-Champaign—to prepare its students for study in the United States. American-educated Chinese scholars led young scholars through an eight-year preparatory program that qualified them to transfer into American universities as juniors. Because Tsinghua's main patron was the United States government, the academy was governed not through the Ministry of Education but by the Ministry of Foreign Affairs, and the American Ambassador to China maintained an implicit power to approve presidential appointments and budget decisions for the academy.[3]

When Tsing Hua College (as it was formally known in English—we will simply call it Tsinghua here) opened its doors on April 29, 1911, its sixteen students could choose from ten available disciplines: philosophy, Chinese literature, world literature, arts and music, history and politics, math and astronomy, physics and chemistry, biology, geology and geography, and athletics and craftsmanship.[4] The curriculum also included linguistic and cultural preparation for the students' future studies in America. The student body quickly expanded, as did ambitions for the institution, which reflected an increasing demand across China for domestic higher education. By 1925 Tsinghua had transformed itself into a university of liberal arts and sciences and was home to China's leading Institute of Chinese Studies, the *Guoxue-yuan*. Its famous "Four Tutors"—Liang Qichao, Wang Guowei, Chen Yinke, and Zhao Yuanren—added international and scientific dimensions to the study of Chinese language, literature, linguistics, and archaeology.

Tsinghua's influence went well beyond China. Its history department, founded in 1926, was chaired for its first decade by T. F. Tsiang (Jiang Tingfu), a recipient of an American liberal arts education at Oberlin and a doctoral degree from Columbia. Tsiang revolutionized the study of China's modern international relations. He would go on to a distinguished diplomatic career, serving as the Republic of China's ambassador to the United Nations from 1946 to 1966. My own mentor in Chinese history, John K. Fairbank, the pioneer of modern Chinese studies in the United States, learned his Chinese history from T. F. Tsiang at Tsinghua in the early 1930s. Tsinghua's influence on Harvard continued: the undergraduate course on Chinese history that Fairbank began teaching at Harvard in 1939 became central to Harvard's General Education programs for more than eighty years; my colleague Peter Bol and I teach a rather different version of it to this day.

Figure 9.1. John K. and Wilma Cannon Fairbank with Liang Sicheng and Lin Huiyin. Courtesy of Holly and Laura Fairbank.

National Tsing Hua University

With the establishment of the Nationalist government led by Chiang Kai-shek in 1927, Tsinghua was renamed National Tsing Hua University under the jurisdiction of the Ministry of Education. The university comprised four schools—Arts, Law, Sciences, and Engineering—which were further divided into seventeen departments. The university offered strong training in the sciences as well as a broader education in liberal arts. In 1929 Tsinghua inaugurated its graduate school. After less than a quarter century, Tsinghua had already gained renown not just for the scope of its programs—by 1935 Tsinghua's ten graduate departments counted for one-third of the graduate departments across China—but also for the excellence of its graduates.[5]

The 1930s witnessed Tsinghua's first golden age. Tsinghua was unusual among the "national" universities of that era in that it was a fully residential (and, after 1929, co-educational) campus in the American style, yet in a historically Chinese and bucolic setting, located well outside the walls of old Beijing and some eleven miles from the city center. Students and faculty comingled in the blue cotton gowns of scholars. The campus grounds and its lakes were maintained almost as a private garden, where students could enjoy recreations such as fishing, ice skating, and romantic liaisons in its quieter quarters. Tsinghua, so well supported by the Boxer Indemnity fund, expanded its campus in style, with a stunning library, a gymnasium filled with imported equipment, an auditorium with the best Western musical instruments, and laboratories stocked with the latest scientific instruments—all of it, as Wen-hsin Yeh has shown, "shipped directly from the United States."[6]

By 1937 Tsinghua had become a research university in the arts and sciences.[7] Because of its Boxer Indemnity funding, Tsinghua was less beholden to government support than institutions such as Peking University or National Central University and therefore more resistant to attempts by the ruling Nationalist (Guomindang) party to exert ideological control over it.

This period of development ended suddenly in 1937 when the Tsinghua campus was occupied by Japanese troops. In 1938 many of its faculty and students marched with the Nationalist government to the interior, where Tsinghua—along with Peking and Nankai Universities—became part of Kunming-based National Southwest Associated University (*Guoli xinan lianhe daxue*, or *"Lianda"*) for the duration of the war. Despite the wartime atmosphere, this period has been recalled as a special moment in Chinese higher education, characterized by a relatively liberal academic environment and close cooperation between the country's top scholars, previously spread across three campuses. Some of Tsinghua's most famous and innovative alumni, such as Nobel laureate physicists C. N. Yang (Yang Zhenning) and C. T. Li (Li Zhendao), completed their studies during this time.[8] Tsinghua's president and the leader of *Lianda*, Mei Yiqi, is remembered still today for his advocacy of liberal education, institutional autonomy, and academic freedom even in the darkest moments of the war. For that he has earned the honor, by alumni who know this history, of being Tsinghua's "eternal president" (*Tsinghua daxue yongyuande xiaozhang*).

The university's return to its Beijing campus in 1946 would offer only a short respite before the onset of civil war and the Communist conquest of China. In December 1948 President Mei Yiqi left Beijing. In 1956 he became president of a renewed and distinguished National Tsing Hua University in Taiwan, leading one part of a divided Tsinghua in a divided China.

Communist Tsinghua University

With the Communist victory on the Chinese mainland, Tsinghua's long-standing ties with the United States were severed, not to be resumed for three decades. The new People's Republic of China (PRC) forged a close alliance with the Soviet Union—the "socialist elder brother" that had founded the Chinese Communist Party in 1921. China's political system was reordered along Stalinist lines and retains still today an indelible Soviet DNA. China's universities, including Tsinghua, were rapidly sovietized. A new Tsinghua campus arose next to the original one. Its thirteen-story Main Building (*Zhulou*), a brutal Stalinist complex of three structures, now dominated the campus. Tsinghua in the 1950s looked less like Urbana-Champaign and more like Moscow State.

In 1952 Tsinghua became a polytechnic university to train engineers. The schools of sciences and humanities, agriculture, and law were all abolished, and their faculty members were scattered to other institutions, primarily Peking University. In return, faculty from the engineering schools of Peking and Yenching Universities were transferred to Tsinghua. Faculty who would not or could not work under the new regime either fled abroad or were purged at home. Tsinghua was now academically more on the model of the East German Humboldt University than any American university. Within the newly combined engineering schools, the curriculum was reorganized to eliminate the credit system and instead provide each student with a structured set of courses according to a specific major chosen upon admittance to the university, leading normally to a specific job in government or a state-owned enterprise, Soviet-style. Anxious to ensure its competitiveness despite losing many of its most famous scholars during the reorganization, the university developed new programs under the engineering umbrella. The number of majors available to students increased from twenty-two in 1952, just after the reorganization, to forty in 1966.

This reorganization positioned Tsinghua for leadership during the PRC's First Five-Year Plan (1953–1958), which was modeled on Soviet five-year plans. Tsinghua trained many of China's subsequent political and technocratic elites, but the relentless politicization of universities under Mao Zedong first weakened, and then nearly destroyed, Tsinghua. The breaking point at Tsinghua came in the summer of 1966, when the campus was a central political battleground in the political and ideological struggle between Mao Zedong, who was the Party and military chief, and Liu Shaoqi, China's president. An early political target was Jiang Nanxiang, who had served not only as president and Party secretary of Tsinghua since 1952 but also as Minister of Higher Education.[9] He was quickly denounced at the onset of the Cultural Revolution in June 1966, and the university government apparatus was entirely suspended by the work team sent to the campus by the central authorities under Mao Zedong. Small-scale clashes occurred on campus for two years before erupting into outright warfare.

China's 1960s were much more violent and bloody than those in Berlin, Boston, or Berkeley. In the "one-hundred-day war" on the Tsinghua campus in 1968, at least eighteen people were killed, thirty permanently disabled, and eleven hundred injured. After the army finally seized control, remaining students and academic staff were "sent down" for physical and ideological rehabilitation to rural farming areas, where more than one thousand of them suffered from schistosomiasis, a parasitic disease. Back on campus, in principle, only students who were workers, peasants, and soldiers were to be enrolled in a proletarianized Tsinghua. (Still there was room for some of the children of the elite, who were neither workers, nor peasants, nor soldiers. One of these was Xi Jinping, who graduated with a degree in chemical engineering in 1977. But even he still had to do farm work while a student.)[10]

The Cultural Revolution even destroyed Tsinghua's iconic gate, replaced for a time by a huge statue of Mao, which was in turn supplanted by a replica of the original gate in 1991. Tsinghua resumed full operation, and even then on a skeletal basis, only in 1978.[11]

Figure 9.2. Red Guards tearing down Tsinghua University's gate. Reproduced from https://xsg.tsinghua .edu.cn/info/1003/2288.htm.

Tsinghua University Reborn

Like China, Tsinghua was revolutionized, traumatized, nearly paralyzed, and utterly immiserated during the first three decades of the People's Republic. It emerged from the Maoist years a shell of its former self. Over the subsequent decades, however, Tsinghua's resurgence was tied closely with that of the era of "reform and opening." Tsinghua became again in fact, if not in name, *national* Tsinghua University. The university received extraordinary government investment and rose rapidly to lead China in engineering, topping the country's first rankings table for "key" engineering universities in 1987.[12] Flush with government aid, Tsinghua built its faculty again and established a series of graduate and professional schools. In 1984 Zhu Rongji, who later served as premier, became the founding dean of the newly established School of Economics and Management, which has become the most selective school in the world for undergraduate admissions. Tsinghua's graduates came to dominate the Chinese leadership elite, counting among them Presidents Hu Jintao and Xi Jinping.[13]

Over the course of the past several decades, Tsinghua has reestablished itself as the comprehensive university it was in Republican China, and more. A School of Humanities and Social Sciences was established in 1993, and in 2012 it was divided into separate schools. Tsinghua's Law School was reestablished in 1995. In 1999 the former Central Academy of Arts and Design became part of Tsinghua, as did Peking Union Medical College in 2006. In November 2009 Tsinghua revived its famous Institute of Chinese Studies. The Tsinghua School of Economics and Management began to lead the university in reforming its general education curriculum. And at the university's one hundredth anniversary in 2011, a magnificent New Tsinghua Academy (*Xin Tsinghua xuetang*) was dedicated not to the fields of engineering, science, and technology, for which Tsinghua has been best known in recent decades, but to the performing arts.

President James of the University of Illinois was convinced, in 1907, that "[e]very great nation in the world will inevitably be drawn into more or less intimate relations" with a rapidly changing China.[14] He imagined a world where China learned from others, not the other way around. But he also conceived of a China that would rise because of its international educational alliances. Today an ever more academically diverse and internationally connected Tsinghua is without a doubt a leader in higher education in China, and, increasingly, in the global higher education market. Tsinghua was ranked fifteenth in the 2021 QS World University Rankings (two spots above Yale University), reflecting Tsinghua's rising research output as well as its increasingly high reputation in academic circles.[15]

By 2020 over 50,000 students studied at Tsinghua under the guidance of over 3,600 faculty members and 2,836 postdoctoral researchers organized into 21 schools. Tsinghua's over 16,000 undergraduate students chose from 82 majors, and studied in an environment that connected them closely with over 19,700 masters and over 17,200 doctoral students.[16]

Tsinghua now aimed to be "world class." While still focusing primarily on engineering and applied sciences, in broadening its offerings, Tsinghua acted on the belief of many scholars that a world-class university had to encompass a wide variety of disciplines.[17] It was not enough to be known (as Tsinghua was) as the "MIT of China" even though institutions in the United States such as the Massachusetts and California Institutes of Technology were regularly considered world-class institutions despite their narrower offerings. If anything, Tsinghua began to look more akin to Stanford, a comprehensive research university with particular strengths in engineering and applied science.

Tsinghua's decades-long pursuit of becoming a comprehensive, world-class university was rooted in long-term planning and shaped by the Chinese government's national development objectives. In 2003, when Tsinghua President Wang Dazhong articulated a "three nine-year, three-step" plan to transform Tsinghua into a comprehensive, world-class university by 2020, he noted that university planning for world-class status had begun in 1993 as a response to the 16th National Congress of the Communist Party of China's goal of "building a well-off society in an all-round way and accelerating socialist modernization."[18] Reconstituting Tsinghua into a truly comprehensive university was the primary objective of this world-class plan's first step in the three nine-year segments, from 1994 to 2002. In unveiling the second step (from 2003 to 2011), Wang identified "striving to be among the world's top universities" as the university's top priority. Tsinghua achieved this objective. By 2011 it ranked among the top one hundred universities in multiple international rankings, and within the top twenty in the *Times Higher Education* ranking of engineering programs.[19] According to Wang, the third step for Tsinghua would run from 2012 to 2020 and would focus on achieving world-class status across multiple disciplines.

Achieving comprehensive, world-class status by 2020 remained at the forefront of Tsinghua's strategic planning as the university entered what

Wang had viewed as its last "step" toward this goal. The 2011–2015 university development plan declared that this was the "key period in accelerating the development [of Tsinghua] as a world-class university." To this end, the administration outlined its many priorities for institutional reform, including everything from comprehensively strengthening academic disciplines to increasing international cooperation. The 2016–2020 development plan took on an even greater sense of mission and urgency, with its introduction declaring that "it is necessary . . . to ensure that [Tsinghua] reaches the level of world-class universities by 2020."[20]

On the face of it, Tsinghua's administration had kept its eye on the prize since first announcing its aim of becoming a world-class university. However, even as Tsinghua rose in global university rankings, navigating competing interest groups within the Tsinghua community and the Party-State proved to be a persistent challenge for university leadership. The 2016–2020 development plan's references to increasing Tsinghua's contributions to industrial policies such as military-civil fusion and Made in China 2025 underscored the Party-State's view of universities as vehicles to advance its own interests, which might not always align with fostering world-class practices at Tsinghua. The 2016–2020 plan acknowledged that obstacles to Tsinghua's institutional reform would persist long after 2020 by laying out goals for becoming "one of the world's top universities" by 2050.[21] As Tsinghua's self-imposed deadline of achieving world-class status by 2020 has now passed, what is the university's track record of adopting international best practices? And how has the Chinese political system shaped Tsinghua's successes and shortcomings?

May a Thousand Talents Bloom

As we have seen, the recipe for a leading university requires at least three ingredients: an exceptional faculty; a talented student body; and means of governance that promote outstanding research and teaching, ideally unencumbered by political constraint. How has Tsinghua fared in these dimensions?

Faculty

The 3,565 faculty members of Tsinghua are an illustrious group. As of 2019 among them numbered fifty-four members of the Chinese Academy of Sciences, forty members of the Chinese Academy of Engineering, and many other winners of accolades. They carry out a wide variety of research in Tsing-hua's 447 research institutions, which in 2020 included many designated as "key" by the national and regional governments.[22] Since Tsinghua's founding, the university administration sought to enhance the quality of the faculty by recruiting foreign-trained Chinese scholars, and this tradition continued throughout the reform era. Qian Yingyi, Dean of the School of Economics and Management (SEM), for example, was recruited to lead SEM after terms on the faculties of Stanford University, the University of Maryland, and the University of California, Berkeley. As dean of one of the most competitive schools at Tsinghua, Qian implemented vast reforms within SEM, both in terms of curriculum—creating a mandatory, two-year, general education core curriculum for undergraduates and reorganizing the graduate programs—as well as in administration—establishing a tenure track and simplifying the salary system.

In its 2011–2015 development plan, the university administration ac-knowledged that "there was still a relatively large distance between the overall level of our faculty and that of the world's elite universities."[23] By many counts, however, that distance was closing fast. Whereas in 1995, only 15 percent of Tsinghua faculty held doctoral degrees, by 2006 this propor-tion had risen to 62.7 percent. By 2020, 91.02 percent of faculty at Tsinghua held doctoral degrees.[24] Yet the 2016–2020 plan noted that Tsinghua still faced a number of challenges in attracting "excellence," including competi-tion for top faculty from "famous" universities outside China. Although Tsinghua aimed to become a world-class university by 2020, the university gave itself until 2050 to build a faculty with an "overall top level," a goal that Tsinghua hoped would coincide with becoming "one of the world's top uni-versities." Older, less productive faculty would be phased (not forced) out with retirement.

Tsinghua also hoped that the government's Thousand Talents Program, announced in 2008, would aid the university's efforts to recruit world-class faculty. The program offered foreign-based scholars—mostly, but not exclu-sively, of Chinese origin—very generous financial packages to join Chinese universities. Tsinghua seized the opportunity. The 2011–2015 development plan noted that Tsinghua would "make full use of the Thousand Talents Pro-gram" in order to "recruit first-class international scholars."[25] By 2016 the university had recruited 111 senior scholars through the program.[26] By 2019 the Chinese government ceased to promote the program publicly, in response to US concerns that it "encourage[d] theft of intellectual property."[27] Indeed, it was Harvard chemistry professor Charles Lieber's participation in the Thousand Talents Program that led to his arrest in 2019. Tsinghua continued to attract scholars through the Thousand Talents Program, albeit at a slower pace. In 2018 nine new "talents" joined Tsinghua, whereas only four were recruited in 2019.[28] As Tsinghua competed with prestigious and well-funded global universities for talent, government financial support for the recruitment of "stars" remained an important resource for the university.

But Tsinghua was still burdened by its socialist past. Hindering Tsinghua's recruitment of high-quality faculty in an international job market were human resource policies that were relics of the planned economy in which an "iron rice bowl" of enduring employment was standard. After 1995 Tsinghua relied in principle on an "up or out" employment policy. An assistant professor (formerly, lecturer) had up to nine years—three three-year contracts—to receive a promotion to the associate professor level. An associate professorship implied entry into the tenure track, although there was no specific time frame at which an associate professor became a full professor. Full professors were expected to sign two more three-year contracts before ultimately being offered a non-time-specified contract, essentially giving them lifetime tenure. Faculty members tended to be promoted almost exclusively from within, competing against others within their department for promotion. Central planning by university administration determined quotas for each level of faculty in each school, leaving schools few means to affect the scope of their hiring processes.

Faculty salaries were calculated on a monthly basis. But the structure of the system made it difficult to recruit outstanding international researchers who were used to annual, rather than monthly, salary systems. When scholars recruited from abroad were eventually offered annual (and higher) salaries, this naturally created intradepartmental tensions.[29]

Nonetheless, SEM, as a kind of "special economic zone" of experimentation, phased in higher annual salaries for faculty members, as well as an international-standard tenure system. Its approach became part of Tsinghua's 2011–2015 overall development plan.[30] But not all schools at Tsinghua were so rich in funding and experimental in attitude. The university's 2016–2020 plan acknowledged that the salary models for faculty would be established "according to what is suitable for each department."[31]

In terms of credentials, Tsinghua valued hiring its own alumni, especially those who had done their undergraduate work at Tsinghua. But as Li Daokui, a renowned economist and the founding dean of the Schwarzman

Scholars program noted, "If a person does not have a foreign PhD, that person will face tremendous trouble at Tsinghua."[32] Tenure awards required ample publications in prestigious, international journals outside of China. Faculty with international doctorates had a clear advantage in the race to publish and achieve tenure, and their work would help Tsinghua in the international rankings with which it and its peers were so obsessed. At the same time, the international focus of these tenure policies had the potential to lure younger professors to focus on research topics that would be well received internationally rather than on issues most relevant to the Chinese scene. For an institution whose motto was "self-discipline and social commitment," this was a challenge.

Students

That English-language translation of the university motto hardly captures Tsinghua's sense of special mission and status. The motto, *Ziqiang bu xi, hou de zai wu,* taken from the *Book of Changes,* calls for the superior person to "self-strengthen without cease" and "with great virtue to take charge of the world." Indeed, Tsinghua's most famous alumni in the PRC era have been those who took charge of the world, or a good part of it: Xi Jinping, president of China, former President Hu Jintao, and former Premier Zhu Rongji all graduated from engineering programs at Tsinghua. Tsinghua continues to draw many of China's most gifted students through one of the most competitive admissions processes in the world. The top humanities division *gaokao* scorers from twenty-eight of the thirty-two provincial-level administrative units on the Chinese mainland enrolled at Tsinghua in 2018. Top scorers in the science division from fourteen provincial administrative units chose to attend Tsinghua as well.[33] From my own lectures and seminars at Tsinghua, and from many visits, I can attest: Tsinghua students are second to none.

Tsinghua clearly attracts some of the best students in the world. But how are they educated once they walk through its iconic gate? Since the revival of Tsinghua as a comprehensive university, it has experimented with multiple approaches to new curricula and pedagogy. All of Tsinghua's schools have some general education requirements, including a nationally required political curriculum as well as university-based initiatives. All students are able to take advantage of freshman seminars, designed to foster more discussion-based and participatory learning. Students can also participate in the Student Research Training (SRT) program, working alongside faculty on specific projects to gain research experience. Tsinghua reports that over 60 percent of its undergraduates participate in more than one thousand SRT projects offered annually.[34] Gifted students who are interested in pursuing careers in academia can apply for the Tsinghua Xuetang Talents program, which offers high-level academic training in a variety of scientific and quantitative fields. Still, despite this growing emphasis on specialized educational opportunities, the average undergraduate class size at Tsinghua is fifty, and only 35.3 percent of undergraduate courses are taught by full professors.[35] With over sixteen thousand undergraduate students, developing a feasible educational program that promotes individualization and creativity is a significant challenge.

Not an institution to shy away from a challenge, in September 2014 Tsinghua built on its existing experience and launched a new undergraduate residential college experience combined with a more rigorous general education curriculum. Students at the new institution, Xinya College, were expected to earn twelve credits from a host of newly designed, seminar-style core courses that emphasized "Chinese and Western civilizations and the interconnectedness between different civilizations and cultures."[36] Students entered Xinya without having been divided into majors and spent their entire first year studying a variety of courses, including general education, before choosing a major in their second year.[37]

A key feature of the program was student life: Xinya students lived together in residential college style, as a multidisciplinary cohort. This was a departure from traditional campus life at Tsinghua, in which students were grouped together and assigned dormitories by discipline, leaving few opportunities for cross-disciplinary interactions within or outside the classroom. Within the Xinya residence, emphasis was placed on student life and activities outside the classroom as well. Students ran festivals and events and established various interest groups with their peers.

By the time this cross-school experiment was first piloted in 2014, those in charge of Xinya College were able to draw on the experience of the School of Economics and Management, which had led the way in curricular reform by instituting its own undergraduate general education requirement in 2009. Here again the figure of SEM Dean Qian Yingyi looms large.

Qian Yingyi is a remarkable man. He passed the college entrance exams the first year they were revived after the Cultural Revolution, when a decade's worth of candidates took the exams for a miniscule number of admission slots. He graduated from Tsinghua in mathematics and went on to receive his doctorate at Harvard in economics. Qian was professor of economics at Berkeley when he was recruited back to Tsinghua by former Premier Zhu Rongji, the founding dean of SEM. Qian then succeeded Zhu in this role, serving as dean of the School of Economics and Management from 2006 to 2018. A scholar who had published in all the leading journals of his field, Dean Qian authored multiple books on China's economic reform and, closest to his heart, on the early, pre-Communist, distinguished history of the social sciences at Tsinghua.[38]

The years of his deanship coincided with a great boom of the Chinese economy and of Tsinghua's reputation. SEM became the destination of choice not only for undergraduates but for executive education MBAs. SEM's parking lot would be filled every weekend with the private vehicles of China's new corporate elite, from Mercedes to Maseratis. Qian, by contrast, parked the only vehicle he owned: an old bicycle so rusty and tired that no one would steal it.

Qian's passion—so unusual for an age consumed with research rankings—was undergraduate education. He had studied the core and general education

Figure 9.3. Dean Qian Yingyi and his bicycle on Tsinghua's campus.
Photograph © William C. Kirby.

curricula at Harvard and other American universities, and I recall long discussions with him on the merits of each. He knew that university-wide reform of undergraduate education at Tsinghua would be a steep, uphill and, possibly, political battle, but he could start more quietly at SEM and set an example. He concluded, "Given . . . that Chinese students are strong in some aspects but very weak in terms of worldview, global vision, and critical thinking, at the very beginning, I realized that undergraduate curriculum is the most important thing to change." Guided by the goal of "training the mind to think," rather than merely helping students acquire knowledge, and working closely with his faculty, Qian built a curriculum of core classes that dominated most of the students' first two years in SEM. As Qian recalled, the general education program "integrated value formation, skills development and attainment of core knowledge of human civilizations, stressing the importance of nurturing curiosity, imagination, and critical thinking. . . . The new curriculum was geared to global needs of the future . . . and placed the development of students at the center of the design."[39]

The impact of this new curriculum was felt in many ways at SEM. One of the central components of the general education curriculum was a course called "Critical Thinking and Moral Reasoning." One day, Qian told me, he heard students say, "'Have you CTMR-ed?' They use this as a verb. I was struck! Because when a company's name becomes a verb, it's a tremendous achievement." While some students clearly warmed to the new curriculum, others were more skeptical. Many students worried that the lack of study in specialized subjects like finance and accounting during their first and second years would make them less competitive candidates for internships. Still, with quiet determination and a carefully cultivated personal legitimacy, Qian was able to successfully implement his envisioned curricular reforms. Each year, he reformed the requirements of a different degree until every program at SEM fit his vision.

Governance: The Case of the School of Economics and Management

Like all public universities in China, Tsinghua was governed by a president (Qiu Yong) who worked in coordination with the Chinese Communist Party Committee (led by Party Secretary Chen Xu). Su-Yan Pan, research assistant professor in the Faculty of Education at the University of Hong Kong, described the relationship between Tsinghua and the government as "semi-independent," wherein the university had "the power to protect itself from external intervention in certain areas, and [could] act upon its own initiative to respond to social needs within the framework of the government's policies."[40] Much like the University of Berlin in Wilhelmine times, Tsinghua's loyalty, or at least adherence, to the ruling system was assumed. As the alma mater of so many prominent Chinese political leaders, Tsinghua had greater autonomy than its more free-spirited neighbor in Beijing, Peking University, where the Party intervened early and often in controlling its leadership. While the university president and Party secretary's interests did not always align, Tsinghua's leadership and the central government were both determined to turn Tsinghua into a world-class university.

Administrative decision-making powers not reserved for the Party Committee were split between the university president and the dean of each individual school. Each school, and indeed each department, also had a Party Committee, but Tsinghua deans had considerable freedom within their fiefdoms, be it on matters of curriculum (as in SEM) or on the allocation of their budgets. The central university administration, on the other hand, maintained some control over each school by setting quotas for the hiring and promotion of professors.

Because salaries were paid out of SEM's budget, the school was able to implement its reforms without requiring more funds from the central university budget. However, this did not mean that the dean was free to take unilateral action. Rather, Qian went through a long, consultative process during which he worked closely with many faculty committees to establish the new salary system. He noted that while in most other countries, salary negotiations normally took place one-on-one between the dean and faculty member, this would be unacceptable in the Chinese context. Rather, the system was reformed so that salaries for each faculty member were reviewed, negotiated, and decided through anonymous vote by a seven-person salary committee.

The tenure system reform exemplified the relative governance roles of the university and individual schools. Changes to the hiring process required university approval as they would affect decisions that were previously under the jurisdiction of the central administration. This was not a case of the "shoot first and ask forgiveness later" strategy that defines so much private enterprise in China today. Innovative as it was, SEM had to keep the central administration well informed of its efforts.

Faculty without administrative roles played a limited role in university governance. The main vehicle for faculty engagement was the Faculty and Staff Representative Assembly, a body drawn from the whole university by school or department, and consisting of no less than 60 percent of faculty. Its meetings bore no resemblance to those of Harvard's Faculty of Arts and Sciences, not to mention Berkeley's Academic Senate. The Assembly, falling under the university's Party-led labor union (which was not a union formed by employees in the European or American sense), had extremely limited prerogatives. Its powers, as laid out in its charter, were at most consultative: listening to and issuing opinions on reports on the workings of the university and its administrators. The Assembly's regulations did not stipulate any mechanism by which these opinions had to be taken into account.[41]

Ultimately, governance issues at Tsinghua in general and at SEM were subject to political winds blowing eleven miles to the south, in the Chinese Communist Party's leadership compound in Zhongnanhai, in the shadow of the Qing Forbidden City. The tightening of censorship and academic control that marked the presidency of Xi Jinping after 2012 led to an enhanced role of the Party in university affairs and greater scrutiny of individual schools. For example, SEM, like all leading Chinese business schools, had a strong executive education program and robust income from it. But from one day to the next, it was announced that state-owned enterprises (SOEs) should not and could not pay the high levels of tuition charged for executive MBA programs. Worse, even if an SOE executive was but one credit from receiving the MBA, he or she had to withdraw from the program. Worse still, for SEM, it was required to refund the *entire tuition* received over many years of SOE executives in its programs.

The Party's Central Commission for Discipline Inspection (CCDI) investigated Tsinghua (as it did all leading universities) in 2017. The CCDI criticized the universities, including Tsinghua, declaring that their "implementation of ideological systems is not strong enough."[42] At Tsinghua, the CCDI sought evidence of corruption of either the monetary or ideological sort. They found none at SEM, but they did discover that Dean Qian's office was a few square meters larger than central regulations allowed. This was a common finding in Chinese university administrative offices, but unlike some of his peers, who hired carpenters to build fake walls to make their offices smaller, Qian simply turned his office into a seminar room (he had already used it as such), and moved across the hall to a space the size of a typical office cubicle.

Tsinghua, Incorporated

In 2020 Tsinghua reported projected expenditures of over US$4.6 billion.[43] Of its total projected income in 2020, 39 percent came from university earned revenue, including student tuition and fees.[44] Tuition levels for undergraduate, MA, and PhD programs are set by the Ministry of Education. Undergraduate tuition varies by program, but in 2020 it was under US$1,000 per year, with the exception of the fine arts program, whose annual tuition was closer to US$1,500. Graduate program annual tuition fell in the US$1,200 to $1,500 range. Tuition for professional degree programs is proposed by the relevant school's administration and negotiated with the Ministry of Education.[45] At over $29,600, tuition for SEM's MBA program was significantly higher than that of other schools.[46] These state-set (or state-negotiated) tuition rates change, however, for international students. The 1,198 full-time international undergraduate students at Tsinghua in 2019 paid tuition of between $2,000 and $5,000.[47]

As one of the primary beneficiaries of Project 211 and Project 985, Tsinghua received extraordinary research and capital improvement funding from the government. However, university accounting of government funds was rather opaque. While an exact figure for the amount of government support Tsinghua receives is unknown, it is surely substantial. Yet senior administration members predicted that absolute support was likely to fall in the coming years as the government started to express more concern for regional equity in contrast with previous policies that funneled government support into a few, select institutions. In addition, the composition of the government funding Tsinghua receives is changing as the state's national development priorities evolve. One of the few areas of government funding for Tsinghua to grow in 2020 was outlays for its science and technology expenditures.

Expanding military-civil fusion research and teaching programs at Tsinghua is one emerging area receiving growing support from the Chinese government. MCF, a national strategy launched in 2015 by Xi Jinping to incentivize contributions to China's defense industrial base by nonmilitary actors, is used to justify "strategic cooperation and resource docking with the military" in Tsinghua's 2016–2020 plan.[48] Since the plan's release, Tsinghua launched new programs educating People's Liberation Army officers, opened laboratories researching MCF technologies, and invested in companies developing MCF-focused projects.[49]

Tsinghua's STEM initiatives have also benefited from incentives created by the government to support the "Made in China 2025" (MIC 2025) industrial policy. Released by the State Council in 2015, MIC 2025 laid out a blueprint for fostering globally competitive and increasingly self-sufficient Chinese industries in technologies such as semiconductors, automobiles, artificial intelligence, and telecommunication equipment.[50] Tsinghua jumped to signal its support for the policy.[51] Behind Tsinghua's early and eager support for MIC 2025 were expectations of immense, new state-backed financial support for higher education research, reported to exceed US$1.6 billion between 2016 and 2020, to be disbursed among all universities.[52] Moreover, the Ministry of Industry and Information Technology named university cooperation a "basic principle" for projects in application materials for MIC 2025 subsidies.[53] Since its release, Tsinghua has initiated a series of research centers and teaching programs in support of MIC 2025.[54]

Tsinghua's financial relationship with the state had both local and national elements. The Beijing municipal government opened applications for subsidies that would fund military-civil fusion projects in Tsinghua's home district of Haidian.[55] Tsinghua played a role in industrial policies in MIC 2025 plans ranging across the country, from Tianjin to Qinghai[56]—operations that continued well after the central government dropped official references to the plan.[57] In 2018 state media reported that since MIC 2025's release in 2015, Tsinghua had received eighty projects and US$288 million in government funding.[58] Although regular government funding for Tsinghua had declined as a proportion of the university's revenue, the rise of special industrial policy projects at Tsinghua suggests that, as an official *Drittmittel* funder in the German context, the state remained the central actor in the composition and allocation of Tsinghua's resources.

Institutional Entrepreneurship

And yet Tsinghua has set out on its own to develop sources of funding beyond government research support and government-controlled tuition. Tsinghua encourages an institutional entrepreneurial culture that is more like Stanford or MIT than Harvard or Berkeley. The university takes stakes in commercial endeavors started at the Tsinghua University Science Park (TusPark), including Tsinghua Unigroup and Tsinghua Tongfang Co., Ltd. As university-based enterprises, both companies receive partial tax exemption.[59]

These companies and TusPark are all part of Tsinghua Holdings Co., Ltd., the investment arm of the university, which at the end of the 2019 financial year held over US$73 billion in assets and had 1,908 subsidiaries.[60] In 2019 *Fortune China* ranked it the 187th largest company based on operating income.[61]

But entrepreneurialism is not always rewarded in Xi Jinping's China. Attempts to diversify Tsinghua's income through commercial enterprises were complicated by the 2017 investigation by the Central Commission for Discipline Inspection into "Party leadership" at twenty-nine Chinese universities. In the CCDI's report on Tsinghua's conduct, the university was told explicitly to strengthen "the leadership of [Tsinghua's] Party committees over holding companies" and to restructure commercial enterprises to reduce investment levels and operational risks.[62] In May 2018 the government doubled down on this position, declaring that universities must institute "state capital management reform" in order to "focus on education."[63] State interference in Tsinghua's investment plans leaves uncertain the role of commercial endeavors in diversifying its income. If Tsinghua follows through on the state's mandate to divest itself of commercial assets, its budget would be ever more reliant on government funding, making Tsinghua more responsive to state interests in the future.

The university also seeks and receives private donations. Tsinghua is home to the People's Republic of China's first university endowment, the Tsinghua University Education Foundation (TUEF), governed by a twenty-five-person board of directors. Founded in 1994 with an initial balance of less than US$3 million, the fund grew to a total value of over US$1.4 billion by 2019 and had a reputation as one of the highest-performing university endowments in China.[64] In 2019 the investments of TUEF earned over US$150 million in investment income (roughly a 12.2 percent return).[65] Annual donations to TUEF have increased steadily; in 2018 the fund received about US$300 million in donations, around one-tenth of which was donated from outside China. Foreign donations proved hard to sustain year-on-year, falling 75 percent in 2019 to account for just 2 percent of total donations that year, while overall gifts to the endowment fell by only around 9 percent.[66] While a small endowment by American standards, TUEF was attempting to build a foundation in a short period for future growth. Following Tsinghua's model, there are now 623 Chinese university endowments. Tsinghua's remains the largest and most successful, earning nearly double the investment income of its closest competitor, Peking University, in 2020.[67]

Like Harvard and many American universities, however, central fundraising was but part of the story and by no means the largest one. Individual schools also housed their own fundraising teams. SEM was the first school at Tsinghua to begin running its own fundraising campaigns, with several other schools following its lead. TUEF played an active role in trying to get more schools to increase their fundraising capacity and form their own development offices.

SEM is again a case in point. Its Advisory Board is perhaps among the most distinguished, in business terms, and surely both the most powerful and the wealthiest, of any board of any part of any university anywhere in the world. Its membership is a Who's Who of Chinese political and Western business elites. Chaired by the former PRC premier and founding dean of SEM, Zhu Rongji, its 2018 Chinese leadership included Vice President Wang Qishan (Xi Jinping's closest supporter); Chen Jining, the former Tsinghua president and now mayor of Beijing; Yi Gang, governor of the People's Bank of China; Jack Ma of Alibaba; Robin Li of Baidu, and on and on. And the foreign members were no slouches, either: Mary Barra, head of General Motors; Lloyd Blankfein of Goldman Sachs; Tim Cook of Apple; Elon Musk of Tesla; Stephen Schwarzman of Blackstone; and the man who would do absolutely anything to have his company legalized in China, Mark Zuckerberg of Facebook. SEM, and its Advisory Board, was for foreign business leaders a privileged port of entry to China's political and business stratosphere.

Out of this came donations to SEM as well. Advisory Board member John Thornton, formerly of Goldman Sachs, established the John L. Thornton China Center both at Tsinghua and at the Brookings Institution in Washington. But some of the biggest fish at Tsinghua, as at most universities, were reserved for the central administration. While Dean Qian of SEM may have imagined what Stephen Schwarzman could do for his school, President Chen Jining had larger ambitions, and the new Schwarzman College at Tsinghua, supported by a half-billion dollar fundraising effort led by Schwarzman, would be Chen's signature program.

These donations, as well as profits from university-affiliated companies, were an important step toward financial flexibility for the university as a whole and for the individual schools because of the many limitations on other fundraising means. The Ministry of Education controlled the levels of tuition, and the government now forbade schools from taking out bank loans to complete capital projects. The mega-gifts from foreigners were a start. But as Qian noted, with the rapid increase in wealthy Chinese individuals, it was likely that private donations from within China would become a fast-growing source of university funding in the future.[68]

Competition at Home and Abroad

Tsinghua has successfully reestablished itself as a leading comprehensive university in China, but it must confront many challenges before it can enduringly be considered among the world's leading universities. Tsinghua's comparative advantage in China, as Li Daokui says, has been the university's position "at the center of national politics, science, technology, development, and education."[69] However, as China's population has become more internationally mobile and aware, international universities are increasingly Tsinghua's stiffest competitors for high-performing Chinese students and top rankings. With one exception.

Tsinghua's fiercest competitor within China for government grants and international reputation may be found just across the street from its own gates. Founded in the center of the capital in 1898, Peking University (PKU) has long been one of China's flagship institutions. It took over the residential campus of Yenching University in 1952, forming with Tsinghua and other universities a cluster of higher education institutions in what is now northwestern Beijing. Yet the two institutions were intended to serve different purposes from their early history. As Li Daokui once explained to me, PKU's "tradition is to be critical of the government . . . far away from politics. . . . Tsinghua, on the other hand . . . it's close to politics. That's the difference."[70]

Like Tsinghua, PKU expanded in the reform era to once again become a comprehensive university, determined to rise to world-class status. Today, both universities have been primary recipients of Project 985 funding, and both compete for other state subsidies. In November 2015 China's State Council announced the "Double First Class" (DFC) program, a national project aimed at building world-leading "first-class universities" with "first-class academic disciplines."[71] In January 2017 Tsinghua was picked for 34 of the total 110 disciplines being considered, slightly behind PKU, which had 41.[72] Moreover, PKU's world-class ambitions led it to share many of the same ambitions as Tsinghua. PKU's Yenching Academy, for example, mirrored many aspects of Tsinghua's Schwarzman Scholars program. Like Tsinghua, PKU seeks to compete with the world's best universities. This pursuit has opened both universities up to new challenges.

With increased mobility and international awareness, growing numbers of high-performing Chinese students are choosing to attend top international universities, forgoing China's leading institutions. Many top-tier Chinese high schools offer special tracks designed to prepare students for international college admissions procedures, rather than the traditional *gaokao*. During the first decade of the twenty-first century, the number of Chinese students pursuing foreign higher education grew by over 20 percent each year, while the number of students taking the *gaokao* declined every year from 2008 to 2013.[73] In 2013, 686 students from mainland China studied at Harvard alone—representing the largest international cohort on that campus.[74] Since opening their doors to fee-paying mainland students in 2002, the well-regarded universities of Hong Kong have also competed with Tsinghua to recruit top students. While China's integration into the international system has transformed Tsinghua's institutional ambitions, the university's international competitors have, if only slightly, diminished one of Tsinghua's key strengths: its ability to recruit the elite of the elite among China's top students.

As Tsinghua gains the vast resources world-class comprehensive universities require, its individual programs must compete with specialized institutions devoted to world-leading status in a single field. While Tsinghua's joint executive MBA program between SEM and the Institut Européen d'Administration des Affaires (INSEAD), a leading European business school, was ranked first among all executive MBA programs in the world by the *Financial Times* in 2015, the full-time MBA program of SEM faced stiff competition from the China Europe International Business School (CEIBS), a joint venture between the Chinese government and the European Union, which ranked eleventh in the 2015 *Financial Times* ranking of full-time, global MBA programs.[75] CEIBS offered a targeted education with an international flavor to Chinese and foreign business students. The relatively small size and focused nature of CEIBS ran counter to Tsinghua's strategy of expansion of disciplines, but its clear results challenged the feasibility and desirability of Tsinghua's vision.

State support fueled Tsinghua's rise to the apex of the country's higher education system, but contributing to Beijing's research priorities for China's universities required Tsinghua to double down on its traditional strengths at the cost of improving in dramatic ways its performance in new or renewed fields. Tsinghua was, of course, among the forty-two universities China's DFC identified as "having the potential to develop into a world-class university."[76] These schools were chosen because of their leading positions in specific academic disciplines in China, and all were expected to build toward leading positions in their chosen fields in the world. Almost two-thirds of Tsinghua's chosen disciplines were in engineering, information technology, and the natural and physical sciences.[77] Government funding, which still makes up a significant portion of Tsinghua's budget, was disproportionately distributed to areas in which Tsinghua already excelled internationally.

For Qiu Yong, Tsinghua's president, the state's support of a discrete and focused number of disciplines limited his capacity to make Tsinghua become more than a world-leading university in any field but engineering. During meetings with university leaders and faculty, Qiu reminded them of the enormous influence Tsinghua once had in China in the humanities and social sciences, through figures such as the Four Tutors.[78] The educational philosophy of Tsinghua was to integrate the "shaping of values," the "cultivation of abilities," and the "transfer of knowledge" to create innovative talent for the country. To do this, he argued, students had to engage deeply across disciplines in the liberal arts and sciences to understand how the leading minds in different fields approached and solved problems. But ultimately the state's emphasis on and investments in Tsinghua's natural and applied sciences left the university's commitment to educating the "whole person" rather unbalanced.

And so, in recent years, Tsinghua has recommitted to raising its already excellent engineering disciplines, rather than the university's comprehensive standing, into leading positions in the world by 2030 and to being at the very top of their fields by 2050. Between 2015 and 2018, Tsinghua led the world in the number of publications in both engineering and physical science and mathematics and computer science. The research done by Tsinghua faculty was not only plentiful but also influential. Of the top 1 percent of the most frequently cited papers in the physical sciences and engineering, Tsinghua faculty authored the third most papers, lagging behind only MIT and Stanford in the same period.[79] Tsinghua was ranked first and ninth in the world in engineering by the 2021 *U.S. News and World Report* and QS subject rankings, respectively.

Spirits Independent?

Surely it is not surprising that a country led by engineers (individuals with engineering educations or backgrounds have dominated China's leadership over the past two decades) would be less enamored with the promotion of the humanities and social sciences. And since 1949 the Chinese Party-State has concerned itself more with the control, censorship, and political mobilization of the humanities and social sciences than with their research excellence. After many oscillations, the political pressure ramped up again after 2012. The 2017 CCDI investigation into Tsinghua required that the university "strengthen political control over textbooks" and "expand supervision of teaching" to help resolve the "issue of lax controls over positions." Moreover, the investigation forced thirteen liberal arts departments to "add requirements for political standards . . . to teaching appointments . . . and [have] academic standards reflect the specific requirements of Chinese characteristics."[80] This political rubric for what was acceptable work in the humanities and social sciences made it difficult for Tsinghua to revive its institutional roots in the liberal arts through "vigorously promoting the 'new humanities,'" as had been called for in the 2016–2020 plan. Yet Tsinghua made it through the CCDI inspection relatively unscathed compared to other Chinese universities, as we will see in the case of Nanjing University.

To be sure, Chinese universities have rich experience in trying to delay, deflect, or ignore untoward state intrusion. They have seen it all before, and worse, in the Maoist years. Take the example of textbooks. A major course at Tsinghua used a leading international textbook on economic issues. The problem was that the textbook contained accurate information about the near-destruction of the Chinese economy under Mao's Great Leap Forward. What to do? Customs and postal censors (yes, there are censors everywhere) offered to allow the book to be used if a few pages were torn out. Fine, said a Tsinghua professor. But then some censor read further, and now it was clear that the book—which had been used at Tsinghua for a decade or more—could not enter the country at all. Miraculously, the international author of the textbook emailed the Tsinghua students a PDF of the book, as a gift. Everyone, except possibly the publisher, was then happy. The censors had done their job, for the physical book had not entered the country. The faculty members had done their job, for their text of choice could now be read. And the author had reached his intended audience. Philanthropy can have its academic virtues.

Tsinghua's participation in state-backed initiatives, such as the Thousand Talents Program, military-civil fusion, and Made in China 2025, presented political risks for the university's international reputation. Universities positioning themselves to receive financial and political support from their government would normally be unremarkable in any country. However, growing distrust of the Chinese government in certain Western countries, such as the United States and Australia, has put Tsinghua's contributions to state policy priorities under a microscope.[81] The Thousand Talents Program has helped Tsinghua recruit world-class scholars who may improve its research output, but, as previously mentioned, concerns about economic competition with China have led some foreign governments to view the initiative as a vehicle for "stealing" intellectual property, as articulated in a US congressional report on the program.[82] The rise of military-civil fusion projects at Tsinghua has led to growing concerns in foreign capitals that some research collaborations between Tsinghua and foreign scholars support the Chinese military.[83]

In my opinion, much of this concern is misplaced. As we have seen in earlier chapters, it is a mark of a great university to recruit and retain the best possible scholars and teachers. A "thousand talents" program would not have suited a Harvard, Berkeley, or Duke—but only because the numbers were too large. The leading American universities, like China's, have as their central mission the recruitment of the best possible faculty. When I expanded the Faculty of Arts and Sciences at Harvard by one hundred faculty members in the first years of this century, one might well have called it a "Hundred Talents Program." And, as we have seen from Harvard's history, the role of universities assisting national militaries is hardly unique to China. Perhaps there ought to be some limits, however. I recall when, in the 1990s, the Harvard Kennedy School hosted a program for colonels from China's People's Liberation Army to meet and study with their American counterparts. I still cringe when I recall a toast offered by the then-director of the Kennedy School program, Ambassador Robert Blackwill: "To the enduring cooperation between Harvard and the People's Liberation Army!" That was a bridge too far for me.

The most immediate challenge to Tsinghua's rise is not geopolitics; it is the resurgence of political repression within China, which has a direct effect on the university community. This is especially the case in the humanities and social sciences. In July 2018 Xu Zhangrun, a professor in Tsinghua's School of Law and one of the Top 10 Young Legal Scholars of China in 2005, published an open letter on the internet entitled, "Imminent Fears, Immediate Hopes."[84] It was a scathing critique of Xi Jinping's grasp for enduring powers by ending term limits for the country's president. Xu feared, not without reason, a return to a state where the Party's leadership demanded absolute political and ideological loyalty. The letter received enormous attention on both Chinese social media and in the international press. Then the reaction set in. It was reported in March 2019 that Professor Xu had been suspended from all his teaching and research positions at Tsinghua. Then in July 2020 Professor Xu was formally detained after having published a further series of essays brutally critical of Xi Jinping's government during the coronavirus pandemic.[85] In one of his last commentaries, published immediately before the convening of the National People's Congress, Xu wrote that "there should be an end to the persecution of university professors who dare to speak out," referring not to himself but to ten Wuhan University professors who had signed a letter demanding free speech protections following the death of Doctor Li Wenliang, a martyr and whistleblower for China's cover-up of its coronavirus outbreak.[86]

Upon Professor Xu's release from detention six days after his arrest, he received notice from Tsinghua that he had been fired. To justify his position's termination, Tsinghua claimed Xu's essays had put him in violation of the "10 standards of professional conduct for teachers in tertiary institutes in the new era," a regulation published by the Ministry of Education in 2018, which made "words and deeds that harm the authority of the Party Central Committee or violate the Party's line" a fireable offense.[87] Yet despite the Tsinghua administration's decision to dismiss Xu, many within Tsinghua were sympathetic to his plight. Nearly six hundred from the Tsinghua community donated over US$14,000 to Xu, who had lost his salary along with his livelihood, but the professor declined their generosity, encouraging them to give instead to those "who are truly in need."[88] Yet, although Xu promised to bear any burden to continue his work, Tsinghua's administration, which I imagine did its best to protect him as long as possible, could no longer hold back the political forces that basically threw Xu out of the Chinese academy.

While scholars at Tsinghua are afforded many privileges because of their institution's prestige and personal connections to China's rulers, the case of Xu Zhangrun shows the real limits, human and intellectual, of Chinese higher education even at the country's university most committed to world-class standing. Tsinghua has risen on the back of its great access to state resources and officials, but it is also, perhaps in some ways uniquely, vulnerable to being caught in the crossfire of political debates.

Here we are reminded of the time, in the Republican era, when Tsinghua was home to four of the most famous scholars in the land. Liang Qichao, Wang Guowei, Chen Yinke, and Zhao Yuanren were all products of both classical and international learning. All were at home in Chinese culture while also cutting-edge scholars in the modern humanities and social sciences. And all were famous abroad as at home. After Wang Guowei ended his own life in 1927, his colleague Chen Yinke inscribed on a commemorative stele on campus in honor of Wang Guowei: "A spirit independent and a mind unfettered" (*Duli zhi jingshen, ziyou zhi sixiang*).

These ten characters are known to every Tsinghua scholar. Tsinghua's faculty—despite all the political turbulence and repression of recent decades—still venerates the virtues inscribed on Wang Guowei's commemorative stele. However, in April 2019, on the 108th anniversary of the founding of Tsinghua University, when Tsinghua faculty and alumni, including Professor Xu Zhangrun, sought to pay respect to Wang Guowei's stele, they found it walled off and "under repair." On the construction wall surrounding the monument, a sardonic poster reframed Chen Yinke's famous inscription: "Tsinghua at 108 years: A self-made barrier against any independent spirit; so thick that no mind remains unfettered." As Tsinghua sought to propel itself into the global elite, its capacity to recruit, support, and protect scholars of "spirits independent and minds unfettered" also seemed under repair.

Abroad at Home: Internationalization at Tsinghua

Tsinghua was founded as a prep school for those looking to go abroad. As a university in Republican China, its faculty and students looked toward the United States. In the early People's Republic, they looked toward Moscow. During Mao's Cultural Revolution, Tsinghua faced inward and went nowhere. From the beginning of the reform era after 1979, Tsinghua was determined to be again part of the larger world of universities.

Weaving through contemporary Tsinghua's approach to excellence in faculty recruitment and research, student achievement, and administration was a renewed push toward internationalization. This had begun with the faculty. As Tsinghua sought to raise its profile on the international stage, it focused on recruiting overseas Chinese scholars, especially Tsinghua alumni, to return to China as distinguished faculty. Both Qian Yingyi and Li Daokui were part of this early wave of returnees. Among Chinese universities, this approach to recruitment was hardly unique to Tsinghua; however, Tsinghua carried the advantage of prestige, funding, and an alumni base both large and elite from which to recruit. For many scholars of Qian and Li's generation, the call to return and serve the motherland was difficult to ignore, particularly during the early twenty-first century, when government incentives and general funding for higher education made faculty positions extremely attractive. Once on board, faculty were expected to publish in international journals and with international coauthors, which would in turn contribute to higher research rankings for the university.

Students at Tsinghua also found themselves among an increasingly international cohort. Tsinghua hosted a total of 3,257 international students in 2019.[89] Nearly 2,000 Tsinghua undergraduate students participated in some form of international experience in 2017, with exchange programs with over 140 universities around the world that had signed official exchange agreements with Tsinghua.[90] The opening of the Schwarzman Scholars program at the newly built Schwarzman College courtyard within the Tsinghua campus in 2016 brought even more international graduate students, professors, and media attention to Tsinghua.

At an institutional level, Tsinghua actively pursued partnerships with universities outside of China as well. In 2014 it announced the opening of the Tsinghua-Berkeley Shenzhen Institute in Shenzhen in partnership with the University of California, Berkeley.[91] In 2015 Tsinghua became the first Chinese university to build major research facilities outside of China when it entered into a partnership with Microsoft and the University of Washington to form the Global Innovation Exchange, a Seattle-based graduate school for technology and innovation.[92]

Tsinghua's international partnerships increasingly extended to the developing world as well, in tandem with the Chinese government's international infrastructure program, the Belt and Road Initiative (BRI). Although infrastructure investments are the heart of the BRI, collaboration in education is also included in the plan to foster people-to-people ties and educate technical elites in countries receiving investments. A white paper released by the Ministry of Education in 2016 declared that "China is willing to work with countries along the route to expand humanities exchanges, strengthen personnel training, and jointly create a better future through education."[93] Tsinghua announced its intention to align with BRI priorities in its 2016–2020 development plan, noting that the university would "promote the 'Belt and Road'" and "make full use of countries" that joined the initiative.[94] Since then, Tsinghua has established a range of BRI offerings, from a BRI-focused think tank and annual forum to increasing enrollment from BRI countries and even a degree in public administration along the BRI.[95]

Tsinghua also engaged in international business. In 2015 Tsinghua Unigroup, a subsidiary of the Tsinghua University-owned Tsinghua Holdings, attempted a $23 billion acquisition of Micron, an American chip manufacturer, more than quadrupling the previous record deal value of a Chinese acquisition of an American company. The deal was blocked, however, by the US government because of alleged national security concerns.[96]

A Special Education Zone: Schwarzman College

The growing political pressures within China and an unpredictable international environment threatened to limit Tsinghua's internationalization at home and its rise globally. But there were new opportunities at home. Just as China's economic "opening up and reform" in the 1980s had begun with special economic zones such as Shenzhen, the first decades of the twentieth century saw a series of what might be deemed "special education zones" through Sino-foreign joint ventures, of which NYU Shanghai and Duke Kunshan University are the best known. Tsinghua created its own special zone, within the gates of the university.

Stephen A. Schwarzman, chairman and CEO of the Blackstone Group, a leading private equity firm, had strong business interests in China ever since China's sovereign wealth fund invested in Blackstone at the time of its initial public offering in 2007. He served on the Advisory Board of Tsinghua's School of Economics and Management. SEM Dean Qian Yingyi had hoped to approach Schwarzman, who as a philanthropist had given generously to the New York Public Library and other institutions, for a major gift. But presidents often steal a dean's best prospects, and President Chen Jining had larger ambitions still. He aimed to work with Schwarzman on a project that he hoped would transform Tsinghua and its place in the world.

After years of negotiation, planning, building, and recruiting both students and faculty, the result was Schwarzman College, an international, residential graduate school of global affairs, located on the Tsinghua campus, aimed at "the next generation of global leaders."

I became involved in this project in late 2011, when Steve Schwarzman came to my HBS office to ask my advice. At that point, Tsinghua's plans for his potential gift were still undefined, except that it was to be large. Very large. Schwarzman, too, had not clarified what he wished to do, save that he wanted it to be transformative, and above all he wanted it to promote the long-term development of Chinese-American relations—to bring the next generations of Chinese and American leaders together to learn with, and from, one another. In his own words, Schwarzman's aim was for students to "study under Chinese and Western professors who would help them find the links between cultures. Each cohort of scholars would be enriched by the experience. Then as they rose to positions of influence in different countries, they would understand each other and their ambitions. They would act out of friendship and reason, not with the kind of suspicions and mistrust that cause countries to stumble into the 'Thucydides trap.'"[97] Within a few months, my HBS colleague Warren McFarlan and I were advising Schwarzman on every aspect of a project that, by American academic standards, began to move with lightning speed.

It is no easy thing to start a new college, anywhere. A new college within a university is perhaps particularly challenging, for the energy and resources devoted to it inevitably come at some cost to existing schools and their deans, who have little to gain from it. But President Chen Jining—and then his successor, Qiu Yong—mobilized the schools and faculty of Tsinghua for this project, for they too believed it to be transformative for the university as a whole, bringing international students, faculty, and standards to the heart of the Tsinghua campus. Everything was up for definition and negotiation, except for the program's intended impact on Tsinghua, China, the United States, and the wider world. Even Schwarzman's Chinese name was given new character, as it were. Formerly, the name Schwarzman had simply been transliterated in Chinese. Chen Jining now gave him a real three-character Chinese name that meant something: *Su Shimin*, that is, Mr. Su, World Citizen.

Both Chen Jining and Schwarzman were men in a hurry. Chen and Tsinghua worked at "China speed," a phrase that conveys the remarkable speed with which things can be built in China today. (There is a bridge at Harvard across the Charles River that recently took six years to repair. A bridge of similar size in China was replaced in forty-eight hours.) But often enough "China speed" was no match for "Schwarzman speed," which moved the project forward at a breathtaking pace. By the end of 2012 fundamental agreement was reached on the nature and funding of the project; a global search for an architect was under way; I had formed and chaired a global Academic Advisory Council; Tsinghua had recruited a founding dean, the charismatic and prolific economist, Professor Li Daokui; and Schwarzman had pledged $100 million of his own funds while he undertook to raise al-most all of the rest. Since few of his acquaintances can turn down Steve

Schwarzman, by 2020 pledges for the program's endowment stood at nearly $600 million.[98]

That level of funding would be needed to build and sustain the program that has become Schwarzman Scholars. The program planned a maximum of two hundred graduate students, for whom everything (tuition, fees, housing, meals, transportation) would be provided gratis. They would reside in a stunning new residential college that housed, in the Oxbridge model, students and (some) faculty, containing also case-study classrooms, an opulent auditorium, open meeting spaces, a gymnasium and, for good measure, a pub. (That was my idea.) In the tradition of early twentieth century Chinese campuses, an American architect, Robert A. Stern, was given the commission. He designed a thoroughly modern campus with Chinese characteristics, including Beijing-style brick and a courtyard.

Schwarzman College, as the physical complex is known, stood in lush contrast to any Tsinghua student residence, with its individual rooms, bathrooms, and suites. (It was built on the site of the public showers used by Tsinghua students whose dorms had none.) It boasted state-of-the-art filtration systems for air and water, protecting its inhabitants from Beijing's often noxious environment. It had its own, dedicated internet service that could transcend the Great Firewall of Chinese censorship. Its library had international newspapers, magazines, and scholarly books—as well as the bound Collected Speeches of Xi Jinping in ten languages.

Figure 9.4. Schwarzman College. Photograph © William C. Kirby.

Was this a new, academic kind of treaty port, with extraterritorial privileges? Certainly in part, although the extensive public programs of the college, featuring Chinese and international leaders from all fields, were open to the university community. Was it also a sign of the direction Tsinghua itself wished to head? Without question. Faced with the inevitable critique of the comparative opulence and openness of the new college, Chen Jining said bluntly that the new college could be a model for Tsinghua's future. (As Deng Xiaoping had said, in inaugurating the first Special Economic Zones decades earlier, it was no betrayal of Chinese socialism if some people got rich first.)

By 2020 the Schwarzman Scholars at Tsinghua University was an unquestioned success, even if temporarily displaced from Beijing by the global pandemic. With its fellowship competition modeled on that of the Rhodes Scholarships, it admitted students from the United States, the Chinese mainland, Hong Kong, Macao, and Taiwan in addition to scholars from a further seventy-four countries around the world. It rapidly became among the most selective of international graduate programs, admitting approximately 4 percent of applicants, and with an admissions yield of 94 percent. Its Masters of Global Affairs degree focuses on politics, business, and science, while immersing students in issues facing China and the world. It has so far been insulated from the growing political oversight of the Xi Jinping era. Led now by a distinguished scholar and administrator, Dean Xue Lan, its faculty includes a stellar list of Tsinghua and international scholars, teaching ambitious cohorts of young people who are told that they shall become "leaders prepared to deepen understanding between China and the rest of the world."

Can Tsinghua Lead?

Within China, Tsinghua already leads in many areas. Tsinghua is China's top comprehensive university in the most prestigious international rankings. In discipline-specific rankings, Tsinghua is world-leading, or nipping at the heels of the world's best. Excellence in STEM has afforded it greater stability than other Chinese universities in its overall budget. Publicly funded science and technology expenditures at Tsinghua rose nearly 30 percent in 2020, while government outlays for Tsinghua's peers declined following the COVID-19 pandemic.[99] However, Tsinghua's reliance on the support of the political system that fueled its rise has not come without cost. Like the University of Berlin in Wilhelmine times, Tsinghua is part and parcel of a rising nation-state that is among global leaders in science and technology. It promotes liberal education and yet remains broadly illiberal in its national politics. Moreover, the state's enormous support for Tsinghua's STEM fields underscores a view that the university serves China's development priorities, not, primarily, the creation and dissemination of knowledge. Will a program such as Schwarzman Scholars suffice for Tsinghua to present itself to be a truly internationalized university in values as well as research?

We shall see. Meanwhile, Tsinghua, an institution founded to send Chinese students away for their education, now hosts proudly what it calls the Rhodes Scholarship for the twenty-first century. After all, why should the best and brightest of the world's young leaders go to Oxford—to a foggy, chilly, self-isolating island, in decline, off the coast of Europe—when they could come to Tsinghua in Beijing, the capital of a rising China? Cecil Rhodes had aimed to educate those with "the potential for leadership." Surely Tsinghua, too, has the potential for leadership.

CHAPTER TEN

The Burden of History

Nanjing University

NANJING, OR Nanking, as it was long known in English, is China's "southern capital." At least, that is what the characters mean. Today, the city of Nanjing occupies an unclear position in China's political and economic hierarchies. With political power headquartered in Beijing, financial might at home in Shanghai, and trade and manufacturing centered in Guangdong, what is Nanjing but one of a growing number of wealthy, industrialized provincial capitals? Of course, that is no minor status: this metropolis of 8.5 million inhabitants is the capital of Jiangsu province, long one of China's commercial and intellectual centers, whose eighty million citizens enjoy one of China's highest standards of living. Certainly, Nanjing occupies a higher place in the hierarchy of Chinese cities than Durham, North Carolina, does in the hierarchy of American cities. But, today, Nanjing University confronts a challenge not unlike that once faced by Duke University: how to punch above its place.

The city of Nanjing, in east-central China on the banks of the great Yangzi River, was once at the absolute center, with a longer and more distinguished history than that of Beijing, which lies at the dusty northern frontier of the North China plain. Nanjing was the capital of multiple Chinese dynasties. Called Yingtian when capital of the Ming dynasty (1368–1644), it may have been the largest city in the world, with a half-million inhabitants in 1400. When the Ming established its "northern capital" in *Bei*jing, Yingtian became *Nan*jing, or the southern (and suddenly secondary) capital. In the Qing dynasty (1644–1912) the city was for a decade in the mid-nineteenth century called *Tian*jing, or the "heavenly capital" of the rebellious Taiping Heavenly Kingdom. When the Republic of China was established in 1912, Nanjing was initially named the capital. And it would be China's national capital, in fact, under the Nationalist regime from 1927 to 1949.

In modern times Nanjing has experienced both tragedy and hope. Massacres of its inhabitants occurred twice during the Taiping Rebellion of the mid-nineteenth century. Thirty thousand imperial troops were stabbed, burned, or drowned when the Taiping forces took the city in 1853. Eleven years later, when imperial troops retook the city, their commander, Zeng Guofan, reported that one hundred thousand rebels had perished. In 1911, when Nanjing fell in a bloody battle to revolutionary forces seeking to overthrow the Qing, the days of the last imperial dynasty were numbered. In 1937 the Japanese "rape of Nanjing" set new standards for military criminality. The seven-week-long mass execution of Chinese soldiers and the slaughter and rape of tens of thousands of civilians took place in contravention of all rules of modern warfare and in the full view of international observers.

Yet when it was China's capital after 1927, Nanjing had dreams of a return to glory. The city's boundaries were vastly expanded to house both the new National Government and an anticipated population of two million (in retrospect, a conservative estimate). Rail connections were to grow and a huge airport to be built. A new government district of nearly ten square kilometers was to be erected on the site just west of the old Ming palace, and south of the Ming tombs was to be an imposing mausoleum for the Nationalist founder, Sun Yat-sen. Located at the district's center would be a modern palace complex situated on a north-south axis, dominated at its northern end by a massive Nationalist Party headquarters, an international architectural marvel combining features of Beijing's Temple of Heaven and the U.S. Capitol in Washington, DC. Beyond all this, the city would be beautified. In Parisian style, trees would line the avenues and electric lights in the shape of Chinese lanterns would line the streets. A system of parkways and boulevards was conceived, dominated by the grand, six-lane Zhongshan Lu, or Sun Yat-sen Road. A "ring boulevard" was to encircle the new capital, but not, as later in Beijing, at the expense of the ancient city wall. Nanjing's great city wall would be retained, perhaps with the thought—times being what they were—that it might be needed. So Nanjing's ring road would run *on top* of the old wall, offering its motorists a parkway with a panorama of city, river, and suburbs.[1]

Not all of these things were built. A few were, however, and they serve today as reminders of what Nanjing was meant to be. Sun Yat-sen Boulevard is the main thoroughfare, leading through the city to Sun's stunning mausoleum. The city walls remain—among the best-preserved in China. And massive numbers of what locals called "French trees" (in fact a hybrid of American sycamore and Oriental plane) were planted. Seedlings imported from France would in time shade a Communist Nanjing.

Inheritances

It was during these years of ambition and revival, before the establishment of the People's Republic of China, that Nanjing University's predecessors, institutions such as National Central University and the University of Nanking, were founded and flourished. Before they merged under the umbrella of Nanjing University, or Nanda, as it became known (distinguishing itself from Beida, or Peking University), each had developed a distinctive institutional culture closely connected with the international trends and models in higher education of their era.[2]

National Central University: Berlin on the Yangzi

Nanjing University's primary predecessor, National Central University (NCU), was itself born out of a series of institutions established during the late Qing dynasty's reform movement. NCU's lineage may be first traced to Sanjiang Normal School, founded in 1902 at the urging of Zhang Zhidong, the reformist Governor General of Liangjiang (today's Jiangsu, Jiangxi, and Anhui provinces). Zhang believed the region needed a modern education system, basing Sanjiang on a Japanese model, which was itself inspired by Western models. The institution changed rapidly in its first two decades. In 1905, just a year after Sanjiang enrolled its first students, it was renamed Liangjiang Normal School, and an expanded curriculum was introduced offering students greater flexibility to specialize. The school was restructured again in 1914, this time as National Nanjing Higher Normal School, and the Japanese-inspired curriculum was replaced with one based on American and European models.[3] Behind this shift was school president Guo Bingwen, a major figure in this era of Chinese education. A recipient of a Boxer Indemnity Scholarship, he studied at the University (now College) of Wooster in Ohio, where he became committed to an education in the sciences and the humanities. Guo was one of the first Chinese nationals to receive a doctorate from an American institution, and he wrote his Columbia doctoral thesis on "The Chinese System of Public Education." As president, Guo introduced reforms based on practices in Euro-American higher education that were considered innovative to China, including offering elective courses and opening the school's doors to women. By 1920 he had transformed the school into a full university. Three years later it was given a name to fit its mission: National Southeast University, the leading institution at the center of the country.

National Southeast University was a major institution for its time. It employed over two hundred faculty and staff, enrolled sixteen hundred students, and housed twenty-seven departments within five schools. The university's curriculum began with a general education program before students declared academic majors and chose elective courses. The university was deeply engaged with the significant intellectual movements of Republican China. In response to the May Fourth Movement and the Peking University–led New Culture movement, which sharply critiqued China's cultural legacy, several scholars at National Southeast University sought to preserve China's "national essence" while infusing it with elements of Western culture. Their "Xueheng School," so named for the journal *Xueheng* (Critical Review), was led by a group of "aggressive, outspoken" young scholars trained at Harvard under Irving Babbitt, whose literary and political writings helped to define American conservative thought in the 1920s and 1930s.[4]

While it left an important mark on Nanda's historical foundations, National Southeast University lasted but four years before being again restructured in the aftermath of the Nationalist revolution of 1926–1927, which brought to power the Guomindang, or Nationalist Party, and the government it led.

The Nationalist government, established in 1927, desired a comprehensive, flagship, *national* university for its new capital, Nanjing. It sought a University of Berlin for its Berlin. It also sought a flagship *Party* university: the Nationalists were heirs to the permanent revolutionary, Sun Yat-sen, the first provisional president of the Chinese republic. Sun died in 1925, but his mission of Party-led national development became the political gospel for his Nationalist successors led by Chiang Kai-shek.

Chiang's rule would emphasize a commitment to political discipline and scientific/technological advancement, in equal measure. National Central University, born on May 16, 1928, of a merger of National Southeast University with eight other institutions, came to life under the direct sponsorship of the ruling party. This new university was then China's largest, with eight schools, 1,762 students, and 346 faculty members—far larger than Tsinghua University at the time. Although the structure of the curriculum stayed initially constant in the transition to National Central University, its content became subject to politicization. Students were required to study English and Sun Yat-sen's famous "Three People's Principles" (nationalism, socialism, democracy, in the short version) from the point of view of the ruling party and also pass military training and physical education courses.[5]

In a period of profound German influence on China's military, industrial, and educational development in the decade before the onset of China's war with Japan in 1937,[6] the presidency (1930–1932) of German-educated geologist Zhu Jiahua aimed to make National Central University China's national model. Higher education was to be "partified" (*danghua*), with an emphasis on alignment with the state's political priorities and a commitment to science. Chiang Kai-shek himself extolled the educational values of Prussia / Germany—values of "patriotism, discipline, honor, and order."[7] He even sent his son, Chiang Wei-kuo, to be a cadet at the Munich *Kriegsschule*, from which he participated in the German *Anschluß* with Austria in 1938. But students, even at National Central University, were more nationalist than Nationalist, and they protested vigorously Japan's recurrent incursions. The Japanese takeover of Manchuria in 1931 led to such student protests in Nanjing that Chiang Kai-shek temporarily suspended the university's operations. At Chiang's request, Luo Jialun gave up his presidency at Tsinghua to run and reform National Central University.

Having studied at the Universities of Berlin, Paris, and London, Luo was determined to make NCU an important player in China's cultural rejuvenation. He focused on recruiting outstanding faculty and raising the bar for full professorship (which did not endear him to the faculty). His second priority was to link the university's academic development to China's social and economic needs. For example, Luo Rong'an of MIT was recruited to build National Central University's mechanical engineering department, which produced China's first aeronautical engineers. Finally, Luo streamlined the university's administrative structure, reducing redundancy, improving efficiency, and cutting costs. The money saved was used to purchase books and remake the university's campus, which included building its iconic Brandenburg Gate in 1933 and auditorium in 1934, modeled after that of the University of Berlin. Luo's most ambitious plan, a new campus to ac-

Figure 10.1. The "Brandenburg Gate" of National Central University.
Wikimedia Commons.

commodate an additional ten thousand students, was permanently derailed
by the Japanese invasion.

When Nanjing fell to the Japanese army in 1937, a Japanese-led Chinese
"puppet" government, now in formal alliance with National Socialist Germany, operated its own National Central University on the site of the original institution. Jiang Zemin, future president of the People's Republic of
China, attended this NCU from 1943 until shortly after the war ended in
1945. There, he became an active participant in anti-Japanese student protests. However, when the war ended and the Chinese government returned
to Nanjing in 1945, the Nationalists refused to recognize the education
given Jiang and others at the Japanese-run NCU. Jiang was forced to finish
his education at Shanghai's Jiao Tong University, where he promptly joined
the Communist Party.[8]

The Nationalist-led NCU reopened in Nanjing in 1946 as China's leading
comprehensive university. Chiang Kai-shek had been named NCU president
during World War II, when the university was relocated to China's southwest. He remained president emeritus after the war, but the university's recovery would be short-lived. Following the Communist military victory in
the Chinese Civil War (1946–1949), the university was once again renamed,
this time as National Nanjing University. Then, after an edict eliminated

"National" from all university names, the institution finally settled on a name that would last: Nanjing University.

The University of Nanking

National Central University may be the most important ancestor of Nanjing University, but Nanda's lineage includes also leading Christian colleges, which were important actors in Chinese higher education during the late nineteenth and early twentieth centuries. They bequeathed to modern Nanda a strong commitment to teaching, which arguably remains stronger at Nanda than at other leading Chinese universities.

The University of Nanking (UNK), a direct predecessor of Nanda, was founded in 1910 as a merger of several institutions operated by American missionaries in Nanjing and was incorporated by the Regents of the University of the State of New York.[9] Why New York? The New York legislature worked to establish "benevolent, charitable, scientific and missionary societies" overseas, guide their development, and give academic recognition to the course work completed.[10]

These Christian aspirations for UNK were reflected in its academic offerings, specializing in disciplines often associated with missionary work in China, such as education, medicine, agronomy, and the humanities.[11] Its curriculum was influenced by American models, focusing on English language, interactive classroom pedagogies, and applied projects.[12] UNK's American ties were also the source of much of its funding, with the founding missionary board providing 65 percent of its budget. The university achieved some repute, ranking eleventh overall in a 1928 study of greater China's undergraduate programs by a University of California, Berkeley, scholar.[13] While UNK's foreign relationships diminished under the scrutiny of the Nationalist government, the institution continued to grow, having a student body of 675 and 214 faculty members divided into three schools and one Center for Research on Chinese Culture by 1934.[14] However, as with National Central University, war with Japan upended UNK's operations as it was moved to Chengdu from 1937 to 1946 by order of the Ministry of Education.

While UNK flourished again in Nanjing immediately after the war's end, the Chinese Civil War prevented it from finding permanent footing. In 1948 UNK had surpassed its prewar size, with 1,100 students and 150 faculty

THE BURDEN OF HISTORY

members. But its good fortune was short-lived. Only a year later, much of the Nationalist governing apparatus and many affiliated institutions fled to Taiwan as the conflict turned in the Communists' favor. UNK's administration chose to remain in Nanjing, a decision that cost the university its independence. In January 1951 UNK was forced by the new PRC's Ministry of Education to cut all ties with its American missionary funding sources and was restructured into the public National University of Nanking. Soon thereafter, it was merged with Ginling College, but the unified institution lasted less than a year before being hoovered up into the newly created Nanjing University.

Ginling College

Nomenclature confusion abounds in the ancestral tree of Nanda. The Chinese name of the University of Nanking was *Jinling daxue,* or Jinling University ("Jinling" or "Ginling" being a historical name for Nanjing). Ginling *College* or, as it was also called in English, Ginling College for Women (*Jinling nüzi daxue*), had a different origin and represents another important branch in Nanda's ancestral tree. Founded in 1912 by five American missionary organizations in Nanjing, Ginling College was a women's liberal arts college modeled after the American "Seven Sisters" and was affiliated with UNK. American missionaries were inspired by the US Progressive Era, in which promoting educational opportunities for women had become a central cause.[15] Ginling was the first college in China to grant bachelors' degrees to women. The college's first president, Matilda C. Thurston, was an alumna of Mount Holyoke College, but Ginling built its strongest relationship with Smith College, with which it exchanged faculty and even received financial support through fundraising by Smith alumnae.[16] Wu Yifang, a PhD from the University of Michigan, served as Ginling's president from 1928 to 1951 and was China's first female college president. In 1937 an acting Ginling president, the American missionary Wilhelmina Vautrin, known as the "Goddess of Mercy," protected ten thousand women and children on the campus during the Nanking massacre.[17] As with many institutions of higher education, Ginling College dispersed during the Second World War but returned, eager to continue the school's mission, in 1946.[18] However, the college would remain independent only for another five years, before finding itself under the new umbrella of Nanjing University.

Figure 10.2. Students at Ginling College. Gamewell, Mary Louise Ninde, *New Life Currents in China*. Missionary Education Movement in the United States and Canada, 1919, page 194 / Wikimedia Commons.

Communist Nanda

With the Communist takeover of China in 1949, Nanjing was suddenly no longer the national capital. National Central University, Nanjing's and the country's most prestigious institution of higher learning, ceased to exist. Like Humboldt University in 1945 and again in the 1990s, it was purged of faculty and administrators deemed most loyal to the *ancien régime*. Once central in every respect and centrally funded, it was now decidedly provincial. Carrying with it the "original sin" of being *the* Nationalist university, the new Nanjing University that took the place of NCU was for decades refused the special resources devoted to institutions in the Northern Capital. Beida and Tsinghua became China's new "national" universities in fact, if not in name.[19] Moreover, the strong missionary connections of several of its ancestors ensured Communist Nanda was in for rough sledding from the start.

Nanda was not only de-Nationalized but reduced in size. It was quickly sovietized and reformed as a purely teaching university with no mandate to pursue new research. Stripped of its programs in engineering, education, and agriculture, Nanda was housed on former campuses of National Central University and Ginling College, and the curriculum focused on the basic sciences and humanities.[20] By 1956 Nanda was home to just ten departments, mainly in literature, languages, and basic math and science. The university lost 36 percent of its teaching faculty in the reorganization, although it retained renowned scholars in math and science, allowing it to retain a leading position in these fields.[21]

NCU, Ginling, and UNK had all had strong relations with Europe or America. Like all Chinese universities, Nanda was now constricted to the Soviet bloc for its international partners. It brought scholars from the "socialist brother countries" to Nanjing and sent Nanda affiliates to the Soviet Union and Eastern Europe, but it was never a leading actor in Sino-Soviet exchanges. Nanda's somnambulance lasted until 1963, when Kuang Yaming, a scholar of traditional Chinese culture and a biographer of Confucius, was appointed president. The ambitious and outspoken Kuang began his tenure during a brief period of political loosening in China, and he tried to make the most of it. He criticized the Soviet model of ultra-specialization. He opened new research institutes, hosted conferences, published academic journals, and sought to put Nanda again at the forefront of research universities in China. He developed ten-year plans to bring Nanda back from the scholarly wilderness. As it turned out, he only had three years.

Kuang Yaming—like every Chinese university president in the modern era—had to be alert to changing political winds. After Mao Zedong openly criticized university education as elitist and out of touch in 1964 and 1965, Kuang moved proactively in early 1966 to show Nanda's loyalty. He sent five hundred students and faculty in the humanities to the countryside for an extended period of "half-farming, half-study." They lived the Maoist ideal in principle. In fact, the working conditions were horrific, and they resented Nanda's engineers who remained home in Nanjing. When the Cultural Revolution broke out on Beijing campuses that summer, these rusticized and begrudged faculty and students led a political attack on Kuang, to which he responded by labeling them reactionaries and "rightists." Kuang was then bizarrely accused by radicals in Beijing of stifling "the student movement," and soon the man who was trying to do what he *thought* Mao wanted was accused by *People's Daily* of "anti-Party and anti-socialist crimes of suppressing the revolutionary mass movement and undermining the proletariat Cultural Revolution."[22]

President Kuang was unceremoniously deposed on June 1, 1966; a few weeks later he and his subordinates were hauled before a mass rally where they were beaten and then paraded around campus. The campus, like the city and indeed the country, descended into factional strife and chaos. Mass movements and struggles arose across Nanjing, while three different Nanda student groups played leading roles in the factional conflicts and lethal armed conflict that continued well into 1967. That same year, in the midst of all this, the university halted admissions and basically shut down. The next class was not enrolled until 1972, when admissions were limited in principle to workers, peasants, and soldiers and, as at Tsinghua, based on recommendations and class identities.[23] Nanda was a shell of its former self and a basket case of a university.

Rebirth

In 1978, after twelve years of chaos and dysfunction, Nanda came back to life. Kuang Yaming was exhumed from his academic tomb to resume the presidency of the university. And he was ready to lead. He abandoned Soviet-era specializations in favor of a more open undergraduate curriculum with a credit system. China's central government established a national system of eighty-eight key universities, of which Nanda was one. With new-found support from the central and provincial governments, and with a newly tolerant perspective on education, Kuang seized the opportunity for higher education presented by China's reform and opening.[24]

Kuang quickly rehired talented scholars who had been purged from the academy during the anti-intellectual tumult of the Cultural Revolution. Because of Nanda's pre-1949 strength in the sciences, which he had enhanced during his first presidency, Kuang started with a strong, if now aging, base. In 1978 Nanda's scientific projects received fifty-four awards at China's National Science Convention, outshining all other Chinese universities. He further sought to retain and reward young talent by promoting junior faculty and by sending them abroad to attend international conferences. His reforms extended to Nanda's curriculum, which, for the first time in the Communist era, introduced an element of "general education," as each department was required to offer at least one "foundational course" open to nonmajors. Kuang himself taught a writing course required of all students. By 1981 Nanda was on the path to be again a comprehensive university when it reopened its graduate school, which then offered twenty-four doctoral programs and fifty-three master's degrees.

Nanda's academic and research culture in this era seemed to absorb Kuang's increasingly independent intellectual instincts. The university's humanities institute received national attention for the work of Hu Fuming, then an associate professor in the politics department. His 1978 essay, "Practice is the Sole Criterion of Truth," was a stunning and forceful renunciation of Maoist infallibility. He famously rebutted the doctrine, promoted by Mao's immediate successor as Party Chairman, Hua Guofeng, that "we must support whatever decisions made by . . . whatever instructions given by" the now-dead Mao Zedong. Hu Fuming's critique made waves nationwide, and it gave theoretical ballast to the return to power of Deng Xiaoping, who became China's paramount leader later that year. Nanda, for once, was now on the winning side of Chinese politics.

Nanda also led a revival of historical studies, a largely forbidden area in the Maoist period, save for the most ideological works. In Chinese historical tradition, every new ruling house writes the official history (*zhengshi*) of the previous dynasty. There are twenty-four such "standard histories" composed over two millennia, the last being the Ming history, completed in 1775.

In Republican China a *draft* Qing history was composed but never completed; after 1949, when the government of the Republic of China moved to Taiwan, competing Qing history projects continued on either side of the Taiwan Strait. The very act of composing an official history is meant to lend legitimacy to the new ruling house, and so the People's Republic was determined to write *its* history of the Republic, thereby consigning it to history. Most of the effort was centered in Nanjing, the old Nationalist capital. A Research Institute for the History of the Republic of China was established at Nanjing University under a courageous and astute historian, Zhang Xianwen, who would also chair its History Department and Institute for Historical Studies. Zhang led a groundbreaking effort beginning in the 1980s to write a defining history of the Republic on the basis of materials housed in the Republic's old *Guoshiguan,* or Academia Historica, which became the home of the PRC's Second Historical Archive, storing materials of the Republican era. Zhang's *Outline of the History of the Republic of China* was acclaimed for its objective analysis and use of primary sources on a topic that had been more the subject of propaganda than sober analysis on both sides of the Taiwan Strait.[25] (The topic was sensitive enough that the writer of its preface admitted that he had not read the book.)

Because of the work of Zhang Xianwen and his colleagues, Nanda became the center of historical research on twentieth-century China. I recall attending many workshops and conferences held by Professor Zhang and his colleagues in the 1980s. With his introduction, I also was among the first foreigners to be granted extensive access to the Nationalist-era documents in the Second Historical Archive. It was, in retrospect, a golden time for work in my field, even if the archives were not yet accustomed to international scholarly norms. (Behind the archivist's desk there was a large set of printed rules on the wall, including a prohibition against accurate footnotes: scholars could cite the full details of a document, but not name the archive; or they could name the archive but not the details. When I asked an archivist why this rule existed, she responded, "Well, then *everyone* would know!")

Zhang Xianwen and Nanda leveraged the attention received by his work on Republican China to establish serious academic exchanges with Taiwan—something illegal in the Maoist period—and even pursued fundraising from Taiwanese businesses.[26] In multiple dimensions, then, Nanda was asserting its leadership to study China's Republican past, when Nanjing and its universities were at the center.

Internationalization

That historical context mattered when Nanda built on its pre-Communist history of international exchanges to reengage with the world in the post-Mao era. It hosted its first post-Cultural Revolution group of international students and scholars in 1979. That same year, Kuang Yaming led the first delegation of Chinese university presidents to the United States since the Communist revolution.[27] While in Maryland, he invited Professor Chih-Yung Chien of Johns Hopkins University, who was a friend of that university's president, Steven Muller, to spend three months in China lecturing at Nanda and other universities.[28] For his part, Muller was interested in opening a Hopkins campus in China, as its School of Advanced International Studies (SAIS) had done in Bologna, Italy. To Muller, even in 1979, "China was the future." Chien returned from his trip to China convinced that Nanjing—not as political as Beijing nor as commercial as Shanghai—was the ideal location for such a venture.

In 1981 Muller traveled to Nanjing to negotiate an agreement with Kuang, which was approved by the Ministry of Education. Construction began in 1984, and in 1986 Nanda opened the Hopkins-Nanjing Center for Chinese and American Studies (HNC) in partnership with Hopkins' SAIS.[29] The Hopkins-Nanjing Center was the first academic joint-venture institution between Chinese and American universities since the founding of the People's Republic. It remains to this day the most rigorous. It was designed as a demanding, joint, interdisciplinary master's degree program in both Chinese and American studies, with intense language requirements on both sides. For example, American applicants typically completed three to four years of college-level Chinese before matriculating. The Americans took classes mostly in Mandarin Chinese, while the Chinese students studied mostly in English. It was designed to serve as the premier gateway to China for aspiring US government officials, businesspeople, and academics and as an opportunity to build relationships between these Americans and their Chinese counterparts. To foster friendships among students of different backgrounds, each dorm room had one American and one Chinese occupant.

Teaching—a historically distinguishing strength of Nanda—was at the core of the Hopkins-Nanjing Center's reputation for academic excellence. From its onset, the student body was small (originally 100, now 170), as were the intensive classes in American and Chinese history, politics, and culture. The Center's pedagogical and intellectual openness was enhanced from the beginning by an open-stack and uncensored library, bountifully stocked with books and periodicals ordered by both partner universities, including academic and media materials otherwise banned in China. (This was, and remains, the only open-stack library I have seen in hundreds of visits to Chinese universities.) The Hopkins-Nanjing Center set the academic bar high for a joint-venture program. Followers, such as NYU Shanghai (in partnership with East China Normal University), Duke Kunshan University (with Wuhan University as its partner), and Schwarzman Scholars (at Tsinghua) would all emulate the standards of academic autonomy first set at HNC. Nanjing, China's national capital in the more internationalist era of Republican China, was back at the center and in the vanguard of China's reentry into global systems.

The success of the Hopkins-Nanjing experiment was not easily won. The political and bureaucratic cultures of SAIS, in Washington, DC, and Nanjing University were strikingly different, and the American codirectors tended to stay for comparatively short tenures. The macrotensions of US-China relations periodically complicated the microproblems of running a bicultural institution. Yet HNC would endure and thrive. It taught the first course anywhere in China on the Cultural Revolution, and it has maintained its early promise of academic autonomy ever since. When formal processes failed, there were other means of addressing problems. I recall visiting and speaking at the Center in 1987 as the guest of the American codirector, Leon Slawecki, a retired foreign service officer who had studied China's foreign relations from a distance and now up close. He knew China well. And he knew that to smooth any problem, a liberal sampling of *baijiu,* the potent white liquor of which the Nanjing region boasted many famous brands, was his most useful diplomatic tool. His apartment held a famous collection of more than two hundred different types of *baijiu.*

There were, to be sure, some unexpected and unhappy outcomes of Nanjing's renewed internationalism. Nanda and other Nanjing universities welcomed a large number of students from Africa in the 1980s, seeking to revive ties from the 1950s that had been cut off by the Cultural Revolution. At a time when admission spots in any Chinese university were still severely limited, there arose resentment against African scholars who were recruited with comparatively large stipends. Added to this was the envy and resentment by male Chinese students of male African students who dated Chinese women. A combination of political and sexual frustrations among Chinese students, plus anti-African racism and anti-foreignism, sparked an incident on Christmas Eve in 1988 on a nearby campus that in turn led to a brawl that led to large student demonstrations at the Nanjing railway station, threatening the African students who were trying to leave the city. (I was introduced to this story by a remarkable Harvard undergraduate, whose 1989 senior thesis, "Anti-Africanism in China," remains one of the best pieces of undergraduate writing I have read. I encouraged her to pursue a doctorate in history. She declined: she wanted to be an actress. Six years later Mira Sorvino won an Academy Award.)[30]

Even the nationwide demonstrations and crackdown of 1989, which played out with such tragic consequences in Tiananmen Square in Beijing, proved to only pause Nanda's push to reinvigorate itself on international standards. Student protests in Nanjing during the spring of that year, while passionate and well attended, were not as large or organized as those in Beijing, nor did they face the same degree of military suppression. This did not mean that 1989 posed no challenges. Some at Johns Hopkins University pushed President Muller to close the Hopkins-Nanjing Center. However, with the aid of Hopkins' SAIS China Studies chair, A. Doak Barnett, Muller convinced the trustees that staying in China, and especially the partnership with Nanda, was the right course, even through tumult and crisis.[31]

Ambitions, Setbacks, and Renewal

Nanda's ambition to return to the center of Chinese higher education and be again a leading comprehensive university continued after Kuang's second term as Nanda's president ended in 1982. His successor, the astrophysicist Qu Qinyue, was another remarkable and remarkably independent leader. Unusually for a PRC university president, he was not a Communist Party member. Even more unusually, he aimed to make Nanjing University a model of the integration of teaching and research. Nanda's curriculum was dispersed nationwide by the publication of hundreds of textbooks. Qu oversaw the revision of undergraduate and graduate education, established a School of Graduate Studies in 1984, and three years later established the first medical school in a Chinese university since the Communist takeover.[32]

Kuang, who remained influential after his presidency, lobbied the central government for support. However, when Deng Xiaoping announced five universities to receive special funding, Nanda was not among them.[33] Deng prioritized investments in Beijing's and Shanghai's top universities as the likeliest candidates to become China's "key" strategic universities.[34] Nanjing was again on the periphery. President Qu lobbied for resources as well, but he failed initially, with the central government increasing investments in fifteen universities but, again, not Nanda.[35] Only in 1993, when Nanda was named among the one hundred universities to receive funding through Project 211 and, in a greater boost to its standing, was later among the nine elite schools, eventually termed the "C9," selected for the second round of Project 985, could the university again aspire to national stature. Yet the national commitment remained small in financial terms. It fell to the Jiangsu provincial government to invest the funds needed to keep Nanda in the national conversation after 1999.[36]

Like Duke in North America, Nanda had to do more with less. It focused resources on faculty recruitment and talent development, the renovation of its central campus in Nanjing's ancient Gulou (Drum Tower) district, and building a new, "independent" campus in Pukou, on the north bank of the Yangzi River, allowing it to expand student enrollment and tuition revenue.

Given its comparatively small size and limited resources, Nanda consistently punched above its weight in research. According to Thomson Scientific's Science Citation Index (SCI), which is widely used in China and around the world to evaluate a university's research prowess in the sciences, Nanda boasted the highest total number of papers published in international scientific journals among all Chinese universities for six consecutive years from 1992 to 1998.[37] However, as competition for talent and resources increased with the rapid development of higher education in China, Nanda found that its academic needs consistently outpaced government outlays. Frustrated by the government's fiscal timidity, President Qu, in a move unprecedented at a Chinese university, resigned his position in 1997, explaining, "If the government does not change its lip service into taking real responsibility, it will be very difficult for the development of education to meet the needs of social change, and the morale of university leaders and faculty and education will be inevitably affected."[38]

A Return to the Center? Massification and the Quest for Global Repute in the Twenty-First Century

In the twenty-first century, the financial gloves came off. Nanjing University rode the dramatic wave of expansion within Chinese higher education, growing far larger while finally regaining its position as one of China's top universities. In 2019 Nanda served 63,876 students across 31 schools and departments, including 13,129 undergraduates, 14,937 postgraduates, 6,996 doctoral students, and 3,205 foreign students. Although Nanda had capped undergraduate enrollment at around 13,000 since 2005, its graduate student population grew eightfold over a period of 25 years, from 2,409 in 1995 to over 20,000 in 2019.[39] International university rankings consistently placed Nanda sixth or seventh within China and in the top 100 to 150 institutions globally. This was a dramatic improvement over the start of this century, when Nanda did not place among the top three hundred international universities in 2004. A two-hundred place improvement within fifteen years would be cheered as a success by most university administrations, and it was at Nanda. But after President Xi Jinping named Nanda as among five universities on track to become "the first famous Chinese institutions of higher education" in 2014, developing Nanda into a world-class university became an inescapable, central tenet of its institutional strategy.

Nanda's thirteenth five-year plan, released in 2016, declared its intent to pursue a development model with "Chinese and world-class characteristics" with the goal of "maintaining a leading position at home while accelerating its pace toward becoming a world-class university."[40] The plan conceded, frankly, that this was "a tough time to join the ranks of world-class universities," but Nanda's leadership declared itself ready for the challenge. The following year, Nanda released its "Plan for Building a World-Class University," which foresaw Nanda jumping to the "forefront of world-class universities to realize the great rejuvenation of the Chinese nation."[41] The "great rejuvenation" was a catch phrase of President Xi's, to whose political agenda Nanda was now increasingly tied. Although Nanda was far from the only Chinese university to have set its sights high, it held a number of distinct institutional advantages.

Teaching Your Way to the Top?

Building on Nanda's inherited traditions of independent intellectualism and the reforms of Presidents Kuang and Qu, the university sought to differentiate itself from national and international peers not only by advances in research but also, and indeed primarily, by focusing on cultivating talented students. "Talent training," according to Nanda's World-Class University plan, "is a foundational part of creating a world-class university."[42] But how does a university improve how talent is "trained"? For Nanda, the answer lay in the classroom.

This was an unusual strategy, in which Nanda sought to differentiate itself from other Chinese universities whose success was determined almost exclusively by research outcomes and where outstanding teaching was seldom rewarded. After all, why not distinguish yourself in teaching, which had long been in Nanda's DNA, especially as no one else is doing it? It is a competition you can win. In 2006 Nanda's small, teaching-intensive Kuang Yaming Honors School was founded to provide science students with an interdisciplinary education.[43] Reforms to university-wide general education followed in 2009. Students could now enter Nanda without having declared a major, as in an American college. Only after completing the general education sequence could students formally declare a major. Reforms to Nanda's general education requirements also included a focus on seminars and the formal evaluation of teaching. The emphasis on teaching and curricular quality echoed the work of Dean Qian Yingyi at Tsinghua. But Qian only had to convince his own unit of Tsinghua to adopt the program. Nanda sought to build a general education program that all students would share. In 2016 Nanda, with a bit of a numerical fetish, set the goal of creating ten courses recognized as world class, one hundred courses that were among the best in China, and one thousand courses that utilized modern, "individualized" pedagogies. So proud was Nanda's administration of its new curriculum that, in 2018, international educators were invited to attend class sessions and see for themselves the education on offer at Nanda.

Building on its signature program with Johns Hopkins, "promoting international exchanges and cooperation" remained a core tenet of Nanda's strategy to build "international resources, reputation, and support."[44] The university committed itself to establishing a new range of foreign exchanges with the strategic purpose of helping the university improve its talent training initiatives, strengthen its academic departments, and raise research standards. At their best, Nanda's internationalization strategies showed an openness to identifying and adopting the highest international standards of academic excellence. By 2020 Nanda boasted student, faculty, or academic exchanges with more than forty European institutions; eight in the UK; nine in Australia; forty across Asia; twenty in the United States; and two in Latin America.

By the end of the second decade of the twenty-first century, however, Nanda's internationalist, cosmopolitan academic culture—aspirationally "world class"—began to come under scrutiny at home. Beijing would remind Nanjing who, at the end of the day, was at the center, and who was in charge.

Serving the State, Pursuing Rankings

Nanjing University's return to respectability in the post-Mao era was rooted in its history: its great inheritance from the Republican era in the liberal arts and sciences. But from the government's perspective, universities were, above all, vehicles for achieving national priorities—and priorities can change. This was as true of the Nationalists in the days of National Central University as it would be for the Communists in the era of reform. For Nanda, this led to a pivot to rebuild departments in engineering and applied sciences that it had lost during the restructuring of Chinese universities in the 1950s. Nanda had nearly merged with Southeast University, which was (re)created out of many of the applied departments lost to Nanda in the 1950s, but this plan was scrapped at least in part due to opposition from the Southeast University faculty.[45] (Even in China, faculty can make serious trouble for administrators.) Surging government funding for engineering became an opportunity for Nanda to realize these ambitions and climb higher in the league tables.

Nanda's thirteenth five-year plan in 2016 was brutally frank, somewhat like a Duke plan. It was noted that the university had not produced "many landmark achievements in response to major national strategic needs." To improve its standing, Nanda committed to being "guided by the major needs of national and regional economic and social development by integrating engineering disciplines and R&D resources."[46]

In now giving priority to applied disciplines, over 40 percent of Nanda's hiring opportunities were for scholars in STEM disciplines.[47] Scholars in STEM recruited through Nanda's "high-level talent" program were eligible to receive salary bonuses, start-up grants, housing stipends, and teams of research assistants.[48] With government funding opportunities in STEM fields proliferating, Nanda had set up the Research Fund Management Center in 2014 to manage grant opportunities, applications, and distributions from cultural, scientific, and military funding sources for the entire university. But while Nanda received accolades from the Jiangsu and Nanjing governments for its contributions to regional development, the university's national rankings in engineering, physics, chemistry, atmospheric sciences, and environmental science all fell in 2017. Success in these realms was a moving target. Worse yet, disciplines that Nanda saw as its strengths, such as foreign languages and literature, fell in the rankings as well. To succeed in the brutally competitive world of Chinese universities, Nanda concluded that it had to get bigger and richer, fast.

Unlike several leading Chinese universities, which had grown in scale and fortune by relentless mergers with regional institutions (for example, Zhejiang University with its seven campuses), Nanjing University was slow to reach its current scale. The one big merger it sought, with Southeast University, had foundered. Vice Secretary Yang Zhong sought to put Nanda in its best light when he explained, "We believe that world-class universities don't rely on scale. . . . The most important thing is to look at the level of quality of your human talent cultivation. A university's greatness isn't in its size, but rather in its way of thinking, in its innovation."[49] Still, Nanda aimed to grow in size and income. In 1998 it opened a new incarnation of Ginling College, officially Jinling College of Nanjing University (*Nanjing daxue jinling xueyuan*). This was a separate but affiliated school in partnership with the state-owned Jiangsu International Trust Corporation, Ltd. The trust provided RMB 100 million in funding, and the school was established with an independent organizational structure, legal status, campus, and budget system.[50] Whereas Nanda's standard undergraduate program was strong in basic research, Jinling College was built to bolster Nanda's "integration of industry, academia, and research" by focusing on attracting and training those talented in the applied disciples, such as engineering, business, and media.[51] The college was relocated to Nanda's Pukou campus in 2009, but enrollment was capped to control the quality of education. This hesitation to increase Nanda and its affiliate's size had an opportunity cost: stagnant revenue from tuition dollars just when the university needed more money with fewer strings attached. By 2020 Nanda seemed eager to square this circle. Jinling College would be moved again, this time to an entirely different city: Suzhou. This, Nanda hoped, would allow Jinling's applied disciplines greater opportunities to thrive in an industrial hub with an entrepreneurial city government.[52] As for Pukou, it would become home to a new center for executive education, another potential revenue generator, with a research and development innovation park to serve Nanjing's regional economy.[53]

This ancillary income aside, the most significant portion of Nanda's income came from government sources. As with other Chinese universities, and as we have seen with Tsinghua, Nanda does not publish a transparent accounting of income the university receives from government appropriations. However, using Nanda's disclosures of how much the university received directly from the Ministry of Finance as a baseline, it is clear that government funding plays by far the largest role in Nanda's budget. In 2019, of the university's projected income of US$1.2 billion, US$402.6 million, or about one-third of the total, came directly from the Ministry of Finance.[54] Yet with a significant portion of these outlays tied to the size of a university's enrollment, as long as the university capped enrollment, Nanda's options to increase state funding were limited largely to competing for subsidies tied to strategic initiatives. Nanda had a policy of limiting the number of new undergraduates each year to around three thousand.[55] Although Nanda's endowment had grown from just over US$34 million in 2009 to over $US163 million in 2017, the Nanda Education Foundation, which managed these funds, earned only around US$7 million from investments in 2017.[56]

University leadership hoped that Nanda's opening of a new campus in Nanjing's burgeoning Xianlin "University City," east of the city's center, in 2009 would help to sustain the university's growth for the next one hundred years. By 2012 Nanda Xianlin was Nanda's principal campus and home to the university's engineering and applied sciences departments, while basic science departments, such as mathematics and physics, and professional schools (business, law, and medicine) remained at Nanda's historic Gulou

Figure 10.3. The new "Brandenburg Gate" commemorating National Central University at Nanjing University's Xianlin campus. zhongwenpan/ Pixabay.

Figure 10.4. Nanjing University's new Xianlin campus. Ozonefrance/Wikimedia Commons/CC BY-SA 3.0.

campus. The physical expansion and redistribution of Nanda split the university, quite literally, into the old and the new. Xianlin would be home to an RMB 5-billion science park to deepen enterprise-university partnerships, which could become a source of innovation and, ideally, revenue.

The Jiangsu provincial government and Nanjing's municipal authorities cheered the move and supported it financially. Nanda's alumni financed part of the project. Xianlin was the physical manifestation of Nanda's determination to rise through investment in policy and political priorities.

Competition Abroad, Attacks at Home

In the twenty-first century, Nanda continued to innovate in its international partnerships. Nanda was chosen as one of the first two Chinese universities to host American students from the U.S. Department of Defense–funded Chinese Language Flagship program.[57] Managed by the National Security Education Program, the Language Flagship program was founded to create cohorts of Americans with advanced language proficiency in "critical languages"—those spoken in countries considered especially important to US national security.[58] When the Language Flagship rolled out an undergraduate program in 2006, Nanda partnered with Brigham Young University, with which it had held exchanges since the 1980s, to open one of two PRC-based Chinese Flagship Centers.[59] Annually thereafter, forty of the top American students from the twelve Chinese Flagship programs at US universities took a semester at Nanda.[60] Unlike the Hopkins-Nanjing Center, Chinese Flagship students enrolled directly at Nanda, choosing among the same courses (all taught in Chinese) as regular Nanda undergraduate and graduate students, a testament to Nanda's growing confidence in its curriculum. As the US-China relationship rose in importance in the twenty-first century, Nanda's early and eager engagement with US universities positioned it to capitalize on the growing American appetite for educational exchanges with China.

The advent of the "America First" administration of President Donald Trump in 2016 threw all this into doubt, as the US government criticized international education cooperation with China. Beginning with the National Defense Authorization Act of 2018, an annual piece of US legislation, universities that housed both Chinese Flagship programs and Confucius Institutes (Chinese language and cultural promotion ventures partially funded by the PRC's Ministry of Education) were required to close their Confucius Institutes to receive Flagship funding. To protect their Flagship programs, six US universities shuttered their Confucius Institutes.[61] There were also signs that the Flagship program was seeking to shift a growing proportion of its operations from mainland China to Taiwan, as US-China tensions rose under Trump. Since the program's start, there had always been two PRC-based Flagship centers, but in 2019 the second campus moved to National Taiwan University. All of this put Nanda, with its Chinese Republican ancestry, suddenly in uneasy and public competition with the Republic of China on Taiwan.[62]

Meanwhile, Nanda's premier international education program, the Hopkins-Nanjing Center, faced competitive pressures from China's most elite institutions. Tsinghua and Peking Universities had charted a different path to attract the world's top students. Unlike Hopkins-Nanjing, Tsinghua's Schwarzman College, announced in 2013, and Peking's Yenching Academy, announced in 2014, were independent ventures, not joint partnerships. Their core differentiators included the unmatched prestige of those institutions and a deep well of funding. Framed as merit scholarships, Schwarzman and Yenching courted comparisons to Oxford's Rhodes Scholarship, as we have seen. They sought to build endowments that rivaled that of the Rhodes. Indeed, the Schwarzman Scholars' $600 million endowment exceeded the Rhodes Trust's $390 million[63] and far exceeded the endowment of *all* of Nanjing University. The Hopkins-Nanjing Center, supported in part through the Johns Hopkins University School of Advanced International Studies, which had its own fiscal challenges, had no such financial firepower.

Schwarzman and Yenching had no Chinese language prerequisites, a central feature of Hopkins-Nanjing. This expanded their potential applicant pool dramatically. In the Schwarzman Scholarship's first year, more than three thousand students applied.[64] Numbers have continued to climb, reaching over forty-seven hundred in the 2019 admissions cycle.[65] Yenching Academy did not report the size of its applicant pool, but it enrolled around 125 students per year with a reported acceptance rate of 2.7 percent, indicating that it also received thousands of applications.[66] Successful admits to these new programs were, on average, of higher academic caliber than those admitted to Hopkins-Nanjing. Competitive applicants to Yenching had undergraduate grade point averages (GPAs) of 3.7 or higher, while the average GPA of a Schwarzman scholar was 3.8.[67] The middle 50 percent of undergraduate GPAs for Hopkins-Nanjing students ranged from 3.30 to 3.77 in 2019.[68] With Schwarzman and Yenching each enrolling more students than Hopkins-Nanjing annually, Nanda's mantle as China's premier provider of graduate-level instruction in Chinese studies to international students, and especially to Americans, seems to have been lost.

The Party Strikes Back

The tensions inherent in building a "world-class" university that also met President Xi Jinping's definition of building one of "the first famous Chinese institutions of higher education," have become painfully apparent in recent years. In Nanda's 2016 five-year plan, achieving world-class status became formally tied to Xi's rhetoric of "realizing the Chinese dream."[69] Yet it was Nanda's inclusion on the list of twenty-nine Chinese universities scrutinized by the Party's Central Commission for Discipline Inspection (CCDI) in 2017 that led the Party and its politics to intrude in dramatic ways on Nanda's leadership and governance.

The CCDI launched its investigation into universities to ensure that the Party retained—or, more accurately in the case of Nanda, regained—its ideological and operational grip over higher education. Wang Qishan, secretary of the CCDI and a top aide to Xi Jinping, presided over the announcement of the investigation, which emphasized examining universities for the strictness of their "political discipline" as well as whether they were abiding by "the core role of the Party's leadership" and adhering to the Party's education policies.[70] CCDI inspectors were deployed to universities in mid-March to conduct their work until May of 2017.[71] President Xi himself took part in this inspection, underscoring the significance of the effort to his political agenda. While surveying the Chinese University of Political Science and Law on the eve of the anniversary of the May Fourth Movement, Xi stated that "university Party committees were responsible for managing both the Party and the schools themselves."[72]

Upon the inspection's conclusion, Nanda's Party Secretary Zhang Yibin and Executive Vice President Lu Jian convened an extraordinary meeting of faculty and staff to express the significance of the CCDI's findings to the future of the university. To fulfill the inspectors' wishes, Secretary Zhang told a packed auditorium that the university must focus on three areas: political consciousness, political discipline, and political responsibilities. Nothing about teaching. Nothing about research. Nothing about outreach. Executive Vice President Lu emphasized that addressing these areas was now Nanda's "biggest political task."[73]

The sense of urgency among these administrators was evident when the CCDI's findings were publicly circulated, revealing that Nanda had performed poorly during the exercise. Regarding the strength of Party leadership at Nanda, the CCDI inspection team concluded that "the outstanding problems . . . are objective, profound, and crucial" and that these results should serve as an "alarm bell" for Nanda.[74]

In short, Nanda, with its Nationalist and internationalist roots, needed "rectification." To address the CCDI's concern, Nanda created a "rectification task list" of over one hundred action items the university committed to implement. Reforms to the policies governing the diffusion of ideology throughout Nanda's staff and classrooms were given prominent treatment in the university's response.[75] Nanda's own "Inspection and Rectification Report," written by a taskforce made up of Nanda Party Committee members, stated that it had released new guidelines for ideological training and supervision with the hope that these would "clarify the content and form of theoretical learning at different levels for schools, departments, and Party members" to ensure the Party's ideology would receive "full coverage throughout learning" at Nanda. The "Inspection and Rectification Report" committed Nanda to release a "Plan for Building a World-Class University," which would "comprehensively implement the Party's education policy, adhere to the guidance for social schools, and strengthen the Party's leadership of the school."[76] In reorienting the role of the Party at Nanda, the university also began the process of limiting its world-class ambitions to be in alignment with those the Party would allow. The severity of the CCDI's criticisms, which all but indicted Nanda of subverting Party leadership of the university, and the sweeping "rectification tasks" now required, suggest that the inspection was another existential crisis for Nanda.

The CCDI inspection's admonishments of Nanda left it more sensitive to changing political winds in China than at any time since the Cultural Revolution. Following the enshrinement of Xi Jinping's "thought" in the Party's constitution in October 2017, Nanda's Party Committee convened a study session to promote greater understanding of these constitutional amendments so that the university would "be in line with the central government." Nanda's president, Chen Jun, also attended the meeting to express the required view that the university would "connect" these constitutional amendments to the "school's development."[77] Nanda's Party Committee then pressed for greater authority over the direction of reforms within the university. In April 2018 Nanda Party Secretary Zhang Yibin laid out the year's key tasks to an audience of Nanda Party members. All involved strengthening Party governance over Nanda, improving adherence to political rules, and not just "consolidating" but also "expanding" the university's response to the CCDI inspection.[78]

Could Nanda have resisted this onslaught? No. As a provincial university of Nationalist heritage, and without the political network of a Beijing-based Tsinghua, Nanda was more than vulnerable to the state's political pressures. Moreover, without a global reputation like that of Tsinghua, the Party could meddle in Nanda's affairs without worrying it would undermine a national treasure.

In December 2017, six months after the CCDI inspection's conclusion, the university released the "Plan for Building a World-Class University," broadly rewriting Nanda's institutional development priorities into closer alignment with the Party's political and economic agenda. If lip service to the "Chinese dream" in Nanda's thirteenth five-year plan might have been excused as pure rhetoric, the same could not be said of this new "world-class" plan. Unlike the plans of Kuang Yaming and Qu Qinyue in earlier decades, this was not an academic plan. It was an ideological call to arms. Now, Nanda's educational aim was to "guide Nanjing University through adherence to Marxism, fully implement the Party's education policy, [and] adhere to socialist governance of schools."[79] Following the Party Committee's constitution study session in November 2017, Xi Jinping Thought was named Nanda's "guiding ideology" in its world-class plan.

The politicization of Nanda's strategy harbored significant consequences for its efforts to pursue excellence in teaching and internationalization. By 2030 Nanda was committed to having "the core values of socialism fully integrated into the whole process of educating people." Teaching and research in the humanities and social sciences, the heart of the university's push to offer all students a broad-based and interdisciplinary general education, needed now to conform to "Chinese characteristics." Teachers and students, Nanda plans now stated, had to be "armed with the latest achievements of the Sinicization of Marxism so that they acted politically and ideologically."[80] While Nanda's general education website continued to state that the program prioritized "students' independent thinking and free development," the boundaries of intellectual independence at Nanda became increasingly limited.

All this had to have an effect on the university's internationalization. Nanda had cultivated partnerships with elite foreign universities to attract top students and scholars. But the arrival of President Xi's Belt and Road Initiative redirected some of Nanda's internationalization efforts toward partnerships with developing countries along the "New Silk Road." Nanda's revised world-class strategy stated that "Building the Belt and Road Initiative was an opportunity to focus on research and the development of academic disciplines on matters useful to the initiative."[81] The university established a Belt and Road research institute, held international symposia to generate ideas for the program, and received government scholarships for students from Belt and Road countries. But few believed that the international future of Nanjing University lay more in Lahore than in London or Los Angeles.

Marx versus "Marxism"

The politicization of higher education spread to many other areas of university life at Nanda. The Party mandated an expanded study of Marxism, in contrast to (presumably other) "Western" values. The CCP had launched a major initiative in 2004 to generate more research on Marxism and produced a series of stultifying Party-approved textbooks that integrated "the new achievements realized by the Sinicization of Marxism," making them "relevant" to China under the CCP's rule.[82] Nanda's Philosophy Department, one of the top five in the country, actively participated in this project. The Nanda *Undergraduate Education Quality Report of 2017–2018* (published in December 2018) prioritized work to "perform political gate-keeping on philosophy and social science textbooks" and "strictly manage the use of original versions of textbooks published outside China" for the future so as to "not allow textbooks that propagate erroneous Western views to enter the classroom."[83]

Students at Nanda took the government at its word and began to read the original, fiery, revolutionary works of Marx. In the autumn of 2014 several enthusiastic students approached faculty members in Nanda's Philosophy Department to start a "Marxist Reading and Research Society" (MRRS). As students and government cadres alike had been officially encouraged (read: told) to study Marxism by Xi Jinping, faculty members agreed to support the students, and one of them sponsored the formal registration of their group on campus. Earlier that year, the Nanda Party Committee had released *Several Opinions on Strengthening and Improving the Construction of Teachers' Morality,* which endorsed an expanded role for Marxist ideology in how Nanda was to educate its student body. The "Opinions" named "promoting the core value of socialism into . . . students' minds" as one of the "main tasks" for the university's faculty.[84] But Nanda's students did not want to be restricted to book learning. To put what they learned in original Marxist texts into action, the students approached cleaning staff and workers in the school's kitchens to help with their work and donated items to improve their lives. The students also organized events around campus to encourage the study of Marx. For these activities, they were praised by the secretary of Nanda's Communist Youth League, the official CCP youth organ.[85]

In July 2018 students of the MRRS learned that workers at a Jasic Technology Company factory in Shenzhen were trying to form independent unions to fight for better wages and working conditions. When the workers' efforts were suppressed by the company with the help of local police, several Nanda students joined students from other leading universities in China, many belonging to similar Marxist study groups, to form a support group for the Shenzhen workers.[86] They protested in front of a local police station involved in the arrest of the labor organizers.[87] In late August riot police broke into the apartments of student activists and arrested them.[88] Many, including students from Nanda, were later released and allowed to return to their schools in September.[89]

When Nanda MRRS students returned to campus, they found they had to reregister their group with the school administration. Their longtime sponsor in the Department of Philosophy was initially reluctant to sponsor them again.[90] After long conversations, MRRS leaders agreed to some changes in their leadership and removed phrases like "paying attention to social realities, discussing current events, and focusing on social practice" from their registration material in exchange for support from their long-time sponsor. In agreeing to support the students again, the sponsoring professor admonished members of the MRRS to "read more books, organize fewer events."[91]

On September 9 several MRRS students met up with student activists from other schools and some Jasic workers at Mao Zedong's birthplace in Hunan to commemorate the anniversary of his death.[92] By mid-September, MRRS's registration material was returned by its sponsor, and the students were informed by the university that the group had to undergo additional evaluation. MRRS leaders then went on a frantic search for a new sponsor, knocking on the doors of every humanities and social science department at Nanda in September and October. In late September MRRS leaders submitted a petition to Nanda Party Secretary and renowned Marxist scholar Zhang Yibin, pleading for him to support the organization, as he had done during its founding. One faculty member in the School of Marxism and another in the School of Social and Behavioral Sciences finally agreed to help, but they backed out after meetings with more senior administrators. Throughout this period, MRRS students continued to organize activities on campus including their signature volunteer program to help cafeteria workers as well as protests against the administrative barriers to their registration as a student group. Some of the students were photographed and followed by plainclothes security agents during and after these events. The student leader of the MRRS was summoned and cornered by staff from the school's security office and police to "answer questions."[93]

On October 23, 2018, the ax fell. A university-wide meeting of faculty and administrators was held, announcing Party Secretary Zhang Yibin's (heretofore unknown) request to step down early from his leadership position and the appointment of Hu Jinbo as the new Party Secretary of Nanda. Zhang was highly praised by representatives of the CCP Central Organization Department, the Ministry of Education, the Jiangsu CCP Committee, the Jiangsu Department of Education, and President Lu Jian, and he was thanked for his service.[94]

Two days later, MRRS students submitted an open letter to the new Party Secretary, asking again for the support of the school leadership. The letter quoted a speech made by Xi Jinping at Peking University in May 2018, asking university faculty to "deepen student understanding of the theoretical and real-life meaning of Marxism, educate them to observe the world and analyze the world using Marxist principles so that they might fully realize the power of Marxist truth."[95] The students felt they were answering the call of the General Secretary, so why were they being mistreated?

The Party had successfully pressured Nanda's administration into ideological lockstep with its priorities, but the students—unexpectedly idealistic in China's reform-era material culture—proved a greater challenge. In 2018 Nanda's students were joined by comrades in Peking and Renmin Universities in organizing labor movements in Guangdong in the summer and protests on campus in the fall.[96] All three universities prided themselves on their strengths in the humanities and social sciences and had top-ranked philosophy departments in China. And in all three universities the students were punished severely, with some arrested, some expelled, and all disciplined in some form.[97] And all three universities saw sudden "retirements" or leadership shuffles of their presidents or senior members of their Party committees.[98] (Bizarrely, in a fit of American political correctness, when the Renmin University students were sanctioned, Cornell University's School of Industrial and Labor Relations suspended its research and exchange program with Renmin, utterly ignorant of how far that university had gone to try to support its students.[99])

New Rules for a "New Era"

Xi Jinping has declared that China has entered a "new era," and that phrase may be found in political pronouncements at every level of Chinese society. For Nanda, it meant a new university charter. Chinese universities had begun publishing charters in 2013, shortly after Xi's ascendence to the role of paramount leader. Nanda's first charter, released in 2015, noted that it was "committed . . . to realizing the Chinese dream and great rejuvenation of the Chinese nation" in the document's second paragraph but did not state its commitment to the Party's ideological construction and to "fully implementing the Party's educational policies" until Article 6 of the charter.[100] This was clearly not enough. The revised charter of 2019 did not beat around the bush. The preamble's second paragraph was amended to open with,

"Facing the future, Nanjing University adheres to the overall leadership of the Party."[101] New powers and prominence for the Party were incorporated throughout the document. Fudan University in Shanghai, often considered one of China's top three institutions of higher education, also released a revised charter in which it removed a commitment to freedom of thought in the preamble, replacing it with a statement supporting "the leadership of the Chinese Communist Party, full implementation of the Party's educational policies, and adherence to the guiding role of Marxism and direction of socialism."[102] Across the country, new university charters were presented as a pledge of allegiance to the Party,

Nanda's new charter afforded the Party new roles in university governance. Article 22 included the Party Secretary among the school executives with the authority to convene special university leadership meetings to discuss pressing administrative matters and challenges at Nanda, a power previously reserved for the president. Nanda's joint Party and government committee would now not simply be charged with "reviewing" and "implementing" the university's development plans but instead specifically be tasked with "formulating work plans" that addressed the "Party's and country's lines, principles, and policies." Moreover, the charter enhanced the roles of those with Party and government leadership positions in Nanda's academic committee, the university's "highest academic body."[103]

In response to student unrest at Nanda in the previous year, the 2019 charter stressed the deepening of the Party's ideology in campus organizations. Article 14 in the latest revision included a commitment to "leading the school's ideological, political, and moral education work [and] maintaining the political stability and safety of campus."[104] However, a new clause was added in 2019 that pledged Nanda would "strengthen the theoretical study of Party members, insist on arming the mind with the Party's scientific theory, and . . . organize Party members to study the Party's line, principles, policies and resolutions."[105]

All these changes were not universally embraced by university communities. The deputy dean of the liberal arts school posted online that the revisions were an "evil act" that challenged the academy's ethical commitments.[106] Other universities saw campus unrest following the publication of the new charters. At Fudan, which had removed its charter's commitment to freedom of thought, students protested these changes in the university cafeteria by singing Fudan's anthem, which includes lyrics that reflected Humboldtian values. Two universities that had long promoted concepts of academic autonomy, East China Normal University and Wuhan University, the joint-venture partners of New York University and Duke University, respectively,[107] both maintained language supporting academic freedom in their charters. Asked about Nanda's charter revisions, a spokesperson for Johns Hopkins University, Nanda's joint-venture partner for the Hopkins-Nanjing Center, stated that the Center "was founded on the principle of academic freedom. . . . Any externally imposed limits or restraints on academic freedom in the class-room or on students' or faculty members' work would be wholly inconsistent with [these] principles."[108]

What Now?

The pressures of expansion and politicization at Nanda placed into question whether the university, with its rich pre-Communist history and its remark-able recovery in the early reform period, could succeed in the contest for world-class standing in a highly politicized homeland. Nanjing, after all, had been the capital of the country. It was now a provincial capital: the capital of a rich province to be sure, but provincial nonetheless. The university that is now Nanda had once been China's National Central University, modeled on the University of Berlin. Its history and legacy enhanced its reputation, but in the twenty-first century it was again forced to kneel to the politics of the day.

Today's Nanda is rich with the seeds for excellence on an international scale. However, its fate has been strongly tied to the ambitions of two Party-States: that of the Nationalists before 1949 and that of the Communists ever since. As the case of Tsinghua University shows, some universities can both serve the Party-State and make their distinctive mark on higher edu-cation in China and internationally. But Nanda is perhaps not so well posi-tioned. As it adheres to an increasingly rigid ideological regimen, it places in question the durability of the confident openness that defined its interna-tional profile when establishing its partnership with Johns Hopkins.

At the very least, the recent politicization of higher education has done the university no favors. Expanding the role of the Party's ideology in the classroom threatens to crowd out curriculum designed to foster the critical thinking skills that had been at the heart of Nanda's distinctive undergrad-uate education. Moreover, the press for ideological purity has fed student un-rest, rather than nurturing stability. As US-China relations nose-dived in the eras of Trump and Xi, flagship exchange programs were threatened by the political crossfire. Pressure to expand its offerings in the applied disciplines has increased Nanda's appetite for resources that it already found hard to come by for existing programs. Nanda's efforts to so visibly align itself with the Party's priorities had yet to do it any good in domestic and international rankings. Once considered among the top three institutions within China, Nanda had fallen to sixth or seventh place, depending on which rankings table was consulted.

The COVID-19 pandemic underscored the precarious position Nanda found itself in. The economic hardship brought on by virus-induced lockdowns reduced the Chinese government's income and reserves, leading it to slash outlays for many budget items. Unlike Tsinghua, Nanda has not been immune from the government's call to "vigorously reduce" public expenditures in response to the pandemic.[109] For the 2020–2021 fiscal year, Nanda's public funding fell by 17.5 percent. The greater strain on Nanda and its future is revealed by the over 50 percent decline in Nanda's science and technology expenditures, funded by the government. Nanda's laboratories experienced a budget reduction of over 60 percent, and the university's expenditures on basic research, traditionally Nanda's strong suit, declined by 55 percent.[110] In short, Nanda's efforts to build out its science and technology offerings still have a long way to go before it can compete with China's top engineering universities. If acceding to state economic priorities pays so little in tough times, how resilient can Nanda's current institutional strategy be?

Hard choices face Nanjing University in the years ahead. Will its strategy of riding the wave of politicization in Chinese higher education begin to pay dividends? As hawkish perceptions of China and its universities proliferate in the United States, will the bilateral partnerships Nanda has relied on to build its international reputation in the United States and elsewhere become more fragile and fraught?

Unlike Duke University, which has been able to overcome its provincial geography to win national repute and status in the United States, Nanda currently lacks the room to innovate, experiment, and plan on its own terms in China. It had done so, remarkably, in the early years of China's reform and opening. That spirit seems suppressed, for now. Yet, as we have seen, Nanda has survived multiple revolutions and endures, if not as a leader, as one of the leading followers in Chinese higher education.

One of the strengths of both the German and American public universities is that they are, to be sure, state funded, but funded by different states: by the *Länder* in Germany and the fifty states of the sometimes United States.

Chinese universities, far flung and different in their origins and capacities, also have—or have had—the capacity for differentiation as great as that of the economies or cuisines of China's many regions and cultures. This was amply demonstrated by Nanjing University's accomplishments in the early reform era, led by truly courageous presidents. But the standardization and synchronizing of the academic and ideological universes under Xi Jinping appear to have called a sharp pause, if not a halt, to regional experimentation.

Tian gao, Huangdi yuan. "Heaven is high, and the emperor is far away." This old phrase, said to date from the Yuan dynasty, implies that the farther away you are from the capital, the greater your capacity to act. But today the emperor, or at least his "thought," is omnipresent, a presence in every provincial university—perhaps especially this one, with its roots in the previous dynasty. The sun may be setting on the prospects for the great and historical university in China's Southern Capital.

CHAPTER ELEVEN

Asia's Global University?

The University of Hong Kong

XIANG ZHANG, the president of the University of Hong Kong (HKU), was told of the Occupy Central movement and its accompanying protests while interviewing for the position in 2017. Born in mainland China and educated both at home and in the United States, where he rose to be a chaired professor at UC Berkeley, Zhang embodied the aspirations of "Asia's Global University." At the time, Zhang recalled, "everybody said that the tensions were gone."[1] Indeed, when Zhang succeeded outgoing president Peter Mathieson in 2018, it appeared that the major protests had subsided in Hong Kong. In what was then a rare moment of calm in Hong Kong, Zhang arrived eager to build on Mathieson's work to internationalize HKU and improve its global standing. The strategic plan Mathieson had crafted, *Vision 2016–2025*, was "a good plan," Zhang said, but he added that the university needed "more concrete and executable steps."[2] Although Zhang was still working through how he would execute this vision, his ambitions for HKU were clear cut and sky high: "We want to be the next Harvard. We want to be the next Cambridge. In twenty or fifty years, we want to say that, yes, we can compete with Harvard in terms of faculty recruiting, or students, or alumni. That is what we will measure."[3] Yet as Zhang tried to unite HKU's many stakeholders around a substantive, long-term agenda for the university, political tensions—of a different sort than those at Nanjing University—were never far below the surface of HKU's campus and city.

For much of its history, HKU was Hong Kong's only university. Although HKU now competes against seven other higher education institutions in Hong Kong for government funding and support, by reputation it was the leading university in Hong Kong and, by accidents of history, the leading Chinese university that was *not* under the guidance of the Chinese Communist Party. Zhang believed that HKU needed to look outward in order to climb higher. Only through internationalization could HKU continue to thrive. He stated that "if you want to be a global university, a world-leading university, you have to look at global issues, important issues, not just the city's issues."[4]

Historically, HKU's unique value lay not only in its monopoly on higher education in Hong Kong but also in its role as a bridge between an inaccessible mainland China and the rest of the world. As mainland Chinese universities gained international reputations and partnerships, HKU's role as an intermediary between East and West came under threat. The *Vision 2016– 2025* plan developed under Mathieson sought to leverage China's renewed global presence while competing with the growing influence of China's top universities. As an English-language institution at the crossroads of China and the wider world, HKU would be "Asia's Global University." Zhang believed that with strong leadership, HKU, located in China's Special Administrative Region of Hong Kong, could ride the wave of China's rise to improve its own standing: "HKU is always among the top three or four universities in Asia. We should not be happy with that, especially as the world order is undergoing transformation."[5]

To achieve this, HKU needed a period of peace and productivity. Yet only one year into President Zhang's tenure, Hong Kong witnessed the largest political protests in its history. HKU's greatest challenges seemed increasingly local. How could HKU deepen its ties with mainland universities at a time when millions were protesting the city's subservient relationship to mainland authorities? How could HKU maintain its position as a top institution linking East and West in an era of growing East-West tensions and in such a volatile metropolis?

An Imperial Project

From its inception, HKU was an institution with many goals. It was intended to link Great Britain, its colonial overlord, with mainland China, while providing high-quality, local educational opportunities for the young men of the British colonies in Southeast Asia and strengthening the capacities of Hong Kong citizens. Its greatest early champion, Frederick Lugard, governor of Hong Kong from 1907 to 1912, envisioned HKU as a key establishment in and accomplishment of the British Empire.[6] Lugard wrote, "What England has done for India and Egypt in mitigation of famine . . . she can help China to do for herself."[7] A longtime diplomat, Lugard did not have extensive experience in the field of education, but he nonetheless believed in the economic and moral merit of establishing a local university.

The sense of competition among imperial powers was also an impetus for the founding of HKU. Already by 1905 newspapers warned that British influence in China was being surpassed by Japan, which was an early destination for Chinese students studying abroad.[8] The British eyed with envy the progress made by Americans, particularly American missionaries, in developing higher education in mainland China. The German establishment of Tongji University in Shanghai in 1907 and plans to develop a research university in Kiaochow (Qingdao) in 1908 further encouraged the British to develop an institution of their own. Indeed, it was the news of the founding of the German school that led Hormusjee Nowrojee Mody, a prominent Parsi merchant who became one of the most generous donors to HKU, to ask Governor Lugard and his wife, "[W]hy cannot we get ahead of them?"[9]

Vocal about the important role the university could play in empire building, Lugard was still unable to gather significant financial support from the British government. Most of the early funding for the university came from the private sector, although the government maintained a high level of involvement in administrative decisions. Mody was an early supporter, sponsoring the construction of HKU's iconic Main Building, with donations ultimately valued at HK$365,000 (approximately £36,500, or US$5.9 million in today's value).[10] More early support was received in May 1909, when the firm of John Swire & Sons announced the donation of £40,000 to the university endowment, which would be worth US$6.7 million in 2021.[11] These gifts initiated enough fundraising from individuals in Hong Kong, mainland China, and overseas Chinese communities in Australia, Malaya, and French Saigon[12] as well as the governments in Beijing and Guangdong—after their fears of a new university as a revolutionary hotbed were assuaged—to build the skeleton of a university just before the end of Lugard's tenure as governor of Hong Kong in 1912.

The first university to be founded in Hong Kong, HKU was preceded by a number of technical and ecclesiastical colleges. One, the Hong Kong

College of Medicine for Chinese, founded in 1887, became HKU's School of Medicine. When the university opened its doors to its first cohort of seventy-five students in the autumn of 1912,[13] it offered courses at its School of Medicine as well as its School of Engineering, joined by the School of the Arts in 1913. The University Ordinance of 1911 established HKU's tripartite governance structure of Court (for government and societal oversight), Council (for administrative matters), and Senate (for academic matters). While responsibilities and power of the three groups shifted over time and the Court grew increasingly ceremonial, the basic structure remained almost unchanged into the twenty-first century.

The ordinance also laid out a nondiscrimination policy, stating, "No distinction of race or nationality shall be permitted, and no test of religious

Figure 11.1. Hong Kong University Main Building, the oldest structure on HKU's main campus, 1912. *Growing with Hong Kong: The University and Its Graduates,* Hong Kong University Press, 2002/Wikimedia Commons.

belief or profession shall be imposed, in order to entitle any person to be admitted as a member, professor, reader, lecturer, teacher, or student of the University or to hold office therein or to graduate thereof or to hold any advantage or privilege thereof."[14] Initially, this ethos was applied much more readily to students than to faculty. Founders of HKU felt that having well-qualified, British lecturers was necessary to bolster the fledgling institution's reputation.[15] This preferential policy was challenged by some of the university administration in 1919 when HKU sought to fill the newly created position of the Chair of Pathology and was torn between a Senate-supported British candidate and the Council-supported Dr. Wang Chung Yik, a graduate of the Hong Kong College of Medicine and Edinburgh University. The withdrawal of the Senate-supported candidate led to the appointment of Dr. Wang, HKU's first ethnic Chinese academic.[16]

During its first decade, the university struggled to remain solvent. By 1919 the Colonial Government finally agreed to help pull HKU out of debt, but only with the expansion of government oversight of the university. Throughout the next few decades, up to and beyond World War II, the university continued to toe a delicate line with the government, gradually gaining more public financial support, but also subjecting itself to increasing government inquiries and reports.

The university's small initial budget limited its research agenda; it was ultimately the provision of sufficient resources—and donor preferences—that transformed HKU into a more research-oriented institution. In 1922 the Rockefeller Foundation, which supported medical education around the world and at several institutions in mainland China, endowed two chairs at the School of Medicine, followed by a third chair less than two years later. This funding allowed the medical school to expand its professoriat and gave the school a stronger research orientation. By 1929 endowment income accounted for 62 percent of HKU's operating funds.

The founding of HKU had been predicated on its ability to keep young men out of radical politics—by which was meant the politics of modern Chinese nationalism. As the Nationalist movement led by the Guomindang grew in power in southern China, it challenged the British colonial presence. A major test of politicization on campus came in 1925 when, following a shooting of Chinese protesters in the foreign concession of Guangzhou on the mainland, a general strike and boycott of British goods spread to Hong Kong. University administrators were relieved to discover that HKU students generally sided with the British, going so far as to step in as assistant caretakers at an insane asylum when workers went on strike.[17] Chinese staff members also supported British interests. From that point forward, there was growing acceptance by the colonial authorities of HKU students as loyal subjects of the British Empire.

By the 1930s HKU was financially stable, helped first by the Rockefeller Foundation, then by funds from the British Boxer Indemnity that were returned to the university in 1931.[18] Yet, it still lacked a role in the educational landscape of greater China. HKU had been founded in the same era when a wave of Western-style higher education institutions was being established in mainland China. By the 1930s mainland China offered a variety of excellent higher education opportunities, many of which were connected with institutions in America, Europe, or Japan. HKU had the tenuous position of offering a more expensive, less convenient education that still lacked the professional and social cache of a Western degree.[19]

In response to this questionable positioning, a commission of colonial government and business representatives was tasked in 1937 with examining the university's role in society and its future development. Their subsequent report drew the ire of many faculty for its suggestions—for example, that HKU faculty need not hold high-level research degrees—that threatened to relegate the university to second-class status. Heated debate over the report's recommendations raged in the HKU Senate as well as the colonial government. The HKU Senate issued a response stating that it was of the "unanimous opinion that research is a necessary and integral function of every university."[20]

Ultimately, Duncan Sloss, the newly appointed vice-chancellor of HKU, used the controversy over the 1937 report to broaden the sense of purpose of HKU and elevate its standards. After arguing for the need to make HKU "a University in the British sense" rather than "a much more modest institution, a superior technical college,"[21] Sloss arranged for the establishment of a committee to draft the *University Development Report* of 1939, which laid out an ambitious plan for improved recruitment of students from mainland China as well as reforms in curriculum and upgrades to the physical plant.[22]

Defeat and Detention

Alas, Sloss built his strategy for growth when China was already two years into the war with Japan. Just two years later, in 1941, all plans came to an abrupt halt when Japan invaded Hong Kong.[23] When the Japanese invaded,

HKU faculty and students dispersed, and Japanese troops transformed the campus into an army base, requisitioning medical and scientific supplies and equipment for military use.

This was a time of unprecedented suffering. The Japanese ruled Hong Kong by martial law. Streets and buildings were renamed in Japanese. Food became scarce and scarcer still when rationing was implemented. Hong Kong suffered its first real famine. Later in the war, it also suffered sustained American bombing. Between deaths and deportations, Hong Kong's population dropped by more than half under Japanese occupation: from approximately 1.6 million in 1941 to little more than 600,000 in 1945. The colony was the site of numerous Japanese war crimes, including the execution of ten thousand civilians.

Many of the European faculty members spent the war in internment camps under desperate and often horrific conditions. Some quietly attempted to continue research and plan for the return of the university. Many others perished. HKU staff, students, and alumni who had the opportunity fled to Free China, that is, to the areas under Nationalist control during the war. Others continued their studies at the top mainland universities, such as National Central University in Japanese-occupied Nanjing. It was a time of uncertain identities and loyalties, as indeed would be the postwar years.

Duncan Sloss was held during the war in the Stanley Internment Camp, on the southern side of Hong Kong Island. After Hong Kong was liberated, and as Sloss prepared to return to London for rest and recuperation in September 1945, he noted in his farewell address to students the promise of a new age with China's survival and indeed victory in an eight-year-long war: "We shall work together to get a University going of which we can all be proud and which, turned toward a new China, shall be a perpetually open line of communication between China and England and equally between England and China. We base our efforts on a realisation of what China can do for Western civilization no less than what Western ideas and standards can do for China."[24]

Postwar Traumas and Opportunities

By the end of World War II, the buildings of HKU were in ruins, its supplies lacking, students scattered, and faculty largely gone. The government of Hong Kong, along with the remaining university administration, went through a period of soul-searching before deciding in 1948 to reopen the university.[25] This decision turned out to be a prescient one, as the landscape of higher education in greater China was soon to be rocked by the Communist victory in the Chinese Civil War and the founding of the People's Republic of China in 1949. Many mainland Chinese scholars fled to Hong Kong, while many local Hong Kong students who in the past would have gone to China for university studies found that path blocked.

The Communist conquest of China proved both a burden and a blessing for Hong Kong. Hong Kong was suddenly inundated with refugees from the mainland, at times at a rate of more than one hundred thousand per month, and its population swelled to more than two million in the early 1950s. It received both extraordinary entrepreneurial talent—business families fleeing Shanghai and other urban centers—and outstanding scholars. And, in much larger numbers, it received people simply fleeing communism, who needed help and education to make their way in a suddenly populous Hong Kong, economically cut off from its Chinese hinterland.

In the 1950s and 1960s HKU expanded as quickly as its limited finances and physical plant would allow to meet a rapidly growing Hong Kong's need for qualified professionals. In 1963 three postsecondary colleges combined to establish the second public university in Hong Kong, the Chinese University of Hong Kong (CUHK).[26] CUHK was born of émigré, anticommunist intellectuals from the mainland and of the desire to set up a comprehensive, Chinese-speaking university in the British colony. In 1965, responding to the growing complexity of the higher education sector, Hong Kong's Legislative Council established a University Grants Committee (UGC), along the British model, to coordinate tertiary education financing in the colony and to serve as the governing body between the government's Education Bureau and the individual campuses.

In the late 1960s, as the Cultural Revolution wreaked havoc on the social order in mainland China, protests spilled over the border to Hong Kong, which suffered the worst riots it would see until 2019. Unlike on the mainland, however, where university campuses became physical battlegrounds and education ground to a halt, HKU remained relatively apolitical. The HKU Students' Union declined to participate in demonstrations.[27] HKU students became more engaged politically in the 1970s, participating, for example, in the 1974 protests that led to the establishment of Chinese as an official language of the colony alongside English.[28]

From Britain to China

By the Treaty of Nanjing (1842), Hong Kong Island, on which HKU is located, was ceded to Great Britain in perpetuity. But the physically largest part of modern Hong Kong, the New Territories, which became part of the colony in 1898 on a ninety-nine-year lease, and where much of Hong Kong's population (not to mention the Chinese University of Hong Kong) is located, was destined to return to China in 1997. Assuming the indivisibility of the colony, the 1984 Sino-British Joint Declaration confirmed the return of *all* of Hong Kong to Chinese sovereignty in 1997. That agreement, negotiated at the height of China's post-Mao promise of political reform, would be rudely followed in 1989 by the brutal military crackdown on student and other protestors in Beijing's Tiananmen Square, setting off a major crisis of confidence for the future of Hong Kong in general, and, on campus, for HKU.

China proposed a "One Country, Two Systems" framework for Hong Kong, promising that, even under PRC sovereignty, "laws currently in force in Hong Kong will remain basically unchanged" until 2047, fifty years following the handover.[29] Anxiety in Hong Kong was high, inspiring British colonial authorities to introduce major public sector investments in the 1990s, not the least in education. Public education enrollment at all levels expanded. From 1989 to 1994, higher education enrollment grew from less than 3 percent to 18 percent of graduating secondary school students. A major new institution, Hong Kong University of Science and Technology, was founded as Hong Kong's third university (and "Hong Kong's MIT") in 1991 under the dynamic leadership of its founding president, Chia-wei Woo, a Shanghai-born, American-educated academic leader. Soon thereafter, several colleges were promoted to university status to absorb the increase in enrollment.[30] As the primary body overseeing publicly funded universities, the UGC oversaw this expansion: it funded universities through block grants, allowing each university to maintain a high degree of academic and administrative autonomy. HKU would continue its role as Hong Kong's flagship university, but in a suddenly more crowded and competitive sector.

It is difficult to overstate the uncertainties gripping Hong Kong in the years preceding the handover. A half-million residents left the colony, and many others found second domiciles abroad. Having governed Hong Kong as a Crown Colony since 1842, the British introduced a series of democratic reforms, including an expanded franchise for elections to the Legislative Council. Even Hong Kong's most privileged residents harbored doubts. I recall a conversation in early 1997 with one of Hong Kong's "tycoons," as the local press labeled the leaders of the richest families. He told me he was leaving Hong Kong "because the communists are coming in." By "communists" he did not mean the Chinese Communist Party—with which he had a good relationship—but rather Hong Kong's Democratic Party, which had vowed to raise taxes on tycoons like him. (He did not leave.)

Anxieties were higher still at HKU. The 1990 "Basic Law" adopted by China's National People's Congress became Hong Kong's *de facto* constitution. It provided that "educational institutions of all kinds may retain their autonomy and enjoy academic freedom." But in the aftermath of the Tiananmen crisis and the subsequent crackdown on mainland universities, HKU's leadership was anxious about how its academic autonomy could be maintained in practice.[31] Several well-known scholars left Hong Kong for positions in Great Britain and Australia, although many ultimately returned to Hong Kong after the stability of the political and economic environment seemed ensured. In June 1997, shortly before Hong Kong's retrocession to China, HKU students attempted to display on campus the *Pillar of Shame,* a pro-democracy sculpture by Danish artist Jens Galschiot, in commemoration of the eighth anniversary of the Tiananmen Incident. Administrators initially refused to allow the display because of "safety concerns." The university was clearly wary of upsetting Beijing on the eve of Chinese President Jiang Zemin's greatest personal triumph: overseeing the return of Hong Kong and putting a final end to the last vestiges of colonial rule on Chinese territory. After students moved the statue on campus anyway, the university agreed to allow its display.[32] The incident foreshadowed what would become growing tensions as the university struggled to balance its role as a public institution under a complex governing system with its commitment to academic freedom and autonomy.

At the same time, Hong Kong's return to China offered new opportunities, new leadership, and new visions for HKU. Having been founded as the premier university in British colonial Asia, HKU's reach had shrunk with the diminution of Britain's empire, of which Hong Kong had been one of the last remnants. In the last years of British rule, facing an increasingly crowded local higher education sector, HKU had become a locally focused institution, concerned primarily with besting its local competitors and educating a student body almost entirely from Hong Kong.

Figure 11.2. *Pillar of Shame*, on "permanent" display outside the HKU Student Union until 2021. Photograph © William C. Kirby.

This relatively narrow vision was challenged and then greatly broadened by new, local leadership with a global outlook. The prominent Hong Kong businessman and former Harvard Business School professor Victor Fung served as a transformative chairman of the HKU Council from 2003 to 2009. Fung had distinguished himself both in business and in public service. He and his brother, William, turned their family firm, Li & Fung, into the world's leader in supply-chain management. Victor Fung also chaired Hong Kong's Airport Authority and oversaw in the final years of British rule (and over intense Chinese opposition) the building of today's extraordinary Hong Kong International Airport, which has proven a key element in Hong Kong's post-handover prosperity. His desire to make Hong Kong a center of Asia's modern development extended to education. As council chair (broadly equivalent to chair of a university board of trustees), Fung spearheaded the re-envisioning of HKU as not just the flagship institution of higher education in Hong Kong but also a leading university in Asia and the world. This new vision was supported by a wide range of major reforms in university governance that promoted modern, streamlined administrative practices. Working closely with Vice Chancellor Lap-Chee Tsui and a reorganized and reinvigorated Council, Fung built faculty and student consensus around this new vision of the university and established the foundation for HKU's continued pursuit of global excellence in the twenty-first century.

The University of Hong Kong in the Twenty-First Century

By 2019 HKU was in many ways still at the apex of eight publicly funded higher education institutions in Hong Kong. As the system's flagship English-language research institution, HKU offered internationally competitive teaching in all fields, as well as internationally competitive research in select areas.[33] HKU was home to over seventeen thousand undergraduate students and thirteen thousand graduate students. From its inception, HKU had sought to attract a regionally diverse population, but its capacity to attract mainland Chinese students was better served in the early twenty-first century than it was a century earlier. In the 2019–2020 school year, 23.5 percent of undergraduate students and 35.5 percent of students overall held mainland or international passports.[34]

HKU's diverse student population studied under an academic staff of nearly two thousand, grouped into ten faculties (its original faculties of Medicine, Engineering, and the Arts, plus Architecture, Business and Economics, Dentistry, Education, Law, Science, and Social Sciences) and a Graduate School.[35] Its programs in medicine, as well as the humanities, social sciences, and business and management, were among its strongest. Across all programs, the employment rate of graduates six months after graduation was 99.3 percent.

In his time as council chair, Victor Fung had determined that HKU should rise to be among the top twenty-five universities in the world. HKU, he argued, should not compare itself with the Chinese University of Hong Kong or the Hong Kong University of Science and Technology. It should vie with Berkeley, Stanford, Harvard, and others for global leadership. When, in 2007, the *Times Higher Education World University Rankings* placed HKU as number eighteen in the world—one position above the nineteenth-ranked Stanford University, HKU seemed on its way.[36]

That rise did not continue, however. Overall in 2019, HKU was ranked twenty-fifth in the world in the QS ranking, thirty-sixth in the *Times Higher Education World University Rankings,* and in the 101–150 bracket in the ARWU ranking. During his term as president, Peter Mathieson had not been overly concerned with this recent drop: "My attitude toward rankings is publicly expressed: I will never set institutional strategy in order to satisfy any particular league table."[37] The task of rising further—or even staying in its current positions—would be challenged by the vortex of local, national, and international politics that would consume the university in the second decade of the twenty-first century. First, however, HKU would attempt to reinvent its education in the liberal arts and sciences.

Curricular Extension and Institutional Expansion

HKU had long been known for graduating those who would quickly find their way in the professions—medicine, law, and government in particular. As in Britain, students were admitted directly into departments for a three-year curriculum. HKU had never been known for liberal education in either the Humboldtian sense or in the American practice. In 2005 the UGC mandated the expansion of undergraduate education at Hong Kong's eight public universities from three to four years. The aim of this reform was to create space in the university curriculum for new general education curricula and to align Hong Kong's universities with the most prestigious global practices. After the reform, students in Hong Kong received six years (as opposed to seven) of secondary education (equivalent to junior and senior high school in the American system), and then, optionally, attended a four-year university program, earning the reform the moniker "3 + 3 + 4."

Planning for this large-scale change commenced immediately, and HKU began to implement some elements of its new general education program as early as 2009.[38] In 2012 HKU welcomed both its first cohort of students in its newly designed four-year program and its last cohort of three-year students. Arthur Li, the former Vice Chancellor of the Chinese University of Hong Kong and former Secretary for Education and Manpower in Hong Kong's government, who oversaw the four-year undergraduate curriculum change in Hong Kong, commented, "The British system was very good if you know what you want to do, right when you are a kid of 18 . . . but if you want more rounded individuals for the twenty-first century, where you have to have multi-tasking, where you have to have flexibility within your workforce, is it such a good thing that you make up your mind so early in life at that point in time?"[39]

The "3 + 3 + 4" plan energized HKU's faculty. After all, how often do you get to argue over what will be taught in a whole extra year in a university? After lengthy discussion and consultation, six Common Core classes introduced four Areas of Inquiry—Scientific and Technological Literacy; Humanities; Global Issues; and China: Culture, State, and Society.

Such a big rethinking of undergraduate education presented academic and financial challenges. HKU needed to recruit and fund a 20 percent increase in faculty positions. It seized the chance to recruit young faculty with a strong research orientation. Funding was more of a burden, as the government provided but 60 percent of the cost of the extra year. This led HKU irretrievably into the world of high-level fundraising.

The impact of such a fundamental change in undergraduate education reached into every department. Each program had to rethink its major requirements and create new course offerings. This proved less of a challenge for faculty members—by 2015 the Common Core already boasted 175 course offerings—than for the students, who, like students everywhere, were focused on their postgraduate careers. Vice President for Teaching and Learning Ian Holliday noted that, while program implementation had largely been successful, there was still a "mismatch of expectations," with students not understanding the reasoning behind a transition that asked them to delay courses in their major until later in their studies.[40]

Finally, there was the physical challenge of providing classroom and living space to many more students. While the physical campus of HKU, located on a rocky hill overlooking the sea on the western edge of Hong Kong Island, had long been circumscribed, the opening of a rapid transit station at the HKU campus in December 2014 eased transportation to the rest of Hong Kong and presented the possibility of housing students on other parts of the island. Advancements in engineering allowed HKU to expand over the reservoir abutting the campus on the west to establish the Centennial Campus. This expansion, part of the school's one hundredth anniversary celebration, included classroom space where the four-year undergraduate degree program would be centered.

A new institution, Centennial College (not located on the Centennial Campus), was an effort at a different kind of outreach: it offered four-year undergraduate degrees and became part of what was now known as the for-profit HKU Group, whose initiatives were primarily financed by student tuition payments, not government subsidies.

Multicultural Environment

HKU had a long history as a diverse campus, and this remained true in the twenty-first century. Since Rayson Huang's appointment as the first ethnic Chinese vice chancellor in 1972, that position had been held by a mix of ethnic Chinese and British administrators.[41] The majority of the faculty remained international, although there had been an increase in the hiring of local scholars after 1997. Even with more balance overall, faculty members from Hong Kong, mainland China, and other countries had differing perceptions of and experiences at HKU. One Chinese faculty member noted the constant need to juggle two systems of behavior, the formal use of the Western system and the informal use of the Chinese one: "Most people will clearly feel the tensions between what I call the formal and informal systems. . . . In my life, I constantly need to adjust myself. In this situation I need to be Chinese, and in this situation, quickly, sometimes, and very dramatically, I need to be a Westerner."[42]

Academic freedom was one issue that could drive a wedge between Chinese and non-Chinese faculty members. The academic environment at HKU was very open; former Provost Roland Chin noted in 2015 that Chinese Communist Party communiqués limiting acceptable topics of discussion "don't apply now. You can argue that there's some self-restraint, but it's not apparent." But by 2047, he warned, "this might change." Thinking about potential future flashpoints at HKU, an American professor noted, "I guess there's the academic freedom issue, which I don't really see as much of an issue. Although, even there, there's a dividing line between foreigners and Chinese."[43] As the HKU campus became increasingly involved in politics, the division between "protected" foreign staff and the more vulnerable local or ethnic Chinese faculty had the potential to become more acute.

While there were inevitable tensions in a professoriat with deep cultural and ethnic divides, the cosmopolitan and international atmosphere of HKU remained one of its distinct strengths. Chin noted that, in recent years, other universities in Hong Kong had tended to become more Chinese and less international. HKU, on the other hand, had worked hard to retain its internationalism. In Chin's eyes, Hong Kong's institutional autonomy was very different from that of the higher education system on the mainland. "In addition, if a university is local and isolated, its value and influence to the world is small. The support from the society and the government would very much depend on the economic and political situation at that time. If it is international and connected, the society would value its existence and diversity."[44] The prolonged anti-government (and, implicitly, anti-Beijing) demonstrations of 2019 would test these assumptions.

One of the challenges that HKU faced in 2019 was how to address the antiquated personnel policies that limited its ability to recruit leading scholars. With the onset of formal government subsidies for HKU in 1952, the pay scales and retirement policies of professors were linked to those of civil servants. In the early 2000s salaries were delinked from the civil service pay scale, allowing HKU to make more competitive offers when recruiting faculty. While this improved HKU's recruiting power, the institution was still hampered by the civil service–influenced retirement age of sixty, which made it nearly impossible to recruit scholars at the height of their academic careers. In 2016 HKU ended its policy of granting rare, ad hoc exemptions to the mandatory retirement age, instead offering faculty turning sixty the option of applying for nontenured positions.[45]

Both the administration and departments with high ratios of teaching-oriented, older faculty, favored keeping the retirement age intact, so as to renew the faculty. Other departments, particularly those in fields like the humanities in which scholars tended to produce their best work later in their careers, were eager to change the policy to aid in recruiting. This was important in recruiting scholars from beyond Hong Kong, who made up nearly 60 percent of the professoriat. HKU could offer impressive salaries, research support, and generous housing allowances. (Where else could a new faculty colleague live inexpensively in a large flat with an ocean view?) But on retirement those benefits ceased, and HKU faculty who had not invested long before in Hong Kong real estate would find themselves competing to buy or rent property in the most expensive housing market on Earth. (In 2020 the average price for a residential property in Hong Kong was US$1.25 million.)

In 2018 members of the University Court, one of the university's governing boards, called on the university to "reconsider whether the current retirement policy at HKU is in line with the best interest of the university."[46] Discontent among the faculty rose as growing numbers applied for new contracts as they turned sixty. Faculty were concerned that nontenured contracts might offer lower pay and renewals subject to vague performance criteria. Some worried that political considerations affected which contracts were renewed, and for how long.[47] In response, HKU's administration held a townhall explaining the rationale for the policy but did not commit to its reform.[48] The retirement age remains unretired.

"Fit for Purpose": Governance and Its Reform

Governance matters for every university, but among the universities of greater China, perhaps nowhere was it more important than at the University of Hong Kong. As the leading university not under the supervision of the Chinese Communist Party, if HKU were to realize its vision as "Asia's Global University," it would need to retain the traditions of academic autonomy and unfettered teaching and research inherited from the latter period of British rule.

HKU had a complex and archaic governance structure that was poorly suited to university-wide academic planning. But the need to set a strategy was palpable. In the transition years of the late 1990s Vice Chancellor Patrick Cheng had to create an ad hoc strategic advisory working group of senior academic staff to discuss the large issues facing the university, including its international and local positioning as well as how to maintain its leadership role. This laid the groundwork for a blue-ribbon commission of leading scholars and businessmen to develop HKU's first modern strategic plan in 2003.

How was the university structured? The university administration was led formally by the chancellor, the chief officer of the university, a position originally reserved for the colonial governor and now for the chief executive (CE) of Hong Kong. The CE served as chancellor at each of Hong Kong's eight public universities, largely in a ceremonial role. In reality, most administrative control at each university lay in the hands of its president (or vice chancellor). The president was "the principal academic and administrative officer of the University," supported by a provost, an executive vice president (administration) and a team of vice presidents, who together with the registrar and director of finance made up the senior management team and reported to the University Council.

The University Council was the chief governing body. It managed financial and human resources as well as strategic planning. The Council was composed of nonuniversity affiliates, HKU administrators, faculty, staff, and students who, by the turn of the twenty-first century, collectively numbered over fifty. This changed during the Council chairmanship of Victor Fung, who engaged a blue-ribbon panel of three experts—Neil Rudenstine, the recently retired president of Harvard; Andrew Li, a former chairman of the UGC and head of the Hong Kong Court of Final Appeal; and John Nyland, former president of the University of New South Wales—to review the governance and management structures of the university. The panel reported their recommendations in the 2003 *Fit for Purpose* report, which put forth seventeen recommendations for good governance, the majority of which focused on the role of the Council. The report recommended the transformation of the Council from its unwieldy, large number into a body of eighteen to twenty-four members, and it reaffirmed the Council as the "de facto supreme governing body of the University."[49] The panel also recommended changes to the membership of the reformed Council, which, under Fung, came to include a greater number of student representatives and, for the first time, included union representatives of senior and junior faculty, as well as of professional staff.

While the Council dealt primarily with administration, political matters, and budgeting, the Senate was responsible for academics and all matters related to education. As such, the Senate was heavily engaged in managing the shift from the three- to four-year curriculum. Its membership consisted of professors, deans, and several student representatives.[50] This body did provide a forum for debate of policy but did not enact any itself.

The third central administrative body was the University Court, which met once a year and served largely useless but charming ceremonial purposes. It was led by the chancellor with a membership of elected representatives from various political and educational bodies.[51]

One of the challenges Vice Chancellor Cheng addressed was the highly compartmentalized academic and financial structure of HKU. Traditionally, the key unit of management was the department, and HKU had over eighty departments, each one of which reported to the central administration. The departments and the schools in which they were organized had neither an organizational mandate nor any incentive to work together. Funding was disbursed to departments based on the number of undergraduates they taught, leading to redundancies in teaching as each department fought to maintain the highest possible student numbers. For example, the civil engineering department might hire a mathematics professor to teach that subject to its students, rather than working with the existing capacity of the mathematics department to meet students' needs.[52]

HKU faced a challenge common to many universities (recall our discussion of Duke): how to bring more resources from the periphery to the center. In a surely unpopular but effective way, Cheng established a new policy of "top-slicing." The majority of funding would continue to be disbursed as it had been in the past, but 10 to 15 percent would be held by the central administration to support strategic initiatives. In principle, this would incentivize departments to be less concerned about their individual numbers and to work together as schools and faculties to plan projects.[53]

The administrative capacity of HKU's schools was further strengthened by the reforms, several of American provenance, enacted during Victor Fung's Council chairmanship. Deans were henceforth appointed by the central administration based on an international search. Previously, deans had been (in the German style) elected by their colleagues, leaving them less accountable to the central administration and unlikely to implement significant but necessary changes that might upset their lifelong colleagues. This was but one of the seventeen administrative changes recommended in the *Fit for Purpose* report and approved for subsequent implementation. It was also under Fung's leadership that faculty and staff salaries were delinked from the civil service pay scale.[54]

HKU was not a young university, but it had never had a formal strategic plan. Fung and Vice Chancellor Lap-Chee Tsui spearheaded the creation of the 2003–2008 strategic plan that prioritized four areas: enhancing academic excellence, raising global presence and visibility, partnering with society and serving the community, and developing and supporting "the university family."[55] Bolstered by a modernized governance system with a streamlined Council, Fung visited each of the HKU faculties in person, meeting with senior faculty at each school and discussing their plans for external benchmarking. This was when Fung set the goal for HKU to make it into the top twenty-five of the *Times Higher Education World University Rankings*. Certainly even Fung did not expect the seemingly instantaneous results of 2007, when HKU jumped from thirty-third in the 2006 rankings to eighteenth.[56]

In 2016 Peter Mathieson launched *Vision 2016–2025*, a strategic plan that built on *Fit for Purpose* by doubling down on internationalization at all levels of university operations. *Vision 2016–2025* committed HKU to increasing opportunities for "learning experiences in mainland China and overseas."[57] HKU, whose identity had been that of a university *not* of mainland China, now experimented with ways to increase its engagement with the mainland, establishing an engineering research institute in Zhejiang and a teaching hospital in Shenzhen, the dynamic new city just to Hong Kong's north.[58]

Faculty and administrators broadly agreed on the lasting effects of the governance and management reforms laid out in *Fit for Purpose*. Feelings about HKU's strategic planning were rather more equivocal. Clearly, HKU's plans did not command the authority of Duke's, on that university's campus. One former senior administrator felt that long-term change had been achieved in the promotion of performance-based evaluation, noting, "The culture of the institution accepted the fact that it was appropriate to measure performance, it was appropriate to reward good performance." At the same time, he noted his amusement at "how [the strategic plans] were, I use the term 'shelved.' The plan was put on the shelf and life went on as normal."

Funding

Whatever its goals, HKU was in a financially enviable position to realize them. The HKU Group—including HKU, Centennial College, and HKU School of Professional and Continuing Education—ended the 2019–2020 academic year with a budget surplus of over US$180 million. Its finance department attributed the surplus primarily to the block funding from the UGC and growing donations to HKU.[59] Funding for the university came from four major sources: government funds, tuition and fees, donations, and investment returns.

As one of the eight publicly funded higher education institutions in Hong Kong, a large part of HKU's operating budget came from the UGC, in the form of triennial block grants, allowing for stability and predictability in financial planning, as well as funding for specific capital projects, research initiatives, or other specific purposes. For example, in 2014 HKU received a new type of funding from the UGC specifically for internationalization and engagement of mainland China.

Tuition and fees were the second largest source of income for HKU. The university offered different tuition scales for local and foreign students. In 2019 one year of tuition for a local undergraduate student was around US$5,400, while all nonlocal students, including those from mainland China, paid nearly US$21,000 per year.[60] Attending Centennial College cost much more for local students (around US$11,300 per year) but less for international students (around US$15,200 per year).[61] In 2015 the university announced that self-financed programs like Centennial College brought in nearly 40 percent of the HKU Group's total tuition and fee income, despite being responsible for less than 15 percent of the group's total expenditures.[62]

Donations and investment returns made up most of the rest of HKU's revenue. Donations included funds dedicated to research, scholarships, and capital expansion. In addition to returns on invested endowment funds, the HKU Group also owned 20 percent stakes in leading firms in Hong Kong's growing medical services industry.[63] With its enviable budget surplus in 2019, HKU had progressed well beyond its financially strained early years. Looking to the future, however, HKU's financial situation appeared less certain. One professor recalled a conversation with a politically connected university administrator, who said, "We have no friends [in the government]. The left wing [i.e., pro-China] politicians hate universities in general because we're not patriotic enough. The democratic ones think we take too many mainland students."[64] High-level administrators expected that funding provided by the government would drop well below 50 percent of the university's operating budget in the future—to be sure an enviable number from the perspective of an American public university, such as Berkeley. To make up the difference, HKU planned to increase fundraising and development efforts. This was the task of Sabrina Lin, vice president of institutional advancement. She would have, even for Hong Kong, a high mountain to climb. One of her projects was to increase the percentage of alumni donors. In 2018 that consisted of just 2.5 percent of alumni.

Hong Kong's Political Order and Disorder

Hong Kong's post-1997 political order, enshrined in the city's Basic Law approved by China's National People's Congress, enabled HKU's growth in the early twenty-first century. The "One Country, Two Systems" model provided Hong Kong's university system with academic freedoms not offered to mainland institutions. As HKU's leadership aspired to create "Asia's Global University," it assumed there would be continuity in both the generous funding and academic autonomy that were hallmarks of HKU under Hong Kong's post-handover polity. Yet it was not clear that Hong Kong's special status in greater China would survive. By 2017 Hong Kong's "high degree of autonomy" promised in the Basic Law had endured basically intact for two decades, but years of political contention and protests left it weakened in the eyes of Hong Kongers and mainland officials.

Hong Kong had an archaic and increasingly dysfunctional political system. Its "prince," or chief executive, was basically appointed by Beijing. The CE enjoyed significant authority but little legitimacy, and the tenure of each CE was rockier than that of the last. The parliament, or Legislative Council, had the trappings of democracy, and because its members were in part directly elected, it enjoyed legitimacy, but it had little real authority. Hong Kong had a strong professional civil service, with an historically independent court system and honest police force. These were stable elements in this volatile mix, although they too would be tested in the extreme in Hong Kong's recurrent crises.

Attempts at political reform in Hong Kong did not reverse rising displeasure among residents about the city's management. By 2013 over 50 percent of Hong Kong residents polled responded that they were dissatisfied with the pace of the city's political development, an increase from just 29 percent in 2007.[65] Support for the "One Country, Two Systems" model also began to crumble. While nearly three-quarters of the city's residents supported that concept in 2007, barely half of those polled in 2012 said they were confident in the system.[66] Beijing seemed to be racing against time to lay the groundwork for gradual political reforms in Hong Kong. Economic inequality was worsening, and demands not only for political reforms but also for a new political identity in Hong Kong were emerging.

Beijing's bid to maintain stability and public support in Hong Kong faced multiple obstacles. Although an influential indicator of quality of life in Hong Kong hit an all-time high in 2008, the trend has since been downward.[67]

Results released in 2012 showed the measure fell below its score for 2003.[68] Restricted voting rights for residents limited outlets for frustrated Hong Kongers. In circumscribing democratic rights, the mainland's cautious approach to political reforms in Hong Kong led Beijing both to exacerbate and be caught in the crossfire of the city's internal social divisions. Dissatisfaction with the mainland's management of Hong Kong's political development contributed to a rising proportion of residents identifying primarily as "Hong Kongers," instead of "Chinese."[69] Growing desire for strong "local," over national, identity heightened the political stakes of debates over democratic and legal reforms in Hong Kong and at HKU.

Since 1997 there had been a gradual increase in conflicts at HKU over engagement with China. In 2000 Vice Chancellor Patrick Cheng and his deputy stepped down amid accusations that they had pressured a university researcher to stop his opinion polling, which had showed declining support for the Beijing-picked chief executive.[70] Because the issue was framed by some as one of academic freedom, it put much academic and emotional stress on the university. In 2011, when Vice Chancellor Lap-Chee Tsui announced his decision to not seek a third term, many speculated that it was related to the accusations of overly harsh treatment of student protestors during the visit of Chinese Vice Premier Li Keqiang.[71] None of these incidents, however, compared to the scale and influence of Occupy Central.

Occupy Central

Beijing had promised Hong Kong that the CE would in time be chosen by universal suffrage. But in 2014 Beijing proposed extending the electorate but limiting the candidates, which sparked intense resistance.

These developments had been followed closely by a group called Occupy Central with Love and Peace, led in part by HKU Faculty of Law associate professor Benny Tai. The group, along with many university and even high school students, launched a civil disobedience campaign in late September 2014, occupying some of Hong Kong's commercial center's busiest streets and demanding full universal suffrage. This movement was galvanized on September 28, 2014, when police used tear gas on demonstrators. This drew attention and sympathy to the demonstrators, whose ranks were ultimately swelled by citizens opposed to any police use of force. The movement, which came to be known as the Umbrella Movement, in reference to the umbrellas carried by protestors to protect themselves from tear gas, continued to occupy the streets of Hong Kong for seventy-nine days.[72] Ultimately, the election format endorsed by the National People's Congress was rejected by the Hong Kong Legislative Council—a dubious victory for the Occupy Central movement, as it left citizens of Hong Kong with no form of popular participation in the 2017 election.[73]

Occupy Central remained a divisive topic in Hong Kong with many fierce proponents and opponents. Because of the high-profile involvement of HKU faculty like Benny Tai (who was later sentenced to sixteen months in prison by a Hong Kong court for "conspiring to commit public nuisance") as well as heavy participation by HKU students, the university seemed inextricably tied to the extended but notably restrained protest movement.[74] (In all seventy-nine days of protest and dispersal, no students were injured.) Government relations with HKU became increasingly tense at a time when the central government of China was already tightening its ideological control over mainland universities, as we have seen at Tsinghua and Nanda.

An early indication of the deteriorating relationship between the Hong Kong and Chinese central governments, on the one hand, and HKU, on the other, was the controversy over Professor Johannes Chan. The public conflict over the delayed confirmation of Chan, a professor and former dean of HKU's Faculty of Law, as vice president of academic staffing and resources lent a concrete form to abstract fears of government interference in university affairs and called into question the role of Hong Kong's chief executive in university administration. In December 2014 a university selection committee nominated Chan for the vice president position, which had been vacant for five years.[75] HKU's Council then delayed responding to the nomination on grounds of waiting until HKU first filled the position of provost, and could then allow the new administrator to weigh in on the decision. It was widely suspected that the delay was due to Chan's connection with Occupy Central—Benny Tai had served as associate dean of the Faculty of Law from 2000 to 2008, overlapping with Chan's deanship for six years.

Seven months later, there was still no response to the selection committee's recommendation. In July 2015 a group of students stormed a meeting of the Council to protest the delay. More than one thousand HKU alumni and over three thousand others then signed an online petition condemning the actions of the students.[76] With the issue still unresolved on September 1, 2015, more than seven thousand HKU staff and alumni called on the Council to confirm Chan within thirty days.[77] On September 29, 2015, the Council voted twelve to eight against Chan's nomination.[78] Following the vote, one of the student representatives on the Council broke confidentiality and published his summary of the meeting. His report indicated that the vote had largely been split between the university-based members of the Council, who voted in favor of Chan's appointment, and the government-appointed members, who had carried the vote against.[79] University faculty and many members of the public believed that his rejection was attributable to political pressure from outside the university's walls.

This led to a constitutional crisis at HKU. How, in fact, was the university being governed? If a deanship approved by a university search committee and the president could be cast aside, what did that portend? This led in turn to scrutiny of the Council and the Chief Executive's right to appoint members, some of whom appeared to be his political allies. For historical reasons, across Hong Kong's universities, only at HKU was the CE entitled to appoint the chair and other members of the Council *without* consultation with the president. Tensions over this power of the CE came to a head with the 2015 appointment of Arthur Li, who was known for his strong leadership style, as Council chairman. Despite protests in 2016, Li's chairmanship was extended for three more years in 2018.[80]

Governance, Reviewed but not Renewed

There was widespread belief that Chief Executive C. Y. Leung had become deeply engaged in HKU university politics, from the very public Johannes Chan affair to the (publicly invisible) selection of HKU honorary degree candidates. The chief executive's position of chancellor (as distinct from vice chancellor or president) had become largely honorific under his predecessors. But Leung took the title literally: he intervened early and often in university affairs.

Under enormous pressure from faculty, students, and staff to ensure the university's academic integrity, the University Council undertook its second major review of governance in the twenty-first century by establishing an independent Review Panel on University Governance in April 2016. Framed as a successor to 2003's *Fit for Purpose* and the 2009 follow-up report, the review panel put forth recommendations aimed to insulate HKU's governance and its academic autonomy from the *Sturm und Drang* of Hong Kong's incessantly contentious politics.

The story of this panel and its work tells us much about the present state of HKU and Hong Kong. It was chaired by Sir Malcolm Grant, chancellor of the University of York in the United Kingdom and the recent president and provost of University College London. A longtime and influential member of Hong Kong's University Grants Committee, Grant also chaired Britain's National Health Service. I was asked to join the review, for I, too, was a former, longtime member of UGC and had a strong commitment to Hong Kong's universities. Sir Malcolm and I were joined by a distinguished senior barrister in Hong Kong, Peter Van Tu Nguyen, former High Court judge of the Hong Kong Special Administrative Region.

Our review was commissioned by HKU's Council with broad terms of reference: to conduct an overall review of the governance structure of the university; to take into consideration other recent assessments (such as *Fit for Purpose*); to meet with all relevant constituencies; to review all ordinances and statutes as to their current appropriateness; and to make recommendations to enhance the university's governance.

We did all that, and more. We solicited confidential, written input from all university stakeholders, including faculty, students, and alumni, and received forty formal written submissions, many quite extensive, all kept confidential to the members of the review panel and its secretary. We held thirty-three meetings with different groups across the university, several in public settings, others in confidence. We indicated at the commencement of each meeting that we would operate under so-called Chatham House rules, meaning that views expressed to us might be quoted directly but would not be attributed to any individual. Our secretary prepared a summary of each meeting, in which speakers were identified only by the order of their speaking and not by name. We reviewed all recent agenda and minutes of the university's governing boards, including the Council.

Our committee met in a "safe" and quiet conference room to review what we had encountered and to make our recommendations. We had reason to assume that our deliberations would in fact be made in confidence, until we were prepared to make them public. But this was Hong Kong. There is good reason why Hong Kong is a frequent locus of John le Carré novels and James Bond films. Nothing stays secret in Hong Kong.

Our review panel made a lengthy report with thirty-five formal recommendations. Many of them were simple housekeeping: how to make things work more efficiently. But others sought to address the great crisis of confidence gripping HKU at the time. The most consequential recommendation was that the chancellorship, held in a hereditary fashion by the chief executive, become clearly honorary, with the chancellor delegating unusual and potentially political powers (such as unilaterally naming Council chairs and members) to the Council itself, and to do the same with other matters, such as the awarding of honorary degrees. Further, we saw distinct advantages of separating the chancellorship from the government, following the current norms in the United Kingdom, Australia, and other countries that had followed British practice.[81] The point was not to accuse the current chief executive of interference in university affairs, but—as he was about to step down—to relieve his successor of the burden of being perceived as acting with political motives toward the university.

We contemplated these recommendations, the three of us, over the course of an intensive week in our private, "sealed" room on the HKU campus. Early in our deliberations we had asked to speak with the chief executive, but his office sent us a curt reply that he had no time. However, before we had come to our (still confidential) conclusions, we were suddenly summoned to Government House to meet with him.

Our room, it seems, was neither sealed nor confidential; it had "ears." When we met with the CE, C. Y. Leung, he was brief on etiquette. He told us, before we had said scarcely a word, "I will never agree to what you are recommending. And Beijing won't allow it." (We had not yet finalized our recommendations.) We reminded him that, as chief executive, he already had very significant power, not the least of the purse, over Hong Kong's universities in general and HKU in particular. He seemed to agree, for he said, "You know, I do not need to be chancellor in order to interfere with the University of Hong Kong." But he was unrelenting in his refusal to accept recommendations that we had yet to set down on paper. He told us as we departed that this was an off-the-record conversation and, indeed, no staff were present. We agreed to keep it among ourselves—until we had dinner that night with Council Chair Arthur Li, who gave us chapter and verse about the "confidential" meeting we had just attended with the chief executive.

What came of all this? The views of the review panel members were reinforced by the brutal meeting with C. Y. Leung, and we agreed unanimously to the first draft of the report in September 2016, which was sent to Arthur Li and Peter Mathieson for their review. Then, however (and here one can only speculate), Nguyen, the only local member of our panel, must have been subject to great pressure, and he ceased all communication with Sir Malcolm and me. He very belatedly endorsed the report nearly in full, save for those recommendations related to the chief executive. For his part, Arthur

Li, the Council Chair, buried the report in Council until the following spring, when a new chief executive was in place, and then eviscerated its main points.

Eventually, the University Council adopted the majority of the review panel's multiple recommendations, but the most significant ones, aimed to improve the Council's transparency and autonomy, were rejected.[82] The rejected recommendations included those making the role of chancellor "largely honorary," with its powers delegated to the Council, including the rights to nominate members and select its chair.[83] After the new CE reappointed Arthur Li as council chair, over thirty student, staff, and alumni groups at HKU issued a joint statement demanding the Council remove the chancellor's powers to appoint members and select a chairman without public consultation.[84] As protests consumed Hong Kong again in the summer of 2019, the Council's ability to effectively govern HKU while protecting its institutional autonomy from political storms would be tested again.

Anti-Extradition Bill Protests

In spring 2019 Hong Kong's government proposed legislation for allowing the CE to determine ad hoc extraditions of suspected criminals on Hong Kong territory to jurisdictions with which it lacked mutual extradition treaties.[85] The bill raised concerns in Hong Kong that it could be used by a pro-Beijing CE to arrest political dissidents and extradite them to mainland China for trial.[86] Responding to criticism, Hong Kong CE Carrie Lam, the successor to C. Y. Leung, introduced an amended bill she argued would limit the threat of its use for political ends and pushed for its swift passage.[87]

Amendments to the bill did not satisfy the public, and Lam's intention to press on sparked enormous protests in June, with many HKU students participating.[88] When Lam suspended the bill, HKU students were among those who declared they would continue to protest until its formal withdrawal.[89] The protests also led to tensions between local students, who largely supported the anti-extradition bill movement and mainland students, who supported Beijing. At an HKU forum held to discuss the protests, mainland students who voiced concerns were jeered.[90] HKU's attempts to convince students that the ongoing protests should not be allowed to affect campus learning were ignored, as student groups opened the academic year with a class boycott.[91] HKU's tradition of student activism had again drawn the university into Hong Kong's protest politics.

As anti-extradition bill demonstrations continued, protester demands expanded and violence grew, placing Hong Kong's political order in jeopardy. In September Lam announced the formal withdrawal of the extradition bill, but by then, protester demands had grown to encompass greater democratic rights and an investigation into police brutality.[92] HKU's student union encouraged their classmates to support these demands, and a survey revealed college-aged and college educated participants were the protests' largest constituency.[93] The turn toward radical politics in protests coincided with growing violence at them. By the end of the summer, over two thousand protesters had been reported injured, and on the seventieth anniversary of the People's Republic of China, the first Hong Kong protester was shot by a police officer.[94] Although China doubled its paramilitary presence in Hong Kong, Chinese President Xi Jinping reportedly did not want to quell protests with military force.[95] Yet, as Hong Kong's municipal government struggled to end the demonstrations, Beijing's patience seemed to be running thin.

In October Xi threatened that "anyone attempting to split China in any part of the country will end in crushed bodies and shattered bones."[96] This poured oil on Hong Kong's fire, and more violent demonstrations ensued.

As student protesters grew fearful that a Beijing-condoned crackdown was imminent, universities became the protests' front line. In mid-November, clashes between protesters and police broke out on the campuses of HKU, the Chinese University of Hong Kong, and Hong Kong Polytechnic University (PolyU) as police sought entry to arrest student protesters.[97] Students and other demonstrators responded by attempting to barricade themselves inside their campuses. Police deployed tear gas in an attempt to disperse protesters and clear the areas, and protesters were reported to have responded with bows and arrows and even javelins to ward off the approaching officers.[98] The police siege of PolyU lasted twelve days and attracted global media attention. When police arrived in armored cars, protesters at PolyU targeted their vehicles with explosive petrol bombs.[99] This latest round of skirmishes set off the most significant crisis universities in Hong Kong had faced since the protests began. University facilities across Hong Kong, including HKU's, were significantly damaged.[100] Many mainland students were reported to have fled the city, and over a dozen foreign universities suspended study abroad programs in Hong Kong.[101] On November 14 the president of HKU announced that classes on the university's main campus were suspended for the rest of the semester.[102]

Figure 11.3. Protests in Hong Kong, June 16, 2019. Studio Incendo / Wikimedia Commons / CC BY 2.0.

With protests reaching a fever pitch in late fall 2019, Hong Kong's government needed a way to dissipate tensions. An opportunity for détente with the city's residents arrived with the November 24 District Council elections. District Council members represent city neighborhoods and do not wield significant political power. However, during a time of political tensions, the District Council's 117 seats on the 1,200-person Election Committee that selects the CE were symbolically important. Pro-democracy parties achieved a stunning victory in the November 24 election, winning 389 of 452 District Council seats with a record 71 percent voter turnout citywide.

CE Carrie Lam told pro-Beijing officials that the election results signaled "dissatisfaction with the government." Despite—or because of—the overwhelming unpopularity of its policies in Hong Kong, Beijing clamped down hard. In January 2020 Luo Huining, former Party Secretary of Shanxi province and before that of Qinghai province, was appointed director of the central government's Hong Kong Liaison Office. In Shanxi and Qinghai, Luo was known for using hardline tactics to bring corrupt officials and dissidents to heel.[103] The first Liaison Office director to have not previously held a Hong Kong-related position, Luo was known to be trusted by Beijing because of his diligent implementation of Xi Jinping's anti-corruption campaign.[104] Under Luo, the Liaison Office became more vocal in its efforts to secure the mainland's control over Hong Kong. In April 2020 the office stated for the first time that Article 22 of the Basic Law, which guaranteed noninterference by mainland departments in Hong Kong affairs did "not apply to the liaison office," undercutting both the legal stipulations and the spirit of the "One Country, Two Systems" policy.[105] Luo himself also urged the Legislative Council to pass controversial national security legislation to defend the city against "violent" protesters and "foreign influence."[106] A similar effort in 2003 had provoked what were then Hong Kong's largest protests posttransition.

The mainland government then moved unilaterally to introduce its own National Security Law for Hong Kong at the May 2020 meeting of the National People's Congress.[107] Beijing had wanted the long-delayed law finally pushed through after the previous year's protests consumed the city, but many expected pro-Beijing forces in the Legislative Council to lead the charge.[108] Instead, the National People's Congress passed a resolution committing the central government to draft legislation for Hong Kong that would ban secession, subversion of state power, foreign intervention, and terrorism as well.[109] This surprise decision sparked a swift backlash, with Hong Kong experiencing its first large protests since the coronavirus lockdown had begun in the winter of 2020.[110] Yet HKU Council chair Arthur Li spoke out in support of the forthcoming legislation and likened the previous year's protesters to a neo-Nazi group.[111] Even HKU's President Zhang tentatively backed the law before a draft had even been publicly released, signing a letter with four other Hong Kong university presidents stating, "We fully support 'One Country, Two Systems,' understand the need for national security legislation, and value the freedom of speech, of the press, of publication, of assembly, and other rights the Basic Law confers upon the people of Hong Kong."[112]

Beijing held the draft's text so close to the chest that not even CE Lam had seen it before the National People's Congress Standing Committee voted the bill into law in the dark of night on June 30.[113] The law was published at 11:00 p.m., Beijing time, the moment it went into force. Why would Beijing resort to such cloak-and-dagger legislating? The reason became clear as the world read the final law in full. Under the law, an expansive national security apparatus, afforded a long leash and reporting ultimately to Beijing, would be set up to pacify Hong Kong. A broad and vague list of offenses (ranging from "disrupting . . . the performance of duties" by the government to "provoking by unlawful means hatred among Hong Kong residents towards" their government) would be deemed national security crimes and carry up to a lifetime prison sentence. Hong Kong's education sector did not escape the law's reach. Under the national security law, "the Hong Kong Special Administrative Region shall promote national security education in schools and universities . . . to raise the awareness of Hong Kong residents of national security and of the obligation to abide by the law."[114] Whereas President Zhang announced his early support for the law prior to its release, neither he nor HKU made any public comment on the law in its wake.

Concerns about the future of academic freedom in Hong Kong gripped scholars at HKU and other universities in the city. The national security law's broad but vague language left HKU's faculty to debate the degree to which academic discussions could run afoul of the bill.[115] Some within HKU's administration, however, seemed to have already decided that constricting academic speech was now a legal requirement. The program director for the humanities and law faculty at HKU's School of Professional and Continuing Education wrote to staff that "[a]ny behavior in eliciting further discussion on sensitive issues MUST be avoided" and warned there would be "zero-tolerance against politics or personal political views brought into class-rooms."[116] HKU responded to inquiries by stating that although this was not an official university policy, classrooms must be "politically neutral." To be sure, the frost settling over academic speech in Hong Kong's universities aligned with the interests of CE Lam, who had criticized universities for allowing "teaching materials" and "classroom teaching" to politicize higher education.[117] Yet it was still unknown whether these were warning shots designed to silence dissident academics and students, or if this uncertainty would give way to greater scrutiny and intrusions into Hong Kong's academic life. Would the universities of Hong Kong be pressed to align themselves with the rules and restrictions governing the mainland's universities?

The dismissal of dissident legal scholar Benny Tai in July 2020 by HKU's University Council was the first concrete signal that the passing of the National Security Law did indeed mark the beginning of a new, less free era for academic life in Hong Kong. Tai had been sentenced to sixteen months in prison in April 2019 for "conspiracy to commit public nuisance" because of his role in the 2014 Occupy Central protests.[118] At President Zhang's behest, HKU initiated an inquiry into Tai's behavior, which found that although his actions did meet the criteria for "misconduct," they fell short of the threshold for dismissal. The HKU Senate, composed mostly of faculty, ratified this recommendation, but it was Arthur Li's University Council, where many members were pro-establishment, that had the final say in the matter. In a vote of eighteen to two, the Council overturned the Senate's recommendations in favor of terminating Tai's employment at HKU. Three members, including President Zhang, declined to cast a ballot. Upon learning of the decision, Tai released a statement that it "marked the end of academic freedom in Hong Kong." Beijing's officers in Hong Kong could not contain their glee. The mainland's Hong Kong Liaison Office cheered HKU for holding Tai accountable for his "evil" actions.[119]

Although Arthur Li, HKU's Council chair, discounted concerns about the Benny Tai case, stating that Tai's sacking was "not a political decision," Hong Kong's government signaled that purging institutions of dissident faculty had become a priority.[120] Hong Kong's Secretary for Security, John Lee, stated that the city had "failed to do a good job with education" since the handover and that his first priority would be to "deal with schools" and their "bad apples" by depoliticizing the education sector.[121] Such an intervention seemed at odds with Article 137 of Hong Kong's Basic Law, which guaranteed academic freedom and autonomy for institutions, but the demands of national security seemed set to subordinate these and many other rights that had been promised to Hong Kong. Benny Tai, for his part, appealed the Council's decision to CE Lam, also HKU's chancellor, potentially forcing a direct and visible political intervention in his case even though, he acknowledged, the chances of Lam reversing the decision were virtually none.[122]

Complacency and Competition

Amid all its political turmoil, HKU still had to focus on its place in an increasingly competitive local, regional, and global landscape for higher education. Mathieson had warned, "There's a real danger of complacency in what, in this part of the world, is a relatively old university. We can't say that because we're 104 years old and we had a good reputation in the past therefore that's fine and we just need to carry on doing what we're doing."[123] These sentiments were echoed by Arthur Li: "I think that will be our biggest enemy at Hong Kong University. It's the complacency. We have always been the top dog. We are good. We are wonderful, you know. There is self-congratulations and so on. And I think that has to be shaken up."[124] The rapid expansion of higher education in Hong Kong in the early 1990s gave students many more options for advanced study. While none of the universities that were established or expanded in recent years were as comprehensive as HKU, some, like the Hong Kong University of Science and Technology, were strong competitors in certain disciplines.

HKU found itself competing not just for human, but also for financial, resources. Government funding for public institutions was increasingly distributed through competitive, project-based grants from Hong Kong's Research Grants Council, stiffening the competition between local universities for faculty and the funding they might attract. HKU was positioned to do well in this competition, so long as it remained apolitical.

For many years, HKU had been the primary beneficiary of the largess of Hong Kong businesspeople, many of whom were not alumni but appreciated the university's contribution to society, particularly to health care and governance. "For sixty years or so, leaders in Hong Kong were all HKU graduates, and this will change," noted former Provost Roland Chin. "Ten . . .

twenty years from now, most of these people will retire, and then the younger generation [will come to power], and they are from [other universities]."[125] HKU was no longer the only respectable, local alma mater for mature professionals and could therefore expect to lose some of its dominance in private funding.

Meanwhile, as we have seen, the mainland Chinese government had begun a concerted effort to nurture world-class universities. Leading institutions such as Peking and Tsinghua Universities were armed with increased funding, more flexible faculty recruiting policies, and low tuition fees to attract the best students. For example, annual tuition for most undergraduate programs at Tsinghua for a mainland Chinese student would be no more than US$1,000. Even for students who would not be considered local at either Tsinghua or HKU, the tuition difference was striking. International undergraduates at Tsinghua could expect to pay annual tuition of around US$4,000 per year, less than 20 percent of the cost of a year of study at HKU.[126]

HKU's tradition of English instruction remained a major differentiating factor between it and the top mainland universities. However, programs like Tsinghua University's School of Economics and Management were beginning to incorporate more English-taught courses and degrees. Victor Fung also observed HKU's diminishing competitive advantage, "We are the only university in China that is taught completely in English. We are the only one. And I think that means something. And, I think the Tsinghuas are getting a lot of resources. I'm sure they will improve and improve and improve. They may exceed Hong Kong."[127] To be sure, before Occupy Central and other demonstrations, HKU had no problem attracting absolutely top students from the mainland who might otherwise have gone to Tsinghua or Beida. But over time, the steady rise of mainland universities, combined with Hong Kong's political instability, meant that HKU would have to work harder to attract mainland students and faculty in the future.

Competition for HKU was not limited to mainland China. In 2012 the National University of Singapore (NUS) overtook HKU in the *Times Higher Education World University Rankings* for the first time, becoming the second ranked institution in Asia after the University of Tokyo.[128] In subsequent years, HKU remained relegated to third place in Asia.[129] NUS in particular was increasingly known for its experimentation with internationalization, including its partnership with Yale University to develop a new liberal arts college, Yale NUS, and with Duke University to found the Duke-NUS

Medical School.[130] Moreover, whereas the Hong Kong government was committed to funding Hong Kong's eight higher education institutions equitably, the Singaporean government had prioritized a few, elite institutions, including NUS; in 2014 NUS received 60 percent more funding from the Singaporean government than HKU did from its government.[131]

Finally, HKU's position in international league tables was never far from the minds of its leaders. Although *Vision 2016–2025* and the *Report of the Review Panel on University Governance* may have helped HKU recover a bit in ratings, the university still lagged behind its peak performance following the release of *Fit for Purpose*. Strategic plans seemed less relevant in a period of deep unrest and anxiety. The media and the public jumped on any dip in the university's performance, and the university itself noted that rankings "are now a permanent part of the higher education landscape and cannot be disregarded in setting institutional strategies."[132] Peter Mathieson noted more general public awareness of international rankings but added that the public's chief interest in such rankings was still the relative position of Hong Kong's universities to each other. Victor Fung recalled a similar dynamic during the initial period of his Council tenure: "The University was beset by rivalry between HKU and Chinese U. This rivalry had no reference, however, to absolute standards of excellence. Should not these schools instead be benchmarked against the top universities in the world?"[133] In the world of higher education, there were competitors everywhere, but HKU, it seemed, had still to truly recognize those beyond Hong Kong's borders. The events of 2019–2020 had not made that task easier.

Facing the Future

The University of Hong Kong was founded on the assumption that its students would steer clear of politics. When HKU was established, the obstacles to fulfilling its role as a flagship higher education institution had been primarily internal—disagreements over the balance of teaching and research, constant dearth of funding, and wavering political support for the institution from a distant ruling power. After 1997, with Hong Kong's return to China under "One Country, Two Systems," HKU sought to seize the opportunity of being arguably the leading university in greater China, with a governance structure unimpeded by Communist Party secretaries. Generously funded by Hong Kong's government and supported by an apolitical University Grants Committee, it faced unmatched opportunities. Under

Victor Fung's dynamic Council chairmanship, it sought to be in reality, as later it would be in slogan, "Asia's Global University," benchmarking itself against the best in the world. In its massive rethinking and expansion of undergraduate education, it showed itself capable of major change. In Peter Mathieson's *Vision 2016–2025* plan, it set out its ambition. On taking office, President Zhang sought to take HKU's globalizing goals further still: "A great university includes a number of dimensions. First, education and transmission of knowledge, as we do in the British system. Research degrees like in the German system. Third one, which the U.S. does, is research innovation. . . . I am also looking at the fourth dimension, societal impact, which U.S. universities talk about."[134] Since the beginning of the twenty-first century, HKU has committed itself to aiming high and charting paths to achieve its ambitions. This determination has helped the university remain upright even as its city was consumed with the politics of protest in the 2010s. Yet the seemingly permanent political crisis of Hong Kong threatened even the best laid plans.

By 2022 HKU faced a much different set of challenges. Not only did it have to compete with a host of excellent higher education institutions within Hong Kong—from whom it had not truly distanced itself—it faced also stiff competition from the increasingly internationalized universities of mainland China, Singapore, and the world. Provost Paul Tam had commented in 2015: "HKU is a global university, but it also has China as a hinterland, so we have to make the best use of our position to ensure that our research is relevant on the world stage and has world reputation, making use of the China factor, but also hoping to help China by bringing in the international aspect."[135] Just five years later, it was not China, but an embattled HKU that seemed isolated and in need of help.

Within the university, its governance issues had grown more acute. In late 2021, HKU withdrew recognition of its student union and ordered the removal of the *Pillar of Shame,* which for nearly a quarter-century had symbolized a commitment to freedom of speech.[136] HKU's Council had become a state-within-the-state, under a strong-willed chairman who at times acted like the former university president and government minister he had been, deeply compromising HKU's capacity for self-governance, let alone self-renewal.

President Xiang Zhang remained resolute. The University of Hong Kong, he told its faculty and students in late 2019, was "a citadel of freedom and knowledge, where we cherish civil and rational debate, and seek to find solutions with knowledge, wisdom, and imagination. I am here to support and promote a diverse and vibrant campus culture premised on openness, civility, and respect. . . . I know many of you are in pain, Hong Kong is in pain. It is time to think differently, to work on solutions and find ways forward together."[137]

Conclusion

Lessons and Prospects

T HIS HAS been a book about the modern research university in three of its most powerful settings— Germany, the United States, and China—and in eight of its leading institutions. I posed a simple question: German universities set in place the foundations of modern universities everywhere in the nineteenth century; American universities had enormous international influence by the end of the twentieth century; what then are the prospects for Chinese leadership in the twenty-first century?

Before we address that final question, we must remember that none of these are static systems, frozen in place and time in earlier centuries. How might we assess, even briefly, the current trajectories of German and American higher education?

A German Reawakening

Over the first two decades of the twenty-first century, German universities have witnessed gradual, consistent, and consequential changes that promise to reshape German higher education. First, the Excellence Initiative has introduced an enduring ethic of competition among leading institutions— places that *know* they are leading because they have been designated "Universities of Excellence." Second, the competition for "third party" funds (*Drittmittel*) has intensified greatly and is changing the landscape of German university funding. Third, a cluster of dynamic and innovative private universities has emerged, challenging the monopoly of state institutions not in numbers but in creativity.

The Excellence Initiative has shocked, energized, mobilized, and organized the modern German university since its announcement in 2005. The system as a whole had become complacent and comfortable with the egalitarian ethos that emerged from the turbulent 1960s and the massification of higher education in the 1970s and 1980s. Now, suddenly, excellence mattered again. It was a jolt when, in the very first set of Excellence awards announced in 2006, venerable Heidelberg was passed over in favor of its upstart neighbor, Karlsruhe, once a sleepy technical school. With strong leadership and Excellence funding, Karlsruhe University became the Karlsruhe Institute of Technology, or KIT, and the MIT at least of Baden-Württemberg. A leading center of nanotechnology, KIT ranked first among German universities in the physical sciences in 2020.[1] "People used to say elite was a dirty word," remarked Heidelberg's rector at the time, Peter Hommelhoff, but thanks to the Excellence Initiative, "the idea of elites is no longer a problem in Germany."[2]

Fifteen years later, it is clear that this nationwide competition and the resources that accompanied it have enabled German universities to attract and retain talent, expand and hone their research profiles, and become innovative, international hubs for research. The fact that the funding is not permanent is a further incentive to remain, in a formal sense, "excellent" or to find other sources of support. In short, the Excellence Initiative has made German universities academically entrepreneurial and, in many fields, newly competitive internationally. In 2017, as the second round of Excellence funding was drawing to a close, a lively debate about the future of the initiative and of German universities themselves took place in the political sphere and in the press. Among the solutions offered was the idea that the federal government establish several elite universities, leaving the others to be run by the states.[3] This would take a page out of the Chinese book, where extraordinary resources are given to Tsinghua and Peking Universities, leaving the rest to fight it out for recognition. But despite—or perhaps because of—the University of Berlin serving as a de facto national university in the nineteenth century, this revived vision did not materialize. Meanwhile, it seems likely that the Excellence funding, now under the title "Excellence Strategy" (*Exzellenzstrategie*), which commenced in 2019, will remain a central part of German higher education. Another opportunity for universities to receive funding under the Excellence Strategy will take place in 2026 and will bring new applicants into the mix. But, as the strategy aims to encourage competition, sustained or permanent funding for all selected clusters, graduate schools, and universities remains conditional on performance. This, in my view, is a very good thing.

The quasi-permanence of the Excellence Initiative funding reflects the directive planning of Germany's Federal Ministry of Education and Research for German universities, which had historically been funded by the individual states. Federal government investment in extra-university institutions has also increased dramatically, in some cases displacing universities as the centers of research excellence. Nonuniversity institutions with long histories, such as the Max Planck Society and the Leibniz Association, carry out research with an international pedigree, untethered to teaching responsibilities. In research published in leading journals in the natural sciences, Max Planck institutes ranked third in the world in 2020—trailing the Chinese Academy of Sciences and Harvard University.[4]

The perpetual competition for resources seems certain to remain a distinguishing feature of the German academy in the future. Third-party funding today increases a scholar's prospects of academic success and supports many of the most innovative projects. The German Research Foundation publishes a "Funding Atlas" (*Förderatlas*) that shows which institutions have received what funding for which projects across German universities, revealing the status of third-party funding as an overall measure of a university's quality.[5] This development has not met with universal praise: critics charge that tying universities to their ability to attract funding makes market-worthiness the distinguishing metric of the academy.[6] Still, the ability to attract external funding remains a significant—if not the most significant—factor in influencing a scholar and a university's standing. It shows no sign of fading.

Where external markets have truly entered the world of German universities is in the private sector. The largest and best-known research universities remain all public institutions. But in the first decades of the twenty-first century, a handful of private universities have sprouted, with specialized and distinguishing offerings. These private initiatives aim to bring to Germany international models of education, be it campus life or truly international degree programs. They are financed through nonprofit foundations (*Stiftungen*). The first of these, Jacobs University in Bremen, was founded in 1999 as the International University Bremen with the support of the University of Bremen, Rice University in the United States, and the City of Bremen and opened its doors to students in 2001. Located in a former Nazi barracks that was used for displaced persons after the war, the university aimed to bring the American campus experience to an international community of students in Bremen, a port city with historic global ties. In 2006, after years of financial trouble and wavering commitment of the city, the Jacobs Foundation rescued the university and took on a controlling stake. "We are small, innovative and agile," its ambitious young president, Katja Windt, told me in 2016. In 2021 the university offered fifteen degree programs in English ranging from BA to PhD, teaching a total of 1,500 students.

Not long after Jacobs was founded, two other private institutions appeared on the scene. In 2003 the Hertie School opened its doors near Humboldt University in Berlin. The school offered English language degree programs, targeting German and international students seeking professional training in public administration and governance. As of 2019, 687 students were enrolled as the school planned its move to a larger campus at the renovated Robert Koch Forum near the Reichstag, a complex of Wilhelmine buildings that were originally the home of the natural scientific and medical institutes of the University of Berlin.[7]

History is inescapable in Germany. The Hertie Foundation that funds the Hertie School stems from the retail chain that founded the modern department store in Germany. Its business was "aryanized" by the Nazis in 1933, the assets seized, and its owners forced into exile. A postwar settlement allowed Hertie stores to return across the West German (and West Berlin) landscape, and the philanthropic foundation was founded in the 1970s.

A different story can be found farther south. Around the same time that the Hertie School opened, on the shores of Lake Constance in the southern state of Baden-Württemberg, another private institution welcomed its first class of undergraduates. At Zeppelin University in Friedrichshafen, hand-picked cohorts of students arrive to study the intersections of business, technology, and culture in modern facilities. Its research focuses on globalization, cultural production, and the computational social sciences. The university is supported by the Zeppelin Foundation, whose funding was derived from the fortune of the airship company founded by Ferdinand Graf von Zeppelin at the beginning of the century. The *Graf Zeppelin II*, named for the late count, was a sister ship of the *Hindenburg* and the last of its kind. When the *Hindenburg* went down in flames in 1937, the company turned to making V-2 rockets to attack England during World War II. Not quite the Hertie story.

Zeppelin University (ZU) aims not to be rooted in the German past but to be "the university of the 21st century" that "bridges business, culture, and politics." Its curriculum stresses interdisciplinarity and innovation, encouraging students and faculty to work closely with businesses and entrepreneurs. Its selective admissions process distinguishes it from German state universities, as it requires a written application and interview. It emphasizes that old principle of the unity of teaching and research and small class size in its fourteen bachelor's and master's degree programs, as well as in its doctoral courses. Its program in economic sciences was ranked first (tied with Frankfurt) among German universities in 2020–2021.[8] Students spend their final "Humboldt Year" on a research project at one of its eighty-five international partner universities. Perhaps taking a swipe at the censorship at leading Chinese universities (remember the "seven forbidden topics" on Chinese campuses?), the first principle of ZU's mission statement is this: a university "has to be a place where every question is allowed." ZU's current president, Klaus Mühlhahn, a former vice president of Free University of Berlin, is a leading historian of modern China.[9]

The three institutions just discussed remain exceptions in German higher education. Their small size and comparatively large endowments allow them a degree of flexibility that eludes their public counterparts. In particular, the small size, English language degree programs, and campus environment offered by the undergraduate bachelor's programs at Jacobs and Zeppelin Universities have made them attractive destinations for German and international students and, perhaps, models for more established universities. In 2012 the University of Freiburg founded the first "university college" in Germany. Freiburg followed a model that has been brilliantly successful in the Netherlands, where, most notably, Amsterdam University College was founded as an elite college of the liberal arts and sciences in partnership with two major research universities.[10] University College Freiburg offers a four-year liberal arts program to undergraduates from across the world, paralleling in many ways the American small college experience but nested within a large research institution. The degree program is conducted in English, and the class size is kept deliberately small: annual intake averages eighty students per year.

In sum, between the Excellence Initiative, with its compelled competition and forced planning; the growing strength of research foundations and the scope of "third party" funding; and the educational start-up culture seen at Hertie, Jacobs, Zeppelin, and Freiburg, the German scene is more dynamic and imaginative than anyone could have predicted two decades ago. German universities were once purveyors of best practices in higher education. They are now among the keenest consumers of the lessons found in global university systems. They are taking the best of the Chinese model of state commitment and financial incentives, and, at the edges, of the American experience of the innovative possibilities of private universities.[11]

German universities may not again dominate the global stage, but they are, once again, centers of excellence and innovation.

The United States: The Trials of Public Higher Education

From most external perspectives—and certainly from the viewpoint of Europe or Asia—American universities remain the envy of the world. Judging from the Academic Ranking of World Universities in 2021, eight of the ten leading universities in the world were American—and seventeen of the top twenty-five. The *Times Higher Education World University Rankings* is similarly generous (eight of the top ten, if only fifteen of the top twenty-five). Even the 2021 QS World University Rankings, historically tougher on the Americans, gives them half of the top ten and twenty-five slots.

Yet within the United States there is a broad and deep anxiety about the future of American higher education. A sizeable cottage industry of books has grown up bewailing the limits, failings, or demise of American universities. The former Harvard president, Derek Bok, has written about *Our Underachieving Colleges.* My learned colleague in Harvard's English Department, Jim Engell, worries about *Saving Higher Education in the Age of Money.* On a similar theme, Duke University's Charles Clotfelter has authored *Unequal Colleges in the Age of Disparity.* The former chancellor of the University of North Carolina, Holden Thorp, has written of the need to "rebuild the partnership between America and its colleges." James Shulman, then of the Mellon Foundation, collaborated with Princeton's former president, William G. Bowen, to study *The Game of Life* and how collegiate sports in the United States have warped educational values. The American Academy of Arts and Sciences, apart from worrying that the humanities are no longer *The Heart of the Matter,* warned about *The Perils of Complacency* in American science and engineering. Oxford's Simon Marginson, invited by Berkeley to give the Clark Kerr Lectures on the Role of Higher Education in Society, concluded that *The Dream is Over.* Others believe that the most important agenda for American education is now *Surpassing Shanghai.* American higher education has become a *Palace of Ashes,* according to another book, the subtitle of which is *China and the Decline of American Higher Education.*[12]

Critiques of access and inequality have become increasingly numerous and sharp. Anthony Abraham Jack describes how even lower-income students given scholarships to elite colleges remain *The Privileged Poor*. Elizabeth Armstrong and Laura Hamilton unmask the social and cultural effects of "Greek" and "party" life for students of lower socioeconomic backgrounds. Sara Goldrick-Rab calls the crisis of affordability and the United States's extraordinary number of dropouts a *Betrayal of the American Dream*. Tressie McMillan Cottom calls American for-profit colleges *Lower Ed* and highlights how they exacerbate inequalities. And Jennifer Hirsch and Shamus Khan, in *Sexual Citizens,* explore the pervasive nature of sexual assault on university campuses.[13]

The critique of leading institutions is a healthy part of American political life. And perhaps there is no market for books about what's right with American universities. But these books, collectively, serve as a powerful early warning system that the age of American ascendency and hubris may be coming to an end, in the world of universities as in other realms.

There is much to worry about in the very uneven state of private colleges and universities in the United States. Our two examples of Harvard and Duke, for all their challenges, should be among the least concerned. To be sure, Harvard, as a historically second-wave innovator and comparatively risk-averse, faces the danger of what Richard Brodhead called "the inertia of excellence." (Harvard has not absorbed the lesson of Duke's Peter Lange that "the greater your reputation, the greater your capacity to take risk.")[14] But it is truly in the realm of public higher education, which we explored in detail in the case of Berkeley, that the United States should be very worried indeed.

Six of the world's twenty-five leading universities in the ARWU tables are public American institutions. All but one of these six have come under severe financial pressure in the past several decades because of a common, nationwide phenomenon: the American disinvestment from public higher education.

We have seen some of the consequences of disinvestment at Berkeley, where a once proud and mission-driven campus devolved into turmoil and backbiting, driven in good measure by an enduring economy of scarcity. What is true at Berkeley is true, in some measure, across the University of California system.[15] The state of California made a commitment in 1911 to fund the UC system in proportion to its growth: as the state expanded and enrollments grew, so too would state support of higher education. Not anymore. The University of California has maintained the commitment in Clark Kerr's Master Plan to admit the top 12.5 percent of California high school graduates. But as enrollments grew from 166,500 in 1990 to 291,200 in 2020,[16] the state scaled back its commitment. Economic downturns in the early 1990s, in 2001, and, especially, in 2008, were each accompanied by cuts in public funding for the UC system. The state spent 18 percent of its budget on higher education in the mid-1970s, but only 12 percent in 2017. The UC itself received 8.1 percent of the state's general funds in 1996–1997; ten years later that figure was 2.5 percent.[17] In the year 2000 the state supported 24 percent of the UC operating budget. By 2014 that number had fallen to 10 percent, and it has fallen further since. In 1988 the state expended approximately $25,000 (in inflation-adjusted dollars) per UC and California State University student; by 2015 it was closer to $10,000. What the state no longer funds is paid for by higher tuition. In-state students at UC Berkeley paid $4,050 in 2000, a figure that had risen to $14,250 in 2019–2020. One could go on and on with such statistics, but they all tell the same story.[18]

California is always a first-mover. It has led in both the rise and decline of public higher education in the United States. What in 2009 Berkeley Chancellor Robert Birgeneau called California's "completely irresponsible disinvestment in the future of its public universities"[19] is now a national phenomenon. Across the country, state support for public colleges and universities (measured as funding per full-time student) declined 30 percent between 2000 and 2014. Whereas nationwide, state appropriations accounted for 32 percent of revenue per public university student in 2000, by 2016 it was but 18 percent. By 2020 state funding for public higher education nationwide remained 9 percent below pre-2008 levels (that is, before the Great Recession) and 18 percent below the level of 2001. In 2009 Birgeneau proposed that the US government pass "a 21st-century version of the Morrill Act" to reinvigorate flagship public universities with federal funds.[20] Nothing came of that. As one analyst of higher education funding noted in 2020, "With every recession, funding for higher ed has had steeper declines and shallower recoveries."[21] We shall see if this is true also for the economic recession induced by the COVID-19 pandemic. With rising tuition making up much of the shortfall, more students incurred debt: 54 percent of public university students graduated with some student loan debt in 2012–2013, with nearly 20 percent owing more than $20,000. Nearly 70 percent of American college graduates in 2019 (here counting both private and public institutions) took out student loans; their average debt was $29,900.[22] The growing debt and its consequences are particularly pronounced for less affluent students of color.[23]

In the financing of higher education, California was by no means the worst performer. By 2020 it was among seven states to return to pre-2008 levels of overall education appropriation per full-time equivalent student (albeit in current dollars). Another seven states were more than 30 percent below their pre-2008 levels of funding. The others were somewhere in between.[24] In short, that means that forty-three of the fifty American states had disinvested in public higher education since 2008.

Why is there so little public support for public universities? It is not hard to understand how leading American private universities can become lightning rods for public criticism. Harvard may be perceived as elite, aloof, and unfathomably rich. Why not tax its endowment? But why do not the citizens of Alabama take as much pride in their public University of Alabama as they do in the success of the Crimson Tide, the university football team? It is a mystery to me. Perhaps it is the result of a renewed American aversion to paying taxes for anything. Public institutions in the United States educate three-quarters of all American university students. They count among their ranks many of the world's leading universities. It is an ongoing tragedy when even the states most historically supportive of public higher education, such as California and Michigan, fail to reinvest in their extraordinary flagship institutions. As the *New York Times* columnist Bob Herbert wrote in 2009, "It will say a great deal about what kind of nation we've become if we let these most valuable assets slip into a period of decline."[25]

Make no mistake: the slow-motion defunding of US public higher education will have consequences also for the private schools, the Stanfords and the Harvards. If the public universities decline, so in time will the private ones, who compete with their public counterparts for the same faculty, graduate students, and senior administrators. There is no greater threat to the leading position of American higher education than America's growing parsimony in the support of public higher education. I had a premonitory shiver in 1991, when I was considering taking a senior leadership position at the University of Washington. I had been invited to a private dinner with the university's president, the late Bill Gerberding. The president was delayed in arriving, being held up in meetings with the legislature on the university's budget. I will never forget his arrival. He came in, wordlessly, and he ordered an enormous Scotch. Then he told me: "You know, Mr. Kirby, this is a much better university than the taxpayers of this state deserve."

Lessons

Before we turn to the future, and the role of Chinese universities, let us think of what we have learned through our case studies on factors that may enhance, or retard, a university's quest to be among the best. For this we should first return to several of the founding principles of Humboldt.

First, we can be reassured that the primary and *new* mission assigned to universities by Humboldt and his successors—the pursuit of *Wissenschaft*, of knowledge pure and applied—has succeeded far beyond his or anyone of his generation's imagination. Ideas and inventions developed in universities have empowered nation-states, such as Germany, the United States, and China, in war and in peace, and the reach of university research has expanded fantastically (to the Moon? to Mars? to an exoplanet?). It is no accident that universities have been at the forefront of the medical, epidemiological, and public health research that has led to treatments, vaccines, and public health strategies for COVID-19 in the third decade of the twenty-first century.

Second, Humboldt's commitment to an education rooted in the arts and sciences—idealistic in his own time, when most university students pursued forms of professional education—has endured, surprisingly, across two centuries of the evolution of the research university. It became, and it remains, the foundation of American undergraduate education in most public and private universities. It has been re-imported into Germany, thanks in part to the Excellence Initiative and its high level of support for the humanities and social sciences; and because of the example next door, in the Netherlands, of university colleges of arts and sciences that have enrolled no small number of German students and which set the stage for experiments such as we have seen at Freiburg.

One of the more striking developments in elite Chinese higher education in the twenty-first century is the independent understanding that the general education of China's students—in the arts and humanities as well as the sciences and social sciences—will be as important as their specialized, professional training. "General education" (*tongshi jiaoyu* and other formulations) is now a cornerstone of curricular reform throughout the People's Republic, as well as in Hong Kong and Taiwan. Nanjing University's efforts are among the most ambitious, requiring all students to complete a shared general education curriculum before choosing their major.

Why are Chinese educational leaders, at least in the elite institutions, experimenting with general education in the arts and sciences? They believe that they need to do this in part because in China, as in the United States, as in Germany, all the pressures are in the opposite direction—on the part of students, who too single-mindedly pursue their careers, and on the part of faculty, whose careers and interests are ever more specialized—leading to a situation in which students and faculty interact on ever-more-narrow ground. It would be nice, as Henry Rosovsky once declared, if it were true that precisely what the faculty wanted to teach was exactly what the students needed to learn. But as Dean Rosovsky knew, that has never been the case, and it is the job of leading universities to ensure that our students learn broadly from the best faculty how to think, to reflect, to analyze, and to become the critical thinkers and problem-solvers of the next generation. For this, in my judgment, a study of the humanities remains essential. And—despite the increased pressures of political oversight on their campuses—this is a view shared broadly by the presidents of China's top universities. Perhaps this is because they know, better than anyone else, what life can be like in the absence of the humanities. For that is part of the tragedy of China's mid-century Maoism, which is deeply remembered, if not much talked about.

Third, governance matters, today as much as in any period. Humboldt's ideal of a university with the autonomy to govern itself, to make its own appointments, set its own curricula, and chart its future insulated from the politics of the day has never come to pass, not the least for universities founded by, and in some sense for, the state. (That would include every one of the universities chronicled in this book, except Duke.) Yet the broad degree of academic independence that characterized the University of Berlin in its first century, where professorial appointments were made largely on the basis of proven excellence or exceptional promise, would come to define how the "tenure-track" system would evolve in the United States and, in recent decades, again in China.

Beyond faculty appointments, there is no single or easy measure of good governance in universities. Harvard is the oldest of the institutions we have studied, with the oldest set of governing boards. Harvard's president, you will recall, is selected by, and is responsible to, not the Commonwealth of Massachusetts but the Harvard Corporation, a self-perpetuating body that consisted of but seven members from 1650 to 2010. This small and secretive structure worked well when it had outstanding leadership (for example, under Robert Stone, a Corporation member from 1975 to 2002). But a crisis of governance and confidence in both the president and the Corporation in 2005–2006 led in time to an expanded (thirteen members), more expert, less clubby board. It is still a remarkably small and private board for an enterprise with an annual budget of more than $5 billion and a community of some forty thousand students, faculty, and staff. Duke University, by contrast, has long had a larger board of trustees (thirty-five in 2021) from a range of professions and industries, and with multiple committees. It has been deeply and publicly engaged in the strategic planning that has come to define Duke.

"Not everything is improved by making it more democratic." This was Henry Rosovsky's first principle of university governance.[26] Surely the experiences of an ultra-democratic and increasingly ungovernable Berkeley would bear out this observation. So too, after the fall of the Berlin Wall, would the experience of the newly democratized Humboldt University, with its revolving-door rectorships and presidencies.

In these universities simplicity and clarity of governance would appear to trump complexity. The dual-governance structure of contemporary Chinese universities, with the Party secretary elevated above the president, and with Party secretaries in every major school alongside the deans, aims to keep universities aligned with Party priorities; but Chinese universities have grown in stature despite, not because of, the intrusion of Party oversight.

Fourth, leadership matters, not only at the presidential level but also at the next and the next levels down. Harvard had Charles Eliot and Berkeley had Clark Kerr, two individuals who profoundly altered the future of their institutions. One might add the name of Friedrich Althoff, who was never rector of the University of Berlin but who, as the de facto Minister of Culture in Prussia, did as much to shape it as an institution as anyone else. There is no shortage of books on presidential leadership in universities, usually written by former presidents—the successful ones presumably.[27] Much less is written about the individuals who run the universities day-to-day, with a long-term perspective on their future.

Free University would likely not be among the leading German universities today were it not for the extraordinary (and extraordinarily quiet) work of Peter Lange, who served the university for three decades, the last fifteen as *Kanzler*, or financial vice president. His cross-Atlantic namesake, Peter Lange of Duke, spearheaded Duke's internationalization as a faculty member and oversaw its academic and financial integration in his fifteen years as provost. In this work he partnered closely with another long-timer, Tallman Trask III, the executive vice president overseeing both administration and finances—a man who, like FU's Peter Lange, knew where the money was and how to get it, quietly.

Every great university has such individuals who do quietly transformative work outside the limelight of the presidency. At Berkeley, Provost George Breslauer kept the lights on and the university running at the depth of the financial collapse after 2009. At Harvard, Provost Harvey Fineberg, who established the position, and two long-term successors, Stephen Hyman and Alan Garber, have had the Sisyphean labor of knitting together a far-flung university of independent kingdoms that share little connective tissue. At Tsinghua, Dean Qian Yingyi was the transformative and long-term dean of the School of Economics and Management, where he experimented with general education reforms that would have an impact on the whole university. His former deputy dean, Yang Bin, has risen to be provost and vice president of Tsinghua and chairman of the Tsinghua University Education Foundation, the university's endowment. Yang Bin's real portfolio includes much more, including Tsinghua's international partnerships at home and abroad. He is provost, vice president, and minister of foreign affairs at Tsinghua, to name only his better-known responsibilities. His long, discrete, and powerfully effective service has made him one of the most trusted and influential voices in Chinese higher education. To this list I must add the name of Hao Ping. He is currently president of Peking University and formerly its Party secretary. Before that, and perhaps most consequentially, he was China's vice minister of education who oversaw—and gave critical support to—all the major joint-venture initiatives between Chinese and international universities: the University of Nottingham Ningbo; Xi'an Jiaotong-Liverpool University in Suzhou; New York University Shanghai; Duke Kunshan University; and Schwarzman College at Tsinghua University. It is not too much to say that Hao Ping is the Friedrich Althoff of the internationalization of Chinese higher education.

Leadership matters also at the board level. I have mentioned the tenure of Bob Stone on the Harvard Corporation, a man who was known, rightly, as "Mr. Harvard" over the course of three university presidencies. Rick Wagoner was a powerfully positive chair of the Duke board when Duke was establishing its campus in China, a place Wagoner knew well from his time as CEO of General Motors. Victor Fung, as chair of the Council of the University of Hong Kong, accomplished more in his tenure than did many presidents in theirs. Fung spearheaded the re-imagination of HKU as a leading university in Asia and the world. He reformed an archaic set of governance boards, making the council leaner and stronger. He reformed

HKU's appointment, promotion, and tenure processes. And, with his unique combination of intelligence, persistence, and personal modesty, he built a new consensus among faculty and students as to what HKU could be. It is sad that so much of his work has been undone by a successor.

Fifth, money matters (a lot), but success is measured in how you plan to use it. Harvard's great wealth allows it to do much more, and at a higher level, than any university on Earth. It maintains a culture of excellence in appointing faculty—the individuals who will be both the recipients and spenders of university funds. Its resources have allowed it to survive its own fiscal mismanagement in and around the recession of 2008. But uniquely among the universities we have encountered in this book, the management and use of Harvard's resources are still widely dispersed across individual schools, with broadly excellent but inevitably uneven leadership. The university still seems to lack the capacity or even the will to do deep, university-wide strategic planning—the kind of planning that has allowed Duke, in certain areas, to do more with much less. Planning has mattered critically, too, to FU's success in the Excellence Initiative. For without the detailed assessment of its own capacities and ambitions, FU could never have been competitive for, much less received, the financial and reputational rewards of being a "University of Excellence." There is wide adoption of strategic planning among Chinese universities, too. This has helped to realize their ambitions to rise in the rankings of global higher education. Yet what Chinese universities plan for, and what they can actually do, may depend on the priorities of the Chinese Party-State—sometimes to their detriment, as in the case Nanjing University.

Planning for higher education at the national level can make a difference. Just compare the roles of today's German Federal Ministry of Education and Research and the (more powerful) Chinese Ministry of Education with the absent or invisible U.S. Department of Education in the funding, promotion, and guidance of higher education.

Berkeley and our two Berlin universities are examples of how great universities can be brought nearly to their knees by financial crises; and of these three, FU stands out as the best managed. Our Chinese universities, by contrast, do not want for resources at present, however unevenly they may be distributed. Their resources and domestic rankings are almost preordained. For the foreseeable future China will have two "number one" universities; seven others content to be in the C9; and everyone else. For all of them, as

I suggested earlier, the test is not how good you are when the funds are flooding in; it is how you fare when they dry up. If history is any guide, that day will come, but we are not there yet.

Can China Lead the World of Universities?

This is the question with which I began this research more than eight years ago. Then, the trajectory of Chinese higher education was unrelentingly upward, in values as in accomplishments. China's was an educational landscape of ambition, with a diversity of institutions. The PRC showed a willingness to take risks, for example by welcoming international partners to found new institutions in China. If, in the first half of the twentieth century, China could build one of the strongest small systems of higher education, how could it not succeed when it addressed the challenge of building at scale—China scale?

As Germany retools and revives its universities, and as America disinvests, at least from its public institutions, China has shown an unmatched ambition to build more of the best, "world-class" universities than anyone else. To this effort it has mobilized both state and private resources, and it has at hand more of the best human capital—Chinese scholars at home or in the diaspora—than any university system in the world.

Chinese universities continue to rise in the various rankings tables, and two of them, Tsinghua and Beida, will surely be among the world's top ten in short order. For their ascent is a factor both of their own growing excellence and the broader geopolitical rise of China.

The rise of China and its modern universities has been coterminous with periods of openness and internationalization. Germany, the United States, and the Soviet Union have at different times and places all played the role of partner. The very short period of Chinese "self-reliance" during Mao's Cultural Revolution was a near-death experience for Chinese universities. There is little question that Chinese universities will continue their international engagement, but in which direction?

A Chinese Model Along the New Silk Road?

In 2021 Chinese universities remain open to the world, but they are also open to official redefinition. As we have seen, President Xi Jinping aspires to build Chinese universities that are singular and distinctive from their international partners: not China's Harvard, but China's Tsinghua, China's Nanda. And Chinese universities have been mobilized for a new national goal: China going abroad along the "New Silk Road" (NSR), presumably to provide Chinese models for higher education in Central Asia, Africa, and even Europe. The NSR metaphor invokes the legacy of land-based trading routes across Eurasia that, at specific points in history, connected East and Central Asian markets to those of the Middle East and Mediterranean. These were famously termed the *Seidenstraße,* or Silk Road, by the German explorer Ferdinand von Richthofen in 1877. In economic terms, the Silk Road has been as moribund in modern times as it was for large stretches of history. Yet President Xi Jinping's 2015 announcement that higher education cooperation was to be an important element of the NSR suggested that the initiative might make the "New Silk Road" a conduit for ideas.

What are the implications of the rise and internationalization of Chinese higher education for the NSR, otherwise known by the less metaphorical name, the "Belt and Road Initiative"? This ambitious concept of multilayered cooperation between China and over 130 Eurasian, African, and Latin American countries is predicated on Chinese institutions "going out" into the world to make their mark, be it in business, infrastructure, or education. By deploying the Silk Road metaphor and legacy to support the initiative, the NSR seems to redirect, at least rhetorically, the trajectory of Chinese higher education's historically Western-focused internationalization.

Chinese universities are expanding abroad, some along a generous interpretation of the Silk Road: Suzhou University in Laos took in its first students in 2012; the Yunnan University of Finance and Economics (YUFE) set up the YUFE Business School in Bangkok in 2014; and Xiamen University established its Malaysia campus in 2015. But larger efforts still have gone toward established centers of higher education. The Beijing Language and Culture University (BLCU) partnered with Japan's ISI Corporation to establish BLCU Tokyo College in 2015. In 2016 the first wholly owned Chinese tertiary institute in Australia, the Global Business College of Australia, welcomed its first class of students. In 2019 Beijing Normal University (BNU) and Cardiff University (CU) in Wales, agreed to build the BNU-CU Chinese College in Cardiff.[28] In 2020 the Peking University HSBC Business School opened the "first [completed] Chinese campus in the developed world," in Oxfordshire, England in a neo-Gothic and modern campus inherited from Britain's Open University.[29] As noted, Tsinghua University and the University of Washington, both partnering with Microsoft, founded a dual-degree program known as the Global Innovation Exchange in 2015 and have completed the first Chinese university research facility in the United States. Its home is the new, one-hundred-thousand-square-foot Steve Ballmer Building, named for the Microsoft co-founder (and Harvard graduate). And in June 2021 Fudan University in Shanghai announced plans to construct its European campus in Budapest.

Chinese students, who have long "gone out" to seek education abroad (more than 700,000 in 2019), have largely flown over or by NSR countries to seek their education in North America, Australia, the United Kingdom, the European Union, or Japan. Students from NSR countries have indeed come to China to study in increasing numbers, and scientists from NSR countries have been recruited to newly established "Belt and Road" laboratories. But at the moment, this is a one-way road. Precious few Chinese find their way to graduate programs in Karachi or Almaty. Aiding China's rise as a destination for international students is the recent surge of nationalism in the United States and United Kingdom, long the top destinations for international students, which has led students to increasingly consider institutions in alternative locations. This development may "internationalize" Chinese universities in new ways. As of 2021 the rhetoric and propaganda of the NSR has outpaced the development of a coherent strategy on the Chinese side. Higher education cooperation along the New Silk Road can make Chinese universities more "international" in their posture, but the nature of such institutional exchanges may do little to aid Chinese universities' pursuit of "world-class status."[30] Just as Richthofen's *Seidenstraße* invented a history of Eurasian exchange that was less robust and coherent than his imagination of it, the implications of the NSR for the internationalization of Chinese education are likely to be less significant than many envision.

The point here is that leading Chinese universities have been, and see themselves as, a part of a web of elite global institutions, and today they measure themselves above all vis-à-vis their counterparts in Europe and North America. They may have ever more students from the New Silk Road countries, but they recruit their faculty from, and focus on building their premier research partnerships with, the leading "Western" universities. Today, the path toward global excellence of Chinese universities still lies clearly in cooperation and competition with European and American institutions.

So, is there a "Chinese model" for universities that may be exported, along the New Silk Road or anywhere else? Is there such a thing as "a university with Chinese characteristics"? The answer is basically no. What distinguishes leading Chinese universities today is how they have grown as part of an international system of higher education and research, now buttressed by enviable financial support from the Chinese state. Like the Americans, who developed universities of a high reputation by plagiarizing the norms of German and British institutions, Chinese universities have learned from other global leaders over the past century, be they European, American, or Soviet. In university governance, for example, the "Chinese model" of the role of Party secretaries is hardly a Chinese invention. One can find the same in every "socialist brother country," as we have seen with Humboldt University in East German times. This is not, in any event, a readily exportable model at present, unless your export market is North Korea.

This is not to say that Chinese universities partake in all of the trends of contemporary international universities. In the United States, along with accessibility, there is increasing focus on issues of diversity and inclusion, particularly regarding students of color. There is no evidence that these issues are front and center in China.[31] As we have seen, the idea of universities as political sites is actively resisted by Chinese authorities. This is doubly true at present, as the Chinese Communist Party renews its attempt to assimilate and "make Chinese" China's multiple ethnic and religious minorities.

Can Chinese Universities Lead?

The greatest challenge confronting Chinese universities today is not the competition they face abroad but the obstruction they encounter at home. In many private conversations with Chinese educational leaders, past and present, I have asked this question: What is your greatest problem? The answer, invariably, is "the Party." The founding ideals of great institutions such as Peking University and Tsinghua University remain in tension with a powerful—and powerfully insecure—Chinese Communist Party, which limits debate in multiple realms of the humanities and social sciences, even as Chinese researchers become recognized as global leaders in the pure and applied sciences. There is enduring anxiety in the Party that universities can be—as they have been throughout modern Chinese history—powerful centers of dissent.

When the founder of China's first modern university, Governor-General Zhang Zhidong, wrote his *Exhortation to Study* in 1898, he stressed that "Chinese learning" (education in the classics) had to remain the foundation, while "Western learning" was for "practical matters." Chinese political leaders today continue to distinguish between "Chinese" and "Western" values. In Chinese government policy today, a new version of "Chinese learning" is often given official pride of place over "Western learning." At least in Zhang Zhidong's day, people knew what Chinese learning—a deep education in the classical canon—meant. Today, it is "socialism with Chinese characteristics" and the "guiding role of Marxism in ideology," according to the former Minister of Education, Yuan Guiren, who suggested that to arm themselves against "Western values," students should study the theories of President Xi Jinping.[32] Compared to the Four Books and Five Classics of the traditional canon, this is thin gruel indeed. As a system born of international influences and massively strengthened by Chinese government support, Chinese higher education faces an ideological tightening not seen since the Cultural Revolution.

At the end of the day, can "world-class" universities—however they are defined—exist in a politically illiberal system? In a country where there are "seven topics" that must never be broached? The answer is yes, if we recall the German university of the nineteenth century, where political orthodoxy was seldom questioned. Yet Wilhelmine Germany was no match for contemporary China in its control of political and historical narratives. Is there room today, for example, in the study of Chinese history, for a Chinese Mommsen or a Chinese Meinecke? Perhaps, but as Cai Yuanpei argued a century ago, only with a significant degree of autonomy within the walls of the university. German universities in the nineteenth century had many political pressures, but they valued traditions of institutional and intellectual freedom. China's universities today boast superb scholars and among the world's most talented students. China's university leaders have been among the best in the world. But in recent ideological campaigns, its students are forced to sit through required courses in Party ideology, and they learn a comic book version of the history of their own nation. Despite excellent new programs of general education, in the realm of politics and history the distance between what students have to learn in order to graduate, and what they know to be true, grows greater every year. In this environment, China's great universities—which have the responsibility to produce leaders for China and the world in the twenty-first century—face the prospect of graduating two kinds of students: cynics and opportunists. For these students know, as do the eminent scholars who teach them, that world-class universities are places where there is not a *single* topic that cannot be addressed, let alone seven.

But let us not end so pessimistically. No civilization has a longer or more enduringly successful record than China of educating, examining, and promoting talent to serve state and society. Over the course of the past 130 years, modern universities have propelled China to the first ranks in science and engineering, while—whenever political circumstances have permitted—also promoting the values of open inquiry that have marked the world's leading institutions of higher learning. After all, it was at a Chinese university (Peking University) that Marxism was introduced to China a century ago.

Chinese universities were founded in the late Qing dynasty, they flourished in the early Republic, and several became notable national institutions of international repute under the Nationalist government. They educated young Chinese leaders from the back country of Free China during World War II. They survived war, civil war, sovietization, and the Cultural Revolution. They have outlived an empire, several republics, and multiple incarnations of the People's Republic of China. They have seen political campaigns, such as the current ones, come and go. They must take the long view. So should we.

The most compelling statement of the principles and values of contemporary research universities was announced at the 2013 annual meeting of China's C9 universities in the city of Hefei, west of Nanjing, home to the University of Science and Technology of China. The statement, now known the world over at the "Hefei Statement on the Ten Characteristics of Contemporary Research Universities," was drawn up in concert with the Association of American Universities, the League of European Research Universities, and Australia's Group of Eight universities.[33] In its commitment to research integrity, academic freedom, and institutional autonomy, the Hefei Statement is a powerful, twenty-first-century articulation of Humboldtian values. For the leaders of Chinese universities in 2021, several of these principles may seem more aspirational than achieved, but they set out, accurately in my view, the shared ambitions of great universities the world over.

Can Chinese universities set global standards in the twenty-first century? Yes, of course. But not alone. Chinese universities have grown and flourished on international models and in partnership with the great institutions of Europe and North America. It is that company that they wish to keep, to compete in, and to lead.

Notes

Preface

1. William C. Kirby, *The World of Universities in the 21st Century: The 2017 Kuo Ting-yee Memorial Lectures* (Taipei: Institute of Modern History, Academia Sinica, 2019).

Introduction

1. *All India Survey on Higher Education 2019-20* (New Delhi: Ministry of Education, 2020), 1.
2. See Wikipedia, "List of Universities in North Korea," https://en.wikipedia .org/wiki/List_of_universities_in_North_Korea.
3. For alternative numbers see "Countries Arranged by Number of Universities in Top Ranks," July 2021 edition, http://www.webometrics.info/en/distribution _by_country.
4. Sheldon Rothblatt, *The Modern University and its Discontents* (Cambridge: Cambridge University Press, 1997), 1.
5. Paul Kennedy, *Rise and Fall of the Great Powers: Economic Change and Military Conflict* (New York: Vintage Books, 1987); David Landes, *The Wealth and Poverty of Nations* (New York: Norton, 1998); Daron Acemoglu and James A. Robinson, *Why Nations Fail* (New York: Crown Business, 2012); Charles S. Maier, *Among Empires* (Cambridge, MA: Harvard University Press, 2006).
6. Landes, *Wealth and Poverty,* 409.
7. Sharan B. Merriam, *Case Study Research in Education: A Qualitative Approach* (San Francisco: Jossey-Bass Publishers, 1988), xiii. See also Robert E. Stake, *The Art of Case Study Research* (Thousand Oaks, CA: SAGE Publications, 1995).
8. See "Teaching by the Case Method," https://www.hbs.edu/teaching/case -method/Pages/default.aspx.

9. L. W. B. Brockliss, "The European University 1789–1850," in *University of Oxford,* VI, Part I, 131–133, cited in *A History of the University in Europe: Volume III, Universities in the Nineteenth and Early Twentieth Centuries (1800–1945),* Walter Rüegg, ed. (Cambridge: Cambridge University Press, 2004), 11.

10. Phillip Altbach, foreword to *Indian Higher Education: Envisioning the Future* by Pawan Agarwal (Thousand Oaks, CA: SAGE Publications, 2009), xi–xii.

11. Arvind Panagariya, "Higher Education: A New Dawn—National Education Policy 2020 Offers Transformative Road Map for Colleges and Universities," *Times of India,* August 19, 2020, https://timesofindia.indiatimes.com /blogs/toi-edit-page/higher-education-a-new-dawn-national-education -policy-2020-offers-transformative-road-map-for-colleges-and-universities/, accessed March 9, 2020.

12. Jamil Salmi, *The Challenge of Establishing World-Class Universities* (Washington, DC: World Bank, 2009), 1–2.

13. Tsinghua University, *Qinghua daxue shiye fazhan shi er wu guihua gangyao* [Outline of Tsinghua University's Twelfth Five-Year Plan] (Beijing: Tsinghua University, 2011), http://www.tsinghua.edu.cn/publish/newthu /openness/attachments/fzgh/fzgh.htm, accessed October 2014. China's large-scale funding efforts began with the announcement of Project 211 in 1995, which ultimately provided increased funding for one hundred universities. The even more elite Project 985 was launched in 1998 and funneled billions of RMB to thirty-seven institutions, including 1.8 billion each to Peking University and Tsinghua University.

14. Philip G. Altbach, "Costs and Benefits of World-Class Universities," *Academe* 90 (2004): 21.

15. Luke Meyers and Jonathan Robe, *College Ranking: History, Criticism and Reform* (Washington, DC: Center for College Affordability and Productivity, 2009).

16. James McKeen Cattell, *American Men of Science: A Biographical Directory* (New York: Science Press, 1906).

17. Meyers and Robe, *College Ranking.*

18. Meyers and Robe, *College Ranking,* 17.

19. David S. Webster, *Academic Quality Rankings of American Colleges and Universities* (Springfield, IL: C. C. Thomas, 1986), 6.

20. Henry Rosovsky, *The University: An Owner's Manual* (New York: W. W. Norton, 1990), 33.

21. Justin Thorens, "Liberties, Freedom and Autonomy: A Few Reflections on Academia's Estate," *Higher Education Policy,* no. 19 (2006): 87–110, cited in Kai Ren and Jun Li, "Academic Freedom and University Autonomy: A Higher Education Policy Perspective," *Higher Education Policy,* no. 26 (2013): 509.

22. James O. Freedman, *Liberal Education and the Public Interest* (Iowa City: University of Iowa Press, 2003), xi.

23. *The Heart of the Matter: The Humanities and Social Sciences for a Vibrant, Competitive and Secure Nation* (Cambridge, MA: American Academy of Arts and Sciences, 2013), 6.

24. See Derek Bok, *Our Underachieving Colleges: A Candid Look at How Much Students Learn and Why They Should Be Learning More* (Princeton: Princeton University Press, 2006).

25. See *Essays on General Education in Harvard College* (Cambridge, MA: President and Fellows of Harvard College, 2004); *On the Purpose and Structure of a Harvard Education* (Cambridge, MA: President and Fellows of Harvard College, 2005).

26. Jonathan R. Cole, *The Great American University: Its Rise to Preeminence, Its Indispensable National Role, Why It Must Be Protected* (New York: Public Affairs, 2009), 8.

27. Jamil Salmi, *The Challenge of Establishing World-Class Universities*, 7.

28. Rosovsky, *The University: An Owner's Manual*, 34.

29. "Lead the Future," Schwarzman Scholars at Tsinghua University, https://www.schwarzmanscholars.org, accessed November 28, 2021.

30. See, for example, Qinghua University Educational Research Institute's "Creating First-Class Universities: Combining National Determination with the University Spirit: Round-Up of an Academic Seminar on the Theory and Practice of Establishing First-Class Universities" in *Chinese Education and Society* 37, no. 6 (Nov/Dec 2004).

31. See, for example, the discussion by Jamil Salmi in *The Challenge of Establishing World-Class Universities*, 6–7.

1. The University in Germany

1. On universities in the contemporary Federal Republic see Christian Bode et al., eds., *Universitäten in Deutschland* (München: Prestel Verlag, 2015).

2. James J. Sheehan, *German History 1770–1866* (Oxford: Clarendon Press, 1989), 135.

3. Charles E. McClelland, *State, Society, and University in Germany 1700–1914* (Cambridge: Cambridge University Press, 1980), 78–79.

4. Daniel Fallon, *The German University: A Heroic Ideal in Conflict with the Modern World* (Boulder: Colorado Associated University Press, 1980), 6.

5. Fallon, *The German University*, 5.

6. McClelland, *State, Society, and University*, 34–35.

7. Quoted in McClelland, *State, Society, and University*, 43.

8. Friedrich Gedike, Report to King Friedrich Wilhelm II of Germany, reprinted with commentary in Louis Menand, Paul Reitter, and Chat Wellmon, eds., *The Rise of the Research University: A Sourcebook* (Chicago: University of Chicago Press, 2017), 14–15.

9. Alternative numbers come from McClelland, *State, Society, and University*, 28; Sheehan, *German History*, 137.

10. Quoted in McClelland, *State, Society, and University*, 79.

11. See McClelland, *State, Society, and University*, 28, 56, 63–64; Fallon, *The German University*, 8.
12. See Fallon, *The German University*, 32–34.
13. Fallon, *The German University*, 5.
14. All quoted in Fallon, *The German University*, 2–3.
15. See also William C. Kirby and Joycelyn W. Eby, "'World-Class' Universities: Rankings and Reputation in Global Higher Education," Case 316-065 (Boston: Harvard Business School, 2015).

2. The Modern Original

1. Christoph Markschies, "Words of Welcome by the President of Humboldt-Universität-zu-Berlin," Conference Program, *HU200: Humboldt's Model: The Future of Universities in the World of Research*, October 7–9, 2010, 6–7.
2. Markschies, "Words of Welcome," 7.
3. The famous first line of Thomas Nipperdey, *Deutsche Geschichte 1800–1866: Bürgerwelt und starker Staat* (München: C. H. Beck, 1983), 11.
4. See also Walter Rüegg, "Themes," in *A History of the University in Europe: Volume III, Universities in the Nineteenth and Early Twentieth Centuries (1800–1945)*, Walter Rüegg, ed. (Cambridge: Cambridge University Press, 2004), 3.
5. See also Max Lenz, *Geschichte der Königlichen Friedrich-Wilhelms-Universität zu Berlin. Erster Band: Gründung und Ausbau* (Halle: Verlag der Buchhandlung des Waisenhauses, 1910), 78.
6. James J. Sheehan, *German History, 1770–1876* (Oxford: Oxford University Press, 1989), 137.
7. Charles E. McClelland, *State, Society, and University in Germany, 1740–1914* (Cambridge: Cambridge University Press, 1980), 115.
8. Sheehan, *German History*, 137–141.
9. See Karl-Heinz Günther, "Profiles of Educators: Wilhelm von Humboldt (1767–1835)," *Prospects* 18, no. 1 (March 1988).
10. David Sorkin, "Wilhelm von Humboldt: The Theory and Practice of Self-Formation (Bildung), 1791–1810," *Journal of the History of Ideas* 44, no. 1 (1983): 55–73.
11. Wilhelm Humboldt, "Der Königsberger und der Litauische Schulplan (1809)," in *Wilhelm von Humboldts Gesammelte Schriften, Band 13*, A. Leitzmann, ed. (Berlin: B. Behr Verlag, 1920), 277.
12. Sorkin, "Wilhelm von Humboldt," 63.
13. McClelland, *State, Society, and University*, 125.
14. See also Brad S. Gregory, *The Unintended Reformation: How a Religious Revolution Secularized Society* (Cambridge, MA: Harvard University Press, 2012), 349.
15. Quoted in Walter Rüegg, "Themes," 5. See also Friedrich Schleiermacher, *Gelegentliche Gedanken über Universitäten im deutschen Sinn. Nebst einem Anhang über eine neu zu errichtende* (Berlin: In der Realschulbuchhandlung, 1808), 32–33.

16. See Daniel Fallon, *The German University: A Heroic Ideal in Conflict with the Modern World* (Boulder: Colorado Associated University Press, 1980), 29.

17. Quoted in Fallon, *The German University*, 19.

18. Johann Gottlieb Fichte, "Über die einzig mögliche Störung der akademische Freiheit: Eine Rede beim Antritte seines Rektorats an der Universität zu Berlin den 19ten Oktober 1811," (Berlin: L. W. Wittich, 1812).

19. Lenz, *Geschichte*, 410.

20. Ilka Thom and Kirsten Weining, *Mittendrin: Eine Universität macht Geschichte: Eine Ausstellung anlässlich des 200-jährigen Jubiläums der Humboldt-Universität zu Berlin* (Berlin: Akademie Verlag, 2010), 43.

21. Sheehan, *Germany History*, 365; Fallon, *The German University*, 25.

22. Fallon, *The German University*, 25–26.

23. Quoted in Fallon, *The German University*, 25.

24. Cited in David McLellan, *Karl Marx: A Biography* (London: Palgrave Macmillan, 2006), 15.

25. Sheehan, *German History*, 575.

26. McClelland, *State, Society, and University*, 164.

27. Sylvia Paletschek, *Die permanente Erfindung einer Tradition. Die Universität Tübingen im Kaiserreich und in der Weimarer Republik* (Stuttgart: Steiner, 2001), 234.

28. McClelland, *State, Society, and University*, 165–167.

29. Thom and Weining, *Mittendrin*, 53; Sheehan, *German History*, 666–668; see especially Heinz-Elmar Tenorth, "Universität im Protest und auf den Barrikaden—Studenten und Dozenten," in *Geschichte der Universität Unter den Linden: Gründung und Blütezeit der Universität zu Berlin, 1810-1918*, vol 1, Heinz-Elmar Tenorth, ed. (Berlin: Akademie Verlag, 2012), 381–424.

30. See also Fritz K. Ringer, *The Decline of the German Mandarins: The German Academic Community, 1890–1933* (Cambridge, MA: Harvard University Press, 1969), 5–6.

31. McClelland, *State, Society, and University*, 221–223.

32. Ringer, *The Decline of the German Mandarins*, 141–142.

33. Robert Proctor, *Value-Free Science? Purity and Power in Modern Knowledge* (Cambridge, MA: Harvard University Press, 1991), 106–107.

34. See also Hartmut Titze, *Datenhandbuch zur deutschen Bildungsgeschichte: Wachstum und Differenzierung der deutschen Universitäten 1830–1945* (Göttingen: Vandenhoeck & Ruprecht, 1995), 81.

35. Einweihung der Ruhmeshalle in Görlitz (29 November 1902). See Ernst Johann, *Reden des Kaisers: Ansprachen, Predigten und Trinksprüche Wilhelms II.* (München: Deutscher Taschenbuch Verlag, 1966), 107.

36. Sheehan, *German History*, 307–309.

37. Nobel Prize winners in the fields of chemistry, literature, medicine, and physics: https://www.hu-berlin.de/en/about/history/nobel-laureates.

38. See McClelland, *State, Society, and University*, 291–299; see also Proctor, *Value-Free Science*, 106.

39. See also Friedrich Lenz, *Beiträge zur Universitätsstatistik* (Halle: Verlag der Buchhandlung des Waisenhauses, 1912), 15; Titze, *Datenhandbuch*, 82.

40. See also Franz Eulenburg, *Der akademische Nachwuchs: Eine Untersuchung über die Lage und die Aufgaben der Extraordinarien und Privatdozenten* (Berlin: B. G. Teubner, 1908), 80–81. See also Ulrich von Lübtow, *Die Rechtsstellung der entpflichteten Professoren* (Berlin: Duncker & Humblot, 1967), 24–25.

41. In 1905–1906, the average salary in Berlin was 7,653 Mark; the average salary for all Prussian universities was 5,825 Mark. See also Lenz, *Beiträge*, 35, table X.

42. Christopher Lasch, *The American Liberals and the Russian Revolution* (New York: McGraw Hill, 1962), 26.

43. Max Lenz, *Geschichte der Königlichen Friedrichs-Wilhelms-Universität zu Berlin*, 5 vols. (Halle: Verlag der Buchhandlung des Waisenhauses, 1910). For the extraordinary volumes published for the bicentenary, see Heinz-Elmar Tenorth, ed., *Geschichte der Universität Unter den Linden*, 6 vols. (Berlin: Akademie Verlag, 2012).

44. Quotes from Charles E. McClelland, "Die Universität am Ende ihres ersten Jahrhunderts—Mythos Humboldt?" in Tenorth, *Geschichte*, vol. 1, 637, 641.

45. McClelland, "Die Universität," 640.

46. McClelland, "Die Universität," 651.

47. See McClelland, "Die Universität," 652–653.

48. Original quote: "Kriegssemester sind die gewonnenen Semester." Thom and Weining, *Mittendrin*, 68.

49. Both quoted in McClelland, *State, Society, and University*, 315.

50. See also Titze, *Datenhandbuch*, 82.

51. See Hans Kohn, *The Mind of Germany* (New York: Scribner's, 1960); Istvan Deak, *Weimar Germany's Left-Wing Intellectuals* (Berkeley: University of California Press, 1968), 44.

52. Censored authors included Erich-Maria Remarque, Stefan Zweig, Sigmund Freud, Erich Kästner, Heinrich Mann, Karl Marx, and Kurt Tucholsky.

53. Heinz-Elmar Tenorth, "Eduard Sprangers hochschulpolitischer Konflikt 1933. Politisches Handeln eines preußischen Gelehrten," *Zeitschrift für Pädogogik* 36 (1990): 573–596; United States Holocaust Memorial Museum, "Telegram Regarding the 'Action against the Un-German Spirit,'" https://perspectives.ushmm.org/item/telegram-regarding-the-action-against-the-un-german-spirit.

54. Jens Thiel, "Der Lehrkörper der Friedrich-Wilhelms-Universität im Nationalsozialismus," in *Geschichte: Der Berliner Universität zwischen den Weltkriegen, 1918–1945*, vol. 2, Tenorth, ed., 465–538.

55. See Lauren Leff, *Well Worth Saving: American Universities' Life-and-Death Decisions on Refugees from Nazi Europe* (New Haven, CT: Yale University Press, 2019).

56. Christian von Ferber, *Die Entwicklung des Lehrkörpers des deutschen Universitäten und Hochschulen, 1864–1954* (Göttingen: Vandenhoeck & Ruptrecht, 1956).

57. Cited in Carlo Jordan, *Kaderschmiede Humboldt-Universität zu Berlin: Aufbegehren, Säuberungen und Militarisierung, 1945–1989* (Berlin: Ch. Links Verlag, 2001), 20.

58. Jordan, *Kaderschmiede,* 14.

59. Author interview with Heinrich Fink, Berlin, October 9, 2015.

60. See also Ilko-Sascha Kowalczuk, "Die Humboldt-Universität zu Berlin und das Ministerium für Staatssicherheit," in *Geschichte: Sozialistisches Experiment und Erneuerung in der Demokratie—die Humboldt-Universität zu Berlin 1945–2010,* vol. 3, Tenorth, ed., 462.

61. "Inoffizieller Mitarbeiter (IM)" *MFS-Lexikon,* Bundesbeauftragte für die Unterlagen des Staatssicherheitsdienstes der ehemaligen Deutschen Demokratischen Republik, https://www.bstu.de/mfs-lexikon/detail/inoffizieller -mitarbeiter-im/.

62. See also Kowalczuk, "Die Humboldt-Universität zu Berlin," 466.

63. Stefanie Endlich, ed., *Gedenkstätte für die Opfer des Nationalsozialismus. Eine Dokumentation* (Berlin: Bundeszentral für politische Bildung, 2002), 111.

64. Hannelore Scholz, "A Free University—Free of Women? Women and Higher Education in Berlin since 1989," in *Berlin in Focus: Cultural Transformations in Germany,* Barbara Becker-Cantarino, ed. (Westport, CT: Praeger, 1996), 38.

65. See also Konrad H. Jarausch, "Umgestaltung von außen, Dezember 1990–März 1994," in *Geschichte,* vol. 3, Tenorth, ed., 653.

66. See Helmut Klein, ed., *Humboldt-Universität zu Berlin: Überblick 1810–1985* (Berlin: VEB Deutscher Verlag der Wissenschaften, 1985), 145–146.

67. Author interview with Heinrich Fink, October 9, 2015.

68. Author interview with Heinrich Fink, October 9, 2015.

69. See also Jarausch, "Umgestaltung," 646–647.

70. Personalabeiltung, file of Prof. Dr. Roland Felber, 1983–2010, Universitätsarchiv der Humboldt-Universität zu Berlin.

71. See also Jarausch, "Umgestaltung," 660, 683.

72. Constitution of Humboldt University, §13 (1).

73. Constitution of Humboldt University, §4 (2).

74. Constitution of Humboldt University, §8.

75. Constitution of Humboldt University, §2 (1).

76. Constitution of Humboldt University, §2 (3).

77. Constitution of Humboldt University, §13 (2), (3).

78. Author interview with Christoph Markschies, Berlin, October 5, 2015.

79. Humboldt-Universität zu Berlin, Personenstatistik-Daten, 1995–2020, https://www2.hu-berlin.de/personalstatistik/components/personal/daten .php#.

80. Author interview with Jan-Hendrik Olbertz, Berlin, December 2, 2015.

81. Author interview with Peter Frensch, Berlin, January 10, 2017.
82. Author interview with Jan-Hendrik Olbertz, December 2, 2015.
83. Author interview with Christoph Markschies, October 5, 2015.
84. Author interview with Jan-Hendrik Olbertz, December 2, 2015.
85. Author interview with Jan-Hendrik Olbertz, December 2, 2015.
86. Author interview with Recardo Manzke, Berlin, January 10, 2017.
87. Öffentlicher-Dienst.info, "Besoldungstabelle Beamte Berlin 2016," http://oeffentlicher-dienst.info/c/t/rechner/beamte/be?id=beamte-berlin-2016&matrix=1.
88. Verordnung über die Lehrverpflichtung an Hochschulen (Lehrverpflichtungsverordnung - LVVO), March 27, 2001, §2, http://gesetze.berlin.de/jportal/;jsessionid=418B777FD7942163F6B45CEC000D0E46.jp26?quelle=jlink&query=LehrVPflV+BE&psml=bsbeprod.psml&max=true&aiz=true#jlr-LehrVPflVBEV2P5.
89. Humboldt-Universität zu Berlin, Personenstatistik-Daten, https://www2.hu-berlin.de/personalstatistik/components/personal/diagram.php.
90. Federal Ministry of Education and Research, "The Path to a Professorship," https://www.research-in-germany.org/en/jobs-and-careers/info-for-postdocs-and-junior-researchers/career-paths/path-to-professorship.html.
91. Humboldt-Universität zu Berlin, Personenstatistik-Daten, https://www2.hu-berlin.de/personalstatistik/components/personal/daten.php.
92. The number had risen from 23 percent in 2015: Statisches Bundesamt, "Frauenanteil in Professorenschaft 2015 auf 23% gestiegen," https://www.destatis.de/DE/Presse/Pressemitteilungen/2016/07/PD16_245_213.html.
93. Statista, "Frauenanteil in der Professorenschaft in Deutschland im Jahr 2020 nach Bundesländern," https://de.statista.com/statistik/daten/studie/197898/umfrage/frauenanteil-in-der-professorenschaft-nach-bundeslaendern/.
94. Humboldt-Universität zu Berlin, "Daten und Zahlen zur Humboldt-Universität," https://www.hu-berlin.de/de/ueberblick/humboldt-universitaet-zu-berlin/daten-und-zahlen.
95. Humboldt-Universität zu Berlin, "Daten und Zahlen zur Humboldt-Universität," https://www2.hu-berlin.de/personalstatistik/components/personal/diagram.php; https://www.hu-berlin.de/de/ueberblick/humboldt-universitaet-zu-berlin/daten-und-zahlen.
96. Statista, "Number of students at universities in Berlin in Germany in the winter semesters from 1998/1999 to 2019/20," https://www-statista-com.ezp-prod1.hul.harvard.edu/statistics/1114450/students-number-universities-berlin-germany/.
97. Source for percentage of female students at Humboldt University (in 2016): https://www.hu-berlin.de/de/ueberblick/humboldt-universitaet-zu-berlin/daten-und-zahlen. Source for percentage of female students in Germany (in 2015): https://www.destatis.de/DE/ZahlenFakten/GesellschaftStaat/BildungForschungKultur/Hochschulen/Tabellen/FrauenanteileAkademischeLaufbahn.html.

98. Humboldt-Universität zu Berlin, "Studierendenstatistik, Studierende nach Bundesland und Hochschulzugangsberechtigung," http://edoc.hu-berlin.de /browsing/series/index.php?l[2]=Einrichtungen&l[3]=Humboldt-Universit %C3%A4t%2C+Studierendenstatistik&c[3][corp_id]=27501&l[4]=Studiere nde+nach+Bundesland+der+Hochschulzugangsberechtigung+-&c[4][series _id]=41035&_=521a552fece06b8245430c05a864183b.

99. Author interview with Christoph Markschies, October 5, 2015.

100. See also Jan-Hendrik Olbertz, *Angelegenheit vier: Abschiedsworte des Präsidenten Christoph Markschies am 18. Oktober 2010*, 7.

101. Humboldt-Universität zu Berlin, "Studierendenstatistik, Bewerbungen und Einschreibungen im 1. Fachsemester in NC-Studienfächern im Akademischen Jahr 2016–17," http://edoc.hu-berlin.de/browsing/series/index.php ?l%5B2%5D=Einrichtungen&l%5B3%5D=Humboldt-Universit%C3%A4t %2C+Studierendenstatistik&c%5B3%5D%5Bcorp_id%5D=27501&_=383 6b3faa3c66a2336969e24a2857081.

102. Author interview with Christoph Markschies, October 5, 2015.

103. Source for percentage of international students at HU (in 2016): Studierendenstatistik, Anteile ausländischer und männlicher Studierender, http:// edoc.hu-berlin.de/browsing/series/index.php?l%5B2%5D=Einrichtungen &l%5B3%5D=Humboldt-Universit%C3%A4t%2C+Studierendenstatistik &c%5B3%5D%5Bcorp_id%5D=27501&_=3836b3faa3c66a2336969e24a28 57081; Source for percentage of international students in Germany (in 2015–16): https://de.statista.com/statistik/daten/studie/222/umfrage/anteil-auslaendischer -studenten-an-hochschulen/.

104. Numbers for 2016–17. Studierendenstatik, Ausländische Studierende in grundständigen und weiterführenden Studiengängen nach Herkunft und Fächern, https://edoc.hu-berlin.de/bitstream/handle/18452/18752/tab_15 _17_Auslaendische_Studierende_in_Programmstudien_nach_Herkunft _und_Faecher.pdf?sequence=1&isAllowed=y.

105. Humboldt-Universität zu Berlin, "Daten und Zahlen zur Humboldt-Universität 2019," https://www.hu-berlin.de/de/ueberblick/humboldt -universitaet-zu-berlin/daten-und-zahlen#personal.

106. Numbers for 2014. Calculated by Deutsches Zentrum für Hochschul- und Wissenschaftsforschung based on Statistisches Bundesamt, in Deutsches Zentrum für Hochschul- und Wissenschaftsforschung and Deutscher Akademischer Austauschdienst, eds., *Wissenschaft weltoffen kompakt 2016: Facts and Figures on the International Nature of Studies and Research in Germany*, fig. 24, 25.

107. "BMBF Initiatives in the Context of the Bologna Process," Federal Ministry of Education and Research (Germany), https://www.bmbf.de/bmbf/en/aca demia/the-bologna-process/initiatives/bmbf-initiatives-in-the-context-of-the -bologna-process.html; Stephan L. Thompson and Johannes Trunzer, "Did the Bologna Process Challenge the German Apprenticeship System? Evidence from a Natural Experiment," IZA Institute of Labor Economics, October 2020, https://www.econstor.eu/bitstream/10419/227333/1/dp13806.pdf.

108. See also International Agenda of the Presidential Committee of Humboldt-Universität zu Berlin, 2015.

109. Humboldt-Universität zu Berlin, Strategische Partnerschaften der HU-Berlin: "Princeton University," https://www.international.hu-berlin.de/de/internationales-profil/strategische-partnerschaften-der-hu-berlin/PU.

110. Source for Sao Paulo: https://www.international.hu-berlin.de/de/internationales-profil/partnerschaften/profilpartnerschaften/universidade-de-sao-paulo. Source for Singapore: https://www.international.hu-berlin.de/de/internationales-profil/partnerschaften/profilpartnerschaften/NUS.

111. Humboldt-Universität zu Berlin, "Daten und Zahlen zur Humboldt-Universität 2019," https://www.hu-berlin.de/de/ueberblick/humboldt-universitaet-zu-berlin/daten-und-zahlen#personal.

112. Author interview with Recardo Manzke, January 10, 2017.

113. Frank Bösch, *A History Shared and Divided: East and West Germany Since the 1970s* (New York: Berghahn Books, 2018), 419.

114. Katerina Selin, "Berlin's Humboldt University Plans Massive Job Cuts," December 19, 2016, https://www.wsws.org/en/articles/2016/12/19/humb-d19.html, accessed January 2021; see also Manzke interview.

115. See William C. Kirby and Joycelyn W. Eby, "'World-Class' Universities: Rankings and Reputation in Global Higher Education," Case 316-065 (Boston: Harvard Business School, 2015).

116. Anja Krieger, "Equality or Excellence," *Nature,* 537 (2016): 12, http://www.nature.com/nature/journal/v537/n7618_supp/full/537S12a.html?WT.mc_id=TWT_OUTLOOK_SLE.

117. The number for 2015 is an estimate. https://de.statista.com/statistik/daten/studie/36284/umfrage/oeffentliche-ausgaben-fuer-hochschulen-nach-koerperschaftsgruppen/.

118. The first phase of the Excellence Initiative provided US$2 (or €1.9) billion of funding. The second phase allocated US$2.9 (or €2.7) billion.

119. Deutsche Forschungsgemeinschaft, "Excellence Initiative General Information," http://www.dfg.de/en/research_funding/programmes/excellence_initiative/general_information/index.html.

120. Deutsche Forschungsgemeinschaft, "Excellence Initiative at a Glance: The Programme by the German Federal and State Governments to Promote Top-level Research at Universities," 16, https://www.dfg.de/download/pdf/dfg_im_profil/geschaeftsstelle/publikationen/exin_broschuere_en.pdf.

121. Author interview with Jan-Hendrik Olbertz, December 2, 2015.

122. Stanford Facts 2016, http://facts.stanford.edu/pdf/StanfordFacts_2016.pdf. Number of students at Stanford in 2015 (page 9): 16,122; annual budget in 2015–16 (page 44): US$5.5 (or €5.02) billion. For Humboldt University: https://www.hu-berlin.de/de/ueberblick/humboldt-universitaet-zu-berlin/daten-und-zahlen. Number of students at HU in 2016: 32,553 (without Charité); annual budget in 2016: US$413 (or €397) million.

123. "Internationale Expertenkommission zur Evaluation der Exzellenzinitiative: Endbericht," (Jan. 2016), https://www.gwk-bonn.de/fileadmin/Redaktion /Dokumente/Papers/Imboden-Bericht-2016.pdf.

124. Stabsstelle Presse- und Öffentlichkeitsarbeit der Humboldt-Universität zu Berlin, ed. *Spuren der Exzellenzinitiative. Die Humboldt-Universität zu Berlin zieht Zwischenbilanz—The Excellence Initiative makes its mark—Humboldt-Universität reviews its successes and looks ahead* (2015) 14.

125. Findings by *Nature* based on an analysis of articles in Scopus database using Elsevier's SciVal tool, http://www.nature.com/news/germany-claims-success -for-elite-universities-drive-1.18312.

126. "Zusammenfassung des Antrags: Berlin University Alliance—Crossing Boundaries toward an Integrated Research Environment," Berlin University Alliance, Exzellenzstrategie, https://www.berlin-university-alliance.de /press/berlin-university-alliance-summary.pdf, accessed January 7, 2020.

127. "The Oxford/Berlin Research Partnership," *Berlin University Alliance—Our Goals,* https://www.berlin-universityalliance.de/en/commitments/international /oxford/index.html.

128. "Wide-ranging new research partnership with Berlin universities," *Oxford Sparks,* https://www.oxfordsparks.ox.ac.uk/content/wide-ranging-new -research-partnership-berlin-universities.

129. Jarausch, "Umgestaltung," 653.

3. Truth, Justice, and Freedom in a Cold War World

1. Remarks of President John F. Kennedy at the Rudolph Wilde Platz, Berlin, June 26, 1963, John F. Kennedy Presidential Library and Museum, Boston, https://www.jfklibrary.org/archives/other-resources/john-f-kennedy-speeches /berlin-w-germany-rudolph-wilde-platz-19630626.

2. Remarks of the President at Free University, West Berlin, Germany, June 26, 1963 (as delivered), https://www.jfklibrary.org/asset-viewer/archives/JFKPOF /045/JFKPOF-045-028.

3. "Henry Ford Building: Construction," Freie Universität Berlin, https://www .fu-berlin.de/en/sites/hfb/geschichte/bau/index.html.

4. Karol Kubicki and Siegward Lönnendonker. *Die Freie Universität Berlin 1948–2007: Von der Gründung bis zum Exzellenzwettbewerb* (Göttingen, Germany: V&R Unipress, 2008), 14.

5. James Tent, *The Free University of Berlin: A Political History* (Indianapolis: Indiana University Press, 1988), 36.

6. Tent, *The Free University,* 65–66.

7. Tent, *The Free University,* 78.

8. Tent, *The Free University,* 81–82.

9. Tent, *The Free University,* 85.

10. Tent, *The Free University,* 95.

11. Tent, *The Free University,* 104.

12. Quoted in Tent, *The Free University*, 106.
13. Quoted in Tent, *The Free University*, 139.
14. Tent, *The Free University*, 141.
15. Taken from the appeal to found the Free University, July 23, 1948.
16. See Tent, *The Free University*, 160–164. Quote from 161.
17. Quote and background from Tent, *The Free University*, 154–155.
18. Full speeches in official booklet on the occasion: *Gründungsfeier der Freien Universität Berlin* (Berlin: Erich Blaschker, 1949); see also Tent, *The Free University*, 166–168.
19. Fritz von Bergmann, "Die Hilfe der USA für die Freie Universität Berlin," 189, in *Freie Universität Berlin 1948–1973: Hochschule im Umbruch, Teil III: Auf dem Weg in den Dissens (1957–1964)*, Universitätsarchiv der Freien Universität Berlin (hereafter, FU Archives).
20. Kubicki and Lönnendonker, *Die Freie Universität Berlin*, 50.
21. Der Präsident der Freien Universität Berlin, ed., *40 Jahre Freie Universität Berlin: Die Geschichte 1948–1988, Einblicke, Ausblicke* (Berlin: Zentrale Universitätsdruckerei der Freien Universität Berlin, 1988), 53.
22. Kubicki and Lönnendonker, *Die Freie Universität Berlin*, 50.
23. See Tent, *The Free University*, 219–220, 244–249.
24. See Tent, *The Free University*, 281–286.
25. Tent, *The Free University*, 303.
26. Tent, *The Free University*, 324–325.
27. Gerhard Göhler, "Politischer Wissenschaftler und Philosoph. Zum Tode von Alexander Schwan," in *Politische Vierteljahresschrift* 31 (1990), Heft 1, 97–100. On the Maoists see Anke Jaspers et al., eds., *Ein kleines rotes Buch. Über die 'Mao-Bibel' und die Bücher-Revolution der Sachzicherjahre* (Berlin: Matthes & Seitz, 2018).
28. See Tent, *The Free University*, 403–407. Quotes are from Tent, *The Free University*, 406–407.
29. Quoted in Tent, *The Free University*, 417.
30. *40 Jahre Freie Universität Berlin*, 53.
31. Tent, *The Free University*, 451.
32. Tent, *The Free University*, 446.
33. Freie Universität Berlin, *Fünfzig Jahre Freie Universität Berlin* (Berlin, 1998), 72.
34. Landeshochschulstrukturkommission Berlin, ed., *Stellungnahmen und Empfehlungen zu Struktur und Entwicklung der Berliner Hochschulen* (Berlin, 1992), 63.
35. "Empfehlungen zur Struktur der Freien Universität Berlin in den Neunziger Jahren" (April 1988), FU Archives.
36. Kubicki and Lönnendonker, *Die Freie Universität Berlin*, 141. Numbers used here are from "Zwischen Wende und Jahrtausendwende: Freie Universität Berlin, 1989–1999. Zahlen-Daten-Fakten," 3, FU Archives.
37. Author interview with Herbert Grieshop, Berlin, June 17, 2015.

38. "Der Unsichtbare Kanzler," *Furios. Studentisches Campusmagazin an der FU Berlin*, Jan. 24, 2011, https://furios-campus.de/2011/01/24/der-unsichtbare -kanzler/.

39. Peter-André Alt, "Rede anlässlich der Abschiedsfeier für den langjährigen Kanzler der Freien Universität Berlin, Peter Lange, am 18. Dezember 2015," full text in FU Berlin *Campus.Leben*, December 22, 2015, https://www.fu-berlin.de /campusleben/campus/2015/151222-abschied-peter-lange/index.html.

40. Interview with Peter Lange, *Berliner Tagespiegel*, Feb. 13, 2016.

41. Jon Marcus, "Germany Proves Tuition-Free College is Not a Silver Bullet for America's Education Woes," *Quartz*, October 18, 2016, https://qz.com /812200/is-free-college-possible-germany-shows-there-are-downsides-to -tuition-free-college/.

42. Information provided by Free University.

43. See also *Struktur- und Entwicklungsplan für die Freie Universität Berlin (Stand 2015)*, https://www.fu-berlin.de/universitaet/media/strukturplan -2015.pdf.

44. Kubicki and Lönnendonker, *Die Freie Universität Berlin*, 142.

45. "Fortschreibung des Struktur- und Entwicklungsplans für die Freie Universität Berlin (Stand 2018)," https://www.fu-berlin.de/universitaet/media /strukturplan-2018.pdf.

46. Data provided by Free University.

47. Deutscher Hochschul Verband, "Grundgehälter und Besoldungsanpassungen," https://www.hochschulverband.de/fileadmin/redaktion/download /pdf/besoldungstabellen/grundgehaelter_w.pdf.

48. Information provided by FU. Data do not include medicine. "Der Besoldungsdurchschnitt für die Freie Universität Berlin ist für das Jahr 2017 durch amtliche Bekanntmachung auf monatlich."

49. *Times Higher Education World University Rankings*, "Free University Berlin," https://www.timeshighereducation.com/world-university-rankings/free -university-berlin.

50. "Leistungsbericht über das Jahr 2018" Professorinnen und Professoren: 559; Sonstige wiss. U. künstl. Beschäftigte: 2,286; Nebenberufliches Lehrpersonal: 953; 35. See https://www.berlin.de/sen/wissenschaft/service/leistungsberichte/.

51. Berlin University Alliance, vi, https://www.berlin-university-alliance.de /excellence-strategy/universities-of-excellence/berlin-university-alliance -proposal.pdf.

52. "Freie Universität Berlin," *U.S. News and World Report*, https://www.usnews .com/education/best-global-universities/freie-universitat-berlin-502084; Freie Universität Berlin, "Facts and Figures," https://www.fu-berlin.de/en /universitaet/leitbegriffe/zahlen/index.html.

53. "Freie Universität Berlin," *U.S. News and World Report*, https://www.usnews .com/education/best-global-universities/freie-universitat-berlin-502084; "Facts and Figures," Freie Universität Berlin, https://www.fu-berlin.de/en /universitaet/leitbegriffe/zahlen/index.html.

54. "Freie Universität Berlin," *U.S. News and World Report.*
55. Deutsche Wissenschafts- und Innovationshäuser (German Center for Research and Innovation), *Annual Report 2018,* 79, https://www.dwih-netzwerk.de/files/2019/08/DWIH-JB_2018_zweiseitig.pdf.
56. Deutscher Akademischer Austauschdienst, *Wissenschaft Weltoffen 2019: Daten und Fakten zur Internationalität vom Studium und Forschung in Deutschland* (Bielefeld: wvb Media, 2019), 136.
57. Kubicki and Lönnendonker, *Die Freie Universität Berlin,* 152.
58. *Wissenschaft Weltoffen 2019,* 82.
59. Data provided by Free University.
60. Alexander von Humboldt Foundation, *Annual Report 2018,* 127, https://www.humboldt-foundation.de/pls/web/docs/F634970970/jahresbericht_2018.pdf.
61. European Commission, UNA Europe, https://ec.europa.eu/education/sites/education/files/document-library-docs/european-universities-factsheet-una-europa.pdf.
62. "International Council," Freie Universität Berlin, https://www.fu-berlin.de/en/sites/inu/network-university/international-council/index.html.
63. "Decision in the German Excellence Strategy," Berlin University Alliance, https://www.berlin-university-alliance.de/en/news/items/20190719-decision-excellence-strategy.html.
64. Author interview with Peter-André Alt, Berlin, June 18, 2015.
65. "Freie Universität Declares State of Climate Emergency," Freie Universität Berlin, https://www.fu-berlin.de/en/presse/informationen/fup/2019/fup_19_398-klimanotstand/index.html.
66. Ibid.
67. Remarks of the President at Free University, West Berlin, Germany, June 26, 1963 (as delivered), https://www.jfklibrary.org/asset-viewer/archives/JFKPOF/045/JFKPOF-045-028.

4. The Rise and Challenges of American Research Universities

1. Henry W. Diederich, "American and German Universities," *Science,* July 29, 1904, 157.
2. "German Universities Left Behind," *Literary Digest,* December 11, 1909, 1067.
3. John S. Brubacher and Willis Rudy, *Higher Education in Transition: A History of American Colleges and Universities* (New Brunswick, NJ: Transaction Publishers, 1997), 3; Samuel Eliot Morison, *The Founding of Harvard College* (Cambridge, MA: Harvard University Press, 1998), 127.
4. Brubacher and Rudy, *Higher Education in Transition,* 4.
5. Arthur M. Cohen, *The Shaping of American Higher Education: Emergence and Growth of the Contemporary System* (San Francisco: Jossey-Bass, 1998), 57.
6. Samuel Eliot Morison, *Three Centuries of Harvard* (Cambridge, MA: Harvard University Press, 1946), 224.

7. Philip Alexander Bruce, "History of the University of Virginia, 1819–1919: The Lengthened Shadow of One Man," vol. 1, 339–342, https://babel .hathitrust.org/cgi/pt?id=coo1.ark:/13960/t48p6m780;view=1up;seq =363;size=150.

8. Edwin Emery Slosson, *Great American Universities* (New York: MacMillan, 1910), 374.

9. Jonathan R. Cole, *The Great American University: Its Rise to Preeminence, Its Indispensable National Role, Why It Must Be Protected* (New York: Public Affairs, 2012), 22.

10. Slosson, *Great American Universities*, 375.

11. Cole, *The Great American University*, 26–27.

12. Slosson, *Great American Universities*, 383.

13. "A Brief History of the University of Chicago," University of Chicago, http://www-news.uchicago.edu/resources/brief-history.html.

14. "A History of Stanford," Stanford University, https://www.stanford.edu /about/history/.

15. Roger Geiger, *American Higher Education since World War II: A History* (Princeton, NJ: Princeton University Press, 2015), 426–427.

16. John R. Thelin, *A History of American Higher Education* (Baltimore, MD: Johns Hopkins University Press, 2011), 199–201.

17. David F. Labaree, *A Perfect Mess: The Unlikely Ascendancy of American Higher Education* (Chicago: The University of Chicago Press, 2017), 106.

18. Labaree, *A Perfect Mess*.

19. Ibid.

20. Geiger, *American Higher Education since World War II*.

21. Thelin, *A History of American Higher Education*, 263.

22. "History and Timeline," U.S. Department of Veterans Affairs, http://www .benefits.va.gov/gibill/history.asp.

23. "The Office of Scientific Research and Development (OSRD) Collection," Library of Congress, https://www.loc.gov/rr/scitech/trs/trsosrd.html.

24. National Science Foundation, "Science The Endless Frontier," A Report to the President by Vannevar Bush, Director of the Office of Scientific Research and Development, July 1945, https://www.nsf.gov/od/lpa/nsf50 /vbush1945.htm.

25. National Science Foundation, "Science The Endless Frontier."

26. "Farewell Address," Dwight D. Eisenhower Library, https://www.eisen howerlibrary.gov/research/online-documents/farewell-address.

27. Charles T. Clotfelter, introduction to *American Universities in a Global Market*, Charles T. Clotfelter, ed. (Chicago: University of Chicago Press, 2010).

28. See, for example, Clotfelter, *American Universities;* James Axtell, *Wisdom's Workshop: The Rise of the Modern University* (Princeton, NJ: Princeton University Press, 2016); or Hunter R. Rawlings, "The Lion in the Path," remarks at Princeton University Alumni Day, February 22, 2014, https://www

.princeton.edu/main/news/archive/S39/33/39I39/index.xml?section=topstories, accessed August 16, 2016.

29. Axtell, *Wisdom's Workshop*, 365.

30. Derek Bok, *Higher Education in America* (Princeton, NJ: Princeton University Press, 2013), 44–46.

31. Bok, *Higher Education in America*, 49.

32. Bok, *Higher Education in America*, 51.

33. Axtell, *Wisdom's Workshop*, 228.

34. Walter Crosby Eells, "The Origin and Early History of Sabbatical Leave," *AAUP Bulletin* 48, no. 3 (September 1962): 253–256.

35. Celina M. Sima, "The Role and Benefits of the Sabbatical Leave in Faculty Development and Satisfaction," *New Directions for Institutional Research* 2000, no. 105: 67–75.

36. "Federal and State Funding of Higher Education," Pew Trusts, June 11, 2015, http://www.pewtrusts.org/en/research-and-analysis/issue-briefs/2015 /06/federal-and-state-funding-of-higher-education.

37. "Historical Trends in Federal R&D," American Association for the Advancement of Science, https://www.aaas.org/programs/r-d-budget-and-policy /historical-trends-federal-rd.

38. Michael Mitchell, Michael Leachman, and Kathleen Masterson, "A Lost Decade in Higher Education Funding," Center on Budget and Policy Priorities, August 23, 2017, https://www.cbpp.org/research/state-budget-and-tax /a-lost-decade-in-higher-education-funding, accessed September 2019.

39. Labaree, *A Perfect Mess*, 7.

40. Melissa Korn, "Giving to Colleges Jumps 7.2% to Record $46.7 Billion," *Wall Street Journal*, February 11, 2019, https://www.wsj.com/articles/giving -to-colleges-jumps-7-2-to-record-46-7-billion-11549861260.

41. Council for Aid to Education, "Colleges and Universities Raise Record $40.30 Billion in 2015," press release, http://cae.org/images/uploads/pdf /VSE_2015_Press_Release.pdf, accessed August 17, 2016.

42. National Association of College and University Business Officers (NACUBO), "Endowment Study," (Boston: Cambridge Associates Inc., 1990), 23; "Number of U.S. Institutional Respondents to the 2019 NTSE, and Respondents' Total Endowment Market Value, by Endowment Size and Institution Type," NACUBO, https://www.nacubo.org/Research/2020 /Public-NTSE-Tables, accessed March 15, 2021.

43. "GDP data," World Bank, United States, https://data.worldbank.org /country/united-states, accessed March 15, 2021.

44. National Association of College and University Business Officers, "Educational Endowments' Investment Returns Decline Sharply to 2.4% in FY2015; 10-Year Returns Fall to 6.3%," *2015 NACUBO-Commonfund Study of Endowments*, http://www.nacubo.org/Documents/2015%20NCSE%20 Press%20Release%20%20FINAL.pdf.

45. "U.S. Educational Endowments Report 5.4 Percent Average Return in FY19," National Association of College and University Business Officers,

January 30, 2020, https://www.nacubo.org/Press-Releases/2020/US
-Educational-Endowments-Report-5-3-Percent-Average-Return-in-FY19.

46. Michael Bloomberg, "Michael Bloomberg: Why I'm Giving $1.8 Billion in
College Financial Aid," *New York Times*, November 18, 2018, https://www
.nytimes.com/2018/11/18/opinion/bloomberg-college-donation-financial
-aid.html.

47. Michael Bloomberg, "Why I'm Giving $1.8 Billion."

48. Phillip G. Altbach, *Global Perspectives on Higher Education* (Baltimore, MD:
Johns Hopkins University Press, 2016), 32.

49. Slosson, *Great American Universities*, 180.

50. "Number of International Students in the United States Hits All-Time
High," Institute for International Education, November 18, 2019, https://
www.iie.org/Why-IIE/Announcements/2019/11/Number-of-International
-Students-in-the-United-States-Hits-All-Time-High, accessed June 2020;
"NAFSA International Student Economic Value Tool," National Association
of International Educators, https://www.nafsa.org/policy-and-advocacy
/policy-resources/nafsa-international-student-economic-value-tool-v2, accessed
June 2020.

51. David Engerman, *Know Your Enemy: The Rise and Fall of America's Soviet
Experts* (New York: Oxford University Press, 2006); Mitchell L. Stevens,
Cynthia Miller-Idriss, and Seteney Shami, *Seeing the World: How US Universities Make Knowledge in a Global Era* (Princeton, NJ: Princeton University Press, 2018).

52. "Announcement: IFLE Awards Over $71 Million in FY 2018 Grants to
Strengthen International Studies, World Language Training, and Global
Experiences for Educators and Students," U.S. Department of Education,
https://www2.ed.gov/about/offices/list/ope/iegps/2018news.html.

53. Nick Anderson, "In Qatar's Education City, U.S. Colleges Are Building
an Academic Oasis," *Washington Post,* December 6, 2015, https://www
.washingtonpost.com/local/education/in-qatars-education-city-us-colleges
-are-building-an-academic-oasis/2015/12/06/6b538702-8e01-11e5-ae1f
-af46b7df8483_story.html.

54. Slosson, *Great American Universities*, 180.

55. Labaree, *A Perfect Mess*, 183–185.

56. Labaree, *A Perfect Mess, 2.*

57. Clark Kerr, *The Uses of the University* (Cambridge, MA: Harvard University
Press, 2001), 7–11; Labaree, *A Perfect Mess*, 13, 73.

58. Kerr, *The Uses of the University,* 1; Labaree, *A Perfect Mess,* 129.

5. Rising through Change and through Storm

1. Samuel Eliot Morison, *Three Centuries of Harvard* (Cambridge, MA: Harvard
University Press, 1946), 253.

2. Morison, *Three Centuries,* 251.

3. Quoted in Morison, *Three Centuries,* 260.

4. This section relies on the superb account of the tercentenary in Morton Keller and Phyllis Keller, *Making Harvard Modern: The Rise of America's University* (Oxford: Oxford University Press, 2001), 3–10.

5. Quoted in Keller and Keller, *Making Harvard Modern*, 8.

6. Keller and Keller, *Making Harvard Modern*, 4–5.

7. Morison, *Three Centuries*, 272.

8. Quoted in Keller and Keller, *Making Harvard Modern*, 10.

9. Gene I. Maeroff, "Harvard of the West Climbing in Ratings," *New York Times*, October 10, 1977, https://www.nytimes.com/1977/10/10/archives /harvard-of-the-west-climbing-in-ratings.html.

10. For a summary, see Eugenia V. Levenson, "Harvard Girl," *Harvard Magazine*, July-August 2002, https://harvardmagazine.com/2002/07/harvard-girl.html.

11. The phrase from the subtitle of Keller and Keller, *Making Harvard Modern*.

12. Morison, *Three Centuries*, 5.

13. See Bernard Bailyn, "Foundations," in *Glimpses of the Harvard Past*, Bernard Bailyn, Donald Fleming, Oscar Handlin, and Stephan Thernstrom (Cambridge, MA: Harvard University Press, 1986), 9.

14. Morison, *Three Centuries*, 22–24.

15. Morison, *Three Centuries*, 14–16.

16. Morison, *Three Centuries*, 69–71.

17. Bailyn, "Foundations," 11.

18. Bailyn, "Foundations," 61.

19. Bailyn, "Foundations," 224–226.

20. Bailyn, "Foundations," 232.

21. Bailyn, "Foundations," 254.

22. Bailyn, "Foundations," 35.

23. Bailyn, "Foundations," 324.

24. Morison, *Three Centuries*, 295.

25. Donald Fleming, "Eliot's New Broom," in Bailyn et al., *Glimpses*, 63.

26. All quotes from Fleming, "Eliot's New Broom," 62–63.

27. Morison, *Three Centuries*, 324.

28. Fleming, "Eliot's New Broom," 65.

29. Morison, *Three Centuries*, 330.

30. Fleming, "Eliot's New Broom," 65.

31. Records of the President of Harvard University, Charles W. Eliot, Addresses, Speeches, and Articles, 1869–1925, 1870 Harvard Commencement Address, Harvard University Archives.

32. Morison, *Three Centuries*, 421.

33. Quoted in Fleming, "Eliot's New Broom," 70.

34. Fleming, "Eliot's New Broom," 76.

35. Fleming, "Eliot's New Broom," 73.

36. Fleming, "Eliot's New Broom," 384.

37. See Ernest P. Young, *The Presidency of Yuan Shikai* (Ann Arbor: University of Michigan Press, 1977), 47–48, 172–176. Quote on 175.

38. Quoted in Richard Norton Smith, *The Harvard Century: The Making of a University to a Nation* (Cambridge, MA: Harvard University Press, 1986), 60.

39. John King Fairbank, *Chinabound: A Fifty-Year Memoir* (New York: Harper & Row, 1982), 155.

40. Keller and Keller, *Making Harvard Modern,* 14.

41. Stephen Steinberg, *The Ethnic Myth: Race, Ethnicity, and Class in America* (Boston: Beacon Press, 2001), 245.

42. Jerome Karabel, *The Chosen: The Hidden History of Admission and Exclusion at Harvard, Yale, and Princeton* (Boston: Houghton Mifflin, 2005), 126.

43. Karabel, *The Chosen,* 88; Steinberg, *The Ethnic Myth,* 245.

44. Keller and Keller, *Making Harvard Modern,* 51. See their subsection "No Women Allowed . . . ," 51–59.

45. Morison, *Three Centuries,* 446.

46. Keller and Keller, *Making Harvard Modern,* 23.

47. Keller and Keller, *Making Harvard Modern,* 24.

48. Keller and Keller, *Making Harvard Modern,* 163–164.

49. John T. Bethell, *Harvard Observed: An Illustrated History of the University in the Twentieth Century* (Cambridge, MA: Harvard University Press, 1998), 34.

50. Bethell, *Harvard Observed,* 278.

51. "It's Complicated: 375 Years of Women at Harvard," Radcliffe Institute for Advanced Study, Harvard University, https://www.radcliffe.harvard.edu /event/2012-its-complicated-exhibition.

52. David S. Webster, *Academic Quality Rankings of American Colleges and Universities* (Springfield, IL: Charles C. Thomas, 1986), 137–139.

53. Keller and Keller, *Making Harvard Modern,* xii.

54. Oscar Handlin, "Making Men of the Boys," in Bailyn et al., *Glimpses,* 48.

55. Bethell, *Harvard Observed,* 198–201; Keller and Keller, *Making Harvard Modern,* 178–183.

56. Quoted in Keller and Keller, *Making Harvard Modern,* 347–348.

57. Johanna Berkman, "Harvard's Hoard," *New York Times,* June 24, 2001, http://www.nytimes.com/2001/06/24/magazine/24HARVARD.html ?pagewanted=all; see also Keller and Keller, *Making Harvard Modern,* 372.

58. Author interview with Neil Rudenstine, New York City, August 26, 2016.

59. Sara Rimer, "Some Seeing Crimson at Harvard 'Land Grab,'" *New York Times,* June 17, 1997, http://www.nytimes.com/1997/06/17/us/some-seeing -crimson-at-harvard-land-grab.html.

60. Sarah Wu, "Lessons from Barry's Corner," *Harvard Crimson,* May 10, 2017, https://www.thecrimson.com/article/2017/5/10/barrys-corner-allston -feature/.

61. Steve Stecklow, "Management 101: Harvard's President, Too Slow to Delegate, Got Swamped in Detail—It's a Uniquely Tough Job, and Rudenstine's Style Made it Even Tougher, Will He Return After a Rest?," *Wall Street Journal,* December 1994.

62. Laura L. Krug, "Allston Tax Extended to 25 Years," *Harvard Crimson,* January 9, 2004, https://www.thecrimson.com/article/2004/1/9/allston-tax-extended-to-25-years/.

63. Daniel J. Hemel, "Summers' Comments on Women and Science Draw Ire," *Harvard Crimson,* January 14, 2005, https://www.thecrimson.com/article/2005/1/14/summers-comments-on-women-and-science/.

64. William C. Marra and Sara E. Polsky, "Lack of Confidence," *Harvard Crimson,* March 15, 2005, https://www.thecrimson.com/article/2005/3/15/lack-of-confidence-in-a-sharp/.

65. Geraldine Fabrikant, "Harvard and Yale Report Losses in Endowments," *New York Times,* September 10, 2009, https://www.nytimes.com/2009/09/11/business/11harvard.html.

66. "$11 Billion Less," *Harvard Magazine,* November-December 2009, http://harvardmagazine.com/2009/11/harvard-endowment-update.

67. Beth Healy, "Harvard Ignored Warnings about Investments," *Boston Globe,* November 29, 2009, http://archive.boston.com/news/local/massachusetts/articles/2009/11/29/harvard_ignored_warnings_about_investments/; Geraldine Fabrikant, "Harvard and Yale Report Losses in Endowments."

68. "Further Financial Fallout," *Harvard Magazine,* January-February 2010, https://harvardmagazine.com/2010/01/harvard-2009-financial-losses-grow.

69. Geraldine Fabrikant, "Harvard and Yale Report Losses in Endowments."

70. Author interview with Lawrence S. Bacow, Cambridge, MA, July 7, 2016.

71. "Looming Layoffs," *Harvard Magazine,* July-August 2009, https://harvardmagazine.com/2009/07/looming-layoffs.

72. Keller and Keller, *Making Harvard Modern,* 64–70; Conant quotation, 65.

73. "The New Tenure Track," *Harvard Magazine,* September-October 2010, http://harvardmagazine.com/2010/09/the-new-tenure-track.

74. *The 68th Annual Harvard Crimson Confidential Guide to Courses at Harvard* (1993), 133.

75. Harvard University Office of the Senior Vice Provost, *Faculty Development & Diversity Annual Report 2013–2014,* https://hwpi.harvard.edu/files/faculty-diversity/files/fdd_annual_report_2013-2014_hq.pdf.

76. "The New Tenure Track."

77. Colin Campbell, "The Harvard Factor," *New York Times Magazine,* July 20, 1986, http://www.nytimes.com/1986/07/20/magazine/the-harvard-factor.html?pagewanted=all.

78. *Faculty Development & Diversity Annual Report 2013–2014*; Julie Chung, "Women at Work," *Harvard Magazine,* March-April 2020, https://harvardmagazine.com/2020/03/jhj-undergraduate-women-at-work, accessed April 2020.

79. Noah J. Delwiche and Daphne C. Thompson, "Yield Remains Steady at 81 Percent for Class of 2019," *Harvard Crimson,* May 15, 2015, http://www.thecrimson.com/article/2015/5/15/class-2019-yield-81-percent/; Tyler Fog-

gatt, "Yield Drops, Diversity Increases for Class of 2019," *Yale Daily News*, September 3, 2015, http://yaledailynews.com/blog/2015/09/03/yield-drops -diversity-increases-for-class-of-2019/; "At 69.4 Percent, Class of 2019 Yield Highest Ever," *The Daily Princetonian*, May 8, 2015, http://www.dailyprinceto-nian.com/article/2015/05/at-69-4-percent-class-of-2019-yield-highest-ever.

80. Victor Xu, "Record 81.1 Percent Yield for Class of 2019," *The Stanford Daily*, June 9, 2015, http://www.stanforddaily.com/2015/06/09/de-vx-record-81-1 -percent-yield-rate-reported-for-class-of-2019/.

81. Susan Svrluga, "Harvard Fencing Coach Dismissed for Conflict-of-Interest Violation," *Washington Post*, July 10, 2019, https://www.washingtonpost.com /education/2019/07/10/harvard-fencing-coach-dismissed-conflict-of-interest -violation/.

82. Derek Thompson, "The Cult of Rich-Kid Sports," *The Atlantic*, October 2, 2019, https://www.theatlantic.com/ideas/archive/2019/10/harvard-univer sity-and-scandal-sports-recruitment/599248/.

83. William L. Wang, "Filings Show Athletes with High Academic Scores Have 83 Percent Acceptance Rate," *Harvard Crimson*, June 30, 2018, https://www.thecrimson.com/article/2018/6/30/athlete-admissions/.

84. "Meet the Class of 2022," *Harvard Crimson*, https://features.thecrimson .com/2018/freshman-survey/makeup/.

85. Max Larkin and Mayowa Aina, "Legacy Admissions Offer and Advan-tage—And Not Just at Schools Like Harvard," NPR, November 4, 2018, https://www.npr.org/2018/11/04/663629750/legacy-admissions-offer-an -advantage-and-not-just-at-schools-like-harvard.

86. Preston Cooper, "The Real Problem with Legacy Admissions," *Forbes*, Feb. 20, 2020.

87. Zohra D. Yaqhubi, "New Admissions Outreach Initiative Seeks to En-courage Low-Income College Applicants," *Harvard Crimson*, October 24, 2013, http://www.thecrimson.com/article/2013/10/24/financial-aid-office -connection/.

88. Camille G. Caldera, "83 Percent of Harvard College Admits Accept Spots in Class of 2023," *Harvard Crimson*, May 10, 2019, https://www.thecrimson .com/article/2019/5/10/class-of-2023-yield/, accessed October 2019.

89. "How Aid Works," Harvard College, https://college.harvard.edu/financial -aid/how-aid-works.

90. Ibid.

91. "Economic Diversity," *U.S. News and World Report*, https://www.usnews .com/best-colleges/rankings/national-universities/economic-diversity.

92. David Leonhardt, "How Elite Colleges Still Aren't Diverse," *New York Times*, March 29, 2011, https://economix.blogs.nytimes.com/2011/03/29 /how-elite-colleges-still-arent-diverse/.

93. *General Education in a Free Society* (Cambridge, MA: Harvard University Press, 1945), 51. As quoted in http://harvardmagazine.com/sites/default /files/GenEd.pdf.

94. See Morison, *Three Centuries,* 446. As cited in http://harvardmagazine.com /sites/default/files/GenEd.pdf.

95. "Financial Administration," Harvard University, https://finance.harvard.edu /financial-overview.

96. "Financial Report FY2021," Harvard University, https://finance.harvard .edu/files/fad/files/fy21_harvard_financial_report.pdf.

97. Ibid.

98. Harvard Management Company, *Annual Report 2021,* "Message from the CEO," October 2021, https://www.hmc.harvard.edu/wp-content/uploads /2021/10/FY21_HMC_Annual_Report.pdf.

99. Doug Gavel, "University Has a Cosmopolitan Flair," *Harvard Gazette,* November 16, 2000, https://news.harvard.edu/gazette/story/2000/11/harvard -gazette-university-has-a-cosmopolitan-flair/.

100. Michael C. George and Alyza J. Sebenius, "Between Harvard and Yale, a World of Difference," *Harvard Crimson,* May 24, 2012, http://www.thecrimson .com/article/2012/5/24/international-harvard-yale-singapore/?page=single.

101. John S. Rosenberg, "Going Global, Gradually," *Harvard Magazine,* November 24, 2015, https://www.harvardmagazine.com/2015/11/harvard-global-institute, accessed June 2020.

102. "About HGI," Harvard Global Institute, https://globalinstitute.harvard.edu /about-hgi, accessed June 2020.

103. Author interview with Barry Bloom, Cambridge, MA, May 25, 2016.

104. "Statistics," Harvard International Office, http://www.hio.harvard.edu /statistics.

105. United States District Court for the District of Massachusetts, "Civil Action No. 1:20-cv-11283," https://www.harvard.edu/sites/default/files /content/sevp_filing.pdf.

106. Camille G. Caldera and Michelle G. Kurilla, "Harvard Affiliates, Other Colleges and Universities File Amicus Briefs in Support of ICE Lawsuit," *Harvard Crimson,* July 12, 2020, https://www.thecrimson.com/article/2020 /7/13/harvard-mit-ice-lawsuit-amici/.

107. Nate Herpich, "The Conundrum for International Students," *Harvard Gazette,* July 31, 2020, https://news.harvard.edu/gazette/story/2020/07/harvard -addresses-the-challenges-for-international-students/.

108. Christine Heenan, "Harvard Center Shanghai Opens Its Doors," *Harvard Gazette,* March 20, 2010, http://news.harvard.edu/gazette/story/2010/03 /harvard-center-shanghai-opens-its-doors/.

109. "Harvard in the World," Harvard Worldwide, https://worldwide.harvard .edu/harvard-world, accessed September 2020.

110. "Summers Visits People's Republic of China," *Harvard Gazette,* May 16, 2002, https://news.harvard.edu/gazette/story/2002/05/summers-visits -peoples-republic-of-china/.

111. Theodore R. Delwiche, "In Beijing, Faust Talks Climate Change with Chinese President," *Harvard Crimson,* March 17, 2015, https://www.thecrimson .com/article/2015/3/17/faust-visits-chinese-president/.

112. Colleen Walsh, "In China, Bacow Emphasizes Common Values," *Harvard Gazette,* March 20, 2019, https://news.harvard.edu/gazette/story/2019/03/harvard-president-speaks-at-peking-university/.

113. Nidhi Subbaraman, "Harvard Chemistry Chief's Arrest over China Links Shocks Researchers," *Nature,* February 3, 2020, https://www.nature.com/articles/d41586-020-00291-2; James S. Bikales and Kevin R. Chen, "Former Chemistry Chair Lieber Indicted on Four Additional Felonies for Tax Offenses," *Harvard Crimson,* July 29, 2020, https://www.thecrimson.com/article/2020/7/29/lieber-tax-offenses-charges/.

114. Kate O'Keefe, "Education Department Investigating Harvard, Yale over Foreign Funding," *Wall Street Journal,* February 13, 2020, https://www.wsj.com/articles/education-department-investigating-harvard-yale-over-foreign-funding-11581539042; U.S. Department of Education, "U.S. Department of Education Launches Investigation into Foreign Gifts Reporting at Ivy League Universities," February 12, 2020, https://content.govdelivery.com/accounts/USED/bulletins/27b7801.

115. Meg P. Bernhard and Ignacio Sabate, "The Founders: The Evolution of edX at Harvard and MIT," *Harvard Crimson,* May 28, 2015, http://www.thecrimson.com/article/2015/5/28/the-founders/.

116. Morison, *Three Centuries,* 371.

117. Morison, *Three Centuries,* 371–372.

118. Virginia Postrel, "Harvard Gets Its Geek On: Can Big-Ticket Gifts Lift Harvard's Engineering Schools to the Top Ranks?," *Bloomberg,* June 18, 2015, http://www.bloombergview.com/articles/2015-06-18/harvard-gets-its-geek-on.

119. Postrel, "Harvard Gets Its Geek On."

120. Jonathan Shaw and John S. Rosenberg, "Engineering a School's Future," *Harvard Magazine,* January-February 2016, http://harvardmagazine.com/2015/12/engineering-a-school-s-future.

121. "Ballmer Boosts Harvard Computer Science," *Harvard Magazine,* November 13, 2014, http://harvardmagazine.com/2014/11/ballmer-boosts-harvard-computer-science-faculty.

122. "Frequently Asked Questions," Harvard John A. Paulson School of Engineering and Applied Sciences, https://www.seas.harvard.edu/prospective-students/prospective-undergraduate-students/frequently-asked-questions-faqs.

123. Meg P. Bernhard, "CS50 Logs Record-Breaking Enrollment Numbers," *Harvard Crimson,* September 11, 2014, http://www.thecrimson.com/article/2014/9/11/cs50-breaks-enrollment-records/?page=single; Melissa C. Rodman, "CS50's First Semester Winds Down at Yale," *Harvard Crimson,* December 16, 2015, http://www.thecrimson.com/article/2015/12/16/cs50-yale-end-semester/.

124. Melissa C. Rodman, "CS50's First Semester Winds Down at Yale."

125. "Best Undergraduate Engineering Programs Rankings 2020," *U.S. News and World Report,* https://www.usnews.com/best-colleges/rankings/engineering-doctorate.

126. "Allston: The Killer App," *Harvard Magazine,* February 5, 2013, https://harvardmagazine.com/2013/02/harvard-moving-engineering-school-to-allston-campus-0.

127. John S. Rosenberg, "Allston Land Company Leads Harvard Commercial Development," *Harvard Magazine,* November 29, 2018, https://www.harvardmagazine.com/2018/11/harvard-allston-land-development-company.

128. *Times Higher Education World University Rankings,* https://www.timeshighereducation.com/world-university-rankings/2020/world-ranking#!/page/0/length/25/sort_by/rank/sort_order/asc/cols/scores.

129. Author interview with Douglas A. Melton, Cambridge, MA, May 24, 2016.

130. John S. Rosenberg, "Allston Land Company Leads Harvard Commercial Development."

131. Jay London, "The Transformation of Kendall Square: The Past, Present, and Future of MIT's Neighborhood," *Slice of MIT,* October 7, 2015, https://alum.mit.edu/slice/transformation-kendall-square-past-present-and-future-mits-neighborhood; Andy Metzger, "Kendall Square: From Dustbowl of 1970s to Tech Hub of Today," *Wicked Local,* April 27, 2012, https://www.wickedlocal.com/article/20120427/News/304279870, accessed September 2020.

132. "Science and Engineering Complex Gets Final Beam," *Harvard Gazette,* November 29, 2017, https://news.harvard.edu/gazette/story/2017/11/final-beam-placed-in-harvards-science-and-engineering-complex/.

133. Brigid O'Rourke, "SEAS Moves Opening of Science and Engineering Complex to Spring Semester '21," *Harvard Gazette,* April 10, 2020, https://news.harvard.edu/gazette/story/2020/04/opening-of-new-science-and-engineering-complex-moves-to-spring-21/.

134. David F. Labaree, *A Perfect Mess: The Unlikely Ascendancy of American Higher Education* (Chicago: The University of Chicago Press, 2017), 13.

6. Public Mission, Private Funding

Epigraph: Nicholas Dirks, "Chancellor's Corner: Traditions of Excellence Worth Maintaining," *The Daily Californian,* February 6, 2015, http://www.dailycal.org/2015/02/06/chancellors-corner-traditions-excellence-worth-maintaining/, accessed December 7, 2015.

1. Will Kane, "Chancellor Christ Sworn in as 600 Graduate during Winter Ceremony," *UC Berkeley News,* December 17, 2017, https://news.berkeley.edu/2017/12/17/chancellor-christ-sworn-in-as-600-graduate-during-winter-ceremony/.

2. "Update on Campus Budget," University of California, Berkeley Office of the Chancellor, April 11, 2016, http://chancellor.berkeley.edu/update-campus-budget, accessed August 3, 2016; "Reducing UC Berkeley's Def-

icit," University of California, Berkeley Office of the Chancellor, http://chancellor.berkeley.edu/deficitreduction, accessed August 3, 2016.

3. Center on Budget and Policy Priorities, "A Lost Decade in Higher Education Funding: State Cuts Have Driven Up Tuition and Reduced Quality," August 23, 2017, https://www.cbpp.org/research/state-budget-and-tax/a-lost-decade-in-higher-education-funding.

4. "Budget 101," University of California, Berkeley Office of the Chief Financial Officer, https://cfo.berkeley.edu/budget-101.

5. "History," UC Berkeley Foundation, https://www.ucberkeleyfoundation.org/history-mission/.

6. Ry Rivard, "The New Normal at Berkeley," *Inside Higher Ed*, January 23, 2015, https://www.insidehighered.com/news/2015/01/23/gov-brown-says-normal-californians-cant-get-berkeley-problem-some-californians-blame, accessed December 7, 2015.

7. Michael Burke and Larry Gordon, "Newsom's proposed budget cuts to higher education force difficult choices ahead," EdSource, May 15, 2020, https://edsource.org/2020/newsoms-proposed-budget-cuts-to-higher-education-force-difficult-choices-ahead/631681; John Aubrey Douglass, "Why Does UC Berkeley Need $6 Billion?," UC Berkeley Blog, March 12, 2020, https://blogs.berkeley.edu/2020/03/12/why-does-uc-berkeley-need-6-billion/.

8. "An Act to Create and Organize the University of California," California State Assembly Bill No. 583, March 5, 1868, http://bancroft.berkeley.edu/Cal History/charter.html, accessed August 18, 2016; "Bylaws," University of California Board of Regents, November 2015, http://regents.universityofcalifornia.edu/governance/bylaws/index.html, accessed August 18, 2016.

9. Patricia A. Pelfrey, *A Brief History of the University of California*, 2nd edition (Berkeley: University of California Press, 2004), 9.

10. Pelfrey, *A Brief History*, v.

11. Pelfrey, *A Brief History*, 11.

12. Pelfrey, *A Brief History*, 14–15.

13. Clark Kerr, *The Gold and the Blue: A Personal Memoir of the University of California, 1949–1967: Volume One: Academic Triumphs* (Berkeley: University of California Press, 2001), 39.

14. Edwin Emery Slosson, *Great American Universities* (New York: MacMillan, 1910), 149; Pelfrey, *A Brief History*, 22.

15. Pelfrey, *A Brief History*, 24.

16. Pelfrey, *A Brief History*, 28–29.

17. Kerr, *The Gold and the Blue: Academic Triumphs*, 140.

18. Jennifer Fenn Lefferts, "From Community College to Harvard," *Boston Globe*, May 23, 2019, https://www.bostonglobe.com/metro/globelocal/2019/05/22/from-community-college-harvard/ff9D4BQZYgsWTFpIo45NGO/story.html.

19. See Belinda Reyes, ed., *A Portrait of Race and Ethnicity in California: An Assessment of Social and Economic Well-Being* (Public Policy Institute of

California, 2001), http://www.ppic.org/content/pubs/report/R_201BRR
.pdf; Deborah Reed, Melissa Glenn Haber, and Laura Mameesh, "The Distribution of Income in California," (Public Policy Institute of California,
July 1996), http://www.ppic.org/content/pubs/report/R_796DRR.pdf, accessed
August 22, 2016.

20. Clark Kerr, *The Gold and the Blue: A Personal Memoir of the University of
California, 1949–1967: Volume Two: Political Turmoil* (Berkeley: University of
California Press, 2001), 28.

21. Kerr, *The Gold and the Blue: Political Turmoil*, 28.

22. Kerr, *The Gold and the Blue: Political Turmoil*, 288.

23. Quoted in "Education: View from the Bridge," *Time Magazine*, November 17,
1958.

24. Kerr, *The Gold and the Blue: Political Turmoil*, 309.

25. University of California Annual Endowment Report 2007, http://regents
.universityofcalifornia.edu/regmeet/mar08/i3attach.pdf, accessed August 18, 2016; University of California Annual Endowment Report 2009,
http://regents.universityofcalifornia.edu/regmeet/feb10/i6attach.pdf, accessed August 18, 2016.

26. Kevin O'Leary, "California's Crisis Hits Its Prized Universities," *Time
Magazine*, July 18, 2009, http://content.time.com/time/nation/article
/0,8599,1911455,00.html, accessed December 7, 2015.

27. Kevin O'Leary, "California's Crisis Hits its Prized Universities."

28. Author interview with George Breslauer, Berkeley, CA, April 28, 2015.

29. Author interview with George Breslauer, April 28, 2015.

30. Mac Taylor, *Faculty Recruitment and Retention at the University of California*,
Report of the Legislative Analyst's Office of California, December 13,
2012, http://www.lao.ca.gov/reports/2012/edu/uc-faculty/uc-faculty-121312
.pdf, accessed December 7, 2015.

31. Author interview with Nicholas Dirks, Berkeley, CA, May 3, 2015.

32. "Announcement of Comprehensive Planning and Analysis Process," UC
Berkeley Office of the Chancellor, February 10, 2016, http://chancellor
.berkeley.edu/announcement-comprehensive-planning-and-analysis-process,
accessed August 18, 2016.

33. Rachel Bachman, "Cal's Football-Stadium Gamble," *Wall Street Journal*,
April 18, 2012.

34. Nanette Asimov, "Cal Scrambling to Cover Stadium Bill," *SFGate*, June 16,
2013, http://www.sfgate.com/collegesports/article/Cal-scrambling-to-cover
-stadium-bill-4604221.php, accessed August 23, 2016.

35. Amy Jiang, "Campus Faculty Urge Review of Investigation into Allegations
Faced by Former Vice Chancellor," *The Daily Californian*, April 21, 2015,
https://www.dailycal.org/2015/04/20/uc-berkeley-faculty-sign-letter-review
-allegations-former-vice-chancellor-graham-fleming/, accessed September 2019.

36. Andrea Platten, "Napolitano Addresses Sexual Misconduct Cases, Orders
Graham Fleming Fired from New Post," *The Daily Californian*, March 13,

2016, https://www.dailycal.org/2016/03/12/graham-fleming-fired-from-role
-as-berkeley-global-campus-ambassador/, accessed September 2019.

37. UC Berkeley Public Affairs, "Berkeley's Budget Challenge: Reduce, Rethink,
Restructure," *UC Berkeley News*, March 11, 2016, http://news.berkeley.edu
/2016/03/11/berkeleys-budget-challenge/, accessed August 9, 2016.

38. Phillip Matier and Andrew Ross, "Fence and Its Costs Rising at UC
Berkeley Chancellor's Home," *San Francisco Chronicle*, August 29, 2015,
http://www.sfchronicle.com/bayarea/matier-ross/article/Fence-and-its-costs
-rising-at-UC-Berkeley-6472768.php, accessed August 8, 2016.

39. Teresa Watanabe, "UC Berkeley Provost Resigns after Criticism of
Handling of Sexual Harassment and Budget Issues," *Los Angeles Times*,
April 15, 2016, http://www.latimes.com/local/lanow/la-me-ln-berkeley
-provost-resigns-20160415-story.html, accessed August 3, 2016; Suhauna
Hussain, "Andrew Szeri Resigns from Position as Vice Provost of Strategic
Academic and Facilities Planning," *The Daily Californian*, June 19, 2016,
http://www.dailycal.org/2016/06/19/andrew-szeri-resigns-position-vice
-provost-strategic-academic-facilities-planning/, accessed August 8, 2016.

40. University of California, Berkeley Academic Senate Spring Division
Meeting, audio recording, May 3, 2016, http://academic-senate.berkeley.edu
/meetings/division/property-0-3, accessed August 9, 2016.

41. Nanette Asimov, "UC Berkeley Chancellor Faces Skeptical Academic Senate,"
SFGate, May 3, 2016, http://www.sfgate.com/news/article/UC-Berkeley
-chancellor-faces-skeptical-Academic-7391798.php, accessed August 8, 2016.

42. Pelfrey, *A Brief History*, 11.

43. Author interview with Sheldon Rothblatt, Berkeley, CA, May 3, 2015.

44. Author interview with George Breslauer, April 28, 2015.

45. Author interview with Nicholas Dirks, May 3, 2015.

46. George Breslauer, "What Made Berkeley Great? The Sources of Berkeley's
Sustained Academic Excellence," University of California, Berkeley Center
for Studies in Higher Education Research & Occasional Paper Series:
CSHE.3.11, January 2011.

47. Author interview with George Breslauer, April 28, 2015.

48. University of California, *Budget for Current Operations Report: Summary of
the Budget Request As Presented to the Regents for Approval 2019–20,* 9,
https://www.ucop.edu/operating-budget/_files/rbudget/2019-20-budget
-summary.pdf, accessed September 2019.

49. Curan Mehra, "Prop. 20 Passes, Midyear UC Tuition Increase Avoided,"
The Daily Californian, November 6, 2012, http://www.dailycal.org/2012/11
/06/fate-of-prop-30-still-unclear/, accessed December 8, 2015.

50. *2013–2014 UC Berkeley Budget Plan,* http://cfo.berkeley.edu/sites/default
/files/2013-14%20UC%20Berkeley%20Budget%20Plan%20-%20Final%20
%289-5-13%29.pdf, accessed December 7, 2015.

51. John Wilton, "Time Is Not on Our Side," Berkeley Administration and Finance, November 29, 2013, part 1, 5–6, http://vcaf.berkeley.edu/sites/default

/files/Time%20is%20not%20on%20our%20side%202%20%2011.29.13%20
FINAL.pdf, accessed December 7, 2015.

52. *Times Higher Education,* "THE World Academic Summit: Nicholas Dirks,"
YouTube video, 46:59, October 2, 2015, https://www.youtube.com/watch?v
=3NkoyHAJiPY, accessed December 7, 2015; Nicholas Dirks, "The Future
of World-Class Universities," *University World News,* no. 385 (October 2,
2015), http://www.universityworldnews.com/article.php?story=2015100100
4022774, accessed December 7, 2015.

53. "Energy Biosciences Institute: About EBI," 2015, Energy & Biosciences,
http://www.energybiosciencesinstitute.org/content/energy-biosciences
-institute, accessed December 7, 2015; Rick DelVecchio, "UC Faculty Critical of BP Deal," *SFGate,* March 9, 2007, http://www.sfgate.com/education
/article/BERKELEY-UC-faculty-critical-of-BP-deal-2611643.php, accessed August 23, 2016.

54. Charles Burress, "Probe of Research Pact at Cal Released," *SFGate,* July 31,
2004, http://www.sfgate.com/bayarea/article/BERKELEY-Probe-of
-research-pact-at-Cal-released-2737385.php, accessed August 23, 2016;
Lawrence Busch et al., *External Review of the Collaborative Research Agreement between Novartis Agricultural Discovery Institute, Inc. and the Regents of
the University of California* (East Lansing, MI: Institute for Food and Agricultural Standards, Michigan State University, 2004); Robert M. Price and
Laurie Goldman, *The Novartis Agreement: An Appraisal,* UC Berkeley Administrative Review, October 4, 2004.

55. Data from the National Center for Education Statistics Integrated Postsecondary Education Data System, http://nces.ed.gov/ipeds/, accessed
August 26, 2020.

56. Author interview with Nicholas Dirks, May 3, 2015.

57. "University Ultra High Net Worth Alumni Rankings 2019," Wealth-X,
https://www.wealthx.com/wp-content/uploads/2019/08/University-Ultra
-High-Net-Worth-Alumni-Rankings-2019.pdf; Chris Parr, "Top 20 Universities for Producing Billionaires," *Times Higher Education,* November 20,
2014, https://www.timeshighereducation.com/news/top-20-universities-for
-producing-billionaires/2017097.article.

58. UC Berkeley Public Affairs, "Campus Sets New Records for Fundraising,"
UC Berkeley News, July 14, 2016, http://news.berkeley.edu/2016/07/14
/campus-sets-new-records-for-fundraising/, accessed August 18, 2016.

59. UC Berkeley, "Light the Way: The Campaign for Berkeley: FAQ," https://
light.berkeley.edu/o/about/, accessed September 2020.

60. UC Berkeley Public Affairs, "At Saturday Event, Berkeley Kicks off $6 Bil-
lion 'Light the Way' Campaign," *UC Berkeley News,* March 2, 2020, https://
news.berkeley.edu/2020/03/02/at-saturday-event-berkeley-kicks-off-6
-billion-light-the-way-campaign/.

61. UC Berkeley, "Light the Way: The Campaign for Berkeley."

62. "Berkeley Operational Excellence: About," http://oe.berkeley.edu/about, accessed December 7, 2015.

63. Logan Goldberg, "Campus Leaders Address 'Painful' Budget Cuts, Other Changes at Staff Forum," *The Daily Californian*, February 24, 2015, http://www.dailycal.org/2015/02/24/campus-leaders-address-painful-budget-cuts-changes-staff-forum/, accessed August 9, 2016; Curan Mehra and Jordan Bach-Lombardo, "Birgeneau Leaves Legacy of Complicated Commitment to Public Mission," *The Daily Californian*, May 3, 2013, http://www.dailycal.org/2013/05/03/birgeneau-leaves-legacy-of-complicated-commitment-to-public-mission/, accessed August 9, 2016.

64. Wilton, "Time Is Not on Our Side," part 1.

65. UC Berkeley Research, "Faculty Excellence," https://vcresearch.berkeley.edu/excellence/faculty-excellence, accessed March 16, 2021.

66. Author interview with Nicholas Dirks, May 3, 2015.

67. Kerr, *The Gold and the Blue: Academic Triumphs*, 8–9.

68. Marc Gould, "UCB Faculty Advancement Slides, 1985–2011 by Discipline," Office for Faculty Equity and Welfare, http://ofew.berkeley.edu/sites/default/files/ucb_faculty_advancement_slides_by_discipline_2011.pdf, accessed August 18, 2016.

69. Author interview with Robert Birgeneau, Berkeley, CA, May 3, 2015.

70. Confidential author interview, April 2015.

71. Author interview with Nicholas Dirks, May 3, 2015.

72. Author interview with George Breslauer, April 28, 2015.

73. Teresa Watanabe, "UC Berkeley Chancellor to Resign Following Widespread Criticism by Faculty," *Los Angeles Times*, August 16, 2016, http://www.latimes.com/local/lanow/la-me-ln-uc-berkeley-chancellor-resign-20160816-snap-story.html, accessed August 18, 2016.

74. Data from the National Center for Education Statistics Integrated Postsecondary Education Data System, http://nces.ed.gov/ipeds/, accessed August 24, 2016.

75. National Center for Education Statistics, "UC Berkeley: Human Resources," https://nces.ed.gov/ipeds/datacenter/Facsimile.aspx?unitid=110635, accessed September 2020.

76. *Review of the Institute of East Asian Studies, University of California, Berkeley, 2011–2012*, submitted January 27, 2012.

77. "Best Colleges, 2020," *U.S. News and World Report*, 2019, http://colleges.usnews.rankingsandreviews.com/best-colleges/, accessed September 2019.

78. Wilton, "Time Is Not on Our Side," part 2, 2–3.

79. Wilton, "Time Is Not on Our Side," part 2, 2; U.S. Department of Education, "Distribution of Federal Pell Grant Program Funds by Institution," https://www2.ed.gov/finaid/prof/resources/data/pell-institution.html, accessed August 26, 2020; "Economic Diversity Among the Top 25," *U.S. News and World Report*, https://www.usnews.com/best-colleges/rankings

/national-universities/economic-diversity-among-top-ranked-schools, accessed August 26, 2020.

80. "By the Numbers," 2015, University of California, Berkeley, http://www
.berkeley.edu/about/bythenumbers, accessed December 7, 2015.

81. "UC Berkeley Fall Enrollment Data," University of California, Berkeley
Office of Planning and Analysis, https://opa.berkeley.edu/uc-berkeley-fall
-enrollment-data, accessed August 26, 2020.

82. "A Semester Unlike Any Other," University of California, Berkeley Division
of Equity and Inclusion, https://diversity.berkeley.edu/news/semester-unlike
-any-other, accessed September 25, 2020.

83. See Gary Y. Okihiro's *Third World Studies: Theorizing Liberation* (Durham,
NC: Duke University Press, 2016) for an in-depth history of the Third
World Liberation Front.

84. The Berkeley Revolution, "The Third World Liberation Front," http://
revolution.berkeley.edu/projects/twlf/.

85. Gino Nuzzolillo and Trey Walk, "You Should Take an Ethnic Studies
Course," *The Chronicle,* January 15, 2019, https://www.dukechronicle.com
/article/2019/01/duke-university-you-should-take-an-ethnic-studies-course.

86. Tyler Kingkade, "Occupy Cal Berkeley Protest Draws Thousands, As Two
Years of Occupation Come Home," *Huffington Post,* November 10, 2011,
http://www.huffingtonpost.com/2011/11/10/thousands-gather-for-occupy
-cal-protest_n_1086963.html, accessed August 18, 2016; Amruta Trivedi,
"Chancellor's Statement to ASUC Senate Cut Short by Calls for Resignation," *The Daily Californian,* December 8, 2011, http://www.dailycal.org
/2011/12/07/chancellors-statement-to-asuc-senate-cut-short/, accessed August 18, 2016; Chloe Hunt and J. D. Morris, "Robert Birgeneau to Step
Down as Chancellor of UC Berkeley," *The Daily Californian,* March 14,
2012, http://www.dailycal.org/2012/03/13/uc-berkeley-chancellor-robert
-birgeneau-announces-he-will-step-down-at-years-end/, accessed August 18, 2016.

87. "The Berkeley Undergraduate Initiative Executive Summary," University of
California, Berkeley Vice Chancellor for Undergraduate Education, March 30,
2016, http://vcue.berkeley.edu/sites/default/files/the_undergraduate
_initiative-_executive_summary_final.pdf.

88. Interview with Nicholas Dirks, May 3, 2015.

89. "CA Demographics," University of California, https://www.university
ofcalifornia.edu/infocenter/ca-demographics, accessed September 2020.

90. "UC Berkeley Fall Enrollment Data," University of California, Berkeley
Office of Planning and Analysis, https://opa.berkeley.edu/uc-berkeley-fall
-enrollment-data, accessed August 26, 2020.

91. Doris Sze Chun, "John Fryer, The First Agassiz Professor of Oriental Languages and Literature, Berkeley," *Chronicle of the University of California,*
no. 7 (Fall 2005): 2, https://cshe.berkeley.edu/sites/default/files/chron7
_excerpt_fryer.pdf.

92. "International Student Enrollment, Fall 2019," University of California, Berkeley International Office, https://internationaloffice.berkeley.edu/sites/default/files/student-stats2019.pdf.

93. "International Student Enrollment Data," Berkeley International Office, http://internationaloffice.berkeley.edu/students/current/enrollment_data.

94. Larry Gordon, "UC Berkeley Studies International Education Campus in Richmond," *Los Angeles Times,* February 24, 2015, http://www.latimes.com/local/education/la-me-uc-richmond-20150224-story.html#page=1, accessed December 7, 2015.

95. UC Berkeley Public Affairs, "Campus Launches Effort to Form New Global Alliance," *UC Berkeley News,* October 16, 2015, http://news.berkeley.edu/2015/10/16/campus-announces-new-global-alliance/, accessed December 7, 2015.

96. Larry Gordon, "UC Berkeley Studies International Education Campus"; Nicholas Dirks, "Open Letter to the Richmond Community from UC Berkeley Chancellor Nicholas Dirks: An Update on the Berkeley Global Campus," May 28, 2015, http://chancellor.berkeley.edu/sites/default/files/UCB-ChancellorDirksOpenLetterRichmond-BGCRB-5-28-15.pdf, accessed December 7, 2015.

97. Wilton, "Time Is Not on Our Side," part 1, 3.

98. Author interview with Robert Birgeneau, May 3, 2015.

99. Author interview with Robert Birgeneau, May 3, 2015.

100. Teresa Watanabe, "UC Berkeley's New Chancellor Brings Optimism—and a World Record—to an Embattled Campus," *The Baltimore Sun,* August 18, 2017, https://www.baltimoresun.com/la-me-uc-berkeley-new-chancellor-20170818-story.html, accessed May 2020.

101. Teresa Watanabe, "UC Berkeley's New Chancellor Brings Optimism."

102. Maxine Mouly and Olivia Buccieri, "Campus Officials Announce Elimination of $150M Deficit," *The Daily Californian,* September 26, 2019, https://www.dailycal.org/2019/09/24/campus-officials-announce-elimination-of-150-million-deficit/, accessed May 2020.

103. UC Berkeley Public Affairs, "Chancellor Christ: Free Speech Is Who We Are," *UC Berkeley News,* August 23, 2017, https://news.berkeley.edu/2017/08/23/chancellor-christ-free-speech-is-who-we-are/, accessed May 2020.

104. Yao Huang, "UC Berkeley Ranks Below UCLA as 2nd-Best Public School in US," *The Daily Californian,* September 13, 2018, https://www.dailycal.org/2018/09/13/uc-berkeley-ranks-below-ucla-as-2nd-best-public-school-in-us/, accessed May 2020.

105. Robert Morse, Matt Mason, and Eric Brooks, "Updates to 5 Schools' 2019 Best Colleges Rankings Data," *U.S. News and World Report,* July 25, 2019, https://www.usnews.com/education/blogs/college-rankings-blog/articles/2019-07-25/updates-to-5-schools-2019-best-colleges-rankings-data, accessed September 2019.

106. UC Berkeley Public Affairs, "UCLA, UC Berkeley Top Publics in *U.S. News* National Rankings," *UC Berkeley News,* September 2019, https://news

.berkeley.edu/2019/09/09/us-news-national-rankings2020/, accessed May 2020; Yao Huang, "UC Berkeley Ranks Below UCLA."

107. UC Berkeley Public Affairs, "In Online Conversation, Carol Christ Gives Budget, Campus Updates," *UC Berkeley News*, May 12, 2020, https://news .berkeley.edu/2020/05/12/in-online-conversation-carol-christ-gives-budget -campus-updates/, accessed May 2020.

108. UC Berkeley Public Affairs, "In Online Conversation, Carol Christ Gives Budget, Campus Updates."

109. "UC Berkeley Announces Plans for Fall Semester," *UC Berkeley News*, June 17, 2020, https://news.berkeley.edu/2020/06/17/uc-berkeley-announces -plans-for-fall-semester/, accessed June 2020.

110. Jessica Ruf, "California Creates Higher Ed Recovery Taskforce to Mitigate COVID-19 Impact," *Diverse Education*, August 10, 2020, https://diversee ducation.com/article/187160/.

111. Interview with George Breslauer, April 28, 2015.

112. "A Semester Unlike Any Other," University of California, Berkeley Division of Equity & Inclusion, https://diversity.berkeley.edu/news/semester-unlike -any-other, accessed September 2020.

7. Outrageous Ambitions

1. This story was first related in Brodhead's inaugural address, "More Day to Dawn," September 18, 2004, reprinted in Richard H. Brodhead, *Speaking of Duke: Leading the 21st Century University* (Durham, NC: Duke University Press, 2017), 19.

2. Brodhead, "Constructing Duke," Freshman Convocation, August 19, 2015, in Brodhead, *Speaking of Duke*, 220.

3. See William C. Kirby, Nora Bynum, Tracy Yuen Manty, and Erica M. Zendell, "Kunshan, Incorporated: The Making of China's Richest Town," Case 313–103 (Boston: Harvard Business School, 2013).

4. Terry Sanford, "Outrageous Ambitions," Address to the Annual Meeting of the Faculty, October 25, 1984, https://dukespace.lib.duke.edu/dspace /bitstream/handle/10161/91/outrageousambitions.pdf?sequence=1.

5. "Facts," Duke University, https://facts.duke.edu, accessed August 2020; "Quick Statistics about Duke University," Duke University Libraries, https://library.duke.edu/rubenstein/uarchives/history/articles/statistics, accessed September 2020.

6. "Global Companies Rank Universities," *New York Times*, October 25, 2012, https://archive.nytimes.com/www.nytimes.com/imagepages/2012/10/25 /world/asia/25iht-sreducemerging25-graphic.html.

7. Brodhead, "More Day to Dawn," in Brodhead, *Speaking of Duke*, 20.

8. On Crowell and the move to Durham, see Robert F. Durden, *The Dukes of Durham, 1865–1929* (Durham, NC: Duke University Press, 1975), 91–96. See also Crowell's memoirs: John Franklin Crowell, *Personal Collections of*

Trinity College, North Carolina, 1887–1894 (Durham, NC: Duke University Press, 1939). The Duke University Archives hold Crowell's papers, including account books and grade books in the collection "John Franklin Crowell Records and Papers, 1883–1932."

9. See Robert F. Durden, *The Dukes of Durham*; on the British-American Tobacco Company's success in China see Sherman Cochran, *Big Business in China: Sino-foreign Rivalry in the Cigarette Industry* (Cambridge, MA: Harvard University Press, 1980).

10. "Washington Duke and the Education of Women," Duke University Libraries, https://library.duke.edu/rubenstein/uarchives/history/articles /washington-duke-women, accessed September 2019.

11. See Nora Campbell Chaffin, *Trinity College, 1839–1892: The Beginnings of Duke University* (Durham, NC: Duke University Press, 1950); Earl W. Porter, *Trinity and Duke, 1892–1924: Foundations of Duke University* (Durham, NC: Duke University Press, 1964).

12. See Robert F. Durden, *Bold Entrepreneur: A Life of James B. Duke* (Durham, NC: Carolina Academic Press, 2003), 155.

13. Robert F. Durden, *The Launching of Duke University: 1924–1949* (Durham, NC: Duke University Press, 2005), 26.

14. "Medical Center History—Overview," Duke University Medical Center Archives, https://archives.mc.duke.edu/history, accessed September 2020.

15. "History of Duke Hospital," Duke Department of Surgery, https://surgery .duke.edu/about-department/history, accessed September 2020.

16. "History of Duke Hospital," Duke Department of Surgery.

17. Cited in Tallman Trask III, foreword to *Duke University: An Architectural Tour* by Ken Friedlein and John Pearce (New York: Princeton Architectural Press, 2015), 11–12.

18. *First Progress Report,* Committee on Planning and Development at Duke University (June 1959), 5.

19. *First Progress Report,* Introductory Statement.

20. Quoted in Robert F. Durden, *Lasting Legacy to the Carolinas: The Duke Endowment, 1924–1994* (Durham, NC: Duke University Press, 1998), 149.

21. Durden, *Lasting Legacy,* 36.

22. Durden, *Lasting Legacy,* 36–37.

23. Durden, *Lasting Legacy,* 32; "Quick Statistics about Duke University," Duke University Library, https://library.duke.edu/rubenstein/uarchives/history /articles/statistics.

24. "Commemorating 50 Years of Black Students at Duke University," Duke University, https://spotlight.duke.edu/50years/.

25. *First Progress Report,* 36.

26. Richard H. Brodhead, "Coming through the Current Challenges," *Duke Today,* February 10, 2010, https://today.duke.edu/2010/02/rhbspeech.html.

27. *Long Range Planning at Duke University: Second Progress Report,* Duke University (1960), 19.

28. *The Fifth Decade,* Duke University (1964); *Duke University in the Decade Ahead (Third Progress Report),* Duke University Committee on Long Range Planning (1961).

29. "Profile of Duke University 1956–1976," Duke University (1976), 15.

30. "Profile of Duke University 1956–1976," 16–18.

31. "Profile of Duke University 1956–1976," 20.

32. "History and Mission," Duke Lemur Center, https://lemur.duke.edu/about /history-mission/.

33. "History and Mission," Duke Lemur Center.

34. John Markis, "From Lemurs to Poisoned Chocolate: The Tale of a Lemur Center Founder," *The Chronicle,* April 23, 2019, https://www.dukechronicle .com/article/2019/04/duke-university-from-lemurs-to-poisoned-chocolate -the-tale-of-a-lemur-center-founder-john-buettner-janusch.

35. Markis, "From Lemurs to Poisoned Chocolate."

36. "History and Mission," Duke Lemur Center.

37. Sanford, "Outrageous Ambitions."

38. Howard E. Covington and Marion A. Ellis, *Terry Sanford: Politics, Progress, & Outrageous Ambitions* (Durham, NC: Duke University Press, 1999), 368–369.

39. Covington and Ellis, *Terry Sanford,* 373; "Meet Terry Sanford," Duke Sanford School of Public Policy, https://sanford.duke.edu/about-us/inside-sanford /meet-terry-sanford.

40. "Summary Report of the University Planning Committee," Duke University (1972).

41. "Summary Report," Duke University (1972).

42. Ibid.

43. Ibid.

44. Terry Sanford, "A Time for Greatness at Duke: The Epoch Campaign," Duke University (1973), 21, https://ia600401.us.archive.org/24/items /timeforgreatness00duke/timeforgreatness00duke.pdf.

45. Sanford, "A Time for Greatness at Duke," 20.

46. *Directions for Progress: A Report to the Duke University Board of Trustees,* Duke University (1980), 1–2.

47. *Directions for Progress,* 2.

48. "History and Quick Facts," Duke Nicholas School of the Environment, https://nicholas.duke.edu/general/history-quick-facts.

49. *Directions for Progress,* 3.

50. *Directions for Progress,* 64.

51. "Academic Plan," Duke University (1987), 15–16.

52. Covington and Ellis, *Terry Sanford,* 421.

53. David Yaffe, "The Department That Fell to Earth: The Deflation of Duke English," http://Linguafranca.mirror.theinfo.org/9902/yaffe.html.

54. *Crossing Boundaries: Interdisciplinary Planning for the Nineties,* Duke University Self-Study (1988), 46.

55. Adam Beyer, "Remembering Keith Brodie: Community Mourns Passing of the Former Duke President," *The Chronicle,* December 6, 2016, http://www .dukechronicle.com/article/2016/12/remembering-keith-brodie-community -fathers-to-mourn-passing-of-the-former-duke-president.

56. Beyer, "Remembering Keith Brodie."

57. "Economic Diversity among the Top 25 National Universities," *U.S. News and World Report,* https://www.usnews.com/best-colleges/rankings/national-uni versities/economic-diversity-among-top-ranked-schools, accessed June 2020.

58. U.S. Department of Education, "Equity in Athletics Data Analysis," https://ope.ed.gov/athletics/#/, accessed June 2020.

59. Niharika Vattikonda, "Duke Athletics' Annual Equity Report Sheds Light on Spending, Coaching for Men's and Women's Teams," *The Chronicle,* April 10, 2019, https://www.dukechronicle.com/article/2019/04/duke -athletics-annual-equity-report-shows-differences-between-mens-and -womens-teams, accessed June 2020.

60. Burton Bollag, "Men's Lacrosse Team at Duke U. Forfeits Games Following Accusations of Rape at Party," *The Chronicle of Higher Education,* March 27, 2006, https://www.chronicle.com/article/Mens-Lacrosse-Team-at-Duke-U /117736, accessed June 2020.

61. Duff Wilson and David Barstow, "All Charges Dropped in Duke Case," *New York Times,* April 12, 2007, https://www.nytimes.com/2007/04/12/us /12duke.html, accessed June 2020.

62. David S. Webster, *Academic Quality Rankings of American Colleges and Universities* (Springfield, IL: Charles C. Thomas Publisher, 1986), 127, 131; citing David S. Webster, "America's Highest Ranked Graduate Schools, 1925–1982," *Change: The Magazine of Higher Education* 15, no. 4 (May–June 1983).

63. "U.S. News & World Report Historical University Rankings," data compiled by Andrew G. Reiter, https://sites.google.com/site/andyreiter/data.

64. Sanford, "Outrageous Ambitions."

65. *Shaping Our Future: A Young University Faces a New Century,* Duke University (1994), 6–8.

66. *Shaping Our Future,* Duke University (1994).

67. *Building on Excellence,* Duke University (2001), 160.

68. "$2 Billion and Counting," *Duke Magazine,* January-February 2003, https:// alumni.duke.edu/magazine/articles/2-billion-and-counting.

69. "$2 Billion and Counting."

70. "Master Plan," Duke Facilities Management, https://facilities.duke.edu /campus/master-plan, accessed March 16, 2021.

71. "Bylaws of Duke University," Duke University Board of Trustees, https:// trustees.duke.edu/governing-documents/bylaws-duke-university.

72. Author interview with Peter Lange, Durham, NC, April 13, 2015.

73. "Minutes of the Regular Meeting of the Academic Council: January 19, 2006," Duke University Academic Council, https://academiccouncil.duke .edu/sites/default/files/AC01-19-061.pdf, accessed June 2020.

74. Ibid.
75. "Bylaws of Duke University."
76. "Minutes of the Regular Meeting of the Academic Council: September 21, 2006," Duke University Academic Council, https://academiccouncil.duke.edu/sites/default/files/AC09-21-06P.pdf, accessed June 2020.
77. Author interview with Peter Lange, April 13, 2015.
78. Author interview with Sally Kornbluth, Durham, NC, April 10, 2015.
79. Author interview with Tallman Trask III, Durham, NC, April 15, 2015.
80. *Building on Excellence*, 160.
81. *Building on Excellence*, 177.
82. Author correspondence with Peter Lange, February 7, 2021.
83. Author interview with Richard Brodhead, Durham, NC, April 15, 2015.
84. "Minutes of the Regular Meeting of the Academic Council: September 21, 2006," Duke University Academic Council, https://academiccouncil.duke.edu/sites/default/files/AC09-21-06P.pdf, accessed June 2020.
85. "Duke's Financial Aid Initiative Raises $308.5 Million," *Duke Today*, January 26, 2009, https://today.duke.edu/2009/01/fai.html.
86. "In Letter to Staff, President Brodhead Outlines Duke's Response to Economic Downturn," *Duke Today*, March 1, 2009, https://today.duke.edu/2009/03/rhbletter.html.
87. "In Letter to Staff."
88. Ibid.
89. Ibid.
90. Ibid.
91. "Memo: Peter Lange Charges Deans to Review Strategic Plan," *Duke Today*, April 29, 2009, https://today.duke.edu/2009/04/stratmemo.html.
92. "Duke University's Endowment: 2015–16 Snapshot," Duke University (2016), https://dukeforward.duke.edu/downloads/Duke_Endowment-2016_D.pdf; Jake Satisky, "University Endowment Rises to Record $8.6 Billion after 'Economic Headwinds,'" *The Chronicle*, September 28, 2019, https://www.dukechronicle.com/article/2019/09/duke-university-endowment-record-board-of-trustees#:~:text=University%20endowment%20rises%20to%20record%20%248.6%20billion%20after%20'economic%20headwinds; "Duke's Endowment Returns Nearly 56 Percent in Fiscal Year 2021," *The Chronicle*, October 15, 2021, https://www.dukechronicle.com/article/2021/10/duke-university-endowment-gain-56-percent-dumac-how-used-financial-aid-faculty-pay-who-manages.
93. Draft of Peter Lange Letter to the Faculty, Duke University Archives, Office of the Provost, Common Archives, 2000–2007.
94. Rachel Chason, "How Brodhead Changed Duke," *The Chronicle*, April 12, 2017, http://www.dukechronicle.com/article/2017/04/how-brodhead-changed-duke.
95. "About DukeEngage," DukeEngage, https://dukeengage.duke.edu/about-dukeengage.

96. Author interview with Noah Pickus, Durham, NC, April 9, 2015.
97. *Building on Excellence,* 165.
98. "About Duke Global Health Institute," Duke Global Health Institute, https://globalhealth.duke.edu/about.
99. *Making a Difference,* Duke University (2006), 45–47.
100. "Interdisciplinarity at Duke: A Brief Inventory of Connections among Schools and University-Wide Institutes, Initiatives, and Centers," Duke OVPIS (2018), https://sites.duke.edu/interdisciplinary/files/2018/09 /interdisciplinarity-at-duke-august2018-1.pdf, accessed September 2019.
101. "Interdisciplinarity at Duke."
102. Ibid.
103. Ibid.
104. Ibid.
105. Ibid.
106. Author interview with Sally Kornbluth, April 10, 2015.
107. Author interview with Richard Brodhead, April 15, 2015.
108. Author interview with Peter Lange, April 13, 2015.
109. Author interview with Haiyan Gao, Durham, NC, April 9, 2015.
110. Author interview with Sally Kornbluth, April 10, 2015.
111. Author interview with Peter Lange, April 13, 2015.
112. *Together Duke: Advancing Excellence through Community,* Duke University (April 2017).
113. *Times Higher Education World University Rankings,* 2017, https://www .timeshighereducation.com/world-university-rankings/2017/world -ranking#!/page/0/length/25/sort_by/rank/sort_order/asc/cols/stats; "QS World University Rankings 2016–2017," QS Top Universities (2017), https://www.topuniversities.com/university-rankings/world-university -rankings/2016; Duke University, Academic Ranking of World Universities, http://www.shanghairanking.com/World-University-Rankings/Duke -University.html.
114. "Best Medical Schools," USNWR Rankings 2019, https://www.usnews.com /best-graduate-schools/top-medical-schools/research-rankings; "Best Law Schools," USNWR Rankings 2019, https://www.usnews.com/best-graduate -schools/top-law-schools/law-rankings.
115. "Best Nursing Schools: Research," USNWR Rankings 2019, https://www .usnews.com/best-graduate-schools/top-nursing-schools/nur-rankings.
116. "Best Business Schools," USNWR Rankings 2019, https://www.usnews .com/best-graduate-schools/top-business-schools/mba-rankings.
117. "Duke Ranks as 6th Best Global University in Environment and Ecology," Duke Nicholas School of the Environment (2016) citing USNWR rankings, https://nicholas.duke.edu/about/news/duke-ranks-6th-best-global-university -environment-and-ecology.
118. *Summary Report of the University Planning Committee,* Duke University (1972), 95.

119. Ibid.
120. Ibid.
121. Lisa K. Childress, *The Twenty-first Century University: Developing Faculty Engagement in Internationalization* (Frankfurt, Germany: Peter Lang Publishing, 2009), 43–44.
122. *Shaping Our Future,* Duke University (1994), 26.
123. *Shaping Our Future,* Duke University (1994), 27.
124. "A Global Vision for Duke University," Duke University Global Priorities Committee (2013), Fuqua Global Executive MBA Program, http://www .fuqua.duke.edu/programs/duke_mba/global-executive/.
125. Fuqua Cross Continent MBA Program, http://www.fuqua.duke.edu /programs/duke_mba/cross_continent/.
126. *Building on Excellence,* 89–90.
127. *Building on Excellence,* 89–92.
128. "About," Duke Global Education Office, https://globaled.duke.edu/about, accessed September 2020.
129. *Duke Global Health Institute 2015–2016 Impact Report,* Duke Global Health Institute (2018), https://globalhealth.duke.edu/sites/default/files/files/dghi _annual-report-2017-2018_final-forweb.pdf.
130. "Duke University and National University of Singapore Advance to Second Phase of Medical School Partnership," November 30, 2010, Duke Health, https://corporate.dukehealth.org/news/duke-university-and-national-university -singapore-advance-second-phase-medical-school.
131. Author interview with Richard Brodhead, April 15, 2015.
132. "Duke-Kunshan Planning Guide," Duke University Office of the Provost and Office of Global Strategy and Programs (2011); Kirby et al., "Kunshan, Incorporated"; See my filmed interview with Party Secretary Guan Aiguo at my online course, ChinaX, Part 10, Section 49.6, "Kunshan Field Trip," https://www .edx.org/course/contemporary-china-the-peoples-republic-taiwan-and.
133. "Duke-Kunshan Planning Guide."
134. "Duke-Kunshan Planning Guide," 20.
135. "Duke-Kunshan Planning Guide," 19.
136. "Senior Leaders Appointed for Duke Kunshan University," *Duke Today,* September 20, 2012, http://today.duke.edu/2012/09/dkuexecs.
137. "Duke-Kunshan Planning Guide."
138. Author interview with Haiyan Gao, Kunshan, China, March 22, 2017.
139. "Undergraduate Curriculum: Liberal Arts in the 21st Century," Duke Kunshan University, https://dukekunshan.edu.cn/en/academics/undergraduate -curriculum.
140. "Trustees Approve Undergraduate Program for Duke Kunshan University," *Duke Today,* December 3, 2016, https://today.duke.edu/2016/12/trustees -approve-undergraduate-program-duke-kunshan-university.
141. New York University, "The Creation of NYU Shanghai," March 27, 2011, https://www.nyu.edu/about/leadership-university-administration/office-of -the-president-emeritus/communications/the-creation-of-nyu-shanghai.html.

142. Sally Kornbluth, "Memo to the Faculty from Provost Sally Kornbluth," March 16, 2016, https://provost.duke.edu/sites/all/files/Duke%20and%20 the%20Development%20of%20DKU%20rev%20Aug%202016%20.pdf, accessed June 2020.
143. Ibid.
144. Ibid.
145. Maria Morrison, "Duke Kunshan University Breaks Ground on 47-acre Expansion," *The Chronicle* August 19, 2019, https://www.dukechronicle.com /article/2019/08/duke-kunshan-university-breaks-down-phase-2-expansion -china, accessed May 2020.
146. "Vincent Price Named Duke University 10th President," *Duke Today,* December 2, 2016, https://today.duke.edu/2016/12/presannouncement.
147. Ibid.
148. Duke Strategic Framework, https://president.duke.edu/wp-content/uploads /2019/04/Duke-Will-Strategic-Framework.pdf, accessed October 2019.
149. Duke Kunshan University, "Duke Kunshan University Welcomes Its First Undergraduate Class," August 14, 2018, http://webcache.googleusercontent .com/search?q=cache:EqrvPB1A45cJ:https://dukekunshan.edu.cn/en/news /arrival-class-of-2022&hl=en&gl=us&strip=1&vwsrc=0.
150. Johns Hopkins University Coronavirus Resource Center, "COVID-19 Dashboard by the Center for Systems Science and Engineering (CSSE) at Johns Hopkins University," https://coronavirus.jhu.edu/map.html, accessed September 2020.
151. Nick Anderson, "China's Coronavirus Crisis Forces Duke Kunshan University to Teach Online," *Washington Post,* February 22, 2020, https://www .washingtonpost.com/local/education/chinas-coronavirus-crisis-forces-duke -kunshan-university-to-teach-online/2020/02/22/311349aa-5333-11ea-929a -64efa7482a77_story.html.
152. Duke Kunshan University, "Coronavirus: Updates on DKU's Response," May 14, 2020, https://dukekunshan.edu.cn/en/news/special-message-novel -coronavirus, accessed June 2020.
153. Matthew Griffin and Carter Forinash, "Duke Limits Fall Housing to First-years and Sophomores, Scaling Back Reopening Plans," *The Chronicle,* July 26, 2020, https://www.dukechronicle.com/article/2020/07/duke -university-email-fall-changes-housing-limited-first-years-sophomore -coronavirus.
154. "A Global Celebration for Duke Kunshan's Class of 2024," *Duke Today,* August 26, 2020, https://today.duke.edu/2020/08/global-celebration-duke -kunshan%E2%80%99s-class-2024.
155. Duke Office of Duke Kunshan University Relations, "Message to Duke '24 International Students: DKU Option for Fall 2020," https://dkurelations .duke.edu/students/duke-students-dku/message-duke-24-international -students-dku-option-fall-2020.
156. Author interview with Richard Brodhead, April 15, 2015.
157. Ibid.

158. "Minutes of the Meeting of the Academic Council: November 17, 2016,"
Duke University Academic Council, http://academiccouncil.duke.edu/sites
/default/files/11-17-16%20minutes.pdf.

8. A Chinese Century?

1. Qi Wang and Nian Cai Liu, "Higher Education Research Institutes in Chinese Universities," *Studies in Higher Education* 39, no. 8 (September 2014):
1488–1498.
2. "Sustainable Development Goals: National Monitoring: Enrolment by Level
of Education: Enrolment in Tertiary Education, All Programmes, Both
Sexes (Number): China," UNESCO, http://data.uis.unesco.org/#, accessed
January 19, 2021.
3. Andrew Jacobs, "China's Army of Graduates Struggles for Jobs," *New York
Times,* December 11, 2010, https://www.nytimes.com/2010/12/12/world
/asia/12beijing.html; Qinying He, Yao Men, and Lin Xu, "Composition
Effect Matters: Decomposing the Gender Pay Gap in Chinese University
Graduates," *Economic Research* (*Ekonomska Istraživanja*) 33, no. 1 (March
2020), https://www.tandfonline.com/doi/full/10.1080/1331677X.2020
.1734850.
4. "College Enrollment in the United States from 1965 to 2018 and Projections
up to 2029 for Public and Private Colleges," Statista, November 5, 2020,
https://www.statista.com/statistics/183995/us-college-enrollment-and
-projections-in-public-and-private-institutions/.
5. National Bureau of Statistics, "China Statistical Yearbook 2001: Number
of Institutions of Higher Education by Region and Type (2000)," China
Statistics Press, http://www.stats.gov.cn/english/statisticaldata/yearlydata
/YB2001e/ml/indexE.htm, accessed January 19, 2021.
6. Guojia tongji ju, "Zhongguo tongji nianjian 2011: gaodeng xuexiao shuliang
(2010)" [National Bureau of Statistics, China Statistical Yearbook 2011:
Number of Schools or Institutions of Higher Education (2010)], China Statistics Press, http://www.stats.gov.cn/tjsj/ndsj/2011/indexeh.htm, accessed
January 19, 2021.
7. William C. Kirby, "The Chinese Century? The Challenges of Higher Education," *Daedalus* 143, no. 2 (Spring 2014): 145–156, https://www.jstor.org
/stable/43297323.
8. UNESCO Institute for Statistics, "School Enrollment, Tertiary (% Gross),"
World Bank, http://data.worldbank.org/indicator/SE.TER.ENRR/countries
/CN-4E-XT?display=graph, accessed May 12, 2020.
9. For an overview of all these trends, see David A. Stanfield and Yukiko
Shimmi, "Chinese Higher Education: Statistics and Trends," in *International Briefs for Higher Education Leaders,* no. 1 (2012): 5–7. On broad trends,
see the annual *Zhongguo jiaoyu fazhan baogao* [Report on China's Economic
Development], edition 21 sheji jiaoyu yanjiuyuan (Beijing: Shehui kexue

wenxian chubanshe, 2011); "Mao ruxue lu da 51.6% gaodeng jiaoyu geng pujile" [The Collegiate Gross Enrollment Rate is 51.6%, Higher Education Has Become More Popular], *Xinhua,* November 26, 2020, http://www .xinhuanet.com/local/2020-11/26/c_1126786875.htm.

10. Kai Yu, Andrea Lynn Stith, Li Liu, and Huizhong Chen, *Tertiary Education at a Glance: China* (Boston: Sense Publishers, 2012), 7.

11. See Ichisada Miyazaki, *China's Examination Hell: The Civil Service Exams of Imperial China,* trans. by Conrad Schirokauer (New Haven, CT: Yale University Press, 1976).

12. Ji Xianlin, as quoted in Hao Ping, *Peking University and the Origins of Higher Education in China* (Los Angeles: Bridge21 Publications, 2013), 384.

13. For a detailed presentation of the Hanlin Academy, see Adam Yuen-chung Lui, *The Hanlin Academy: Training Ground for the Ambitious 1644–1850,* (Hamden, CT: Archon Books, 1981).

14. Gu Ming-yuan, *Cultural Foundations of Chinese Education* (Leiden, Netherlands: Brill, 2014), 108–113.

15. Benjamin A. Elman, *Civil Examinations and Meritocracy in Late Imperial China* (Cambridge, MA: Harvard University Press, 2013).

16. Frank J. Swetz, "The Introduction of Mathematics in Higher Education in China, 1865–1887," *Historia Mathematica* 1 (2, 1974), 169.

17. Richard A. Hartnett, *The Saga of Chinese Higher Education from the Tongzhi Restoration to Tiananmen Square* (Lewiston, NY: Edwin Mellen, 1998), 7.

18. See Timothy B. Weston, *The Power of Position* (Berkeley: University of California Press, 2004), 81ff.

19. Cai Yuanpei, "Daxue jiaoyu" [University Education], in *Cai Yuanpei quanji* [Collected Works of Cai Yuanpei], vol. 5 (Beijing: Zhonghua shuju, 1988), 507–508.

20. Hu Shi, "Guoli daxue zhi zhongyao" [Important Features of National Universities], in *Hu Shi sanwen* [Hu Shi's Essays], Yao Peng and Fan Qiao, eds. (Beijing: Zhongguo guangbo dianshi chubanshe, 1992), 191–192.

21. See Ruth Hayhoe, *China's Universities 1895–1995: A Century of Cultural Conflict* (New York: Routledge, 1996), 47.

22. See Wen-Hsin Yeh, *The Alienated Academy: Culture and Politics in Republican China 1919–1937* (Cambridge, MA: Harvard University Press, 1990).

23. For a critical—and American—response, see Stephen Duggan, "A Critique of the Report of the League of Nations' Mission of Educational Experts to China," *Institute of International Education* 14, no. 3 (January 1933).

24. William C. Kirby, "The Internationalization of China: Foreign Relations at Home and Abroad in the Republican Era," *China Quarterly,* no. 150 (June 1997): 455.

25. "Recent Conditions of Chinese Universities, Colleges, and Libraries," *China Institute Bulletin* 3, no. 2 (November 1938): 51–62; John Israel, *Lianda: A Chinese University in War and Revolution* (Stanford: Stanford University Press, 1998), 15.

26. Israel, *Lianda: A Chinese University in War and Revolution*, 376.

27. Hayhoe, *China's Universities 1895–1995*, 78.

28. Robert Taylor, *Education and University Enrolment Policies in China, 1949–1971*, (Canberra: Australian National University Press, 1973).

29. See Andrew G. Walder, *Fractured Rebellion: The Beijing Red Guard Movement* (Cambridge, MA: Harvard University Press, 2009).

30. Joel Andreas, *Rise of the Red Engineers* (Stanford: Stanford University Press, 2009), 189.

31. Andreas, *Rise of the Red Engineers*, 210.

32. Chen Zhili, "Gaige kaifang ershinian de Zhongguo jiaoyu" [China's Education in the Past 20 Years of Reform and Opening Up], Zhonghua renmin gongheguo jiaoyubu [Ministry of Education of the People's Republic of China], http://www.moe.gov.cn/jyb_xwfb/xw_zt/moe_357/s3579/moe_90/tnull_3161.html, accessed May 12, 2020; Suzanne Pepper, *China's Education Reform in the 1980s* (Berkeley, CA: Institute of East Asian Studies), 69.

33. Pepper, *China's Education Reform in the 1980s*.

34. "Zhagen Zhongguo dadi fenjin qiangguo zhengcheng xin Zhongguo qishinian gaodeng jiaoyu gaige fazhan licheng" [Rooted in China's Land and March Towards a Powerful Country: The 70-Year History of Higher Education Reform and Development in New China], Zhonghua renmin gongheguo jiaoyubu [Ministry of Education of the People's Republic of China], http://www.moe.gov.cn/jyb_xwfb/s5147/201909/t20190924_400593.html, accessed May 12, 2020.

35. Wanhua Ma, "The Flagship University and China's Economic Reform," in *World Class Worldwide: Transforming Research Universities in Asia and Latin America*, P. G. Altbach and J. Bal, eds. (Baltimore, MD: Johns Hopkins University Press, 2007), 32.

36. Colin Norman, "China to Get $200 Million for University Expansion," *Science* 213, no. 4506 (1981): 420–421.

37. Martin King Whyte, "Deng Xiaoping," *China Quarterly*, no. 135 (September 1993): 515–535.

38. Ruth Hayhoe, "China's Universities and Western Academic Models," *Higher Education* 18, no. 1 (1989): 49–85.

39. Pepper, *China's Education Reform in the 1980s*.

40. Chen Zhili, "Gaige kaifang ershinian Zhongguo jiaoyu."

41. Ruth Hayhoe, "China's Universities since Tiananmen: A Critical Assessment," *China Quarterly*, no. 134 (June 1993): 291–309.

42. Guojia tongji ju, "Zhongguo tongji nianjian 2007: xuexiao shuliang (2006)" [National Bureau of Statistics, China Statistical Yearbook 2007: Number of Schools by Level and Type of School (2006)], China Statistics Press, http://www.stats.gov.cn/tjsj/ndsj/2007/indexeh.htm; National Bureau of Statistics, "Number of Institutions of Higher Education by Region and Type (1999)," http://www.stats.gov.cn/english/statisticaldata/yearlydata/YB2000e/T16E.htm, accessed January 19, 2021.

43. Li Lixu, "China's Higher Education Reform 1998–2003," *Asia Pacific Education Review* 5, no. 1 (2004): 14–22.
44. Xiaoyan Wang and Jian Liu, "China's Higher Education Expansion and the Task of Economic Revitalization," *Higher Education* 62, no. 2 (August 2011): 213–229."
45. Li Lixiu, "China's Higher Education Reform 1998–2003."
46. "Gaodeng jiaoyu xuexiao shuliang" [Number of Higher Education Schools (Institutions)], Zhonghua renmin gongheguo jiaoyubu [Ministry of Education of the People's Republic of China], http://www.moe.gov.cn/s78/A03/moe_560/jytjsj_2019/qg/202006/t20200611_464789.html, accessed June 2020.
47. "2019 nian quanguo gaoxiao mingdan" [2019 National College List], Zhonghua renmin gongheguo jiaoyubu [Ministry of Education of the People's Republic of China], http://www.moe.gov.cn/jyb_xxgk/s5743/s5744/201906/t20190617_386200.html, accessed August 2019.
48. Huiqing Jin, "China's Private Universities," *Science* 346, no. 6208 (2014): 40, http://www.sciencemag.org/content/346/6208/401.full, accessed August 13, 2015.
49. See William C. Kirby, Michael Shih-ta Chen, Keith Chi-ho Wong, and Tracy Manty, "Xi'an International University: The Growth of Private Universities in China," Case 309-074 (Boston: Harvard Business School, 2009).
50. Kirby, "The Chinese Century?"
51. "2019 nian quanquo gaoxiao mingdan."
52. "Vision and Mission," Xi'an Jiaotong-Liverpool University, https://www.xjtlu.edu.cn/en/about/overview/vision-and-mission.
53. William C. Kirby, Nora Bynum, Tracy Yuen Manty, and Erica M. Zendell, "Kunshan, Incorporated: The Making of China's Richest Town," Case 313-103 (Boston: Harvard Business School, 2013).
54. "Sanshinian qiande Zhongguo daxue paiming yilan, ni zenme kan? [What Do You Think of the Rankings of Chinese Universities 30 Years Ago?], *Sohu,* May 23, 2020, https://www.sohu.com/a/397252209_523175.
55. "Education: Enrolment by Level of Education: Enrolment in Tertiary Education, All Programmes, Both Sexes (Number)," UNESCO Institute for Statistics, http://data.uis.unesco.org/#, accessed May 12, 2020.
56. Hayhoe, *China's Universities 1895–1995,* 119.
57. Mei Li and Rui Yang, "Governance Reforms in Higher Education: A Study of Institutional Autonomy in China," in *Governance Reforms in Higher Education in Asia: A Study of Institutional Autonomy in Asian Countries,* N. V. Varghese and M. Martin, eds. (Paris: International Institute for Educational Planning, UNESCO, 2013), 70.
58. Zhongguo shehui kexue wang, "Zhong ban yinfa gaoxiao dangwei lingdao xia de xiaozhang fuze zhi shishi yijian" [Chinese Academy of Social Sciences, Opinion on the Implementation of the Principal Responsibility System under the Leadership of the University Party Committee], Oc-

tober 16, 2014, http://www.cssn.cn/zx/yw/201410/t20141016_1364866
.shtml, accessed August 2019.

59. Yao Li et al., "The Higher Educational Transformation of China and Its
    Global Implications," National Bureau of Economic Research, Working
    Paper 13849 (March 2008), 22–24.
60. Sun Yan, "Qinghua daxue jiaoyu jijinhui cheng licai gaoshou," [Tsinghua
    University Education Foundation Becomes a Master of Fundraising],
    CNTV Online, October 19, 2010, http://igongyi.cntv.cn/20101019/100856
    .shtml, accessed October 2014.
61. Hayhoe, *China's Universities 1895–1995,* 95.
62. Zhonghua renmin gongheguo jiaoyubu, "211 gongcheng jianjie" [Ministry
    of Education of the People's Republic of China, Introduction to Project
    211], https://web.archive.org/web/20121110220139/http://www.moe.edu.cn
    /publicfiles/business/htmlfiles/moe/moe_315/200409/3799.html, accessed
    March 3, 2021.
63. Yao Li et al., "The Higher Educational Transformation of China and Its
    Global Implications," 20.
64. Zhongguo xuewei yu yanjiusheng jiaoyu xinxi, "C9 lianmeng gaoxiao
    mingdan" [China Academic Degrees & Graduate Education Information,
    List of 'C9 Alliance' Universities], https://www.cdgdc.edu.cn/xwyyjsjyxx
    /xwsytjxx/yxmd/274942.shtml, accessed January 19, 2021.
65. Guowuyuan, "Guifan xiao ban qiye guanli tizhi zhongdian wenti de tongzhi"
    [State Council, Notice of Standardizing Issues of School-Run Enterprise
    Management System], November 1, 2001, http://www.gov.cn/zhengce
    /content/2012-12/14/content_5832.htm.
66. "Difang putong benke gaoxiao xiang yingyong xing zhuanbian de zhidao
    yijian" [Opinions on Guiding Some Local General Undergraduate Colleges
    and Universities to Transform into Application-Oriented Institutions],
    Zhonghua renmin gongheguo jiaoyubu [Ministry of Education of the
    People's Republic of China], October 23, 2015, http://www.moe.gov.cn
    /srcsite/A03/moe_1892/moe_630/201511/t20151113_218942.html.
67. Yao Li et al., "The Higher Educational Transformation of China and Its
    Global Implications," 19–21.
68. dxsbb.com [College Student's Essential Network], "2020 nian Qinghua
    daxue xuefei shi duoshao? Ge zhuanye shoufei biaozhun" [How Much Is the
    Tuition Fee of Tsinghua University in 2020? Fee Standards for Each Major],
    September 9, 2020, https://m.dxsbb.com/news/52163.html; Zhejiang daxue
    chengshi xueyuan, "Zhejiang daxue chengshi xueyuan 2020 nian xuefei shi
    duoshao? Shoufei biaozhun" [City College of Zhejiang University, How
    Much Is the Tuition Fee of City College of Zhejiang University in 2020?
    Fee Standards], January 14, 2020, https://www.szedu.com/data/r264225/;
    Daxuesheng bi bei wang, "Xi'an guoji daxue 2020 nian xue zafei shi duo-
    shao? Ge zhuanye shoufei biaozhun" [College Student's Essential Net,
    How Much Are Annual Tuition and Fees for Xi'an International University

in 2020? Fee Standards for Each Major], September 16, 2020, https://m
.dxsbb.com/news/56603.html; "Xuefei he jiangxuejin" [Tuition and Scholar-
ships], NYU Shanghai, https://shanghai.nyu.edu/cn/zsb/cost, accessed January 19, 2021.

69. Shanghai shi zhengfu, "2018 nian shanghai keji daxue yusuan an" [Shanghai
Municipal Government, ShanghaiTech Budget 2018], http://www.shanghai
.gov.cn/Attach/Attaches/201802/201802131116415044.pdf, accessed March
2019.

70. Sheng Yunlong, "Qinghua daxue jiaoshi xueli yu xue yuan jiegou de bianqia"
[Changes to Tsinghua University's Teaching Qualifications and Structure],
Tsinghua daxue jiaoyu yanjiu [Tsinghua Journal of Education] 29, no. 2
(April 2008): 92–98.

71. Ibid.

72. Lin Jie, "Zhong Mei liang guo daxue jiaoshi jinqin fanzhi zhi bijiao"
[Comparison of "Inbreeding" between Chinese and American University
Teachers], *Gaodeng jiaoyu yanjiu* [Higher Education Research] 30, no. 12
(December 2009): 39–51.

73. Guojia waiguo zhuanjia ju, "Gongzuo Zhongguo zhaopin waiguo zhuanjia
jihua: 1000 ren gao cengci waiguo zhuanjia rencai jihua" [State Administration of Foreign Expert Affairs, Work China Recruitment Program of
Foreign Experts: 1000 Talent Plan for High-Level Foreign Experts], http://
1000plan.safea.gov.cn/index.php?s=Cont&id=12742321, accessed August 28,
2015; Liz Gooch, "Chinese Universities Send Big Signals to Foreigners,"
New York Times, March 11, 2012, http://www.nytimes.com/2012/03/12/world
/asia/12iht-educlede12.html, accessed August 28, 2015.

74. Gooch, "Chinese Universities Send Big Signals to Foreigners."

75. Sharon LaFraniere, "Fighting Trend, China Is Luring Scientists Home,"
New York Times, January 6, 2010, http://www.nytimes.com/2010/01/07
/world/asia/07scholar.html, accessed August 28, 2015.

76. Kai Yu, *Diversification to a Degree: An Exploratory Study of Students' Experi-
ence at Four Higher Education Institutions in China* (Bern, Switzerland: Peter
Lang, 2010), 62, https://books.google.com/books?id=6VZHgCf3SEoC&pg
=PA62&lpg=PA62#v=onepage&q&f=false, accessed August 27, 2015.

77. Yiqun Fu, "Gaokao Statistics 2014," *TeaLeaf Nation*, https://docs.google
.com/spreadsheets/d/1XgT5uoO31m5gPnPXRpAQfc26LIlJHDCrhsl6a
sgm-WM/edit#gid=0, accessed August 28, 2015.

78. Kong Defang and Yao Chun, "China to Overhaul Exam, Enrollment
System by 2020," *People's Daily Online*, September 4, 2014, http://en.people
.cn/n/2014/0904/c90882-8778889.html, accessed August 28, 2015; Song
Rongrong, "Wo guo gaokao zhidu gaige shi da yaodian" [Ten key points
of China's college entrance examination system reform], *IFeng Talk*, September 4, 2014, http://edu.ifeng.com/a/20140904/40787450_0.shtml, accessed
August 28, 2015.

79. Kirby et al., "Kunshan, Incorporated."

80. "MOE closes 234 Chinese-Foreign Joint Education Institutions and Programs," Ministry of Education of the People's Republic of China, July 5, 2018, http://en.moe.gov.cn/News/Top_News/201807/t20180710_342467.html; Emily Feng, "China Closes a Fifth of Foreign University Partnerships," *Financial Times*, July 17, 2018, https://www.ft.com/content/794b77e8-8976-11e8-bf9e-8771d5404543.

81. "Jiaoyubu jiedu Zhongguo zhongyang, guowuyuan 'Zhongguo jiaoyu xiandaihua 2035' he 'shishi fang'an'" [Ministry of Education Statement on the 'China Education Modernization 2035' and 'Implementation Plan' of the Central Committee of the Communist Party of China and the State Council (with full text)], *Sohu*, February 24, 2019, https://www.sohu.com/a/297290631_473325.

82. "More Chinese Study Abroad in 2018," Ministry of Education of the People's Republic of China, March 28, 2009, http://en.moe.gov.cn/news/media_highlights/201904/t20190401_376249.html.

83. "Georgia on Their Minds," *The Economist*, February 21, 2015, https://www.economist.com/china/2015/02/19/georgia-on-their-minds, accessed August 28, 2015; Institute of International Education, "International Student Totals by Place of Origin," https://www.iie.org/Research-and-Insights/Open-Doors/Data/International-Students/Places-of-Origin, accessed May 12, 2020.

84. "The Unveiling Ceremony of the China-Italy Design Innovation Hub and the Tsinghua Arts and Design Institute in Milan," Tsinghua University, https://goglobal.tsinghua.edu.cn/en/news/news.en/lgR56myTb, accessed October 9, 2019.

85. "Ground-Breaking of the Tsinghua Southeast Asia Center in Indonesia," Tsinghua University, http://eng.pbcsf.tsinghua.edu.cn/portal/article/index/id/1421.html, accessed October 9, 2019.

86. Coco Liu, "Belt and Read: How China Is Exporting Education and Influence to Malaysia and Other Asean Countries," *South China Morning Post*, July 30, 2017, https://www.scmp.com/week-asia/politics/article/2097965/belt-road-and-books-how-chinas-trying-soft-power-outreach.

87. "Hungary Agrees to Open Chinese University Campus in Budapest by 2024," *Euronews*, February 5, 2021, https://www.euronews.com/2021/05/02/hungary-agrees-to-open-chinese-university-campus-in-budapest-by-2024.

88. *Times Higher Education World University Rankings*, 2020, https://www.timeshighereducation.co.uk/world-university-rankings/, accessed May 12, 2020; Academic Ranking of World Universities, "Academic Ranking of World Universities 2018," http://www.shanghairanking.com/ARWU2018.html, accessed January 19, 2021; QS Top Universities, "QS World University Rankings 2021," https://www.topuniversities.com/university-rankings/world-university-rankings/2021.

89. Calculated based on data from "Double First-Class University and Discipline List Policy Update," Australian Government, Department of Educa-

tion, Skills and Employment (December 14, 2017), https://international
education.gov.au/International-network/china/PolicyUpdates-China/Pages
/Double-First-Class-university-and-discipline-list-policy-update.aspx, accessed March 2018.

90. Zhonghua renmin gongheguo zhongyang zhengfu, "Guojia zhong chang qi
jiaoyu gaige he fazhan guihua gangyao (2010–2020 nian)" [The Central
Government of the People's Republic of China, Outline of the National
Medium and Long-Term Education Reform and Development Plan (2010–
2020)], July 29, 2010, https://www.gov.cn/jrzg/2010-07/29/content_1667143
.htm.

91. dxsbb.com [College Student's Essential Network], "How Much Is the Tuition
Fee of Tsinghua University in 2020? Fee Standards for Each Major," Sep-
tember 9, 2020, https://m.dxsbb.com/news/52163.html; City College of
Zhejiang University, "How Much Is the Tuition Fee of City College of
Zhejiang University in 2020? Fee Standards," January 14, 2020,
https://www.szedu.com/data/r264225/, accessed January 19, 2021; College
Student's Essential Network, "How Much Are Annual Tuition and Fees
for Xi'an International University in 2020? Fee Standards for Each Major,"
September 16, 2020, https://m.dxsbb.com/news/56603.html, accessed January 19, 2021; "Tuition and Scholarships," NYU Shanghai, https://shanghai
.nyu.edu/cn/zsb/cost, accessed January 19, 2021.

92. "Annual Per Capita Disposable Income of Rural and Urban Households in
China 1990–2019," *Statista,* November 20, 2020, https://www.statista.com
/statistics/259451/annual-per-capita-disposable-income-of-rural-and-urban
-households-in-china/.

93. Zhongguo jiaoyu zai xian [China Education Online], June 9, 2020, https://
news.eol.cn/xueshu/202006/t20200609_1732373.shtml.

94. "Zhongguo gaodeng jiaoyu jinru pujihua shidai" [China's Higher Education
Has Entered the Era of Popularization], *Xinhua,* October 13, 2020,
http://www.xinhuanet.com/politics/2020-10/13/c_1126597896.htm.

95. Tom Mitchell, "China University Rule Change Sparks Protests in 4 Provinces," *Financial Times,* May 23, 2016, http://www.ft.com/intl/cms/s/0
/6a6c8b18-20be-11e6-aa98-db1e01fabc0c.html#axzz4AXbTFtYk, accessed
June 3, 2016.

96. "Ge ji xuexiao shaoshu minzu xuesheng renshu" [Number of Minority Students in Schools of All Levels], Zhonghua renmin gongheguo jiaoyubu
[Ministry of Education of the People's Republic of China], 2010, http://
www.moe.gov.cn/s78/A03/moe_560/s6200/201201/t20120117_129611
.html.

97. "Ge ji xuexiao shaoshu minzu xuesheng renshu" [Number of Minority Students
in Schools of All Levels], Zhonghua renmin gonghequo jiaoyubu [Ministry
of Education of the People's Republic of China], 2020, http://www.moe.gov
.cn/s78/A03/moe_560/jytjsj_2019/qg/202006/t20200611_464796.html;
"Zhonghua renmin gongheguo 2010 nian renkou pucha," Zhongguo tongji

chuban she [2010 Population Census of the People's Republic of China, China Statistics Press], http://www.stats.gov.cn/tjsj/pcsj/rkpc/6rp/indexch .htm.

98. Qinghua daxue, "2019–2020 xuenian benke jiaoyu zhiliang baogao" [Tsinghua University, 2019–2020 Academic Year Undergraduate Education Quality Report], December 2020, https://www.tsinghua.edu.cn/__local/C/24 /2D/B7896456DF4989A6A6CF192E2D1_515D4FF2_1B3A98.pdf; "939 suo gaozhong, 4,326 ren Beijing daxue 2020 nian luqu qingkuang ji shengyuan jiegou fenxi" [939 High Schools and 4,326 Students: A Structural Analysis of Peking University's 2020 Admissions Decisions and Accepted Students], September 2, 2020, http://m.mxzzzs.com/news/104886.html.

99. "Ge ji xuexiao shaoshu minzu xuesheng renshu," 2020.

100. Association of American Universities, "Hefei Statement on the Ten Characteristics of Contemporary Research Universities," https://www.aau.edu/sites /default/files/AAU%20Files/Education%20and%20Service/Hefei_statement .pdf.

101. "Document 9: A ChinaFile Translation," ChinaFile, November 8, 2013, https://www.chinafile.com/document-9-chinafile-translation.

102. Zhu Shanlu, "Yi peiyu he hongyang shehuizhuyi hexin jiazhiguan wei yinling zhashi zhua hao xin xingshi xia gaoxiao xuanchuan sixiang gongzuo" [Guided by the cultivation and promotion of core socialist values, begin incorporating propaganda and ideology into colleges and universities], *Zhongguo jiaoyu xinwen wang* [China Education News Online], Zhonghua renmin gongheguo jiaoyubu [Ministry of Education of the People's Republic of China], February 3, 2015, http://paper.jyb.cn /zgjyb/html/2015-02/03/content_430445.htm?div=-1, accessed September 10, 2015, trans. Joycelyn Eby.

103. "Xin shidai gaoxiao jiaoshi zhiye xingwei shi xiang zhunze" [Ten Guidelines on Professional Behavior of College Teachers in the New Era], *Zhongguo jiaoyu xinwen wang* [China Education News Online], Zhonghua renmin gongheguo jiaoyubu [Ministry of Education of the People's Republic of China], November 14, 2018, http://www.moe.gov.cn/srcsite/A10/s7002 /201811/t20181115_354921.html.

104. Emily Feng, "Chinese Universities Are Enshrining Communist Party Control in Their Charters," NPR, January 20, 2020, https://www.npr.org/2020 /01/20/796377204/chinese-universities-are-enshrining-communist-party -control-in-their-charters.

105. Philip Wen, "Demand for Absolute Loyalty to Beijing at Chinese Universities Triggers Dissent," *Wall Street Journal*, December 18, 2019, https://www .wsj.com/articles/demand-for-absolute-loyalty-to-beijing-at-chinese-univer sities-triggers-dissent-11576674047?mod=article_inline/.

106. White House, "President Donald J. Trump Is Protecting America from China's Efforts to Steal Technology and Intellectual Property," May 29, 2020, https://www.whitehouse.gov/briefings-statements/president-donald-j-trump -protecting-america-chinas-efforts-steal-technology-intellectual-property/.

107. Emily Feng, "As U.S. Revokes Chinese Students' Visas, Concerns Rise About Loss of Research Talent," NPR, September 23, 2020, https://www .npr.org/2020/09/23/915939365/critics-question-u-s-decision-to-revoke -chinese-students-visas.

9. From Preparatory Academy to National Flagship

1. Keith Bradscher, "$300 Million Scholarship for Study in China Signals a New Focus," *New York Times,* April 21, 2013; and "Oxford and the Rhodes Scholarship," http://www.rhodesscholar.org, accessed June 2013.

2. Edmund J. James, "Memorandum Concerning the Sending of an Educational Commission to China" (1907), cited in Mary Brown Bullock, "American Exchanges with China, Revisited," in *Educational Exchanges: Essays on the Sino-American Experiences,* Joyce K. Kallgren and Denis Fred Simon, eds. (Berkeley: Institute of East Asian Studies, 1987), 26.

3. Su-Yan Pan, *University Autonomy, the State, and Social Change in China* (Hong Kong: Hong Kong University Press, 2009), 71.

4. Qinghua daxue xiaoshi yanjiushe [Tsinghua University School History Research Office], *Qinghua daxue jiushinian* [Ninety Years of Tsinghua University] (Beijing: Tsinghua University, 2001), 9.

5. Yoshi S. Kuno, *Education Institutions in the Orient with Special Reference to Colleges and Universities in the United States, Part II* (Berkeley: University of California Press, 1928), 55–56.

6. See Wen-hsin Yeh, *The Alienated Academy: Culture and Politics in Republican China, 1919–1937* (Cambridge, MA: Harvard University Asia Center, 1990), 207–210, 224.

7. See Qian Yingyi and Li Qiang, eds., *Lao Qinghua de shehui kexue* [Social Sciences in Old Tsinghua] (Beijing: Qinghua daxue chubanshe, 2011).

8. See John Israel, *Lianda: A Chinese University in War and Revolution* (Stanford: Stanford University Press, 1998).

9. Israel, *Lianda,* 38.

10. See Andrew G. Walder, *Fractured Rebellion: The Beijing Red Guard Movement* (Cambridge, MA: Harvard University Press, 2009).

11. See Tang Shaojie, *Yi ye zhi qiu: Qinghua daxue 1968 nian "bai ri da wudou"* [A Single Leaf Heralds Autumn: Tsinghua University's 1968 "Hundred Days of Great Violence"] (Hong Kong: Zhongwen daxue chubanshe, 2003); and William Hinton, *Hundred Day War: The Cultural Revolution at Tsinghua University* (New York: Monthly Review Press, 1972).

12. "Sanshinian qian de Zhongguo daxue paiming yilan, ni zenme kan? [What Do You Think of the Rankings of Chinese Universities 30 Years Ago?], *Sohu,* May 23, 2020, https://www.sohu.com/a/397252209_523175.

13. See Cheng Li, *China's Leaders: The New Generation* (Lanham, MD: Rowman & Littlefield, 2001), 87–126.

14. James, "Memorandum Concerning the Sending of an Educational Commission to China."

15. QS Top Universities, "QS World University Rankings 2021," https://www
.topuniversities.com/university-rankings/world-university-rankings/2021.

16. "Tongji shuju" [Statistical Data], Tsinghua University, https://www.tsinghua
.edu.cn/xxgk/tjzl.htm.

17. Samuel Eliot Morison, *The Development of Harvard University Since the Inauguration of President Eliot, 1869–1929* (Cambridge, MA: Harvard University
Press, 1930), 329.

18. "Zhonggong Qinghua daxue weiyuanhui guanyu xunshi zhenggai qingkuang" [Tsinghua University Committee of the Communist Party of China
on the Inspection and Rectification], Tsinghua University, August 27, 2017,
http://news.tsinghua.edu.cn/publish/thunews/11062/2017/201708270933
52932836560/20170827093352932836560_.html.

19. "Tsinghua University," University Rankings, https://www.universityrankings
.ch/results?ranking=Times&region=World&year=2011&q=Tsinghua
+University, accessed May 12, 2020; *Times Higher Education World
University Rankings*, "Tsinghua University," https://www.timeshighereducation
.com/world-university-rankings/tsinghua-university, accessed May 12,
2020.

20. Tsinghua University, "Shisanwu fazhan guihua gangyao" [Outline of Development Plan for the Thirteenth Five-Year Plan], July 2016, http://www.moe
.gov.cn/s78/A08/gjs_left/s7187/zsgxgz_sswgh/201703/W0201703103325
81867931.pdf.

21. Ibid.

22. "Keyan jigou" [Scientific Research Institutions], Tsinghua University,
https://www.tsinghua.edu.cn/kxyj/kyjg1.htm, accessed January 19, 2020.

23. Tsinghua University, "Shisanwu fazhan guihua gangyao."

24. "Qinghua daxue 2019–2020 xuenian benke jiaoxue zhiliang baogao"
[Tsinghua University 2019–2020 Academic Year Undergraduate Teaching
Quality Report], Tsinghua University, http://tsinghua.edu.cn/jwc/info/1018
/1072.htm; Sheng Yunlong, "Qinghua daxue jiaoshi xueli yu xueyuan jiegou
de bianqian" [Changes to Tsinghua University's Teaching Qualifications and
Structure], *Tsinghua Journal of Education* 29, no. 2 (April 2008): 92–98.

25. "Shi'erwu fazhan guihua gangyao" [Outline of the Development Plan for
the Twelfth Five-Year Plan], December 2011, Tsinghua University,
https://www.tsinghua.edu.cn/publish/newthu/openness/jbxx/fzgh.htm.

26. Tsinghua University, "Shisanwu fazhan guihua gangyao."

27. Yuan Yang and Nian Liu, "China Hushes Up Scheme to Recruit Overseas
Scientists," *Financial Times,* January 9, 2019, https://www.ft.com/content
/a06f414c-0e6e-11e9-a3aa-118c761d2745.

28. Quanguo gaoxiao sixiang zhengzhi gongzuo wang, "Qinghua Daxue" [Na-
tional University Ideological and Political Work Net, Tsinghua University],
October 28, 2019, http://www.sizhengwang.cn/zt/7102/2019scxmz/sfgx
/2019/1028/2923.shtml.

29. Qian Yingyi, "Daxue renshi zhidu gaige: Yi Qinghua daxue jingji guanli
xueyuan wei li" [Faculty Personnel System Reform: The Case of Tsinghua

University School of Economic and Management], *Qinghua daxue jiaoyu yanjiu* [Tsinghua Journal of Education] 34, no. 2 (April 2013): 1–8.
30. Tsinghua University, "Shisanwu fazhan guihua gangyao."
31. Ibid.
32. Author interview with David Daokui Li, Beijing, March 23, 2015.
33. "2018–2019 xuenian benke jiaoyu zhiliang baogao" [2018–2019 Academic Year Undergraduate Education Quality Report], December 2019, Tsinghua University, https://www.tsinghua.edu.cn/__local/D/51/C4/9C31C0CC9287 C56A7E246B71ED7_32475816_81794.pdf?e=.pdf.
34. "Shijian jiaoxue" [Practical Teaching], Tsinghua University, https://www .tsinghua.edu.cn/publish/newthu/newthu_cnt/education/edu-1-5.html, accessed May 12, 2020.
35. "2018–2019 xuenian jiaoshou benke kecheng zhan bi . . ." [The Proportion of Undergraduate Courses Taught by Professors in the 2018–2019 Academic Year . . .], Tsinghua University, https://www.tsinghua.edu.cn/xxgk/jxzlxx /zjbkkcdjs.htm, accessed January 19, 2021.
36. Li Cao, "The Significance and Practice of General Education in China: The Case of Tsinghua University," in *Experiences in Liberal Arts and Science Education from America, Europe, and Asia: A Dialogue across Continents,* William C. Kirby and Marijk van der Wende, eds. (New York: Palgrave, 2016).
37. "Qinghua daxue 2014–2015 xuenian benke jiaoxue zhiliang baogao" [Tsinghua University 2014–2015 Academic Year Undergraduate Teaching Quality Report], Tsinghua University, https://www.tsinghua.edu.cn/jwc /bkpy/zlbg.htm.
38. Qian Yingyi, *How Reform Worked in China: The Transition from Plan to Market* (Cambridge, MA: MIT Press, 2017); Qing and Li, *Lao Qinghua* [Old Tsinghua].
39. Tsinghua University School of Economics and Management 2013–2014, Tsinghua University brochure (Beijing, 2013), 41.
40. Pan, *University Autonomy*, 183.
41. "Qinghua daxue jiao zhigong daibiao dahui" [Tsinghua University Staff Congress], Tsinghua University, December 2012, http://www.tsinghua.edu .cn/publish/newthu/openness/jbxx/jzgdbdhgd.html.
42. Emily Feng, "China Universities Accused of Ideological Weakness," *Financial Times,* June 19, 2017, https://www.ft.com/content/88191d36-54b4-11e7 -9fed-c19e2700005f.
43. "Qinghua daxue 2019 nian bumen yusuan" [Tsinghua University 2019 Departmental Budgets], Tsinghua University, April 2019, https://www .tsinghua.edu.cn/publish/newthu/openness/cwzcjsfxx/cwyc_2019.htm.
44. "Qinghua daxue 2020 niandu yusuan" [Tsinghua University's Annual Budget 2020], Tsinghua University, https://www.tsinghua.edu.cn/publish /newthu/openness/newsml/cwyc_2020.htm.
45. dxsbb.com [College Student's Essential Network], "2020 nian Qinghua daxue xuefei shi duoshao? Ge zhuanye shoufei biaozhun" [How Much Is the

Tuition Fee of Tsinghua University in 2020? Fee Standards for Each Major], September 9, 2020, https://www.dxsbb.com/news/52163.html.

46. Tsinghua University SEM, "Feiyong he jiangxuejin" [Expenses and Scholarships], http://gmba.sem.tsinghua.edu.cn/content/page/expensesscholarship .html, accessed May 2020.

47. "Tongji shuju" [Statistical Data], Tsinghua University, https://www.tsinghua .edu.cn/publish/newthu/newthu_cnt/about/about-6.html, accessed May 12, 2020; College Student's Essential Network, "How Much Are the Tuition and Fees for Tsinghua University in 2020? Expenses for Each Major," September 9, 2020, https://www.dxsbb.com/news/52163.html.

48. Tsinghua University, "Shisanwu fazhan guihua gangyao."

49. Jun wang, "Qinghua daxue kaishe junmin ronghe gaoduan rencai zhuanxiu ban" [Military Net, Tsinghua University Launches Special Training Class on Military-Civilian Integration of High-End Talents], September 21, 2018, http://military.cnr.cn/zgjq/20180921/t20180921_524366936.html; Elsa B. Kania, "In Military-Civil Fusion, China Is Learning Lessons from the United States and Starting to Innovate," August 27, 2019, https://www .realcleardefense.com/articles/2019/08/27/in_military-civil_fusion_china _is_learning_lessons_from_the_united_states_and_starting_to_innovate _114699.html.

50. Guowuyuan, "Guowuyuan guanyu yinfa Zhongguo zhizao 2025 de tongzhi" [State Council, Notice of the State Council on Printing and Distributing Made in China 2025], May 8, 2015, http://www.gov.cn/zhengce /content/2015-05/19/content_9784.htm.

51. Tsinghua University, "Shisanwu fazhan guihua gangyao."

52. Kexue wang, "Zhongguo zhizao 2025 tian bai yi zijin 25 xiang renwu ruwei" [Science Net, Tens of Billions in Funds for 25 Shortlisted Tasks Available through Made in China 2025], October 12, 2017, http://news .sciencenet.cn/htmlnews/2017/10/390819.shtm.

53. Zhongguo qiche gongye xiehui, "Gongye he xinxi hua bu guanyu fabu 2017 nian gongye zhuanxing shengji (Zhongguo zhizao 2025) zijin (bumen yusuan) xiangmu zhinan de tongzhi" [China Association of Automobile Manufacturers, Notice of the Ministry of Industry and Information Technology on the Issuance of the 2017 Industrial Transformation and Upgrade (Made in China 2025) Funding (Departmental Budget) Project Guidelines], May 24, 2017, http://www.caam.org.cn/policySearch/con_5210981.html.

54. "Qinghua daxue shuju kexue yanjiu suo gongye da shuju yanjiu zhongxin chengli" [Tsinghua University Data Science Research Institute Industrial Big Data Research Center established], Tsinghua University, October 28, 2015, https://news.tsinghua.edu.cn/publish/thunews/9650/2015/2015 102916041690 9874073/20151029160416909874073_.html; "Qinghua daxue 'Zhongguo zhizao 2025' yu 'shisanwu' Zhongguo zhizao qiye fazhan zhanlue di si qi gaoji yanxiu ban" [Tsinghua University's "Made in China 2025" and "Thirteenth Five-Year Plan" for Chinese Manufacturing Enter-

prises' Fourth Advanced Seminar], Tsinghua University, March 16, 2017, http://www.tsinghua-tj.org/news/3376.html; Tsinghua Shenzhen International Graduate School, "Xianjin zhizao xueyuan" [Faculty of Advanced Manufacturing], https://www.sigs.tsinghua.edu.cn/xjzzxb1/index.jhtml, accessed May 12, 2020.

55. Beijing shi haidian qu renmin zhengfu, "2018 Niandu haidian qu min ronghe zhuanti shenqing zhinan [Beijing Haidian District People's Government, 2018 Haidian District Military and Civil Integration Special Fund Application Guide], http://www.bjhd.gov.cn/ztzl2014/zxzt/Afour/sbzn/QYHXJZL /jmhz/201804/t20180417_1504152.htm, accessed May 12, 2020.

56. Qinghai sheng zhengfu, "Qinghai xing renmin zhengfu guanyu yinfa Zhongguo zhizao 2025 Qinghai xingdong fang'an de tongzhi" [Qinghai Provincial Government, Qinghai Provincial People's Government Notice on Printing and Distributing the Made in China 2025 Qinghai Action Plan], June 27, 2016, http://www.maqin.gov.cn/html/3142/241618.html, accessed May 12, 2020; *Tianjin ribao*, "Tianjin zhineng zhizao shuiping buduan tisheng," [Tianjin Daily, Tianjin's Smart Manufacturing Continues to Improve], May 8, 2018, http://www.gov.cn/xinwen/2018-05/08/content _5289067.htm.

57. Tom Holland, "Beijing's 'Made in China 2025' Plan Isn't Dead, It's Out of Control," *South China Morning Post*, April 8, 2019, https://www.scmp.com /week-asia/opinion/article/3004900/beijings-made-china-2025-plan-isnt -dead-its-out-control.

58. Xintangren dianshitai, "Fouren fangqi: Zhonggong guanmei pilu zhizao 2025 jingfei fenpei" [New Tang Dynasty Television, Disclaimer: the Chinese Communist Party's Official Media Disclosure of Funding Plan for Made in China 2025], November 13, 2018, https://www.ntdtv.com/gb/2018 /11/13/a1399033.html.

59. Wanhua Ma, "The Flagship University and China's Economic Reform" in *World Class Worldwide: Transforming Research Universities in Asia and Latin America*, Philip G. Altbach and Jorge Bal, eds. (Baltimore, MD: Johns Hopkins University Press, 2007), 39.

60. Zhang Di, "Qinghua konggu 'da shoushen': zichan die po wuqian yi gaige shangwei wancheng" [Tsinghua Holdings 'Slims Down': Assets Fall Below 500 Billion, Reform Has Not Been Completed], *Zhongguo jingying wang* [China Business Net], May 26, 2020, http://www.cb.com.cn/index/show/zj _m/cv/cv13487671267.

61. Tsinghua Holdings, "2019 caifu Zhongguo 500 qiang: Qinghua konggu lianxu liunian wen ju jisuanji hangye qian san" [2019 Fortune China's Top 500: Tsinghua Holdings Co., Ltd. Has Steadily Improved Its Ranking for Six Consecutive Years, Ranking Top 3 in the Computer Industry], July 15, 2019, https://www.thholding.com.cn/news/show/contentid/2847.html.

62. "Zhonggong Qinghua daxue jilu jiancha weiyuanhui" [Tsinghua University Committee of the Communist Party of China for Discipline and

Inspection], August 27, 2017, http://news.tsinghua.edu.cn/publish/thunews /11062/2017/20170827093352932836560/20170827093352932836560_.html.

63. "Xi Stresses Coordinated Efforts in Central, Local Institutional Reform," *Xinhua*, May 12, 2018, http://www.xinhuanet.com/english/2018-05/12/c _137172840.htm.

64. Yan Sun, "Qinghua daxue jiaoyu jijinhui cheng licai gaoshou" [Tsinghua University Education Foundation Becomes a Financial Expert], *CNTV Online*, October 19, 2010, http://igongyi.cntv.cn/20101019/100856.shtml, accessed October 2014; Qinghua daxue jiaoyu jijinhui, "Qinghua daxue jiaoyu jijin weiyuanhui 2018 nian gongzuo baogao" [Tsinghua University Education Fund Committee 2018 Work Report], March 25, 2019, http://www .tuef.tsinghua.edu.cn/sites/pdf/infomation/2018ndgzbg.pdf.

65. Tsinghua University Education Fund, "Qinghua daxue jiaoyu jijin weiyuanhui 2018 nian gongzuo baogao."

66. Ibid.

67. "Gaoxiao ju'e juanzeng bian shaole: hou yiqing shidai, gaoxiao yaoguo jin rizi? [Huge Donations to Colleges and Universities Have Decreased: In the Post-Epidemic Era, Do Colleges and Universities Have to Live a Tight Life?], *Sohu*, December 17, 2020, https://www.sohu.com/a/438929037_608848.

68. Author interview with Qian Yingyi, Beijing, March 23, 2015.

69. Author interview with David Daokui Li, March 23, 2015.

70. Ibid.

71. William C. Kirby, Joycelyn W. Eby, Yuanzhuo Wang, "Higher Education in China: Internationalization in Turbulent Times," Case 316-066 (Boston: Harvard Business School, 2019), 8.

72. Kirby, Eby, and Wang, "Higher Education in China," 22.

73. Zhongguo guojia tongji ju, "yanjiusheng he liuxue renyuan tongji" [National Bureau of Statistics of China, "Statistics on Postgraduates and Students Studying Abroad"], *China Statistical Yearbook 2019*, http://www.stats.gov.cn /tjsj/ndsj/2019/indexeh.htm; Gao Hongmei, Hu Yiwei, Zhao Hong, Zhao Lei, "Qi zhang tu zhu ni liaojie Zhongguo gaokao" [Seven Charts to Help You Understand China's Gaokao (National College Entrance Exam)], CGTN, June 8, 2018, https://news.cgtn.com/news/3d3d414f776b544f7745 7a6333566d54/share_p.html.

74. Alexis Lai, "Chinese Flock to Elite U.S. Schools," CNN, November 26, 2012, https://www.cnn.com/2012/11/25/world/asia/china-ivy-league -admission/index.html.

75. Laurent Ortmans, "What the 2015 Executive MBA Survey Reveals," *Financial Times*, October 18, 2015, https://www.ft.com/content/14c11226 -570e-11e5-9846-de406ccb37f2; "Global MBA Ranking 2015," *Financial Times*, http://rankings.ft.com/businessschoolrankings/global-mba-ranking -2015.

76. Australian Government, Department of Education, Skills and Employment, "Double First-Class University and Discipline List Policy Update,"

December 14, 2017, https://internationaleducation.gov.au/International
-network/china/PolicyUpdates-China/Pages/Double-First-Class-university
-and-discipline-list-policy-update.aspx.

77. Kirby, Eby, and Wang, "Higher Education in China," 22.

78. "President Qiu Yong Visited the School of Humanities," Tsinghua University, April 1, 2015, https://news.tsinghua.edu.cn/info/1006/52325.htm.

79. CWTS Leiden Ranking, "CWTS Leiden Ranking 2020," https://www
.leidenranking.com/ranking/2020/list, accessed January 19, 2021.

80. "Zhonggong Qinghua daxue jilu jiancha weiyuanhui."

81. Kathrin Hille and Richard Waters, "Washington Unnerved by China's 'Military-Civil Fusion,'" *Financial Times,* November 8, 2018, https://www.ft
.com/content/8dcb534c-dbaf-11e8-9f04-38d397e6661c; Elsa B. Kania, "In Military-Civil Fusion, China Is Learning Lessons from the United States and Starting to Innovate."

82. Permanent Subcommittee on Investigations of the United States Senate, "Threats to the U.S. Research Enterprise: China's Talent Recruitment Plans," November 18, 2019, https://www.hsgac.senate.gov/imo/media/doc
/2019-11-18%20PSI%20Staff%20Report%20-%20China's%20Talent%20
Recruitment%20Plans.pdf.

83. U.S.-China Economic and Security Review Commission, *Technology, Trade, and Military-Civil Fusion: China's Pursuit of Artificial Intelligence, New Materials, and New Energy,* 116th Cong., 1st sess., 2019, https://www.uscc.gov
/sites/default/files/2019-10/June%207,%202019%20Hearing%20Transcript
.pdf.

84. Geremie R. Barmé, "Xu Zhangrun's Fears and Hopes, July 2018–July 2020," *China Heritage,* July 26, 2020, https://chinaheritage.net/journal/xu-zhangruns
-fears-hopes-july-2018-july-2020/.

85. Chris Buckley, "Seized by the Police, an Outspoken Chinese Professor Sees Fears Come True," *New York Times,* July 6, 2020, https://www.nytimes.com
/2020/07/06/world/asia/china-detains-xu-zhangrun-critic.html?smid=em
-share.

86. Geremie R. Barmé, "Remonstrating with Beijing—Xu Zhangrun's Advice to China's National People's Congress," *China Heritage,* May 21, 2020, http://chinaheritage.net/journal/remonstrating-with-beijing-xu-zhangruns
-advice-to-chinas-national-peoples-congress-21-may-2020/.

87. Josephine Ma and Guo Rui, "Chinese Professor Known for Challenging the Party Leadership Sacked by University," *South China Morning Post,* July 18, 2020, https://www.scmp.com/news/china/politics/article/3093769/chinese
-professor-known-challenging-party-leadership-sacked; Zhonghua renmin gongheguo jiaoyubu, "Jiaoyu bu yinfa xin shidai gaoxiao jiaoshi zhiye xingwei 'xin shidai zhong xiaoxue jiaoshi zhiye xingwei shi xiang zhidao yijian'" [Ministry of Education of the People's Republic of China, Ministry of Education on Printing and Distributing the Professional Behavior of College Teachers in the New Era: Ten Guidelines for the "Professional Behavior of

Primary and Secondary School Teachers in the New Era"], November 14, 2018, http://www.moe.gov.cn/srcsite/A10/s7002/201811/t20181115_354921 .html.

88. Geremie R. Barmé, "Responding to a Gesture of Support—Xu Zhangrun," *China Heritage,* July 19, 2020, http://chinaheritage.net/journal/responding -to-a-gesture-of-support-xu-zhangrun/.

89. "Tongji Shuju" [Statistical Data], Tsinghua University, https://www.tsinghua .edu.cn/xxgk/tjzl.htm.

90. "2018–2019 Academic Year Undergraduate Education Quality Report," Tsinghua University, December 2019, https://www.tsinghua.edu.cn/__local /D/51/C4/9C31C0CC9287C56A7E246B71ED7_32475816_81794.pdf?e= .pdf.

91. Karen Rhodes, "UC Berkeley and Tsinghua University Launch Research and Graduate Education Partnership," *Berkeley News,* September 6, 2014, http:// news.berkeley.edu/2014/09/06/uc-berkeley-and-tsinghua-university-launch -research-and-graduate-education-partnership/, accessed July 20, 2015.

92. Nick Wingfield, "University of Washington and Chinese University Unite to Form Technology Institute," *New York Times,* June 18, 2015, http://www .nytimes.com/2015/06/19/business/university-of-washington-and-chinese -university-unite-to-form-technology-institute.html, accessed July 20, 2015.

93. Zhonghua renmin gongheguo jiaoyubu, "Jiaoyubu guanyu yinfa tuijin gong jian yidai yilu jiaoyu xingdong fang'an de tongzhi" [Ministry of Education of the People's Republic of China, Notice of the Ministry of Education on Printing and Distributing the Education Action Plan for Promoting the Belt and Road Initiative], July 15, 2016, http://www.moe.gov.cn/srcsite/A20 /s7068/201608/t20160811_274679.html.

94. Tsinghua University, "Shisanwu fazhan guihua gangyao."

95. Beijing Net, "Qinghua daxue quanqiu gongtong fazhan yanjiuyuan ruxuan 'yidai yilu' yanjiu tese zhiku" [Tsinghua University Global Common Devel- opment Institute Selected as a Special Think-Tank for "Belt and Road" Re- search], November 18, 2019, https://www.yidianzixun.com/article/0Nob AQ9l?s; Tsinghua University, "Qinghua daxue juban di si jie 'yidai yilu' dawosi luntan" [Tsinghua University Holds the Fourth "Belt and Road" Davos Forum], January 23, 2020, http://news.tsinghua.edu.cn/publish/thunews /10303/2020/20200123162907289119592/20200123162907289119592_ .html; Tsinghua University, "Yidai yilu" guoji gonggong guanli shuoshi (IMPA-BRI) xiangmu 2020 nian zhoasheng jianzhang" [Belt and Road International Master of Public Administration (IMPA-BRI) project 2020 Admissions Guide], http://www.sppm.tsinghua.edu.cn/xwjy/IMPABRI/, accessed May 12, 2020.

96. Eva Dou, "Who is Tsinghua Unigroup, the Firm Preparing a $23 Billion Bid for Micron," *Wall Street Journal blog,* July 14, 2015, http://blogs.wsj.com /digits/2015/07/14/who-is-tsinghua-unigroup-the-firm-preparing-a-23 -billion-bid-for-micron/, accessed July 17, 2015; Paul Mozur and Quentin

Hardy, "Micron Technology Is Said to Be Takeover Target of Chinese Company," *New York Times,* July 14, 2015, http://www.nytimes.com/2015 /07/15/business/international/micron-technology-is-said-to-be-takeover -target-of-chinese-company.html, accessed July 17, 2015; John Kang, "Why China Wants U.S. Memory Chip Technology—And What Washington Is Doing About It," December 6, 2016, https://www.forbes.com/sites/johnkang /2016/12/06/china-beijing-u-s-washington-memory-chip-semiconductor -technology/#7fd7305a46f9.

97. Stephen A. Schwarzman, *What It Takes: Lessons in the Pursuit of Excellence* (New York: Avid Reader Press, 2019), 291.

98. Keith Bradsher, "$300 Million Scholarship for Study in China Signals a New Focus," *New York Times,* April 20, 2013, http://www.nytimes.com /2013/04/21/world/asia/us-financier-backs-china-scholarship-program .html, accessed July 20, 2015.

99. "Qinghua daxue 2020 nian bumen yusuan" [Tsinghua University 2020 Departmental Budget], Tsinghua University, July 2020, https://www.tsinghua .edu.cn/publish/newthu/openness/newsml/cwyc_2020.htm.

10. The Burden of History

1. William C. Kirby, "Engineers and the State in Modern China," in William P. Alford, Kenneth Winston, and William C. Kirby, eds., *Prospects for the Professions in China* (New York: Routledge, 2011), 286–287. Also see Charles D. Musgrove, *China's Contested Capital: Architecture, Ritual and Response in Nanjing* (Honolulu: University of Hawaii Press, 2013).

2. This section draws heavily on Wang Dezi, ed., *Nanjing daxueshi* [History of Nanjing University] (Nanjing: Nanjing daxue chubanshi, 1992) and Wang Dezi, Gong Fang, and Mao Rong, eds., *Nanjing daxue bainian shi* [One-Hundred Year History of Nanjing University] (Nanjing: Nanjing daxue chubanshi, 2002).

3. Wang, Gong, and Mao, *Nanjing daxue bainian shi,* 53.

4. Guy S. Alitto, *The Last Confucian: Liang Shu-ming and the Chinese Dilemma of Modernity* (Berkeley: University of California Press, 1979), 6–7; Laurence Schneider, "National Essence and the New Intelligentsia," in Charlotte Furth, ed., *The Limits of Change: Essays on Conservative Alternatives in Republican China* (Cambridge, MA: Harvard University Press, 1976), 58–75, *passim.* Description of Xueheng scholars from Schneider, 73.

5. Wang, *Nanjing daxueshi,* 134.

6. See William C. Kirby, *Germany and Republican China* (Stanford: Stanford University Press, 1984).

7. See Wen-hsin Yeh, *The Alienated Academy* (Cambridge, MA: Harvard University Asia Center, 1990), 179, and chap. 5, *passim.*

8. Robert Lawrence Kuhn, *The Man Who Changed China: The Life and Legacy of Jiang Zemin* (New York: Crown Publishers, 2004), 42.

9. See Augustus S. Downing, "Report on Higher Education for the School Year 1918–19," in *Sixteenth Annual Report of the Education Department: University of the State of New York, Volume III* (Albany: University of the State of New York and State Department of Education, 1919), 60–66, https://books.google.com/books?id=CdpJAQAAMAAJ&lpg=PA190&ots=jw3g2a YwjX&dq=new%20york%20state%20department%20of%20education%20 university%20of%20nanking&pg=PA62#v=onepage&q=nanking&f=false, accessed November 19, 2015.

10. Ibid, 63.

11. Wang, *Nanjing daxueshi*, 466–468.

12. Wang, *Nanjing daxueshi*, 476–477.

13. Yoshi S. Kuno, *Educational Institutions in the Orient with Special Reference to Colleges and Universities in the United States, Part II* (Berkeley: University of California, 1928); Wang Dezi, *Nanjing daxueshi*, 480.

14. Wang, *Nanjing daxueshi*, 498.

15. Mrs. Lawrence Thurston and Ruth M. Chester, *Ginling College* (New York: United Board for Christian Colleges in China, 1955), 2–3; Downing, "Report on Higher Education," 61–62, 71–74.

16. Ellen Widmer, "The Seven Sisters and China, 1900–1950," in *China's Christian Colleges: Cross-Cultural Connections, 1900–1950*, Daniel H. Bays and Ellen Widmer, eds. (Stanford: Stanford University Press, 2009), 88.

17. Hua Ling Hu, *American Goddess at the Rape of Nanking: The Courage of Minnie Vautrin* (Carbondale: Southern Illinois University Press, 2000).

18. Thurston and Chester, *Ginling College*, 135.

19. See Jun Li, Jing Lin, and Fang Gong, "Nanjing University: Redeeming the Past by Academic Merit," in Ruth Hayhoe, Jun Li, Jing Lin, and Qiang Zha, *Portraits of 21st Century Chinese Universities: In the Move to Mass Higher Education* (Dordrecht, NL: Springer, 2011), 135–136.

20. Widmer, "The Seven Sisters and China," 94.

21. Wang, Gong, and Mao, *Nanjing daxue bainian shi*, 305.

22. "Nanjing daxue jiu chu fan dang fan shehuizhuyi de fangeming fenzi Kuang Yaming. Jiangsu sheng wei jueding chexiao Kuang Yaming yiqie zhiwu, shoudao relie yonghu" [Nanjing University Uncovered Kuang Yaming as an Anti-Party and Anti-Socialist Counter-Revolutionary. The Jiangsu Provincial Party Committee's Decision to Remove Kuang Yaming from All Positions was Warmly Supported], *Renmin ribao* [People's Daily], June 16, 1966, http://www.morningsun.org/chinese/library/19660616.html.

23. A superb source on Nanda during the early stages of the Cultural Revolution is Dong Guoqian and Andrew G. Walder, "Factions in a Bureaucratic Setting: The Origins of Cultural Revolution Conflict in Nanjing," *The China Journal*, no. 65 (Jan. 2011), 1–25, esp. 11–18.

24. Li, Lin, and Fang, "Nanjing University," 137–138.

25. See Zhang Xianwen, *Zhonghua minguo shigang* [Outline History of the Republic of China] (Zhengshou: Henan renmin chubanshe, 1985).

26. Guido Samarani, "Studies on the History of Republican China in the PRC and the Nanjing Research Center," *Revue Bibliographique de Sinologie*, 14 (1996): 153–158.

27. Norton Wheeler, "Educational Exchange in Post-Mao U.S.-China Relations: The Hopkins-Nanjing Center," *The Journal of American-East Asian Relations* 17, no. 1 (2010): 56–88, http://www.jstor.org/stable/23613332.

28. Maria Blackburn, "Professor Chien, Diplomat," *Johns Hopkins Magazine*, June 10, 1986, https://pages.jh.edu/jhumag/0607web/chien.html.

29. Katie Pearce, "Trailblazing Chinese-American Grad Program Celebrates 30 Years in Nanjing," Johns Hopkins University, June 2016, http://hub.jhu .edu/2016/06/16/hopkins-nanjing-center-30th-anniversary, accessed October 2016.

30. Mira Sorvino, "Anti-Africanism in China: An Investigation into Chinese Attitudes toward Black Students in the PRC" (Undergraduate Honors Thesis, Department of East Asian Languages and Civilizations, Harvard College, December 1989).

31. Maria Blackburn, "Professor Chien, Diplomat."

32. Li, Lin, and Fang, "Nanjing University," 139–140.

33. "'211 gongcheng' he '985 gongcheng' yuan yu '835 jianyi'" ['Project 211' and 'Project 985' Originated from '835 Suggestions'], *Zhongguo Jiangsu wang* [Jiangsu Net], October 11, 2019, http://www.jiangsucc.com/5703-1.html.

34. Ibid.

35. "Dailing Nanjing daxue chengwei guonei dingjian gaoxiao de qian Nanda xiaozhang—Qu Qinyue [The President Who Led Nanjing University to Be at the Apex of Domestic Universities—Qu Qinyue], *Nanjing daxue xiaoyou wang* [Nanjing University Alumni Net], September 9, 2020, https://alumni .nju.edu.cn/8b/02/c21703a494338/pagem.htm.

36. *Nanjing daxue nianjian 1999* [Nanjing University 1999 Yearbook] (Nanjing: Nanjing daxue chubanshe, 2000), 10–21.

37. Naomi Ching, "Fame Is Fortune in Sino-science," *Nautilus*, September 19, 2013, https://nautil.us/issue/5/fame/fame-is-fortune-in-sino_science.

38. As quoted in Li, Lin, and Fang, "Nanjing University," 141.

39. Jun Li, et al., "Nanjing University," 142; Zhongguo tongji nianjian 2006 he 1991 [China Statistical Yearbook for 2006 and 1991], http://tongji.cnki.net /overseas/engnavi/YearBook.aspx?id=N2005120321&floor=1### and http://www.stats.gov.cn/tjsj/ndsj/2006/indexeh.htm; http://xiaoban.nju.edu .cn/687/list.htm.

40. Nanjing daxue, "Shisanwu fazhan guihua" [Nanjing University, 13th Five-Year Development Plan], July 2016, 12, http://webcache.googleusercontent .com/search?q=cache:udOp7NP9pk8J:fzghc.bnu.edu.cn/docs/2018112017 0123477926.pdf+&cd=1&hl=en&ct=clnk&gl=us.

41. Nanjing daxue, "Yiliu daxue jianshe guihua" [Nanjing University, World-Class University Development Plan], December 26, 2017, https://webcache .googleusercontent.com/search?q=cache:x7oX2S5vVtcJ:https://xkb.nju.edu

.cn/_upload/article/files/72/cf/56c3661c41d1b7bd0eceb2fd6d57/e27d8fad
-5d2d-4020-9b62-b1651aebea01.pdf+&cd=2&hl=en&ct=clnk&gl=us.

42. Ibid.

43. "School Profile," Kuang Yaming Honors School, Nanjing University,
https://dii.nju.edu.cn/kym_en.

44. Nanjing daxue, "Yiliu daxue jianshe guihua."

45. Li, Lin, and Fang, "Nanjing University," 152.

46. Nanjing daxue, "Shisanwu fazhan guihua."

47. Manhan Education, "Nanjing daxue 2019–2020 nian jiaoyan gangwei
rencai yinjin yu zhaopin jihua" [Nanjing University's 2019–2020 Teaching
and Research Post Talent Introduction and Recruitment Plan], *Zhihu*,
July 24, 2019, https://zhuanlan.zhihu.com/p/75070993.

48. Nanjing daxue xinwen wang, "Nanjing daxue qidong xin yi lun 'shandi
rencai zhichi jihua,' xuanba qingnian rencai ke xiangshou youdai" [Nanjing
University News Net, Nanjing University Has Launched a New Round of
"Mountain Talent Support Plan" and Selected Young Talents Can Enjoy
Preferential Treatment], Beijing Zhong Gong Education, May 15, 2018,
http://bj.offcn.com/html/2018/05/131161.html.

49. Author interview with Yang Zhong, Nanjing, March 30, 2015.

50. "History of NJU," Nanjing University School History Museum, https://web
.archive.org/web/20170504075303/http://museum.nju.edu.cn/univerhistory
/index_02.asp?column=01.

51. "Xuexiao jianjie" [School Profile], Nanjing University Jinling College,
https://www.jlxy.nju.edu.cn/xygk/xxjj.htm.

52. "Nanda jinling xueyuan xiaoyou xiao kule, san ben zhuan she wei 985
xiaoyuan chengwei Nanda xiaoyoule" [Alumni of Nanjing University's Jinling College Laughed and Cried as the Three Independent Colleges Were
Converted to a 985 Campus, and They Become Alumni of Nanjing Univer-
sity], Cunman Entertainment Network, July 19, 2020, http://www.cunman
.com/new/492725cfaef94e7a8f1795ef1c8f48f9.

53. "Nanjing daxue jinling xueyuan banqian hou pukou xiaoqu jiang bian cheng
zheyang" [After the Relocation of Nanjing University's Jinling College,
Pukou Campus Will Look Like This], 360 Kuai, May 14, 2019, https://www
.360kuai.com/pc/95688776f821940e5?cota=4&kuai_so=1&tj_url=so
_rec&sign=360_e39369d1.

54. "Nanjing daxue 2016 nian bumen yusuan" [Nanjing University 2016 Departmental Budget], Nanjing University, May 2016, http://xxgk.nju.edu.cn
/_upload/article/files/54/1a/20d4a9e8486997b264c51d78243f/9350f5b8
-ab18-4d53-a997-58dbbe667b6c.pdf.

55. "Nanjing daxue xiao shi" [Nanjing University School History], Nanjing University, https://web.archive.org/web/20160304030017/http://museum.nju.edu
.cn/univerhistory/index_02.asp?column=01; "Nanjing daxue benke jiaoxue
zhiliang baogao, 2013 niandu" [Nanjing University 2013 Undergraduate
Teaching Quality Annual Report], Nanjing University, http://xxgk.nju.edu.cn
/07/15/c199a1813/page.htm.

56. Nanjing daxue, "Nanjing daxue jiaoyu fazhan jijin hui gongzuo baogao, 2017 niandu" [Nanjing University, Nanjing University Education Development Foundation 2017 Annual Report], February 28, 2019, https://njuedf.nju.edu.cn/43/ae/c4443a279470/page.htm.

57. "The Flagship History," The Language Flagship, https://www.thelanguageflagship.org/content/flagship-history, accessed August 2020.

58. U.S. Department of Education, Office of Postsecondary Education, "Enhancing Foreign Language Proficiency in the United States" (Washington, DC, 2008), https://nsep.gov/sites/default/files/nsli-preliminary-results.pdf.

59. Joel Campbell, "BYU Trying to Recall Group from Nanjing," *Deseret News,* June 6, 1989, https://www.deseret.com/1989/6/6/18809954/byu-trying-to-recall-group-from-nanjing; The Nanjing Chinese Flagship Center, "About the Nanjing Chinese Flagship Center," https://chinesefs.byu.edu/, accessed August 2020.

60. William A. Stanton, "Arrival of Flagship in Taiwan Significant for US-Taiwan Relations," *Taiwan News,* October 13, 2019, https://www.taiwannews.com.tw/en/news/3794865.

61. Elizabeth Redden, "3 More Universities Close Confucius Institutes," *Inside Higher Ed,* May 1, 2019, https://www.insidehighered.com/quicktakes/2019/05/01/3-more-universities-close-confucius-institutes.

62. William A. Stanton, "Arrival of Flagship in Taiwan Significant for US-Taiwan Relations."

63. "Donors," Schwarzman Scholars, https://www.schwarzmanscholars.org/donors/, accessed August 2020.

64. "Schwarzman Scholars Announces Inaugural Class," Schwarzman Scholars, January 11, 2016, https://www.schwarzmanscholars.org/news-article/schwarzman-scholars-announces-inaugural-class/.

65. "Schwarzman Scholars Announces Class of 2021," Schwarzman Scholars, December 4, 2019, https://www.schwarzmanscholars.org/news-article/schwarzman-scholars-announces-class-of-2021/.

66. "Degrees of Danger," Week in China, August 30, 2019, https://www.weekinchina.com/2019/08/degrees-of-danger/; "FAQ," Yenching Academy of Peking University, https://yenchingacademy.pku.edu.cn/ADMISSIONS/Frequently_Asked_Questions.htm, accessed August 2020.

67. "Schwarzman Scholars: Global Leadership for the 21st Century," Schwarzman Scholars, December 2018, https://www.schwarzmanscholars.org/wp-content/uploads/2018/12/Schwarzman-Scholars-Brochure.pdf; "Fellowship Program Information Sheet—Yenching Scholarship," Smith College, https://www.smith.edu/fellowships/docs/1.YEN.2.001_Fellowship_Info_Sheet_Yenching.pdf, accessed August 2020.

68. "Class Profile: Hopkins-Nanjing Center," Johns Hopkins School of Advanced International Studies, https://sais.jhu.edu/hopkins-nanjing-center/class-profile-hopkins-nanjing-center, accessed August 2020.

69. Nanjing daxue, "Shisanwu fazhan guihua."

70. Shanghai Observer, "Zhongyang jiang dui Qinghua Beida deng 29 suo gaoxiao kaizhan xunshi. Wang Qishan: xunshi yao qizhixianming jiang zhengzhe" [The Central Government Will Conduct Special Inspections of 29 Universities, Including Tsinghua University and Peking University. Wang Qishan: The Inspections Must Take a Clear Stand and Speak to Politics], February 22, 2017, https://www.jfdaily.com/wx/detail.do?id=45466.
71. Emily Feng, "Ideological Purge Hits China Universities with Western Ties," *Financial Times*, April 24, 2017, https://www.ft.com/content/8a7552d8-1f68-11e7-a454-ab04428977f9.
72. "Xi Jinping zai Zhongguo zhengfa daxue kaocha" [Xi Jinping Inspects China University of Political Science and Law], *Xinhua*, May 3, 2017, http://www.xinhuanet.com//politics/2017-05/03/c_1120913310.htm.
73. Nanjing daxue zhonggong jiwei, "Nanjing daxue dangwei xunshi fankui qingkuang ji zhenggai luoshi gongzuo ganbu dahui zhaokai" [Nanjing University CCP Disciplinary Inspection Committee, Nanjing University Party Committee's Inspection Feedback and Rectification Implementation Work Cadre Meeting Held], *Nanjing daxue xinwen wang* [Nanjing University News Net], June 27, 2017, https://jwb.nju.edu.cn/29/01/c8317a207105/page.htm.
74. Zhonggong Nanjing daxue dangwei, "Nanjing daxue xunshi zhenggai tongbao: dui weiji zhongceng ganbu yi cha daodi" [Nanjing University Committee of the Communist Party of China, Nanjing University Inspection and Rectification Bulletin: A Thorough Investigation of Middle-Level Cadres Who Violate Discipline], *Sina News*, August 28, 2017, http://news.sina.com.cn/c/nd/2017-08-28/doc-ifykiurx2388342.shtml.
75. Ibid.
76. Ibid.
77. Nanjing daxue zhonggong jiwei, "Xiao dangwei zhongxin zu zhuanti xuexi xin dangzhang" [Nanjing University CCP Disciplinary Inspection Committee, The School Party Committee Leading Group Holds Special Meeting to Learn New Party Constitution], Nanjing daxue xinwen wang [Nanjing University News Net], November 2, 2017, https://jwb.nju.edu.cn/6f/85/c8317a225157/page.htm.
78. Nanjing daxue zhonggong jiwei, "Nanjing daxue xinwen 2018 nian quanmian cong yan zhi dang gongzuo huiyi" [Nanjing University CCP Disciplinary Inspection Committee, Nanjing University Holds the 2018 Comprehensive Party Governance Work Conference], Nanjing daxue xinwen wang [Nanjing University News Net], April 13, 2018, https://jwb.nju.edu.cn/eb/c1/c8317a256961/page.htm.
79. Nanjing daxue, "Yiliu daxue jianshe guihua."
80. Ibid.
81. Ibid.
82. "Makesi zhuyi lilun yanjiu yu jianshe xiangmu" [Marxist Theory Research and Construction Project"] *Zhongguo gongchandang xinwen* [Communist Party of China News], September 25, 2008, http://cpc.people.com.cn/GB

/134999/135000/8105941.html; "Zhonggong zhongyang guowuyuan yinfa
guanyu jinyibu jiaqiang he gaijin daxuesheng sixiang zhengzhi jiaoyu de
yijian" [The Central Committee of the Communist Party of China and the
State Council Opinions on Further Strengthening and Improving the Ideological and Political Education of College Students], Zhonghua renmin
gonghequo jiaoyubu [Ministry of Education of the People's Republic of
China], October 14, 2004, http://www.moe.gov.cn/s78/A12/szs_lef/moe
_1407/moe_1408/tnull_20566.html.

83. "Nanjing University 2017–2018 Undergraduate Education Quality Report,"
Nanjing University, December 20, 2018, https://xxgk.nju.edu.cn/e4/f7
/c15434a320759/page.htm, accessed August 2020.

84. Zhonggong Nanjing daxue weiyuanhui, "Nanjing daxue guanyu qieshi jia-
qiang he gaijin shi de xuefeng jianshe de ruogan yijian" [Nanjing University
Committee of the Communist Party of China, About Nanjing University:
Several Opinions on Strengthening and Improving the Development of
Teachers' Ethics and Style of Study], May 17, 2018, https://hr.nju.edu.cn/1d
/cc/c12918a269772/pagem.htm.

85. Nanjing daxue Makesi zhuyi yuedu yanjiu she, "Nanda ma hui zhi Nanjing
daxue dangwei shuji Hu Jinbo de gongkaixin" [Marxist Reading and Research Society, An Open Letter from a Nanjing University Club to the Secretary of the Nanjing University Party Committee Hu Jinbo], October 16,
2018, https://njured.wordpress.com/2018/10/16/.

86. Ran Ran, "Zhongguo zuoyi qingnian de chengzhang he guanfang de daya"
[The Rise and Official Suppression of China's Left-Wing Youth], BBC
News, December 28, 2018, https://www.bbc.com/zhongwen/simp/chinese
-news-46616052.

87. "Shenzhen Jasic Workers' Rights Defense: Left-Wing Youth and Political
Aspirations," BBC News, August 16, 2018, https://www.bbc.com/zhong
wen/simp/chinese-news-45204596.

88. "Shenzhen jia shi weiquan: Shengyuan tuan chengyuan pilu bei jingfang dai
zou guocheng" [Shenzhen Jasic Rights Defense: Members of the Support
Group Disclose the Process of Being Taken Away by the Police], BBC
News, August 29, 2018, https://www.bbc.com/zhongwen/simp/chinese
-news-45341005.

89. Ran Ran, "Zhongguo zuoyi qingnian de chengzhang he guanfang de daya."

90. Nanjing daxue Makesi zhuyi yuedu yanjiu she, "Nanda ma hui zhi Nanjing
daxue dangwei shuji Hu Jinbo de gongkaixin."

91. Nanjing daxue Makesi zhuyi yuedu yanjiu she, "Nanda Makesi zhuyi yuedu
yanjiu hui julebu baoming shijian (09.12–11.05)" [Marxist Reading and Research Society of Nanjing University, Nanda's Marxist Reading and Research Society Club Registration Timeline (09.12–11.05)], November 2,
2018, https://njumarx.wordpress.com/2018/11/02/.

92. Voice of America, "Shenzhen jia shi weiquan huodong renshi zai zao jingfang yanli zhenya" [Shenzhen Jasic Rights Activists Are Severely Suppressed

by the Police Again], November 11, 2018, https://www.voachinese.com/a
/China-Rounds-Up-Uni-Labor-Campaigners-20181111/4653698.html.

93. Nanjing daxue Makesi zhuyi yuedu yanjiu she, "Nanda Makesi zhuyi yuedu
yanjiu hui julebu baoming shijian (09.12–11.05)."

94. "Zhongong zhongyang ziyuan Hu Jinbo wei Nanjing shuji" [The Central
Committee of the Communist Party of China Appointed Hu Jinbo as Secretary of the Party Committee of Nanjing University], *Nanjing daxue
xiaoyou wang* [Nanjing University Alumni Net], October 23, 2018, https://
alumni.nju.edu.cn/90/17/c276a299031/pagem.htm; Yan Hongliang, "Zhang
Yibin xieren Nanda dangwei shuji: zhudong tichu cong lingdao gangwei tui
xia" [Zhang Yibin Stepped Down as Secretary of the Nanda Party Committee: Voluntarily Proposed to Retire from the Leadership Position], *Sina
News*, October 24, 2018, https://news.sina.com.cn/o/2018-10-24/doc
-ihmxrkzw0005437.shtml.

95. Nanjing daxue Makesi zhuyi yuedu yanjiu she, "Nanda ma hui zhi Nanjing
daxue dangwei shuji Hu Jinbo de gongkaixin."

96. Ran Ran, "Zhongguo zuoyi qingnian de chengzhang he guanfang de daya."

97. He Haiwei, "Zhongguo duo ming changdao gongren quanli de nianqing
huodong renshi shizong" [Several Young Activists Advocating for Workers'
Rights in China Have Disappeared], *New York Times* (Chinese Edition),
November 12, 2018, https://cn.nytimes.com/china/20181112/china-student
-activists/.

98. Wen Yuqing, Han Jie, and Luisetta Mudie, "China Replaces Head of Peking
University with Communist Party Chief," Radio Free Asia, November 25,
2018, https://www.rfa.org/english/news/china/university-party-102520
18143652.html; "Zhu Xinkai ren Zhongguo renmin daxue dangwei chan-
gwei, fu xiaozhang" [Zhu Xinkai Serves as a Member of the Standing Committee of the Party Committee and Vice President of Renmin University of
China], *Renmin ribao* [People's Daily], November 28, 2018, http://renshi
.people.com.cn/n1/2018/1128/c139617-30429118.html; "Qi Pengfei ren
Zhongguo renmin daxue dangwei fu shuji" [Qi Pengfei Is Appointed Deputy
Secretary of the Renmin University of China Party Committee], *Xinhua*,
June 27, 2019, http://www.xinhuanet.com/renshi/2019-06/27/c_1124678988
.htm; "Zhongong zhongyang ziyuan Hu Jinbo wei Nanjing shuji."

99. Javier C. Hernández, "Cornell Cuts Ties with Chinese School after Crackdown on Students," *New York Times*, October 29, 2018, https://www
.nytimes.com/2018/10/29/world/asia/cornell-university-renmin.html.

100. Beijing daxue jiaoyu fa yanjiu zhongxin, "Nanjing daxue zhangcheng" [Pe-
king University Research Center for Education Law, Charter of Nanjing
University], October 12, 2015, http://www.educationlaw.cn/plus/view.php
?aid=160.

101. "Jiaoyubu guanyu tongyi Fudan daxue zhangcheng tiaokuan xiugai de pifu"
[Reply of the Ministry of Education on Agreeing to the Revision of Some
Articles of Fudan University's Charter], Zhonghua renmin gongheguo

jiaoyubu [Ministry of Education of the People's Republic of China], December 5, 2019, http://www.moe.gov.cn/srcsite/A02/zfs_gdxxzc/201912 /t20191216_412276.html.

102. Ibid.

103. Ibid.

104. Beijing daxue jiaoyu fa yanjiu zhongxin, "Nanjing daxue zhangcheng."

105. "Jiaoyubu guanyu tongyi Fudan daxue zhangcheng tiaokuan xiugai de pifu."

106. Philip Wen, "Delete 'Freedom' and Emphasize 'Loyalty': Chinese Colleges and Universities Revise Their Statutes, Raising Objections," *Wall Street Journal,* December 20, 2019, https://on.wsj.com/3qI9uE8.

107. Emily Feng, "Chinese Universities Are Enshrining Communist Party Control in Their Charters," NPR, January 20, 2020, https://www.npr.org/2020 /01/20/796377204/chinese-universities-are-enshrining-communist-party -control-in-their-charters.

108. Douglas Belkin and Philip Wen, "American Colleges Watch for Changes at Chinese Universities," *Wall Street Journal,* December 27, 2019, https://www .wsj.com/articles/american-colleges-watch-for-changes-at-chinese-univer sities-11577474706.

109. "Jiaoyubu 2020 nian bumen yusuan" [Ministry of Education 2020 Departmental Budget], June 11, 2020, Ministry of Education of the People's Republic of China, http://www.moe.gov.cn/srcsite/A05/s7499/202006/t20200611 _465019.html.

110. "Nanjing daxue 2020 nian bumen yusuan" [Nanjing University 2020 Departmental Budget], Nanjing University, July 3, 2020, https://xxgk.nju.edu .cn/63/fb/c15419a484347/page.htm.

11. Asia's Global University?

1. Author interview with Xiang Zhang, Hong Kong, October 15, 2019.

2. Ibid.

3. Ibid.

4. Ibid.

5. Ibid.

6. *London Gazette,* no. 28024, May 24, 1907, 3589, https://www.thegazette.co .uk/London/issue/28024/page/3589, accessed December 9, 2015; Peter Cunich, *A History of the University of Hong Kong, Volume 1: 1911–1945* (Hong Kong: Hong Kong University Press, 2012), 80.

7. From an article by Lugard published in the October 1910 issue of *The Nineteenth Century and After,* as quoted in Bernard Mellor, *Lugard in Hong Kong: Empires, Education and a Governor at Work, 1907–1912* (Hong Kong: Hong Kong University Press, 1992), 1–2.

8. Cunich, *A History of the University of Hong Kong,* 82.

9. Bert Becker, "The 'German Factor' in the Founding of the University of Hong Kong," in *An Impossible Dream: Hong Kong University from Foundation*

to Re-establishment, 1910–1950, Lau Kit-Ching Chan and Peter Cunich, eds. (Oxford: Oxford University Press, 2002), 29.

10. Cunich, *A History of the University of Hong Kong,* 86.
11. Cunich, *A History of the University of Hong Kong,* 120.
12. Mellor, *Lugard in Hong Kong,* 3.
13. Cunich, *A History of the University of Hong Kong,* 185.
14. University of Hong Kong Calendar, 1955–1956. (Hong Kong: Cathay Press, 1955), 11.
15. Cunich, *A History of the University of Hong Kong,* 169.
16. Cunich, *A History of the University of Hong Kong,* 262.
17. Cunich, *A History of the University of Hong Kong,* 301.
18. Cunich, *A History of the University of Hong Kong,* 312.
19. Brian Harrison, "The Years of Growth," in *University of Hong Kong: The First 50 Years, 1911–1961,* Brian Harrison, ed. (Hong Kong: Cathay Press, 1963), 54–55.
20. Cunich, *A History of the University of Hong Kong,* 335.
21. Sloss, as quoted in Cunich, *A History of the University of Hong Kong,* 335.
22. Cunich, *A History of the University of Hong Kong,* 340.
23. Cunich, *A History of the University of Hong Kong,* 388–389.
24. As quoted in Cunich, *A History of the University of Hong Kong,* 433.
25. Francis Stock, "A New Beginning" in Harrison, *University of Hong Kong,* 86.
26. "Milestones through the Decades," Chinese University of Hong Kong, 2015, http://www.cuhk.edu.hk/ugallery/en/zone-a.html, accessed December 9, 2015.
27. *Faculty of Arts 100: A Century in Words and Images* (Hong Kong: University of Hong Kong Faculty of Arts, 2014), 100.
28. *Faculty of Arts 100,* 33.
29. Chinese Central Government, "Full Text of Sino-British Joint Declaration," Government of China, June 14, 2007, http://www.gov.cn/english/2007-06/14/content_649468.htm, accessed October 22, 2019.
30. Phoebe H. Stevenson, "Higher Education in Hong Kong: A Case Study of Universities Navigating through the Asian Economic Crisis" (dissertation, University of Pennsylvania, 2010), 14–15.
31. "The Basic Law of the Hong Kong Special Administrative Region of the People's Republic of China," Government of Hong Kong, accessed October 22, 2019, https://www.basiclaw.gov.hk/en/basiclawtext/images/basiclaw_full_text_en.pdf; "Wang Gungwu, Historian and Former Vice-Chancellor of the University of Hong Kong, Shares Life Memories and His Views on Hong Kong's Future," *South China Morning Post* video, September 7, 2019, https://www.scmp.com/video/hong-kong/3026052/wang-gungwu-historian-and-former-vice-chancellor-university-hong-kong.
32. "University Allows Display of Democracy Sculpture," *The Globe and Mail,* June 7, 1997, http://search.proquest.com.ezp-prod1.hul.harvard.edu/docview/1140556689?accountid=11311, accessed September 24, 2015.

33. University Grants Committee, *Hong Kong Higher Education: To Make a Difference, To Move with the Times,* January 2004, http://www.ugc.edu.hk/eng/doc/ugc/publication/report/policy_document_e.pdf, accessed December 9, 2015.
34. "Quick Stats," University of Hong Kong, http://www.cpao.hku.hk/qstats/, accessed October 28, 2015.
35. "Staff Profiles," Quick Stats, University of Hong Kong, https://www.cpao.hku.hk/qstats/staff-profiles, accessed November 2020.
36. Mimi Lau, "Global HKU is on Top of the World," *South China Morning Post,* November 10, 2007, http://www.scmp.com/article/615037/global-hku-top-world, accessed January 26, 2016.
37. Author interview with Peter Mathieson, Hong Kong, October 20, 2015.
38. University of Hong Kong Strategic Planning Unit, *University of Hong Kong Strategic 2009–2014 Development,* November 2009, 6, http://www.sppoweb.hku.hk/sdplan/eng/images/doc.pdf, accessed December 9, 2015.
39. Author interview with Arthur Li, Hong Kong, October 15, 2015.
40. Author interview with Ian Holliday, Hong Kong, May 12, 2015.
41. Rayson Huang, *A Lifetime in Academia* (Hong Kong: Hong Kong University Press, 2000), 102.
42. Author interview with anonymous source, Hong Kong, May 15, 2015.
43. Author interview with Roland Chin, Hong Kong, May 11, 2015.
44. Ibid.
45. "Terms for Re-appointment beyond Retirement Age," Human Resources of HKU, September 13, 2018, https://www.hr.hku.hk/news/internal_communication/announcement.php?id=428, accessed October 22, 2019.
46. Cindy Wan, "HKU court calls for review of retirement age," *The Standard,* December 18, 2018, http://www.thestandard.com.hk/section-news.php?id=203359&sid=11, accessed October 22, 2019.
47. Kris Cheng, "HKU grants 2-year contract extensions for liberal profs Johannes Chan and Petula Ho instead of 5," *Hong Kong Free Press,* August 10, 2018, https://www.hongkongfp.com/2018/08/10/hku-grants-2-year-contract-extensions-liberal-profs-johannes-chan-petula-ho-instead-5/, accessed October 22, 2019.
48. Karen Zhang, "HKU academic staff express discontent over retirement at 60 in forum with management and alumni," *South China Morning Post,* November 20, 2018, https://www.scmp.com/news/hong-kong/education/article/2174164/hku-academic-staff-express-discontent-retirement-60-forum, accessed October 22, 2019.
49. *Fit for Purpose Report,* 2003, http://www.hku.hk/about/governance/purpose_report.html, accessed February 11, 2016.
50. "The Senate (Membership)," University of Hong Kong, 2015, http://www.hku.hk/about/governance/governance_structure/the-court/senate_membership.html, accessed December 9, 2015.

51. "The Court (Membership)," University of Hong Kong, 2015, http://www
    .hku.hk/about/governance/governance_structure/the-court/court_member
    ship.html, accessed December 9, 2015.
52. Author interview with John Malpas, Hong Kong, May 12, 2015.
53. Ibid.
54. Ibid.
55. The University of Hong Kong—Strategic Development 2003–2008, "Trans-
    forming the University for the 21st Century," https://www.sppoweb.hku.hk
    /sdplan/2003_08/english/fs-transform.htm.
56. The University of Hong Kong, "HKU Ranked 18th amongst the World's
    Top 200 universities," https://www.hku.hk/press/news_detail_5651.html.
57. "Asia's Global University: The Next Decade: Our Vision for 2016–2025,"
    The University of Hong Kong, https://www.sppoweb.hku.hk/vision2016
    -2025/index.html.
58. "About ZIRI," Zhejiang Institute of Research and Innovation, http://www
    .ziri.hku.hk/en/about.html; LKS Faculty of Medicine, The University of
    Hong Kong, "The University of Hong Kong-Shenzhen Hospital," https://
    fmpc.hku.hk/en/Clinical-Services/The-University-of-Hong-Kong
    -Shenzhen-Hospital.
59. *University of Hong Kong Financial Report, 2018*, http://www.feo.hku.hk
    /finance/information/annualreport/publications/2018/HTML/index.html
    accessed October 21, 2019.
60. "Undergraduate Admissions," University of Hong Kong, 2019, https://aal
    .hku.hk/admissions/international/admissions-information?page=en/fees
    -and-scholarships and http://www.als.hku.hk/admission/mainland
    /admission/overview#, accessed October 22, 2019.
61. "Centennial College," University of Hong Kong, 2019, https://www
    .centennialcollege.hku.hk/en/faq, accessed October 22, 2019.
62. University of Hong Kong Financial Report, 2014, http://www.feo.hku.hk
    /finance/information/annualreport.html?v=1449761272864, accessed De-
    cember 10, 2015.
63. University of Hong Kong Financial Report, 2018, http://www.feo.hku.hk
    /finance/information/annualreport/publications/2018/HTML/index.html,
    accessed October 21, 2019.
64. Author interview with anonymous source, Hong Kong, May 15, 2015.
65. "People's Satisfaction with HKSARG's Pace of Democratic Development
    (Half-Yearly Average)," HKU Public Opinion Programme, https://www
    .hkupop.hku.hk/english/popexpress/sargperf/demo/halfyr/demo_halfyr
    _chart.html, accessed January 2020.
66. "People's Lack of Confidence in HK's Future, People's Lack of Confidence
    in China's Future and People's Lack of Confidence in 'One Country, Two
    Systems,'" HKU Public Opinion Programme, accessed January 2020, https://
    www.hkupop.hku.hk/english/popexpress/trust/conhkfuture/combine_no
    /combine_no_halfyr_chart.html; "People's Confidence in HK's Future,

People's Confidence in China's Future and People's Confidence in 'One Country, Two Systems,'" HKU Public Opinion Programme, https://www.hkupop.hku.hk/english/popexpress/trust/conhkfuture/combine/combine_hfyear_chart.html, accessed January 2020.

67. "CUHK Hong Kong Quality of Life Index Reveals Continuous Improvement of Quality of Life for Hong Kong," CUHK Communications and Public Relations Office, https://www.cpr.cuhk.edu.hk/en/press_detail.php?id=487&t=cuhk-hong-kong-quality-of-life-index-reveals-continuous-improvement-of-quality-of-life-for-hong-kong, accessed January 2020.

68. "CUHK Hong Kong Quality of Life Index: Quality of Life in Hong Kong Declined," CUHK Communications and Public Relations Office, https://www.cpr.cuhk.edu.hk/en/press_detail.php?id=1351&t=cuhk-hong-kong-quality-of-life-index-quality-of-life-in-hong-kong-declined, accessed January 2020.

69. "Categorical Ethnic Identity (per poll)," HKU Public Opinion Programme, https://www.hkupop.hku.hk/english/popexpress/ethnic/eidentity/poll/eid_poll_chart.html, accessed January 2020.

70. "Hong Kong Controversy Strikes University Officials," *Wall Street Journal*, September 7, 2000, http://search.proquest.com.ezp-prod1.hul.harvard.edu/docview/398878047?accountid=11311, accessed December 9, 2015.

71. Peter So, "University Chief Vows Truth on Police Action," *South China Morning Post*, September 6, 2011, https://global.factiva.com/redir/default.aspx?P=sa&an=SCMCOM0020110906e7960000z&cat=a&ep=ASE, accessed December 10, 2015; Dennis Chong and Tanna Chong, "Tsui Denies He Was Forced to Quit University," *South China Morning Post*, October 27, 2011, https://global.factiva.com/redir/default.aspx?P=sa&an=SCMP000020111026e7ar0000p&cat=a&ep=ASE, accessed December 10, 2015.

72. Reuters, "Explainer: What Was Hong Kong's 'Occupy' Movement All About?," April 23, 2019, https://www.reuters.com/article/us-hongkong-politics-occupy-explainer/explainer-what-was-hong-kongs-occupy-movement-all-about-idUSKCN1S005M.

73. Hong Kong Special Administrative Region, "Decision of the Standing Committee of the National People's Congress on Issues Relating to the Selection of the Chief Executive of the Hong Kong Special Administrative Region by Universal Suffrage and on the Method for Forming the Legislative Council of the Hong Kong Special Administrative Region in the Year 2016," August 31, 2014, http://www.2017.gov.hk/filemanager/template/en/doc/20140831b.pdf.

74. Harry Ong, "What Is HKU's Murky Role in 'Occupy Central'?," *China Daily*, November 4, 2014, https://www.chinadaily.com.cn/hkedition/2014-11/04/content_18861375.htm.

75. Kris Cheng, "Explainer: The HKU Pro-Vice-Chancellor Debacle," *Hong Kong Free Press*, September 30, 2015, https://www.hongkongfp.com/2015

/09/30/explainer-hku-council-rejects-johannes-chan-appointment-to-pro-vice-chancellor/, accessed December 10, 2015.

76. "Thousands Sign Petition against HKU Students," RTHK News, August 5, 2015, http://news.rthk.hk/rthk/en/component/k2/1203053-20150805.htm, accessed December 10, 2015.

77. RTHK, "7,000 HKU Alumni Favor Johannes Chan," *The Standard,* September 2, 2015, http://www.thestandard.com.hk/breaking_news_detail.asp?id=66171&icid=3&d_str=, accessed December 10, 2015.

78. Michael Forsythe, "Vote at Hong Kong University Stirs Concern over Beijing's Influence," *New York Times,* September 30, 2015, http://www.nytimes.com/2015/10/01/world/asia/hong-kong-university-votes-against-promoting-johannes-chan.html, accessed December 10, 2015.

79. Billy Fung, "Zhuanzai: Feng Jing'en jiu yue ershijiu xiaoweihui huiyi zhi geren shengming quanwen" [Reprint: Billy Fung's Personal Recollection of the September 29 University Council Meeting], *Post 852,* September 29, 2015, http://www.post852.com/2015/09/29, accessed December 10, 2015.

80. Jeffie Lam, "More than 3,000 March against Arthur Li's Appointment as Chairman of HKU Governing Council," *South China Morning Post,* January 4, 2016, http://www.scmp.com/news/hong-kong/education-community/article/1897821/more-3000-march-against-arthur-lis-appointment, accessed February 11, 2016.

81. See *The Report of the Review Panel on University Governance* (University of Hong Kong, February 2017), http://www.gs.hku.hk/Grant_Report_and_Addendum.pdf, accessed October 22, 2019.

82. Working Party on the Recommendations of the Review Panel on University Governance, *Report of the Working Party* (University of Hong Kong, June 2017), http://www.gs.hku.hk/Report_of_Working_Party.pdf, accessed October 22, 2019.

83. *The Report of the Review Panel on University Governance.*

84. "HKU Groups Condemn Reappointment of Arthur Li," RTHK News, January 1, 2019, https://news.rthk.hk/rthk/en/component/k2/1435945-20190101.htm, accessed October 22, 2019.

85. *Fugitive Offenders and Mutual Legal Assistance in Criminal Matters Legislation (Amendment) Bill 2019* (Hong Kong Legislative Council, March 2019), https://www.legco.gov.hk/yr18-19/english/bills/b201903291.pdf, accessed October 22, 2019.

86. Fion Li and Carol Zhong, "Everything You Need to Know About the Extradition Bill Rocking Hong Kong," *Washington Post,* June 13, 2019, https://www.washingtonpost.com/business/everything-you-need-to-know-about-the-extradition-bill-rocking-hong-kong/2019/06/11/12a7907c-8c26-11e9-b6f4-033356502dce_story.html, accessed October 22, 2019.

87. James Pomfret and Farah Master, "Hong Kong Pushes Bill Allowing Extraditions to China Despite Biggest Protest Since Handover," Reuters, June 9, 2019, https://www.reuters.com/article/us-hongkong-extradition/hong-kong

-pushes-bill-allowing-extraditions-to-china-despite-biggest-protest-since -handover-idUSKCN1TB08W, accessed October 22, 2019.

88. "Hong Kong Protest: 'Nearly Two Million' Join Demonstration," BBC, June 17, 2019, https://www.bbc.com/news/world-asia-china-48656471, accessed October 17, 2019.

89. Hillary Leung, "Hong Kong University Students Reject Invitation to Meet City's Leader for Closed-Door Talks," *Time*, July 5, 2019, https://time.com /5620905/hong-kong-student-unions-reject-carrie-lam-meeting/, accessed October 22, 2019.

90. Alvin Lum, "University of Hong Kong President Zhang Xiang Calls for 'Every Corner of Society' to Mend Political Divide through Talking as City Gears up for More Marches," *South China Morning Post*, July 18, 2019, https://www.scmp.com/news/hong-kong/politics/article/3019223/university -hong-kong-president-zhang-xiang-calls-every, accessed October 22, 2019.

91. Yojana Sharma, "Students Defy University Warnings with Classes' Boycott," *University World News*, September 3, 2019, https://www.universityworldnews .com/post.php?story=20190903181638206, accessed October 22, 2019.

92. Center for Communication and Public Opinion Survey, "Onsite Survey Findings in Hong Kong's Anti-Extradition Bill Protests," Chinese University of Hong Kong, August 2019, http://www.com.cuhk.edu.hk/ccpos/en /pdf/ENG_antielab%20survey%20public%20report%20vf.pdf.

93. Ibid.

94. Li Xinxin, "Yuan Guoyong, "Fan xiuli shiwei chongtu shoushang renshu keneng yu 2000 ren" [Yuan Guoyong: The Number of Injured in the Anti-reform Demonstrations May Exceed 2,000], RTHK News, August 15, 2019, https://news.rthk.hk/rthk/ch/component/k2/1474890-20190815.htm, accessed October 22, 2019.

95. Greg Torode, James Pomfret, and David Lague, "China Quietly Doubles Troop Levels in Hong Kong, Envoy Says," Reuters, September 30, 2019, https://www.reuters.com/investigates/special-report/china-army-hongkong/, accessed October 22, 2019; Andrew J. Nathan, "How China Sees the Hong Kong Crisis," *Foreign Affairs*, September 30, 2019, https://www.foreign affairs.com/articles/china/2019-09-30/how-china-sees-hong-kong-crisis, accessed October 22, 2019.

96. Cannix Yau, Wendy Wu, and Gary Cheung, "Chinese President Xi Jinping Warns That Anyone Trying to Split Any Part of Country Will Be Crushed," *South China Morning Post*, October 13, 2019, https://www.scmp.com/news /hong-kong/politics/article/3032741/chinese-president-xi-jinping-warns -anyone-trying-split-any, accessed October 22, 2019.

97. "Clashes Spread to Different Hong Kong Universities," RTHK, https:// news.rthk.hk/rthk/en/component/k2/1491306-20191111.htm, accessed January 2020.

98. Mary Hui, "Photos: Hong Kong Police and Students Are Fighting a War in One of the City's Top Universities," *Quartz*, https://qz.com/1746924/police

-students-battle-in-chinese-university-of-hong-kong/, accessed January 2020.

99. Wenxin Fan and Dan Strumpf, "Hong Kong's Harrowing University Siege Ends Not with a Bang but a Whimper," *Wall Street Journal,* https://www.wsj .com/articles/hong-kongs-harrowing-university-siege-ends-not-with-a-bang -but-a-whimper-11574942822, accessed January 2020.

100. Chan Ho-him, "Hong Kong Protests: City University Reveals Bill to Fix Vandalised Campus Will Run to Hundreds of Millions of Dollars," *South China Morning Post,* https://www.scmp.com/news/hong-kong/education /article/3040062/hong-kong-protests-city-university-reveals-bill-fix, accessed January 2020.

101. Jinshan Hong, "Mainland Students Flee Hong Kong Campus Clash with China Aid," *Bloomberg,* https://www.bloomberg.com/news/articles/2019-11 -13/mainland-students-flee-hong-kong-campus-standoff-with-china-help, accessed January 2020; Theo Wayt, "U.S. Universities Suspend Hong Kong Study Programs amid Deadly Protests," NBC News, https://www.nbcnews .com/news/us-news/u-s-universities-suspend-hong-kong-study-programs -amid-deadly-n1084046, accessed January 2020.

102. "Teaching and Learning Arrangements for the Remainder of the Semester," The University of Hong Kong, https://www.hku.hk/press/press-releases /detail/20219.html, accessed January 2020.

103. Christian Shepherd and Sue Lin-Wong, "Luo Huining: Beijing's enforcer in Hong Kong," *Financial Times,* January 7, 2020, https://www.ft.com/content /c95614f6-3063-11ea-9703-eea0cae3f0de.

104. "Key Facts about New Head of China's Liaison Office in Hong Kong," Reuters, January 5, 2020, https://www.reuters.com/article/us-honkong -china-liaison-factbox/key-facts-about-new-head-of-chinas-liaison-office-in -hong-kong-idUSKBN1Z50AS; Natalie Lung, Iain Marlow, and Cathy Chan, "China's New Hong Kong Liaison Confident City Will Stabilize," Bloomberg, January 4, 2020, https://www.bloomberg.com/news/articles /2020-01-04/china-announces-new-top-liaison-official-for-hong-kong?sref =8JkQ65qI.

105. Natalie Wong, Gary Cheung, and Sum Lok-kei, "Beijing's Liaison Office Says It Has Right to Handle Hong Kong Affairs, as Provided by Constitution and Basic Law," *South China Morning Post,* April 17, 2020, https://www .scmp.com/news/hong-kong/politics/article/3080506/beijings-liaison-office -says-it-has-right-handle-hong-kong.

106. Helen Davidson, "China's Top Official in Hong Kong Pushes for National Security Law," *The Guardian,* April 15, 2020, https://www.theguardian.com /world/2020/apr/15/china-official-hong-kong-luo-huining-pushes-national -security-law.

107. Anna Fifield, Tiffany Liang, Shibani Mahtani, and Timothy McLaughlin, "China to Impose Sweeping Security Law in Hong Kong, Heralding End of City's Autonomy," *Washington Post,* May 21, 2020, https://www.washingtonpost

Chan Ho-him, "University of Hong Kong Governing Council Sacks Legal Scholar Benny Tai over Convictions for Occupy Protests," *South China Morning Post*, July 28, 2020, https://www.scmp.com/news/hong-kong/politics/article/3095043/university-hong-kong-governing-council-sacks-legal-scholar.

Ibid.

Chan Ho-him, "University of Hong Kong's Governing Council Chief Defends Benny Tai Sacking, Rejects Allegations of Outside Interference in the Decision," *South China Morning Post*, July 31, 2020, https://www.scmp.com/news/hong-kong/politics/article/3095411/university-hong-kong-governing-council-chief-defends-benny.

"First Priority Is to Get Rid of 'Bad Apples' in Education: Hong Kong Security Chief," *Apple Daily*, July 30, 2020, https://hk.appledaily.com/us/20200730/XP6ZJSHFIONFE6G3UOZ7XNA27E/.

Chan Ho-him, "Sacked Legal Scholar Benny Tai to Challenge Hong Kong's Leader Carrie Lam over Dismissal," *South China Morning Post*, July 29, 2020, https://www.scmp.com/news/hong-kong/politics/article/3095120/sacked-legal-scholar-benny-tai-challenge-hong-kongs-leader.

Author interview with Peter Mathieson, October 20, 2015.

Author interview with Arthur Li, October 15, 2015.

Author interview with Roland Chin, May 11, 2015.

Qinghua daxue jiaoyu shoufei hongshi [Tsinghua University Tuition Fee Publication], Tsinghua University, http://www.tsinghua.edu.cn/publish/newthu/openness/cwzcjsfxx/sfxm.html, accessed December 10, 2015; University of Hong Kong, "Fees and Scholarships: Tuition Fee & Cost of Living Reference," University of Hong Kong International Undergraduate Admissions, 2019, http://www.aal.hku.hk/admissions/international/admissions-information?page=en/fees-and-scholarships, accessed October 22, 2019.

Author interview with Victor Fung, Hong Kong, October 21, 2015.

Times Higher Education World University Rankings, 2012–2013, https://www.timeshighereducation.com/world-university-rankings/2013/world-ranking#!/page/0/length/25/sort_by/rank/sort_order/asc/cols/undefined.

See *Times Higher Education World University Rankings*, https://www.timeshighereducation.com/world-university-rankings/2021/world-ranking#!/page/0/length/25/sort_by/rank/sort_order/asc/cols/stats.

Kelly Ng, "Yale-NUS and Duke-NUS Offer New Route for Liberal Arts Students to Become Doctors," *Today Online*, January 16, 2018, https://www.todayonline.com/singapore/yale-nus-and-duke-nus-offer-new-route-liberal-arts-students-become-doctors.

National University Singapore, "National University of Singapore and its Subsidiaries: Full Financial Statements for the Financial Year Ended 31 March 2014," https://www.nus.edu.sg/docs/default-source/annual-report/nus-financialreport-2014.pdf; University of Hong Kong, "An Extract from

.com/world/asia_pacific/china-signals-plan-to-take-full
-realigning-citys-status/2020/05/21/2c3850ee-9b48-11
_story.html; Keith Bradsher, "China Approves Plan to F
Defying Worldwide Outcry," *New York Times,* May 28,
.nytimes.com/2020/05/28/world/asia/china-hong-kong

108. Chris Buckley, "China Vows Tougher Security in Ho
Than Done," *New York Times,* November 6, 2019, htt
/2019/11/06/world/asia/hong-kong-protests-china-n

109. Nectar Gan, "China Approves Controversial Nationa
Hong Kong," CNN, May 28, 2020, https://www.cnr
/china-npc-hk-security-law-intl-hnk/index.html.

110. James Griffiths and Helen Regan, "Hong Kong Prot
tional Security Law Met with Tear Gas," May 24, 2(
.com/2020/05/24/asia/hong-kong-protest-national-s
/index.html.

111. CGTN, "Arthur Li Voices Firm Opposition to Exte
HKSAR affairs," May 28, 2020, https://news.cgtn.c
/Arthur-Li-voices-rejection-to-external-interference
-QR5cYpmMYo/index.html.

112. Wong Tsui-kai, "Hong Kong University Heads Rele
They 'Understand' New National Security Law," *Sou*
June 1, 2020, https://www.scmp.com/yp/discover/ne
/3086981/hong-kong-university-heads-release-state

113. Chris Buckley, "What China's New National Securi
Kong," *New York Times,* June 28, 2020, https://www
/28/world/asia/china-hong-kong-national-security-l

114. "English Translation of the Law of the People's Rep
guarding National Security in the Hong Kong Spec
gion," July 1, 2020, *Xinhua,* http://webcache.google
?q=cache:fTYutlWet2cJ:www.xinhuanet.com/english
_139178753.htm+&cd=1&hl=en&ct=clnk&gl=us.

115. Chris Lau, "National Security Law: Hong Kong Ac
Self-Censorship to Protect Themselves, Law Dean \
Morning Post, July 15, 2020, https://www.scmp.com
/politics/article/3093337/national-security-law-hon
-choose-self.

116. Jerome Taylor and Su Xinqi, "Security Law: Hong I
Academic Freedom," *Hong Kong Free Press,* July 15,
fp.com/2020/07/15/security-law-hong-kong-schola
-freedom/.

117. Kelly Ho, "Hong Kong's Carrie Lam Says Educatio
Media for 'Negative, Smearing' Coverage," *Hong K(*
2020, https://hongkongfp.com/2020/07/13/hong-k
-education-is-politicised-blames-media-for-negative

118

119
120

121

122

123
124
125
126

127
128

129

130

131

18. See Douglass and Bleemer, *Approaching a Tipping Point?*, 12–13, 21–23; UC Berkeley Office of Undergraduate Admissions, "Estimated Student Budget, 2019–2020," https://admissions.berkeley.edu/cost, accessed March 14, 2021.

19. Quoted in Bob Herbert, "Cracks in the Future," *New York Times,* October 3, 2009.

20. Robert J. Birgeneau and Frank D. Yeary, "Rescuing Our Public Universities," *Washington Post,* September 27. 2009.

21. Emma Whitford, "Public Higher Ed Funding Still Has Not Recovered from 2008 Recession," *Inside Higher Ed*, May 5, 2020, https://www.insidehighered .com/news/2020/05/05/public-higher-education-worse-spot-ever-heading -recession, accessed March 10, 2021. Quotation is of Sophia Laderman, a senior policy analyst at the State Higher Education Executive Officers Association.

22. American Academy of Arts and Sciences, *Public Research Universities. Recommitting to Lincoln's Vision: An Educational Compact for the 21st Century* (Cambridge, MA, 2016), 6–10; "A Look at the Shocking Student Loan Debt Statistics for 2021," Student Loan Hero, updated Jan. 27, 2021, https://student loanhero.com/student-loan-debt-statistics/, accessed March 14, 2021.

23. Laura T. Hamilton and Kelly Nielsen, *Broke: The Racial Consequences of Underfunding Public Universities* (Chicago: University of Chicago Press, 2021).

24. State Higher Education Executive Officers Association, "State Higher Education Finance FY 2019 Report," April 2020, 10, https://shef.sheeo.org/wp -content/uploads/2020/04/SHEEO_SHEF_FY19_Report.pdf, accessed March 10, 2021.

25. Herbert, "Cracks in the Future."

26. Henry Rosovsky, *The University: An Owner's Manual* (New York: Norton, 1990), 262.

27. See William G. Bowen and Harold T. Shapiro, eds., *Universities and their Leadership* (Princeton, NJ: Princeton University Press, 1998), especially the chapters by Shapiro and Hanna Gray, 65–118; Scott Cowen, *Winnebagos on Wednesdays: How Visionary Leadership Can Transform Higher Education* (Princeton, NJ: Princeton University Press, 2018).

28. See Australian Government, Department of Education, Skills and Employment, "Chinese Universities Establishing Programs and Campuses in Foreign Countries," September 6, 2016, https://internationaleducation.gov.au /news/latest-news/Pages/Chinese-universities-establishing.aspx, accessed March 10, 2021.

29. See Peking University HSBC Business School website, https://uk.phbs.pku .edu.cn/index.php?m=content&c=index&a=lists&catid=21, accessed March 10, 2021.

30. See William C. Kirby, "The International Origins and Global Aspirations of Chinese Universities: Along the New Silk Road," in Marijk C. van der Wende, William C. Kirby, Nian Cai Liu, and Simon Marginson, eds., *China and Europe on the New Silk Road: Connecting Universities across Eurasia* (Oxford: Oxford University Press, 2020), 18–32.

31. Amy Binder and Kate Wood, *Becoming Right: How Campuses Shape Young Conservatives* (Princeton, NJ: Princeton University Press, 2014); Norimitsu Onishi, "Will American Ideas Tear France Apart? Some of Its Leaders Think So," *New York Times*, February 9, 2021, https://www.nytimes.com /2021/02/09/world/europe/france-threat-american-universities.html, accessed February 21, 2021; Norimitsu Onishi, "Heating Up Culture Wars, France To Scour Universities for Ideas That 'Corrupt Society,'" *New York Times*, February 18, 2021, https://www.nytimes.com/2021/02/18/world /europe/france-universities-culture-wars.html, accessed February 21, 2021.

32. "Education Minister Warns against 'Wrong Western Values,'" *Global Times*, February 3, 2015, https://www.globaltimes.cn/content/905557.shtml.

33. Association of American Universities, "Hefei Statement on the Ten Characteristics of Contemporary Research Universities," (2013) https://www.aau .edu/sites/default/files/AAU%20Files/Education%20and%20Service/Hefei _statement.pdf.

Index

Italic page numbers refer to figures or tables.

Chinese universities (*continued*)
governance, 15, 244, 247–248, 250–252, 262–265, 387; Harvard and, 116, 146, 157–158, 259, 293; international engagement, 243, 391–392; international partnerships, 90–91, 248–249, 258–259, 315, 388; key, 245, 313, 317; liberal arts, 228, 241, 248–249, 257–258, 270, 292, 309; number of, 1, 236, 246, 247, *247*, 248; political interference, 246, 262–265, 276, 283, 284, 393–394; private, 248–249, 252, 257, 261; rankings, 249–250, 389–390; science and technology, 245, 249–250, 252, 253–254, 306, 321; strategic planning, 389; student activism, 241–242, 246; tuition, 254, 261, 285; Western influences, 5, 14, 239–241, 242, 243, 305. *See also* Nanjing University; Peking University; Tsinghua University
Chinese University of Hong Kong (CUHK), 344, 345, 365, 373
Chongqing University, 249
Christ, Carol, 167–168, 186, 191, 195, 197–198, 199
CIA. *See* Central Intelligence Agency
Clark, Kim, 152
Clark University, 9, 100
Clay, Lucius D., 46, 68
climate issues, 96, 155
Clotfelter, Charles T., 381
Cogswell, Joseph, 121
Cold War: area studies in American universities, 109, 128; Berlin blockade and airlift, 71; division of Berlin and Germany, 45–46, 47, 63, 65–68, 71, 74
Cole, Jonathan R., 14, 99
College of California, 169–170, 172
Columbia University, 14, 103, 121–122, 149, 177, 259, 305
Conant, James Bryant: on German universities, 24; as Harvard president, 113–114, 115, 125, 127–129, 141–142; portrait, 138; Redbook, 128–129, 150, 151–152; SAT and, 117
Conceison, Claire, 213

Confucius Institutes, 91, 325
Cornell University, 100, 110, 170, 332
Council for Aid to Education, 107
COVID-19 pandemic: in China, 233, 294, 300, 335; scientific research, 385; in United States, 110, 117, 156, 165, 169, 199, 233–234, 383. *See also* online learning
Crispi, Angela, 152
Crowell, John F., 203–204
CUHK. *See* Chinese University of Hong Kong

DAAD. *See* German Academic Exchange Service
de Gaulle, Charles, 143
Deißmann, Adolf, 42
Deng Xiaoping, 157, 244–245, 246, 300, 313, 317
Deutsche Forschungsgemeinschaft (DFG). *See* German Research Foundation
Dewey, John, 241
Diederich, Henry W., 97
Dirks, Nicholas: as Berkeley chancellor, 168, 174, 177–182, 183, 193; Berkeley Global Campus, 177–178, 180, 194–195, 198; on faculty, 187–188, 189; speeches, 184–186
diversity: faculty, 145; student, 148–149, 191, 193, 210, 212, 223
DKU. *See* Duke Kunshan University
DLC. *See* Duke Lemur Center
Document 9, 263; *See also* seven forbidden topics
Doyle, Frank, 161
Drake, Michael V., 183
DUHS. *See* Duke University Health System
Duke, James Buchanan, 204, 205
Duke, Washington, 204
Duke Kunshan University (DKU): academic autonomy, 228, 316; Advisory Board, 201, 229; campus, 202, 226, 231–232, *232*; challenges, 234–235; curriculum, 229–230; governance, 228;